"At last a book that really explains adolescence! 'You just don't get me' is a common refrain from teenagers to their parents and teachers. Adolescents who read this book will discover that Daniel Siegel gets them. Siegel has long been the go-to person for parents who want to understand their young children's minds and relationships. Now he applies his powerful mindsight tools to the turbulent years of adolescence. Siegel sees adolescence not as a problem to be solved or a hardship to be endured, but rather as a wellspring of courage and creativity."

—LAWRENCE J. COHEN, PH.D., author of *The Opposite of Worry: The Playful Parenting Approach to Childhood Anxieties and Fears*

"This book is filled with validation, vision, and clarity to help us navigate the seas of an often overwhelming time in life—the teenage years. It is chock-full of cutting-edge knowledge as well as a deep compassion for teenagers, the adults they will become, and the teenagers in all of us."

—ALANIS MORISSETTE, Grammy Award–winning singer and songwriter

"Daniel Siegel debunks myths of 'hormone-crazed teenagers' and replaces them with a more constructive narrative about age-related 'remodeling in the brain.' This book offers mind-opening brain science alongside practical tools that teens can use to navigate the emotions and relationships they encounter each day."

—BARBARA L. FREDRICKSON, PH.D., Kenan Distinguished Professor of Psychology, University of North Carolina, Chapel Hill, and author of *Positivity* and *Love 2.0*

"The information that Dr. Siegel shares not only is invaluable for understanding your growing child's brain, but also helps build more compassion and patience. A gift for us all."

—GOLDIE HAWN, Academy Award–winning actress, producer, director, and founder of MindUP™

"Dr. Siegel aptly characterizes the teen years as the most powerful life phase for activating courage, purpose, and creativity. A visionary and a guide, Siegel knows that if we treat teenagers with the respect and understanding they deserve, they are more likely to live up to their greatest capacities."

—LAURA S. KASTNER, clinical professor of psychiatry and behavioral sciences, University of Washington, and author of *Wise-Minded Parenting*

Praise for *Brainstorm*

"Siegel emerges as a bighearted writer, fully convinced that we all possess the fundamental virtues to navigate the choppy waters of adolescence—and he is hugely convincing of the intense engagement and creativity that often accompany this time period in a person's life. Smart advice . . . on providing the most supportive and brain-healthy environment during the tumultuous years of adolescence."
—*Kirkus Reviews*

"By the end of this book, the teenager has been transformed from a monstrous force into a thinking, feeling, and entirely approachable human being."
—*Publishers Weekly*

"A much-needed guide to the perils—and *promise!*—of adolescence, *Brainstorm* is full of practical tips for fostering happiness and success throughout the teen years. A must-read for all those with adolescents in their lives."
—Christine Carter, Ph.D., author of *Raising Happiness* and director of Greater Good Parents at the Greater Good Science Center, University of California, Berkeley

"Siegel gives us a fresh and insightful examination of adolescence from his point of view as an expert on the brain. The book also shows him to be a thoughtful parent, a compassionate guide, and a very fine writer. I strongly recommend *Brainstorm* to teens and to those who care about them."
—Mary Pipher, Ph.D., author of *Reviving Ophelia: Saving the Selves of Adolescent Girls* and *The Green Boat: Reviving Ourselves in Our Capsized Culture*

"*Brainstorm* recognizes the power, courage, and creativity of the next generation of change makers and invites us on a reflective and experiential journey of living life to the fullest, through adolescence and beyond. It is essential reading for all those interested in creating a better world for themselves and others."
—Craig Kielburger, cofounder of Me to We and Free the Children

"*Brainstorm* is eye-opening and inspiring, a great gift to us all—teens, parents of teens, and anyone who wants a full and rich life on this planet. Daniel Siegel shows how the supposed downsides of the teen years all have upsides, and that the lessons for living that await teens are lessons any of us, at any age, can learn from. Teens and their parents stand to benefit immensely from reading this book, separately or together."
—Daniel Goleman, author of *Emotional Intelligence*

"Dr. Siegel aptly characterizes the teen years as the most powerful life phase for activating courage, purpose, and creativity. With his usual personal and compassionate delivery, he illustrates how we can all become more aware, empathetic, and understanding of teenagers and ourselves. A visionary and a

guide, Siegel knows that if we treat teenagers with the respect and understanding they deserve, they are more likely to live up to their greatest capacities."
—Laura S. Kastner, Ph.D., clinical professor of psychiatry and behavioral sciences, University of Washington, and author of *Wise Minded Parenting: 7 Essentials for Raising Successful Tweens + Teens*

"At last a book that really explains adolescence! 'You just don't get me' is a common refrain from teenagers to their parents and teachers. Adolescents who read this book will discover that Daniel Siegel gets them. My favorite thing about this book is that Siegel sees adolescence not as a problem to be solved or a hardship to be endured, but rather as a wellspring of courage and creativity. This respectfulness is why the book works so well as a manual for adolescents, as well as their parents and mentors."
—Lawrence J. Cohen, Ph.D., author of *The Opposite of Worry*

"This book is filled with validation, vision, and clarity to help us navigate the seas of an often overwhelming time in life—the teenage years. Dan Siegel illuminates where there was mystery, empowers where there was fear, and inspires where there was trepidation. I am indebted to Dan for his deep kindness and ability to so articulately share his scientific, psychological, and social intelligence. This book is chock-full of cutting-edge knowledge as well as a deep compassion for teenagers, the adults they will become, and the teenagers in all of us."
—Alanis Morissette, Grammy Award–winning singer and songwriter

"A positively refreshing twist on the age-old topic of adolescent behavior. In a captivating conversational tone suited to teens (or those who work with or care for them), author Dan Siegel debunks myths of 'hormone-crazed teenagers' and replaces them with a more constructive narrative about age-related 're-modeling in the brain.' This book offers mind-opening brain science alongside practical tools that teens can use to navigate the emotions and relationships they encounter each day."
—Barbara L. Fredrickson, Kenan Distinguished Professor of Psychology, University of North Carolina, Chapel Hill, and author of *Positivity* and *Love 2.0*

"*Brainstorm* is a necessary look at why adolescents do what they do that can put parents in an emotional frenzy. The information that Dr. Siegel shares not only is invaluable for understanding your growing child's brain, but helps build more compassion and patience. A gift for us all."
—Goldie Hawn, Academy Award–winning actress, producer, director, and founder of MindUP™

"The teen years don't have to be filled with turmoil! In *Brainstorm*, Dan Siegel serves up a rich blend of smart insights and nitty-gritty tips to guide teens and the adults who care for them through this amazing period of creativity, conflict, and love."
—Harvey Karp, M.D., FAAP, author of *The Happiest Toddler on the Block*

ALSO BY DANIEL J. SIEGEL, M.D.

Mindsight:
The New Science of Personal Transformation

The Developing Mind:
How Relationships and the Brain Interact to Shape Who We Are
(now in its second edition)

Pocket Guide to Interpersonal Neurobiology:
An Integrative Handbook of the Mind

The Mindful Brain:
Reflection and Attunement in the Cultivation of Well-Being

The Mindful Therapist:
A Clinician's Guide to Mindsight and Neural Integration

Parenting from the Inside Out:
How a Deeper Self-Understanding Can Help You Raise Children
Who Thrive (with Mary Hartzell)

The Whole-Brain Child:
12 Revolutionary Strategies to Nurture Your Child's
Developing Mind (with Tina Payne Bryson)

No-Drama Discipline:
The Whole-Brain Way to Calm the Chaos and Nurture Your Child's
Developing Mind (with Tina Payne Bryson)

Daniel J. Siegel, M.D.

Brainstorm

The Power and Purpose
of the Teenage Brain

JEREMY P. TARCHER/PENGUIN

a member of Penguin Group (USA)

New York

JEREMY P. TARCHER/PENGUIN
An imprint of Penguin Random House LLC
375 Hudson Street
New York, New York 10014

First trade paperback edition 2015

Most Tarcher/Penguin books are available at special quantity discounts for bulk
purchase for sales promotions, premiums, fund-raising, and educational needs.
Special books or book excerpts also can be created to fit specific needs.
For details, write: SpecialMarkets@penguinrandomhouse.com.

The Library of Congress has catalogued the hardcover edition as follows:

Siegel, Daniel J., date.
Brainstorm : the power and purpose of the teenage brain / Daniel J. Siegel, M.D.
p.   cm.
Includes index.
ISBN 978-1-58542-935-6
1. Adolescent psychology.   2. Brain.   3. Cognition in adolescence.   I. Title.
BF724.S49   2013   2013029724
155.5—dc23

ISBN 978-0-399-16883-3 (paperback)

Printed in the United States of America
1   3   5   7   9   10   8   6   4   2

Book design by Ellen Cipriano

Names and identifying details of some individuals have been changed.

To Madeleine and Alexander,
for illuminating the vital essence of adolescence.

To Caroline,
for being a compassionate companion along this wild and
wonder-filled journey.

And to my mom,
for keeping your inner adolescent alive and well and being an
inspiration to us all.

Contents

Part II. Your Brain ▪ 65

Part IV. Staying Present Through Changes and Challenges ▪ 217

Preface

Thank you for picking up this book written for and about adolescents. Why might you consider reading it? Perhaps it will be helpful if I offer you a snapshot of a few of the ideas that are covered in the pages to follow, in the hopes that you can determine if this book will be useful for you.

I wrote this book because my own two children, now in their twenties, were passing through their adolescent years and I wanted to make sense of what in the world was going on. There was a revolution taking place in terms of our understanding of how the brain changes from the preteen years on into the mid-twenties, and I was fascinated to learn more. As a psychiatrist who works with children, adolescents, and families, I also wanted to see if the things I had learned from those I had worked with in my clinical practice might be combined with these new scientific insights to formulate a road map for navigating this period of life for both adolescents and those who love them.

When I set out to write this book, I was faced with a confusing set of challenges. One was that the common things we are taught, as parents and as physicians, in our schools and in our society, were basically wrong. That's right, wrong. How could that be? Isn't adolescence just a period of "immaturity" that teenagers just need to hurry up and get through? Isn't the impulsive, risk-taking behavior that takes place during this time of life simply a result of "raging hormones"? And doesn't the adolescent period end when the teenage years end? No, no, and no. I wanted to explore each of these myths and other misguided views, so that these erroneous, and oftentimes harmful, perspectives could be debunked.

But who would this book actually be written for?

I went to the online and brick-and-mortar sources for books and found essentially nothing written about these myths of adolescence, nor anything written for adolescents to understand their own brains. There was also essentially nothing that a parent, teacher, therapist, coach, or any other adult supporting the development of an adolescent could draw upon that made this new science both understandable and useful.

At first I tried to write a book just for adolescents, but felt that the adults in their lives needed something, too, if this might be helpful to all concerned. And then I tried to write a book where there were two independent parallel conversations going on side by side, so that an adult might peek over to what I was discussing with the adolescent, and the adolescent could take a look at what I was saying to the adult. That was head-spinning, and also didn't work. So I decided to try writing one direct discussion of these important issues, addressed to *both* the adolescent and the adult. I had done this in my clinical practice for nearly thirty years, and, with my wife, had the experience discussing these kinds of issues directly with our two adolescents, so why not stick to one conversation in the book?

I reviewed the existing science and wove it together with true stories of actual people I worked with or knew in my personal and professional lives. I then sent the manuscript out to many adolescents and adults to read. The first version got a lot of harsh criticism, mostly from the teens, who wanted something written more directly for them. So I rewrote the whole thing and sent it out to them and to a new group as well. This time the feedback was more positive, but it still needed something more. By the third pass, once there were practical Mindsight skill-building sections included in each of the four parts, and once the conversations were connecting fully to both adolescent and adult, the feedback was all reassuring. The book now had science, stories, and practical life-empowering and brain-developing skills that could be taken in in any order the reader felt worked best. Now the question was: Would such an unusual book—that spoke directly to both generations—be of interest to anyone who might read it and find it helpful?

The response across the generations has been enthusiastically positive, from adolescents in their preteen years to adolescents in their twenties, and for adults who either care for and support the development of adolescents now, or even because they simply were adolescents once themselves. The book has helped people understand this important period of life in a new and transformative way. I had hoped to keep the ideas cutting-edge and strong and the stories clear and useful so that the book could bring science to life in an interesting and practical way. Since the book's release, I've been giving talks around the country to schools—directly teaching adolescents themselves, as well as their parents and teachers, about the ideas and practices of *Brainstorm*. It's all been deeply rewarding, and a lot of fun.

Some adolescents who've read the book have let me know how it has changed their lives. Let me offer you a few examples of what they have said.

A journalist friend of mine ran into a nineteen-year-old boy on a plane trip, and when she saw that he was reading the book she asked what he thought of it. He told her, and when she then said that she was my friend, he asked if he could send me a message. Here is what he said: "Can you please tell Dr. Siegel that I'm serious when I say this book is changing my life. I'm not kidding. Before I found it, I was really down, really lost. I felt like it was me against the world. I wasn't really into anything, I had no real friends that knew me or cared about me that much. I was drifting. I had no idea that there was an 'essence' to me or to my life. I didn't know what my life was about or what the point was, or what I had to offer that mattered . . . and then I read about the book somewhere, can't remember, and picked it up. I see myself differently now. Everything. I just have this deep, deep excitement and hope that wasn't there before. It's like putting on glasses, I can see everything more clearly. Will you tell him that?" And as my friend's e-mail to me went on to state, "Uh . . . yes. Yes I will. Gulp. My eyes welled up actually. 33,000 feet paradigm shifts!! ☺"

A fifteen-year-old said this: "If every teen in every high school in every country and every parent and every teacher understood the ESSENCE of adolescence, they would realize that they've been looking at things in the wrong way all this time. Instead of looking at teens as people with problems, they would see people with potential. Instead of teens feeling misunderstood and inadequate, they would feel significant. They could take their lives by storm—by Brainstorm!"

And a thirteen-year-old sent me a handwritten note (so old-school!) that said, "Mr Siegel: Thank you <u>sooo</u> much for your book.

After reading it I felt more important as a teenager, and it made me feel more purposeful. I never knew a book about the brain could be so interesting!! Not only did this book make me feel like a more important teen, but it also opened my eyes up to neurology . . . Thank you so much again!"

As an author, these notes have been a deep source of inspiration for me.

The "essence" that those teens are referring to you'll discover in depth in the pages ahead, but here let me simply say that the "remodeling" that goes on in the teenage brain has the potential to inspire so much more than just "immature" or rash behavior. This time of transition in the brain also inspires emotional spark, social engagement, novelty seeking, and creative exploration that can be optimized to empower adolescents to live their lives to the fullest. Without awareness, each of these elements has a downside, for sure. But with knowledge and the skills taught in this book, we can turn potentially negative aspects of adolescence into positive growth.

There is a power and purpose to the adolescent period that can transform lives, but first it must be identified and developed so that these forces can be harnessed in a positive direction.

And, amazingly, it turns out that this essence of adolescence doesn't have to end at twenty-four. If we adults can rediscover these tendencies within ourselves, this is a sure way to support optimal living on into the final stages of our lives. Whether you are now in your adolescence or once were an adolescent, it is never too late to put on new glasses and see everything differently, as that wise teen suggests.

We have so much to learn from each other, adolescent from adolescent, adult from adolescent, adolescent from adult. Let's make our lines of communication wide open with respect and collaboration, harness the essence of adolescence to empower ourselves from the inside out, and use science and practical skill-building tools to bring more health and connection to our lives.

That's the power and purpose of adolescence, and the potential and promise of *Brainstorm*. I hope you'll join me in the journey ahead. Welcome!

PART I

■

The Essence of Adolescence

Adolescence is as much a perplexing time of life as it is an amazing one. Running roughly between the ages of twelve and twenty-four (yes, into our mid-twenties!), adolescence is known across cultures as a time of great challenge for both adolescents and the adults who support them. Because it can be so challenging for everyone involved, I hope to offer support to both sides of the generational divide. If you are an adolescent reading this book, it is my hope that it will help you make your way through the at times painful, at other times thrilling personal journey that is adolescence. If you are the parent of an adolescent, or a teacher, a counselor, an athletic coach, or a mentor who works with adolescents, my hope is that these explorations will help you help the adolescent in your life not just survive but thrive through this incredibly formative time.

Let me say from the very start that there are a lot of myths surrounding adolescence that science now clearly shows us are simply not true. And even worse than being wrong, these false beliefs can actually make life more difficult for adolescents and adults alike. So let's bust these myths right now.

One of the most powerful myths surrounding adolescence is that raging hormones cause teenagers to "go mad" or "lose their minds." That's simply false. Hormones do increase during this period, but it is not the hormones that determine what goes on in adolescence. We now know that what adolescents experience is primarily the result of changes in the development of the brain. Knowing about these changes can help life flow more smoothly for you as an adolescent or for you as an adult with adolescents in your world.

Another myth is that adolescence is simply a time of immaturity and teens just need to "grow up." With such a restricted view of the situation, it's no surprise that adolescence is seen as something that everyone just needs to endure, to somehow survive and leave behind with as few battle scars as possible. Yes, being an adolescent can be confusing and terrifying, as so many things during this time are new and often intense. And for adults, what adolescents do may seem confounding and even senseless. Believe me, as the father of two adolescents, I know. The view that adolescence is something we all just need to endure is very limiting. To the contrary, adolescents don't just need to survive adolescence; they can thrive *because* of this important period of their lives. What do I mean by this? A central idea that we'll discuss is that, in very key ways, the "work" of adolescence—the testing of boundaries, the passion to explore what is unknown and exciting—can set the stage for the development of core character traits that will enable adolescents to go on to lead great lives of adventure and purpose.

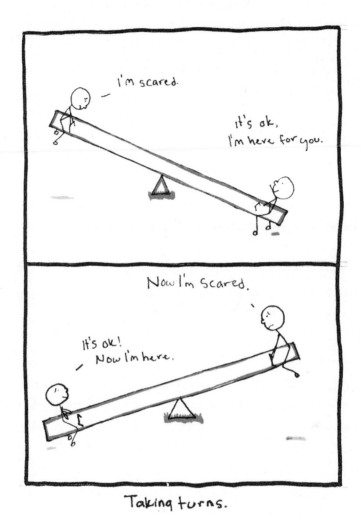

Taking turns.

A third myth is that growing up during adolescence requires moving from dependence on adults to total independence from them. While there *is* a natural and necessary push toward independence from the adults who raised us, adolescents still benefit from relationships with adults. The healthy move to adulthood is toward interdependence, not complete "do-it-yourself" isolation. The nature of the bonds that adolescents have with their parents as attachment figures changes, and friends become more important during this period. Ultimately, we learn to move from needing others' care during childhood, to pushing away from our parents and other adults and leaning more on our peers during adolescence, to then both giving care and receiving help from others. That's interdependence. In this book we'll explore the nature of these attachments and how our need for close relationships continues throughout the life span.

When we get beyond the myths, we are able to see the real truths they mask, and life for adolescents, and the adults in their lives, gets a whole lot better.

Unfortunately, what others believe about us can shape how we see ourselves and how we behave. This is especially true when it comes to teens and how they "receive" commonly held negative attitudes that many adults project (whether directly or indirectly)— that teens are "out of control" or "lazy" or "unfocused." Studies show that when teachers were told that certain students had "limited intelligence," these students performed worse than other students whose teachers were not similarly informed. But when teachers were informed that these same students had exceptional abilities, the students showed marked improvement in their test scores. Adolescents who are absorbing negative messages about who they are and what is expected of them may sink to that level instead of realizing their true potential. As Johann Wolfgang von Goethe wrote, "Treat people as if they were what they ought to be and you help them become what they are capable of being." Adolescence is not a period of being "crazy" or "immature." It is an essential time of emotional intensity, social engagement, and creativity. This is the essence of how we "ought" to be, of what we are capable of, and of what we need as individuals and as a human family.

Brainstorm is set up as follows: The first part examines the essence of adolescence and how understanding its important dimensions can create vitality now and throughout the life span. The second part explores the way the brain grows during adolescence so that we can make the most of the opportunities this period of life creates for us. The third part explores how relationships shape our sense of identity and what we can do to create stronger connections with others and with ourselves. In the fourth part, we dive into the ways in which the changes and challenges of adolescence can be best navigated by being present, by being receptive to what is happening so that we can be fully aware of the inner and interpersonal aspects of these experiences. I'll also provide practical steps along the way, in the Mindsight Tools sections, which offer science-proven ways to strengthen our brains and our relationships.

Because we each learn most effectively in different ways, you may want to experience this book in whatever approach is best for you after reading Part I. If you enjoy learning by blending concepts and facts with science and stories, reading the book from front to back might be best. If instead you learn best by doing, by actual practice, then the four Mindsight Tools sections would be a useful place to start; you can explore the science and stories later. I wrote the book in such a way that if you want to dive into a particular topic, you can do so by reading that part first—for relationships that would be Part III, while for the brain that would be Part II. If you learn best by story-driven discussions, you might read Part IV first, and the earlier sections and practice entries later. Mix it up and find what works best for you. The Parts and the Tools sections fit together as a whole; it's up to you how to sample them in a way that meets your needs.

This book is all about understanding and nurturing the essential features of adolescence to bring the most health and happiness into the world regardless of what age we are.

The Benefits and Challenges of Adolescence

The essential features of adolescence emerge because of healthy, natural changes in the brain. Since the brain influences both our minds and our relationships, knowing about the brain can help us with our inner experience and our social connections. In our journey I'll show how this understanding, and learning the steps to strengthen the brain in practical ways, can help us build a more resilient mind and more rewarding relationships with others.

During the teen years, our minds change in the way we remember, think, reason, focus attention, make decisions, and relate to others. From around age twelve to age twenty-four, there is a burst of growth and maturation taking place as never before in our lives. Understanding the nature of these changes can help us create a more positive and productive life journey.

I'm the father of two adolescents. I also work as a physician in the practice of child, adolescent, and adult psychiatry, helping kids, teens, adults, couples, and families make sense of this exciting time in life. In addition to working as a psychotherapist, I also teach about mental health. What has struck me in each of these roles is that there is no book available that reveals the view that the adolescent period of life is in reality the one with the most power for courage and creativity. Life is on fire when we hit our teens. And these changes are not something to avoid or just get through, but to encourage. *Brainstorm* was born from the need to focus on the positive essence of this period of life for adolescents and for adults.

While the adolescent years may be challenging, the changes in the brain that help support the unique emergence of the adolescent mind can create qualities in us that help not only during our adolescent years, if used wisely, but also as we enter adulthood and live fully as an adult. How we navigate the adolescent years has a direct impact on how we'll live the rest of our lives. Those creative qualities also can help our larger world, offering new insights and innovations that naturally emerge from the push back against the status quo and from the energy of the teen years.

For every new way of thinking and feeling and behaving with its positive potential, there is also a possible downside. Yet there *is* a way to learn how to make the most of the important positive qualities of the teenage mind during adolescence and to use those qualities well in the adult years that come later.

Brain changes during the early teen years set up four qualities of our minds during adolescence: novelty seeking, social engagement, increased emotional intensity, and creative exploration. There are changes in the fundamental circuits of the brain that make the adolescent period different from childhood. These changes affect how teens seek rewards in trying new things, connect with their peers in different ways, feel more intense emotions, and push back on the existing ways of doing things to create new ways of being in the world. Each of these changes is necessary to create the important shifts that happen in our thinking, feeling, interacting, and decision making during our adolescence. Yes, these positive changes have negative possibilities, too. Let's see how each of these four features of the adolescent brain's growth has both upsides and downsides, and how they fill our lives with both benefits and risks.

1. *Novelty seeking* emerges from an increased drive for rewards in the circuits of the adolescent brain that creates the

inner motivation to try something new and feel life more fully, creating more engagement in life. **Downside:** Sensation seeking and risk taking that overemphasize the thrill and downplay the risk result in dangerous behaviors and injury. Impulsivity can turn an idea into an action without a pause to reflect on the consequences. **Upside:** Being open to change and living passionately emerge, as the exploration of novelty is honed into a fascination for life and a drive to design new ways of doing things and living with a sense of adventure.

2. *Social engagement* enhances peer connectedness and creates new friendships. **Downside:** Teens isolated from adults and surrounded only by other teens have increased-risk behavior, and the total rejection of adults and adult knowledge and reasoning increases those risks. **Upside:** The drive for social connection leads to the creation of supportive relationships that are the research-proven best predictors of well-being, longevity, and happiness throughout the life span.

3. *Increased emotional intensity* gives an enhanced vitality to life. **Downside:** Intense emotion may rule the day, leading to impulsivity, moodiness, and extreme, sometimes unhelpful, reactivity. **Upside:** Life lived with emotional intensity can be filled with energy and a sense of vital drive that give an exuberance and zest for being alive on the planet.

4. *Creative exploration* with an expanded sense of consciousness. An adolescent's new conceptual thinking and abstract reasoning allow questioning of the status quo, approaching problems with "out of the box" strategies, the creation of

new ideas, and the emergence of innovation. **Downside:** Searching for the meaning of life during the teen years can lead to a crisis of identity, vulnerability to peer pressure, and a lack of direction and purpose. **Upside:** If the mind can hold on to thinking and imagining and perceiving the world in new ways within consciousness, of creatively exploring the spectrum of experiences that are possible, the sense of being in a rut that can sometimes pervade adult life can be minimized and instead an experience of the "ordinary being extraordinary" can be cultivated. Not a bad strategy for living a full life!

While we can brainstorm lots of new ideas inside us that we can share collaboratively during the creative explorations and novelty seeking of adolescence, we can also enter another kind of brainstorm as we lose our coordination and balance and our emotions act like a tsunami, flooding us with feelings. That's when we get filled with not only mental excitement but also with mental confusion. Adolescence involves both types of brainstorms.

In a nutshell, the brain changes of adolescence offer both risk and opportunity. How we navigate the waters of adolescence—as young individuals on the journey or as adults walking with them—can help guide the ship that is our life into treacherous places or into exciting adventures. The decision is ours.

Maintaining the Power and Purpose of the Adolescent Mind into Adulthood

Too often I hear adults in my practice say that their life is in a rut. They feel "stuck" or "empty," have lost their novelty-seeking drive, and are filled with the boredom of just doing the same old things over and over again. They also find their lives filled with a lack of social connectedness—they feel isolated and alone. And for many, life has lost its emotional intensity, things feel lackluster, even boring. This ennui can lead to apathy or even depression and despair. Nothing seems to matter; nothing seems to feel alive or vital. When adults stop using their potential for creative exploration, the way they reason and approach life's problems becomes simply a repeated familiar routine and imagination goes out the window. Life can become, well, lifeless. When adults lose the creative power of the adolescent mind, their lives can lose vitality and become meaningless.

The playfulness and humor that emerge from the creation of new combinations of things are essential to keep our lives full of vitality. Hang out with teens and you'll often hear laughter and hysterics. And sometimes you'll hear a lot of crying. So emotional intensity can bring joy, and it can bring tears, for sure. Hang out with many adults, and you'll often hear predominantly serious talk. Yes, life is serious. But we can bring joy and humor to these lives we lead. We need to live with humor and zest, not in spite of the world's problems but because of them.

Yet when adults lose the four distinguishing features of adolescence, when they stop cultivating the power of novelty seeking, social engagement, emotional intensity, and creative exploration, life can become boring, isolating, dull, and routinized. Who would intentionally choose to live like that? Most likely no one. But it happens all the time. It seems we adults are prone to just cruise on auto pilot. Why? It can be difficult coping with life's circumstances, to face the world's stresses. Sometimes it's easier to just shut down these essential aspects of a vital life that come during adolescence and instead try and stay in "survival mode" as we develop a routine we can rely on to function. But allowing ourselves to lose our vitality will only make life harder—and it also can lead to not keeping the brain as strong as it could be as we age.

So I'm suggesting that what adolescents have going for them that is both a challenge and a gift is actually what adults need in order to maintain vitality in their lives. Here's another myth. People tend to assume that the brain stops growing after childhood. But that's not true. The brain not only grows and changes during childhood and adolescence, but continues to grow throughout the life span. My proposal to you is that the four features of adolescence are exactly what we need to not only live a vital life as teens, but also to keep our brains growing throughout our lives.

Here's a way to remember this "essence" of the brain changes in adolescence. I love acronyms, much to my students' either delight or dismay. So if this acronym is helpful for you, great. Here it is: The essence of the adolescent brain changes that are the essence of healthy ways of living throughout the life span spell the word *essence* itself:

> **ES:** *Emotional Spark*—honoring these important internal sensations that are more intense during adolescence but serve to create meaning and vitality throughout our lives.
>
> **SE:** *Social Engagement*—the important connections we have with others that support our journeys through life with meaningful, mutually rewarding relationships.
>
> **N:** *Novelty*—how we seek out and create new experiences that engage us fully, stimulating our senses, emotions, thinking, and bodies in new and challenging ways.
>
> **CE:** *Creative Explorations*—the conceptual thinking, abstract reasoning, and expanded consciousness that create a gateway to seeing the world through new lenses.

This is the essence of living well during adolescence and during the adult years: *Emotional Spark—Social Engagement—Novelty—Creative Explorations*. Adol-ESSENCE. Or: *Adolescence is Adult-ESSENCE.*

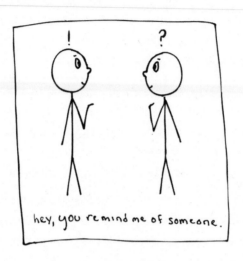

hey, you remind me of someone.

I wonder if some of the tension that I see in parents as a reaction toward adolescents is at times a deep longing for these very features they themselves may have lost. Not having an emotional spark can make a teen's exuberance threatening. Not being socially engaged can make an adult feel disconnected in the face of a teen's social life. How many new friends did we make at ages thirty, forty, or fifty? All the drive for new things in an adolescent's life can make an adult's daily routines seem dull. And the creative explorations that drive a teen into all sorts of new ways of thinking and behaving can make the humdrum and predictability of adult life at times seem too controlled and too limiting.

Perhaps if adults could recapture some of this vital essence the gap between the generations would lessen. What I mean by this is that sometimes what we see in others can remind us of what we are missing in ourselves, and this reminder makes us frustrated, disappointed, angry, or sad. As a therapist, I see this all too often, when, for instance, parents cannot stand some aspect of their child's personality because it reminds them of something that bugs them about their own life. If we take a deep breath and realize we are all lifelong learners, then an adult's intense emotional reaction to a teen, for example, can serve as a reminder for us to explore our own inner lives and not simply react outwardly.

Adults have things to learn from adolescence as a period we went through and from adolescents as the ones going through that developmental period right now. Adolescents can remind us of what we have a right to experience in our lives. Similarly, as adolescents we have things to learn from adults, as adults share with us their experiences as they support our development toward independence.

Learning to use the power of the adolescent mind can help us have a positive experience as it emerges during this period of intense change. When navigated well, these brain changes can lead to positive outcomes later on. Holding on to the essential power of the teenage mind into later adolescence and beyond, into the adult years, can enable us to continue lifelong learning and recognize the important life-affirming sense of adventure, vitality, and courage that adolescence brings. Learning to use the power of the emerging adolescent mind well is as important for us as adolescents as it is for us as adults!

Adolescence from the Inside Out

We'll be exploring the essence of adolescence from an "inside out" approach. What this means is that we can learn how understanding our own or others' inner workings can help us understand the outer behaviors of ourselves and of others. This inside-out understanding can help us create the life we want, not simply settle for what we are given. To take on this inside-out approach, we'll learn about how the brain, self-awareness, and relating to others all help create the experience of who we are—how they help create our minds—so that we can be better equipped for this period of life.

We'll also explore important and relevant scientific ideas and reveal how to apply science in helpful ways. This book is written so that it feels like a conversation between me as author and you as reader. My hope is that reading it will make you feel as if we are actually talking together, in person, about this important period of life.

I'm excited to invite you to join with me in this conversation-like exploration to put yourself in the experience, to reflect on what is going on in your own life. With two adolescents in my personal life now, one in his early twenties and the other in her late teens, I am presented every day with the opportunities and challenges of being a parent of two individuals going through this period of life. And being their father also recalls the memories and meanings of my own adolescent years. I'll share with you as we go along some of these inside-out reflections that are directly relevant to the topics we'll be focusing on.

For you as an adolescent, these discussions can invite you to think about your own life now. If you are an adult reading this, you may find yourself reflecting on what is going on now or what went on in your own adolescence. Your reading experience—like my writing experience—is intended as an invitation for us to become actively involved in a conversation with each other and for you to reflect on your own experiences with me. You may find it helpful to keep a personal journal to capture your own reflections, a process that may feel good and also one that has been shown to support the ability to make sense of things. If you are looking for a journey of discovery where what you learn and what you reflect on can help you travel through the adolescent years and harness the creative power of this period and hold on to its essence with more knowledge, insight, and understanding, you've come to the right place.

We never stop discovering who we are or what has meaning in life. Our minds continually emerge in ways that can support a healthy, exuberant life as we grow and develop throughout our lives. So this is truly an exploration I am asking you to join me in, not some download of facts and figures, not just a bunch of opinions and mandates on what you should do. And whether you are in adolescence or adult years, this exploration can help your mind emerge in helpful ways. Since this is a conversation, it means we'll be asking questions, basic questions, that we'll wrestle with as we attempt to answer them. The fact is that we don't know the final answers to a lot of questions about the brain or the mind, but asking them and searching for the answers are essential steps for us to take.

My own kids ask me why I like teaching so much, and I say it is because I am always learning when I connect with people in educational experiences. I feel it's an important stance to take—that we are lifelong learners. To have an understanding of where another person is coming from during this developmental period helps everyone navigate it well and continue to grow.

During childhood, parents are often seen as the be-all and end-all of role models. In fact, adolescence is a time when we begin to see our parents as actual people, not heroes, who have their own flaws and limitations. Perhaps seeing parents in this way helps us leave them and go out into the world. As Mark Twain once said, "When I was a boy of fourteen, my father was so ignorant I could hardly stand to have the old man around. But when I got to be twenty-one, I was astonished at how much the old man had learned in seven years."

Naturally, pushing away from the status quo is a fundamental way to create novel experiences. And novelty seeking is both a part of the push back and inherently rewarding. Adolescence is also a time filled with new ideas. In many ways, seeking novelty is rewarding as it fills experiences, behaviors, perceptions, thoughts, ideas, intentions, and beliefs with the spirit of adventure.

This striving for novelty is a creative power that can be harnessed for the benefit of everyone, *if* we see this move toward new things and independence in a positive way. On the other hand, if adults fight against these fundamental features of adolescence, it's like fighting against the natural push of a waterfall. The force of adolescence will find some way to manifest itself in a teen's external actions and internal mental shifts. You cannot stop a waterfall, but you can learn to direct its course and harness its power.

The good news is that the developmental state of adolescence does not have to be experienced as a war between the generations. If adults try to block the flow of adolescence, it is likely that communication, so important to relationships, will be tainted with tension and disrespect. Disconnection, secrecy, isolation, and many other negative and hurtful social responses can emerge. The key is for the adolescent and the adult-who-once-was-an-adolescent to recognize these important brain changes and learn to navigate these years constructively and collaboratively in order to keep communication open between them, to optimize life for everyone, and to avoid tragic endings of risky behaviors. The challenge is not easy, but it at least should be made clear.

This is our balancing act, for adolescents and adults alike: making the push toward independence, the drive for reward, and the passion for novelty result in positive outcomes in life.

The brain is our enabler—our control center—and the good news is that when we understand the brain, we can harness its powerful drives to make positive choices and constructive changes in our lives. Understanding how the brain links its different circuits, how it becomes integrated with development, is a useful way of seeing how we can help promote optimal functioning in our lives during adolescence and beyond. This integration is altering the linkage of different areas in the brain, and even between people, that can help us understand and optimize the important changes in adolescence.

Here is the powerful finding from science: You can learn the steps to make your brain more integrated and to strengthen it. You can learn how to improve the way your mind functions and make your brain healthier and your relationships more rewarding. These are the basic things we'll explore in the pages ahead. You'll learn through stories and science about these important aspects of your life; and you'll be offered practices to create more integration in your life. And if you learn these things, they can make the rest of your life better. No kidding.

Risk and Reward

While most measurable aspects of our lives are improving during adolescence, such as physical strength, immune function, resistance to heat and cold, and the speed and agility of how we respond, we are three times more likely to suffer serious injury or death during this time than we were in childhood or than we will be in adulthood. This increase in risk is not "by chance"—scientists believe it comes from the innate changes in how the brain develops during this period.

The question is whether we can support the exploration of new things while we also minimize the chance of permanent harm. That's the issue, and that's one of the challenges we'll address in the pages ahead.

Just before my son's first birthday, he and I were walking around the block near our apartment, gathering stones we could toss around (a favorite pastime of his), when I noticed a line of cars jammed along what was usually a pretty quiet street. When we got home, I heard from some neighbors who had been stuck in the traffic that there had been a terrible accident just a mile from our apartment.

That evening I was horrified to find out what had happened.

My favorite teacher during my psychiatric training program was pulling out of his driveway with his wife that late afternoon, headed for a Friday night dinner and a movie. I'll call my teacher Bill. (As in all the true stories you'll read about, I've changed the names and identifying features of the people in these nonfiction narratives to honor their privacy and protect the confidentiality of all concerned— except, naturally, I've left my own details and those of my family members.) As Bill and his wife left for the evening, his wife later told me, they were excited to go out together. Bill drove his car to the corner of their residential street, looked both ways, and when the coast was clear carefully drove his car across the westbound lanes to head east toward the restaurant, a trip he and his wife had been taking for nearly a half century. But this time was different. In that brief time crossing over the lanes, a car suddenly appeared headed west and barreled into them. Before they knew it, their car was hit head-on, split in half, and Bill was killed instantly. Amazingly, Bill's wife and the driver of the speeding car were unharmed, physically at least.

The driver was a nineteen-year-old young man in a brand-new sports car. Two months earlier, after crashing into a tree, he had been arrested for speeding down that same twisty boulevard. His parents replaced that wrecked sports car with another. Bill's wife told me that the investigators at the scene later estimated that the teenager had been driving at least ninety-five miles an hour. I traced the path of that teen's car in my mind over and over again, trying to make sense of this senseless accident. At that speed and with those curves, Bill could never have seen the car approach before crossing those westbound lanes to head east, and the oncoming teenage driver at that speed would never have seen Bill's car crossing his path until it was too late.

I did whatever I could to support Bill's family, friends, and colleagues in the memorial services at the university and at the clinical institutions where Bill had taught for so many years. I reflected on what he had taught me as an expert in development and the mind—how our early experiences shape who we are, shape who we become; how so much of our behavior is driven by mental processes outside our awareness. Just a few weeks before his tragic death, Bill and I had met to talk about some of the research I was starting to do on attachment and memory. "That's so fascinating!" Bill said. "Tell me more!" He was such an inspiring teacher, someone who would listen closely to what was going on inside me, support my interests, encourage me to pursue my passions. And at that meeting I told him so. "Thanks, Dan, but you know I think of you more as a peer now, a colleague." I thanked him, and felt honored to be connected to him however he defined our relationship. I wondered how Bill's life devotion to exploring why people do what they do might help all of us comprehend this reckless and fatal accident.

When I began to look into the facts about the adolescent period, I was shocked to find that though teenagers are more physically fit and healthier than children or adults, they actually make up the largest group with avoidable causes of death. By avoidable I mean that risky or dangerous behaviors lead to permanent injuries or fatalities. With accidents, drug use, wounding from weapons, suicide, and

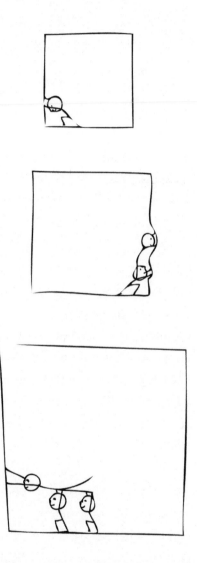

Pushing boundaries.

murder, the period from twelve to twenty-four is the most dangerous time of our lives. Bill's death fit with well-established statistics.
The reality is that many teenagers—like this nineteen-year-old—act
in extreme ways that risk life and limb, harming their own and others' lives in irreversible ways.

Why do such risk-taking, limit-testing, sensation-seeking behaviors happen? With my one-year-old son there by my side around the
time of Bill's death, I wondered if there was anything I could do as
his father to prevent him from participating in such destructive behavior. If that was possible, I wanted to figure it out and share it with
my patients and the mental health community so that tragedies like
the one that ended Bill's life might be avoided.

Adolescence is a time of great boundary pushing that can be
challenging and create catastrophes; but this pushing-back propensity can also be a remarkably positive, essential part of our lives. Our
challenge is to engage and explore ways to push at life's boundaries
without driving a hundred miles an hour down a public street and
killing someone in our path. For males especially, who seem to bio-
logically need to court danger, in some fashion to "come of age" as
young men, to test limits and face risk to prove they can come out
alive, there must be some culturally sanctioned rites of passage we
can reinvent that don't involve a two-ton weapon barreling down
the road with innocent victims in its wake. When an adolescent ga-
zelle runs up close to a cheetah to inspect its potential predator, it is
risking its own life, not the life of its fellow gazelles, adolescents or
adults. As modern human beings who share with other mammals
this adolescent drive toward danger, cars and alcohol make accidents
one of the top killers in this otherwise healthy period of life.

In the twenty years since Bill's death, the tragic school shootings
and public explosions we bear witness to have often been carried out
by males in their adolescence. There is an increasing disconnect in

today's world and we need to do something to help teens so that such destructive behavior can be understood and made less likely to happen.

Rather than simply wondering what is going on, it would be much more productive to explore the nature of adolescence with individuals in their teens and twenties and with the adults who help support them in such a way that maybe, just maybe, the chances of these destructive actions occurring might be lessened, even if in some small but personally significant way. I think Bill would be happy if understanding the adolescent processes leading to his tragic death could help avoid such tragedies for others in the future.

Pushing Away

In broad terms, the adolescent push against what is known, safe, and familiar is a two-sided coin. Yes, that adolescent pushing away from adults seems to be built into our genes. It's what gets us to drive outrageously fast down a public street. That is the destructive side of the adolescent coin, a side we should try to control so the adolescent can grow well and stretch his or her wings but minimize damage to self or to others.

Yet there is a constructive side that can be used, too.

With awareness, the power of the adolescent mind can be utilized to benefit oneself and others. It is this constructive side that has led to so many innovations that have transformed our modern world in art, in technology, in music. This period of the teenage years and early twenties is a time of great potential and of great constructive power. The push against traditional ways of doing things and of thinking about reality can yield ways of thinking outside the box that enable new and creative ways of doing things to emerge.

With the problems our world faces today—the energy crisis, changes in the environment, overpopulation, war, poverty, and threats to the availability of healthy food, water, and air—never before have we so desperately needed a way to think beyond our usual strategies to create innovative ways of sustainable living on our precious planet. My suggestion to you is that the power of the adolescent mind has just that spark of emotion and social drive, just that push to explore new solutions to old ways of doing things, that may save life on our planet.

The key is how to discover these hidden positive aspects of adolescence and work together as adolescents and adults to make them work for us rather than against us.

Even if we don't buy into the idea that adolescents will save the world, at least understanding brain science may help explain how we can encourage a teen to decide to call home or come in by one in the morning instead of three. We may be more open to the notion that brain science shows how the very essence of adolescence can help individuals be healthier and happier. But the truth, too, is that these essential features also can help improve our planet.

Let me say here that if you as an adolescent begin to grasp the science behind the changes in your brain during your teenage years, your adolescence and your adulthood will be better. And if adults can gain insight into these same fundamental aspects of the adolescent mind, they, too, will have healthier and happier lives. We have a lot to learn from the adolescent mind as it emerges in these years and about how we can hold on to its essence throughout our lives. Whether you are a teenager or an older adolescent, or you are an adult making sense of adolescents in your life now or wondering what happened to you when you were this age, these essential features are an important part of the unfolding of your individual life history.

The Timing of Puberty, Sexuality, and Adolescence

Two changes happen universally in our human adolescence. One is that as puberty hits we begin to experience changes in the body and changes in our emotions. The second is that we push away from our parents, hanging out with our peers more and trying to do things in new ways.

With puberty, our sexual organs develop and create changes in hormone levels and in our secondary sexual characteristics, such as breasts in girls and facial hair in boys. For many of us after puberty, our feelings of sexuality begin to emerge. We become attracted to others in new ways that can be intense, wonderful, and frightening all at once. Puberty and sexual maturation often mark the onset of adolescence. For some individuals, the brain changes of adolescence may occur even before puberty, in cases, for example, of delayed sexual maturation.

Whenever puberty occurs, the new emerging sexuality gives rise to fertility—the ability to reproduce. A hundred years ago, the time between the onset of adolescence and the taking on of adult responsibilities of working and having and raising children was very short, a couple of years. In those days, puberty in girls happened around age fifteen or sixteen, and just a few years later teens would create a new family home. What has changed is that now there is a longer duration between puberty and the "end of adolescence," a transition that has no clear end point. The time for setting up a new family and becoming employed in many modern cultures can be a decade or two. With the onset of puberty now at a younger age than ever before—in girls, often before the teen years—and the later timing of setting up a home and assuming other adult responsibilities, adolescence is now quite extended.

While pushing away from adults is universal, what also may be unique to modern life is the increasing number of adolescents who respond to these challenges by completely excluding adults from their lives. For both adolescent and adult, keeping the lines of communication open is the most basic principle of navigating these years well.

In all cultures throughout the world the years that fall between childhood and adulthood are considered a distinct period of life. Interestingly, scientists have noted that it is a marked period in the animal kingdom as well—dogs and cheetahs, parrots and finches all experience adolescence as a distinct life stage. It's possible that this adolescent period, then, is something encoded in our genetic material; it's in our genes.

If we continued to do things just like they did in previous generations, we would be using the same old-world strategies that may not work in a new environment created by a constantly changing world. By pushing away from adults and hanging out more with peers during our adolescence, we can find new ways of dealing with the world and create new strategies for living. In the "adapt or die" realities of evolution, adolescents are our adaptive force.

Yet adults sometimes forget their own adolescence and settle into the status quo, feeling more comfortable with the way things are. While that sense of familiarity in a stressed life of adult responsibilities is understandable, as we've seen, it may also be a reason why the adult-adolescent relationship is filled at times with tension. Adults desire things to stay the same; adolescents are driven to create a new world. This is part of the source of what can become intense friction, sometimes destructively so, that can create pain in everyone, adolescent and adult alike.

We'll explore in great detail how our relationships shape our identity as we move from the important attachment relationships with our parents to the relationships we begin to cultivate more with our peers during adolescence. As we push away from adults during adolescence we begin to associate much more with peers. Associating with our peers during this time is vital for our survival. There is safety in numbers as we "leave the nest" and help one another brave this new world. This increased social engagement also helps us collaborate with our peers, with whom we'll set up a whole new world.

Throughout human history, we stayed together as communities, with adolescents exploring and establishing independence while maintaining a range of important and instructive interactions with their adult elders. Those strands of connectedness are being stretched in today's world, sometimes severing them with negative consequences of isolation and alienation. We are meant to live in a community, meant to live in connection with others. So if the pushing away from adults leads a teen to become isolated even from his or her peer group, then that total disconnection can be quite disorienting. Remember, adolescents pushing away from others is natural; shutting others out totally is not helpful (nor is it natural) for anyone. An important take-home message is that it is vital to keep the lines of connection and communication open and to remember that we all—adolescents and adults—need to be members of a connected community.

The Stress and Distress of Our Extended Adolescence

I sat recently with a group of older adolescents and young and older adults to brainstorm some new approaches to education and the Internet. In order to get the conversation going, we focused on what our teenage years were like and took on a group exercise to offer one word that captured a sense of those years. Here are the words these individuals offered to the group: *isolated, crazed, confused, a mess, alone, terrified, wild, out of control, lost, seeking,* and *frightened.*

I myself offered the word *disconnected,* which I felt, and right away I wondered if the word was too abstract, too intellectual, too disconnected itself from my own emotional experience or theirs. Such doubt, as we'll see later on, may be a part of our temperament, as it is with me. But the adolescent years are also filled with a sense of uncertainty by nature. Why? Because this is a time of great transition. We move from the relative safety and familiarity of the home nest to a temporary period—one that may last decades—of having no real home base. So right there we have two reasons for distress: losing the familiar and safe, and gaining the unfamiliar and dangerous. You never know what lurks in the world outside the home nest, do you?

In facing such newness, adolescence is a tough time. It can be disorienting, disturbing, discombobulating, and distressing. We can become disengaged, disenchanted, and discouraged. Maybe you can think of some other terms that describe these "dis-" states, like the feeling you've disappeared or are dissolving. These are the distasteful aspects of the transition from dependency and the nest-home life of childhood to the come-what-may years that lie ahead in the outside world before the more settled interdependency of adult life.

One source of not just comfort but basic survival is to identify more with your peers than with your parents, to connect with other adolescents and push away from adults. By being a part of an adolescent group, you get companionship on this transitional trek, as well as safety in numbers: Predators will be intimidated by a large group, and you can lose yourself in the group mass. That is one reason why for many but not all teens, fitting in can feel so important—it's an evolutionary holdover of life or death. You can feel comforted by membership in the group, strengthened by membership in the group, and even more creative in the collective intelligence of the group.

While group collaboration can certainly be a source of collective intelligence, it can also get you to jump off a cliff or drive too fast. And that's probably why some form of continued connection to the adults and their adult perspectives still exists in traditional cultures, and even in our animal cousins. Without adults around, young adolescents can literally go wild.

In many cultures the period of adolescence is marked by a culturally sanctioned rite of passage. For boys, there is often a sense of danger and actual risk taking, with the successful completion marked by a ceremony welcoming the youth into the adult world of responsibility. For girls, adolescence is a time of acknowledgment of fertility, the ability to bear children and care for them, so girls are welcomed into the community as new members ready to become a part of the adult generation. These rites of passage are formal acknowledgments of this important transition in life.

In modern culture, our rites of passage are often missing or minimized in importance. We seem to have lost many of our communal and sanctioned ways of taking risks and acknowledging the transition from childhood to adulthood. Human adolescents—and even adolescents of many other mammal species—leave the home and move away from those to whom they are genetically related. Some argue that the biological benefits of such geographical migration make commingling similar genes among our relatives less likely. From a group point of view for humans, there needs to be a clear separation of the dependency of the child and the responsibility of the adult.

With a lack of jobs and a great deal of uncertainty about participating in contemporary society, however, the adolescent period may in many ways be even further prolonged. Because modern cultural practices do not offer transitional relationships with non-parental adults to help acknowledge and facilitate the adolescent period, we have some major challenges as adolescents in our modern times. This might be something we may want to change in the future in our evolving cultural practices.

With this perspective, perhaps collectively we can create a cultural rite of passage, a way in which adolescents are connected to new adults who can help support them in risk-taking and novelty-creating experiences that minimize danger yet optimize the essence of adolescence. There is a lot of power in the emotional spark of this period. And with some adult involvement, the social engagement during this important time can fuel the drive for novelty and the creative explorations that emerge. The key is how we can all work together, across the generations, to honor this essence of adolescence, to discover and cultivate the hidden power and purpose of the adolescent mind.

Adolescent Transitions and the Centrality of Our Relationships

As I embark upon this conversation with you, I am also living these transitions in my own life. The weight of it all, but also the beauty, hit me recently on the morning my daughter was preparing to leave us to go off to college. I want to share this experience with you, as I hope it will speak to your own experiences as both adolescents and parents going through these changes.

The sun is rising slowly on an overcast day here in this desert city by the sea. Los Angeles is where I grew up, and this is where my wife and I have raised our two kids—now twenty-two and eighteen years of age. Clothes are folded in piles along the walls in the hallway outside our daughter's room. I wake early this morning, restless in bed, tumble out in the hazy light, and step into the hall that for eighteen years has been our passage to her room.

She was born four and a half years after her brother, whose room, empty since he moved away to college, has long become the repository of boxes of things to be sorted out and stored in his closet like memories of years now past. A lot has been happening all at once in our family in the past few months.

My father's recent passing, the first death in our immediate family in decades, marks the unfolding of the generations with a finality that underlines the flow of this life we call being human. Life is constantly changing, continually moving forward in time, no matter how much we may want things to simply stay as they are. This is the last day in our home before our daughter will take all those piled clothes, pack them up in boxes and suitcases, put them in her brother's car, and then drive off to college.

So much is happening, all at once, that I can't seem to grasp and hold on to it all. I think of a dear family friend, an Irish poet named John O'Donohue, who died suddenly just after he turned fifty-two. John was an accomplished, insightful author and philosopher, who left behind magnificent books on life and love. In an interview shortly before his death, he was asked if there was anything that still bothered him, something he could not deal with. John said that no matter how much he thought, no matter how much he wrote, he had a nagging feeling that time was like fine sand that he could not hold on to, however tightly he tried to grasp it—it just ran through his fingers.

And that's how I feel now. So much happening, so much life and death and change, and no matter what I do, I can't hold on to any of it. It just slips onward, ever forward.

To be aware, to awaken to the momentous time of it all, to feel its weight, to sense the inevitability of these tides of life, this flow of birth, childhood, adolescence, emergence into adulthood, transition, illness, death. To be aware of our dependence on one another, on our individual development from the earliest days into maturity—whenever that actually is—to a life filled with discovery, connection, growth, and then dissolution. When John and I would teach together, he'd always laugh and say that the "pain level is dropping now" and that the "joy level is rising rapidly" when we'd greet each other after a long time apart. Love fills these moments with laughter and light even in the face of this transience of our being.

When I was a teen, I first started wrestling with some of these notions of life and death, trying to make sense of how we could live lightly in life while knowing the heaviness of its finality. The streets of this city were my playground, where I'd ride my bike for hours, reflecting on this wild journey and how we should be aware of the reality of what it means to be awake, to be human. I came back here after leaving for my own education, returning to these streets and to this coastal city where the shore meets the sand, letting the waves of the sea be my companion all these years later.

Our own children have walked those same sandy paths, their footprints as light and temporary as mine decades ago. The waves washing away our steps through life, the tides moving in and out with the cycle of our days. Their childhood joys, and sorrows, as real and alive for them as they were then for me, as they are for each of us now. No matter our age, we are on this life journey together.

I feel the weight of time here and now. Is this the sadness of her leaving? The sadness of my father's dying? Is this some sense of helplessness at the uncertainty of it all, of the only certainty in life being change itself? I, too, cannot grasp the sand in my hands, cannot stop time from moving forever forward. I sit here, now, filled with it all.

I look at my daughter's clothes and I also see in my mind's eye a young toddler's toys strewn in this same hallway. I feel the rhythm of the music she and I would play in her preschool years, when on Wednesdays I'd take the afternoon off from work to pick her up from school and then we'd dance the afternoon away. We'd twirl in tempo, her feet dancing in air, my toes clinging to carpet as I swung her round and round. "More . . . More . . . More!" she'd cry out, and round and round we'd go, collapsing on the couch, exhausted, exhilarated, giggling, together.

I can see, too, an excited kindergarten kid holding her sweater as she carried her shoes downstairs, tied her laces just so, and picked up her lunch box as she bounded out the front door. If patients' appointments permitted, I'd run home for her arrival at the end of the day and see that boundless energy of excitement as she recounted the day's events. I'd head back to work, seeing people in therapy whose attachment to their own parents was often filled with strife. We'd work to make sense of their lives, their histories, their struggles. And I'd be working to make sense of my own, to embrace the profound importance of our relationships with one another.

How do we find a balance between our adolescents' personal decisions and our parental regulation, our concerns? Structure with empowerment is how my wife and I would think of our strategy of parenting. How could we support our adolescents while also allowing them to find their own voices? And how at the same time could we set the limits and cautions our own years of living had taught us?

Science would call this "authoritative parenting," a helpful approach that is filled with warmth, limit setting, and honoring of autonomy in age-appropriate ways. Such a stance is also the balanced approach of secure attachment: lending support while supporting separation. In fact, attachment is all about this way in which we provide a safe haven while also encouraging exploration. Attachment is all about both security at home and security in the world. We did our best to supply the basic S's of attachment, letting our kids be *seen*, be *safe*, be *soothed*, and feel *secure*. It is from this foundation of secure attachment that adolescents can then ride the white-water rapids of this tumultuous journey with the best hopes of balance and agility.

Since those earliest days raising our son, after my teacher Bill had been killed by that need-for-speed racing teen, I always thought in the back of my mind that providing secure attachment would be the best we could do as parents to create the kind of self-awareness in our son and daughter that would minimize the chances for such prevent- able destructive behaviors. Challenging to create in a busy life but crucial. As our kids each grew into their own adolescence, that secu- rity of childhood seemed to disappear, on the surface, and was re- placed with emotional tension, quick reactivity, and sense of disrespect and disregard. When the studies came out that many adolescents ex- perience more distress and negative emotional states, it made sense for how our own kids' experiences were unfolding during those early teen years. And as a young adult student once said to me about what he learned from his own adolescence, we need to remember that teens are changing a lot, and sometimes they'll be one way, with one kind of identity, feeling a lot and feeling intensely, and sometimes they'll be another way, feeling nothing and not interacting much. "Just let them be who they are at the time, not who you expect they should be" was his great advice.

Fortunately, the tectonic shifts in emotion and identity of those early adolescent years give rise to a more stable state for many teens as they leave the middle school years.

High school is the ultimate testing ground for such balancing acts of relationships, tests of attachment to us and new attachments to friends. Parenting adolescents is an emotionally challenging task when facing the decision to speak or not speak, to constrain or permit, to hold close in times of uncertainty, to give comfort when things don't go right. Finding a network of supportive relationships for parents seems crucial in giving us the reflective space to move through adolescence. When we realize that in our evolutionary past we raised children collaboratively and close family or friends or other designated and trusted individuals in our tribe cared for our offspring, we realize how unnatural being isolated as a parent, or as a family, truly is. When it comes to village life for the teen, during the time he or she is pushing against parents, there would be other adults in the tribe to whom the teen could turn for security and connection. But when the only close adult is your parent, the natural way to go in adolescence is entirely toward other adolescents.

As we grow through development, our needs for attachment do not end when our childhood emerges into adolescence; we transfer those needs for supportive connections with others to our friends and life partners. We need to be seen by our friends who serve as important attachment figures in our lives; we need to be safe with them; we need to be soothed by them; and we need to feel secure with them. My wife is my secure attachment figure, and I am hers. We seek comfort from the other at times of stress and internalize the sense of the other to bring an internal sense of security throughout the day.

The last three years of our daughter's adolescence has been a test, for her and for us, in patience. As with her brother's development, this middle period of adolescence feels like a preparation for physical departure and emotional separation. From fifteen to eighteen years old, our daughter, like other teens during this period, has found her way from experiencing life's moments of decision as struggles for clarity to sensing them as moments of expressing her identity. She, and we, have moved from eye rolls and intense emotional wrestling over issues of what she wears, how long she stays out, and what movies she can see and with whom, to finding a mutual space of respect where we can say what we are concerned about and she can state what she needs, what she wants, and what her thinking is regarding these day-to-day decisions as well as major life choices.

It took a while, but after a lot of tearful conflicts on all sides, we learned that by saying what was going on inside our own minds— what each of us was feeling, thinking, hoping for, how we were seeing things, and what we were hearing—we could then listen closely to the other's inner life and the intention behind what often had become simply proclamations of action, if not outright declarations of war. That's reflection, that's reflective conversation. Without such reflective dialogues with one another, the experience of these years would have been so different.

Our daughter's clothes are neatly folded along the wall of the hallway; her plans for these next twenty-four hours before her brother drives her and the packed car up to school, where we'll fly north to meet them, are laid out and include time spent mostly with her friends; and I stand here, feet heavy on the floor, eyes glued to her door, my heart in awe of her, of her growth, and of who she has become. She is ready to go. But like so many parents at this moment, I am not so sure if I am ready to see her leave.

As parents we can only do the best we can. It is helpful to realize that sometimes, in more than a third of us at least, there is active, intentional reflective and relational work to be done to move from a history of insecurity to a present life of security. Such a conscious presence on our part can help bring integration into our children's lives, to bring security to them as they push away and push on into their adolescence, so they'll carry the best intentions and connections from us that we can offer. That is a gift we can give to our children, and one we can offer to ourselves as well.

The intention, all the effort to live and to learn and to love from the inside out, that parents cultivate in their home lives will indeed provide the formative experiences to help our children thrive as they live their adolescence well and hold on to its essence as they emerge into their adult years. If you are an adolescent preparing to leave home or are already out on your own, I hope you will know that there is the possibility of having a secure home for you to return to any time you wish, or you will find your way to creating one that will serve as a home base for you in the future. This inside-out approach is what this book is all about: creating the secure base that enables us as families to turn the changes and challenges of the adolescent period into strengths we will draw on together as we navigate this journey that is our life.

MINDSIGHT TOOLS #1

■

Seeing and Shaping the Sea Inside

In the Mindsight Tools sections we'll explore practical ways you can strengthen your mind, make your brain more flexible and resilient, and improve your relationships. As we've seen in Part I, the changes during adolescence are not something to just get through; they are qualities we actually need to hold on to in order to live a full and meaningful life in adulthood. The practices we'll dive into will strengthen these essential qualities of living well throughout our lives.

In this first practice entry, we'll focus on what I refer to as "mindsight." Mindsight is the ability to truly "see" or know the mind. It's a word I created years ago in medical school when I found that many of my professors lacked this ability— or at least didn't exercise it well with their patients, or their students. I needed some word to remind me that seeing the mind, being empathic, compassionate, and kind, were important in all relationships, especially the one between a physician and a patient. It turns out that the greater our ability to understand the workings of our minds, the healthier our internal worlds become. This is because when we focus our attention on the mind, it's possible to build specific circuits in our brains. The mind is truly "plastic"—changeable through experience— and it is possible at any age to move it toward greater health and harmony.

Mindsight includes three fundamental skills.

The first is *insight*, the ability to sense your own inner mental life. Insight lets you know who you are now, who you've been in the past, and who you'd like to be in the near future. Insight connects past, present, and future and so it includes a mental time-travel ability that can give you a full and clear sense of who you are.

The second aspect of mindsight is *empathy*, or the ability to sense the inner mental life of another person. Empathy enables us to "see" from the other person's perspective, and to imagine what it's like to walk in their mental shoes. Empathy is a gateway to compassion and kindness, and it is also a key to social intelligence, as it allows us to understand others' intentions and needs so we can interact in a mutually satisfying way.

The third component of mindsight is *integration*, the ability to link different parts of something into an interconnected whole. Integration enables us to make our relationships rewarding as we honor differences and promote compassionate connections in how we communicate. Integration inside ourselves helps us link the different aspects of memory together connecting our past, present, and future in a coherent way so that we have a life story that makes sense of who we are. Integration also helps us link different aspects of the brain and body so that we are healthy and function well. Integration creates coordination and balance in our inner and interpersonal worlds. Integration is the basis for living a healthy life, and so the skill of mindsight with its insight, empathy, and integration enables us to create health in our bodies, our relationships, and our minds.

The highest region of the brain, the cortex, makes "maps" or patterns of firing neurons—the basic cells of the nervous system—that create an image or representation of various things. The back of the cortex makes maps of what we see, and the side areas make maps of what we hear. In the frontal area we make many kinds of maps, including a map of past events and a map of possible future experiences. The most forward part of this frontal area, the prefrontal cortex, makes a map of the mind itself. This is how we sense and imagine another person's feelings, thoughts, and memories, among the many aspects of our mental life. I call these "mindsight maps" because they enable us to perceive that others have a mind just as we do. When we sense the mind of another person, we are making a map in our brains of what we imagine that person's internal mental experience is at that moment. It is this ability to make maps of one's mind and of the minds of others that I refer to as mindsight, an important skill that powerfully changes how we understand ourselves. Mindsight is the key ability at the core of both emotional and social intelligence. And mindsight is something that we can learn, and learn well, to make our lives stronger.

Every person has feelings and thoughts and memories. But having mindsight empowers us to have a picture, a map of the mind so that we can use those feelings, thoughts, and memories in new and helpful ways. For example, mindsight enables us to go beyond "being sad" or "being angry" and to recognize that we have these feelings of sadness or anger, see that they are not the totality of who we are, accept them for what they are, and then allow them to transform so they do not lead to depression or anger and rage.

A mindsight map is a kind of picture inside ourselves of our inner mental life—the feelings and thoughts and perspectives—of others, or of ourselves.

Three Basic Kinds of Mindsight Maps

We have mindsight maps of *me* for insight, sometimes called self-awareness or self-knowing awareness. We have mindsight maps of *you* for empathy or other-knowing. We even have a mindsight map of *we* for the way we think, imagine, reason, and behave knowing we are a part of a larger whole, a part of a "we." This mindsight map of we enables us to live with morality as we consider the larger social good. Insight, empathy, and morality emerge from mindsight mapping in our brains.

As teens we can make these maps in new and evolving ways. The more we grow our ability to make these mindsight maps of me, you, and we, the freer, fuller, and more flexible our lives will be. An important aspect of our journey during adolescence is developing a more intricate way of understanding ourselves and others.

Mindsight is a skill. But we don't need to go to a training camp to start building this important integrative ability in our lives. We can simply start the regular practice of reflection and reflective conversations that we'll explore throughout the mindsight tools sections. One of the most exciting things to remember as we set out to learn these skills is that science suggests that such training of a skill grows connections among our neurons that help create a more integrated set of circuits in the brain. And these integrated circuits support how we balance our emotions, focus our attention, understand others and ourselves, approach problems, and interact with others. This is why integration is so helpful to create. Mindsight skills build integration in your brain.

As we've seen, learning mindsight skills means three things. One is seeing the mind of oneself for insight. The second is seeing the minds of others for empathy. And the third means moving our own minds and those of others toward integration. That's mindsight in a nutshell.

Seeing Inside the Sea Inside

When we reflect on things going on inside us, in our inner subjective mental life, we develop the mindsight mapmaking circuits of the brain. That's right. As we practice mindsight skills, we activate those prefrontal circuits and help them grow stronger. Since this region in the brain helps coordinate and balance our inner and interpersonal life, developing mindsight skills can help you understand what is going on and help you make what is going on work best.

But how does what we do with our mind's awareness, how we become conscious of our own subjective mental life and then make mindsight maps of our sea inside, change the physical structure of our brains? This happens because of a process called neuroplasticity, the way the brain changes its connections in response to experience. And experience here means how you focus your attention. When we pay attention to our inner mental life, we grow those important fibers that help us understand ourselves and others. That's what mindsight maps can do for us. They help illuminate the sea inside ourselves and others.

But what is this inner mental sea?

This rich inner world includes your feelings, thoughts, perceptions, memories, images, and sensations, as well as your intentions, attitudes, beliefs, hopes, dreams, and desires. Even though that's a long list of inner mental processes, you can imagine that there are even more things in our inner mental sea that we can be aware of, like motivations and longings and impulses.

These mental activities, the content of our mental life, can occur even without our being aware of them. But when we pay attention to these inner experiences, when we place them in awareness, something very important happens. When our mental lives become something we are aware of, we can develop the mindsight ability to sense this sea inside and to transform our inner life in a positive direction.

How can mindsight actually change our mental lives? To learn how this can happen and to learn how to make it happen for us, we need to ask a basic question about what the mind is. If this is a topic that is of special interest to you, please read an in-depth exploration of the mind in my *Pocket Guide to Interpersonal Neurobiology*, in which I discuss in great detail what we'll discuss in practical ways here. If you'd like to explore how these skills can be used to face various challenges across the life span, please see the range of examples illustrating this approach in my book *Mindsight*.

What is the mind? There is no single answer to this question. And many science fields actually have no answer to this simple but challenging query. Odd as that might seem, it's true. Here we'll explore the practical applications of what I think the mind is in ways that I hope will empower your life.

While the term "mind" is often used to mean our inner, subjective experience of life and the process of being aware or conscious, the mind also regulates the flow of energy and information. The mind regulates how energy moves both within us (embodied energy) and between us and others (relational energy). And since regulation entails both monitoring and modifying, the mind tracks and changes how that energy and information flow over time. A representation or map shows the pattern of energy regarding a specific image, memory, or thought in what is called information flow.

Recognizing the mind's role in regulating energy and information allows us to learn to direct their flow in a positive way. In order to move in a healthy direction, we must engage our minds in integration—linking different aspects of our inner and interpersonal worlds into a more harmonious and functional whole.

It is important to note that (1) the mind affects not just your internal processes, but your relationships with others as well, and (2) the mind is a regulatory process that is self-organizing in that it enables us to sense and then shape how energy flows within us and with others. This is how mental activities are formed.

What are mental activities, really? What do they all have in common?

Mental activities like feelings and thoughts can be described as patterns of energy and information that flow inside us. Energy comes in many forms, like light that enables us to see these words or the sound energy that we use to hear them. In the brain, ions flowing in and out of the membranes of its basic cells, the neurons, lead to the release of chemicals that allow these neurons to communicate with one another. That's electrochemical energy. At its most basic level, whatever its form, energy is the capacity to do stuff.

Certain energy patterns have information in them. When patterns of energy contain information, it indicates that the pattern means something beyond just the sensation of the energy itself. When I write "Golden Gate Bridge," that energy of the light of the letters or of the sound waves for hearing the words is not the bridge over the San Francisco Bay. Words are carried on energy patterns, yes, but they are patterns that contain information. Information is when energy flow represents something—it re-presents it to us. And this movement across time, this flow that we are saying is an aspect of the mind, is all about energy and information and how it changes across time.

Insight enables us to sense this flow of energy and information inside ourselves. How do we see this inner world? We begin with sensing energy and information flow by directing our attention inward. Attention, by the way, is defined as how we direct the flow of information. So consciously paying attention to our inner mental life means focusing the information of our minds into awareness. With awareness, we can learn to navigate our internal worlds, to see clearly and to move easily within the sea inside. This is how mindsight empowers us to develop more inner understanding and inner strength.

MINDSIGHT PRACTICE A: Insight and SIFTing the Mind

Right now, try closing your eyes and simply ask yourself, what am I *sensing* right now in my body? You may feel tension in your muscles or you may sense your heart beating, your lungs breathing, or simply a wash of sensations from the body as a whole.

What *images* come up in my mind's eye? Images may take many forms, including the familiar visual ones. But you can also have images of sounds and touch, an image of a time of your life or some hope for the future. Images may be hard to put into words, but don't worry about that—simply being aware of these inner mental experiences is what matters now.

And what *feelings* are inside me? Emotions can involve bodily sensations, yes, but they also link our bodies to our thoughts, to our memories, and to our perceptions. Becoming aware of your emotional feelings can fill you with a wash of energy that may be challenging to name, which is fine. Just becoming aware of your emotional state is a great starting place.

And now, what *thoughts* are streaming through my consciousness? It's funny, but no one really knows exactly what a thought or thinking really is! So don't worry if it's hard to define what you mean when you say you are thinking this or that. Some experience an inner voice that they can hear, others just a sense that has no words. It is fine however thoughts emerge; you just need to let yourself be aware of whatever comes up for you right now.

This is the basic way we can SIFT our sea inside to see what is going on. When we SIFT through our minds, we check inwardly on the *s*ensations, *i*mages, *f*eelings, and *t*houghts going on inside ourselves at any given moment. "Sift" is an apt term to describe the process, of course, because all of the many sensations, images, feelings, and thoughts that may come up in awareness are often connected to one another in a free-flowing process.

We don't need to worry about putting words to these inner experiences; simply becoming aware of our internal world is the essential component for this SIFTing practice. As we become more familiar with it, we can try journaling as a means for further exploration.

Physical Sight of the Material World Versus Mindsight of the Inner World

The way we interact in the world can be divided between two views of reality, one a view of the mind we call mindsight, another view into the physical nature of the world of objects.

Modern life often depends more on physical sight rather than on honoring the mental inner view. This lack of focus on the inner subjective world is a concern because not seeing the mind can lead to people treating others without respect or compassion. Since the experiences we have shape who we are, at home with family or friends, at school with teachers and peers, and in our interactions with the larger social world of culture and society, how we attend to those experiences can promote mindsight or discourage it. So if most of these experiences are externally focused, harnessing only our physical-object perceptual system, then we won't be developing our skills to see and shape the personal world of our inner and our interpersonal life.

When we close one eye, we can see the world in only two dimensions. Then, with both eyes open, we can see in binocular vision with the three dimensions that surround us. That shift in perception from 2-D to 3-D is a subtle analogy for how we move from object vision to mind vision. When we have mindsight, we see the mind within our human lives in its full dimensions. Without it, our perception is limited to the surface level of object-filled physical spaces that surround us, and we do not see the sea inside.

I once began working with someone who was in his early nineties, someone I'll call Stuart, who, sadly, lacked much mindsight ability. He lived mostly in a flat, physically defined reality. Stuart was not prepared to face some of the many challenges and changes in his life at that age, including his emerging illnesses and those of his wife of sixty-five years. As he has learned mindsight skills, his life has gotten fuller and freer and is now imbued with a deep sense of gratitude and joy.

How could Stuart learn a new skill? By focusing his attention, he could stimulate the activity of his brain in new ways.

And when the brain gets activated, it can change the connections among neurons in a helpful way. Focusing the mind can change the structure of the brain no matter our age.

As we move through life, the brain can be the driver in charge of which direction we take. For Stuart, that meant living in a flattened world he had grown accustomed to. His brain called the shots. Our brains can create automatic behaviors, automatic thinking, and automatic responding. The brain can run the show, for sure. But our minds can get our brains to fire and grow in new ways that we choose. That sounds pretty wild, but it is true. Science has clearly shown that how we focus our attention will grow our brains in specific ways. Amazingly, when we learn to see inside the sea inside with more depth, we can use the mind to change the brain toward a more integrated function and structure. Integration in the brain is what creates health and flexibility in our lives.

This is the key to mindsight's power. We can learn the skills that can place us in the driver's seat of our life's journey. We can do that by understanding the brain, as we'll see in Part II, and by learning how to use communication with others in a more effective way, as we'll see in Part III. And we can learn the skills of seeing the mind more clearly so that we might shape it in a way we choose that can change the brain's firing and even the physical connections that make up its wiring. That's what we'll be doing in all of these mindsight-building practice entries.

If we spend a lot of time learning a musical instrument, that encourages those activated parts of our brains to grow. If we spend a lot of time focusing our attention on a sport, the regions of the brain involved in that athletic activity will grow.

And likewise, the kinds of social media and video games we engage in on the Internet will shape our brains as well. The good news is that with balance, our brains can learn many skills, not just one. The key is to find things we love and develop those passions in our lives. Taking some time each day to see inside the sea inside will help us develop our mindsight circuits.

MINDSIGHT PRACTICE B: Mindsight Illuminated

Look around where you are now and locate an inanimate object, like a chair or a rock. If you are outside, see if you can notice something moving, like a cloud or a stream. Now try watching people walking down the street or in a television program or in a photograph, and imagine them only as objects moving through space, objects without an internal mental life. This is your physical sight that allows you to notice the surface features of objects. Now turn on your mindsight and look at those same people and imagine what they might be experiencing in their minds.

The energy we receive from those same images of the people can be processed inside us in two ways. We can see them as just images of objects—that's our physical perceptual system that makes a map of the physical world in time and in space. And we can turn on the mindsight perceptual system that enables us to map the mind of the other person. This is how we can "see" or sense the inner mental life of another person.

If you've never done much mindsight looking around, this may be new for you, so please be patient with yourself. If you've already learned a bit of this, there are always new skills you can develop as we go. And if you've spent a lot of time sensing the mind, then this will be a great review and strengthening of your skills.

Empathy

When we use our ability to make mindsight maps of ourselves, we call this insight. And when we use this same ability to sense and respect the inner mental life of someone else, to make a mindsight map of another person, that can be called compassionate understanding or simply empathy. The way we cultivate empathy can make the difference between a relationship that is rewarding for both people and one that is frustrating and unfulfilling.

But what exactly is a relationship?

When you speak with a friend, you are sending energy in the form of air molecules moving from you to your friend. Her eardrum picks up that energy and the nerve in her ear translates that energy of air molecules moving into electrochemical energy that streams now into the brain itself. The patterns of that energy flow contain within them information that stands for the sounds you are sending, the words that have meanings attached to them. Because you speak the same language, your friend gets the information in the energy patterns you've sent. That energy and information flow shared between people is really how we communicate with each other.

So a relationship can be defined as the *sharing* of energy and information flow.

When that sharing includes information about the mind itself, when you are interested in what is going on within the sea inside your friend, you are *attuning* to her inner life. That attunement is how you create a mindsight map of her inside you. And that is the essential aspect of empathy.

Instead of simply responding to the physical things someone does in their behavior, mindsight enables you to map out the inner mental life of your friend revealed by their physically sent signals, by their communication. Mindsight enables you to sense the mind that is creating the behavior.

You may have noticed that there are three elements to relational communication. One is sensing what is going on between you and another person. A second is being in touch with what is going on inside you, or insight. The other is what is going on inside another person, or empathy. For the "between" sense of your relationship, you can feel how communication is happening between you and another person. This means that signals being sent match what is being received. Does someone hear what you are really saying? Is he paying attention to you or is he distracted? Is he trying to make sense of what you say? And is this friend making an inner map of who you are and of your mind, not just what your behavior is. When we feel that another person feels our feelings, that can be called "feeling felt." This feeling is one of the most important aspects of a close and supportive relationship.

On the empathy side of relationships, we can map out those internal mental experiences we imagine are going on from what we are receiving as signals from other people. These signals include what they say with words and what non-verbal signals are being communicated. These non-verbal signals include eye contact, facial expressions, tone of voice, posture, gestures and touch, and timing and intensity of responses. Such nonverbal signals are often a direct clue as to what is happening in the mind before and beneath the world of words. Paying close attention to these signals can be a key to making mindsight maps of another's mind.

MINDSIGHT PRACTICE C: Empathy

Focusing on non-verbal signals can give us a feeling inside that may be difficult to describe with words, but it is an important way of turning on our mindsight circuits. A fun practice is to try turning off the sound on a television show or film and seeing if you can soak in the feelings being conveyed by the non-verbal signals on the screen. Try a foreign film in a language you don't understand, without subtitles, and leave the sound on so you can also take in the tone of voice of the characters in the story. Just let your mind SIFT the imagined world of the character, exploring in your own mindsight mapmaking view what the sensations, images, feelings, and thoughts might be of the characters in each scene. Don't worry about how accurate you are. Just inviting yourself to imagine the mind of another person activates those prefrontal regions in your brain that will become strengthened by such a perspective-taking practice as you try to see through the mental lens of another person.

Integration

Mindsight is not only the ability to sense the internal sea of others with empathy or of ourselves with insight; mindsight also cultivates integration, a skill that empowers us to coordinate and balance the internal world of others or of ourselves, and the relationships we have with one another.

What does integration really mean, and why does it cultivate clarity from confusion, calm from chaos?

Integration is the linkage of different parts of something. When we integrate within a relationship, for example, we honor differences between ourselves and the other person. Then we promote linkage through compassionate understanding and communication. In the brain, integration happens when we honor the differences between our higher and lower regions and then link them, or between our left and right sides, and then link them.

When we are integrated, a system such as a relationship or a nervous system with its brain and whole body moves into a flexible and harmonious flow. Integration creates harmony. Integration is created as parts of a system are allowed to be unique and specialized, like you and me in a relationship or like members of a choir singing in harmony. The differentiated parts retain their unique aspects and they also become linked. The left and right sides of the brain work in a coordinated and balanced manner, and the communication between you and me honors differences and promotes compassionate connection so our relationship flourishes.

If either differentiation or linkage does not occur, then something very specific happens. When integration is blocked, a system moves toward one or both of two possible extremes: chaos on the one hand, and rigidity on the other.

I think of this like a river. The central flow is one of integration and the harmony it creates. One bank outside this central harmonious flow is chaos; the other is the bank of rigidity. When things are chaotic, they are out of control, wild, overwhelming, completely unpredictable. And when things are rigid, they are stuck, unchanging, boring, and completely

The River of Integration

The river of integration represents the movement of a system across time. When the system is integrated, it is adaptive and harmonious in its functioning. When linkage of the differentiated elements (integration) does not occur, the system moves to rigidity or chaos, or some combination of both. From Daniel J. Siegel, M.D., *Mindsight: The New Science of Personal Transformation*, copyright © 2010 by Mind Your Brain, Inc. Adapted with permission.

predictable. Life has a natural movement toward, rather than getting stuck on, the banks of chaos and rigidity as we wind our way down the river of life, the river of integration.

You may be asking, "Where does this integration take place?" And you may be wondering what exactly is being integrated.

Great questions. Integration takes place inside you and between you and others. This is where the mind is—within us and between us. The mind is both embodied and it is relational. So what is being integrated? The core elements of the mind as we've been defining it: energy and information.

The process of mindsight has insight in which we look inward and honor our differentiated experiences and link them within awareness. Mindsight includes empathy with which we honor our differences with others and make maps of our minds within our own differentiated self. That's linking differentiated parts within an empathic relationship. And so we can see how insight and empathy naturally support the third fundamental power of mindsight to promote integration. Where? Within and between.

Now here's another amazing finding. People who use their minds to reflect on the inner nature of their mental lives grow circuits in the brain that link widely separated areas to one another. This linkage, called "neural integration," creates the coordination and balance of the nervous system. Another term that some researchers often use for this is "self-regulation." In the nervous system, regulation is created through neural integration. And not only can people who develop the skill of mindsight promote self-understanding and empathy, they create integration and regulation within themselves, within their relationships, and within others.

If we actively use our attention to explore the inner world, we can begin to see how mindsight can have positive effects that help make life, especially during adolescence, a more positive experience.

As we'll see in the next part, adolescent brain growth is all about increasing levels of neural integration. So with these practices that cultivate mindsight, we'll actually be creating more integration in our own brains and in those of others!

When we learn to use mindsight skills, we learn to focus our attention in a way that grows the important fibers in the brain that link widely differentiated areas to one another. You may see this repeating idea here: Mindsight is a way of focusing attention that integrates the brain! And that's why learning mindsight skills is such an empowering thing for us to do at any age.

MINDSIGHT PRACTICE D:

Sensing the Harmony of Integration

For this practice, you'll be learning to detect various states of integration. When a relationship you have with another person, or even with yourself on a given day, is working well, can you sense the feeling of connection you have? Try to observe how a state of harmony has the qualities of being flexible, adaptive, connected, energized, and stable. If you are considering your connection with another person, see if you can sense how your differences are being honored and compassionate communication is being cultivated between you. If you are focusing on your own inner life, then see if at this harmonious time you've enabled different aspects of yourself to be respected and then linked by how you've given time for the various needs you may have. For example, in my own life, I, like many people, have different states of mind, different "parts" of myself that have different needs. One part likes being social while another distinct part really loves and needs solitude. What can I do? It is literally impossible to satisfy my differentiated needs all at the same time. So the solution to create harmony in my life is to set out time during the day when each of the conflicting needs can be met separately. That coordination and balance of my various needs create a deep sense of being *f*lexible, *a*daptive, *c*onnected, *e*nergized, and *s*table inside me. If a part of you likes acronyms as much as I do, you might enjoy noticing that this collection of words can spell FACES. And it is this FACES flow that describes an integrated harmonious state.

When Integration Is Not Present: Chaos or Rigidity

Mindsight enables us to not only detect integration and harmony but also feel when integration is not occurring. We each can have moments of losing our temper; of saying things we shouldn't say, of reacting in a negative and sometimes hurtful way. We are all human. The key to living an integrated life is to embrace the human reality of these moments of impaired integration and make a repair, to take responsibility for what we've done, acknowledge those actions, and move toward a more integrated way of being back on a high road and repair the connection to others and to ourselves. When we realize, as do many people in workshops I teach, or patients I treat, or friends I know, that feeling disconnected feels bad and making a reconnection feels good, these feelings let us know the inner sense of harmony that emerges with integration. When your system—which is your body and its brain, *and* it is your relationships—honors differences and promotes linkages, when it creates integration within us and between us, that is the harmony of integration. And that feels good.

When the energy and information flow that is in chaos or rigidity in this non–integrated state are not brought into balance, our inner and interpersonal worlds are not very pleasant, to say the least. Inwardly we can feel like we've lost our minds. Interpersonally we can feel out of control and terrify not only others but ourselves as well. These abrupt emotional explosions are when we've "flipped our lids" or "gone down the low road." The actions that can happen down the low road are not necessarily "the real person revealed," as some people argue. They are the older areas of the brain, our primitive mammalian circuits and old reptilian brains, as we'll see in Part II, that are now acting without the oversight of the prefrontal region.

For some people, the time between a triggering event and the low road can be short. Those people need to work to identify the internal cues that reveal the low road process is starting. For others, the time between is longer, but the awareness that a process is unfolding, leading to the impairment of the prefrontal cortex and flipping our lids, is just not accessible. In retrospect, the trigger can be understood but not as it is happening.

MINDSIGHT PRACTICE E: Name It to Tame It

Repair of disintegrated low-road states starts with the self-reflection of mindsight. What was the trigger? What is the meaning of that hot button issue for you? What were the signs that let you know something was being triggered in you? Once down the low road, did you take a break and if possible leave the scene? Could you feel your way to lowering your nervous system's chaotic flooding or rigid shutting down? Drinking a glass of water, stretching, getting some fresh air, moving around the room are all ways of changing your present state of agitation or withdrawal.

Of course if you are the recipient of such low-road states,

in that moment there may be little you can do except to re-move yourself from a situation. Out of the heat of the moment, it may be extremely useful to name this process "low road" or "flipping out." These are reactive states, far from the receptive state we need to truly connect with others. And so, even stat-ing that "I am reactive now, I need a short break" is better than simply exploding.

In the brain, naming an emotion can help calm it. Here is where finding words to label an internal experience be-comes really helpful. We can call this "Name it to tame it." And sometimes these low-road states can go beyond being un-pleasant and confusing—they can even make life feel terrify-ing. If that is going on, talk about it. Sharing your experience with others can often make even terrifying moments under-stood and not traumatizing. Your inner sea and your interper-sonal relationships will all benefit from naming what is going on and bringing more integration into your life.

MINDSIGHT PRACTICE F:
Detecting Chaos or Rigidity and Balancing the Mind

Try to recall a time when your life became filled with chaos or rigidity. This may have been within some interaction with an-other person in which you felt the chaos of being flooded with an emotion, like anger or sadness or fear. Or it may have been a time of rigidity, in which some repeating thought kept at you without changing, or you felt yourself withdrawing from interactions with others. If this memory is about a specific in-cident, can you detect any triggering event that may have been a part of a non-integrated experience? Was differentiation not occurring, such as someone was insisting on things being done their way and not respecting your viewpoint? Or was linkage absent, such as being ignored, misunderstood, or excluded? Notice how such blockages to integration put you in a period of chaos or rigidity.

If such a time was more extended, try to sense what might have been going on in your life then, when you may have been in a rigid, unchanging state of feeling bored or down in the dumps. Or chaos may have been your extended state, flooding you with emotions or thoughts or images or memories out of your control. Try to sense how some fundamental integration may have been missing at that time of your life and how you tried to pull yourself out of those uncomfortable states.

The key to this practice is to first detect chaos or rigidity. Next you can explore what aspect of your life may have been non-integrated in that it was not enabling differentiation or linkage to occur. One simple practice to try when you feel distressed by the memory of this chaotic or rigid time is to do the following physical positioning of your hands. When the memory of some chaotic or rigid time is in the front of your mind, try placing one hand on your chest—over your heart region—and one over your abdomen. Place a small amount of pressure from each hand and see how you feel. Now try moving the hand on your chest to the belly, and the other hand now up to your chest. Apply some gentle pressure and simply notice how you feel. Now place your hands in the positions that felt the best. What do you notice? Did you feel a calming sensation? Could you tell the difference between left on top or right on top?

I've offered this practice to many people in workshops with some fascinating results. For reasons we don't yet understand, this positioning of the hands on the body is calming for the majority of individuals who try it. And about three-quarters of people prefer the right hand over the chest, one-quarter the left hand. This preference seems to be independent of whether the person is right- or left-handed. I did a small study of one subject, showing that for me this movement (I'm a left-on-top person) created more integration, more coordination and balance, in my nervous system as assessed by some physiological monitoring of my heart. One possibility suggested by this single-person "study" is that the prefrontal region is activated to balance the brakes and accelerator of our bodies—the parasympathetic and sympathetic branches of the autonomic nervous system—and then soothes the heart and creates the state of calm in our minds, as we'll see more in Part II. Though we don't yet know exactly how or why this practice works, for so many it is helpful to bring calming within, and so I invite you to use this whenever your inner world becomes stuck on those banks of chaos or rigidity outside the flow of integrative harmony.

In Part II we'll dive into the brain's functions and how we can understand how to promote integration to achieve these balanced states. Then, in Part III, we'll explore how our attachment relationships may have shaped integration during our development so that we can become familiar with ways to make more harmony out of chaos and rigidity in our lives now.

Mindsight Strengthens the Mind, the Brain, and Our Relationships

As we move through these various practice entries, we'll be building the skills of mindsight to support the development of insight, empathy, and integration in our lives. Since the mind is both within us and between us and others—it is embodied and it is relational—then we can see how knowing about our body's brain and knowing about our relationships are both fundamental to strengthening our minds. In the pages that follow, we'll find important concepts that can help bring integration into our inner lives and our interpersonal lives. That's using mindsight to create a strong life for ourselves from the inside out.

PART II

■

Your Brain

A seventeen-year-old senior in high school, Katey looked terrified as her stomach was being pumped in the local hospital emergency room after a night of heavy drinking. She was writhing in pain from the emetic-induced vomiting, and still drunk from the seven shots of tequila and four glasses of wine she had consumed at an end-of-summer gathering that evening. At least that was her parents' version of what had occurred based on what Katey's friends had told them. For her part, Katey couldn't remember much of what had occurred that evening.

As it turns out, Katey brought the hard liquor to the party, shared it with her classmates, and even coaxed the host of the event—the daughter of the director of their school—into the drinking spree.

Katey was expelled from school the following week, which was the week she came in for her first therapy session. In speaking more with her about what happened, I learned that she had planned to "have fun" at the party even though it was at the home of the director of her school.

Katey knew how "off" it all sounded.

"What were you thinking before that party?" I asked her. She looked sheepish, glancing away with the beginnings of a smile appearing on her face. "What did you think might happen after the party when the school rules state that there is 'zero tolerance' for alcohol at school-related functions?" Katey looked at me, her eyes wide open and locked with mine, her half-smile widening, suggesting that perhaps her anxiety was increasing or that she was somewhat amused at the whole situation.

"Well . . ." she began, her smile now wide across her face. "I *did* think about it." She paused and looked around the room as if someone might be listening, and then she turned back to me. "I knew what might happen, I guess, but the *fun* of getting completely smashed at the director's own house just seemed like too much to turn down." Her eyes shone with a sparkle of delight.

The fact that Katey herself admitted that she had "planned" what would happen at the party even in the face of knowledge about the potential outcomes resonates in recent studies revealing that teenagers usually have awareness of the risks of potentially dangerous behaviors. As teens we are often not oblivious to the negative consequences of our actions. Instead, even though the negative consequences—the cons—are fully known, we place more emphasis on the potential positive aspects—the PROS—of an experience: the thrill, the shared experience, the fun, the excitement of breaking the rules. That emphasis on the positive, we now know, is a result of shifts in the brain's structure and function during the adolescent period.

Dopamine, Decisions, and the Drive for Reward

Katey's enhanced focus on the positive was in fact a natural consequence of the increased reward drive in the adolescent brain. The brain is a collection of cells that communicate with one another using chemicals called neurotransmitters. During adolescence there is an increase in the activity of the neural circuits utilizing dopamine, a neurotransmitter central in creating our drive for reward. Starting in early adolescence and peaking midway through, this enhanced dopamine release causes adolescents to gravitate toward thrilling experiences and exhilarating sensations. Research even suggests that the baseline level of dopamine is lower—but its release in response to experience is higher—which can explain why teens may report a feeling of being "bored" unless they are engaging in some stimulating and novel activities. This enhanced natural dopamine release can give adolescents a powerful sense of being alive when they are engaged in life. It can also lead them to focus solely on the positive rewards they are sure are in store for them, while failing to notice or give value to the potential risks and downsides.

The brain's increased drive for reward in adolescence manifests in teens' lives in three important ways. One is simply increased *impulsiveness*, where behaviors occur without thoughtful reflection. In other words, impulse inspires action without any pause. Pausing enables us to think about other options beyond the immediate dopamine-driven impulse pounding on our minds. Telling that impulse to chill out takes time and energy, so it's easier just not to do it. This said, with the drive for reward stronger and more pressing than ever when we are teens, taking the time needed for processing—for reflection and self-awareness—becomes very important. If any notion turns immediately into an action without reflection, we are living our lives all gas pedal and no brakes. This can be very stressful for adolescents and the adults who care for them.

The good news is that such impulses can be put on hold if certain fibers in the higher part of the brain work to create a mental space between impulse and action. It is during the time of adolescence that these regulatory fibers begin to grow to counteract the revved-up "go" of the dopamine reward system. The result is a decrease in impulsivity. This is sometimes called "cognitive control" and is one important source of diminished danger and reduced risks as adolescents develop. As we'll see shortly, there are ways to enhance the growth of those regulatory fibers that create a pause, and they can be developed at any age.

A second way in which increased dopamine release affects us during adolescence is the documented increase in our susceptibility to addiction. All behaviors and substances that are addictive involve the release of dopamine. As teens not only are we more likely to experiment with new experiences, we are also more prone to respond with a robust dopamine release that for some can become part of an addictive cycle. A drug, alcohol for example, can lead to release of dopamine, and we may feel compelled to ingest beer or wine or hard liquor. When the alcohol wears off, our dopamine plummets. We then are driven to use more of the substance that spiked our dopamine circuits. Studies reveal that foods with a high glycemic index—those, like processed foods or even the simple carbohydrates of potatoes or bread, that lead to a rapid rise in blood sugar—can also lead to rapid rises in our dopamine levels and activity in the reward circuits of the brain. Sadly, in the United States such addiction to foods with high caloric but low nutritional value is thought to be responsible for the dangerous epidemic of obesity in adolescents, a medical crisis created and reinforced by our society's supplying us with just this type of addictive food. As with any addiction, we continue to engage in the behavior despite knowing its negative impacts on our health. That's the power of the dopamine reward centers.

A third type of behavior shaped by the increased reward drives of the adolescent brain is something called *hyperrationality*. This is how we think in literal, concrete terms. We examine just the facts of a situation and don't see the big picture; we miss the setting or context in which those facts occur. With such literal thinking, as adolescents we can place more weight on the calculated benefits of an action than on the potential risks of that action. Studies reveal that as teens we are often fully aware of risks, and even at times overestimate the chance of something bad happening; we simply put more weight on the exciting potential benefits of our actions.

What happens with hyperrational thinking is not a lack of thought or reflection as happens with impulsivity, and it's not a matter of merely being addicted to a particular behavior or something we are ingesting. Instead, this cognitive process comes from a brain calculation that places a lot of weight on the positive outcome and not much weight on possible negative results. By weight I mean that the evaluation centers of the brain downplay the significance of a negative outcome, while at the same time they amplify the significance given to a positive result. The scales that teens use to weigh out their options are biased in favor of the positive outcome. PROS far outweigh the cons, and quite simply, the risk seems worth it.

This positively biased scale can be activated especially when teens hang out with other teens or believe their friends will somehow observe their actions. The social and emotional context we experience as teens sets the stage for how our brains will process information. While that's true for any person whatever their age, the influence of peers is especially strong during adolescence.

In other words, in Katey's situation her brain focused on the rewarding images of the thrill, the core of sensation seeking, and she disregarded the potential negatives. The emotional meaning of her actions was woven together with her ability to plan and she hyperrationally calculated that this was a PRO thing to do. Katey's behavior was not impulsive—she planned her evening long ago in a hyperrational way.

As our teen years unfold, we move from the literal thinking of hyperrationality to the broader considerations called "gist thinking." With gist thinking, we consider the larger context of a decision and use intuition to aim for positive values we care about rather than focusing primarily on the immediate dopamine-driven reward.

So as you can see, it is not as simple as saying that teens are just impulsive. And it's also not as simple as saying, "Oh, raging hormones," as is sometimes stated. Research suggests that risky behaviors in adolescence have less to do with hormonal imbalances than with changes in our brain's dopamine reward system combined with the cortical architecture that supports hyperrational decision-making creating the positive bias that is dominant during the teen years.

When your dopamine circuitry is turned way up, it's like an amplifier with its gain turned up. Enhanced dopamine release drives us toward reward and satisfaction. The gain is turned up for how attention is drawn to the PROS, putting us at risk of deemphasizing the cons during these years.

Hyperrationality can be illustrated in the extreme example of Russian roulette, a game played with one bullet and six chambers of a pistol. You have five out of six chances to make the $6 million offered to you if you win. That means, overall, if hundreds of people play this game, then the average you are most likely to get, statistically winning five out of six times, is five-sixths of $6 million, which is $5 million overall. Let's go for it! The problem is, of course, if you are the one in six, you are dead. And for that one person in six, it is a hundred percent certain that life is over. You can see the challenge. It is true that "most likely" you'll get millions of dollars. If your brain circuits focus on that positive outcome, the PROS, and minimize the smaller chance of the risk, the cons, you'll take part in the activity. "Why not?" Yes, that seems like math gone mad. But to *not* jump into this probability assessment, the trap of "What is most likely to happen so I'll do it," requires a gut feeling, the intuition that is the basis of gist thinking, that lifts you out of hyperrational calculations. With development and the growth of the brain, a gut feeling rises and we get a feeling that the Russian roulette game makes no sense.

Paradoxically, intuition plays a very important role in making good decisions. This is because our intuitions, or gut feelings and heartfelt sensations, tend to focus on positive values, like the benefit of staying in school or driving at the speed limit or keeping fit. Many teens can be too rational, and need to incorporate the non-rational input of their intuitive gut feelings and heartfelt sensations, feelings that enable them to focus on positive values versus mythical rewards that, in reality, are often just out of reach. Learning to experience life from this standpoint is not about inhibiting impulses like driving fast or eating junk food, but rather about embracing positive goals that intuitively mean something to us. Katey's behavior was not impulsive and it was not intuitive or gist-like. It was dopamine-driven and hyperrational. She needed to work on being more aware of what her intuitive gut and heart feelings could tell her about the potential downsides to reckless behavior.

Family, Friends, and Fooling Around

Another important factor that contributed to Katey's decision making is that she was quite preoccupied with how her friends would react if she pulled this escapade off, literally, under the school director's nose, and with his daughter, no less! Here we see another aspect of the teenage brain. On top of the emotional spark and drive for the reward of novelty, intense social engagement with peers is also part of the essence of adolescence. Unfortunately, risk behaviors often significantly increase in the company of peers, as demonstrated in experiments that have measured how teens do when driving on a simulated automobile program when alone and when with their friends.

My son's friend Benji, now in his mid-twenties, tells the story of when he lived in southern Spain with his family as a thirteen-year-old. A half-dozen boys of the same age were running around the cliffs near the beautiful coastal town where he was staying. One of the locals decided to jump the fifty feet or so off the edge of the cliff and into the sea. Then, one by one, the group dynamics lured each of them to jump. When Benji jumped, he may have been just a few feet over from where the others entered the water, he told me, or perhaps it was because none of the local boys had remembered to tell him, as apparently they knew, that he ought to bend his legs right after entering the water. Straight in he went, hurtling toward the bottom and hitting a rock beneath the surface, severely fracturing his right leg. Struggling to the surface with the shock of such a crushing injury, he was losing consciousness when he was rescued by two of the boys and carried a mile back to the town to be hospitalized for much of his remaining time in Spain that summer. If those boys were not there in the water, Benji would not have been telling me the story.

I asked Benji if he thought he would have jumped if he was on his own. "Are you out of your mind?" he said. "No way."

The collective process of being with our friends, or even imagining the impact on our friends, as in Katey's planning stage of her escapade, increases the drive toward reward, the drive toward novelty, and the drive to take risks, and these reduce the focus on weighing the potential risks. So with peers we are much more likely as teenagers to engage in behaviors that may work out most of the time, but if they don't, they may have serious, sometimes irreversible, consequences. Benji's and Katey's behaviors were not impulsive. They both had plenty of time to see what was in the offing and change course. Their decisions were a combination of reward drive, peer process, and hyperrational, non-gist thinking. That's the nature of risky behaviors emerging from the teenage brain.

So the two broad ways that risky behavior emerges in adolescence are hyperrationality, the downplaying of the cons of an action, and impulsivity, or simply flying off the handle, as we'll discuss later. Katey did not, and generally does not, show a tendency to be impulsive. Neither does Benji. In Katey's case, this is what drove her parents mad when they picked her up. Katey is not impulsive, so why such a seemingly impulsive act?

Hyperrationality combined with an increase in her dopamine drive is the cause. And sometimes there are other things at play, such as the dopamine-dependent onset of addiction, that are not limited to being an adolescent but may also be influencing such behaviors, as we'll discuss for Katey and adolescents in general regarding drug use and abuse in Part IV.

The Purpose of Adolescence

In recent years, surprising discoveries from brain imaging studies have revealed changes in the structure and function of the brain during adolescence. As we've seen, interpretations of these studies lead to a very different story than the old raging-hormone view of the teenage brain. A commonly stated but not quite accurate view often presented by the media is that the brain's master control center, the prefrontal cortex, at the forward part of the frontal lobe, is simply not mature until the end of adolescence. This "immaturity" of the brain's prefrontal cortex "explains immature teenage behavior." And this notion also explains why rental car companies generally won't let someone younger than twenty-five take out a car. But this simple story, while easy to grasp, is not quite consistent with the research findings and misses an essential issue.

Instead of viewing the adolescent stage of brain development as merely a process of maturation, of leaving behind outmoded or nonuseful ways of thinking and transitioning to adult maturity, it is actually more accurate and more useful to see it as a vital and necessary part of our individual and our collective lives. Adolescence is not a stage to simply get over, it is a stage of life to cultivate well. This new and important take-home message, inspired by the emerging sciences, suggests that the changes that occur in the adolescent brain are not merely about "maturity" versus "immaturity," but rather are vitally important developmental changes that enable certain new abilities to emerge. These new abilities, as we've discussed, are crucial for both the individual and our species.

Why should this matter to us, whether we are teens, in our twenties, or older? It matters because if we see the adolescent period as just a time to wade through, a time to endure, we'll miss out on taking very important steps to optimize the essence of adolescence. When we see our emotional spark, our social engagement, our novelty seeking, and our creative explorations as positive and necessary core aspects of who adolescents *are*—and who they might become as adults if they can cultivate these qualities well—this period becomes a time of great importance that should be not just survived but nurtured.

Yes, there are challenges in staying open to the "work" of adolescence. Important opportunities for expansion and development during this time can be associated with stress for teens and for the parents who love them. For example, the pushing away from family that adolescents tend to do can be seen as a necessary process enabling them to leave home. This courage to move out and away is created by the brain's reward circuits becoming increasingly active and inspiring teens to seek novelty even in the face of the unfamiliar as they move out into the world. After all, the familiar can be safe and predictable, while the unfamiliar can be unpredictable and filled with potential danger. One historical view for us as social mammals is that if older adolescents did not leave home and move away from local family members, our species would have too much chance of inbreeding and our genetics would suffer. And for our broader human story, adolescents' moving out and exploring the larger world allows our human family to be far more adaptive in the world as the generations unfold. Our individual and our collective lives depend on this adolescent push away.

Hard as it is for parents to worry about their teen's potentially risky behavior, the positive bias of hyperrational thinking helps adolescents take on risks that they'll *need* to embrace if they are to leave the nest and explore the world. As we've seen, the drive to have increased social connections can keep us safe as we associate with our adolescent peers who are also making the journey out into the unfamiliar world. Our increased sensitivity to our own heightened emotional states and to our peers' influence—our emotional spark and social engagement—are fundamental to this journey as well. Seeking out novelty and creating new ways of doing things also helps our species adapt to the ever-changing world. If the brain throughout the life span is indeed a "work in progress," as recent studies suggest, then the work that occurs during adolescence is so much more than simply a process of moving from immaturity to maturity. The essence of adolescence enriches our lifelong journey to embrace life fully.

What we are coming to see is that there is a crucial set of brain changes during our adolescence creating new powers, new possibilities, and new purposes fueling the adolescent mind and relationships that simply did not exist like this in childhood. These positive potentials are often hidden from view and yet they can be uncovered and used more effectively and more wisely when we know how to find them and how to cultivate them. We can learn to use cutting-edge science to make the most of the adolescent period of life. It's a pay-it-forward investment for everyone involved.

For the teen, the growth of the body itself, with alterations in physiology, hormones, sexual organs, and the architectural changes in the brain, also can contribute to our understanding of adolescence as an important period of transformation. Changing emotions revolutionize how we feel as teens inside, making more complex the ways of processing information and our ideas about the self and others, and even creating huge developmental shifts and transitions in the inner sense of who we are and who we can become. This is how a sense of identity shifts and evolves throughout adolescence.

From the inside, these changes can become overwhelming, and

we may even lose our way, and feel that life is just "too much" to navigate at times. From the outside, such changes may at times seem like we are lost and "out of control." Our adolescent years, a time of life filled with challenges that can strengthen who we are, can be challenging for sure. But the great news is that with increased self-awareness of our emotional and social lives, and with an increased understanding of the brain's structure and function, the powerful positive effects of the complex changes that occur during adolescence can be harnessed with the proper approach and understanding.

Making Decisions

Throughout adolescence, different areas of the brain link together, a process we've discussed called "integration." One outcome of integration is the growth of fibers of cognitive control that ultimately decrease impulsivity. As a result, adolescents are afforded more and more space in the mind to pause and consider other options of response than an initial impulse. Another outcome of this integrative growth is sharpened gist thinking, whereby the adolescent is able to rely more and more on intuition to see the larger picture of a situation and therefore make wiser decisions.

Let's see how a better focus on developing gist thinking in our earlier example of the car accident might have helped a teen make better decisions, decisions that could have saved a life. If the teen or his parents were able to acknowledge his longing for speed as a natural dopamine reward drive, then the urge could have been channeled in a constructive way. There are many options, including taking part in athletics where competition and speed and power are parts of the sport—racecar driving, running, bicycling, skiing—risky and adventurous activities that don't put innocent bystanders in harm's way. For example, when my son was in his early teens, we'd spend hours on the weekends racing long skateboards down closed multi-level parking garages at the university where I work. When we'd get to the bottom, we'd take the elevator back up and race down again. Having helmets on and wearing hard gloves to keep our skin from scraping on the concrete as we made those sharp turns helped minimize the damage to our bodies, most of which I seemed to get, not him. There's nothing wrong with the drive for thrills—the issue is how to harness those drives so as to minimize harm to oneself or others. The idea here is to respect the dopamine-driven need for speed or other risky activities, but then channel this drive in helpful ways. If we can instill awareness of the positive sides of these drives, and then find constructive approaches to addressing them, tragic outcomes like my teacher's death might be avoided. Not only might Bill still be alive, but the young man would not have the burden of living with the feeling of responsibility for that accident.

Sadly, instead of addressing a potentially dangerous problem with their son, his parents may have unintentionally rewarded his earlier risky behavior with a brand-new car. So why wouldn't he try something dangerous again? That's how risky behavior without a negative consequence can reinforce itself to happen again and again. Many of us know of other examples of reckless teen behavior that went unaddressed: driving a car without a license and losing the ability to drive later on, taking the chance of having unprotected sex and risking getting a disease or getting pregnant, trying combinations of street drugs without knowing their potentially lethal effects, or getting a tattoo from a disreputable source and risk getting hepatitis. There are even more minor risks, like not taking the time to sleep before an exam because you are talking with friends on the phone late into the night, or getting lost in social media and posting an insulting comment about someone's looks or a drunk party photo of yourself that a college admissions officer later sees. In all these situations the teen is seeing the PROS and de-emphasizing the risks. That's the positive bias of the adolescent mind.

Honoring the important and necessary changes in the adolescent mind and brain rather than disrespecting them is crucial for both teens and their parents. When we embrace these needed changes, when we offer teens the support and guidance they need instead of just throwing up our hands and thinking we're dealing with an "immature brain that simply needs to grow up," or "raging hormones in need of taming," we enable adolescents to develop vital new capacities that they can use to lead happier and healthier lives.

Gist thinking emerges with both experience and programmed brain development. In other words, the timing of the development of the brain is shaped by both experience-induced neural activation and by genetic information. Experience shapes the connections in the brain itself even if it cannot affect the general timing of such maturation. And studies suggest that gist thinking emerges from the growth of integration in our brains as teens. The timing may be in part genetically determined, but we can shape the degree of development of integration in our brains. Experience shapes our development during our adolescence and the rest of our lives. And experience can promote more integration in the brain, more connecting of its different parts so that they work in a coordinated manner. So how we set up our lives and the contexts we live in, what we do and whom we are with, can shape not only how the brain is activated but also how the brain will grow its integrative circuits. For these reasons, knowing the basics about the brain can be helpful in our lives because we can shape our brain's growth of integration in ways that are helpful for us now and for the future.

"Don't Do It" Doesn't Do It:
The Power of Promoting the Positive

Gist thinking draws on the gut feeling and heartfelt sense of a positive value, of aiming *for* something rather than inhibiting something. So instead of trying to shut down an impulse by inhibiting it, adults with adolescents in their lives and adolescents themselves should focus on a positive factor to promote. Choosing not to get a tattoo at an unknown place because you value your health is very different from saying, "I won't do it because my mother told me not to." In contrast, hyperrational thinking considers the impulse and senses the reward drive to realize the positive thrill, the sensation-seeking speed-driven adrenaline rush of getting a tattoo with some friends. And it doesn't hurt that you are also breaking your parents' rules.

Public health advocates' efforts to reduce teen smoking are powerful examples of how appealing to the adolescent's emerging strength in terms of gist thinking can help promote healthy behaviors. The adolescent period is, as we've seen, a time of great vulnerability to becoming addicted to various substances, including cigarettes. It's not just that teens smoke more, but also that the changing teen brain itself is open to becoming addicted in part because of its enhanced dopamine response. If people are going to smoke cigarettes, they most likely start during their teenage years. The same is true with drug addiction. The most effective strategy to get adolescents to avoid smoking was not offering teens medical information or trying to frighten them with images of graveyards, two strategies that did nothing to reduce teens' taking up smoking or continuing to smoke. The strategy that worked was to inform them about how the adults who owned the cigarette companies were brainwashing them to smoke so that they could get their money. Rather than getting teens to say no to smoking because some adult was frightening them into it, this strategy focused on the positive value of being strong in the face of manipulative adults out to get rich. When this embracing of how the adolescent mind worked was taken up by public health advocates, the rate of teen smoking dropped. Simply saying "Don't do it" wasn't enough. Aiming for a positive value, like not letting someone—especially an adult—brainwash you, worked.

Knowing about these understandable and genetically based changes in the teenage brain can help adults support the adolescent's need for pushing back on the adult status quo and the exploration of new possibilities. Encouraging the reflection on values and on gut instinct, not simply the inhibition of impulses, is the difference between turning down a compelling impulse and embracing a thoughtful belief and value.

Integrating Your Brain

In many ways, how we decide to do things in life reveals who we are at that moment. When we understand how the brain changes during our adolescence, we can understand how the decision-making process changes, too. The brain changes during this period in two dimensions. One is how it *reduces* the number of the brain's basic cells, the neurons, and their connections, the synapses. This decreasing of neurons and synapses is called "pruning" and appears to be genetically controlled, shaped by experience and intensified with stress. How can we tolerate losing some neurons? During childhood there is an overproduction of neurons and their synaptic connections. The blossoming of our neuronal populations begins in utero and extends to our prepubertal period, to about eleven years of age in girls and twelve and a half in boys. Some pruning begins early as we learn and develop skills, but the removal of our overall number of neurons and their connections reaches its peak during the robust remodeling period of adolescence. In adolescence we prune those excess connections away, leaving the ones we've been using and discarding the ones we don't seem to need anymore.

Experience shapes which neural circuits—the neurons and their synaptic connections—will be pruned away. So if you want to have a musical skill, best to start it early, before the end of adolescence. And if you want to be a gold-medal Olympic athlete, best to start in your field before adolescence begins. Even if you're not aiming for athletic prowess, it's simply important to remember that your brain will respond to how you focus your attention in your activities. Attention streams energy and information through specific circuits and activates them. The more you use a circuit, the stronger it gets. The less you use a circuit, the more likely it may get pruned away during adolescence.

How you focus your attention throughout life, and especially during the adolescent period, plays an important role in shaping the growth of your brain. Attention maintains and strengthens existing connections, and as we'll see, it helps grow new connections and make those connections more effective. Our mindsight tools sections are all about learning to focus your mind's attention to integrate your brain's connections.

A second way the brain transforms during this period is that it lays down "myelin," a sheath covering the membranes among interlinked neurons. This myelin sheath enables the passage of the electrical flow, the "neuronal activations" among the remaining linked neurons, to allow faster and more synchronized information to flow. When that flow is fast and coordinated, it makes for a more effective and efficient process. As we learn specific skills and acquire knowledge, we grow new connections and even new neurons. Once we've established these new synaptic linkages, we can lay down myelin to make that circuit quicker, more coordinated, and more effective.

These two fundamental changes—pruning and myelination—help the adolescent brain become more integrated. Integration, the linking of different parts, creates more coordination in the brain itself.

We develop gist thinking as this pruning and myelination creates integration in the brain.

These more precise and efficient connections in the brain make for wiser judgment and discernments based not on the small details that are without a larger context but on the overall gist that sees the big picture. We use our intuition to guide our decisions as we aim for positive values, honoring what matters to us. That is gist thinking, one of the many things that the growth of integration in the brain during our adolescent years creates.

As we'll see, the very specific forms of change in the architecture of the brain enable us as adolescents to start to use judgment based on gist thinking, which is informed by experience and intuition rather than reliant on the reward drive and the literal calculations of our earlier years.

Think of it this way: With those neural connections from childhood that were so numerous, lots of details filled our minds. That's what we needed as children soaking up facts and figures from school. With adolescence, we have an increased reward drive and increased emotional reactions and increased sensitivity to social engagements. This combination means that we'll have lots of details still filling our minds before pruning, and intense emotions and heightened concern about our acceptance by peers will drive either impulsive behavior or reward-driven hyperrational decision-making that is based mainly on literal calculations. The upside of this period of functioning is the positive bias we need to take the necessary risks to get ready to explore the world as adolescents. From a decision-making perspective, the process looks like this: Details without perspective from experience win the day as probabilities are assessed and the Russian roulette gun is fired. Chances are most likely that all will be fine. But sometimes it is not. Just think of some of the things you may have tried in your younger years, or what you are trying out now. When you think about those risks you took, you may even shake your head in disbelief that you actually did those things. If your gist thinking and intuitive wisdom are at work, you may reflect on those times and wonder what in the world you were thinking. Now you know.

We can see why parents can be very concerned about the adolescent tendency to seek thrills. The tripling in accidental injuries and mortality during this otherwise very healthy period is not just in a parent's imagination; it is a statistical fact. It may be hard for you as an adolescent to have empathy for what your parents are facing, but in the big picture this understanding may be helpful not just for them but for you, too. When you communicate with your parents about these statistical matters, and then deal with your individual needs and plans, everyone can feel heard and more effective ways of coming to a decision can be created.

We need to increase our communication about these issues, honoring the healthy and necessary essential aspects of our adolescent years and learning to channel this power in more helpful ways. Knowing about the specific circuits in the brain that create this more integrated way of functioning can help us envision a more constructive approach to how we live and make our decisions as adolescents and as adults.

A Handy Model of the Brain

The reason to know some basic details about the brain is simple. When we know something about the parts of our brains, we can learn to direct our attention in new ways that help those parts work in a more coordinated and balanced way. What we know about the brain can help us grow our brains in integrative ways. That's it. And that's pretty useful.

We will look into the brain not only because it is what is chang-

Handy Model of the Brain

The brain in the palm of the hand. This "handy model" depicts the major regions of the brain: cerebral cortex in the fingers, limbic area in the thumb, and brainstem in the palm. The spinal cord is represented in the wrist. From Daniel J. Siegel, M.D., *The Developing Mind: How Relationships and the Brain Interact to Shape Who We Are,* copyright © 2012 by Mind Your Brain, Inc. Adapted with permission.

ing in us as adolescents, but also because knowing about it can help us optimize the opportunities of adolescence. This understanding can help you think, feel, and behave in ways that help you get along better in your life, feel better, and be more the person you want to be. We won't need a plastic model or big poster of the brain for this exploration. We're about to get to know a very handy model of the brain, one you can take with you wherever you go.

If you fold your thumb into your palm, and then fold the fingers over your thumb, you'll have facing you a useful hand model of the brain. Give it a try right now and let's see how these parts fit together. In this model the area of your fingernails facing you is just behind the face—and the back of your hand is where the back of the brain at the back of your head would be.

The highest part of the brain, represented by your fingers, is just under your scalp within your skull. This is the *cortex* or outer bark of the brain. We think and reflect, perceive and remember, plan and make decisions with our cortex. Awareness comes, in part, from what happens in the cortex, and so self-awareness comes from this cortical region. If you lift your fingers, you'll see below them the thumb, which represents the emotion-generating *limbic area* of the brain. The limbic area is in charge of a lot of things, including what motivates us, how we focus our attention, and how we remember things. Lift the thumb, and you'll find in your palm the lowest and oldest area of the brain, the *brainstem*. This ancient region is involved in keeping us awake or letting us sleep. And it's the part of the brain that can interact with the thumb region above it, the limbic area, to create reactive states of being angry or scared. Since the brainstem and limbic areas are below the cortex, we call these the "subcortical regions." Lift your fingers and put them back over the thumb and palm and you'll see how the cortex literally sits on top of these two subcortical regions.

The brain itself sits atop the spinal cord, represented by your wrist. Input from this neural tube within the backbone, along with other neural inputs from the body and from the body's organs such as the heart and intestines, enables the processes of our organs, muscles, and bones to directly influence the neural firings in the skull itself, neural activity within the subcortical and cortical parts of the brain. Not represented here directly is the *cerebellum*, which would be just behind the limbic area and plays an important role in balancing the body's motions and also balancing the interaction of our thoughts and feelings. A band of neurons, called the *corpus callosum*, links the left and right sides of the brain to each other and coordinates and balances their activities.

This is a leftward-facing model of the right side of the brain. The brainstem and the cerebellum are part of the "hindbrain" and regulate basic processes like heart rate and states of alertness. Connecting the two sides of the brain is a band of tissue called the corpus callosum. The amygdala and hippocampus, which are part of the old mammalian region called the limbic area, form the "midbrain" and help with functions such as emotional balance and memory processes. The cortex, also known as the "forebrain," makes representations or images of things. The front-most part of the cortex is the prefrontal cortex, which coordinates and balances the functions of many areas by linking input from the cortex, limbic area, brainstem, body, and social interactions. The insula is a circuit that connects bodily processes to the prefrontal area for self-awareness. From Daniel J. Siegel, M.D., *The Developing Mind*, 2nd edition, copyright © 2012 by Mind Your Brain Inc.

The cortex helps us be conscious in our lives, to think clearly about things, to assess a situation and reason through it, to remember other events, and to pause and reflect on what is going on. Those are a lot of important functions, and it's why the cortex, especially the front part, is called the executive region. It is the master control center that coordinates and balances the whole brain and the body itself.

The forward part of the cortex, the frontal lobe, develops a lot during infancy and toddlerhood, and it continues to grow during the remainder of childhood. When our adolescence begins, even more dramatic changes in this frontal region occur. The reason this area is so important is that it participates in the linkage of different neural regions to one another. In this way, the cortex has an integrative role as it coordinates and balances much of what happens throughout the brain, and even in the nervous system throughout the body as a whole.

As we'll see, the frontal areas of the cortex also link our own neural firing to the activity of other nervous systems, to other brains within other people. In this way, the frontal area is involved in both the shaping of our own internal mental processes such as thinking and decision making as well as the social processes such as empathy and moral behavior. So when we speak about changes in the adolescent brain, we'll see that many of these important changes involve increasing levels of integration, especially carried out in the cortex. This increased cortical integration enables such diverse abilities as cognitive control, emotional regulation, gist thinking, self-understanding and social functions to change and emerge throughout adolescence.

One of the central hubs that link the nodes of our larger cognitive, emotional, and social networks of circuits into a functional whole is in the frontal region of the cortex. A network contains many different parts, or nodes, and a hub is the aspect of the network that links those different nodes to one another. A node in the nervous system, for example, might be collections of neurons in the limbic area or in the cortex. One important nervous system hub that links the nodes together is just behind the forehead. Because it is at the front of the frontal areas, it is called the prefrontal cortex. Notice how in your hand model this integrative prefrontal region, located at the ends of your fingers, your prefrontal-fingernail region, connects the cortex to the subcortical limbic-thumb and brainstem-palm regions. In addition, this prefrontal region links input from the body itself and from other people. Energy and information from the cortex, limbic area, brainstem, body, and social world are coordinated and balanced by the prefrontal region. It is this integrative role, connecting and coordinating many differentiated inputs, that makes the growth of the prefrontal cortex so central to our understanding of how we change and become more integrated as adolescents.

Adolescence as the Gateway to Creative Exploration

In a nutshell: The overall movement of the brain's development is to become more *integrated*. What that means is that areas will become more specialized and then interconnected to one another in more effective ways. That's what the pruning down of connections and the myelination of remaining connections create—the differentiation of specialized regions and then their coordinated linkage. The result of such a process is to have more efficient and specialized processing of information. This is consistent with our discussions of the gist-based thinking that sees through all the details to find the wisest judgment about a situation. What are the basic ways such a transformation of thinking can occur? What are the basic units of the brain's structure that support such reconstructive and integrative changes in adolescence?

As we've seen, both our genes and our experiences contribute to how synaptic connections will form and interconnect the various parts of the network into circuits. What this means is that the changes in the brain will be due in part to genetic information we've inherited and in part to experiences we engage in. Experience streams energy flow through particular neurons and strengthens their connections with one another. It is important to know about our neuronal connections because they shape how we feel, think, reason, and make decisions.

Because this pruning and myelination restructures the brain's networks of connections, it is often called "remodeling." The remodeling changes in the integrative frontal areas of the cortex are responsible for the finding that as teens we begin to become aware of ourselves and to think about life in conceptual and abstract ways. Our emerging adolescent minds begin to consciously and creatively explore the deeper meanings of life, of friendships, of parents, of school, of everything. Even the ability to reflect on our own personalities emerges during the years of adolescence. While genes determine some of the timing of these changes, experience—what we think about, what we discuss with friends, how we spend our time— will help expand on this new way of thinking about the world. For example, some teens may not engage in such reflective thoughts or conversations with their friends or with their family. In this situation, their interpersonal experience of cultivating self-awareness may not be so well developed.

What we focus our attention on and what we spend time doing

directly stimulate the growth of those parts of the brain that carry out those functions.

Rather than the concrete way of thinking and the fact-based learning that dominates in children during the elementary school years, the learning curve for us as teens involves a focus on more complex concepts. Our literal experience of being aware of life ex-

who's under there?

plodes with new visions of what is real, visions that in childhood may not have even crossed our minds. This is why adolescence is such an amazing time. The growth of the frontal lobes permits us to experience our human ability of knowing about knowing—of reflecting on how we think, how we feel, why we do what we do, and how we might do things differently. As Dorothy said in *The Wizard of Oz*, "We're not in Kansas anymore."

I remember that when I was a teen, this new awareness was overwhelming. I went from smiling a lot during my childhood to being more grumpy, more inward, more confused and pensive. When I first hit my teens, my father would ask me why I didn't smile anymore, and I just didn't know what to say to him. When I got older, I saw the film *Harold and Maude* with some friends and couldn't stop thinking of Cat Stevens's lyrics in the classic song "If You Want to Sing Out, Sing Out": "Well, if you want to sing out, sing out. And if you want to be free, be free." There were a million things I could be, the song said, and I could do whatever I wanted, I could make things come true. I used to sing it in my head, over and over; it played like an endless tape. When I listen to the song now as an adult, I can see that those lyrics capture the essence of our journey into those teen years. It's a coming-of-age song, of letting adults go into the background as we create a new world as adolescents.

This emergence of the adolescent mind is our birthright as human beings.

Our species name is *Homo sapiens sapiens*. *Sapiens* means "knowing." So with the double knowing we are the ones who not only know, but *know* we know. And this knowing we know emerges first in adolescence. Creative and conscious explorations of conceptual thinking and abstract reasoning enable the brain to approach old problems in new ways. A fifteen-year-old isn't simply a ten-year-old with five additional years of experience. Brain development means

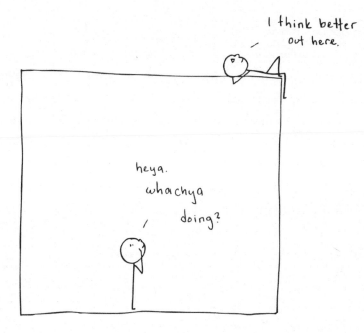

that as adolescents we can think in conceptual and abstract ways a ten-year-old cannot even imagine. One aspect of this exploration can be divergent thinking, a way of approaching problems creatively to "think outside the box." We can approach problems in new ways, and we can approach our self-understanding in new ways never before possible. This creative exploration encompasses ways of perceiving and reasoning and problem solving with abstract capacities and thinking strategies and reflective capabilities that permit us to tackle life's challenges in more innovative ways.

The changes in how we think and expansions in our awareness are because of the brain's remodeling and are a healthy part of our adolescence. The reconstruction of the cortex enables conceptual thinking and creative explorations to emerge and blossom.

With this expanded capacity of consciousness, we are entering a potentially new way of approaching the world and how we fit into it. Instead of the old pattern of just going along with earlier knowledge sponged up from adults when we were elementary school–aged children, as adolescents our brains now permit this new form of thinking that can challenge old ways of doing things. This new conceptual thinking even enables us to see that the old way of doing things embedded in our brains is just one approach—and we can now come up with another approach that may be just as good or perhaps even better.

The power of the adolescent mind emerges from these brain changes, which permit us to solve problems in new and innovative ways. We might even say that this is also the primary work and purpose of the adolescent period—the essence of adolescence.

As we've seen, many revolutionary ways of interpreting and shaping our world—in music and art and in the recent creation of our digital age—emerge during the emotionally vibrant, socially connected, novelty-seeking adolescent period. Adolescence is a golden age for innovation because it is during this time of growth and change that the brain's developmental shifts in the reward centers and in the cortex encourage creative thought and drive adolescents to explore the world in new ways.

So abstract and conceptual thinking, increased reward drive, and enhanced novelty seeking are three sources of the potential and passion for creative thought. These capacities need to be blended with disciplined study, naturally, to allow knowledge to inform innovation.

Yes, these years can be challenging to navigate because in addition to innovation, they also involve risk and rebellion, as we've seen. Impulsivity and hyperrational thinking enable us to drive too fast, take on unnecessary risks, and endanger ourselves and others. We jump off cliffs into the sea and get hurt. But there is a middle ground, a place to honor the drive for novelty and the creation of new explorations. If we as adults push back severely against these natural changes, rejecting adolescents as they reject us, the result can be a shutting down of all communication between the generations.

The call is to increase empathetic understanding and respectful communicating, creating integration across the generations.

Just as when adolescent elephants are deprived of their male elders in a herd and then run wild and become destructive without the adults' presence, total isolation of adolescent humans from the adult community can be an unhelpful standoff. Technology's products—cars, synthesized drugs, weapons, the worldwide web—make the stakes higher. So an important lesson for adults and adolescents is this: Adolescents' pushing away is not the same as shutting completely out. If both sides of the generational divide understood each other more fully, perhaps these important years of innovation and transition could be navigated better, helping adolescents grow into the people they have the power and potential to become.

Our challenge, simply put, is to see the power and potential of the teenage brain and the emerging adolescent mind as assets rather than liabilities.

Creating Collaboration Across the Generations

In middle school, my son and his fourteen-year-old band mates once stacked up all the amplifiers in their music practice room to see how huge a "wall of sound" they could make with all the instruments being played at the same time through the same system. On the floor above the practice room were the school's administrative offices. Needless to say, the nearly shattered windows in the building were an incentive for the head of the school to come down on my son and his friends with severe consequences. One of those consequences was to bar them from using the practice room for three months. The result was that those adolescents, not being able to have their creative outlet of music at school, started doing even more egregious things. The cycle of pushing back by the teens and then pushing back by the adults began. At a meeting, I suggested that the administrators, as the adults in the cycle, try to see through the vicious feedback loop and consider the drive for novelty and exploration that the amplifier-stacking experiment was really meant to be.

Fortunately, one of the administrators remembered her own brother's experience of a similar cascade of events. She suggested they try a different approach. The school administrators brought the band mates in, told them the negative effects of their actions, gave them back their privilege of using the practice room, and said they could keep that privilege if they didn't violate the basic rules of the school. All of their "conduct problem" behavior disappeared for the next five years.

The key to this creative solution was honoring the natural adolescent drive for innovation and the creation of new ways of doing things. Honoring does not mean setting no limits. It means acknowledging the intention behind the actions. Adolescence is all about experimentation. If adults shut that down, the passion for novelty will be thwarted, the teens will become disillusioned and disconnected, and no one will benefit. I felt grateful that those administrators could think in creative and collaborative ways, as they drew on the essence of their "inner teenager," to come up with a developmentally appropriate, behaviorally and psychologically effective plan. They understood that the waterfall was going to flow, so they used their adult skills to channel its path. It was a win-win situation for everyone. And the band went on to create and perform some really fine music.

Sometimes as adults we see the adolescent drive toward experimentation to create novelty as only a negative change, as only a problem, as a sign of teens being "crazy." As an adult and as a parent, I understand the idea behind this sentiment. But perpetuating the notion that these natural and healthy pushes toward novelty mean teens are only "out of their minds" is not a helpful message for anyone. We are moving out of our old minds and into new ones as adolescents, and our adolescent mind is full of positive power and the potential for creativity. And this power is something we all need to honor. The key as an adolescent or as an adult is to tap into that potential and help cultivate that power.

Vulnerability and Opportunity

Adolescence can be seen as a transformative period in which individuals go from being open to everything (in childhood) to becoming expert at a few things (in adulthood). We've seen that one aspect of this remodeling is pruning, or letting go of the connections in the brain that are not needed. Pruning in general can lead to important changes in how we function as teens—and sometimes it can unmask potential problems. This is why a number of mental health challenges, like mood difficulties such as depression and bipolar disorder, or thinking difficulties such as schizophrenia, may emerge more in adolescence than in childhood. Pruning, along with hormonal changes and alterations in how genes are expressed, shapes our neural activity and synaptic growth and makes the brain's functioning change dramatically during the teenage years.

If there is any vulnerability in the brain's makeup during childhood, adolescence can reveal those brain differences because of the paring down of the existing but insufficient number of neurons and their connections. Such vulnerability may have a wide array of causes, from genetics to toxic exposures to adverse childhood experiences such as abuse or neglect. This developmental view proposes that the vulnerability of the adolescent period happens because the pruning of childhood circuits that may have been "at risk" leads to the unmasking of those deficiencies. The new activation of genes during adolescence, which shape how neurons grow and how they interact with other neurons, may also influence the vulnerability of a teenager's brain. Even if average pruning occurs, what remains may be insufficient to enable mood to be kept in balance or for thought to be coordinated with reality. If stress is high, this pruning process may be even more intense, and more of the at-risk circuits may be diminished in number and effectiveness. The result is the unmasking of underlying vulnerability during the pruning of adolescence. The brain's integrative growth will not occur optimally, and depending on which circuits are affected, impaired coordination and balance in the brain can happen.

During high school and the college years, major psychiatric disorders, such as depression, bipolar disorder, or schizophrenia, can express themselves for the first time, even in otherwise well-functioning individuals. When mood or thought becomes dysfunctional, filled with rigidity or chaos that disrupts adaptive functioning for long periods of time, it is possible that a teen is experiencing not simply the unavoidable intense emotions of adolescence but something more. Perhaps there is simply a period of impaired integration during remodeling in the brain that temporarily leads to such chaos and rigidity and further development may correct that impairment. But sometimes that onset of severe behavioral issues is the sign of a disorder that may be appearing and that needs evaluation and treatment, as with a mood disorder, a thought disorder, or an anxiety disorder with obsessive-compulsive or panic behavior. Since some of these serious psychiatric conditions go along with suicidal thoughts and impulses, seeking help to figure out the significance of such changes in yourself, in your friend, or in your teen, can be extremely important. I myself have a friend whose daughter developed such a mood condition in college, and no one in the dorm helped her find support. She was just called "nuts" and became isolated, and no one reached out to help her until it was too late.

Naturally, with impaired integration in the brain, the mind will not be as flexible or as resilient. Sometimes that lack of integration can respond to therapy with a psychotherapist, sometimes it may also require a medication, but always it should begin with an open mind and a good evaluation. When your own mind stops working well, it can be very distressing for yourself and for others. And the stress of having a tumultuous mind can itself create more stress. Here, remodeling has uncovered an underlying vulnerability, and the dysfunction that ensues from the impaired integration may create its own intensification of the pruning process. This is why getting help can be very important to reduce stress and reduce excessive pruning. The key that is being explored now in research is how this pruning process, intensified by stress, may create inadequate ways in which the connections in the brain can function.

Clearly, early interventions to create a stable life experience for the individual and reduce stress are essential to support the healthy growth of the brain during this period of change and development. This is not an "all-or-none" proposition in which a genetic vulnerability always becomes a psychiatric disorder. The reality is far more complex. Even identical twins who share the same genetic makeup do not have one hundred percent probability that both of them will develop a disorder. Experience plays a big role in how the brain develops, even in the face of genetic or other risk factors. We can look at genes and other important variables as some of the many factors that contribute to a larger picture of brain growth. Genes may influence some aspects of neural growth, but there is a much fuller set of factors that contribute to our well-being than genetics alone. How the mind unfolds, how relationships are supportive, how people feel a sense of belonging to a larger group all influence how the brain achieves and maintains integrative development at the root of our pathway toward health.

During adolescence, the pruning and myelination and the re-modeling that they create happen primarily in the cortical regions. While one of those areas is the prefrontal cortex, it is important to keep in mind that this most forward part of the frontal cortex is not super-special by itself; it is more accurate to say that the prefrontal region and related areas are important because they coordinate and balance other regions of the brain. In this way, we can say that the prefrontal cortex is integrative as it links differentiated areas to one another. This integration enables the "whole to be greater than the sum of its parts." With this integration we achieve more complex and useful functions. As we've seen, examples of these include self-awareness, empathy, emotional balance, and flexibility.

As the prefrontal region serves as a master integrative hub, what some might call a master control center or an executive region, its rewiring during the adolescent period permits a more extensive form of integration to be achieved in the transition from childhood to adulthood. As we've noted earlier, this hub is both for the networks within the brain and body as a whole, and for the networks of inter-connecting brains we call relationships. Here we see how the integration of our inner networks and our interpersonal networks shapes our experience of mind. The mind is embodied within us and it is embedded between us. Our mind is within us and between us.

The Remodeling Brain and Flipping Our Lids

Under the active influence of various drugs including alcohol, our minds can stop functioning well because our prefrontal region is no longer able to carry out its coordination and balance of the streams of information from within our bodies and from the outside world. While various drugs can shut off our brain's integrative functioning in the short run and chronic drug usage can distort that coordination and balance in our lives in the long run, we can also be prone to losing integration in other ways that don't involve drug use. Sometimes we can simply "flip our lids" and have the prefrontal integrative fibers of our brains stop coordinating our whole system. Since the prefrontal area is in a state of reconstruction during adolescence, it may be especially prone at certain times to temporarily lose its integrative functioning in linking separate areas to one another.

Even when we are developing well, sometimes during this remodeling period the prefrontal region's ability to carry out the coordination and balance of its integrative role may not function optimally. Remodeling in the brain is a necessary part of its development and builds integration through the adolescent years. This remodeling involves different phases, with females and males undergoing pruning and myelination in different regions at different times. And remodeling is energy consuming. But while trajectories do differ between the genders, where this remodeling process ultimately ends up is actually quite similar across the genders.

The brain functions in a state-dependent way, meaning that while it is in a calm state, certain integrative functions may work well and efficiently. But in other situations, those same functions may not work so well. For many of us, by the middle of adolescence, when we are away from our peers and our emotions are in balance we can be as efficient as adults. But under settings with increased emotion or in the presence of peers, reasoning can become skewed. The context we are in and the internal emotional state of our minds directly shape how sensitive we are to losing certain functions. This can be interpreted as being "too emotional" or "too swayed by peers," but another view is that our emotional sensitivity and interest in peers is adaptive. This is not immaturity but a necessary step in human development. We need to listen to our peers in order to become a part of that vital survival group as we leave our family home.

From a family point of view, this increased emotionality and social influence can become disruptive to life at home. An extreme form of this is when we get really agitated and "flip our lids" or "fly off the handle." Such a state of non-integration can happen abruptly in anyone, but in our early adolescence we may be especially prone to being this way under certain conditions, as when our parents interrupt us when they know we are busy, or when a friend does not call even though she said she would.

If you put your hand model together and then suddenly lift up your fingers, you'll see the anatomic way we can symbolize how we lose the integrative role of the prefrontal cortex. Without the calming influence of that cortical region, sudden outbursts of limbic lava and bursts of reactivity—the ancient reactions of fight, flight, freeze, or faint—can emerge suddenly, sometimes without warning to anyone. These are our early, primitive, subcortical reactions to threat. Since the cortex is a center for awareness, these lower brain areas can become active without our conscious mind's knowing what is stirring deep inside the brain. Then *wham!* Out comes a set of reactions we didn't even know were cooking inside us. Sound familiar? It happened to me a lot when I was a young teen. And it can certainly happen to us as adults, too. It is at these moments when a vulnerable prefrontal cortex is not at the top of its game monitoring and managing the subcortical world that such "low road" reactions can erupt. If we haven't slept well, haven't eaten, are under pressure, or feel some underlying emotional agitation, the prefrontal cortex's calming influences may not work so well and we can flip our lids. Adolescent or adult, this is a part of being human.

Now, when it comes to teenagers, this flipping one's lid is often seen as being a "crazy teenager." But let's make an agreement not to call this crazy; let's call it what it is—remodeling and shifts in integration. In a construction site, sometimes the previously working plumbing and electricity are temporarily disabled. We don't have to call that a faulty building—it's just a reconstruction project. Remodeling has its inevitable downsides, for sure. For a short time, or for bursts of time, those utilities on the construction site are off-line. No effective electricity, no plumbing, no workable staircase. These are all temporary shifts in what works well. The good news is that remodeling is a process that will create new and improved ways of functioning. Remodeling is necessary to adapt the structure of our neural foundation to adjust to new needs, and remodeling in adolescence is necessary to adapt our human family to the new needs of a changing world. New levels of integration are being created and new capacities are being established and strengthened. Remodeling constructs new integration.

That said, sometimes the remodeling comes with challenging ways of thinking and feeling and interacting that are par for the course in neural remodeling.

The reconstruction zone of the prefrontal cortex in particular means that many of the functions that this frontal area of the brain enables through its integrative role—balancing emotions, planning for the future, having insight and empathy—are more easily thrown off-line with intense emotions and peer influence. They may be more fragile, more easily disrupted, than they will be in the years ahead. In fact, one of my friends, whose son is a few years younger than my son, once said that it felt like night and day when his son went from nineteen to twenty years of age. After his son completed his first year of college, my friend told me that he "seemed to have returned to the world of normal human interactions." Now what did he mean by that? His son's balancing of emotions had been turned off, planning for the future was not happening, insight into himself—or empathy for others—seemed not to have been displayed, at least to this young man's dad. How can we make sense of this common experience?

When you understand that the prefrontal region is necessary for each of these important functions to occur, then you can understand why the change toward a settling in after some intense periods of remodeling feels so different—likely because the remodeling period is stabilizing and the prefrontal region can do its thing.

What is that thing exactly? This region coordinates and balances the whole brain with the whole body, and even our inner networks with the social world. Yes, this region behind the forehead connects all the parts of the brain in the skull to one another, and links those functions to what is going on in the body (signals from the heart, intestines, muscles). Then those connected signals are woven together with the input from other people. That's a lot of integration, the linkage of different parts. So as adolescents we need to cut ourselves some slack, and as adults we need to give respect to the remodeling adolescents are going through. That doesn't mean the shop is closed, it means we make adjustments for the fact that the adolescent mind is shaped, at times, by a construction zone.

Adolescence Builds Integration in the Brain

Take a look at your hand model of the brain. Put your limbic-thumb area over your brainstem-palm area. Those are the lower parts of the brain, the ones that generate emotion and reactivity and reward drive, among other things. Now put your fingers over your thumb, and take a look at the middle two fingernails. This is the prefrontal region. Notice how when you lift up your fingers-cortex and put them back down, you can see how this prefrontal-fingernail area is connected to the cortex; it sits on top of the limbic-thumb, and also connects directly to the brainstem-palm. In addition, signals from the body itself—from muscles and bones, from the intestines and heart—all come up to this prefrontal region, too. And if that was not enough, this prefrontal region also makes maps of what is going on inside other people's nervous systems. That's right! The prefrontal region maps the social world. It is this prefrontal area that creates our mindsight maps of you for empathy and of us for morality, as well as a mindsight map of me for insight.

So let's review this now with your hand model in mind. Five separate areas of information flow are coordinated and balanced by the prefrontal region. Here they are. The cortex. The limbic area. The brainstem. The body proper. And the social world. When these separate sources of information flow are linked together, we call that "integration." And integration is what creates the master functions of self-awareness, reflection, planning, decision making, empathy, and even morality—thinking about the larger social good.

When the prefrontal region achieves a new state of being remodeled, those important functions become more dependable and stronger. Integration can now happen more consistently and reliably. Brain, body, and social world are woven together into one whole by the prefrontal cortex. Knowing about how this prefrontal remodeling happens can help us as adolescents and as adults not only to understand better what is going on inside the brain but to do something about it that is constructive, as we'll soon see. In fact, the mindsight practices we'll explore throughout the book can promote the growth of these integrative regions of the brain. Yes, it turns out that we can cultivate the growth of the integrative fibers of the prefrontal cortex. Positive interactions with others and self-reflection are two ways to increase prefrontal integration. That's right: You can grow those fibers if you choose to learn how to do that!

The Emotional Lower Brain

Did you know that along with these prefrontal changes, the lower brain areas below the cortex (your limbic-thumb and brainstem-palm in the hand model) are more active in adolescents than they are in children or in adults? What this means is that emotions can arise rapidly and intensely without the calming influences of the prefrontal cortex. The prefrontal region can send soothing circuits, called "inhibitory fibers," down to these lower areas and keep their firing calmed.

Brain scans reveal that when teens are shown a neutral face in

a photograph, a major area of the limbic region, the amygdala, becomes activated, whereas in adults the same photograph merely activates the reasoning prefrontal cortex. The result for teens can be an
inner sense of conviction that even another person's neutral response
is filled with hostility and he cannot be trusted. A blank expression
or a bump in the hallway can be interpreted as intentional, and a teen
may respond with an irritated remark even if the look or bump was
completely innocent. Knowing this scientific finding has helped me
as a parent to understand the often intense reactions of my own adolescents to statements I made that, in my view, were pretty neutral,
but they experienced as aggressive.

There are two routes that send information to the amygdala. One
is a slow route, in which the higher cortex sifts through information,
reasons, reflects, and then informs the amygdala in a calm and rational
way. There's a second route, one that bypasses the cortex and simply
sends incoming streams of perception directly to the amygdala. This
is the fast route. Studies of adolescents reveal that even under calm
conditions, the fast route to amygdala activation often occurs more
readily in teens than in adults; the slow route is used more in adults.
What this means is that the intense emotions of a pure amygdala response may rise up even when nothing is shutting off the cortex, as
when we've flipped our lids in an agitated, chaotic state or in a shut-
down, rigid state. As teens we may simply have a more immediate
emotional response that is not filtered by cortical reasoning. That's
the fast route in action. This is what we mean, in part, when we say
that adolescence is a period of more emotional intensity, more emotional spark. The fast route to the amygdala is more readily activated
during this period than it ever was, or ever will be.

For all of us, as teenagers or adults, when intense emotions erupt
in our minds, we need to learn to feel them and deal with them. As
Fred Rogers used to say on television, if feelings are mentionable,

they can become manageable. As we have seen in the Mindsight Tools #1, we can use the notion of "Name it to tame it." Learning to deal with emotions means being aware of them and modifying them inside us so that we can think clearly. Sometimes we can name it to tame it and help balance our brain's emotional intensity by putting words to what we feel. If we say the name of an emotion inside our own minds, it can help. There are even some brain studies that show how this naming process can activate the prefrontal cortex and calm the limbic amygdala! Learning to manage our emotions in adolescence is an important part of becoming independent of our parents and becoming strong in life. In the mindsight tools sections, we'll explore the many helpful emotion-balancing strategies that can support our growth in this way during adolescence and beyond.

Hardwired for Adventure and Connection

When we compare our own adolescent period with the similar transition of other animals, we find some amazing parallels. In *Zoobiquity*, a book on the subject of how we have a lot in common with our animal cousins, Barbara Natterson-Horowitz and Kathryn Bowers write: "A similarly lowered risk threshold—indeed, a new *pleasure* in risk taking—likely propels nearly grown birds out of nests, hyenas out of communal dens, dolphins, elephants, horses, and otters into peer groups, and human teens into malls and college dorms. As we've seen, having a brain that makes you feel less afraid enables, perhaps encourages, encounters with threats and competitors that are crucial to your safety and success. The biology of decreased fear, greater interest in novelty, and impulsivity serve a purpose across species. In fact, it could be that the only thing more dangerous than taking risks in adolescence is *not* taking them."

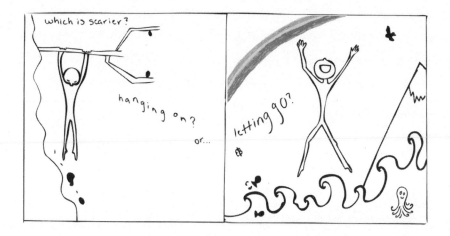

Indeed, the natural process of moving away from the nest is filled with risk. The risk of not taking risks that Natterson-Horowitz and Bowers are referring to is that the individual will not be able to take the chances needed to leave the nest, and with such stagnation our species will not survive. Risk breathes new life into rigid ways of doing things. We can see that deep in our brain's structure, we may have the urge to take on risky behaviors that can feel as if they are matters of life or death. For the health of our family across the generations, they are essential. And for our species as a whole, they in fact *are* a matter of our survival. The adolescent brain sets up a positive bias, emphasizing the PROS and majorly de-emphasizing the cons in order to preserve our human family.

We might be driven as well to connect with our peers, who are also moving out into the world, because in groups we can find the safety of belonging. More eyes to watch for predators, more compatriots to join in our shared journey away from home, more companions to connect to as we create a new world that is necessary for the survival of our species.

I once had a patient come into my office with his pants' waistline beneath his rear end. It was quite the fashion a few years back (it may still be), and it puzzled me. I couldn't stop myself from asking about it. So with curiosity, but also I believe quite respectfully, I asked, "Why do you wear your pants below your butt like that?" I'll never forget his frank response: "I need to wear these pants like this so I can be like everyone else who is trying to be different. I am trying to be like everybody else who is trying not to be like everyone else." Exactly.

So that helps us understand the situation. Teens often feel that they need one another much more than they need adults. Adolescents are our future, and it is through their courage and their sometimes outrageous but creative efforts "not to be like everyone else" that our species has been adaptive. If we are to survive on this fragile and magnificent planet, we are going to need all the ingenuity of the rebellious adolescent mind to find solutions to the grave problems that our and previous adult generations have created in this world.

As a parent, I have tried to take to heart these lessons from science about adolescence. I take a deep breath and try to remind myself the best I can that their push-back behavior is embedded not just in *their* brains but in all *our* DNA. Their push back now was our push back then, when we were adolescents. With this universal human quality in mind, the challenge at a minimum is to find a way to help adolescents navigate these years without seriously harming themselves or others. That can be a foundational goal: *At least do no harm.* After that, everything is icing on the cake. But naturally we can start there and have much greater expectations. Another central goal is to keep the lines of communication as open as they can be. This view sets a framework that can help the most challenging situations become a bit more manageable and make this period a time of collaboration as best we can across the generations.

MINDSIGHT TOOLS #2

■

Time-In

Want to create integration in your brain? Taking time to reflect inwardly is the science-proven way to do that. I call this taking "time-in."

We've been discussing how an integrated brain gives you a strong mind and enables you to have healthy relationships with others. If you are interested in developing integration in your own brain, taking time-in to focus your attention on your internal world has been shown in research to grow those important prefrontal fibers that integrate your life. This mindsight tool will teach you how to grow the integrative fibers of your brain by learning how to focus your attention in very practical ways.

Time-In, Mindsight, and Mindful Awareness

"Time-in" is a term I use to describe the time we can take—be it a minute a day, ten minutes a day, or throughout the day—to intentionally focus our attention on the inner world of our mental, subjective experience. Much of what happens in families and in schools, and even on the Internet with social media, pulls our focus of attention to the outer world. Think of how much time many of us spend on smartphones, iPads, and other devices absorbing an endless stream of information. For many adolescents who've grown up with the Internet, e-mailing, chatting via text, and surfing the Net are just a regular part of life. And while there are a lot of great connections we can make through social media that enhance friendships and social connections in general, the danger is that we fail to pay attention to other aspects of our lives. Hours and days can go by without our taking time-in to just be with our inner life, the life of our own mind.

Why is that an issue? you may ask. Because without at least some time spent exercising our mindsight circuits focusing on the inner world—of ourselves or others—those circuits won't remain healthy and strong. To move our lives toward integration, we can't focus solely on the outside world of physical objects. We need mindsight to develop the integration in our inner lives that cultivates our insight and empathy.

Taking time-in on a regular basis is helpful because it exercises the mindsight circuits that can integrate our brains and empower our lives. One way of taking time-in is to develop mindful awareness, ways of training the mind that help us develop the ability to be present with what is happening in the moment and to let go of judgments and focus instead on accepting life as it is rather than on how we expect it to be. The way we focus attention to train the mind in general is called "meditation," and studies of mindfulness meditation show how it supports healthier functioning in the body, in the mind, and in relationships. For example, research has shown that the more present we are in life, the higher the level of the enzyme telomerase in our bodies, which maintains and repairs the life-preserving ends of our chromosomes, called telomere caps. With the day-to-day stresses of life and the natural progression of the aging process, these chromosome caps are slowly whittled down. Building up more telomerase can help us be healthier and live longer. Some people have come by presence naturally; others may learn it through mindfulness training. For those who were taught to train their mind to be mindful, their ability to be present was increased, their immune system functioned better, and their level of telomerase increased. Amazing, but true: How you focus your mind's attention inwardly can change molecules in your body that make you healthier and make your cells live longer.

With presence, too, our ability to be aware of our emotions and make them work for us instead of against us will be improved. And our ability to focus attention so we can learn what we want to learn will be strengthened. As if that were not enough, other studies of mindfulness meditation show that we will be able to approach, rather than withdraw from, challenging situations and actually feel more meaning and fulfillment in life. Some people call that happiness. It is a way of living a life of meaning, compassion, and purpose. Simply put, time-in helps us to be at our wisest.

For our relationships, time-in and the mindful awareness it creates will help us become more empathic with others. Not only is the compassion that arises from such a skill set directed at being aware of others' feelings and helping them feel better, it also helps us feel more compassionate toward ourselves.

So, yes, time-in is a fundamental part of having mindsight. And time-in is a win-win-win situation, helping our bodies and brains, our minds and inner lives, and our relationships with others. It even helps how we relate to ourselves in a kinder and more supportive way.

Why, then, isn't every school teaching time-in practices? Teachers could expand their focus beyond the traditional three R's of reading, 'riting, and 'rithmetic to teach reflection, relationships, and resilience. I think this is generally not being done because people are simply not aware of these scientifically proven outcomes of such inner practices. And teaching such internal education in schools would mean taking a step back from routines and busy schedules and creating a new approach to education overall. Yet there is a lot of research to suggest that taking time-in and developing the mindsight foundations of social and emotional intelligence enhance academic achievement. Schools can embrace these findings and support adolescents in developing this prefrontal program that supports a healthy mind. A number of innovative programs are being adopted in some schools to bring this new approach of internal education into the classroom. Since presence has been proven to promote happiness, the presence that such a time-in curriculum fosters may even make a happier set of students, and probably teachers, too.

And as families, we can make time-in a part of our daily lives. In many ways, parents are their children's first teachers. So why not have this internal education begin at home for everyone in the family?

There is no better place to begin than with ourselves. Mahatma Gandhi had a great saying: "We must be the change we wish to see in the world." And with this idea in mind, I invite you to join me in developing these basic time-in practices so you can become a mindsight maven and develop more presence in your life. Whether you are beginning your adolescence or are in the middle of it, whether you are at the end of adolescence or deep into adulthood, these time-in practices can work to bring presence into your life, catalyze integration in your brain, and strengthen your mind.

Getting Started

First, I'd like you to think of time-in as a regular daily practice you are doing to activate the mindsight circuits of your brain. A bit like brushing your teeth for oral hygiene, time-in should be a daily habit that you just do because it is a needed part of a healthy life. When we exercise a muscle, the repeated tightening then relaxing, tightening then relaxing of the muscle ultimately strengthens it. There is no muscle in the brain, but the practice of activating and strengthening a part of your body is the same idea for strengthening the brain. Here the practice is not moving a muscle but focusing your attention.

How you focus your attention drives energy and information flow through your nervous system. Where attention goes, neural firing in the brain occurs. Where neural firing happens, neural connections are strengthened. Attention is the way we activate specific circuits in the brain and strengthen them. And when you strengthen neural connections that are linking differentiated areas of the brain to one another, you are creating integration in the brain.

Put simply: Focusing your attention in regular time-in practice can integrate your brain.

Time-in and the mindful awareness and presence it creates will enable your brain to literally grow more integrative fibers that create your ability to regulate emotions, attention, thinking, and behavior, and your sense of well-being and connections to others will be optimized. If carefully conducted scientific studies did not reveal this, I myself would look at this list and say, "That is too good to be true!"

- john   o'donohue -

But these positive outcomes have all been shown to be true.

So the simple question is this: Are you ready to get started? And if you are, please take your time, but let's get ready now to dive into time-in.

Being Present for What Is Happening as It Is Happening

Taking time-in can happen at any moment of the day. If I am washing the dishes, I can simply create the internal stance, called an "intention," to let this be a time to mindfully wash the dishes. What this means is that I will let the internal sensations of the experience fill my awareness. When my mind wanders and I begin to think about what I did last week, or what I'll be doing next month, then I am no longer being aware of the present-moment experience, no longer taking in the sensations of the water or the dish soap or the dish in my hands at that very moment, no longer allowing my mind to be filled only with awareness of the sensations of that moment. Taking time-in and being mindful mean being present for what is happening as it is happening.

You might be wondering: Couldn't awareness of one's thoughts about the past or the future be what is happening at that present moment? If so, isn't this taking time-in because your thinking about the past and future is *inside* you right now? And because it is what is "happening as it is happening," doesn't this also mean that you are being mindful of your thoughts at that very moment? These questions have yes answers if we are *intending* to let our minds wander on purpose and are then open to whatever arises in our thought processes. But if our intention is to focus on the sensations of the experience of washing the dishes and our minds *unintentionally* get distracted as our attention wanders and our awareness becomes filled with the uninvited focus on the past or the future, then no, this is not being mindful, and no, this is not what we mean by time-in practice.

When we take time-in, we intentionally focus on some aspect of our inner world. We are SIFTing our minds as we focus at least on some aspect of our sensations, images, feelings, and thoughts. This is how we strengthen our ability to be present, to be aware of what is happening as it is happening. Learning to be present in life, at any age, will help us become more resilient. Resilience means being flexible and strong in the face of stress, and it is what we need to approach any of the challenges of life and rise above adversity, learn from the experience, and move on with vitality and passion. These are some of the likely reasons that, research has shown, presence creates happiness and well-being in our lives.

Before we can take the steps to be present with strength and reliability, we need to learn the first step of presence, which is to use awareness to stabilize our attention. This is how we strengthen the monitoring ability of the mind.

MINDSIGHT PRACTICE A: Breath Awareness

Here are the basic instructions for this time-in practice with breathing. The task is to focus on the sensation of the breath. When the mind gets distracted, take note of that and redirect attention to the sensation of the breath.

That's it.

This universal mindfulness of the breath approach can be done sitting down or standing up. It can be done in two minutes or twenty minutes. You can do this once a day or many brief times a day. Many people like to have a regular time to carry out this breath practice and find the mornings are a great time to do this. Some researchers suggest that the key to long-term benefits is regular, daily practice. Some have said that for adults a minimum of twelve minutes seems to be important each day. But it's better to do a couple of minutes each day if those daily dozen are not possible. Just as with aerobic exercise, while thirty to forty-five minutes a day is ideal on a regular basis, if you don't have that time, it is better to do something each day rather than nothing.

Great. So now what do you do with your body while you're focusing your mind? Some people like to sit comfortably in a chair, feet flat on the floor, legs uncrossed, back straight but comfortable. Some like to sit on the floor, legs crossed. And if you can keep from falling asleep, some with back troubles like to lie flat on the floor, legs elevated either on the seat of a chair or on a cushion to ease the tension on the lower back and knees. Whatever works for you is fine.

And what do you do with your eyes? Some like to keep their eyes open, some partially closed, and others fully closed. Do whatever works well for you to focus on the breath's sensations. Since the focus is on time-in, turn off any digital objects and try to have some time when you won't be easily distracted or interrupted. You can do this alone, or you can do this with others. Whatever works is fine!

When it is new to you to focus on the sea inside, it can be challenging. So while I am saying this is simple, it doesn't mean it is easy. One challenging aspect of this experience is that we are so used to focusing on the outside world of stimulating sounds and sights that focusing on the internal world of sensations can be less captivating. In short, you may get bored!

Part of the practice is to monitor if you are falling asleep from boredom. Please don't become discouraged, but if you do feel discouraged, or anything else for that matter, just be open to whatever feelings arise. That's what being present is all about. If any particular feeling gets in the way of your focus on the breath, name it to tame it by simply saying something like "feeling discouraged" or "feeling anxious" or simply "feeling, feeling" and then let the feeling cease to be the focus of your attention by returning to the breath. The key is not to try to get rid of something, like a feeling of discouragement, but rather to be open to it, sense it as simply an object of attention, and then let your mind redirect attention to the sensation of the breath.

Being mindful has a sense of kindness, a positive regard toward yourself and others. Some people call this self-compassion, meaning you are patient with yourself and realize that you are just human. The mind has a mind of its own, and getting distracted is just what it means to be a person. Welcome to the human family! So instead of beating yourself up for being "bad" at taking time-in, you should simply acknowledge that your attention wandered to the conversation in the hallway, and then lovingly and gently redirect the attention toward your breath. Again and again, one breath at a time.

Mindful practice has the elements of COAL—that is, being *c*urious about what's happening, being *o*pen to what is going on, *a*ccepting that this is the present moment and letting go of judgments about it, and having a *l*oving stance toward the experience, and yourself. This is the COAL that warms the experience of time-in.

Let's Begin

(You may want to either have someone read this to you as you try the practice, or simply record it yourself and listen to your own voice. If you want to listen to me speaking a version of the Time-In with the Breath Awareness practice, go to my website, DrDanSiegel.com, and click on the Resources tab and the everyday mindsight tools and you'll find the breath awareness practice.)

The first time you do this, get started with a focus on the visible outside world. With your eyes open, let your attention focus on the middle of the room. Now send your attention to the far wall or ceiling. Now direct your visual attention to the middle of the room again. And now bring your attention to about book reading distance, as if you have a book or magazine in your hands. Notice how you can direct the focus of attention.

For this practice, let the sensation of the breath be the object of attention. Let's begin at the level of the nostrils with the subtle sensation of the air coming in and going out. Ride the wave of the breath, in and out, and just sense that sensation. Now notice how you can direct attention from the nostrils to the chest. Let the sensation of the chest rising and falling fill awareness. Up and down, simply ride the wave of the breath in and out. Now redirect attention to the abdomen. If you are new to this abdominal breathing, you can place a hand on the belly and simply notice how the abdomen moves out when air fills the lungs, and the abdomen moves in when air escapes the lungs. Simply ride the wave of the breath by focusing attention on the sensation of the abdomen moving out and moving in.

For this breath awareness practice, just let awareness become filled with the sensation of the breath wherever it feels most natural. It may be the abdomen moving in and out, the chest rising and falling, or the air at the nostrils. Or it may simply be the whole body breathing. Just let the sensation of the breath fill awareness wherever you feel it most readily.

As you ride the wave of the breath, in and out, let's take a few moments to focus on an ancient story that's been passed down through the generations. The story goes like this. The mind is like the ocean. And deep beneath the surface of the ocean, it is calm and clear. From this place of clarity beneath the surface, it is possible to just look up and notice whatever conditions are at the surface. It may be flat, or choppy with waves, or there may even be a full storm, but no matter the conditions, deep beneath the surface it remains calm and clear.

The mind is like the ocean. And just sensing the breath brings you beneath the surface of the mind. From this deep place in the mind, it is possible to notice whatever surface activity is happening in the mind, such as feelings or thoughts, memories or ideas. From this deep place beneath the surface of the mind, it is calm and clear. And just sensing the breath brings you to this place of clarity and tranquility.

Now let's return to a focus of attention on the sensation of the breath wherever you feel it most readily. Just ride the wave of the breath, in and out.

For this basic mindfulness of the breath practice, we'll take time-in to simply let the sensation of the breath fill awareness. When something distracts attention away from the breath and you've come to notice that awareness is no longer filled with the sensation of the breath, just notice the distraction and then let it go, returning the focus of attention to the breath and filling awareness with the sensation of the breath.

We'll practice this mindfulness of the breath now for a few minutes. (If you have a timer, you can set it to whatever duration you like, five minutes, a dozen, twenty.) As you experience the practice, you may find your attention goes to something other than the breath. For some, naming the distraction helps to let it go. For others, such naming is itself a distraction. If you choose to give this a try, it is often helpful to give the distraction the same general name as the kind of distraction that took your attention away. So if a memory of being at the beach distracts your attention, then you can simply say quietly in your mind, "Remembering, remembering, remembering," and let the memory go. For some, this can be helpful to strengthen their ability to release a distraction and return the focus of attention to the breath. For others, it is not helpful and may even be distracting. Find what works for you.

Remember, in addition to the task of simply focusing on the breath, it is recommended that you consider regarding yourself with kindness as you go through this practice. Everyone's mind wanders at times, and that is just what it means to be human. In fact, part of the strengthening aspect of this practice comes from the redirecting of attention, which is like contracting a muscle. The unintentional distractions are like relaxing a muscle, the refocusing on the breath is the tightening of the muscle. Focus, distraction, refocus, distraction, refocus again. That's how we work out our minds with this time-in practice. This time-in can be new to many, focusing on the internal sensations of our mental lives. If you find yourself getting sleepy, you can always open your eyes a bit if they are closed. And if that doesn't help to energize the mind, you can try this exercise standing up. Same practice, only now you are vertical.

Let's give this a try.

After a designated period of time, when you are ready, you can take a more intentional and perhaps deeper breath and let your eyes come open, if they are shut, and we'll bring this time-in breath awareness practice to a close.

How was that for you? If you are new to this, welcome! As we said, this may be simple, but it is not easy for most of us. The mind does get distracted easily, and that is just part of the reality of having a human mind. To carry out this practice, we train our minds to be present. With repeated practice, this mind-training exercise has been shown to grow important parts of the brain that are connected not only with attention but with emotion and empathy as well. These are integrative circuits, and so this basic mindfulness of the breath practice helps integrate the brain. It is a form of brain health, a way of creating mental resilience and well-being.

Building Mindsight's Lens

We can think of taking time-in as a way of building the lens that enables us to see the sea inside with more stability so that what we see is in better focus and gives us more detail and depth. Think of mindsight as having a metaphoric lens, one that is stabilized with a tripod. Each of its three legs represents an aspect of what time-in creates for us. Having a sense of these three factors of a stabilized attention can help us as we practice time-in and strengthen our mindsight skills.

The first tripod leg is *openness*. This is the openness in our COAL work, how we are simply open to whatever arises as it arises. This is an invitation to let happen whatever will happen, a deep presence to the moment that embraces whatever may stream into our awareness from attention.

The second leg is *objectivity*. This is akin to the acceptance of our COAL acronym in which we just accept the object of attention into our awareness. We don't try to distort what we think is happening; we simply let into our awareness whatever is happening at the moment and then see it as an object of our attention, as a known in the larger knowing of conscious experience. When we do our next mindsight practice, this distinction between knowing and known will become the focus of our experience.

From Daniel J. Siegel, M.D., *Mindsight: The New Science of Personal Transformation,* copyright © 2010 by Mind Your Brain, Inc. Adapted with permission.

The third leg of the tripod that stabilizes mindsight's lens is *observation*. When we are tracking our designated goal for a practice and paying attention to our intention, we are observing our experience.

Interestingly, two distinct circuits have been identified in the brain. One is a sensing circuit that streams sensations directly into awareness. Another circuit is an observing circuit that enables us to bear witness to an event and to then be able to narrate that moment of time in our lives if we choose. This observing capacity gives us a bit of distance from direct sensation so that we may be more flexible in how we respond. As one of my students pointed out, this is how we "own" an experience—observe, witness, and narrate.

It is this observing capacity that lets us do something like this during a time-in practice of the breath: Ummm. Interesting conversation in the hallway. I need to talk to Steve. . . . Oh, whoops [observing distraction] . . . That's right . . . I want to talk to him, but this is a time-in practice on the breath [witnessing] . . . listening, listening, listening [narrating] . . . [observing circuit now redirects attention to breath on purpose] . . . Now: Sensation of breath fills awareness as it engages the sensing circuits that fill awareness with the input of simply the sensations of the breath. Observer feels satisfied that we are now following the intention of this time-in practice to focus on the breath by being aware of the sensations of the breath. Now we've "owned" the time-in practice!

This distinction between sensing and observing may seem subtle, but it turns out to be quite important. Time-in builds both circuits, empowering us to simply be in the flow of sensations, and also to observe our inner workings, such as our focus of attention, so that we can modify them as needed depending on our intention. Being mindful embraces at least these two streams of awareness, sensing and observing. To build the capacity for both abilities, we'll turn now to the next practice and explore more about how to build our mindsight skills.

Integrating Consciousness with the Wheel of Awareness

A time-in practice that is specifically designed to integrate consciousness is called the Wheel of Awareness. In our daily lives there are many aspects of our conscious experience, of what we are aware of and the nature of our awareness itself. When we allow these different aspects of consciousness, of being aware, to be seen for their unique qualities—like distinguishing vision from hearing, sensing the body from thinking—and then we connect them through systematically focusing attention on each within awareness, we develop a more coherent sense of ourselves. This is what I mean when I say integrate consciousness. It's the linking of the different elements of being aware into a harmonious whole. It is quite simple but quite empowering as it integrates our minds. The wheel practice is more elaborate than the breath practice offered in the prior practice entry, but taken together, they make a good pair of mind-strengthening time-in exercises. My suggestion to you is that if you have not worked on the time-in with the breath awareness

Wheel of Awareness

The hub represents the experience of knowing within awareness; the spokes are focused attention; the rim is the known, including sensations and other mental processes. The sectors of the rim are as follows: first through fifth (outer world), sixth (body), seventh (mental activity), and eighth (relationships) senses. From Daniel J. Siegel, M.D., *The Mindful Brain*, copyright © 2007 by Mind Your Brain, Inc. Adapted with permission.

practice for a week or so, you may want to do that before trying out the wheel practice. Some just dive in and it goes well, but this practice is both a bit longer—it can take about twenty minutes or so in its full form—and a bit more elaborate.

In my office at work there's a table with a glass center and an outer wood rim. When you look through the glass, the legs of the table appear like spokes connecting this center hub to the outer rim. One day that table seemed to be a good metaphor for consciousness. As an image, the hub could represent the sense of knowing in consciousness, the rim could stand for the known (like a feeling or thought or memory), and the spokes could be the process of attention that streams the known into the knowing.

As integration is the differentiation and then linkage of parts of a system, how can we integrate consciousness? At a minimum, consciousness or being aware has two components: our sense of knowing and that which is known. We can use attention to link these differentiated aspects of consciousness to each other. It is also possible to differentiate the different elements of the known, represented in our metaphoric wheel on the rim, into four segments. This process of creating a linkage of the differentiated parts of being aware creates a powerful state of integration in our minds and can soothe anxiety, create clarity, and open us up to being present in life with strength and resilience. The first segment of the rim represents the first five senses, sight, hearing, smell, taste, and touch. The second segment of the rim contains the interior of the body—what is called the "sixth sense"—that includes the inner sensations of our muscles and bones, and of the internal organs such as intestines, lungs, and heart. A third segment represents our mental processes of feelings, thoughts and memories, intentions, beliefs, and attitudes—our "seventh sense." And a fourth segment can also be differentiated and represents a kind of relational sense, our "eighth sense," where we perceive the connections we have with other people and with our natural environment, our planet.

How could these various knowns of the rim actually be connected to the knowing of the hub? That would be the distinct but related process of attention. Attention is the process that directs the flow of energy and information. We focus attention from the hub of knowing in awareness toward the rim of the known. And when we do this in a systematic way, a "rim review," we then link the differentiated elements of consciousness. That is how the Wheel of Awareness practice integrates consciousness.

So I offer this wheel practice to you as an invitation to explore your own inner life—and to integrate consciousness. The wheel has been vetted by my mindfulness colleagues as a mindfulness practice, but it was not designed to be that. Preliminary research suggests it also has powerful positive effects on how we regulate our emotions and helps develop a clear mind—two outcomes of integration. The Wheel of Awareness was created to integrate consciousness and offer a systematic way of exploring the sea inside.

MINDSIGHT PRACTICE B: The Wheel of Awareness

You can record this practice yourself and listen to it, or you can simply go to DrDanSiegel.com and download it. This practice takes about twenty minutes, so it certainly offers you one variation on doing your daily dozen. If you don't have the twenty minutes, you can also do one segment of the rim review only, tailoring it to your needs as you go. And there is even a way to move more quickly through the rim if needed, covering it all but making the practice more like a dozen minutes, by letting alternate breaths be your guide for timing the movement of your spoke in reviewing the sensations of the outside world and body. I suggest starting with the full timing to get familiar with the wheel and then modifying your practice to fit your needs. You choose what works best for you.

We'll begin the practice here.

In the illustration of the Wheel of Awareness (p. 129), you'll find a drawing of the table in my office that serves as the wheel for our practice. Take a look at the wheel, and let's review its parts. The hub represents the experience of knowing within awareness. The rim represents anything you can be aware of, such as sights or sounds, thoughts or feelings. And the spokes represent attention, the way you can stream energy and information from the rim into the hub.

Let's focus on the breath for a few waves of the in breath and the out breath. If you've been practicing time-in with the breath, you'll be ready to sense the breath wherever you feel it most naturally. Now that deep place beneath the surface of the mind, the place where sensing the breath can take you to notice whatever arises on the surface, is like the hub of the wheel. And just sensing the breath brings you to the hub of the mind. Now let the breath go, and simply visualize or imagine the idea of the Wheel of Awareness, with its central hub of clarity, the spokes of attention, and the rim. We'll now begin our rim review to explore each of the segments of the rim.

Imagine sending a spoke of attention to the first segment of the rim, that part that has sight, hearing, smell, taste, and touch. Let's begin with hearing, letting any sounds in the room fill awareness . . .

Now move the imaginary spoke over a bit in this first segment and let the light coming in through your eyelids, or slightly opened eyes, fill awareness . . .

Now move the spoke again and let any odors fill awareness . . .

And now move the spoke to the sense of taste, letting any tastes fill awareness . . .

Now let anywhere where skin is touching something, touching clothes, touching a chair, touching skin, let the sense of touch fill awareness . . .

Now taking a bit of a deeper breath, we'll let this first segment of the rim go and move the spoke over to the second segment of the rim. Let's begin by focusing attention on the facial area. Let the sensations of the muscles and bones of the face fill awareness. Now move attention to the scalp, and let the sensations from the top of the head fill awareness. And now focus attention on the back of the head and sides, filling awareness with those sensations. Now moving attention to the muscles and bones of the neck and throat, fill awareness with their sensations.

Let attention now go to the shoulder area, letting the muscles' and bones' sensations fill awareness. And now stream attention down both arms, to the elbows . . . wrists . . . and the ends of the fingers . . . Now bring attention to the muscles and bones of the upper back and the chest . . . And now to the lower back and the abdomen . . . Now send attention to the hips, and down both legs to the knees and the ankles and the ends of the toes . . .

Now bring attention to the pelvic area, filling awareness with the sensation from the genitals . . . and now move attention inward, to the intestines, letting these gut sensations fill awareness . . . Now let attention go to the stomach . . . and now up to the interior of the throat. . . And now let attention move to the interior of the lungs . . . And now center attention in the heart region, and just let those heartfelt sensations fill awareness . . .

And now let awareness become filled with the interior of the whole body, from head to toes . . .

Knowing that the body's signals are a deep source of wisdom always available to you, we'll let this segment of the rim go as you take a deeper breath and move the spoke of attention over to the third segment of the rim. This is the segment that represents your mental life of feelings and thoughts, memories and intentions. Whatever the mind can create is represented here. For this aspect of the rim review, we'll have two parts.

In the first part, you'll send the spoke from the hub to the third segment of the rim. Then you'll simply invite into awareness in the hub whatever may arise, whatever comes up to enter awareness. In many ways, this is the opposite of the breath-awareness practice where you intentionally focus on the breath, and when a mental process—like a thought or memory—distracts attention, you let it go and return the focus of attention to the breath. Here you are simply being open to whatever mental life may or may not come into awareness. It's like an internal open stance of "Bring it on." Just sense whatever may arise in awareness. Let's do that for a few minutes . . .

For the second part of this aspect of the rim review, we'll again invite anything into awareness from this third segment of the rim. Now, though, I'll invite you to also study the ways in which a mental activity is experienced in awareness. How does it first come into awareness? Does it come suddenly or gradually? From one side or another? And once it is in awareness, how does it stay there? Is it constant or vibrating, is it steady or intermittent? And then how does it leave awareness? Suddenly, or gradually, or is it just replaced by another mental activity, another thought or memory or feeling or image? If it is not replaced by another mental activity, what does the space feel like between two mental activities in awareness?

So for this part of the rim review, I'm inviting you to become a student of the architecture of your own mental life. Let's begin that practice now for a few minutes . . .

Now I invite you to find the breath, in and out, and take a deeper breath as we let this segment of the rim go for now and move the spoke over, one more time, to the fourth segment of the rim. This is the part of the rim that represents our sense of connection to others and to our environment. First, if there are people in the room near you, let the sense of closeness to them fill awareness. Now let that sense of connection expand to your relationships with friends and family . . . Now let that sense of connection move out to your classmates if you are in school, or to your work colleagues . . . And now let that sense of connection open to all those who live in your community . . . in your city . . . in your state or province . . . in your country . . . on your continent . . .

Now let that sense of connection open up to all people

who share this home we call planet Earth . . . And now see if you can expand that sense of connection to all living beings, animals and plants, who share our common home, this planet, together . . .

Knowing that scientific research has validated what wisdom traditions throughout the world have taught for centuries, that positive intentions and wishes for the well-being of others lead not only to positive changes in the world but also to health benefits to yourself, I invite you to imagine sending wishes of kindness for health and happiness, safety and well-being to all living beings on Earth . . . And now, taking a bit of a deeper breath, sending kindness and compassionate wishes of health and happiness, safety and well-being to your own inner self . . . Now let's find the breath and ride the wave of the breath, in and out . . . And taking now a more intentional and perhaps deeper breath, we'll bring this Wheel of Awareness practice to a close for today.

Reflecting on the Wheel

One amazing thing about the Wheel of Awareness practice is that each time you do it, it is different. People from all walks of life from all over the planet have shared the challenges and the benefits of the practice. You can see for yourself what doing this practice is like, and only you can say if it is useful to you in some way.

When adolescents have reported on their experience with the wheel, they've told me that the sense of the hub has given them a kind of freedom from whatever might be coming up on the rim. One twenty-one-year-old said that her anxiety about being with other people was greatly reduced because her "nervousness and worries just became points on the rim that I could sense from that calmer place on the hub." And she is not alone. Many people, adolescents and adults alike, have reported all sorts of relief from painful emotions and even painful bodily sensations when they've strengthened the hub of their mind.

There is a more advanced practice, Wheel of Awareness III (with the hub-on-hub practice included), in which you are invited to experience sending the spoke out from the hub, only this time it is bent back to return to the hub itself. This is how you are focusing attention on awareness, and experience what awareness of awareness feels like.

For people new to time-in practices of reflection inwardly, such an advanced awareness of the awareness part of the wheel may be too much at first. Rather than frustrating someone new to this important reflective work, I just leave out that more advanced step for the initial experience. But if you've been practicing the breath awareness for a while and feel that it works well for you, and if you've tried out the wheel for a while and feel ready for a more challenging aspect of that process, you may be ready to try out Wheel III.

I suggest that if you feel ready, go ahead to the website and give it a try. That bending of the spoke to come back to the hub is generally done after the fourth segment of the rim is reviewed, just before the end of the whole practice. It's best to do the whole wheel first, and then add this hub-on-hub part at the end so that your mind is prepared. Just let yourself sense whatever focusing attention on awareness itself feels like. After a couple of minutes, let yourself find the breath again, in and out, and then, when you are ready, take a more intentional and perhaps deeper breath and let your eyes come open if they're shut, and let the wheel practice come to a close.

◼

There are many other forms of taking time-in on a regular basis, including focusing on being more compassionate with yourself and others in a systematic way. Even when you are in motion there are ways to take time-in. You can mindfully walk by focusing on the internal sensations from the bottoms of your feet with each step. And you can do other mindful movement practices that encourage you to focus on your intentions, awareness, and sensations. Focusing attention on your intention, being aware of your awareness, and staying present with a stance of kindness and compassion are the essential elements of time-in practices. Each of these practices offers a research-proven way to empower your life. Many studies suggest that taking time daily, even just three minutes several times each day, to focus mindfully on your breath can greatly support your well-being. Time-in integrates your brain, improves your relationships, and strengthens your mind. In so many ways, taking time-in on a daily basis is the powerful starting place to create more integration in your life.

PART III

■

Your Attachments

Close relationships shape us across the life span. Learning about the fundamental ways our connections to others can enrich our lives as they support a healthy mind and likely promote integration in our brains can guide us in creating the relationships that are best for us no matter our age. Our experiences in the first dozen or so years of our lives have a powerful impact on the people we become. Friendships, experiences in school, activities we participate in, and relationships with family members all influence how our brains develop during the years leading up to adolescence. But even after these early years, relationships continue to play a crucial role in our growth and development. In this part we'll explore how the ways we relate to our caregivers shape how our minds develop to reveal some basic guiding principles of relationships. The great news is that by under-standing what happened to you and how you responded to those experiences in the past, you can open your life now to more produc-tive and healthy ways of relating to others, and even to yourself.

Especially influential in terms of how the brain develops—and, in turn, how we learn to calm our emotions, how we understand ourselves, and how we relate to others and the larger world—are our experiences during infancy. The relationships we have with our par-ents and other people who care for us when we are very young most directly shape who we become. But it is crucial to keep in mind that our minds are continually emerging, our brains continually growing in response to experience, and whether you are an adolescent or an adult now, how you make sense of your life and understand these patterns of connecting with others can empower you to optimize how you live.

If you are an adolescent still living with a parent, you may feel intense and complex emotions as you explore these ideas about fam-ily life still going on in the present. I also know, from personal expe-rience as a parent, that reflecting on ways we parent our children and adolescents can be challenging as we face some at times non-ideal patterns of communicating that have been present in our parenting approach. Naturally, we want to do well with our kids. But doing well may sometimes elude us if we've had challenging experiences in our own past. So much of what I've tried to explore in earlier books is how important it is for us to be honest with ourselves and open to the important continuing growth we can model for our offspring. There is no such thing as perfect parenting. But there is a way to make sense of our lives so that we move toward authentic ways of relating that are supportive of our kids and ourselves. So please keep this in mind: It is never too late to course correct, to come to a deeper understanding and enhance the way we connect in our families with the people we love and care so deeply about. If change were not possible, there wouldn't be much reason to dive into this material. But science and experience reveal that with self-reflection and understanding, non-ideal patterns we've adopted from our own pasts can be transformed. Be patient with yourself and with your family members. With kindness and understanding, to yourself and to others, change can be nurtured and good things can emerge.

Connections with others, our relationships, come in many forms. These important connections with our parents or other caregivers are called "attachment relationships." We carry these selective few attachment relationships forward inside us in what are called "models of attachment." The term "model" broadly means the mental way, shaped by brain-firing patterns, that we summarize across experiences and generate a schema that lets us anticipate what is happening next, how we should behave, what emotions we will have, and how we filter our perceptions. Models are really useful in learning and knowing how to behave, and they often influence our ways of seeing and being in the world without our awareness.

An attachment model is in effect the way in which our brains remember the attachment relationship(s) we have had, or still have, and how we have adapted to these formative attachment experiences. The models we carry with us in our minds are very influential in terms of how we feel, how we think, how we behave, and how we connect with friends, teachers, and later on, our romantic partners as we move through our lives. And since we can have more than one model if we've had more than one attachment figure, then each of these brain states, these models, can influence how we behave and react in different situations.

Our attachment models get activated in specific situations that may resemble the particular kind of attachment relationship we had in the past, and then they shape how we interact in that present moment. If we are with an assertive older female friend, for example, we may begin acting as we did with our mother, who, too, may have been an assertive personality. In contrast, if we adapted to a mild-mannered father with our own withdrawal, with a quiet male friend we might find ourselves becoming withdrawn and not even know the reason why. Models become engaged automatically, without our awareness or intention. For all of us, adolescents and parents, under-standing what kinds of attachment models we constructed in our early childhood can greatly help us understand how our lives are unfolding now, and how we might create a new way of living that frees us from any kind of limitations such models may be making in our lives.

There are two broad types of models, one secure and the other non-secure. Secure models support our living with flexibility, self-understanding, and ease of connection with others. Non-secure mod-els come in several forms we'll explore here, and each of these in some ways challenges our ability to be flexible, understand ourselves, and connect with others. Because we can have many models and their activation is dependent on the situation we find ourselves in, we can seem quite different in different settings with different people.

In many ways, developing secure attachment models is an impor-tant way to support the ESSENCE of adolescence. With security our emotional spark can be freed to enrich our lives with passion rather than pushing us toward states of being chaotically overwhelmed or rigidly shut down. With secure models, too, we can have social en-gagements that are mutually rewarding and enable us to feel both differentiated and linked within the integrative social connections that help us thrive as adolescents. We will see that secure attachment is as much about offering a safe harbor of support, to turn to when we are distressed or tired, as it is about supporting how we go out and explore the world. With such a secure launching pad, we can

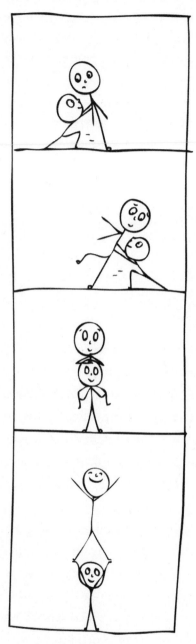

I support you.

take on our drive to seek novelty with more gusto and strength. Security supports the development of a resilient mind. And as our minds find new ways of experiencing how we think and reflect on life during adolescence, having secure attachment models can support our creative explorations during this new period of our growth.

In this part we'll explore what your experiences with attachment figures in your life have been and what attachment models you may have now. We'll then see how we can use this understanding and specific strategies to develop secure attachment models that set the foundations of resilience and support the ESSENCE of adolescence to help you create a life that's best for you, whatever your age.

Safe Harbor and Launching Pad

I have an aquarium in my office and I love to sit and stare at the fish as they swim about. Interestingly, while some fish do care for their young, my fish are typical of most fish (and reptiles and amphibians, for that matter) that fertilize their eggs, deposit them in the sand, and leave them to fend for themselves after they hatch. We mammals are very different. A key feature of our mammalian heritage is that our young require the close care of an adult figure, often the mother, who provides safety and nurturance. That's attachment.

One important feature of human child rearing is that we don't just have one attachment figure as most mammals do. We humans practice what is called alloparenting, which means "other parenting," sharing child rearing with other trusted adults or older children. This ability is crucial for us as a social species and may have shaped how we evolved as a species in general in terms of our unique abilities for communicating and building collaborative relationships. Alloparenting also means that we can have attachments to more than just our mother; we can form attachments to a selective few older, stronger, and hopefully wiser individuals to whom we turn for protection and comfort.

As complex social creatures, we have a very extended period of dependency on our attachment figures. The human brain needs the relationships with our attachment figures and other adults to shape how it grows. Our childhood period of dependency goes on for a good 15 percent of our lifetime—a really long time in mammalian terms. And if we include the period of adolescence, now extended into the twenties, that percentage before we reach adult status in our society is higher still, approaching a third of our lives.

Human attachment can be understood as involving four S's. We need to be *seen*, *safe*, and *soothed*, in order to feel *secure*. Being seen means that our inner mental life is sensed beneath our behavior. Our caregiver hears our cry, figures out what our inner need is, and then offers us something that meets that need. Being safe means we are both protected from harm and not terrified by our caregiver. To be soothed means that when we are distressed, our caregiver's response makes us feel better. When we need comfort, we get a hug. And all of this—being seen, safe, and soothed in a reliable way—gives us an overall sense of security in the relationship.

These ways our attachment figures treat us give us a sense of a safe harbor in which we can feel secure. But attachment relationships also serve as a launching pad from which we can take off and explore the world. When we have a secure attachment model, we have the security to venture out into all that lies ahead in the world beyond our home. And when we are tired, or distressed, or just need to touch base, we return to the safe harbor of our attachment home, our relationships with our attachment figures.

As we grow from infancy into toddlerhood, this sense of security in our relationship is internalized in our brains in a "state of mind"

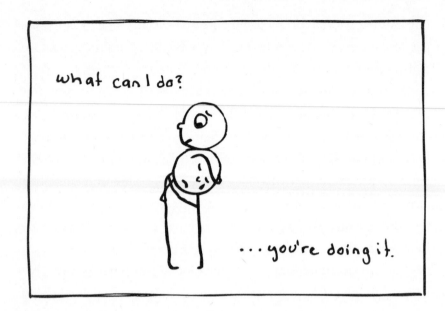

that is secure. We feel good about ourselves, good about connecting with others, and feel that our needs will be met. Even more, in a humble and solid versus demanding and entitled way, we feel we'll be able to have connections with others who will see our minds, feel our feelings, and meet our needs. This is the solid sense of self that emerges for those with secure attachment models.

When we hit adolescence, having a secure attachment model can be a real blessing as we go out into the world and experience all the many changes that becoming an adolescent means and what the journey toward adulthood may entail. If we've had secure attachment in our earlier childhood, then we enter these early adolescent stages with a more secure model, a state of mind that is filled with many of the prefrontal functions that emerge with integration strong and well-developed. Science has shown that secure attachment is associated with the integrative prefrontal functions that include regulating the body, attuning to others and ourselves, balancing our emotions, being flexible, soothing our fears, having insight into ourselves and empathy for others, and having a good grounding in a sense of morality.

To put this proposal in a nutshell, when we've had secure attachments, our relational experiences have supported the development of integration in the brain and resilience of our mind. When we have had insecure attachments, the development of our non-secure models reflects states of non-integrated brain functioning. You can see the basic idea here: If you've had a history of insecure attachment, to grow toward security happens by moving from non-integrated brain functioning to the development of integration in your brain. And that development can potentially happen at any age.

Secure attachment confers resilience as it likely stimulates the growth of integrative connections of the prefrontal cortex. Recall that the prefrontal region links cortex, limbic area, brainstem, body, and even the social world into one coordinated and balanced whole. This is the power of attachment relationships to create healthy and adaptive functions in our lives, functions that emerge from integration in our brains.

While entering adolescence with a secure model of attachment makes it more likely that the adolescent period will be smoother, it does not guarantee it. Resilience is important, but it does not confer absolute immunity to the many curve balls life sends our way. As we've seen, the remodeling period of development that occurs in adolescence can play a role in the emergence of many challenges to well-being, including the onset of various psychiatric conditions such as mood, anxiety, and thought disorders, as well as drug abuse and addiction. These conditions are not caused by attachment and their onsets are not necessarily prevented by secure attachment. Any of these can emerge even with a history of secure attachment, as many other factors in life influence our development besides attachment, such as our temperament, our extended social relationships, our socioeconomic status, our genetics, and our use of dopamine-activating substances. Studies suggest, for example, that certain variations in our genetic makeup that influence ways we process dopamine, serotonin, or oxytocin may have a direct effect on how we respond to certain challenging experiences in life. Attachment is one important element of our lives, but not the whole story. Still, since attachment influences so much, and because we can actively empower our lives as we shape our attachment models in a positive way, knowing about attachment is vital for any of us. You may not be able to alter your genes, but you can alter your mind and your behavior to change your brain. In other words, your attachment models are changeable, and knowing about your attachment models is crucial so that you can move them toward security whatever your age.

For about one-half to two-thirds of the general population, secure attachment is where we start out in life. If that is mostly where you've come from, you've got a great starting place to enter adolescence, a boost in your ability to be resilient when life throws challenges your way. But for about one-third to one-half of us, which means about 150 million people in the United States alone, we have had attachment relationships that were not secure. These insecure attachments don't necessarily mean that we are insecure on the whole as people, it simply means that we didn't consistently receive those S's of being seen, safe, and soothed, and so did not feel secure in our primary attachment relationships. Our non-secure models of attachment reflect how we had to adapt to this insecure relationship when we were younger. And these models of attachment persist throughout our lives. They are changeable, yes, but only if we come to understand them.

With a history of insecure attachment, our brains may not enter the adolescent period with the same baseline integrative growth that a securely attached person has been able to develop in childhood.

The great news is that it is never too late to develop integration in our brains! We can move from non-secure models of attachment, those states of non-integrated brain functioning, to secure, integrated models by developing integration in our brains. One way we can do this is to make sense of what has happened in our lives. Making sense moves us from a non-secure, non-integrated model of attachment to a place of security and an integrated model of attachment.

In this part, we'll explore your life history and try to make sense of the different kinds of attachment that you may have experienced in your childhood and the attachment models that may now be a part of your internal world. Whether you are an adolescent still living with your attachment figures, your parents or others, or you are an older adolescent or adult living away from your attachment figures, making sense of your life is a science-proven way to move from non-secure to secure models of attachment. It's a way of integrating your brain and empowering your life.

The Ways We Attach

There are four broad ways we become attached to our parents or others who care for us. For simplicity, I will usually use the term "parent," even though you may have had a number of caregivers, be they your mother and father, relatives, friends, or others who took care of you and to whom you turned when you needed comfort and protection. As we've seen, our brains are capable of maintaining several different models of attachment, one for each relationship to a given attachment figure. So as we explore these four ways of being attached to our caregivers, keep in mind that you, like many of us, may actually have more than one of these models inside you shaping your inner sense of self and how you relate to others. The setting you are in, how people respond to you, and how people remind you of one of your attachment figures can all directly influence which of these models becomes activated at a particular time.

The Secure Model

If you had a relationship with a parent who in a somewhat consistent way provided you with a sense of being seen, feeling safe, and being soothed, then you will have a model of secure attachment. This secure model lets you balance your emotions, understand yourself well, and engage with others in mutually rewarding ways. Attachment continues across the life span, but to give you a sense of how the fundamental research is done, here's a brief summary of how attachment is assessed during infancy: After about a three-minute separation from the caregiver, the one-year-old infant seeks contact with the caregiver during their reunion, touches base for comfort, and then readily returns to exploring a room filled with toys. The researchers view this interactive behavior as evidence of a secure attachment model in the child that is activated in the presence of this particular parent. The idea is that the parent has provided both a safe haven and a launching pad; the child feels seen, safe, soothed, and secure with this parent. This learned model is then activated so that the child makes contact, feels secure, and launches out to explore the world of new toys in the room.

From infancy on, we carry these models forward as they help us organize our approach to relationships throughout the life span.

The Avoidant Model

If you had a similar experience growing up to about 20 percent of the general population, you had a relationship with one or both parents that was filled with repeated experiences of your not being seen or soothed. Here the form of insecure relationship is called "avoidant attachment." This term comes from research findings in which investigators observed one-year-old infants who were separated from their father or mother later avoiding that parent when he or she returned, rather than reconnecting and seeking comfort from the parent, as happened in the secure relationships. Here the notion is that the child's experience of not being seen or soothed over the first year of life with this parent has led to the development of a non-secure model of attachment—in this case, an avoidant model. In the presence of that parent, the child activates a model of avoidance. This is a learned response quite adaptive for the child's survival.

It's important to note that in these studies it was also seen that several of the infants who avoided one parent actually sought comfort and closeness with the other parent. In other words, if you have an avoidant attachment model as a result of your relationship with one parent, this doesn't mean that you can't have a secure attachment with your other parent, enabling you to go through life knowing what a truly secure relationship feels like. But with avoidant models and the avoidant relationships they grow from, you've learned something very different. With a repeated set of experiences where interacting with that parent, say your father, is not soothing when you are distressed, and not connecting when you feel unseen, then the model you develop says something like, "I don't need this person for anything, because I have learned that he gives me nothing when I need connection or comfort." You learned to minimize your attachment needs. Having this avoidant model as your model for close relationships can potentially lead you to feel disconnected from others and also from your own emotions and needs. That's the disconnected self of avoidant attachment.

Let's highlight again here that your attachment model is a summary of how you've adapted to the relationships you've had with important people in your life. It's not, however, a sign of some problem you have inside you—it's merely a reflection of a learned response to real-life events, to your actual relationship in your early days. Furthermore, it does not mean you are now devoid of a need for closeness and comfort. While these models may be cortical adaptations that shape our external behaviors and our awareness, studies reveal that the limbic area that mediates attachment still retains a deep drive for connection with others. We all need to feel close to the people around us and know that we can rely on them for comfort. That's just being human. In this respect, the self-knowledge that comes from realizing you may have been living your life following an avoidant model can be very empowering. It can allow you to search the quiet, often hidden signals inside you that you may want closer connection with others. Sensing these signals may help you release your avoidant model so you can seek out from others what you need in life as you mature and age. The avoidant model was good and useful during your early years; now it needs updating. Reflecting on these patterns can be one important step in enabling you to transform your non-secure attachment models toward security.

The Ambivalent Model

A third type of relationship is when a child experiences inconsistency or intrusiveness with a parent, as occurs in around 15 percent of the general population. Being seen, safe, and soothed does not happen in a reliable way. When the parent returns after a separation, you go to her, but you cling to her because you are uncertain whether she'll meet your needs for comfort. Maybe she will, but maybe she won't. Better hold on! Your ambivalent model of attachment does not allow you to become soothed as you never know what to expect—she is not a reliable safe harbor. And her feelings and emotions flood your own inner world as well. For example, if you feel hungry, instead of your mom just figuring that out and feeding you, she gets flooded with her own anxiety and fears about whether she will be an effective mother for you. Since the human brain is composed of "mirror neurons" that soak up the feelings of others around us, you naturally sponge up her anxiety and fear. All you were feeling was hunger, but after interacting with your mom you now also feel fearful and anxious. Whose feelings are whose? That's the confused self created within ambivalent attachment relationships. You amplify your attachment needs with ambivalence because of the history of intrusiveness and inconsistency. Maybe this time she can soothe you, but maybe not, but maybe so, but maybe . . . That's ambivalence.

The Disorganized Model

The fourth kind of attachment can occur within the setting of the other three—secure, avoidant, or ambivalent. Besides those baseline experiences of attachment, something else is going on. For a variety of reasons, your parent, say your mom, is terrifying to you. This could be because she is depressed and irritable and runs after you, yelling at you when you get home from school. This could be because she is screaming at your father or your siblings and not at you. And this could be because she just looks terrified herself and you *sponge* her terror up inside you. The problem with being terrified of an attachment figure is that it activates two different circuits in your brain that just don't work together. One is the ancient brainstem circuit that mediates a survival reaction. This circuit gets you to flee or freeze in reaction to being terrified. Get away from this source of terror! But the second circuit is the limbic-based attachment system that motivates you if you are terrified to go toward your attachment figure to be protected and soothed. The problem is you cannot go both toward and away from the same person. After separation, the infant shows behaviors of attempting to both approach and withdraw from the parent, a very disorganized approach to the reconnection.

So when an attachment figure is the source of terror, we become fragmented. This disorganized attachment makes us vulnerable in many ways. We can have a tough time balancing our emotions, having good relationships with others, and even thinking clearly under stress. Even more, a disorganized attachment makes it likely that we'll have a fragmentation of the continuity of consciousness, called "dissociation." Found in about 5 to 15 percent of the general population even without a history of abuse, and in about 80 percent of children in high-risk families with trauma and neglect, disorganized attachment and the dissociation that accompanies it can be very challenging to our well-being. When we dissociate, we dis-associate different aspects of ourselves, such as separating feelings from memories, thoughts from actions. We can feel unreal and broken apart. This is the source of a fragmented self that emerges with a disorganized model of attachment.

Reactive Attachment

When a secure attachment is not available, we can experience a range of ways that we adapt and do the best we can, including avoidance, ambivalence, and disorganization. But there are a number of situations in which our attachment may not be simply secure or insecure. At one extreme of our human spectrum of experiences is the complete absence of attachment, in which there is no consistent figure that we can attach to. In this case, a dysfunctional condition called reactive attachment may arise and we may have trouble with our emotions and relationships, establishing rapid connections with a wide array of individuals in childhood, in adolescence, and into our adulthood. Reactive attachment can be thought of as the best a child can do with the absence of any attachment figure—not a response to forms of security or insecurity. This absence and the "disorder" that emerges with it are distinct from the variety of insecure forms of attachment we are exploring here. If you know individuals who've experienced this absence of attachment, or if you've been through this yourself, please refer to some of the important work in the professional literature on this situation as helpful resources for healthy growth.

Earning Secure Attachment and Integrating the Brain

When Gail's son, Steven, was leaving home for college after his eighteenth birthday, he was excited to begin this next phase of his life. Many of his friends were leaving California for the East Coast, but he decided to stay in the West and attend a school about five hours away from his home in Los Angeles. His mother had gotten ill in his last year of high school, and he wanted to be able to return home and see her more frequently than a cross-country college would have enabled him to do. He felt close to his mother, and like his brother and sister, he was very distressed with her diagnosis of cancer. He did his best to support her during her radiation and chemotherapy, but she insisted he continue to go out with his friends during that senior year and get ready for this new time of his life. It was Steven's decision to stay close—but not that close. In fact he felt completely supported by his mother in his decision not to attend UCLA, a wonderful option for him just a few miles from his family's home.

Gail had herself been through a lot in her own childhood. Her mother died when she was fifteen, and her father had been an actively drinking alcoholic during much of her childhood. The death of Gail's mother "woke her father up," and he began a life of sobriety after that time and has stayed sober ever since. Her family seemed to get closer in the face of that tragedy of her mother's passing. For much of her adolescence, Gail was in turmoil about how she could leave her two sisters and her father when it was time to graduate from high school. She decided to go to a community college near home and help out her father, a decision she was glad to make then. But before she got married to Steven's dad, she spent a lot of time thinking about how upsetting her father's alcoholism had been in her childhood. When he'd come home drunk, he was terrifying. His fits of rage and drunken stupors led everyone to scramble for cover—everyone except her mother, who would take him on. Gail would witness her father berating her mom, and sometimes physically abusing her. She didn't know then but knows now that witnessing abuse is itself a form of abuse, a form of trauma. You might imagine that Gail's early attachment experiences with her dad being filled with terror led her to have a disorganized attachment to him. His drunken states were terrifying. His berating and beating her mom were terrifying. And her feeling of being unable to protect her two younger sisters made her feel terrified and helpless.

During Gail's later adolescence in her early twenties, she decided to try psychotherapy. This is when I first met her. We worked on her history of insecure attachments, including a disorganized attachment model and the accompanying tendency of her mind to fragment in dissociative states. These dis-associations of usually connected processes could come out when she was upset and felt like she was "not put together" and "unraveling at the seams." She'd go down the low road frequently with her boyfriend and her father, yelling at them, feeling intense and "overblown" emotional reactions to small things they'd do. Or these dissociative moments could emerge and she would feel blank and a have a difficult time remembering things or paying attention. When she was a teen, for example, there were times when she couldn't seem to hold on to her memories of her mother after she died, the loss being overwhelming and her relationship with her father still terrifying. We gathered from her attachment assessment that she had what is called an ambivalent history with her mom, who had been preoccupied about her competence as a mother and a wife. Her mom had been warm and caring, but it was a relationship that Gail said was "loving but a confusing mess." Dealing with her feelings toward this confusion was challenging in the face of her grief about her mother's passing. In some ways, there were elements of unresolved loss around her mother, too. Reflecting on that important loss in her life could help her resolve that grief and gain more access to her feelings about their complicated relationship.

Gail generally did pretty well in her emotional and social life as therapy went on, and she was grateful for these changes. Because she had an ambivalent pattern of insecurity with her primary caregiver— her mother—she needed to do some basic work on sensing her own integrity, clarifying from the confusion who she was, what she felt, and how she could hold on to her own inner compass in the face of interacting with others. This transformation from her insecure ambivalent attachment model toward security meant that she could feel her feelings and balance them well. And that meant that she could have mutually rewarding relationships with friends and romantic partners. Our attachment models contain the important ways we've learned to connect to others and know ourselves. When we make sense of our lives, we can move these models from non-security to security.

When Gail met her husband, fell in love, and started her family in her late twenties, some of the paternally related issues of disorganization began to emerge in her life and in their relationship. When they'd have arguments, as most couples do, she would flip out and feel terrified. Instead of standing her ground and expressing her needs, she'd sink into a hole that to her felt like quicksand, and as she struggled to get out she'd dissolve away. This repeating pattern revealed the rigidity of Gail's being stuck and the chaos of her falling apart that were aspects of her non-integrated models of attachment. Some of this pattern may have been a result of her ambivalent history and sense of loss with her mom, and perhaps a fear of losing her present attachment figure, her husband. But in the setting in which these experiences arose, they also seemed to have elements of a response to being terrified and to be related to the dissociation from her disorganized attachment with her dad. Fortunately, these times of becoming fragmented were infrequent, and they emerged only in the close connection she had with her husband. Gail would find herself simply withdrawing from him in ways that dismissed her own needs for closeness. This pattern of disconnecting had the quality of an avoidant model, one that was clearly a part of her relationship with her father. With friends and her work colleagues, such disconnection and such dissociation never occurred. We can see this as her avoidant and disorganized models of attachment being activated only in the setting of her relationship with her husband. Such state-dependent activation of an attachment model is just how our human brain works. What was a problem, though, was that such disconnection and dissociation made her unable to have a solid sense of herself in connection with her husband. Whichever models were being activated, they were preventing her from having the kind of integrated relationship in which differences could be honored and compassionate connections created that would make her life more fulfilling and at ease with her husband.

Through making sense of her past and working on being present even in the face of her terrifying feelings—with her loss of her mom, with her memories of her dad, and with her fear of her husband's anger when they'd fight—Gail gained the integrative ability to simply hold in awareness whatever she was experiencing. She went through the painful process of reflecting on her relationship with her drunken father, about the terror, about her sense of helplessness. And in that process, she came to make sense of what had been non-sense at that time in her life. What this meant was that she could now see the impact that those terrifying experiences with no solution had on her at that time and how they'd continued to affect her now.

Gail would also practice a way of being mindful, of being curious and open about her own internal experiences without judgment. In the face of a fragmented consciousness with disorganized attachment, it became essential that we work to integrate consciousness itself. We did many of the practices you can learn in this book, like the Wheel of Awareness and breath practice, which strengthened her mind and integrated her brain. With this new sense of clarity, she could feel her own needs for closeness, her attachment needs, with openness and acceptance rather than the earlier confusion or dismissal. With the empowerment of these practices, too, her dissociation became less frequent and less intense and transformed into her ability to simply be aware of a sense of "wanting to fall apart" but able to resist that impulse. All of this reflective work enabled her to transform these non-secure attachment models into one of security.

By the time Steven was a young boy, Gail had taken the time to develop what researchers call "earned security." We could also call this "learned security." Over the years since Gail was initially in therapy, she'd come in for check-ins periodically and I'd hear about Steven's development. When Gail was diagnosed with cancer, I also saw her to support how she could deal with her fears during this terrifying time. With her earned security, she was in a new integrative position not to withdraw, become confused, or fragment her mind.

And with this earned security, over these years she could also be a source of secure attachment for Steven. She was able to be a soothing safe harbor for him and a solid launching pad.

So as Steven approached his own time to leave the nest, he came to this adolescent turning point with the integrative resilience of a secure attachment model with his mom. Research has shown clearly that no matter our challenging past, if we make sense of how our early experiences have shaped us and learn our new models of security, we can offer our children security of attachment. Steven happened to have security with his dad, too, so he was feeling solidly ready to leave home. His closeness with his mother in the face of her illness made him feel the need to stay close enough to home to come back whenever she might need him to be there, but not so close that he didn't realize the deep inner drive to explore the world that he could now launch into with security.

Reflecting on Your Attachments and Making Sense of Your Life

Whether you are an adolescent or an adult, it is important to make sense of what your early attachment relationships were like in your childhood. Given the nature of memory development before the age of five or so, it can be hard to recall in any continuous way from this very early period in our lives. This said, even the faintest impressions can be quite helpful. And research shows, too, that a set of questions that support your exploration of what you can recall can help reveal certain patterns that are helpful in your journey to get a broad sense of the attachment models you may have now in your life. The fantastic news is that if you can make sense of your childhood experiences—especially your relationships with your parents—you can transform your attachment models toward security. The reason this is important is that your relationships—with friends, with romantic partners, with present or possible future offspring—will be profoundly enhanced. And you'll feel better with yourself, too!

In science we use a formal Attachment Interview to figure out how a person has made sense of his or her attachment experiences. Hundreds of studies reveal that these patterns are helpful to gain insight into our attachment models. My own work in that field led me to develop a way to help people make sense of their lives and propose how this process may integrate their brains in psychotherapy, and I figuring it out...

MY Life

...One piece at a time.

published that approach in a couple of books, including *Mindsight* and *Parenting from the Inside Out*. The latter book includes a set of questions that I've adapted here for you to use as a guide for reflecting on your own experience, whether you are an adolescent or an adult. Let me invite you to read over these questions, and afterward we'll go through each of the models of attachment and the kinds of responses they tend to include, and then we'll see how you can understand them and move them toward security. Remember, you may have many models of attachment, one for each relationship you have had with your caregivers. You may want to write your responses down in a journal, or simply reflect on them in your own way. Because you may still be living with your attachment figures, your parents or others, or you may have moved away from them, the questions are both in the present tense and in the past tense. Just focus on whichever one applies to your situation now.

Understanding yourself is a basic mindsight tool for integrating your life. Self-understanding is how you connect your past from memory with your present experience. This is an important step in learning how to have secure attachment models in our lives. When we create a narrative of who we are, we link past and present so we can become the active author of a possible future, too. So self-understanding helps us with "mental time travel" as we create a coherent view and integration of ourselves across the past, present, and future.

Questions for Reflection on Attachment

Background

What is (was) it like growing up in your family?

Who is (was) in your family?

What is (was) your parents' philosophy about raising children?

What do (did) or don't (didn't) you like about being raised in your family?

Would you raise (Are you raising) your own children in a similar way, or differently?

Relationships

Do (Did) you get along well with your parents and others in your family?

How do (did) your family members get along with one another?

How have your relationships in your family changed over
time?

If you have two parents, how are (were) your relationships
with each parent similar or different?

State a few words that reflect your relationship with each
parent from your earliest years.

Are there ways you have tried to be like or not like each
of your parents?

Are there any others in your life who have served as
parenting figures to whom you feel attached? If so,
please answer the above questions regarding that person
or those persons.

Separation

Can you remember your first time being separated from
your parents? What was that like and how did it affect
you and your parents?

Did you ever experience a long separation from your
parents in your childhood? What was that like for you
and for your parents?

Discipline

What ways do (did) your parents respond to your
behaviors to teach you how to behave?

Do (Did) your parents use punishment in their discipline?

How have these strategies of being disciplined influenced
your development?

Fear and Threat

Have you ever felt threatened by your parents?

Have you ever felt rejected by your parents?

Have there been any other experiences that may have
been overwhelming in your life? What were these, and
how do you feel they have influenced your life?

Do any of these experiences feel like they are still very
much alive now in your life?

Loss

Has anyone significant in your life died?

Has anyone significant in your life left?

What impact have these losses had on you and your family?

How do these losses affect you now in your life?

Emotional Communication

How do (did) your parents communicate with you when
you are (were) happy and excited?

What happens (would happen) when you are (were)
distressed, unhappy, injured, or ill?

Does (Did) each parent respond with different patterns of
connecting to you when your emotions are (were)
intense?

How do you communicate with others now when
emotions run high?

Safe Harbor

Are (Were) there relationships you can (could) turn to, or
places you can (could) go, that you can (could) rely on
to help you feel comforted at difficult times? Did such a
safe harbor exist when you were a child?

How do you feel those sources of a safe haven affect
(affected) your life?

Do (Did) you feel seen, safe, and soothed by your parents?

Launching Pad

How do (did) your parents support your explorations
  away from them or outside the home?

How are (were) your interests supported by your parents?

Did you feel secure as a child to go out and explore the
  world?

Now

What is your relationship like now with your parents?

Why do you think your parents act (acted) the way
  they do (did)?

Do you try to not do things because of how your parents
  treat (treated) you?

As you reflect on all of these experiences, how do you
  think they influence the ways you relate to other
  people?

How do you feel all of these things we have been
  exploring have influenced who you are now as a person
  and how you have come to be the way you are?

Future

What would you wish for yourself in your future
  relationships?

How do you imagine the experiences from your
  attachment relationships and early childhood may shape
  the person you can become?

Are there any factors from your past that are restricting
  you in the present and limiting who you can be in the
  future?

What do you see as your "growth edge" for things you'd
  like to change in yourself so that you can become freed

up to be the person you would like to be in the
future?

Any other questions we should have covered or that
you may have now?

You're worth figuring out.

How was responding to these questions for you? Sometimes reflecting on these questions can be quite draining. Sometimes what
comes up can be surprising, even shocking. And sometimes you already know how you will respond and it is not a big deal.

Interestingly, researchers who collectively have studied over ten
thousand formal Attachment Interviews featuring questions and topics similar to those above uncovered universal patterns. I'll present
you with the general findings next so you can get a feel for what may
be going on with you. Please keep in mind, however, as you read
these broad groupings and their narrative patterns, that the key to
reflecting on them is not to lump yourself in one category or an-

other, but rather to find helpful insights into your own life that you can weave together into a coherent narrative of your own. Research reveals that the more coherent a narrative we have of our own attachment issues in childhood, the more we've made sense of how our early life experiences have shaped us, the more likely our children will have a secure attachment to us and the more rewarding in general our interpersonal relationships will be. With our own coherent life story, we'll be more likely to consistently provide the four S's of attachment. And as securely attached children grow up, they'll be more likely, too, to have a way of making sense of their lives and creating a coherent life narrative. They'll have a coherent sense of who they've been, of who they are now, and of who they'd like to become. And they'll have a coherent way of being themselves while also having close, meaningful relationships with others. That's what making sense of your life can help bring into your world. That's what secure attachment can offer—whatever age you are when you develop that integrated way of making sense of your life.

Our Attachment Narratives and the Two Sides of the Brain

While the details of each of the Attachment Interviews scientists have conducted vary from person to person, when looked at as a whole across individuals, patterns emerge. Attachment Interviews are tape recorded and then transcribed. The written document is then analyzed for its language use and the ways in which the interviewee communicates with the interviewer (the researcher). In this way, the "narrative analysis" is really a discourse analysis that looks at how one person is communicating with another. The interview findings reveal that individuals with secure attachment models generally reflect in a coherent way on the good and bad parts of what may have happened during childhood. We can't know the accuracy of the facts that are recalled, of course, but we can assess how the responses fit together in a coherent manner—how they make sense, how they are open and flexible in reflecting on various aspects of the past, and how they are reflective and in the present moment with the questions and not just offered as a pre-programmed set of responses.

Even when experiences may have been difficult, or even frightening, a *secure narrative* reveals this quality of the person being present for whatever comes up in the interview. This state of presence is the hallmark of secure attachment, both in how we connect with others and how we connect with our own life story. We are present, meaning we are open and accepting to whatever is happening as it is happening. And this presence in our life story, this attachment security, comes along with narrative coherence, how we've come to terms with the positive and negative of our early relationships, and how we've made sense of our lives.

In others with avoidant attachment histories, or the parents of those with avoidant attachments, the narrative is quite different. The hallmark of these *avoidant narrative* reflections is that the individuals insist that they do not recall anything about family life and that their family life did not influence how they developed. That is a form of incoherence in that if you don't remember something, how do you know that this something did not affect you? The adults with this narrative are said to have a "dismissing" state of mind—they dismiss the idea that their past relationships may have had an impact on who they are. In short, they appear to "avoid" placing importance on the relationships in their lives possibly because this is the best adaptation they could come up with in the face of the emotional desert that is an avoidant attachment relationship.

To understand what may be going on in the pathway from specific forms of attachment relationships in childhood to corresponding attachment narratives in adolescence and adulthood, it is helpful to turn to studies of the brain in creating a working framework. In this view, non-secure attachment models emerge from non-integrated states of brain functioning. In many ways, the communication between parent and child that does not honor differences and promote linkage—that is, patterns of communicating in non-integrated relationships—leads to blocked integration in the child's developing brain. Simply put, this view suggests that integrated communication stimulates the growth of integration in the brain. Non-integrated communication leads to non-integrated brain development.

My proposal, drawn from clinical work and scientific reasoning, suggests that there is an underdevelopment of the right hemisphere of the brain in individuals with avoidant attachment. It is the right side that stores autobiographical memory and holds our raw emotional needs and feelings. In this way, the avoidant model enables us to not feel our needs, and we also don't recall our lived experiences of family life. That explains not only the narrative findings, but also the way avoidant models shape our behavior in relationships where we ignore the non-verbal communication from others, signals that are both sent and received by the right side of the brain.

Personal reflection in the cortex is a process that draws on autobiographical mappings in the brain's cortical region, dominant on the right side of the brain. Such autobiographical reflection is the way we look inward to the meanings and events of our lived experience. Interestingly, even our gut reactions and heartfelt sensations, signals arising from the intestines and the neural circuitry around the heart, arise and end up primarily on the right side of the brain, as it is the right prefrontal cortex that receives such bodily input. These sources of knowing are generally not experienced much by individuals with avoidant attachment.

While both sides of the brain usually work together, they do have differentiated functions. These functions influence not so much what we do as the ways we perceive the world and our ways of being in the world.

The left side of the cortex is dominant for language, logic, linear and literal thinking, and even making lists, like this one! Notice, too, that in English this is a convenient and easy-to-remember list because each word starts with an *l*, as in "left-sided." Many studies also suggest that facts are dominant on the left side, while our autobiographical recollections of episodes of experience are right-side dominant.

(I'd like to ask you to focus on using your left hemisphere's skills to take in some of these scientific details we're about to dive into. The reason to do this is that when we understand some of the fascinating and relevant brain facts in a logical, linear way, we actually can then use that knowledge to hyperdrive the ways we can transform our non-secure attachment models toward security. You'll need your right hemisphere's talents, too, in order to fully grasp the context and personal meaning of some of these brain notions. You can feel the sense of what we're about to explore, and you can track its logic as well. So at this very moment, we'll be calling on both sides of your brain to take in the details of what we're about to explore. In the following three sections, we'll use the gist of all this foundation to examine how each of the non-secure attachment models can be transformed by focusing the mind to integrate the brain and your relationships. Don't worry about recalling every detail, they're all here and you can review them whenever you want. The key is that soon we'll explore how we'll apply them in your own life. Just let the sense of these logical connections fill both sides of your brain and get ready for some continuing integrative work!)

The right side of the cortex is not only a primary source of our autobiographical knowledge; it is also dominant for receiving more direct input from the lower subcortical areas in addition to the body as a whole. And yes, you may have guessed that the right side is often considered "more emotional" in that subcortical and bodily input shape our emotional life more directly and perhaps more spontaneously and robustly. The right side of the cortex maps out the whole of the interior of the body; but the left does not do this. This means that intuition, how we receive the wisdom of the body's input from our muscles, our hearts, our intestines, likely first influences our right cortex. The left side of the cortex has emotion, too, but it may be experienced in a different way, as that side is not so powerfully influenced by the subcortical regions as the right is.

So you can see how different the two sides are in how they focus our attention and how they enable us to be in the world. They differ in other fundamental ways, too, as we'll see now.

The left side of the brain has one frontal region that when activated creates an "approach state" that empowers us to go out in the world and face challenges. In contrast, the right side has areas that create a withdrawal response to new things. This approach to the world goes along with what some summarize in this general way: The left looks outward to the world, while the right looks inward, in the self and others. For this reason, it shouldn't be such a surprise that the left side of the brain specializes not only in language but also in keeping track of our "social display rules," the culturally sanctioned ways we are supposed to communicate with one another. In this way, the left can track what others expect and govern what words are spoken to meet those expectations.

Let's pause for a moment and just sense what this means for our lives. One side, the left, has an outward focus of what it is concerned about, what it is interested in, what it enables us to do in terms of interacting with others. What does the right side help us with in connecting with others?

The right side of the cortex also communicates, but it specializes in non-verbal communication. What is this? This includes the following signals, which my left cortex would like to list for you here in a logical, linear, literal, linguistic fashion. Here's the list—thank you, left—of the right-sided dominant non-verbal signals that are both sent from and perceived and made sense of by the right side of the brain:

1. Eye contact

2. Facial expressions

3. Tone of voice

4. Posture

5. Gestures and touch

6. Timing of signals

7. Intensity of signals

In our narratives, the left side of the brain is thought to be the drive for telling our story. But the autobiographical goods are on the right. So in a nutshell, the coherent narrative of security is reflected in the way that the left and right are differentiated well and then linked.

The two sides can work together, or they can be functioning somewhat in isolation. When I first read about all this, I began to wonder how it might be a foundation for understanding the different attachment patterns of behaving and of telling our life story. What was amazing was that by understanding the brain, by taking on some of these basic brain facts, you could explain a huge amount of the research-established psychological and relational findings. Then you could use that information to catalyze more effective interventions to help people move toward security. It wasn't only helpful to understand the data, it was effective in helping people change.

Recall that the ambivalent attachment model has an amplification of attachment needs. How might that relate to right-left brain findings? Could it be seen as an overreliance on the right side of the brain rather than being balanced with the left? When the two hemispheres do not work in a coordinated fashion, one may become excessively dominant in the absence of the other because the two sides of the brain balance each other. In this case, the characteristic finding of the *ambivalent narrative* output is a flood of autobiographical details that are not directly related to the questions asked. This intrusion of images and emotions has the quality of an excess of right-sided activation without the balancing of the left side's role in keeping track of the language output. The left side is thought to be the source of the narrative drive, using words in a linear, logical way that explains the cause–effect relationship among events. But when those events are autobiographical, the left needs the cooperation of the right to tell a coherent story.

With ambivalent attachment narratives, it is as if the right is overwhelming the left's answering of the questions. In the research literature on adults and adolescents, this is called "preoccupied" attachment and a person is simply assigned one category of attachment. But in actual life we can have many models that shape our narratives in different ways, so we'll just stick with the baseline term of "ambivalent" model of attachment to permit us to realize that we have many models across all the categories of the basic childhood attachment groupings, not just one model. In other words, we are not just preoccupied or dismissing; as individuals, we can have ambivalent models and we can have avoidant models.

Okay. Avoidance seems to rely on the left mode of being in the world as a way of adapting to a disconnected emotional life. This explains the findings in the narrative of a lack of access to autobiographical memories and an insistence that relational matters don't matter. Ambivalence draws more heavily on the right side with a flood of feelings and memories that emerge in the attachment narrative, and in life. What if your attachment model is also disorganized? How can we understand that?

For the disorganized model of attachment we see times in the *disorganized narrative* when the responses become disorganized or disoriented. This disorientation usually occurs when addressing the questions of loss or of threat. If someone has died, for example, the person may lapse into talking about that person as if she were still alive. In the case of threat, a sense of terror may emerge in the person's responses as if he were being terrified right then. For example, I might say about my drunk father, "Well, he wasn't really terrifying, no, I mean, he would drink, and I guess at those times he would come home and, well, you can smell the alcohol in the room, and he comes in and I run, but he's too fast and I . . ." Notice how the discourse moves from the past tense to the present tense and gets disoriented, even disorganized. These features can be subtle or severe, but they reveal a non-integrated brain's functioning. As the left tries to tell the story, it becomes disoriented and loses track of the topic or the focus of time. The right side of the brain may send elements of the lived past over to the left in a jumbled fashion that cannot be easily decoded by the left. A sense of time, mediated by the prefrontal cortex that works with both left and right, gets lost and the past merges with the present. Raw forms of what are called "implicit memories" may pound my consciousness with a sense of my body and emotions, images, and even behavioral impulses that feel as if they are happening in the present. These are each the outcomes of overwhelming experiences that may be unresolved in our lives. This non-integrated state happens when the narrative focuses on loss or trauma. In these moments, the individual is filled with a blockage across many systems, including left working with right, the linkage of layers of memory, and prefrontal coordination and balance. The research term for this is "unresolved trauma or loss—disorganization," but we'll simply call it a "disorganized" model of attachment.

The great news is that unresolved trauma or loss can be resolved through integrating the processes of memory and narrative, and the person can move from non-secure to secure models of attachment. In terms of the left and right brain, disorganization may occur when the flood of bodily sensation and autobiographical memories of the right are not easily taken in and sorted through by the linear left trying to tell its story with words. So at a minimum, disorganization and the unresolved loss or trauma it reveals can be seen as an impaired coordination of the two hemispheres. With reflection, we can transform raw implicit memories into explicit memories of facts in the left and autobiographical memory in the right so that they do not enter our minds in various forms of intrusive emotions or memories and instead become part of a coherent narrative of who we are. Ambivalence likewise can be transformed into security as the left and right hemispheres are brought into balance by developing more of the left hemisphere's role in the person's inner life. Avoidant models can be moved to security by developing more of the right hemisphere's role, accessing those important healthy needs for connection that have been shut down in the past.

At a baseline level, then, we look to the notion of integration in the brain to gain insights into how to move toward security. Understanding how the left and right hemispheres each contribute important but different ways of being and seeing can help guide you in making sense of your life and moving toward a more integrated way of living.

Avoidance, Emotional Distance, and the Left Side of the Brain

If your responses to the reflection questions revealed a sense of disconnection from the experiences with your caregivers, there may be elements of avoidance in your history. Let's dive into what that may have been like, and what you can do about that now.

A parent with whom a child has an avoidant attachment often

does not perceive—or at least does not readily respond to—the non-verbal signals of distress, such as crying or facial expressions. There is a sense in the interaction between parent and child that the internal world of the mind of the child is just not important, or at least not seen. This is a lack of well-developed mindsight and reveals that life for this parent-child relationship is more about managing behaviors rather than empathically feeling another's feelings.

If your sense is that you had an avoidant attachment, you may have had experiences in which attention was repeatedly paid to the physical nature of life but not much of a focus was put on the life of the mind. Reflect on your relationship then, or now, and see if "mentalese," or mind language, was or is a part of your relationship. This would be conversations that lacked words and phrases such as "I was feeling . . . ," "That must have felt for you like . . . ," "I wonder what he was thinking at that moment . . . ," "I imagine that he viewed this as . . . ," "From her point of view it may have seemed . . . ," and "Her belief doesn't make sense to me, but I can understand why she thinks that way. . . ." Each of these phrases reveals an individual who has enough mindsight to communicate either his or her own internal mental state, or to take on, and ask about, the internal mental state of another.

If you were raised by caregivers who were not only missing in their use of mindsight but somewhat distant emotionally in their ways of being with you, it may be that mindsight was not something that these attachment figures helped you develop. In studies of attachment, the teachers of kids with avoidant attachment—who didn't even know the child's attachment history—treated them as if they didn't need help even when they did. Does this sound familiar in your life? For many with avoidant attachment, there seems to be difficulty expressing inner needs, or of reaching out to depend on others to meet those needs. As one person said to me, "I needed to be autonomous from a very young age given how disconnected my mother was. Why would I ever allow myself to need help from anyone?"

If we did an attachment interview on the parent with whom you had this avoidant attachment, we'd be very likely to find a narrative that reveals a lack of access to autobiographical memory and an insistence that relationships are not important in shaping who they are. If that is the way you've come to make sense of your own life, then relationships will not be high on your priority list. It isn't that the parent doesn't love the child, it's just that the adaptation the parent had to make in his or her own childhood minimized attachment needs then, and that adaptation continues now. If you are an adolescent still living with your parents reflecting on this, please keep in mind that parents often do what they do because of how they've adapted to their own childhood experiences. Finding ways to connect more fully can happen, but it just takes time, understanding, patience, and intention. This non-secure model of attachment that helped the individual survive is one of being disconnected from others. So if this is your relationship, please don't measure this as a lack of love. It is really a lack of skills to connect. And in many ways, it is a survival mechanism from the past to disconnect from the need for closeness that simply needs to be updated now in the present.

Another part of this journey for you is to realize that parental presence may seem in short supply in avoidant attachment, that the surface of behaviors is the focus of attention, and that attuning to the internal world of the mind, of the child or even of the self, is simply not often engaged. In this setting, you may have developed with a minimal sense of your own mind, too. The effective strategy to begin with is for you to get in touch with the side of your brain that lets you focus on the internal world—of yourself and of others. That is the right side of the brain.

Since emotions and our bodily sensations fill us with the vitality that makes life rich and meaningful, this avoidant pattern of relating from the left side may have created a disconnected sense of self that is short on the internal joie de vivre, that spirit of being alive, that gives life its zest. This lack of experiential nurturance leads, I believe, to an underdevelopment of the right side of the brain.

So here's a strategy. Integration is about honoring differences and promoting linkages. If you've had a hefty dose of avoidance, the left hemisphere may be in charge because it allowed you to develop in the face of an emotional desert. That was a great adaptation for your past. But what about now? What does that mean for your mental life?

Hold on to your hat as we slowly take in the science-established notion of what "being in the left" is like. When only the left is activated and dominant, then our ways of being tend to be externally focused, logical, "de-contextualized," and characterized by what is called a "linear way" of being in the world. "Linear" means one thing following another. "De-contextualized" means missing the big picture into which something fits. So rather than flowing with the context of a situation as it emerges, moment by moment, a left dominant way of being is to expect things to unfold in a linear sequence, in a specified order, that can be contained, predicted, understood, taken apart and dissected, analyzed, and, ultimately, logically understood. If that was a starting place for you as a child raised with primarily an avoidant attachment history, then adolescence might be particularly challenging with its fill of bodily, emotionally, and interpersonally intense experiences. These components of life—the body, the emotions, and the interpersonal world of other minds—each have a dominant role in right hemisphere ways of being. If you've been given the relationship setting to develop primarily the left and not the right, this would be a great time to balance yourself and develop both sides of the brain well. That's what integration is all about.

The great news is that whatever your age, it is never too late to bring both hemispheres into development and activity. Take a look at the story of Stuart earlier in the book (p. 49) and you'll find a ninety-two-year-old man with avoidant attachment history who made great strides integrating the two sides of his brain after nearly a century without it. With an emotionally and a bodily distant mode of living, he had to learn to develop his right side and then link these new capacities with his well-developed left. If Stuart can do this, it's very likely you can, too.

Just because parents didn't offer secure attachment does not mean you are doomed to stay with a non-secure model of attachment. In the case of an avoidant history, if you find that you have been "leaning to the left" in your experience of avoidant attachment with your caregiver, then the exercises within the tools sections on mindsight, time-in, and the Wheel of Awareness will be useful in integrating your two sides so that you can overcome whatever unbalanced adaptations you need to.

Here are some basic practices if you've had a history of avoidant attachment:

1. Practice becoming aware of your internal bodily states. The Wheel of Awareness rim review on the sixth sense, the bodily sensations, can be a very helpful place to start. If focusing attention on both limbs at the same time is difficult, try to first focus on the right side and then on the left.

2. Become aware of non-verbal signals. Try watching television shows with the sound off or foreign language films without subtitles in a language you don't understand. These experiences will enable you to let your left-sided language centers take a break and your right-sided non-

verbal signal perceiving circuits become more active. Recall that these signals include eye contact, facial expressions, tone of voice, gestures, posture, and the timing and intensity of responses.

3. Learn to use non-verbal expressions. Try looking in a mirror or taking a video of yourself and watching the recording. Try to exaggerate the sending of these important right-sided signals.

4. Autobiographical memory is also a specialty of the right side of the brain. Begin by simply writing down the details of what you did today. Start with the specifics of how you got out of bed, what you did with your body as you got dressed, how you ate your breakfast. See if you can sense those experiences as you are recalling them. After these recent memories have been recounted, try more distant autobiographical reflections, also with details. Don't worry if you can't recall childhood experiences, as these may be quite difficult to access, and some may not have been encoded into your memory as well.

5. Emotions are felt on both sides of the brain, but they may be more direct or spontaneous on the right. When you are ready, you can find a friend who can partner with you in sending and receiving non-verbal expressions of differing emotions. Try out these basic nine: joy, excitement, surprise, sadness, fear, anger, disgust, guilt, and shame. See also if you can simply notice the emotions as they rise up, even fleetingly. Let the sensation of emotion fill you, and don't try to analyze it or even name it.

6. Context is something that the right hemisphere specializes in as well. Context means reading between the lines.
   It is like the spirit of the law rather than the letter of the
   law. It is context, rather than text. Context has a texture
   to it that is more subtle than the clearly demarcated definitions of things that the left hemisphere loves. Some
   compare the left hemisphere to a digital processor, with
   zeroes and ones, and clearly demarcated definitions such
   as up versus down, right versus wrong, in versus out. In
   contrast, the right is analogic, with a wide spectrum of
   values not separated into clearly boxed meanings as on
   the left side. So here you are simply letting yourself get an
   initial glimmer of the meaning behind words and their
   non-verbal components. An exercise you can perform is
   simply to say a neutral sentence with differing contexts
   embedded in the tone of your voice and the timing of the
   words. Here are two of an infinite variety of sentences
   you can try using this technique: "I expected you to
   come to my party on time," or "You always do what you
   say you will do." Try emphasizing each word in turn
   with different tones of voice, and see if you can sense how
   this changes the meaning of the message.

7. Recall that studies have shown that even if there is an
   outer focus on independence, there is often an inner sense
   of needing closeness that is beneath awareness. With this
   in mind, consider trying to tune in to any inner hints,
   however subtle, that you may feel a desire to be closer to
   people in your life. Being aware that avoidance was an
   important adaptation for you, go slow. Reaching out to
   another person to express your feelings in a gesture of

wanting more time to connect can be an important starting place. Since we each participate in creating our relational worlds, you can have a say in how to form new
kinds of relationships in your life now.

As you develop a more integrated way of being, you may find
that things begin to feel different inside you. Even the way that you
sense how you are connecting with others may change as you find
yourself sponging up their inner lives through their non-verbal signals. The presence that emerges now may seem overwhelming at
times, filled with an enriched sense of being alive. While this new
way of being in the world can seem unfamiliar at first, see if you can
rest at ease with the knowledge that integration brings a new way of
simply experiencing being alive.

In many ways, integration creates more integration.

In development we call this a "recursive" aspect of something—a
reinforcing set of recursively influencing factors that continually re-
instate the initial state of mind. In the case of insecure attachment
and non-secure attachment models, we wince and the world winces
back at us, we disconnect and the world disconnects from us. In the
case of security and integration, we smile and the world smiles back
at us.

Ambivalence, Emotional Confusion, and the Right Side of the Brain

Your responses to the reflection questions may have revealed that
your attachment history involves the polar opposite of the frozen
emotional distance that produces the avoidance of attachment. For
you, childhood was more like a hot cauldron of emotional confu-

sion. If avoidance is living in an emotional desert, ambivalence can be like living in an emotional fog if not at times an outright storm.

If this form of ambivalent attachment is in your history, then emotional inconsistency and intrusion by your parents may have been frequent. Keep in mind that your parents likely were doing the best they could, and that this way of being is most helpfully seen as their adaptations to challenges in their own childhood relationships or to other aspects of their lives. The leftover issues of their own parents (your grandparents) may have flooded their ability to be present and open in a clear and receptive way to what was happening within you. If this was the case, it is important to know that your own inner sense of self may be in need of strengthening.

In many ways, children can become an unintended receptacle for their parents' flooding emotions. The confusion that arises for the child is that at the same time he feels he is not being seen clearly for who he is, that he is in some ways invisible, he is also having to absorb emotions that have nothing to do with what he is actually feeling. It's a double challenge. And it's just plain confusing.

In responding to the self-reflection questions, you may have found that certain topics brought up a sense of something being raw or unfinished. In the formal interview, an individual with a history of ambivalent attachment may seem preoccupied with certain experiences from the past; for instance, the leftover emotional issue of a sibling favored by a parent may feel fresh and quite alive. It isn't disorienting as in unresolved trauma or loss, but it is preoccupying and upsetting. As ambivalent attachment amplifies attachment needs, there may be a sense of feeling alone or unseen that remains from childhood and gets experienced often in the here and now in ongoing relationships as a sense of anxiety and uncertainty. There may be a feeling that one's needs may never be met, and that if they are met, they can vanish in an instant. That's the amped-up attachment system that finds no relief, no security, with the ambivalent model. There is no reliable internal sense that things will work out in relationships.

As we take our attachment models with us when we move out into the world and recursively reinforce the very models we used to adapt to our earliest relationships, our learned adaptations evoke from the world similar patterns of interaction that we've grown up with. Studies reveal, for example, that if we've had ambivalent attachment at home, our teachers likely perceive us as less competent than we might really be, offering help when we may not have needed it and, in turn, stifling our independence. What we've acquired at home we carry forward out into the world. This is how the synaptic changes in the brain that developed in childhood as adaptations and models of attachment can persist and perpetuate in adolescence and adulthood, revealing themselves as a specific environment (like school or a new romantic relationship) evokes our unfulfilled attachment needs.

If you have experience with this self-reinforcing cycle of ambivalent attachment, it is important that you gain an understanding of how your brain works so that you can explore new ways of seeing and experiencing your relationships and your life in general.

If you often find yourself flooded by your own emotions without left-sided balance, you may have been struck by your emotional state when you were responding to the reflection questions. Research findings show that individuals with the ambivalent attachment model often respond to attachment interview questions by appearing to feel "intruded upon" by the narrative reflections they inspire. This can be explained on the level of brain science by the additional finding that these individuals display what could be seen as a right-sided excess without the calming effect of the left. The left portion of the brain cannot sort through the bombardments from the excessively active right hemisphere, and as a result, images, feelings, bodily sensations, and fragments of unsorted autobiographical recollections may inhibit the left's attempt to provide some kind of linear, language-based, logical telling of their personal narrative. The right hemisphere's autobiographical memory of your mother favoring your sibling intrudes on your left's keeping track of the question at hand, your body fills with tension, and your emotions influence the clarity and coherence of what you say. Beyond the scope of the research laboratory, what this means in real life is that individuals with the ambivalent attachment model often feel overwhelmed by interpersonal interactions that they experience as "flooding" or "stressful." Fear and anger mingle with the need for security and comfort.

Here are some simple practices if you've had a history of ambivalent attachment:

1. Cultivate the ability to name your internal emotional states. "Name it to tame it" is a starting place for building your left hemisphere's important language abilities and linking them to the more raw and spontaneous emotions of the right side of the brain. You can simply describe what you feel; you don't need to explain it.

2. Journal writing can be an incredibly valuable activity for you. Using your left hemisphere's drive to tell a linear, logical, language-based story will build this important narrative skill. Narrating your life can become an important integrative tool to build the connections between your two hemispheres.

3. Practice the Wheel of Awareness. Integrating consciousness will enable you to strengthen the hub of your mind.

It is in this strengthened hub that you may find the mental space in which to sort through your sensations, images, feelings, and thoughts before you choose to express them to others. This is how you can use your left hemisphere to actively participate in the SIFTing of your internal mindscape.

4. Know your emotions. For many, knowing that feelings are not facts helps to sort through the sometimes intense and rapid internal emotional world that may arise, especially in the face of relationship challenges. Feeling rejected, for example, can activate the same neural circuitry in the right side of the brain that represents bodily pain. Knowing this, you can use your "Name it to tame it" skills to acknowledge the pain of a feeling of disconnection and recognize that it may feel overwhelming but actually is not—in fact, it is something you can learn to reflect upon and calm.

5. As you develop the ability to use your growing left hemisphere to work closely with your right, see how you can connect with others in close relationships in a more satisfying way for all of you. Keep in the front of your mind whatever feelings arise, knowing that feelings are indeed not facts. You may at times have sensitivity to others' signals that makes their feelings enter you more fully and flood your sense of being a differentiated individual. There may be other moments when an internal sensation in you makes you feel that you can't rely on others. While these may be accurate assessments, they may also be clouded by an attachment system on "overdrive," based

on vigilance for connection in order to be safe. Working on the mindsight practices in the first two tools sections of this book may help bring an internal state of calm as you focus on observing these patterns of emotional response with others.

6. Attachment can feel like a life-or-death matter. When we are very small, we rely on our parents or other caregivers for everything—for food, for water, for protection. If we were cared for by unpredictable caretakers, we may still feel, as adolescents or adults, incredibly frightened and unprotected when something stressful happens in our lives. The increased attachment needs of this form of ambivalent attachment can feel, literally, like a matter of life or death. Knowing this can greatly help you to name this sensation, see it for the attachment-based emotional reactive state it is, and then not take it so personally as you acknowledge the emotion without allowing it to swallow you up.

7. Strengthen your internal observer. Developing a part of your mind that can observe, witness, and narrate your experiences can be a powerful way to "own" what you are going through within relationships. When you realize that your past experiences may have been foggy or stormy not because of something "wrong" with you, but simply a reflection of the kinds of emotional communications with your caregivers, then you can see how such emotional weather patterns now may simply be echoes from the past. Having your observing mind narrate how this is all unfolding can give you the emotional space to

calm your internal state and see what is happening in your ongoing relationships with more clarity.

You can grow the integrative circuits of the brain throughout life. As you move through this process of developing greater integration, you may find that your newfound sense of balance and equilibrium, even in the face of stresses that used to make you feel confused, can become a kind of safe harbor for you. As well, your growing inner security can become a solid launching pad from which you can draw strength as you interact with others and explore the world.

Disorganized Attachment and a Dissociating Brain

As a baseline, we have one or some combination of the three "organized" attachment models including security with its integrative functioning, avoidance with its overemphasis on left-sided functioning and the minimization of attachment needs, and ambivalence with its right-sided development and the maximization of attachment needs. For some of us, terrifying experiences with our caregivers can result in disorganized attachment and the tendency to fragment our minds in dissociation. Just as in our childhood these terrifying experiences could find no resolution and we have a disorganized model, so, too, in the present moment our behaviors and language output can become disorganized. In the narrative responses, we've seen that when disorientation occurs, it reveals a state of unresolved trauma or loss. If this is part of your experience, there is help ahead. Fortunately, the challenges of dissociating, balancing your emotions, maintaining clear thinking in the face of stress, and having mutually rewarding relationships, which are each a part of the disorganized model, can be healed.

The research is quite clear. When we make sense of events in our lives that made no sense, the mind can become coherent, our relationships more fulfilling, and our brains function in a more integrated manner. That's the movement from disorganized attachment with its unresolved states to resolution and security.

One way to think about unresolved trauma or loss is this. The brain first embeds experience in those implicit layers of memory that form the foundation of how we remember things. These building blocks include our emotions, our perceptions, our bodily sensations, and even our behavioral responses. We summarize these foundations as schema or mental models that help us get ready to respond to future events in a process called "priming."

Under normal conditions, these building blocks of implicit memory become integrated by a limbic region, the hippocampus, into the two forms of explicit memory of facts and autobiographical recollections. Dominant on the left, factual memory lets us know that something happened even though we may not know when or have the feeling of being in that experience. Autobiographical memory is dominant on the right and has the qualities of a sense of self at some point in time in the past.

I've proposed that one aspect of dissociation and unresolved trauma or loss is that the movement from implicit memory to explicit is blocked. When this blockage occurs, implicit memory in its pure, un-integrated state has the important characteristic of not being labeled as coming from some time in the past. So when a person with disorganized attachment and unresolved trauma or loss is trying to respond to questions about those experiences, the raw implicit memories are retrieved and the individual is flooded with sensations, emotions, images, or behavioral impulses that feel as if they are happening now. There is no sense that these are images or feelings from the past. That is what unresolved trauma or loss can create, and it feels intrusive, confusing, and even terrifying. Sometimes it may feel like a full-on flashback of the event without a sense that it is from the past, but more often it may simply be an intense image or emotion, bodily sensation, or impulse. These are each part of what can cause disorientation during the narrative responses. Simply living life, too, can recall elements of those times of loss or trauma—like someone getting mad at you as your parent perhaps used to—and that trigger evokes not only these intense implicit emotions and sensations, but also that fragmentation of your own inner experience, or dissociation.

Knowing about these processes of implicit and explicit memory, of unresolved trauma and loss, and of disorganized attachment and dissociation can be an essential starting place on the road to healing. Since these forms of non-integrated memory can be in fact integrated, the brain can move from unresolved states to resolution and healing. Here are some suggestions of steps you may consider in helping yourself transform disorganized attachment toward security.

Following are some simple practices to develop greater security and resolution if you have had a history of disorganized attachment in your life:

1. Keep a journal and be sure to write about times when your internal world may have felt it was fragmenting. What were the triggers that preceded such dissociation? How did you first know you were beginning to "unravel"? What enabled you to go from this state into a more integrated return to your usual functioning? The journal entries will be of great value as you reflect on what the common triggers were across different episodes in your life.

2. Knowing that disorganized attachment is a model that you may have had in response to terrifying and disorienting experience of trauma or loss in your life, it can be quite helpful to review those attachment questions that evoked particularly strong reactions from you in the process of reflection. Returning to those questions and diving more deeply into your present and past responses can illuminate which areas may be left unresolved. SIFT your mind for sensations, images, feelings, and thoughts that may arise as you ask yourself about any times you felt terrified in your childhood, any times you felt rejected or abandoned, and any losses you experienced. Focusing on the breath for a few minutes can help you as you explore these in your experiences.

3. RAIN heals the pain: Psychologists Tara Brach and Jack Kornfield use a wonderful acronym about being open to our internal experience that can help in bringing unresolved issues to resolution. We *recognize* the trauma or loss, *accept* that it has occurred and may be in a state of not being resolved, *investigate* the nature of the experience in our past and present lives, and have *non-identification* with the experiences, meaning that we don't let those events define our identity. Bringing a RAIN approach to those internal sensations, images, feelings, and thoughts that reveal unresolved trauma or grief is a helpful stance to take in healing your mind and moving toward resolution and integration in your life.

4. In SIFTing through your internal experience, there may be times when you feel that you are getting overwhelmed and are moving toward chaotic states of flooding of emotions or images, or shutting down in a rigid state of disconnection. Various approaches may be helpful at these times when you move out of the more flexible flow of integration. In Part I's Mindsight Practice F, we explored how putting one hand on your chest and another on your abdomen can be soothing for many. You can also try a research-established approach of putting a hand on each shoulder, left to right, then right to left, and then alternately tapping each shoulder in what is called a "butterfly hug," used effectively in helping those who have experienced the trauma of natural disasters. Another science-proven strategy that might be of help is the time-in with the breath practice (Part II's Mindsight

Practice A), which can also help bring calm to your mind as you explore distressful memories of the past.

5. If you find that particular areas in your explorations continue to be terrifying, sometimes seeking professional support can be helpful to move from unresolved to resolved trauma and loss. Think of it this way: A loss or trauma can be like a splinter in your foot during a hike. Once there, it becomes difficult to walk and the splinter becomes more irritated. The longer you try to simply ignore the situation and adjust to the splinter, the more you may limp along the trail. Taking the time to remove the splinter, either by yourself if you can reach it, or with someone's assistance if it is out of your reach, can greatly help your journey. Sometimes a trauma or loss is simply not so easy to reach with your own reflections. Having a supportive professional help you remove that unresolved splinter can empower you to begin the healing process.

6. If you are still living with or interacting with someone with whom you feel you have unresolved issues, when you feel strong and clear inside yourself, it can be very healing to go to that person and attempt to make a repair. Please keep in mind that the other person may not be in the same state of mind to make a reconnection with you, and being rebuffed because of this may lead to even more painful rejection or anger. Nevertheless, simply knowing that repair can be quite healing, just imagine that this may someday be possible when you and the other person

are feeling able to carry out such a reconnecting and healing process.

7. Whether or not the other person is able to communicate with you about these issues of terror and loss, the growth really begins and ends with your own internal work. If you find that implicit memories of past experiences of loss or trauma still intrude on your life, you can work on your journal writing, in conversations with close and trusted friends, or with a therapist to help bring these unresolved issues toward resolution. I will share with you this knowledge from working over the last thirty years with people who have lacked resolution: Healing is possible no matter what happened to you. Though all forms of insecure attachment may be accompanied by a sense of shame, that painful feeling that there is something wrong with you, please know that shame is an emotion that can arise especially with being disconnected and terrified. We all heal in different ways and in our own time, but beginning the process by seeing what happened and acknowledging how it has influenced your life, including any senses of shame that might be present, is a huge and important starting place on the journey to integrate your life and create the relationships with yourself and others that will be fulfilling and further support your healing and growth!

8. Disorganized attachment and its unresolved trauma and loss, like the other non-secure models of attachment, can be transformed through your relationships and your reflections. If you are a parent and have had the opportu-

nity to reflect on how such experiences in your own past may have led to some terrifying behaviors that frightened your offspring, it is never too late to make a repair. Begin with your own internal work, and then move to make a reconnection with your teen or older adolescent. I've even worked with adult children whose parents have had the courage to reconnect with them after decades following such disconnecting experiences. Sooner is better than later, but making the move when you are ready to acknowledge what has happened and bring the issue into the dialogue with your offspring can be a crucial step toward healing for everyone involved in what is often a cross-generational passage of disorganized attachment. You can end that legacy now with your own reflections and reflective conversations.

Creating a Safe Harbor and Launching Pad for Adolescents

The mind is shaped by changes in our relationships and in our brains throughout the life span. As adolescence involves so much exploration and change—of different interests, compatibilities and types of relationships—it is an extremely vital and formative time of life. If we add to these changes and challenges the attachment models that are non-secure, we can see how what could have been just rocky waters sometimes turns into overwhelming tempests.

Working on the impact of attachment during the adolescent period, for both adolescent and adult, is essential. Navigating the shifting needs for attunement and attachment as adolescence unfolds, riding the changing tides of the relationships between parent and adolescent and peer with peer can be a tricky challenge. Ideally, the adult will have the presence of mind to create the mental space so that he or she can continue to serve as a secure home base, a refuge in the storm that can be life, so that the adolescent knows that a safe harbor always exists. It is essential for both the adult and adolescent to "always keep the channels of communication open"—a statement that can apply as much to your relationship with others as it does to your relationship with yourself.

As I watched my eighteen-year-old daughter getting ready to leave for college, I felt the echoes of my own childhood—the attachment models I formed based on the manner in which I was raised and how these models have evolved as I strove to become a secure attachment figure for my son and daughter. Letting the transitions unfold as my children got older has somehow required that I care for a younger part of me, that collection of states of mind of all the various attachment models I have had from my own youth, so that I can feel clear in having her, our last child, leave home. The mind works to help us assimilate the many brain states, our states of mind, that we have developed in various ways and at various stages as we grow and go through life. The challenge is to find a way to connect with those brain states and take care of their various needs. That's a form of "state integration," which is a healthy part of living. And right now, I need to differentiate that younger state of mind, that younger me, and weave that inner aspect of myself more fully into my life, to prepare to no longer be the father with a child at home, and yet continue to care for my own inner needs for nurturance and connection.

I have had to take the meanings of parenting from the inside out on two levels. I have had to make sense of my own childhood so I can provide the kinds of connections needed to create secure attachments for my children. And I have had to parent myself from the inside out, meaning I have had to acknowledge that a younger part of me with states of mind that needed to be seen, safe, soothed, and secure in my own childhood is still alive and well inside me. Taking care of the needs of that part of me came naturally while caring for my son and daughter as they grew up in our home. That part of me somehow felt comforted by an older part of me caring for my own kids. But to get ready to see each of them go, to serve not just as a safe harbor but as a launching pad, I have had to be sure to directly nurture that inner place of my own attachment needs that is my birthright as a human being. We all have needs for connection. And as we move through life we have the opportunity to both receive that care in our youth and to receive and give that care as we move through adolescence and adulthood.

Watching our adolescents get ready to leave home brings up all these issues of nurturance and care, of attachment and connection. This is the "empty nest" period that we as parents hear so much about. I like to think of it as the "flexibility phase," but I have to admit that when our daughter first left for college, it felt sad, overwhelming, and exhilarating all at once. I try to simply be present with all of this life, aware and accepting of all these layers of experience, letting these days unfold while taking in the majesty of it all.

MINDSIGHT TOOLS #3

■

Time-Between and
Reflective Conversation

In this entry we'll be focusing on the reflective skill of mapping the inner worlds of others and the nature of our communications with one another. Such a tuning in to another's feelings, thoughts, memories, beliefs, attitudes, and intentions will enable others to "feel felt" by you. And this feeling, this sense of joining, which I call "time-between" is the key starting place to make close relationships work well. As we also focus on how we are communicating, we are attending to the quality of connection we have with other people and making it possible to improve our relationships.

For adolescents, the self is naturally changing a lot as they encounter and become adept at navigating more and more differing facets of life. Finding a strong inner sense of who you are in your connection with others is one of the major goals for this time of life. This is perhaps why friendship is so incredibly important to adolescents: It becomes a means for self-awareness and self-invention.

Relationships in which you feel felt by another person—when you sense that your internal world, your mind, is taken in by another and respected—are the building blocks of health. You may find that some of your connections with your friends feel this way and are wonderful in your life. You may find other relationships are rarely like that, or worse, they make you feel bad about who you are.

When we reflect on the inner life of others, when we participate in reflective conversations and attune to another person's mind beneath behaviors, we join with others and our sense of self is expanded. Life feels full. A positive sense of love and caring emerges between us, and within us. Feeling felt is the fundamental experience of a secure relationship, whether it is between friends, romantic partners, teachers and students, or parents and their offspring, older adolescents included. It is reflection that enables us to create that crucial feeling-felt experience in our lives.

A primary way we can connect with others in an integrative way can be called a "reflective conversation" or "reflective dialogue." Much of what happens in schools, and even in the busy lives of many modern families, does not offer an opportunity for such important conversations. Whether you are an adolescent or an adult, having these reflective skills in your life's tool kit is a great addition. Let's first examine how the patterns of relating to our attachment figures from early on may have shaped how we connect with others now.

Making Sense of How
Our Models Shape Our Present

Our attachment experiences with our own parents create a starting place where we learn the first lessons on how to be with our own emotions, how to reflect on our inner life, and how to have reflective conversations with others. In many ways, these attachment relationships shape the initial direction of how we'll sail out on our journeys. With these earlier lessons having shaped the deeper parts of the brain, our emotional circuitry, we set our course as adolescents into the wider world. Reflecting on those relationships can free us, at whatever age, to make the life we choose rather than live a life that has been chosen for us.

It makes sense for you as an adult and as an adolescent to make sense of your life history so you can be as fully present as possible in your relationships. What this means is reflecting on your relationships in the past in your own family life and asking yourself how those experiences influenced your development. How you've come to understand who you are and how you got to be that way is important not only for your own well-being but for how the well-being of your relationships with others, including with your own children, present or future, will unfold in your life.

For someone with an avoidant model of attachment, depending upon others may make him or her feel like a weak person. This model creates an inner stance of isolated thinking, of being analytical without feeling very much. If the adults around us have been ignoring our inner life—if they don't show interest or kindness for what we are going through—it can be very painful and even induce a feeling of shame. As with each of the attachment models, shame may arise when we don't have connections to our caregivers in a reliable way. While shame can shut down our freedom to connect, we can move past that, knowing that it may simply be an emotional response to misconnections in the past.

In many ways, reflecting on our own journey gives us a chance to do things differently with our own children. Without these important reflective conversations, people can simply feel alone and disconnected. Emotions can serve as our compass on life's journey—letting us know when to turn and, ultimately, where to go. Whether they flood us in the moment of interacting with an adolescent home from school for the holidays and moping about, or flood us as an adolescent trying to get our parents to agree to an adventure we are eager to embark upon, these internal measures of what has meaning can come from places we may not even be aware of. Sometimes we have major blocks to knowing what these emotions are. If we've used an adaptation to block feelings, as about one-fifth of the population does with an avoidant history, it has a big impact on how we can know our own internal worlds— and the worlds of others.

For others with a history of ambivalent attachment, we've seen that the flood of feelings from the lower regions of the nervous system moving up into the non-verbal right hemisphere can create a sense of being overwhelmed. If this is your history, we've seen that reflecting on your past and building the balance of the left hemisphere's more distant, analytical approach to weaving your life story can be an important and life-changing strategy. The amplified attachment system with an ambivalent history can at times make interacting with others filled with intense anxiety about how reliable this present connection will be. Taking the time to reflect on this model and how it is an adaptation from your own intrusive or inconsistent past relationships can help give you the internal ballast to engage openly in reflective conversations now.

Having a history of disorganized attachment experiences in which you may have felt terrified of your attachment figure may have left you with a tendency to dissociate—to disassociate your usually fluid flow of thoughts, feelings, and memories as you interact with others and reflect inwardly within yourself. Be patient with yourself. Dissociation is a developmental outcome of being terrified, and it can itself be terrifying. Journal writing, reflection, and being open about what is happening internally can all be helpful starting places on the journey to heal and to connect with others. Knowing that the brain continues to change across the life span and that healing relationships of all sorts, including the one you have with yourself, can support the growth of new integration can help give you a sense of strength, hope, and direction. If you need time to simply collect yourself when things get intense, find a way to request that with a mutual understanding that this is simply what you need while engaging in reflective conversation.

In avoidance, we can't just block out one kind of feeling: When we shut off a feeling, we usually shut off all our feelings. And with ambivalence and being flooded by feelings, we also become unable to connect with others and be fully present with them as well. If we have a tendency to fragment in response to intense interactions, to dissociate with a history of disorganized attachment, then learning how to befriend our own internal emotional world is an important starting place for being open to the feelings of others. Clearly, each of these non-secure attachment models has emotions at its core. And emotion itself is a process that happens not only within us, but also between and among us. So don't be surprised if having a non-secure attachment model, or models, makes reflective conversations challenging. That's okay! The key is kindness and patience. Reflecting on feelings in ourselves guides our decisions and even lets us know what things mean in our lives. Reflecting on feelings with others helps us to join minds, to connect with others in deeply meaningful ways.

The questions for self-reflection in Part III will be an important review in finding a way to enhance your time-between skills. How we have learned to relate to our own emotional life is a crucial starting place to having deep understanding and the possibility for growth.

MINDSIGHT PRACTICE A: Reflecting on How Your Attachment Models Shape Your Reflective Conversations

For this practice, let's return to the mindsight questions on your attachment experiences from Part III (see pp. 163–167). Consider the attachment model or models that you have experienced in your life, be they secure, avoidant, ambivalent, or disorganized. You may have had mostly one, or some of all four. Whatever your set of attachment models, I invite you now to consider how those attachment experiences and the models you developed in response shape how you now connect with others. How have these attachment models influenced your ability to be present for yourself or others? How do these models influence your skills of attuning to your own inner world—or the inner worlds of others? Do you have the experience of feeling felt? Do you feel connected to others in a way that supports the feeling of trust emerging?

These reflections can be an important exercise to heighten your awareness of the contribution you may be making to the quality of communication with others. I'll invite you to now consider that you have the knowledge to play a more vital role in your relationships than perhaps you had up to this point. Remember, your attachment models may shape how you connect and communicate with others, but these models are changeable! So the great news is that with your new self-awareness, you can develop the tools to have more fulfilling ways of connecting with others, and with yourself.

Reflection, Integration, and the Origins of Empathy

Time-in promotes internal integration. And time-between catalyzes interpersonal integration. As we've seen, one of the major experiences during adolescence is that the brain becomes more integrated. The key is that while such integrative changes seem to develop in their own time and we may not be able to alter this timing much, we can in fact stimulate the brain as it is undergoing these genetically programmed and experientially shaped changes to actually grow in more richly integrative ways! A similar process is possible in terms of interpersonal integration.

What happens in a family, with friends, at school, and even in the culture of our communities and larger society can shape the way the brain develops.

But how do you create more integration in your relationships with others?

By now you know one important strategy: reflection.

Reflection may not change the timing of integrative growth, but it can change the depth and richness of that growth.

And the great thing is that, as with internal integration, whether you are a teen or in your nineties, these time-between practices reinforce integration in your relationships no matter what your age.

When you take time-in, you are reflecting on your inner mental life. That means you sense and are aware of the sensations of the body, you feel your feelings, think your thoughts, remember your memories. Whatever arises in your subjective experience, you let it enter awareness and simply be present as it emerges. That's inner reflection. When you did the time-in practices of breath awareness and the Wheel of Awareness earlier, you got a feeling of how focusing the mind on its internal subjective experiences can feel.

Now we'll explore how we can reflect on the inner world

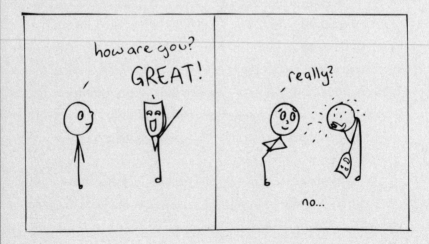

of others, and on our connections with them. One of the principal means for creating time-between is engaging in a reflective dialogue or conversation that focuses on the inner experience of everyone in the communication. In reflective conversations each person can share what they are feeling, thinking, remembering, hoping, dreaming, believing, or perceiving. These conversations connect us to one another so that we can feel felt and seen—so that we can feel authentic and real. Reflective conversations make life meaningful and enable us to feel a part of something larger than our isolated sense of self.

Is there anything off-limits in a reflective conversation? I believe that anything from the inner worlds of the people in conversation brought out in a respectful and kind way is fair game. Why respectful and kind? Respect entails that we honor differences between ourselves and others. And respect means that we do not push people who are different from us away but instead work to promote linkage despite differences. With kindness we honor and support one another's vulnerabilities, creating a safe space where we can open up in an authentic way. Showing respect for one another and being kind are two essential ingredients in effective reflective conversations.

Another important aspect of reflective conversation is that we observe patterns in how we are communicating and connecting with one another. Studies of the brain clearly show that reflection, inward or in communication with others, stimulates the activation and development of the prefrontal cortex toward its integrative growth. When we study the mechanisms at work for such inner self-knowing awareness and other-directed awareness, we find that what is activated are the integrative prefrontal regions and related areas, including the mirror neuron system that let us sponge up the feelings of others inside ourselves and enable us to resonate with someone else.

When we attune to another person and allow our own internal sensations to be shaped by that other person's feelings, we create "resonance." When we resonate with someone, we come to feel their feelings at the same time as we become more aware of our own. This awareness includes our bodily sensations as well as our own emotions. We become more self-aware. When we tune in to the inner life of another, we can create compassionate communication, one filled with empathy and caring. This connection is the essence of a healthy, supportive relationship filled with mutual respect, kindness, and compassion. Reflective conversations make it possible to join with others from the inside out.

Learning to be more reflective can help anyone, regardless of age, develop a more integrated brain. For adolescents going through these important years when the brain is influenced by experience to lay the foundations of integration, working on these skills can be especially beneficial. Learning how to relate to others in meaningful ways using time-between reflective conversations can help adolescents become more resilient to life's changes and challenges—and resilient is a good thing to become as early on in life as possible! So let us now explore a mindsight practice that can help adolescents and adults alike develop the skills to be reflective conversationalists and mindsight mavens.

MINDSIGHT PRACTICE B: Reflective Conversations

Think of a person in your life who you feel brings out the best in you. Let the way you two interact fill your awareness. Now think of another person who brings out the worst in you. Reflect on the nature of your communication with that person. And now compare the two patterns you have in each of these relationships. How do reflective conversations play a role, or not play a role, in each relationship? How has honoring differences and cultivating connections been a part—or not been a part—of your relationship with each of these two people in your life.

In the first part of this practice, reach out to the person who brings out the best in you. See if you can find some time to simply express to them your gratitude for your relationship. You can SIFT your mind and let this person know how you feel and what your connection means for you. Let the positive sense of connection just fill you by taking time to soak in this sense of closeness. Being grateful is a powerful source of reinforcing the positive experiences we have in life. Sharing that gratitude with another person is a powerful way of amplifying the positive interpersonal connection.

Now imagine how you might try to improve the relationship with the person who brings out the worst in you. What would you do differently? How might you communicate with this person in a way that would be more in line with reflective conversation and integration? Do you think you could try to initiate such a new approach to your relationship? For your first go at this, try picking someone with whom you've perhaps had a long-standing relationship, one that in the past may have been filled with trust but recently has had some change that needs an attempt at course correction. It might be a misunderstanding or a missed opportunity to connect. Keep in mind that sometimes reaching out can be hard. But while making a change in how you communicate can be helpful, sometimes it just doesn't work well. So be prepared by embracing the uncertainty inherent in any relationship: We just don't know exactly how another person may respond. But time-between gives you a focus on the process, and that is an important place to begin. Consider writing down some of the thoughts that occur to you before and after you do this exercise. And remember, you can always choose how to be in your relationships with others. It's never too late to make improvements.

The PART We Play in Creating Ourselves in Relationships

We all have a role, or part, we play in creating the quality of our interpersonal relationships. Here's an acronym that can help us remember the essential role or part we play in cultivating healthy relationships with others. PART means that we are *p*resent, *a*ttune, *r*esonate, and create *t*rust. This is the PART we play in helping create the most balanced mental life for ourselves and the others with whom we are connecting.

Our mental lives will thrive if we take this PART we play seriously. This doesn't mean in a heavy-handed way but playfully and with intention! When adolescents are treated with this respectful PART we play as adults, they are given an invitation to enable their own minds to thrive. And when adults are treated by us adolescents with presence and attunement, when we are open to resonating with what is being communicated by the adults in our lives, then trust can be created across the generations. It is a two-way experience.

Being a PART of others' lives may not come easily at first if this was not a part of your own early life experience. Not only does learning to be present in this way help relationships with others; recent studies show that being present improves our own physiological health, too. This may sound more like science fiction than science fact, but carefully conducted research reveals that if we can be present for our experience, if we can be aware of what is happening as it is happening, then we'll improve our subjective sense of well-being and enhance the way our immune system functions and even make our cells live longer! Learning to be present reduces stress and even reduces the effects of aging on those caps at the ends of our chromosomes, our telomeres. Another aspect of these studies amazingly finds that learning to be present makes us not only healthier but happier. Our cells will thank us as we learn to be more present in life!

So this is a win-win situation. Not only will our bodies and minds be in better shape with presence, but this way of being open and reflective to others in the PART we play in communicating will also make our relationships thrive as well. Body, mind, and relationships are enhanced with presence—that's the win-win nature of learning to be present in life.

Reflection is the key to creating presence and connection.

MINDSIGHT PRACTICE C: Repairing Ruptures

If you have an argument with a friend or family member, it can be extremely helpful to reflect on what happened and then make an attempt to make a repair. In this practice, reflect on your ongoing relationships and think of one in which a rupture has recently occurred. It may be subtle or intense, but this disconnection between you and the other person may be in need of repair. Let me walk you through some basic ideas about repair, and I invite you then to reach out to this person to engage in a reflective conversation to reconnect.

When you repair a rupture in a relationship, it means making a move toward the person and reconnecting with them. If you have an open rupture with friends or family members, think of ways you might go back and reconnect with them. Before you share your own experience, see if you can imagine a way to explore their experience. One effective way to begin is by making a statement about your interest in connecting again; this can break the ice and set things in motion.

Sometimes as parents we do things that create a rupture in our otherwise close connection with our child or adolescent. It is our duty to reflect on such ruptures and make the effort to repair and reconnect after we've apologized for our contribution to the conflict. Another lesson is that sometimes we do things that we don't really want to do. The brain has its higher, prefrontal part that helps us be aware of things. But sometimes the lower limbic, brainstem, and bodily areas directly influence our behaviors without the intervening prefrontal filtering or calming influences. We can flip our lids and go down the low road. In the Low Road section in my book *Parenting from the Inside Out*, I discuss the importance of rupture and repair with regard to younger kids. Let me say that being reflective is essential to repair ruptures with those we care about at any age. In fact, during adolescence, because there can be so many challenges, it should be a central theme to maintain open lines of communication, especially when the inevitable ruptures in that connection occur.

Looking upon ruptures as an opportunity to connect again and not just a burden or a problem in life can help us approach these challenging moments as occasions to create integration when integration is broken. I know with my own two adolescents, doing so has allowed our connections to stay really strong. And it has also taught them through our interactions to develop mindsight in their own lives. Having the power of reflective conversation gives us a basic tool, an essential way to connect around things that really matter, that makes the way we relate to one another have a deep and authentic quality to it.

So here's the idea. When you are ready, you can check in with the other person and see if this is a good time to speak with him or her about what is going on. You can state that

you'd like to reconnect and when it's time, you can find a quiet place to engage in a reflective dialogue. Listen to what is being said, don't judge. Being open to the other person is essential to let the person feel felt and for you to truly understand what might be going on. One of the hardest elements may be to let go of the notion that you are right, and the other person is wrong. Listen, take in the other person's perspective, and realize that understanding each other is the road to reconnection. When it's time, you can share in a non-judgmental way your own experience, using "I" language like "I felt that . . ." or "I thought that . . ." rather than "You made me feel . . ." or "You didn't do . . ." Letting each person in the dialogue have space to express and be heard fully is essential.

Though repair is not easy—and further rupturing can feel painful—it is worth trying. Be sure you are in that receptive hub of your mind before you start, so you can be open to whatever arises in the conversation. There are no rights and wrongs in repair, simply a sharing of each person's experience.

PART IV

■

Staying Present Through Changes and Challenges

I n this fourth part we will explore various ways that as an adolescent or as an adult we can stay open and accepting to the changes
and challenges of adolescence. This period of life is filled with new
ways of seeing the world, interacting with others, experiencing the
body, making decisions, and taking responsibility. All of these
changes mean it can be a challenge for adolescents to maintain internal balance. And as adults supporting adolescents, such changes
may challenge us to be open to what is happening, to be receptive
and responsive instead of reactive, to connect rather than correct.

If I had to summarize in one word all of the research on what kind of parenting helps create the best conditions for a child's and adolescent's growth and development, it would be the term "presence." As we've discussed throughout our conversation together, being present means being open to what is. Presence involves being aware of what is happening as it is happening, being receptive to our own inner mental sea, and attuning to the inner life of another person. Being present for others means we resonate with what is going on in their inner worlds, creating the essential way we feel their feelings. This feeling felt sensation is at the heart of how we can help one another feel seen, safe, soothed, and secure. Feeling felt is the basis for secure attachment. It is also the essence of healthy relationships in all domains of our lives.

So often we want to help the people we love fix their problems. We want to show them how to solve a dilemma, resolve a conflict, or get rid of painful emotions. But in order to give them what they need most of all, which is to make them feel felt and connected with us, we need to *not* do these well-intended things first and instead simply be present for our loved one. If we can stay attuned to this person and allow the SIFTing that emerges to enter us, we can truly resonate with what this other person is sharing about their experience. This is the part that may be the most challenging, especially for adolescents and parents who are experiencing different feelings about all the changes that are occurring in the adolescent's life and perhaps not seeing eye to eye. Resonance requires that we let someone's internal feelings enter us and change us. If, for example, the feeling that arises is something we cannot handle, then we'll automatically, without conscious intent, shut down the attunement process. If I am unable to be open to a sense of excitement about my daughter's plan to go on an adventure and travel to another country with friends, it becomes quite difficult for me to simply take in her feelings about her plan and sense what is happening in her world in that moment.

In an attempt to problem-solve about how she might avoid any danger in her travels, I might fail to simply be present to her experience and, in so doing, miss a great opportunity to connect. Understanding does not mean going along with every idea or plan; it means starting with connection and then exploring together what might be the steps she could take to remain safe on her journey to see the world.

The problem with putting up such initial blockades to presence is that trust between adolescent and adult will likely be damaged. Presence, attunement, and resonance, on the other hand, create trust. Remember our mindsight tools on time-between (see pp. 201–216)? This is the PART we play in helpful communication. PART means that we are *p*resent, *a*ttune, *r*esonate, and create *t*rust.

In any close relationship, connection means becoming a PART of the communication in that moment.

Honoring the Person an Adolescent Is Becoming

As parents we cannot control the people our adolescents are becoming. As adolescents, we can try to be open to the many internal and interpersonal experiences that emerge in our lives as our teens and early twenties unfold. This adolescent period is by definition one of intense change, and the potential for intense challenge—for adolescent and adult—is great. The key for both generations is to be open to what is unfolding, to honor the person an adolescent is becoming through all of the many unpredictable stages and experiences this time entails.

Honoring means being present for what is happening and being open and accepting so that we can play an important PART in our adolescent's life. And honoring our own changes as an adolescent means, too, that we can be present for what is happening as it "we'll wait for you here."

happens. I cannot control my life, but I can be present for it in my teens and twenties so that I can best support my own emerging development.

In many ways, the essence of adolescence can serve as our guide to knowing how this becoming process is working. The emotional spark of adolescence means that the feelings that arise will be intense and sometimes challenging, for ourselves and for others. While this passion can fuel a full life, sometimes wide swings in emotions can be exhausting and make life difficult. Social engagement means that our peers play a sometimes crucial role in how we feel and how we make decisions. Depending on who our friends are, sometimes those influences may be good for us, and sometimes they may not be in our best interest. Novelty seeking is a wonderful part of our adolescent journey, filling us with new experiences that are enriching and challenge our learning. But focusing in on one passion, having discipline to stick with difficult projects like learning a musical instrument, a foreign language, a sport, or an academic subject, can require singular focus of attention that may be challenging. Embracing this tension and realizing the need for focused efforts is part of the "work" of adolescence in addition to taking on new experiences. Finally, our creative explorations that are fueled by new ways of seeing life can often be an exhilarating journey into exciting new ways of approaching the world. Not every exploration is easy to understand or accept, but for adolescent and adult alike, focusing on this internal drive for creativity can be an important way of staying present on the journey itself.

In the sections that follow, we'll explore a number of specific changes and challenges that confront us through the adolescent period, such as romance, sex, drug use and abuse, and the experiences of leaving the family and returning home. Naturally there are an endless number of challenges that can arise during adolescence, such as dealing with divorce, the demands of school, the distractions of an increasingly "online, all the time" world, and finding employment. The selected examples we'll explore here offer us an opportunity to build on our earlier conversations and mindsight tools to illuminate how staying present for whatever arises, as an adolescent or an adult, is the essential foundation for a healthy and productive journey through adolescence no matter what issues we are experiencing. What follows are stories blended with science that offer us ideas and facts about how to stay present and maintain an open relationship as we move through these important times.

Leaving Home

I first met Sara when she was twelve. She came in for therapy to discuss her anxiety about being at a new school and making new friends. She ended up making the transition well but came back to therapy several years later as a senior in high school because she was anxious about starting college across the country. She was excited to study biology at a challenging school but was nervous about being far away from her parents. She would be the first to leave home, leaving two brothers back with her parents, who were happy she had found a passion in her life. In therapy this time Sara learned to do some basic time-in practices, such as breath awareness and the reflective exercise of the Wheel of Awareness (see pp. 131–136). With some practice she soon was able to calm her anxiety: She made space in her mind to hold in awareness whatever feelings arose and then just to accept them for what they were. She used the acronym RAIN to remind herself to *r*ecognize, *a*ccept, *i*nvestigate, and *n*ot identify with her anxiety when defining who she was. From a Wheel of Awareness point of view, she came to sense her anxiety as simply a point on the rim, a feeling she could be aware of but was not completely immersed in. She was able to center herself in the now more spacious and strong hub of her mind. These time-in practices strengthened her mind and empowered her to approach this moment of leaving home with more ease and enthusiasm.

I am finding the antidote to "overwhelm" not by completing more or doing less but by falling *madly* in Love with Stillness

When we move from the comfort and familiarity of our family home out into the unknown of the wider world, it is quite natural for anxiety to emerge. When the mind tries to predict what will happen next and everything is new and unfamiliar, it is natural to feel nervous and uncertain. However, depending on how one responds to these natural feelings, either they can move to the background and be stabilized or they can take center stage and be amplified, absorbing us in the intensity of feeling worried and concerned.

Ironically, when we fight what we feel, the feeling gets bigger, not smaller. When Sara came in for therapy, she was understandably in the midst of trying not to feel anxious. But that effort only intensified her anxiety. Acceptance of what is, being present for life as it emerges, moment by moment, is the key to mindfulness and the essence of presence. With such mindful practice on the breath and immersion in the Wheel of Awareness exercise, Sara learned to transform her anxiety into a sense of openness to what was.

During this time at the close of her last year in high school, we also explored what her relationships with friends and family were like. She was close to her parents, and felt that they supported her and understood who she was for the most part. Though her mother never went to college, and her father, an accountant, was not interested in science and initially thought she should go into business, both her parents were open to her getting a college education in biology if that was what she wanted. With her younger brothers, one a freshman in high school and the other just beginning middle school, Sara felt annoyed at times, but mostly she felt close to them, and even proud and protective of them when they weren't "invading" her life with their joking around.

Sara had a close social support network, with an extended group of classmates she would hang out with on the weekends and with a few very close friends she considered her best friends. Sara had dated a lot in her last two years of high school but had no ongoing intimate relationship, no romantic interests, during her senior year.

Nothing stuck out in Sara's history to make me worry about a major psychiatric illness like depression or an anxiety disorder. We all have a temperament, which means the innate predisposition of our nervous system to react in certain ways. Temperament includes our sensitivity to input from the environment, the intensity with which we react to inner or outer stimuli—like our own feelings from the inside or sounds or sights from the outside world. These inborn characteristics also include the qualities of having a generally positive attitude toward life and whether we enjoy or react negatively to change and novelty. One way to describe personality is that we can have a general tendency to activate one of three major emotional states of distress: fear and anticipatory anxiety, sadness and separation distress, and anger and rage. For much of Sara's life, she described a tendency to lean toward fear and anticipatory anxiety when she felt stressed, rather than to the other two modes.

We could see, especially after Sara's parents came in with her for a few sessions, that her reactions to leaving home for school likely were related to her temperament, not to her specific attachment to her parents. Attachment, as we've seen in Part III, is how a child connects with parents, a form of relationship that shapes us in many ways. According to her parents, Sara was "always," for as long as they could remember, a person who had an intense reaction to the world, especially toward changes in her routine, but she also had a generally positive demeanor. She was an upbeat child and now seemed to be the same way as an adolescent.

Sara was very sensitive to things, meaning that small amounts of input (sounds, sights, smells) would get a significant response from her, and that response would be big. Another temperament characteristic was that Sara generally did not like new things. Perhaps *like* is not the right word. Sara had a big, negative, automatic reaction to novelty and change such that new things seemed to evoke a feeling of anxiety and fear at first. After a while, when she could figure out what was happening, she'd warm up and dive into the new activity with some reserve but ultimately with gusto. Some would call Sara "shy," and that would be a fair term; others might prefer to use the phrase "slow to warm up."

We all have a temperament, an inborn propensity of how we respond. And this was simply Sara's way of being in the world. With adolescence, the changes that emerge may intensify some of those earlier characteristics from our childhood as we face the challenges that arise. But for many of us, in fact for the majority, our childhood temperament does not predict how we'll be in our teenage years or beyond. It's a fascinating issue, but realizing that we change and evolve based on our experiences as well as our temperaments is important as we create the life we want to have.

Attachment experiences and temperament interact to form our personality. And personality is what is being shaped during our childhood and adolescence. If we are open as adults, we can even create changes in who we are throughout our lives.

While attachment is based on our interactions with our caregivers and is not related in a significant way to our genes, temperament is inborn and is related to our genetic factors or other issues unrelated to experience. For the majority of us, the externally observable features of our temperament, when not in the extreme, in fact do not predict how we become later on. For about 80 percent of children, their temperamental characteristics are in the "middle range" of values, and experience plays a larger role in shaping their paths. For 20 percent, 10 on either end of a spectrum of typical temperamental characteristics, the extremes of their temperament seem to be associated with the persistence of nervous system tendencies such as sensitivity or aversion to novelty. Experience plays a role in the development of these individuals as well, but the unfolding of personality for this 20 percent is shaped in a greater way by the propensities of the nervous system based on inborn temperament.

For Sara, if her nervous system had an intense degree of reactivity, sensitivity, and withdrawal from novelty (she is slow to warm up), then her internal experience would be intense as she went through life. Fortunately, her attachments appeared to be secure as a child, so her ability to regulate her own internal state—her emotions and reactivity—would be optimized because those integrated relationships would have cultivated integration in Sara's brain. And integration is the basis for flexible regulation. That's what attachment does: Our parents provide the scaffolding when they attune to us with their presence, which shapes how we learn to calm our own reactivity and soothe our own distress and balance our own emotions. Interactive attunement in attachment leads to internal regulation.

So Sara had started life with the secure relational world to optimize her self-regulation. That's a great start. But she also had a temperament at the extreme, suggesting that these propensities toward fear and anxiety might persist and might intensify as she approached the adolescent challenge of leaving home.

Sara did not seem to have a disorder of her mood, her thinking, or her bodily image and eating. She also did not have the clinical presentation of someone with an anxiety disorder, such as panic or obsessive-compulsive disorder. Like the majority of adolescents, Sara was experiencing the common challenges of moving from childhood to adulthood but did not have a formal psychiatric disorder. She was experiencing the challenges of adolescence, not the emergence of a disorder in need of specific treatment interventions such as medications or intensive psychotherapy.

But if you have an inborn proclivity to be reactive, sensitive, and novelty distressed, then even with a history of secure attachment, life will continue to be distressful and challenging. You may not have a formal disorder, but you may be experiencing significant and real distress. So using the mindsight tools (in the form of mindfulness of the breath and the Wheel of Awareness practices) to help her learn for herself how to calm her innate nervous system reactions worked well for Sara, and off to school she went.

The lesson for Sara was that even if you have a temperament that is inborn, a particular personality propensity you are living with, you can still use ways to strengthen your mind to improve your life. Rather than trying to ignore her internal experience, Sara could learn to be present with her propensities so that she could become more resilient in life.

Now here we were in her first year of college. She loved her classes. She loved being at the dorm even if the first few weeks were filled with the unavoidable feelings of loneliness and homesickness. Sara had learned to create a space in her mind, the strengthened hub of her Wheel of Awareness, to reflect on her feelings so that she did not let her feelings take over, so that she was not lost on her rim. She could give her emotions the space to arise, fill her awareness, and then just float away as other feelings came up.

Remember that after ninety seconds an unimpeded emotion will begin to transform on its own. It is often how we fret over a feeling that creates suffering and maintains the intensity and duration of that feeling in our lives. Fretting can involve attempting to avoid a feeling and it can mean vigilantly clinging to that feeling out of fear. Fretting can involve us saying, "I should not feel that feeling—go away!" but the feeling just gets stronger. And fretting can also involve a rapid shutting down of being aware of a feeling even though the emotion remains beneath our consciousness. Just giving space to a feeling without fretting about it lets us make it "mentionable and manageable," as Fred Rogers used to say. Mister Rogers was so right.

As Sara learned to name her internal state of worry as a natural human concern about newness and uncertainty, she could simply be present for this initially uncomfortable feeling and then let it lessen in intensity so that she could move on to live her life. That's the power of presence to bring freedom and vitality to how we live.

Puberty, Sexuality, and Identity

When Sara first came in as a sixth-grader and just turning twelve, she had entered puberty. Puberty is marked by the development of the body and its changes in secondary sexual characteristics (growing genitals and larger muscles in boys; widening hips and budding breasts in girls). This sexual maturation anatomically is associated with increases in chemicals that are distributed throughout the body, hormones of various sorts that help regulate growth and activation of the sexual regions of the body. Changes in the brain itself may not correlate directly with the timing of these changes in the body, so we can't state that mental changes necessarily go along with these sexual changes. But the increase in circulating sex hormones following the onset of puberty creates new and intense sexual drives, feelings of attraction, and erotic arousal.

This increase in pubertal sexuality in the setting of sometimes later brain maturation with delayed impulse inhibition and other executive cognitive functions becomes an important issue in modern times. Many studies suggest that adolescents' sexual maturation used to be much later, in the later teen years, sixteen or seventeen. In earlier cultures adolescents becoming sexually mature at that age would then be very near the time when they'd become not only sexually active but domestically ready to settle down to raise a family. For a variety of reasons, including nutritional intake, children are sexually maturing at earlier ages, especially girls—sometimes before hitting their double digits—but their brains are not maturing at this same rate. Sara was typical of this trend, entering puberty before she was a teenager.

On top of this earlier onset of puberty in modern culture, establishing an independent home life and reaching sexual maturation associated with bearing children will not generally occur for another decade or two after puberty. That is a long transition period to be sexually mature but domestically non-responsible, a duration that has never existed, as far as we can tell, in our human history. This is the modern experience of a substantially longer adolescent period of time between childhood and adulthood.

To understand the changes of sexuality and romance and the challenges they present to both adolescent and adult, we need to explore how these physiological factors influence both our internal experiences and our relationships during this time. Being present for these issues as they arise is greatly aided by understanding what is happening in the body and in our social worlds. Brain changes are rarely demonstrated directly to the visible eye, but parents and teachers can tell when the mind's capacity for abstract thinking begins during this period of early adolescence. As teens, we begin to see the world with conceptual patterns beyond the concrete facts we've been learning throughout elementary school. As we've discussed, such abstract reasoning and thinking include seeing ourselves and others from a bit of a distance, seeing general patterns about life set out in stories within novels and films, and beginning to wrestle with issues about life and death and the meaning and purpose of why we are here on Earth. The notion of personal identity—who we are and what really matters to us—will begin to become a central theme in our inner thoughts, in our journal writing, in our conversations with friends, and in our academic work.

At this age, too, adolescents begin to act in very distinct ways with different groups of people. They may have one "persona" or way of being with fellow teammates in soccer club, another with friends from school, and another with siblings or with parents. During this early adolescent period, studies show, there is often little awareness of these distinct "ways of being" or "states of mind" that can dominate and distress teen and adult alike. It can seem that people have many divided states that they are not even aware of having. I know for myself, as a fourteen-year-old, when I moved past this early adolescent time into mid-adolescence, I felt as if I were split up, as if I had many personalities that seemed to be activated in different ways depending on whom I was with. Those shifts were confusing at best. Who was I really if I could be feeling and acting in such different ways?

In addition to these experiences of changing identity and its various manifestations internally and interpersonally, the impact of increased levels of sexual hormones in both boys and girls has an effect on an adolescent's overall physiology and neurological functioning such that feelings of sexual attraction and arousal begin to arise within awareness. Now we develop a sexual self, a new identity filled with novel and powerful sensations. Some of these feelings may have been present earlier in life, but they were usually less intense, less persistent, and less available to conscious reflection during those years. For many reasons, then, adolescence is marked by an increased awareness of sexual sensations.

For some individuals, this new awareness is exciting; for some, feeling sexually aroused in general or attracted to one person in particular may feel very uncomfortable and "out of control"; for others, awareness of these new sensations can be outright terrifying.

Sara did not share with me much of her inner experience of attraction to some of the boys at school, perhaps because I am a male therapist. She would mention them to me in passing, and then move on to other issues, often about her finding new girlfriends at school. By the time she felt acclimated to her new middle school experience, she was ready to stop therapy.

For any adolescent, the new sensations of romantic interest and sexual arousal can be uncomfortable. When they first arise, their newness and their intensity can be confusing. These feelings can be powerful and exciting but also overwhelming. And when sexual feelings intensify, they can feel like just too much to handle. Given Sara's extreme of temperament toward sensitivity and novelty, we can imagine that these new feelings might be especially overwhelming. Feeling out of control, feeling helpless, feeling that something is "taking over" are all natural responses to the hormonal and neurological alterations that emerge during this period.

Let's think about this for any of us as adolescents: We've gone from an intense interest in the world *around* us—people, activities— to a new state of huge feelings *inside* us. That change alone is a major shift in the origin of both the quantity of sensations and the specific quality of them. Now add to this the reality that these emotional sensations are doing exactly what emotions do, they are getting us to "evoke motion," e-motion. They create a state of mind in which our whole system, our brain and whole body, is being readied to take action. And the action that sexual feelings prime us to take is to move toward the persons to whom we are attracted and connect with them. That's a drive, an impulse, a deep motivation. It fills our awareness automatically, it activates our behaviors automatically, and it colors the way we feel automatically.

When the emotional state is attraction, the drive is to connect. Talking to that person is a start. Getting to know them, holding their hand, kissing them, fondling them, engaging with them sexually, having intercourse are all sometimes hidden (and sometimes not so hidden) desires and images of what may unfold. The kinds of images and degrees of drive vary from person to person, dependent upon individual differences, maturation level, access to emotional states within consciousness, social settings, and culturally sanctioned norms of behavior. Sexual attraction captures our imagination too, weaving the content of our attraction into the daydream-like quality of fantasies. Sexual drives, sexual fantasies, sexual behaviors, these are all a part of what we mean when we say that following puberty as adolescents we experience the maturation of our sexuality. We become sexual beings.

Emotions drive us to move, to take action, to satisfy a need, and adolescence is filled with these new emotions that drive us to fulfill these new needs. It's a lot of new feelings, images, and impulses. And if cultural practices inhibit those internal sensations from being expressed as actions, there may be a lot of gestures without engagement. But in cultures where engaging in sexual behaviors is permitted, or even encouraged as in the modern cultural practice of "hooking up," such sexual activities may be frequent. Our biological legacy is to move from sexual immaturity during the pre-adolescent years to sexual maturity in the adolescent and adult years. How we experience and express those sexual feelings will be shaped by our temperament, our family, our friends, and our culture.

Let's remember, too, that in our evolutionary past, there was a much quicker transition that bridged the divide between sexual immaturity and adult responsibility. By the time physiological sexual maturity happened in the middle to late teens, we were socially set up to make sexual connections with others and ready to make babies.

Now we have a prolonged period of adolescence in which sexual feelings emerge with maturation but pair bonding (finding a mate and creating a new family home) does not occur until much, much later. In modern cultures today, these informal sexual connections sometimes shape how an adolescent first realizes his or her sexual life.

Hooking Up

The last two years of high school for Sara had been filled with learning about her sexuality by experimenting through "hooking up" with boys at parties and after school in casual encounters that felt good to her body but hard on her mind. Sara would find herself wanting more from these boys, at least most of them, and would then feel rejected when a boy she had hooked up with would not reach out to spend more time with her in the days and weeks after or, sometimes, even completely ignore her when they crossed paths at school. In some settings, there is an implied if not outright stated rule that two people hooking up should in fact not get involved with each other emotionally. That can work for some people but not others. And when that doesn't work out for only one member of a pair, it can be painful for either or both of them.

If you are in your adolescence now, you may feel a social pressure to hook up, as if it is an expected way of behaving in social settings. But remember, times are always changing, and your parents may remember feeling quite the opposite societal pressures: that casual sex was unacceptable or taboo. Even if the adults in your life don't seem to "get" what you're going through, keep in mind that getting sexually involved outside the context of a trusting relationship can have significant challenges. Sex without commitment can feel less rich, and even if neither party is looking for a lasting relationship, it can lessen the deep, intimate connection that is a component of any sexual encounter.

As we'll explore in the next section on romance, there are three major ways we can connect with others in deep ways. One is as friends in an attachment-based connection where we feel close and connected, receiving and giving care, creating a sense of security through seeing the inner life of a friend and soothing them when they are distressed. Another is simply being erotically aroused and feeling physically attracted to someone. And a third way of connecting is through romance, feelings of being "in love" and wanting to be around a person as much as we can.

One challenge of hooking up is that sometimes there can be an imbalance in what each person expects. If two people simply want the sexual activity, assuming that pregnancy and diseases are being prevented, then it can be straightforward. The fact that sex without commitment can lessen the deep, intimate connection is something to consider, for sure, as we'll discuss in the next section. Sometimes, however, the falling-in-love circuits become active only in one person and then it's painful for both. If this is happening with a friend, then the friendship may become in jeopardy because one of you wants more of a commitment than the other. Then even the friendship may not be able to survive.

During her senior year, Sara's parents were more concerned about the possibility of her getting pregnant or contracting a sexually transmitted disease than Sara becoming frustrated in her romantic interests. As for Sara, even though she was nervous about her future of leaving home, she would get swept up in her sexual feelings of attraction for boys and lose her concerns and sometimes her caution.

The culture in which Sara was growing up made these informal sexual liaisons an expected part of her teen life. From kissing and fondling to oral sex and sexual intercourse, over her junior and senior year Sara learned a lot about being erotically involved with boys but not much about romance or long-term relationships. She would learn of these things later. Many of her friends had boyfriends, but she said it was "a little ridiculous" because those same boys would be hooking up with other girls at parties all the time. That was a betrayal Sara said she did not want to experience in her life, so she had no interest in such a "fake" setup.

For Sara, there were times when her hooking up at parties was enjoyable for her; at other times she felt it was simply her "duty" to be a part of her clique at school and a way to feel attractive. While she mostly enjoyed her sexual experiences, by the end of her senior year her conflicting feelings were making her think that she'd like to try something different. When she went off to college, I was able to keep in touch with her by phone for that first year. I'd see her in person on breaks from school and was happy to see how well she adjusted to her new life. After her first year of college, though, things changed.

Romance and First Love

Sara's tears slowly welled from her reddened eyes and trickled down her cheeks as she told me how horrible her situation was during her summer break after her freshman year. At the end of her first semester, she had fallen in love with a sophomore at school and they decided to spend their summer together, working at jobs during the week that they were fortunate enough to get in town, and then being with each other and friends on the weekends. It had been an ideal summer and Sara could not believe it was over. So what was the problem?

Jared, her boyfriend, was going to South America for his junior year abroad. He'd be living in the dormitory there with other ex-change students from around the world. Sara was worried that Jared would find another love.

Sara's relationship with Jared began at the end of her first semes-ter. I was relieved that she hadn't met him earlier, as I had hoped she would be able to experience the strength of her newfound ability to soothe her own innate reactivity without the assistance of a boy-friend. Her last year of high school enabled her to move away from her emotional dependence on her parents as she relied more and more on friends for support. That's part of the adolescent journey, to connect more with peers than parents. During her high school senior year "freak-out" about leaving home, it was a natural state, given her temperament, to feel that leaving her friends and leaving her parents was just "too much." Now she had learned, with some internal edu-cation, that she could calm herself. That was a great step in strength-ening her mind.

Jared entered the scene at a school party one weekend. The two met and Sara began to feel feelings she had heard about from friends and movies and books, but in all of her dating and hooking up had never experienced. When she saw Jared at the dorm event, she felt an immediate sense of attraction to him. Jared was a sweet and sensitive person. Unlike Sara, he seemed not to be reactive in the ways that she was, fortunately, so he could approach her and the newness of her with calm and focus. They made a "great pair," Sara told me. The end of that semester was fun for them both. They got closer and closer, and soon their dancing and talking and going out together became "romantic."

Sara told me that though she had hooked up with other boys in college as she had in high school, they never really meant that much to her. Jared was the first guy who she really liked, who she really cared about. It somehow seemed different to her than the informal sexual encounters she had had in high school. This really mattered to her, she said, and she wanted to wait until she knew Jared for a while before things became sexual. And Jared, too, was patient enough to wait until things happened naturally.

Throughout the second semester of her freshman year, Sara and Jared were sexually intimate with each other. Sara went to the college health clinic and started birth control pills, and both of them got checked for AIDS and other sexually transmitted diseases before engaging even in condom-protected sexual intercourse. I was surprised by their conscientious approach to such an important issue that Sara would have treated before with casual disregard. Somehow a more reflective and thoughtful part of her was being engaged with her sexual life now that these new feelings were emerging.

When Sara's parents found out that she had a steady boyfriend, her mother was overjoyed, but her father was nervous, Sara said. Not until her dad met Jared in person did he seem to relax. "He just needed to see who Jared is so he could know I wasn't being hurt by this guy." As a father I know that feeling of wanting to be protective while also wanting to support. It's the parental challenge of being a safe harbor and a launching pad all at once. It's not so easy sometimes.

In many ways, this was an ideal way to get into the experience of romance for Sara. She learned that she could have intense feelings of attraction that were mutually shared by her partner. She learned that her timing for moving from feelings of attraction to getting to know Jared to becoming sexually involved with him could be discussed openly and respectfully. This was the longest lasting relationship Jared had had, too, so he was also learning a lot of new things about romance and emotional involvement.

And now it was August.

I said to Sara that I imagined she might be feeling a very intense sense of loss over what was going on right now. She had become very attached to Jared, I explained, and that was beautiful. Our romantic life is intimately interwoven with our attachments. Some researchers, like Helen Fisher, suggest that at least three kinds of love exist, which I mentioned briefly in the last section.

When we are romantic we "fall in love" and have a deep sense of longing to be with someone, think about the person when he or she is not around, and feel a deep sense of loss when they leave. When the committed relationship ends, or threatens to end, we can feel absolutely bereft. It's like a part of us is being amputated. We are ripped apart. We become not whole. Something is missing.

That's the "addiction" part of love that drives poets and songwriters to devote so much time and energy to trying to express the pain and pleasure of romance. Like other forms of addiction, scientists think dopamine may be the main neurochemical involved in this aspect of love. On one level, this is a "healthy addiction" that creates happiness in our lives. On another level, when the relationship is ending or uncertain, it can create huge pain within us. The very parts of the brain that register bodily pain also represent the pain of a severed relationship. It can feel like we are being stabbed and are dying.

Then there's the sexual or erotic aspect of love, the attraction and arousal. This libido or sexual energy is a natural part of our experience. It doesn't always come along with romance, so these two feelings can be somewhat independent. This form of love may be primarily mediated by androgens, a form of hormone associated with increases in sex drive. In fact, hooking up, as Sara had learned, often involves sexual arousal and not romantic engagement. "One-night stands" are good examples of the passionate engagement of this erotic form of a "loving" experience.

For some, sexual intercourse involves not only the androgens that help mediate arousal but also the secretion of oxytocin, the hormone that generally intensifies our feelings. Some of this intensification can be to enhance a sense of bonding and connection. But be aware that this intensification can be, especially for males, an intensification of jealousy and aggression. For others, especially intense for females, sexual intercourse is associated with oxytocin release; the person one is with becomes the person of one's bonding. This bonding can be in the form of romance. In this case, sexual involvement can create an intensification of romantic dopamine-driven obsession. At times, that obsession may not be shared, and such imbalance may be quite distressing.

Oxytocin release can also be a part of the next form of love, attachment.

Attachment, the third form of love, is what we feel in our close friendships and it is what we feel toward our parents and may involve primarily the serotonin system. Attachment is the kind of love in which we want to offer the nurturance that others need to help them feel safe, seen, soothed, and secure. When we are distressed, going to an attachment figure soothes us. Being around a secure attachment figure calms our inner turmoil and gives us a feeling of being "home" and at ease. This is why children can be soothed by an attachment figure with whom they have a secure attachment. And this is why connecting with a close friend is soothing. This is why even our romantic partner and our sexual companion who is *also* our attachment figure can be so soothing. It is possible to have all three forms of love shared with one person.

When one individual is your romantic partner (you are in love with someone), your sexual companion (you love making love together), and your attachment figure (you love being around this person and go to him or her at times of distress or when you want to share something positive), it's a relationship jackpot.

Not all romantic, sexual, and attachment relationships work out like this. We can imagine all the combinations that can exist: having relation ships.

all three, just two, or only one form of love present. When it's not balanced between two people, it can be really upsetting for one person who wants more, and even for the person who wants less. But when the balance is all there, it's one of the most rewarding experiences we can have. Jared was all three for Sara. And Sara was all three for Jared. Jackpot.

For me, Sara began to look much like she did her senior year of high school just a year and a half earlier. She was filled with sadness and separation distress, the emotional state that was her "go-to" default mode of temperament when she was upset. What had happened to all of the growth and progress she had made? Why was she now so "dependent" on Jared?

Yes, you may say, she is in love with him and doesn't want to leave him. Maybe she should take off and go down to South America with him? Well, I can understand the romantic sensibility of that suggestion, but I don't agree. At this age, during the important adolescent period of time of growing into who you are becoming, I believe that it makes more sense to find your own equilibrium and direction without changing plans to maintain a romantic relationship. And believe me, I'm a pretty romantic guy. It's like what an older adolescent in her twenties recently suggested: "Tell your reader not to get committed too early. If it is going to work out, it will work out."

If you've seen the films *Before Sunrise* and *Before Sunset,* by the director Richard Linklater, you've seen up close and personal the dilemma someone in his adolescent years has when he meets up with a "soul mate" with whom he feels so aligned, so connected, so bonded. I know from personal experience how the timing of such connections makes a huge difference. I know, too, many people who meet up at this age and don't give themselves the space to create their own identity, and then years and sometimes decades pass by and it comes back to haunt them. There is an important maturation during adolescence that requires a freedom of emotional life, thinking, planning, and plain old self-discovery that committed relationships can sometimes curtail.

Please don't get me wrong: I would not be surprised if Jared and Sara ultimately find a lifelong commitment to each other. It's very possible. I just don't think they should make that serious commitment right now at this time in their journeys. I think they both would come to resent that decision and each other.

But how could I help Sara get through this period? In therapy I don't tell people what to do, I try to be present with them to help them figure out how to figure out what to do. The following sections offer examples of a few steps parents and other adults attempting to offer encouragement to adolescents can take to help support them through the intensity of first love and the endings of relationships.

First Be Present

What seemed to help Sara a lot was for me to first connect with exactly where she was. What this means is that I focused on just what was going on inside Sara, helping her to SIFT her mind by sensing, observing, and describing her sensations (what she feels in her body), her images (what she hears and sees in her mind's eye), her feelings (what emotions she is aware of), and her thoughts (in the form of ideas or concepts and word-based thinking). When we help others to SIFT their minds, we are helping them create a focused space in which they can explore their own inner sea. This mindsight skill is by no means the domain only of therapists such as me. Anyone who is willing to stay present for another person can do it.

In any close relationship, connection means becoming a PART of the communication in that moment. By being present for what is happening as it is happening, attuning to the inner experience of what is going on with the other person—not just to their external behaviors but actually resonating with their internal experience—a trust is born. That state of trust between us turns on what Steve Porges calls the "social engagement system." This system calms the internal storms, relaxes a state of distress, and creates a sense of openness to new experience. This is a fundamental way in which being present not only allows us to understand another person, but also allows that connection to create clarity and calmness inside that person.

Once Sara could share the sensations of heaviness in her chest and the empty pit in her stomach, the images of being alone in her sophomore year and of Jared with other women in Argentina, her feelings of fear and rejection, and her thoughts that she'd never find another love like him, we had SIFTed through the contents of her mind at this moment in her life and she was able to feel truly felt.

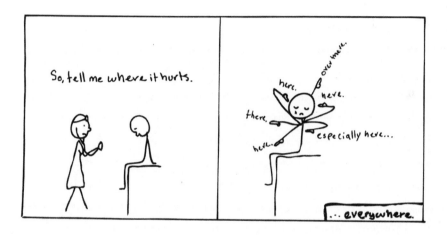

You might ask what words I said, if any, during our connection. Mostly my words were aimed at showing her that I understood her feelings, that I could imagine what she might be feeling because I had experienced some of these feelings myself. I said that I understood what she was saying and could feel how painful this was, and how it seemed there was no solution to this situation but loss. After we spoke for a while about this sense of being stuck, and of how ironic it was that an experience so powerfully good could change and create such powerfully painful feelings, I said something about our common human predicament. To feel such elation means we sometimes will feel intense loss. They go hand in hand.

A common and parallel metaphor I shared with Sara seemed to

help and goes like this. If you take a teaspoon of salt and put it into a small cup of water, that water will taste too salty to drink. But if you imagine putting that same teaspoon of salt into a lake, the water will remain clear to the taste. That's like the difference between getting lost on the rim of the Wheel of Awareness and experiencing life from the hub. Opening the hub of the wheel enables whatever feelings that arise to be experienced within a deep reservoir that gives us resilience. That's the clear taste of diluting the salt in the larger body of water. We can feel whatever feelings arise, not fret over them, and stay fully present as we embrace a wider awareness of knowing beyond only the one feeling or thought or idea. That's how the wheel practice strengthens the mind to be present as we open the hub and become empowered to embrace our experiences with more clarity.

This kind of presence is at the heart of what it means to be your own best friend. You are available to yourself as an attachment figure, as a close companion, as a support, and as a guide. Anything that comes up, you can share. This is what you do with your social best friend; this is what you do with yourself as best friend.

Presence enables us to develop resilience. I focused now with Sara on reinforcing this skill that we had worked on earlier when she was in high school and found the wheel practice to be so helpful and empowering. I also now wanted her to have the knowledge about the three forms of love. In particular, I wanted her to consider this possibility. Jared had become an attachment figure for her, alongside his being a romantic partner and a sexual companion. Three forms of love in one relationship—bingo. No wonder she loved being with him and didn't want to lose this relationship. But as an attachment figure, Jared may have become the person she now relied on for all of her soothing. So while she made the transition to college well, learning to rely on herself to soothe her intensely reactive temperament in an excellent way, perhaps her relationship with Jared after that first semester—being with him essentially all the time for the last nine months—had made her not practice being her own best friend. Perhaps Sara had given up her own inner resilience for the compelling nature of her new love.

Changes and Challenges to Integration

I described to Sara how integration is the linkage of differentiated parts—like connecting the different aspects of ourselves, or like honoring differences with another person in a relationship and then connecting with that person. And well-being emerges from integration. When our inner mental experience and our interpersonal relationships are integrated, harmony emerges. Without integration we move toward chaos or toward rigidity. Sara's "stuck" response to the prospect of Jared being away for a year was, in a sense, rigid and inflexible. What was not being integrated in Sara's life now? What was not being differentiated and linked? Sara was not letting Jared differentiate himself from her. He had his own ideas for the next step in his life journey to fully experience a year abroad, and she was fantasizing about how to join him and not allow him to have that individualized journey unfold. Sara and Jared had been very linked. Now, so early in their lives, it was time to allow more differentiation between them.

Sara had her own work to do, too. She had given up some of her friendships in order to spend more and more time with Jared. Relationships, I told Sara, are like a garden. They need tending to keep growing and thriving across time. Close relationships need devotion and dedication, yes. But they also thrive if they have the balance of differentiation and linkage. Too much of one over the other and integration is not created. You can always tell a relationship that is out of balance because one or both people appear in a repeated state

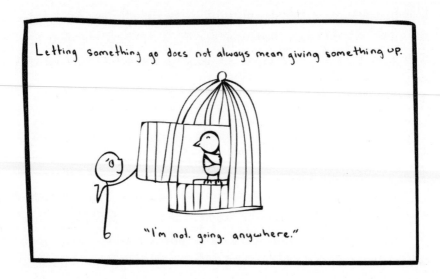

of chaos, with fits of rage. And they can reveal rigidity, too, and sometimes display a sense of enveloping boredom and loss of vitality. While all relationships meander at times toward chaos or, the seeming opposite, boredom, with integration there is a feeling of harmony and energy, openness and vitality.

I told Sara that at this stage perhaps she feared too much differentiation and losing Jared. And I explained why at their young age, the old adage "If you love someone, set them free" had special relevance.

The other issue for Sara was that her attachment system was triggered by her relationship with Jared. To a certain extent, she had been relying on him as an attachment figure, as if he were a parent and she his young child. Of course this meant that his moving away for a year was absolutely terrifying. Sara needed to learn to soothe the "younger Sara" inside her by speaking directly to that young side of herself, that young state of mind, and letting that part of herself know that everything would be okay, that she would not be ignored or forgotten. As we've seen in Mindsight Practice F in Part I, for some people placing one hand on the chest and one hand on the abdomen, applying some gentle pressure and closing the eyes, can be comforting and a source of soothing as well. This helped Sara to find a way to comfort her feelings of longing and distress and find an inner sense of peace.

Fortunately, these ideas and suggestions, as well as her past experience with practices like the Wheel of Awareness when she was anxious about leaving home for college, helped Sara a lot. She was able to face her intense fears and distress head-on and to soothe herself. She also understood that she could feel whatever she was feeling and just let that be where she was at that very moment. That's presence, and that's what created a pathway for Sara's sense of clarity and empowerment. She is currently missing Jared but not fretting over him as she has been able to find an internal balance and continues to cultivate integration in the garden of her life.

Acceptance, Letting Go of Expectations, and Sexual Orientation

As we have discussed, presence is the most fundamental gift that we can give our children in terms of creating a positive environment for them to develop and grow. One of the greatest challenges we may face in our work to stay present for our children, however, is our own expectations for them. Whether you are an outgoing parent who has a shy or introverted child, or an athletic parent who has an artistically inclined teen who steers clear of sports, this issue of how to be present for who your adolescent actually *is* creates the most important starting point for all of us as parents.

Fear and *anger* are words that don't quite describe the emotions that Andy's parents expressed to me on their first visit to my office after their fourteen-year-old son told them in our family session that he might be gay. I had been seeing Andy for issues related to anxiety and poor academic performance for over a year. Andy was a bright young eighth-grader who had come to psychotherapy at the suggestion of his school counselor and upon the insistence of his parents. Initially uninterested in being in an office with a stranger, Andy soon warmed up to the idea that he and I could just talk about whatever came to mind.

Andy and I initially spoke about his friends at school, many of whom he had known since preschool days. He, like virtually all of us, could not recall those times before elementary school very well but had a sense that he had been happy in those early years and that his life and his friendships had been "fine."

I was interested to see if Andy could tell me anything about his understanding of why he was so anxious at school. He recalled doing well in elementary school, recounting his interest in all his classes and sports and art after school. He had a love of drama and a fascination with science and seemed to be a Renaissance man, interested in many dimensions of life and excelling in lots of things. Andy was a person with deep passions about the world around him. During those earlier elementary school days, he told me, he "wasn't anxious, just happy."

When sixth grade came along, things began to change. He moved from a small local public elementary school to a much larger middle school farther from his home. He recalled making this transition without much problem, making new friends, and even continuing to do well with his classes in school. But by the middle of that year, he felt a pit in his stomach when Sunday night would come around. He began to dislike the idea of going to school, and on Monday mornings he often felt as if he was coming down with the flu or some kind of food poisoning. He felt sick to his stomach. His parents soon noticed this pattern of Monday distress, and after a few months of his grades falling and their trying to figure out with his teachers what might be going on, they followed his teachers' advice and brought him in to see me toward the end of that academic year.

My own experience of Andy during seventh grade was that his Monday morning anxiety was more about his social life than about his academics. He had continued to enjoy his classes, worked diligently to keep up with his homework and assignments, and committed himself perhaps to too many activities but ones he really enjoyed. He loved soccer, was excited about drama, loved his art classes after school, and enjoyed just being with his friends.

What slowly became clear during that seventh grade year, however, was that Andy was becoming aware of feelings inside him that were new. Like most adolescents, the physiological changes in his primary sexual organs—testicles for a boy and ovaries for a girl— gave rise to a number of secondary sexual changes. Andy's body was physically changing, and so were his internal sensations.

One day Andy described to me the feeling of being attracted to a particular player on his soccer team. While his teammates would be gawking at some of the girls' soccer team players down the field, Andy found his eyes turning toward his own teammates, and one in particular. When this direction of his attention kept happening, when feelings of interest and arousal arose inside him, he began to feel scared. He said to me that he "knew that wasn't right" but that it was simply what he felt.

Emotion is a deep process that not only gives us the subjective sense of our feelings, but also orients our attention and lets us have a felt sense of "This is important." In this way, Andy was having an emotional experience that let him know what mattered to him. He did not intentionally create this emotional response, he did not choose to focus his attention on boys or on that one boy, it was simply what his body's brain was creating inside him.

For me to help Andy's parents learn to be present for him, I needed to help them be open to what Andy was going through. While Andy's sexual maturation was happening at the same time as the majority of young people in our society, Andy was in the minority of individuals whose sexual orientation was not toward someone of the opposite gender. Andy was having sexual and romantic fantasies about other males. Decades ago, this orientation would have erroneously been called an "illness," but now we know that homosexuality is not a disorder. Just as people who are left-handed are in the minority and this is (usually nowadays) not seen as evidence of a "problem," having a sexual orientation that is in the minority does not make homosexuality a dysfunction. There are still some individuals who view homosexuality as a condition that should be altered clinically or otherwise, but these are mistaken views from a not-so-distant past. Being sexually attracted to people of your own gender is not a "condition" to be treated professionally.

So let's keep track of that as we see how Andy's parents could be present with him and who he truly is so that they can support him living as an authentic self.

Being present is what Andy's parents needed to become. Presence is a way of keeping trust alive and keeping connections strong and communication wide open. That doesn't mean becoming permissive parents, where anything goes. Authoritative parenting where structure is apparent but connection and communication are equally valued is the goal.

But Judy and Peter, Andy's parents, though they claimed to be open-minded people, were each in their own way not open to Andy's sexual orientation. As the majority of individuals in the population are heterosexual, it is understandable that, by simple statistics of probability, no parents would expect that their child would have a homosexual orientation. And this is exactly the point: To be present we need to be open to life, to be open to things occurring that are beyond what our expectations created for us. Being present enables us to become freed from the "shoulds" of life, letting go of expectations and being open to what is actually happening. In mindful awareness, we let go of expectations and are open to what is. Remember the COAL combination of curiosity, openness, acceptance, and love from our time-in practices in Mindsight Tools #2? This COAL state is the stance we take when we are present.

Presence cultivates authenticity in how we live.

Naturally we come to life with expectations. This is just the way the brain works. It is an anticipation machine, setting up from prior experiences a neurological filter that enables us to get ready for the next thing. We survive in the world because of these filters. We make sense of the world and then get ready for what the world is likely to dish up for us. That's what expectations empower us to do. But the downside of such expectations is that they can make it difficult for us to clearly see what is in front of us, or even inside us.

In simple terms, there is no such thing as "immaculate perception."

We can work on being present in an approach that lets go of our expectational mind-sets, our previously created judgments or "pre-judgments," and we bring into perceptions a more direct, unfiltered input of what is. In this way, being present, learning to intentionally let go of expectations, enables us to become mindfully aware of what is happening. This is the receptive perceptual stance we can take when we are present in life.

The mind-set that a child will have a heterosexual orientation is understandable given the statistics (that is, it's more likely to be the case), but it is an innate bias, an expectation, that made it difficult for Andy's parents to see Andy for who he is. If this mental model inside them of what is expected turned into a rigid model of what "should" happen, then presence would be impaired. When we have fixed expectations, we cannot see clearly. Our prior learning (what the society and our family and our own individual experiences have taught us) can create mental models that are the perceptual filters that skew our view of present experience through a lens that biases what we see in the moment. Expectations become fixed, and mental "shoulds" distort what we are open to seeing and accepting.

Even if we think we don't have these biases and expectations, our facial expressions and tone of voice may reveal disappointment and disapproval. We as parents need to be very conscious of the depths of our responses to unexpected developments with our children so that we don't unwittingly make them feel judged, condemned, or even invisible. All of these things can inhibit our ability to be present and can threaten trust in our relationship with our child.

Studies of temperament, for example, reveal that the ultimate developmental outcome for children is not in what temperament the child has, but how accepting the parent is to that child's individual characteristics. If you feel loved for who you are as a child or adolescent by your parent (or for any of us in all of our relationships!), you will have the foundation you need to thrive. Being seen and accepted for who you are makes you feel good about yourself and helps give you a resilient mind. Your home base is strong as a safe harbor, and your home base serves as a solid launching pad from which to move out and explore the world.

When I joined the girls' modern dance class in high school, my father was very upset. He told me that he was worried "everyone would think you are a homosexual." I asked him why that mattered, and he could only look at me with a frightened and angry look on his face. For myself, I knew that joining the class was what I wanted to do. I loved to dance, and found the activities in the boys' physical education program uninteresting. I didn't really enjoy being shoved around on the football field, even though I was one of the fastest runners at my high school and usually didn't get caught as a wide receiver. And I was short, so basketball was forever frustrating. Dance was a way to feel free, and I loved girls, and many of them were in that dance class, so it was a "no brainer" for me to transfer into that activity for my physical education requirement. It was physical, and wow, was that a great education.

I felt a deep sense of being real, of being truly myself, of being authentically there in that class. It was a powerful and life-changing step to ignore my father's reaction and my peers' expectations and simply be me.

Like my father, Andy's parents were afraid that his peers would humiliate him. But also like my father, there was something more. I asked Andy's parents what they felt about Andy's feelings of being attracted to boys, and Peter, Andy's father, had a terrified look on his face. "Being a homosexual just isn't right. There must be something wrong here . . . (long silence) . . . Those feelings just aren't okay. . . . What happened to you?" he asked Andy with a stern voice and terrified look on his face.

What "isn't okay" about having a feeling that you authentically have? Peter wasn't alone when it comes to men having what generically can be termed "homophobia"—not only a fear of others' being homosexual and of homosexuality in general, but also a fear that he himself might be gay. Some of that fear may arise from the spectrum of sexual feelings that are quite natural to have in mammalian life. Sexual urges awaken, genitals become engorged with blood, impulses and sensations emerge, behaviors to move toward individuals to whom we are attracted start to "take over" our external movements, sometimes even before we are aware of them. We can know what we feel by how our bodies behave. And for a young teen, sometimes those feelings surface for a wide range of people—same age, younger or older, same gender or different. Sexuality is a natural feeling, and the sense of attraction arises along a spectrum. Unlike our external genitals and chromosomes that are usually (there are some rare exceptions) either male or female, our sexual arousal can be generated from interacting with a wide array of individuals. That's just human nature.

Yet this uncertainty of the object of our sexual attraction can create anxiety for some people. Mindsight helps us see that this spectrum of sexual feelings is quite different from the internal—often hidden—mental model most of us have of a fixed sexual orientation. That is, many people have a belief that you should be attracted only to people of the opposite gender. The violation of this expectation can agitate some people. In fact, having sexual arousal toward someone of the same gender can create panic. And having sexual arousal toward people of both genders can be befuddling. I have met many patients whose natural spectrum of their own feelings freaks them out. They "clamp down" on their own inner experience in order to conform to the mental model they've learned from family and society that says boys like girls and girls like boys. No exceptions to this rule. Period.

We've seen that a violation of expectation can create profound anxiety and a cascade of internal and external reactions. The internal reactions to such a violation can include shutting down freedom of feeling, creating a cascade of thought processes that condemn such ambiguity of feelings in the self and others, and even a deep fear reaction that becomes a complex web of anger toward anyone else who may evoke such a spectrum of sexual feelings within the person. You can imagine perhaps how such internal reactions are an attempt of the mind to reduce the anxiety of uncertainty. But the irony is that the rigid response to such initial chaotic reactions to a natural spectrum of feelings also shuts the individual into a prison of their own making.

Anger "projected outward" onto others who show a deviation from the societal norm is a primitive defense that is an ineffective and sometimes violent attempt to shut down awareness of the initial spectrum of internal feelings that created the now forgotten anxiety. That anxiety may have been about one's own internal experience and identity. For some, the initiating anxiety may be simply about not knowing what to do with those feelings. Fantasies, dreams, bodily sensations, and impulses directed toward same-gender people may evoke confusion, anxiety, and fear. Rather than simply feeling these feelings, there is a set of reactions against having them. These unexpected and therefore uncomfortable feelings can be "defended" against by being shifted into outward directed emotions and behaviors: fear of others' homosexual feelings, not one's own; anger toward others' homosexuality, not one's own. These projected feelings and reactions are often so automatic that the projecting individual has no conscious idea that such homophobic reactivity is coming from their own inner sense of vulnerability. Quite the contrary, being aware of one's own vulnerability is often the last thing on the angry, fearful person's mind.

With all of these possibilities in mind, I gently tried to align myself with Peter's experience. I had to be present with him, to be open to what his experience was right at that moment in time. With Andy's permission (and relief), I took some time alone with Peter and Andy's mom, Judy, to help give them all the space away from one another they needed to explore some of these issues and whatever might be going on in each of them.

Judy was able to state that she herself was mostly frightened of AIDS and the social exclusion Andy might experience by being gay. Her fears were quite understandable, and as we discussed together the notion that "being gay" was not a choice but a biological reality, she was able to sense that the work she needed to do was to embrace these challenges of his new reality. She still felt scared, scared that he could get ill or be ostracized, but she was open to the fundamental idea that what Andy really needed was her love and support. This love could be expressed by her learning to be present for him—to be curious, open, accepting, and loving.

Peter listened to this discussion silently, his face appearing terrified as we spoke. As the conversation turned toward him, his fear quickly mutated into fury. At first he blamed Judy for being "too doting" over Andy when he was a baby. Then he turned his anger toward me, saying that "therapy brainwashes people" and that I failed to help Andy by making him "too soft" with this "therapy crap" and that I pushed him toward this "gay stuff." As Judy and I let him express his viewpoints, Peter said that this was the "worst thing that could have happened to him."

As a therapist, part of the challenge is to blend the need to give people the space to find out their own inner truths with the need to clarify what is scientifically known about how we develop. I acknowledged to Peter and Judy that there is indeed a "controversy" in this and many other fields. I let them know that some small group of therapists would try to convince Andy that he is not gay. I invited them to find such therapists if they wanted to. But in my scientific and clinical opinion, research and experience suggested instead the approach that people should be given the support to discover who they actually are. I talked to them about the spectrum of feelings and the need to explore those sensations in a safe way so that both the body and the mind remain healthy. When a family pushes for only one set of feelings or identities to be "permissible," authentic feelings and identifications simply go underground, they don't disappear. I talked to them more about presence and Andy's need to feel their acceptance and support. Knowing that Andy was my primary patient and that I wouldn't have much time with his parents beyond a session or two, I then brought up the possible source of Peter's fury.

What amazed me about that extended session was that by using mindsight skills of seeing the inner world of self and others with more stability, Peter's response was actually quite open. We did some breath-awareness practices to let them simply be with their own internal world. And then we let whatever feelings and concerns that were there simply be expressed and explored. Perhaps it was Judy's readiness to help him change, perhaps it was the sense of inevitability of Andy's identity, and perhaps it was his true love for his son and family that contributed to the opening of Peter's mind. Whatever elements, the time felt right and we dove in.

By examining the general issues—the ways the brain works and how relationships support the emergence of our minds—we could then focus on the specifics with a neutrality that was a crucial starting place. This was no longer just about Andy or their family, it was about being human. Embracing the universal is a part of self-compassion, as researchers like Kristin Neff define it. We see that we are not alone, that we are a part of a larger, universal human drama. Being compassionate to ourselves also comes along with being present and mindful of the moment, as well as being kind to ourselves and being gentle and caring.

As mentioned earlier, kindness can be seen as the way we are supportive and honoring of one another's vulnerability. So my whole inner intention was to be kind. Now in many ways, integration made visible is kindness and compassion. So to promote integration, I needed to empower Andy's parents to explore their own differentiated views, and then to help them link to Andy's experience.

To be supportive of Peter's mind, to let him be differentiated in our session, I needed to suspend my own judgments and expectations of "how a father should be" and instead embrace exactly where he was. I needed to know my own inner mental sea, to differentiate myself, and so I reflected within myself on the experiences I have had, including the journey through girls' dance and my father's fearful reactions to that, even before the days of AIDS. With that inner knowing open in myself, I could be ready to be open to Peter's inner mental sea.

I remembered then what you and I have been reviewing in our conversation of the fundamental stance we can take: Chaos and rigidity emerge from impairments to integration. When we are integrated, we are in harmony. When we are not integrated, we are in states of chaos (wild, unpredictable) or rigidity (stuck, paralyzed, unchanging). Peter's response to Andy's experience was to become both rigid and chaotic. He was clearly not in an open state of presence, not in a state of integration. My goal needed to be open to where he was, and then to help him see a way to move toward a more integrated way of being himself.

With all of this in mind, my intention was to simply use mindsight to be present with Peter, attune to his inner experience, resonate with those inner states within myself, and then allow trust to emerge naturally. Remember that mindsight has these three components of seeing inside yourself, seeing inside another, and promoting integration. Mindsight is what I could offer to Andy's family, and it is what any parent can cultivate with their adolescent. And naturally, it is what an adolescent can learn to do with others as well.

Peter struggled mightily with his own fears and his own memories of being a young boy in the competitive, sports-focused world of his family. His father had particularly emphasized his three sons' participation in contact sports, especially football. As we gave Peter the space in the session to speak the truth, his truth, of his own upbringing, he then could move toward finding a new way of approaching his son. The idea in my mind was to be present and enable differentiation to flourish before we might move on to the linkage that Andy so desperately needed at this vulnerable time with his family.

It was tentative at first, but you could see the love both parents had for Andy shining through when we had our next session with the three of them together. Peter told Andy that he was trying to be open to what he was saying, open to who he was, and that he understood Andy was just "being himself" and that he would stand by his side. There was a moment of silence that just hung in the air, unmoving, and then Peter got up and walked over to Andy's chair and without a pause Andy rose and the two hugged each other in an embrace that felt suspended in time. Peter told Andy that he would do his best to be the father Andy deserved.

None of us knew exactly where Andy's life would go, but setting up this presence of his parents was a crucial step for him to feel em-

Building Trust

powered to become the most fulfilled and free, to become the most authentic Andy that he could become.

Time has unfolded well for Andy in the years since those initial sessions. I feel deeply grateful that Peter and Judy were able to open their minds to seeing Andy for who he was at that time and for his courage to continue to become the wonderful human being that he is. Andy is supported in his childhood home by his loving parents, and that has made all the difference in his rewarding and authentic life.

Drug Use or Abuse?

One of the greatest challenges for adolescents and their families can be the potential for the use of mind-altering chemicals, which include alcohol and other recreational drugs. Staying present as a parent in the face of an adolescent's drug involvement can be difficult, especially if you think that this use is a form of abuse or addiction. For adolescents, while it may feel very common and therefore "safe" to be involved with drugs, it is important to acknowledge that drug use can lead to powerful changes in your internal experience and social relationships. If your own activity with mind-altering substances feels like it is becoming something that is controlling you rather than your controlling it, understanding these issues can be essential. In order to stay fully present for the meaning of drugs in your life so that you can make decisions that are best for your own well-being, having some of the basic facts about the brain and drug use is crucial. While these facts could occupy an entire book, here I'll present a fundamental framework that I hope will put drug use in perspective.

As the drive to explore new ways of experiencing reality emerges during adolescence, the use of drugs that alter brain function can be very intriguing. We all have differing emotional reactions to drug use, from excitement and interest to fear and repulsion. Whatever the science or the laws are about using substances that alter our mental state, adults and adolescents alike may use various ingested and inhaled chemicals to alter their experience of consciousness, including alcohol and marijuana, psychedelic mushrooms and cocaine.

There are at least four fundamental drives that can motivate our increased use of drugs during the adolescent period. These include experimentation, social connection, self-medication, and addiction. Let's review each of these in turn so we can understand how the use of mind-altering substances may affect our adolescent growth and social life, now and for our life in the future.

Alcohol is a common drug used legally by adults and illegally by individuals under legislated minimum ages. For an adolescent whose dopamine release is already revved up, drugs, including alcohol, that directly increase the release of this transmitter create an especially challenging mix of drug-enhanced dopamine levels on top of an already activated adolescent dopamine system. In other words, adolescence is a period not only of drug experimentation to explore novelty, but also of vulnerability to becoming physiologically drawn to using and becoming addicted to alcohol and other drugs.

As discussed in Part II, the dopamine system is more reactive in a teen, with heightened release that drives our reward and sensation-seeking behaviors. Even in the face of this enhanced release, as mentioned earlier, the baseline levels of dopamine during adolescence are actually *lower*. What this means is that teens may be prone to feeling "bored" unless they are engaging in novelty-seeking behaviors. An adolescent's dopamine profile has lower troughs, higher peaks. That's the activated reward system of the adolescent brain and one source of the lows and highs of the adolescent mind. So when we realize that many drugs are chemicals that increase dopamine release, we can see how such substances would be attractive to raise ourselves out of the boredom of a trough. That's just the nature of adolescence that may make us especially prone at this time to use dopamine-enhancing substances.

We've seen that adolescence is a time of experimentation, of trying new things. So the drive to alter consciousness and experience new ways of perceiving and feeling and thinking is a natural outcome of a push for novelty and the experience of new sensations. Novelty itself is rewarding and also activates our dopamine release. One aspect of this experimentation is simply to try something new. Another dimension is to widen our understanding of reality by altering the usual patterns of perception that shape our commonly held views of reality. This is sometimes referred to as an exploration of consciousness or a spiritual search and may involve psychedelic drugs such as peyote or psilocybin, which have been used for thousands of years in various cultures. Some drugs used for the purpose of altering consciousness do not involve dopamine, and because of this they may influence a person's life but not be addictive. This drive to expand consciousness and see life with new eyes is important for some drug users, adolescents or adults, but for others it is merely a drive to experience something new without a search to understand new meanings of life.

Experimentation with novelty is likely a prime reason why a majority of teens have been found to use mind-altering substances no matter what their parents may think or have as rules of the house. Parents of high school students are often surprised at surveys revealing that the majority of the juniors and seniors in high school have used alcohol and marijuana. It is important for adults to realize that this "norm" of teenage life does not make it right or permissible; it does not make it safe or legal; it simply makes it very likely that it is happening. To deny such a reality as parents is to put our heads in the sand. It's also important to remember that how we approach this aspect of our teen's life will shape our relationship with our child for the years ahead.

The experimental aspect of the use of alcohol can be an important dimension that drives an initial interest in drinking and getting drunk. For some, there can be the emergence of an intense interest in using alcohol in one's social life. Recall from the story of Katey, in Part II, that drinking alcohol became an important part of her life and motivated her to make decisions that got her expelled from high school. Katey's drinking had also become a central part of her social life, a way she connected with friends and organized her relationships. But in the setting of group alcohol use, the tendency to engage in binge drinking, consuming large amounts of alcohol in short amounts of time, is an especially risky behavior adolescents may be prone to engage in. From the social point of view, it is a group activity, done with a sense of camaraderie and of accomplishment—who can consume the most booze? From the mind point of view, the decision to limit intake depends on executive functions that become suspended after a couple of drinks. And from the brain development perspective, alcohol poisoning has been clearly demonstrated to kill brain cells and their connections, especially in regions that control attention and memory. Repeated bingeing damages the brain.

Group binge behavior reveals the second major reason people use drugs: to be part of a common social fabric, part of a shared experience. In some social circles and in certain social settings such as parties or concerts, drinking alcohol or smoking marijuana may be an expected behavior. The lowering of social anxiety and the lowering of defenses make many people feel more at ease in social settings, and so these drugs are used as a "social lubricant" that facilitates communication. While Katey didn't feel nervous in social situations, she did enjoy the "fun in getting smashed" with her friends. She enjoyed the shared experience and always drank with someone, never by herself. At least that was true while she was in high school.

A third drive for drug use is in its role as self-medication for a primary psychiatric condition or a painful situation. For example, someone with depression may feel so down in the dumps that she wants to "go numb" by frequently using alcohol or she may get herself "revved up" by using amphetamines. Someone with mania as a part of manic–depressive or bipolar illness might use alcohol or barbiturates to slow himself down. A person with schizophrenia might use alcohol to quiet the hallucinations and delusions that are terrifying for him. For others with attention deficit difficulties, the use of stimulants may temporarily increase the focus of sustained attention. And for individuals with social anxiety, taking alcohol may decrease their concerns in social situations, whereas smoking marijuana may inadvertently lead to an increase in their panic. Katey did not have any of these underlying psychiatric conditions, and it did not appear that she was treating any post-traumatic symptoms with alcohol use. It's crucial to be sure that alcohol or street drugs are not being used to treat some underlying challenge to an individual's mental health. Katey was not self-medicating as far as I could tell.

A fourth drive involved in drug use, one that can emerge after drug use begins, is addiction. Katey showed some early signs that were of concern to me regarding her becoming addicted to alcohol, as she needed to use increasing amounts of alcohol to get a "buzz," a state of mind she began to crave. This need to increase the amount of an ingested substance to achieve a certain effect may have been a sign of her developing tolerance to the drug, possibly because her brain was getting used to it or her liver was more rapidly metaboliz-ing it. Tolerance isn't necessary for addiction, but it can be present and be an important sign of a larger issue unfolding. Katey also be-came obsessed with the use of alcohol in ways that felt more like an addiction than just a pastime interest or a part of her social life. She seemed to have a craving that was more than simply an enjoyment; it had the quality of withdrawal from the alcohol. This made me concerned that an addiction was developing in her. We began to discuss whether her preoccupation with alcohol and bringing the li-quor to the party that got her expelled from school was more than just "being a teenager," as she had suggested. When I asked her at the time she just shrugged her shoulders and said, "I don't know . . . but I don't think so."

Addictive substances and addictive behaviors, like shopping or gambling, involve the reward circuit's major transmitter, dopamine. As we've seen, this is the transmitter that is already revved up in its reactivity in adolescence. Dopamine is released from a brainstem-related area, the nucleus accumbens, and influences our limbic emo-tional, motivational, evaluative, and memory systems, and even pushes up into our cortex to influence our thinking, decision making, and behaviors. Alcohol can activate the dopamine system in anyone, leading to surges in this reward-based brain chemical.

Beyond stimulating a dopamine surge that is especially intense in adolescents, alcohol and other drugs have an impact on the way our minds see reality, as they dampen cortical functioning and alter our conscious experience of the world. Substances that alter our state of mind also alter our capacity to responsibly manage a large vehicle as it hurls through space, or manage our own body as our consciousness fails to keep us alert. Some substances, too, especially if taken in excess or in combination with other substances, can kill you. I have two friends who lost an adolescent son and daughter because of such experimental excesses, one in a fatal car accident, the other breathing in her vomit and dying alone in her college dormitory room.

So when adults get agitated about substance use, adolescents should keep in mind that the adults may naturally be concerned about their safety. One approach is to insist on total avoidance of such substances, a position many parents like Katey's and her high school took. From the adolescents' perspective, such a policy may make no sense and seem unrealistic, rigid, and unfair. Other parents take the position that if teens are going to participate in such activities, using substances that alter their state of mind, they should do so in a responsible way. The hopeful aim of such a policy is to save lives. "Call if you need a ride home, no questions asked." "Learn to use alcohol in moderation." "Avoid mixing substances." Helping kids manage their drug-related activities, so that when they are out of the house they don't' "go wild with the freedom they've been waiting to have" and drink themselves into oblivion, can be a crucial first step in helping adolescents navigate this challenging terrain.

Addressing the possibility of addiction at this time in life is important. Adolescence is a period of great risk for not only using mind-altering drugs but also abusing them and becoming addicted to them. As adolescents we begin to experiment with many drugs that activate the dopamine system, and it is during our adolescent period that the brain is most sensitive to becoming addicted to a substance. Our changing adolescent brain is especially vulnerable to respond to drug use with the onset of a cascade of behavioral and physiological responses that can contribute to addiction. Such vulnerability to addiction is due to both the activation of certain genes and the altering of neural functioning, making the dopamine release dependent on drug use. The earlier in adolescence we are exposed to alcohol and drugs, the more likely we are to develop an addiction.

Think of it this way. Addiction is where we get used to the dopamine surge an activity or substance creates in the brainstem and limbic regions that pushes our cortex to make decisions regarding our behavior to continue to do things that may be destructive to us. In fact, a simple way of defining an addiction is when people continue to do something that is destructive even after they know it is hurting their life. The boundary between drug abuse and addiction can be quite hazy.

In Katey's situation she was discovering that she could not stop drinking, even after that party and her expulsion. And she could not stop drinking after just one drink, either. It is true that once you are intoxicated, the very prefrontal regions that would help you decide to stop drinking go off-line. Even one drink, for some individuals, can create sudden and intense shifts in judgment—like the discerning judgment not to drive a car while intoxicated. For some, just one drink can change their personality, and they may not even remember what happened to them. Others can experience a blackout after a lot of drinking. This is different from passing out in that when you are in a blackout, you are aware, more or less, of what is happening. But while you were drinking, your limbic memory region, the hippocampus, had so shut down that, afterward you simply don't recall what happened to you.

Even when Katey was not actively under alcohol's direct effects, alcohol was still influencing her life during high school. She didn't have blackouts, she could "hold her liquor," and she didn't drink alone. Yet Katey's interest in alcohol felt like something more than just an interest in exploring other states of consciousness with her friends; it was more than experimental and more than social.

There was something in the way she talked about getting "smashed" that had the sense of some intense dopamine-driven-reward circuit speaking through her. She was intensely focused on alcohol and its effects on her life. For some individuals who experiment with drugs and alcohol to alter their state of mind temporarily, such dopamine-surge-driven behaviors lead to an alteration in their lives in long-term ways.

Some studies suggest that in those at risk, and especially during our adolescent period, a gene inside our brain's motivational circuitry is activated when a particular substance is ingested. Once this gene activation occurs, the dopamine circuit locks on to a certain "substance of choice" and an intense focus of attention, thought, energy, and behavior is directed to the substance. Alcohol, cocaine, amphetamines, barbiturates, and heroin can all activate that circuit. Rats given cocaine, for example, will choose that dopamine-stimulating drug over food and then die of starvation. With people, studies reveal that this dopamine surge is released not only when *taking* the substance but even when *planning* to take it, when *thinking* about it, when being around people with whom it has been taken, when in similar rooms where it was taken, when getting ready to take it. In short, the intense release of dopamine, which gives you the feeling of urge and the drive for reward, occurs both with the ingestion and with the intention behind use of that substance.

That's the cycle of addiction.

The broader story of the role dopamine plays in our lives goes like this. When we work hard at something and finally finish it, like writing an essay or a book, creating a painting, learning a piece of music, constructing a model airplane, practicing a sport, or going for a long hike, dopamine rises and that disciplined effort is rewarded. There is no sudden peak, no dopamine surge, but there is a gradual rise in dopamine levels above baseline that gives us a feeling of deep satisfaction, a fullness, a pride in our accomplishment. We get lost in the flow of something we love, and we get pleasure in doing it. That flow is how we lose ourselves in an activity and become at peace and content in our experience. Different people have flow in different activities. The key is to discover what our own particular passions are and cultivate them in our lives. We can enjoy an experience of flow and that feeling of a job well done, of hard work completed, of an accomplishment well earned.

When a substance or behavior of addiction happens in those at risk, then there is a surge in dopamine that feels thrilling and compelling and good and rewarding and something that needs to be repeated, and repeated soon. Not all of us may become addicted, but some of us will with exposure, especially with early exposure. With the precipitous drop from the surge's peak, we have a relative plummet in our dopamine levels, and after a while this drop feels really bad. We've gotten used to the dopamine thrill of the peak, and we've become bored with the dopamine trough. And boring becomes so dull and painful in contrast to the surging peak that we need to repeat the dopamine surge-releasing behavior soon, like very soon, like now. Given that the adolescent trough is already low, we can see how this period of time may be especially vulnerable to developing an addiction to the surging dopamine peaks.

Research reveals, as mentioned earlier, that even anticipating and planning for the act of ingesting a drug captures our intentions and focus on the addiction, and these mental processes themselves release the dopamine surge. It's not just the drug's ingestion. It's imagining the drug and the ingestion of it. What this means is that addiction is a life-consuming challenge, not just something we do because we are choosing it. Once a substance becomes an addiction and not just an experimentation we choose to do, the addiction is in charge. But even if we don't get addicted to a drug, studies show that chronic use of a substance like alcohol, for example, can damage the liver and damage the brain.

When we think of Katey's description of her planning, we realize that the excitement and the thrill that felt compelling to Katey may have been more than simply adolescent hyperrationality with dopamine-driven reward amplification. Naturally, Katey is a teen, and so these elements were there. But could it be that this focus on alcohol was also further amplifying the PROS of her dopamine drive because she had inherited her family's legacy of addiction, which included alcoholism?

There is no specific test for that possibility at this point, but I brought it up with Katey and we discussed the issue, and we discussed her lack of concern about it. All we could do at that moment was raise her awareness about addiction as a possibility beyond adolescent experimentation. And this awareness was exactly what she had been missing before her expulsion. That risk of addiction, like all the other cons her mind was minimizing, was just filed away as not that important even as we did our work at the end of high school. She continued to drink at parties during her senior year. All I could do was to help her become more and more aware of herself as the year went on. I was in the role of the non-parental adult who could support her during this period of her life, helping her get ready to carry this new self-awareness with her as she left the safe harbor of her home.

Katey was developing a new sense of herself, one with a great sense of humor, and one with an understanding of who she was and who she could become, even as her drinking continued. Knowing that those reflections emerge from the integrative prefrontal regions of her brain helped me feel as if we were building the important skills of self-awareness that could continue to develop in the months ahead.

Just before she went off to college, Katey was doing pretty well and was ready to stop therapy. At that point she was aware that her use of alcohol might become an issue in her life and what it might mean in the long run if she ended up being consumed by her drinking. I saw Katey periodically during her first year of college. It took several reminders in the course of her active social life, with its many forays into binge drinking during this freshman year, for Katey to discover and admit to herself that she likely had a serious problem with alcohol abuse, and possibly even addiction. When she told me she was having blackouts, that she could not remember things that happened at parties when she had been drinking, and that she had started drinking by herself before she went out, we both knew it was time to consider a different strategy for her life.

Katey is in the midst of trying to stop drinking, at least for now. I've told her that research suggests working with a twelve-step program, like Alcoholics Anonymous, would be the most helpful and effective way to support her efforts to stay sober. But at this point, she says she is reluctant to participate in "something as ridiculous as that." Even the notion of seeing alcohol as a food allergy, like something she just shouldn't eat, seemed "dumb." Time will tell how she'll hold out, and how she'll let her brain recover from the continual dopamine-surging alcohol bath that she's soaked it in over this past year and a half since her expulsion from school. That's a brain, Katey admitted to me, that's gotten "really used to partying hard." That's a brain, too, I told her, that needs a break to think clearly. We've talked to each other on and off over these last few months, and Katey told me recently that she feels challenged by not drinking but is trying to find new ways of focusing her mind during parties and when out with friends in other settings.

What I really needed to have Katey learn is a way to focus her attention to integrate her brain and give her the strength to calm her cravings and clear her mind. Those are skills she should learn to increase her self-awareness and reclaim her life. As with Sara, I've encouraged Katey to take on the mindsight tools we've been learning here. We'll see if she's open to strengthening her mind and integrating her life from the inside out. But with this particular challenge, if she could also find support in a group like Alcoholics Anonymous, it would be great—if she would just go. Let's keep our hopes up that she'll be open to these known ways to improve her life. I know her parents are trying their best to support her, but we all know that at this point it is up to Katey to take the initiative to empower her life.

Returning Home: Reflection, Realignment, and Repairing Ruptures

Moving out of the house is a change and challenge, a powerful transition for adolescent and adult alike. After moving away, many adolescents find themselves coming back home for extended periods of time before they establish their own financially independent lives. In the United States in recent times, one-third to one-half of "grown children" move back in with their parents. This trend is influenced by our stressful financial times, so living at home saves money. But this trend also has its emotional side, in which parents and the parental home provide needed support during this period of stressful transition and employment uncertainty. The emotional impact of older adolescents' returning home needs to be addressed directly and reflected upon internally for this period of time to go well for all concerned.

This returning home has its own challenges for all of us. Whichever side of the generational divide you may find yourself on now, I invite you to try applying your mindsight skills to understanding the experience of both the adult and the adolescent in the following story.

"If you don't like the rules of the house, you can go out and find a job, earn some money, and move into your own apartment."

How many times have these words been said from a frustrated parent to an assertive adolescent? When things arrive at this point in a relationship between a parent and an older adolescent, it doesn't feel good for anyone. I know because I said these very words to my son in a moment of intense frustration and irritation. My saying them was heavy-handed, and as they came out of my mouth I already felt bad in my heart. My son had just graduated from college. He, like many his age, had come back home following his four years away. His plans were uncertain: He might be with us for just a few months over the course of the summer and then start his career in Southern California, or he might move back up to Northern California where he'd gone to college and start his work there. We had all been getting along very well, having meals together, going for walks, watching television, going to concerts. It was, in so many ways, quite wonderful. But a number of times when my wife and I came home, the place was a bit of a mess. It was probably cleaner than his cooperative housing at school, but for us, it was a mess. Pots from morning breakfast were still on the stove, unmoved. Plates filled with food were strewn around the counter; pieces of vegetables and other reminders of earlier meals lay on the floor.

In all honesty, the place was cleaner than when I was there on my own, when my wife was traveling and I was a bachelor "empty nester," with our daughter away for her first year of college. But when I came in from walking the dogs and heard my son say to his mom that it wasn't a big deal to have some plates around, I immediately felt frustrated.

I had learned long ago that life goes well in our household when our cleanliness standards were based on the "highest" expectation of each individual sharing the space. My standards are quite low, I'll admit, and my wife's are high. And we've worked out that tension, or continue to try to work it out, in a way that I think works well for us in our partnership in life. So when our son was, in my view, talking back to my life partner, I found myself getting protective of her. A twenty-two-year-old male back at home can be like a young wolf returning to the pack he'd left, and my alpha male wolf hackles were raised when this young wolf was "threatening" the alpha female of our den. That's the backstory happening deep in my limbic-thumb and brainstem-palm areas. In my cortex-fingers I said to myself, "Don't gang up on him—she can state for herself the case for needing him to clean up after himself. Don't double up on him!"

However, that very morning my wife had given our son a polite but clear talk about our standards of clean and asked him to respect those values. So when we'd come home after a night out and found stuff still around from the morning, it was frustrating. Before I'd left to walk the dogs, my wife and I saw the mess and reflected with each other on what it was like to have a college graduate back at home, about how we'd have to work out some new rules, some new ways of all getting along after his years of living without our oversight. My son and his friends must have come in while I was out with the dogs. My wife and I had agreed earlier not to just blurt out demands but to take a more sensitive approach with our son. At that moment as I stood in the kitchen, it was like saying to myself "Don't think of a pink elephant" and being able to think only of that pink elephant. When the brain is given instructions to be sure *not* to do something, it keeps on checking that thing to keep an "eye" on it. That tracking just primes the thing, making it more likely to be activated. So out of my mouth came some words I shouldn't have said about his needing to clean up, and then when he said that it was not really a big deal to leave a few cups and plates around, I became frustrated. "Look," I told him, "you are back from college and this can happen. You've been living on your own, and with your own rules. And we have *our own* standards. So understandably you may see things differently than we do. But here's the deal: This is our house, not yours. And these are our rules. If you want to live here, you'll need to respect our requests." And then I said those words about his getting his own apartment.

Now, you may be thinking that all this sounds fine. If you are an adult reading this you may feel that way, but as an adolescent reading this you may not. I don't know. But *I* felt terrible right away. That evening I felt heavy and drained and irritated with myself. It wasn't so much about the issue of rules and cleanliness, it was the proclamation that this was not his home. That was just plain insensitive and over the top. It was just wrong. The economy is tough, unemployment is high, college graduates abound, he works hard, and the fact is, this is his home, too. The next morning and throughout the day at work, I couldn't stop thinking about what was really going on inside me that got me to say the part about this not being his home. Why had I gotten so mad *so* fast?

When I came home from work that next day, my son and I had a big discussion about what it was like to be at his stage of life, twenty-two years old and transitioning from college to working life, about going from being a kid at home to an adult in the world.

I apologized for what I had said: "This *is* in fact *your* home. I am sorry for what I said. Yes, you need to keep the place clean, but I was out of line to tell you to go out and get your own apartment. You may want to do that in the future, but you have just graduated after four long hardworking years at school, and I shouldn't have said something so harsh." He thanked me for the apology, and said that he felt that I was probably irritated by something else going on in my own life.

That's mindsight in action. He was right . . . and that something else is what I needed to reflect upon. Our experiences with our attachment figures, our parents, can affect us even as we are parents ourselves. Making sense of those experiences helps us become more present, more self-aware, and better able to connect with others. I had to reflect on my own internal meanings of this period of life so that I could remain present with him as we all moved along on this life journey.

This brief story brings up a number of issues at the heart of adolescence and life in general. One is that sometimes as parents we do things that create a rupture in a close connection. It is our duty to reflect on such ruptures and make the efforts to make a repair, to reconnect after we've apologized for our contribution to conflict. A second lesson is that sometimes we do things that we don't really want to do. The brain has the higher, prefrontal part that helps us be aware of things and creates conscious intentions. But sometimes the lower limbic, brainstem, and bodily areas directly influence our behaviors, motivating our actions and filling them with feelings that shape our non-verbal tone of voice, timings, and facial expressions without the intervening prefrontal inhibition or filtering.

In this case, the output of my using words with him was pretty mild, but sometimes, as we've seen, we can flip our lids and go down the low road with more force. In some of my other books (in *Mindsight*, the chapter "Crepes of Wrath," and in *Parenting from the Inside Out*, the section on the Low Road), the importance of rupture and repair is explored in detail regarding younger kids, including my own. So my son has grown up knowing that if there is a rupture, there ought to be a repair. That's how we can acknowledge that there is no such thing as a perfect way of behaving in a relationship, which is simply the mindsightful way of recognizing when a rupture has occurred and making efforts to reconnect in the repair. But let me say here that being reflective is essential to repair ruptures with those we care about at any age. We've practiced repair in the Mindsight Tools #3, and making a reconnection is crucial at any age. During adolescence, it is a central theme of this period to maintain open lines of communication, especially when the inevitable ruptures in that connection occur. The changes and challenges of this period make it imperative that we work on our own self-understanding as parents and work on repairing ruptures when they inevitably occur. I had to examine my protective stance toward my wife in response to what our son was doing. And I had to reflect on what went on at home when I was an older adolescent, too. So looking upon ruptures as opportunities to reflect internally and then connect interpersonally again, to create integration when integration is broken, is a helpful inner stance to take. My hope was that my son would be able to forgive me, and to experience my apology as an example of how to respond in the face of conflict.

Since this experience, our connection has been really strong. Mindsight gives us the way to be open to our inner lives and maintain an empathic connection with those we care about. Even when our outward behaviors make a rupture in our communication, mindsight can guide us back to connection. It is through the full spectrum of these mindsight moments that our relationships can truly be integrative, honoring differences and cultivating compassionate connections. I love the ways my son and I can communicate with each other now as he moves through his later adolescent years; our connection grows deeper and stronger the older he becomes. Having the notion of staying present through these many changes in his life and the challenges that they have raised has been a guiding principle for us all. Using the power of mindsight's reflective conversations also gives us a basic tool, an essential way to connect around things that really matter, that makes the way we relate to each other have a deep and authentic quality and makes these challenging moments truly opportunities to deepen our connections with one another.

MINDSIGHT TOOLS #4

■

The Mindsight Simple Seven

In this tools section, I'd like to introduce you to seven activities you can do on a daily basis that are scientifically proven to keep your body healthy, your mind strong, and your brain continuing to grow in integrative ways throughout your life. Research into the brain's ability to change and develop in response to experience, what is referred to as "neuroplasticity," reveals that regular practice of these activities can activate the growth of neural connections, and even new neurons. As you may have noticed by now, I like to enlist acronyms to help readers (and myself!) remember important concepts with regard to how our brains and emotional worlds work. In this spirit, I offer here SNAG—stimulate *n*euronal *a*ctivation and *g*rowth. Scientific investigations have shown that when we do the seven activities that follow, we SNAG the brain toward growth, and that growth is often in the direction of integration. I put these seven processes in a visual image with a colleague, David Rock, at the time the United States Department of Agriculture was putting out a new set of suggestions in the form of a food plate revealing what were the recommended daily food groups to keep the body healthy. David and I thought it might be useful to make the same kind of plate for the mind, which we call "The Healthy Mind Platter," a set of seven activities that promote optimal brain matter.

The Healthy Mind Platter

SLEEP TIME   PHYSICAL TIME   FOCUS TIME

TIME-IN   DOWNTIME   PLAYTIME   CONNECTING TIME

The Healthy Mind Platter for Optimal Brain Matter

MINDSIGHT PRACTICE A: Time-In

You'll see that these seven include time-in, which we've explored in depth in Mindsight Tools #2. Time-in is how we reflect on the inner nature of our mental lives and our bodily sensations. It enables us to perceive our feelings, thoughts, memories, and beliefs, and our intentions, hopes, dreams, attitudes, and longings. Time-in practiced on a regular basis has been shown to stimulate the growth of many fibers in the brain, especially the integrative ones that help regulate attention, emotion, and thinking. It also improves empathy and compassion.

Taking time-in means reflecting on your inner world. A simple way to do this is to SIFT the mind, paying attention to your sensations, images, feelings, and thoughts. You can go to my website, DrDanSiegel.com, and explore the breath awareness practice for a simple mindfulness exercise. And if after strengthening your ability to focus your attention for a few weeks, you are ready for something a little more comprehensive that integrates your consciousness, try out the Wheel of

I'm investing in myself.

Awareness practice, too. These are all various ways of giving yourself a time-in that supports the growth of your brain and the well-being of your mind. It's not bad for your relationships, either!

Amazingly, the mindful awareness of time-in that supports your being present for whatever arises in your life also helps to increase your levels of the enzyme telomerase, which repairs and maintains the ends of your chromosomes that help keep your individual cells alive and healthy. That's not a joke—taking time-in makes your cells healthier! In addition, your immune system will function better and you'll have more energy, and even develop a more resilient way of approaching life's challenges because of specific ways your brain will change. Not bad for a simple daily practice of taking time-in and reflecting on the inner world!

MINDSIGHT PRACTICE B: Sleep Time

Another daily activity that has been shown to increase the way your brain continues to grow in an integrative way is the time you sleep. In our modern times, digital displays and electrical lights keep us stimulated and awake long after we'd naturally be falling asleep. Since the time we need to wake up in the morning does not change much, this means that we will be getting less sleep than we may need for optimal brain growth. When you add to that the reality that the teenage brain's cycle of waking and sleeping is on a different schedule than adults or children, with staying up later being a natural outcome for many adolescents, the early time of school makes this setup a chronic source of not getting enough sleep.

Think of the following amounts as a ballpark starting point for thinking about your own sleep hygiene. According to the United States National Sleep Foundation, most teens need about eight and a half to nine and a quarter hours and most adults need seven to nine hours of sleep each night. When I write the word *need*, what I mean is that for optimal brain growth, for optimal memory consolidation of the day's learning, for optimal insulin function and food metabolism to keep fit, for optimal immune function to fight off disease, for optimal response to stress to deal with life's hassles, and for optimal mental functioning with effective abilities for focusing attention, thinking, remembering, problem solving, handling your emotions, and connecting with others in relationships, you need at least the lesser amount of your range of sleep. How much uninterrupted sleep a night are you getting?

Without adequate sleep, each of these important neural, physiological, and mental processes is in jeopardy of not functioning well. What's the outcome of inadequate amounts and quality of sleep? The brain doesn't grow well, memory is not consolidated and you don't remember what you learned, insulin doesn't work right and becoming overweight is more likely, stress hormones rise and make you feel lousy, immune functions don't work well and you can get sick more easily, and your mind won't be as sharp for paying attention, thinking, and problem solving. Plus you may simply have less energy, feel bad, become irritable more easily, and get frustrated with others more frequently. In short, you can become moody and not much fun to be around. You may come to feel out of sorts and not even realize that this state of being is because of your sleep habits.

The great news is that you are in control of your sleeping.

Here is a list of simple daily sleep habits you can practice that will help you get enough sleep soundly throughout the night:

1. Turn off digital objects and electronic screens at least an hour before you go to bed. These objects—computers, smartphones, televisions— keep your brain thinking it should be wide awake.

2. If you have trouble falling asleep, try turning down the lights a bit in the half-hour before you get into bed.

3. Try not to do work or homework in bed. The bed should be for restful activities, not associated with working.

4. Be mindful that caffeine in soda, coffee, or tea can keep some people up at night. This also includes chocolate, unfortunately. So watch when you drink and eat these substances, and make sure you are not consuming too much overall or too late in the day for you to easily fall asleep and maintain sleep through the night.

5. Some people like to take a warm bath before bed. Others like to drink a glass of milk or some other beverage containing calcium, which can help you sleep.

6. Some like to write out the day's events in a journal so that they are not worried about things when

they fall asleep. If that works for you, great! Keep in mind that journal writing has been shown to improve the immune system, and it helps resolve challenging issues in your life. Others find journal writing right before bed too stimulating. Naturally this is true if you are keeping a digital journal on a back-lit screen, so try using a paper journal for evening reflections. See what works for you.

7. The amount of continuous sleep you get matters. So set up the evening accordingly, keeping in mind when you need to get up the next morning. Eight to nine hours is a range to aim for. See what your natural needs are, no matter your age. Over a week's time, give yourself plenty of time to sleep.

MINDSIGHT PRACTICE C: Focus Time

The brain grows not only when we sleep but also when we focus our attention in a continuous way without frequent distractions. In fact, learning is the way our attention streams energy through our brain's circuits, creating information in certain areas that become activated, and then linking those activated neurons with brain growth. That's neuroplasticity, how the brain changes in response to experience. The brain is built to focus on one thing at a time, processing it into more elaborated forms, connecting it to similar items, linking it to others, and then consolidating all of the neural firing into long-term structural changes.

Focus time refers to those periods of time when we focus intently on one thing at a time. Unlike when we are multitasking, such as reading a book while texting or surfing the Web while speaking on the phone, focus time means doing only one thing at a time.

When we focus intensely, we do three things in the brain. One is that the part of the brain just above the brainstem-palm secretes an important chemical, acetylcholine, throughout the brain. A second thing is that paying close attention intensely activates specific circuits. When neurons fire together, they wire together. And this brings us to the third: When we pay close attention to one thing, the acetylcholine bathing those activating circuits works with the localized release of another neurochemical, brain-derived neurotrophic factor, or BDNF, to optimize how genes become expressed to produce the proteins necessary to strengthen the connections among those firing neurons. In short, when you pay close attention, you optimize neuroplastic changes that are the basis for learning.

I know of adolescents who say they are having trouble with schoolwork. They cannot remember, they tell me, what they read or what they studied. And, indeed, all of the homework and studying they are doing just doesn't seem to have a lasting impact on their test performance. When I ask how they study, they reveal that they are often involved in multitasking. So what happens is that the person sits with a book but her attention is constantly being divided. This division of attention toward non-school material, in the form of chatting, texting, blogging, and Web surfing, continually disrupts the neuroplastic conditions necessary to make those studies turn into synaptic change in the brain. Without the lasting structural changes in the brain, no long-term learning can occur. The exam comes and goes, just like the divided attention that prevented any synapse growth from occurring.

These digitally enhanced disruptions to paying close attention compromise long-term learning for both adolescents *and* adults. In fact, many adults who are not involved in some lifelong learning program, like book clubs or discussion groups or adult educational courses, have a serious potential problem. If we don't have focus time on a regular basis, our brains stop doing what they were born to do—continue to learn and grow and make new connections throughout our lives. Adults without the projects that enable them to closely pay attention to something can begin to feel like life has become a rut, unchanging, and boring. Lifelong learning should be seen as an opportunity to keep challenged, to keep the brain growing, and to keep ourselves engaged in learning.

Sadly, school for many of us becomes a burden, not a pleasure. The emphasis on competition instead of collaboration, on achievement rather than creative exploration, makes many of us turn off to the learning experience. Focus time reminds us that we need to keep our minds well honed and to keep on learning throughout our lives.

MINDSIGHT PRACTICE D: Downtime

While focusing attention in an uninterrupted manner helps the brain grow, you may also be relieved to know that we don't need to do that all the time. In fact, giving yourself a break and varying what you do is the whole idea of these simple seven daily mind activities. Every day we can have some downtime to enable our minds to unwind and our brains to sort themselves out. Downtime is when we have no plans, nothing we are trying to accomplish, nothing that needs to be done. During this period the brain seems to recharge its batteries, allowing the mind to intentionally be given a break.

Downtime is quite different from unintentional mind wandering. If the task at hand is to focus on something, like a conversation with someone or an assignment or talk at school, letting our minds wander off task without the choice to do that can be pretty disruptive to what we're trying to achieve. Some studies even suggest it's not good for our health and happiness.

Instead, downtime means that we designate a time to just chill out, to have nothing on the calendar, to let our imaginations go wherever they will. Vacations are a great time to just hang out. But on a daily basis, it's also good to set aside some time to take a brain break, to relax and unwind. Give yourself permission to do this intentionally. That's the goal of downtime, when we intentionally have no set goal. Sounds ironic, I know, but research reveals that it's really important, even in limited amounts, each day.

MINDSIGHT PRACTICE E: Playtime

The term "play" may make you think of childhood experiences on the playground, but we're discovering that participating in the spontaneous exploration of life with others in engaging, pleasurable, and non-judgmental ways is actually crucial for a healthy and fulfilling life throughout our life span. Laughing is a serious matter when it comes to brain matter. When we are spontaneous and having fun, the brain grows. It's as good for adolescents as it is for the adults who less frequently engage in play or just hanging out or goofing around. Giving ourselves the time and the permission to engage in activities, by ourselves and with others, where we are simply creating new and unexpected ways of being—in how we feel, in things we say and things we do, in ways we interact with others—is great to let the mind feel free and accepted for whatever it comes up with. It also lets the brain become active in new and unpredictable ways that are good for it to grow and solidify new connections. That's the basis of creativity and innovation. That's the pleasure of presence and connection.

Sadly, kids in school are scheduled for mostly goal-directed activities in which they are being judged and evaluated, compared with others, and asked to compete and beat their rivals. Whether it's in the controlled setting of a didactic lesson or exam in a classroom, or being on a team on the athletic field, those structured times are not what we mean by playtime. Instead, imagine an interaction where there is no winner, an interactive activity where there are no rigid rules, a time when laughing and creating and goofing around are accepted and people are engaged and silly and having a great time, without judgment, without a winner or loser. That's playtime.

I never stop surprising myself

Many adults forget how to play. The social engagement system of the brain, a set of circuits that make learning facilitated and fun, becomes rusty and out of shape and can shut down. Activities become routine, and the spontaneous exploration of life and the world becomes a thing of the long distant past. In fact, the kind of creative thinking that emerges with such open and accepting engagement decreases dramatically once we get into elementary school. That divergent thinking enables us to "think outside the box" because we see life with fresh eyes and are not worried about being punished or embarrassed for getting something wrong—because there is sharing and exploration, not control and humiliation. A young child in preschool will be filled with curiosity about life and the world. But once that child gets to elementary school, the standard approach is to say that there is a right or a wrong, and if you study well, you'll get the right answer on the test or book report or essay or lab assignment. Nothing is wrong with learning to spell well. But we don't need to shut our spontaneity into little boxes, imprisoned in the routine of studies and tests and studies and tests. Creativity is often out the elementary window, and the rest of our school experience too frequently becomes filled with a non-playful seriousness that can kill spontaneity. And it can stifle the courage to be creative, to take a chance and imagine something new. That's part of why people can come to feel that school life is oppressive and uninspiring. When that's not the case, teachers often may have found a way to instill the spirit of play in the daily life of the classroom.

When I came to realize that as an adult playtime was not a part of my life, I signed up for an improvisational acting class for non-actors to join with others in just cracking up and having a good time. I love it. And though it is only once a week, I try to bring the joy of that experience into my daily life. I also started roller blading around the neighborhood on my own, listening to music and rolling and rocking down the street. The odd thing for me was that not only did I have to give myself permission to have fun, but for the serious part of my adult mind, I had to convince myself that it was actually good for my brain to let myself goof off. It's a win-win situation—my brain grows and I have a good time.

Playtime corrects the usual seriousness trend of school and adult life, giving us a daily time for being spontaneous and creative, feeling accepted and connected, alive and joyful, and having a whole lot of laughter and fun.

MINDSIGHT PRACTICE F: Physical Time

Moving your body grows your brain.

Aerobic movement that involves getting your heart rate up for over thirty minutes, preferably closer to forty-five, is a great start. Lifting weights or doing other activities that strengthen muscles with, for instance, stretch bands also supports how our brains function.

In the school district where I live, the loss of school funds and the emphasis on pure academic achievement led to physical education being disbanded and recess time for kids being shortened. On top of those changes, art and music and drama and dance were cut down as well. Something is off in these priorities, especially when you simply look at this from a brain perspective. Art and music and drama and dance support the creative explorations that playtime facilitates. And physical activity supports all our learning. When we move our bodies, neuroplasticity is enhanced. We remember more, we grow more connections in the brain, and we solidify those connections. Moving the body is crucial for not only brain health but also mental health. Aerobic exercise enhances our mood even if we are prone to becoming depressed. I know many a friend whose moodiness was evened out when exercise became a daily part of their lives.

For adults and for adolescents, physical time, if medically possible, is an important part of your daily brain and mind health. Ask your doctor how intense you can be with your physical activity if there are any medical issues that may limit your movements. Working up a sweat can be great, and finding variation in what you do can be essential in creating fitness and avoiding injuries. The key is to warm up, stretch, work out, stretch, and cool down.

Remember that daily movement of your body is your choice. No one can make you do it but you. But it's a win–win situation. You'll feel better, your brain will grow better, and you'll become more fit and healthy. Not bad for a daily workout.

MINDSIGHT PRACTICE G: Connecting Time

Numerous research studies reveal that the way we connect with others makes our lives more meaningful, healthy, wise, and happy. In Mindsight Tools #3, we explored how time-between and reflective conversations help us connect with others in supportive ways that are mutually rewarding. When we have supportive relationships, we are not only happier, we are healthier and live longer! Other studies show that when we are out in nature, we feel more grounded and our moods are more stable. So connecting time is when we connect to other people and the planet.

I try to remember the qualities of connecting time with the strange term "3G-2P." I know that isn't so memorable, but at least it has the core features of this important daily practice. 3G stands for the gratitude we have for being alive on this precious planet, the generosity we can bring to others in connecting with them, and the giving back (or gifting back) we can practice each day as we serve the well-being of others. And the 2P? You may have guessed. We bring gratitude, generosity, and giving back to other people and to the planet.

People and the planet. When we connect with other people in these positive ways, when we wish others to be happy, to be successful at what they do, to have joy and health in their lives, we bring a compassionate stance that supports something called "empathic joy"—getting joy from another's well-being. I know that sounds quite different from the usual competitive environment that modern society cultivates. But just try it out and I think you'll see that it's a win-win situation again. Studies of how we function as people reveal that we are built to collaborate with one another. When we work together in these supportive ways, the collective intelligence created is much more powerful than the solo person trying to beat out others.

On a simple level, connecting time means taking time to be with friends or family, hopefully face-to-face. The signals we get from others that are non-verbal, like eye contact and facial expressions, tone of voice, posture, gestures, timing and intensity of responses, and the human act of friendly and appropriate touch, are unavoidably missing in our digital means of communicating. If we mostly communicate with others via texting or digital chatting, there is a whole lot of important brain real estate not being engaged. If you can, try to make a daily practice of connecting time in person so that you engage your friends face-to-face when possible.

And the planet? How we take time to be in nature can shape our mood, help us focus attention, and give us a feeling of renewal and pleasure. If you live in a city, it may seem hard to get out in nature on a daily basis. But getting to a park or looking out at trees and clouds and the sky and moon is a good start. We come from the planet, and nature is our original home. Connecting with the planet can also mean doing more than simply being in nature, it can mean taking care of our environment. Picking up litter when we see it, and not littering ourselves, is a great start. Finding ways to avoid waste by recycling and being mindful about how we use energy can all be important ways each of us can connect to our common home, this planet Earth.

Connecting time can help us feel the truth that we belong to a larger whole than the body we live in. We may walk with our own two feet on this planet, but we are not alone. The Earth is our common home, other people our tribe, and all living beings our relatives.

CONCLUSION

■

MWe and the Integration of Identity

We have come a long way in our conversation about adolescence. I cannot know how you are feeling about this exploration coming to a close soon, but I myself am feeling sad it's ending yet exhilarated by the territory we've covered.

Our adolescence is a time of great integration—integration of the many aspects of ourselves. During this important period in our lives, the second dozen years, we explore the very nature of who we are. And as we weave the essence of adolescence—the emotional spark, the intense social engagement, the novelty seeking, and the drive toward creative exploration—into who we are becoming, we are undergoing a fundamental life process that does not, by any means, end when we are twenty-four. Integration of identity is a lifelong journey of defining what has meaning in your life now and for all the years to come.

Some time ago I began to think about the great human need we are facing at this moment in our history to move our focus from "me" to "we." I believe that as inhabitants of this planet the world *needs* us to stop being so self-involved and to instead transform in a way that is giving back, or gifting back, to the planet. I believe it is our duty to help other people and to protect the Earth. Interestingly, numerous studies support this idea that the more we help others, the healthier and happier we ourselves become.

At a lecture I gave on this subject, one of my seminar students became quite upset with this notion of "me to we." She said she was working hard on the various aspects of her personal integration, like finding a way to make sense of her attachment history and create both integration of her memories and a coherent narrative of her early life experiences. She said that she didn't want to give up finding a way of making sense of her individual life and instead focus on a "we." I listened closely to her concerns, and realized that the phrase "me to we" might imply something more extreme than what was intended. So I suggested to her that this notion was more like moving "from only me to also we." While such a phrase may not rhyme so well, at least it embraced the integration intended at its core, one that could embrace the importance of our individual, personal life as well as our interdependent, connected life.

Still, I started wondering how this idea of a bodily-defined self, a "me," opening itself up to and becoming a part of a larger self beyond, a "we," might be described in one word. I offered this young woman the following term, which I'll share with you as well:

MWe.

This is a term I have come to use to succinctly describe the integration of identity. It embraces the notion of breathing across our individualized, bodily defined self and linking all of us together as members of a larger whole, a we-defined self. *MWe* as a word itself, and as a concept, is defined by me and we, so we don't need to give up the important differentiation of a personal self and of an interconnected self. Each is different, each is important. Linking them together in our lives is a key that may help in our journey toward the integration of identity.

But why do we need the notion of MWe in the world?

Studies show that the more individualized and isolated our sense of self is, the less happy and less healthy we'll be. When we define a "self" as limited to the boundaries of our skin-encased bodies, we limit our sense of belonging and meaning in life. Yet so much in our modern culture, on the Internet, in our busy contemporary lives, reinforces this view that the self is a bodily defined aspect of who we are. Studies reveal clearly that when we are in supportive relationships and engage in helping others, we are happier and we are healthier. Even research on people who are given money demonstrates that they will have more long-lasting happiness when they use that money to benefit others rather than keeping it all for themselves.

Embracing MWe also means that we experience the sense that we are a part of a larger whole, a part of a larger purpose in life than just our own personal journey. MWe embraces notions of spirituality and that there is a deeper meaning to life directly. But it is important to note that being connected to something larger than ourselves does not mean that we must discard our private self. We simply need to expand it to include an interconnected self as well. That's integration. That's MWe.

Another aspect of MWe is crucial to mention here. People and our planet are in a painful state of needing care. When we look at the increases in the human population and the challenges for healthy food, air, and water, and the ever-increasing need for medicine, clothing, and shelter for our human family, and when we realize how other living creatures are suffering and disappearing because of what we humans are doing to the planet, we realize that there are a lot of problems we need to try to collectively solve.

Adolescents have so much to offer our world in this regard with their drive and ingenuity to find new solutions to these important global problems. But to do this, younger people need the support of elders; they need to be honored for their emerging minds' drive to push back and find creative explorations that may just open our minds up to new ways of dealing with these challenging times.

Working creatively and collaboratively in their communities and with their families and schools, the emerging generation will have the vision to move away from the mere memorization of facts and figures to create more imaginative and meaningful ways to inspire their generation and the generations that follow. We will be able to create the necessary changes for this new era through education and through the important role of our family life, the message of adolescence then moving out into our communities and the larger society in which we live. There is plenty to tackle, but when we pit our wits against the complex problems of global hunger, disease, and violence, pollution, climate change, and the loss of plants and animals in our ecosystems, we will succeed. By collaborating rather than trying to only surpass or annihilate one another, we will prevail as a human society living in an interconnected world.

When we bring our individual skills and passion and knowledge for the benefit of the larger whole, we are maximizing our chances of solving the world's practical and moral problems. I say "moral" here because it is a moral imperative to find a way to work together to solve our collective challenges. We share the same air, the same water, the same home, our planet Earth. A good planet is hard to find, so let's collectively take care of this one now. It is time to find a new identity to face these crucial times together.

As an adolescent these may seem like lofty ideas, I know. They may even seem irrelevant. I say them as we get ready to say goodbye, because I believe so deeply that our individual needs for meaning and belonging in order to feel happy and fulfilled in life can actually be satisfied by expanding the way we define the self. This is a win-win situation. Developing toward a MWe will make us happier, and it will give the world a fighting chance to become healthier as well. I believe that the world's challenges can most effectively be addressed by helping expand our sense of identity beyond a separate self.

Albert Einstein once said that the notion of an isolated self was "an optical delusion" that leads to all sorts of problems in the world and in life. A delusion is a false belief, a view that is not consistent with reality. When we see ourselves as separate, we are not facing the reality of our interdependent, interconnected nature. We are not integrating our identity with the larger world that we are fundamentally a part of. It just may be that many of our biggest challenges individually and collectively are in fact revealed as the chaos and rigidity of such impaired integration, a state created by our human sense of a separate self that assumes happiness comes from material acquisitions alone and that infinite consumption is possible on our resource-limited planet.

Integrating our identity reminds us to differentiate our bodily self and our interconnected self, and then to link them. It reminds us that our minds emerge as much from our bodies and brains as from our relationships with one another and with our planet. Why would an adolescent or an adult really care about integrating identity? For all of us, these second dozen years of life—whether we are in them now or are learning to hold on to their essence in our lives—carry the core qualities that just may be what we need to move the course of our planet's health in a positive direction. The integration of MWe can draw upon the essence of adolescence to harness the emotional spark that fuels our vital sense of being alive in our journey of life, not just while we are teenagers but throughout our later adolescence and into our adult years. We can harness the power of our social engagements to brainstorm ideas and find deep, meaningful connections that sustain and enrich our lives. With our search for novelty, we can make life an adventure that transforms the ordinary into the extraordinary, finding the unique aspects of our experience within each day of our lives. And with the creative explorations that inspire our inquiring minds to think in new ways, perceive with new eyes, and innovate with original contributions to our world's basic challenges, we can confront the problems ahead with a new sense of potential, purpose, and possibility. So this small word, *MWe*, lets us see the power of differentiation and linkage. And it reminds us of where we can go together as we encourage and expand the essence of adolescence throughout our lives.

E. B. White wrote: "If the world were merely seductive, that would be easy. If it were merely challenging, that would be no problem. But I arise in the morning torn between a desire to improve the world and a desire to enjoy the world. This makes it hard to plan the day."

To improve the world is a great intention, but if we see that as a pressure to "save" the world, it can become too overwhelming, too distant a goal. Instead, perhaps we can simply think of *serving* the world, of helping the planet and other people one relationship and one interaction at a time. The potential outcome of improving or saving can be a broad intention, but cannot be guaranteed; the act of serving is a goal we can grasp, something we *can* achieve. The other urge White felt is equally important. We should honor our desire to create joy in life, and we must never stop *savoring* the world. And so perhaps a way to embrace these two natural drives side by side can be our integrated approach: *Savor and serve*. Integrating our lives is about differentiating and linking these two goals that, though in many ways are separate, contribute to a full life of enjoyment and connection, pleasure and purpose. We can enjoy ourselves and one another; we can have fun and explore this life, this world, these relationships. And we can find ways to help others, to reduce suffering, to heal our planet. Savor and serve. MWe can help us achieve this balance.

The poet Maya Angelou, paraphrasing an old Chinese proverb, reminds us that we don't have to wait to have all the solutions before we express ourselves, before we participate in sharing this collective story of our lives. "A bird doesn't sing because it has an answer, it sings because it has a song." As we develop into adolescence and beyond, it is time for us to connect with one another, to share our songs of life, as we move through this journey of MWe together.

How can we know as adolescents if we are succeeding in living our lives fully? How can we know as adults that we are successfully supporting the emerging minds of the new generation well—and even carrying the essence of adolescence forward in our own lives? A poem by Bessie Anderson Stanley offers insights into what a successful adolescence might look like, how the essence of adolescence can enrich the rest of our lives:

SUCCESS

To laugh often and love much;
To win the respect of intelligent persons and the affection of children;
To earn the approbation of honest critics and endure the betrayal of
*   false friends;*
To appreciate beauty;
To find the best in others;

To give of one's self;

To leave the world a bit better, whether by a healthy child, a garden patch or a redeemed social condition;

To have played and laughed with enthusiasm and sung with exultation;

To know even one life has breathed easier because you have lived—
This is to have succeeded.

As we come to our final moments together, I wish for you all the vitality and authenticity that adolescence offers to those still in this period of life and those who have passed through it but have the opportunity for the rest of their lives to embrace its essence. May you be successful in letting the essence of adolescence thrive throughout your life. May an emotional spark fuel your life; may social engagement encourage collective intelligence and collaborative action; may the drive for novelty let you hold on to the privilege and thrill of this adventure of life; and may your creative explorations empower you to imagine and construct a world of tomorrow that all of us will be proud to live in for generations to come. I hope you will find ways to savor and to serve, to share your life's songs, and to integrate yourselves in new and authentic ways in your life ahead. Enjoy!

Q&A with
Daniel J. Siegel, M.D.

1) **What are people most shocked by when they read your book?**

Adolescents and adults are shocked by the notion that instead of "raging hormones" ruling an adolescent's life, adolescent changes stem from how the brain is actually remodeling itself, pruning some connections and laying down new pathways that increase the communication among remaining connections. This remodeling is shaped by how we focus our attention and live our lives. In effect, there are ways that adolescents—and adults—can actually learn to make the brain stronger and healthier.

2) **What is the greatest myth around the teenage brain?**

The greatest myth is that adolescence is an "immature period of life," one "we need to just get through and survive." The truth is that it is an important and necessary transformative period that can allow us to thrive—not just in adolescence, but in adulthood as well. The scientific truth is that the "essence" of adolescence is something we can learn to cultivate in our lives. This essence is the crucial foundation for living a full life in adulthood as well. This essence = emotional spark (ES), social engagement (SE), novelty seeking (N), and creative exploration (CE). These things, which are all critical points of development, are vital to living well during adolescence and to keeping your brain functioning well as an adult.

3) People don't often think of brain health daily. How important is brain health to a great life?

Our brains shape how we feel, how we think, how our body functions, and how we interact with others. When we learn the key to keeping our brain healthy with daily activities, we not only strengthen our mind, feel better, and engage with others in more rewarding ways, but we actually make our body healthier. How? By strengthening the brain, we help fight off chronic disease, repair the important caps of our chromosomes, and even improve our immune function. These are all skills that I try to teach both adolescents and adults in *Brainstorm*.

4) What can an individual do to keep their brain healthy and active?

Science shows that there are at least seven fundamental daily activities that have been proven to keep the mind strong, the brain healthy, the body working well, and our relationships thriving. These practices include having time each day to move the body, to be out in nature and connect with other people, to focus on one thing at a time, to relax and unwind, to sleep well, to be spontaneous and playful, and to take "time-in" to focus on your inner experiences of Sensations, Images, Feelings, and Thoughts. That's how you can "SIFT" your mind each day to keep your brain healthy.

5) What are five of your favorite facts about the brain?
There are so many, but here are my five favorites:

1. Your brain continues to grow across the life span.

2. How you focus your mind changes the function and the structure of your brain.

3. The brain is the social organ of the body—and relationships shape and are shaped by the brain.

4. The brain's remodeling in adolescence leads to a more integrated and highly functional brain—remodeling is necessary and can be cultivated by both adolescents and adults.

5. You can choose at any age to keep your brain strong and healthy. We can learn these important skills in adolescence and then hold on to the Essence of Adolescence throughout our adulthood to keep our brains vital.

Top Myths About
Teen Behavior

MYTH: Raging hormones are to blame for teenagers "going mad" or "losing their minds."

FACT: Hormones do increase during this period, but it is not "raging" hormones that determines what goes on in adolescence. We now know that what adolescents experience is primarily the result of changes in the development of the brain.

MYTH: Adolescence is simply a time of immaturity, and teens just need to "grow up."

FACT: To the contrary, adolescents don't just need to survive adolescence; they can thrive *because* of this important period of their lives. The "work" of adolescence—the testing of boundaries, the passion to explore what is new and exciting—can lay the stage for the development of core character traits that will enable adolescents to go on to lead great lives of adventure and purpose.

MYTH: Growing up during adolescence is all about moving from dependence on adults to complete independence from them.

FACT: While there *is* a natural and necessary pushing away from the adults who raised us, adolescents still benefit from relationships with adults. The healthy move to adulthood is to interdependence, not complete "do-it-yourself" independence. The nature of the bond adolescents have with their parents as attachment figures changes, and friends become more important during this period.

MYTH: It's my responsibility as a parent to help my child solve any conflicts that emerge as they navigate the often rocky road that is adolescence.

FACT: So often, we want to help the people we love fix all their problems. What adolescents need most of all, however, is to feel connected with us, to know that we are still there to listen and help them sort through their problems versus automatically stepping in and solving them as we might have done when they were younger.

MYTH: The most dramatic brain development occurs during the teenage years—once my child is off to college things should settle down.

FACT: The important "work" of adolescence in terms of brain development actually begins at age twelve and extends into one's twenties (into the mid-twenties generally). Thus, it's important as a parent to continue to patiently support and help guide your adolescent's ever-evolving sense of self beyond the teen years—even as you respect their newfound independence.

MYTH: Things are so different today than when I was growing up—there isn't really much of a relationship between my experiences in adolescence and those of my child.

FACT: Attachment research reveals that our experiences with our own parents growing up create a vital starting place for learning important lessons. Digging deep into the landscape of your own childhood and making sense of how those experiences shaped your own development can yield important benefits in terms of showing you how to maintain close bonds with your children throughout their adolescence and on into adulthood.

Acknowledgments

A book is like life: it depends on so many to nurture its essence as it grows and develops. In the journey to come to life, this book has had many individuals who have contributed to its various ages and stages. The experiences working with the many teens and parents over the years as a child and adolescent psychiatrist has been invaluable in gaining insights about the inside-out experience of the adolescent period. I would like to thank the adolescents and adults who have read various drafts of *Brainstorm* and offered insightful comments, questions, and suggestions that have been important in making the messages as accessible and useful as possible. These thoughtful people include Kayla Abrams, Michele Chaban, Jonathan Fried, Lorna Gallant, Mahayla Galliford, Mike Galliford, Laura Hubber, Laura Kastner, Scott Kriens, Lynn Kutler, Maria LeRose, Sally Maslansky, Mike McKay, Mary Pipher, Ellen Ridgeway, Rebecca Shahmoon Shanok, Maddi Siegel, Rich Simon, and Jamie Zimmerman. I thank you all for your time, energy, and wisdom in helping with the creation of this work.

I have also been fortunate to have a team of wonderful people at the Mindsight Institute, including Eric Bergemann, Tina Bryson, Adriana Copeland, Stephanie Hamilton, Teresa Reilly, Ashish Soni, and Whitney Stambler, who work tirelessly to bring into the world these scientific and practical ideas about our relationships, minds, and brains and about compassion, connection, and community. Special thanks to Caroline Welch for her visionary leadership in guiding our institute and creating a culture of creativity. I am grateful for the professional and personal support of Douglas Abrams as the literary agent representing this work from the start.

Leah Pearlman of Dharmacomics.com was a dream to work with as we selected from her joyous and loving illustrations to illuminate the ideas and feelings of the book, finding parallel passions as we went along. It has also been a pleasure to work with my thoughtful and incisive editor at Tarcher/Penguin, Sara Carder, a wonderful companion in shepherding the ideas and their expression into their final form. Also part of the terrific team at Tarcher are Joanna Ng and Brianna Yamashita, who have worked hard to help this book see the light of day. I thank you all.

I could never be the person I am, or the person who put "pen to page" to help this book be born, without the support and inspiration of my family at home: Alex and Maddi Siegel and Caroline Welch. I do not have the words to express the gratitude and love I feel for the three of you. Thank you for our adventures and for being you.

Index

Page numbers in *italic* refer to illustrations.

Excerpt from
Parenting from the Inside Out
by Daniel J. Siegel, M.D., and
Mary Hartzell, M.Ed.

AN INSIDE-OUT APPROACH TO PARENTING

How you make sense of your childhood experiences has a profound effect on how you parent your own children. In this book, we will reflect on how self-understanding influences the approach you bring to your role as a parent. Understanding more about yourself in a deeper way can help you build a more effective and enjoyable relationship with your children.

As we grow and understand ourselves we can offer a foundation of emotional well-being and security that enables our children to thrive. Research in the field of child development has demonstrated that a child's security of attachment to parents is very strongly connected to the parents' understanding of their own early life experiences. Contrary to what many people believe, your early experiences do not determine your fate. If you had a difficult childhood but have come to make sense of those experiences, you are not bound to re-create the same negative interactions with your own children. Without such self-understanding, however, science has shown that history will likely repeat itself, as negative patterns of family interactions are passed down through the generations. This book is designed to help you make sense of your own life, both past and present, by enhancing your understanding of how your childhood has influenced your life and affects your parenting.

When we become parents we are given an incredible opportunity to grow as individuals because we ourselves are put back into an intimate parent-child relationship, this time in a different role. So many times parents have said, "I never thought I'd do or say the very things to my children that felt hurtful to me when I was a child. And yet I find myself doing exactly that." Parents can feel stuck in repetitive, unproductive patterns that don't support the loving, nurturing relationships they envisioned when they began their roles as parents. Making sense of life can free parents from patterns of the past that have imprisoned them in the present.

WHO WE ARE

The authors bring to this book their own distinct professional experiences in working with parents and children, Dan as a child psychiatrist and Mary as an early childhood and parent educator. Both are parents, Dan with children now beyond their teens, Mary with grown children and grandchildren.

Mary has worked as an educator with children and families for over forty years, directing a nursery school; teaching children, parents, and teachers; and consulting individually with parents. All of her experiences have provided her opportunities to share in the lives of families and to learn a great deal about the frustrations, and joys, parents experience in this sometimes daunting task. In developing her parent education course, Mary found that when parents had an opportunity to reflect on their own childhood experiences they could make more effective choices in raising their own children.

Mary and Dan first met when Dan's daughter attended the nursery school that Mary directed. The school's approach incorporates a profound respect for the child's emotional experience and fosters dignity and creativity among the children, parents, and teaching staff. During that time, Dan worked on the parent education committee and gave a few lectures on brain development for the parents and faculty. When Mary and Dan realized how parallel their approaches to parenting were, they decided to work together to create an integrated seminar.

Dan's interest in the science of development along with his work as a child psychiatrist offered a different but complementary perspective. For more than two decades Dan has worked to synthesize a wide range of scientific disciplines into an integrated developmental framework for understanding the mind, the brain, and human relationships. This convergence of scientific perspectives has been called "interpersonal neurobiology" and is now being incorporated into a number of professional educational programs focusing on mental health and emotional well-being. When his book *The Developing Mind:*

Toward a Neurobiology of Interpersonal Experience (Guilford Press, 1999/2012) was first published, Mary and Dan were teaching their integrated course. The enthusiastic feedback from parents inspired them to begin collaboration on this book. Many parents in the seminar mentioned how useful these ideas were in helping them to understand themselves and to make meaningful connections with their children. "Why don't you write something together so that others can get some of that exciting science and wisdom—and energy—that you brought to our seminar?" numerous parents urged.

We are thrilled to have the chance to share this approach with you. We hope this book conveys in an enjoyable and accessible way some of these practical ideas about the art and science of nurturing relationships and self-knowledge. It is our hope that this book will help you and your child find more joy in each other each day.

BUILDING RELATIONSHIPS AND SELF-UNDERSTANDING

The way we communicate with our children has a profound impact on how they develop. Our ability to have sensitive, reciprocal communication nurtures a child's sense of security, and these trusting secure relationships help children do well in many areas of their lives. Our ability to communicate effectively in creating security in our children is most strongly predicted by our having made sense of the events of our own early life. Making sense of our life enables us to understand and integrate our own childhood experiences, positive or negative, and to accept them as part of our ongoing life story. We can't change what happened to us as children but we can change the way we think about those events.

Thinking about our lives in a different way entails being aware of our present experiences, including our emotions and perceptions, and appreciating how the present is affected by events from the past. Understanding how we remember and how we construct a picture of ourselves as a part of the world we live in can help us to make sense of how the past continues to impact our lives. How does making sense of our lives help our children? By freeing ourselves from the constraints of our past, we can offer our children the spontaneous and connecting relationships that enable them to thrive. By deepening our ability to understand our own emotional experience, we are better able to relate empathically with our children and promote their self-understanding and healthy development.

In the absence of reflection, history often repeats itself, and parents are vulnerable to passing on to their children unhealthy patterns from the past. Understanding our lives can free us from the otherwise almost predictable situation in which we re-create the damage to our children that was done to us in our own childhoods. Research has clearly demonstrated that our children's attachment to us will be influenced by what happened to us when we were young if we do not come to process and understand those experiences. By making sense of our lives we can deepen a capacity for self-understanding and bring coherence to our emotional experience, our views of the world, and our interactions with our children.

Of course, the development of the child's whole personality is influenced by many things, including genetics, temperament, physical health, and experience. Parent-child relationships offer one very important part of the early experience that directly shapes a child's emerging personality. Emotional intelligence, self-esteem, cognitive abilities, and social skills are built on this early attachment relationship. How parents have reflected on their lives directly shapes the nature of that relationship.

Even if we have come to understand ourselves well, our children will still make their own journey through life. Although we may supply them with a secure foundation through our own deeper self-understanding, our role as parents serves to support our children's development, not guarantee its outcome. Research suggests that children who have had a positive connection in life have a source of resilience for dealing with life's challenges. Building a positive relationship with our children involves being open to our own growth and development.

Through the process of reflection, you can enhance the coherence of your life narrative and improve your relationship with your child. No one had a "perfect childhood" and some of us had more challenging experiences than others. Yet even those with overwhelmingly difficult past experiences can come to resolve those issues and have meaningful and rewarding relationships with their children. Research has shown the exciting finding that parents who themselves did not have "good enough parents" or who even had traumatic childhoods can make sense of their lives and have healthy relationships. More important for our children than merely what happened to us in the past is the way we have come to process and understand it. The opportunity to change and grow continues to be available throughout our lives.

ABOUT THIS BOOK

This is not a how-to book—it is a "how we" book. We will explore new insights into parenting by examining such processes as how we remember, perceive, feel, communicate, attach, make sense, disconnect and reconnect, and reflect with our children on the nature of their internal experiences. We will explore issues from recent research on parent-child relationships and integrate these with new discoveries from brain science. By examining the science of how we experience and connect, a new perspective emerges that can help us deepen our understanding of ourselves, our children, and our relationships with each other.

The "Inside-Out Exercises" at the end of each chapter can be used to explore new possibilities for internal understanding and interpersonal communication. The reflections encouraged by these exercises have helped parents deepen their understanding of current and past experiences and enabled them to improve their relationships with their children.

You may find that writing your experiences of these exercises in a journal will provide an opportunity for deeper reflection and self-knowledge. Writing can help to free your mind from the entanglements of the past and to liberate you to better understand yourself. Your journal entries can include anything you would like, such as drawings, reflections, descriptions, and stories. Some people don't like to write at all and may prefer to reflect in solitude or to talk with a friend. Others like to write in a journal each day or when they feel motivated by an experience or an emotion. Do what feels right for you. The value of the exercises will come from an open attitude and thoughtful reflections.

The shaded "Spotlight on Science" sections at the end of each chapter provide the interested reader with more information about various aspects of research findings that are relevant to parenting. These sections are not essential to understand and use the ideas in the main body of the book. They offer expanded, in-depth information but reader-friendly discussion that provides more on the scientific foundation for many of the concepts in the book and we hope you will find them thought provoking and useful. Each of the Spotlight on Science sections relates to the main text but also stands on its own and can be read independent of other Spotlight entries. Reading all of the Spotlight sections will offer an interdisciplinary view of aspects of science relevant to the process of parenting.

There is a saying in science that "chance favors the prepared mind." Having knowledge about the science of development and human experience can prepare your mind to build a deeper understanding of the emotional lives of your children and of you yourself. Whether you read the Spotlight sections after completing each chapter or choose to explore them after finishing the main text of the book, we hope that you will feel free to take an approach that respects your own unique style of learning.

Wilbur Smith

The World's Greatest and Most Popular Writer of Epic Adventure

'Wilbur Smith rarely misses a trick'
Sunday Times

'The world's leading adventure writer'
Daily Express

'Action is the name of Wilbur Smith's game and he is a master'
Washington Post

'The pace would do credit to a Porsche, and the invention is as bright and explosive as a firework display'
Sunday Telegraph

'A violent saga set in Boer War South Africa, told with vigour and enthusiasm ... Wilbur Smith spins a fine tale'
Evening Standard

'A bonanza of excitement'
New York Times

' . . . a natural storyteller who moves
confidently and often splendidly in
his period and sustains a flow of
convincing incident'
The Scotsman

'Raw experience, grim realism, history
and romance welded with mystery
and the bewilderment of life itself'
Library Journal

'A thundering good read'
Irish Times

'Extrovert and vigorous . . . constantly
changing incidents and memorable
portraits'
Liverpool Daily Post

'An immensely powerful book,
disturbing and compulsive, harsh yet
compassionate'
She

'An epic novel . . . it would be hard to think of a theme that was more appropriate today . . . Smith writes with a great passion for the soul of Africa'
   Today

'I read on to the last page, hooked by its frenzied inventiveness piling up incident upon incident . . . mighty entertainment'
   Yorkshire Post

'There is a streak of genuine poetry, all the more attractive for being unfeigned'
   Sunday Telegraph

' . . . action follows action . . . mystery is piled on mystery . . . tales to delight the millions of addicts of the gutsy adventure story'
   Sunday Express

'Action-crammed'
   Sunday Times

'Rattling good adventure'
   Evening Standard

The novels of Wilbur Smith

The Courtney Novels
 When the Lion Feeds
 The Sound of Thunder
 A Sparrow Falls
 The Burning Shore
 Power of the Sword
 Rage
 A Time to Die

The Ballantyne Novels:
 A Falcon Flies
 Men of Men
 The Angels Weep
 The Leopard Hunts in Darkness

Also:
 The Dark of the Sun
 Shout at the Devil
 Gold Mine
 The Diamond Hunters
 The Sunbird
 Eagle in the Sky
 The Eye of the Tiger
 Cry Wolf
 Hungry as the Sea
 Wild Justice
 Golden Fox
 Elephant Song

The Sound of Thunder

Wilbur Smith was born in Central Africa in 1933. He was educated at Michaelhouse and Rhodes University.

He became a full-time writer in 1964 after the successful publication of *When the Lion Feeds*, and has since written twenty novels, meticulously researched on his numerous expeditions worldwide.

He normally travels from November to February, often spending a month skiing in Switzerland, and visiting Australia and New Zealand for sea fishing. During his summer break, he visits environments as diverse as Alaska and the dwindling wilderness of the African interior. He has an abiding concern for the peoples and wildlife of his native continent, an interest strongly reflected in his novels.

He is married to Danielle, to whom his last nineteen books have been dedicated.

WILBUR SMITH

The Sound
of Thunder

Mandarin

A Mandarin Paperback
THE SOUND OF THUNDER

First published in Great Britain 1966
by William Heinemann Ltd
This edition published 1992
by Mandarin Paperbacks
an imprint of Reed Consumer Books Ltd
Michelin House, 81 Fulham Road, London SW3 6RB
and Auckland, Melbourne, Singapore and Toronto

Reprinted 1992 (three times), 1993 (twice), 1994

Copyright © Wilbur A. Smith 1966

A CIP catalogue record for this title
is available from the British Library

ISBN 0 7493 0635 1

Phototypeset by Intype, London
Printed and bound in Great Britain
by Cox & Wyman Ltd, Reading, Berks

This book is for my children –
SHAUN and LAWRENCE
and CHRISTIAN LAURIE

1

Four years of travel in the roadless wilderness had battered the wagons. Many of the wheel-spokes and *disselbooms* had been replaced with raw native timber; the canopies were patched until little of the original canvas was visible; the teams were reduced from eighteen to ten oxen each, for there had been predators and sickness to weed them out. But this exhausted little caravan carried the teeth of five hundred elephant; ten tons of ivory; the harvest of Sean Courtney's rifle; ivory that he would convert into nearly fifteen thousand gold sovereigns once he reached Pretoria.

Once more Sean was a rich man. His clothing was stained and baggy, crudely mended; his boots were worn almost through the uppers and clumsily resoled with raw buffalo hide; a great untrimmed beard covered half his chest and a mane of black hair curled down his neck to where it had been hacked away with blunt scissors above the collar of his coat. But despite his appearance he was rich in ivory, also in gold held for him in the vaults of the Volkskaas Bank in Pretoria.

On a rise of ground beside the road he sat his horse and watched the leisurely plodding approach of his wagons. It is time now for the farm, he thought with satisfaction. Thirty-seven years old, no longer a young man, and it was time to buy the farm. He knew the one he wanted and he knew exactly where he would build the homestead – site it close to the lip of the escarpment so that in the evenings he could sit on the wide stoep and look out across the plain to the Tugela River in the blue distance.

'Tomorrow early we will reach Pretoria.' The voice beside him interrupted his dreaming, and Sean moved in the saddle and looked down at the Zulu who squatted beside his horse.

'It has been a good hunt, Mbejane.'

'Nkosi, we have killed many elephant.' Mbejane nodded and Sean noticed for the first time the strands of silver in the woolly cap of his hair. No longer a young man either.

'And made many marches,' Sean went on and Mbejane inclined his head again in grave agreement.

'A man grows weary of the trek,' Sean mused aloud. 'There is a time when he longs to sleep two nights at the same place.'

'And to hear the singing of his wives as they work the fields.' Mbejane carried it further. 'And to watch his cattle come into the kraal at dusk with his sons driving them.'

'That time has come for both of us, my friend. We are going home to Ladyburg.'

The spears rattled against his raw-hide shield as Mbejane stood up, muscles moved beneath the black velvet of his skin and he lifted his head to Sean and smiled. It was a thing of white teeth and radiance, that smile. Sean had to return it and they grinned at each other like two small boys in a successful bit of mischief.

'If we push the oxen hard this last day we can reach Pretoria tonight, Nkosi.'

'Let us make the attempt.' Sean encouraged him and walked his horse down the slope to intercept the caravan.

As it toiled slowly towards them through the flat white glare of the African morning a commotion started

2

at its rear and spread quickly along the line, the dogs clamoured and the servants shouted encouragement to the rider who raced past them towards the head of the caravan. He lay forward in the saddle, driving the pony with elbows and heels, hat hanging from the leather thong about his neck and black hair ruffled with the speed of his run.

'That cub roars louder than the lion that sired him,' grunted Mbejane, but there was a fondness in his expression as he watched the rider reach the leading wagon and drag the pony from full run down on to his haunches.

'Also he spoils the mouth of every horse he rides.' Sean's voice was as harsh as Mbejane's, but there was the same fond expression in his eyes as he watched his son cut loose the brown body of a springbok from the pommel of his saddle and let it drop into the road beside the wagon. Two of the wagon drivers hurried to retrieve it, and Dirk Courtney kicked his pony and galloped down to where Sean and Mbejane waited beside the road.

'Only one?' Sean asked as Dirk checked the pony and circled back to fall in beside him.

'Oh, no. I got three – three with three shots. The gunboys are bringing the others.' Offhanded, taking as natural that at nine years of age he should be providing meat for the whole company, Dirk slouched down comfortably in the saddle, holding the reins in one hand and the other resting negligently on his hip in faithful imitation of his father.

Scowling a little to cover the strength of his pride and his love, Sean examined him surreptitiously. The beauty of this boy's face was almost indecent, the innocence of the eyes and faultless skin should have belonged to a girl. The sun struck ruby sparks from the mass of dark

3

curls, his eyes spaced wide apart were framed with long black lashes and overscored by the delicate lines of the brow. His eyes were emerald and his skin was gold and there were rubies in his hair – a face fashioned by a jewelsmith. Then Sean looked at the mouth and experienced a twinge of uneasiness. The mouth was too big, the lips too wide and soft. The shape of it was wrong – as though it were about to sulk or whine.

'We are making a full day's trek today, Dirk. No *outspan* until we reach Pretoria. Ride back and tell the drivers.'

'Send Mbejane. He's doing nothing.'

'I told *you* to go.'

'Hell, Dad! I've done enough today.'

'Go, damn you!' Sean roared with unnecessary violence.

'I've only just come back, it's not fair that – ' Dirk started, but Sean did not let him finish.

'Every time I ask you to do something I get a mouthful of argument. Now do what I tell you.' They held each other's eyes; Sean glaring and Dirk resentful, sulky. Sean recognized that expression with dismay. This was going to be another of those tests of will that were becoming more frequent between them. Would this end as most of the others had? Must he admit defeat and use the *sjambok* again? When was the last time – two weeks ago – when Sean had reprimanded Dirk on some trivial point concerning the care of his pony. Dirk had stood sullenly until Sean was finished, and then he had walked away among the wagons. Dropping the subject from his mind, Sean was chatting with Mbejane when suddenly there was a squeal of pain from the laager and Sean ran towards it.

In the centre of the ring of wagons stood Dirk. His face still darkly flushed with temper, and at his feet the

4

tiny body of one of the unweaned puppies flopped and whimpered with its ribs stoved in from Dirk's kick.

In anger Sean had beaten Dirk, but even in his anger he had used a length of rope and not the viciously tapered *sjambok* of hippo hide. Then he had ordered Dirk to his living-wagon.

At noon he had sent for him and demanded an apology – and Dirk, uncrying, with lips and jaw set grimly, had refused it.

Sean beat him again, with the rope, but this time coldly – not for the sake of retribution. Dirk did not break.

Finally, in desperation Sean took the *sjambok* to him. For ten hissing strokes, each of which ended with a wicked snap across his buttocks, Dirk lay silently under the whip. His body convulsed slightly at each lash but he would not speak, and Sean beat him with a sickness in his own stomach and the sweat of shame and guilt running into his eyes, swinging the *sjambok* mechanically with his fingers clawed around the butt of it, and his mouth full of the slimy saliva of self-hatred.

When at last Dirk screamed, Sean dropped the *sjambok*, reeled back against the side of the wagon and leaned there gasping – fighting down the nausea which flooded acid-tasting up his throat.

Dirk screamed again and again, and Sean caught him up and held him to his chest.

'I'm sorry, Pa! I'm sorry. I'll never do it again, I promise you. I love you, I love you best of all – and I'll never do it again,' screamed Dirk, and they clung to each other.

For days thereafter not one of the servants had smiled at Sean nor spoken to him other than to acknowledge an order. For there was not one of them, including Mbejane, who would not steal and cheat and lie to ensure that Dirk Courtney had whatever he desired at the exact moment he desired it. They could hate anyone, including Sean, who denied it to him.

That was two weeks ago. And now, thought Sean watching that ugly mouth, do we do it all again?

Then suddenly Dirk smiled. It was one of those changes of mood that left Sean slightly bewildered, for when Dirk smiled his mouth came right. It was irresistible.

'I'll go, Dad.' Cheerfully, as though he were volunteering, he prodded the pony and trotted back towards the wagons.

'Cheeky little bugger!' gruffed Sean for Mbejane's benefit, but silently he queried his share of the blame. He had raised the boy with a wagon as his home and the veld as his schoolroom, grown men his companions and authority over them as his undisputed right of birth.

Since his mother had died five years before he had not known the gentling influence of a woman. No wonder he was a wild one.

Sean shied away from the memory of Dirk's mother. There was guilt there also, guilt that had taken him many years to reconcile. She was dead now. There was no profit in torturing himself. He pushed away the gloom that was swamping the happiness of a few minutes before, slapped the loose end of the reins against his horse's neck and urged it out on to the road – south towards the low line of hills upon the horizon, south towards Pretoria.

He's a wild one. But once we reach Ladyburg he'll be all right, Sean assured himself. They'll knock the nonsense out of him at school, and I'll knock manners into him at home. No, he'll be all right.

*

That evening, the third of December, 1899, Sean led his wagons down the hills and laagered them beside the Apies River. After they had eaten, Sean sent Dirk to his cot in the living-wagon. Then he climbed alone to the crest of the hills and looked back across the land to the north. It was silver-grey in the moonlight, stretching away silent and immeasurable. That was the old life and abruptly he turned his back upon it and walked down towards the lights of the city which beckoned to him from the valley below.

2

There had been a little unpleasantness when he had ordered Dirk to stay with the wagons; in consequence Sean was in an evil mood as he crossed the bridge on the Apies and rode into the city the following morning. Beside him Mbejane ran to keep pace with his horse.

Deep in his own thoughts Sean turned into Church Street before he noticed the unusual activity about him. A column of horsemen forced him to rein his horse to the side of the road. As they passed Sean examined them with interest.

Burghers in a motley of homespun and store clothes, riding in a formation which might imaginatively have been called a column of fours. But what excited Sean's curiosity was their numbers – By God! there must be two thousand of them at least, from lads to greybeards each of them was festooned with bandoliers of ammunition and beside each left knee the butt of a bolt-action Mauser rifle stuck up from its scabbard. Blanket-rolls tied to the saddles, canteens and cooking-pots clattering, they filed past. There was no doubting it. This was a war commando.

From the sidewalk women and a few men called comment at them.

'*Geluk hoor*! Shoot straight.'

'*Spoedige terugkoms.*'

And the commandos laughed and shouted back. Sean stooped to a pretty girl who stood beside his horse. She was waving a red scarf and suddenly Sean saw that though she smiled her eyelashes were loaded with tears like dew on a blade of grass.

'Where are they going?' Sean raised his voice above the uproar.

She lifted her head and the movement loosed a tear; it dropped down her cheek, slid from her chin and left a tiny damp spot on her blouse.

'To the train, of course.'

'The train? Which train?'

'Look, here come the guns.'

In consternation Sean looked up as the guns rumbled past, two of them. Uniformed gunners in blue, frogged with gold, sitting stiffly to attention on the carriages, the horses leaning forward against the immense weight of the guns. Tall wheels shod with steel, bronze glittering on the breeches in contrast to the sombre grey of the barrels.

'My God!' breathed Sean. Then turning back to the girl he grasped her shoulder and shook it in his agitation. 'Where are they going? Tell me quickly – where?'

'*Menheer*!' She bridled at his touch and wriggled away from it.

'Please. I'm sorry – you must tell me.' Sean called after her as she disappeared into the crowd.

A minute longer Sean sat stupefied, then his brain began to work again.

It was war, then. But where and against whom?

Surely no tribal rising would call out this array of strength. Those guns were the most modern weapons Sean could conceive.

No, this was a white man's war.

Against the Orange Republic? Impossible, they were brothers.

Against the British, then? The idea appalled him. And yet – and yet five years ago there had been rumours.

9

It had happened before. He remembered 1895, and the Jameson Raid. Anything could have happened during the years he had been cut off from civilization – and now he had stumbled innocently into the midst of it.

Quickly he considered his own position. He was British. Born in Natal under the Union Jack. He looked like a burgher, spoke like one, rode like one, he was born in Africa and had never left it – but technically he was just as much an Englishman as if he had been born within sound of Bow bells.

Just supposing it was war between the Republic and Britain, and just supposing the Boers caught him – what would they do with him?

Confiscate his wagons and his ivory certainly, throw him into prison perhaps, shoot him as a spy possibly!

'I've got to get the hell out of here,' he mumbled, and then to Mbejane, 'Come on. Back to the wagons, quickly.' Before they reached the bridge he changed his mind. He had to learn with certainty what was happening. There was one person he could go to, and he must take the risk.

'Mbejane, go back to the camp. Find Nkosizana Dirk and keep him there – even if you have to tie him. Speak to no man and, as you value your life, let Dirk speak with no man. It is understood?'

'It is understood, Nkosi.'

And Sean, to all appearances another burgher among thousands of burghers, worked his way slowly through the crowds and the press of wagons towards a general dealer's store at the top end of the town near the railway station.

Since Sean had last seen it the sign above the entrance had been freshly painted in red and gold. 'I. Goldberg. Importer & Exporter, Dealing in Mining Machinery, Merchant & Wholesaler, Purchasing Agent: gold, precious stones, hides and skins, ivory and natural produce.'

Despite this war, or because of it, Mr Goldberg's emporium was doing good business. It was crowded and Sean drifted unnoticed among the customers, searching quietly for the proprietor.

He found him selling a bag of coffee beans to a gentleman who was plainly sceptical of its quality. The discussion of the merits of Mr Goldberg's coffee beans as opposed to those of his competitor across the street was becoming involved and technical.

Sean leaned against a shelf full of merchandise, packed his pipe, lit it and while he waited he watched Mr Goldberg in action. The man should have been a barrister, his argument was strong enough to convince first Sean and finally the customer. The latter paid, slung the bag over his shoulder and grumbled his way out of the shop, leaving Mr Goldberg glowing pink and perspiring in the flush of achievement.

'You haven't lost any weight, Izzy,' Sean greeted him.

Goldberg peered at him uncertainly over his gold-framed spectacles, beginning to smile until suddenly he recognized Sean. He blinked with shock, jerked his head in a gesture of invitation so his jowls wobbled, and disappeared into the back office. Sean followed him.

'Are you mad, Mr Courtney?' Goldberg was waiting for him, quivering with agitation. 'If they catch you . . . '

'Listen, Izzy. I arrived last night. I haven't spoken to a white man in four years. What the hell is going on here?'

'You haven't heard?'

'No, damn it, I haven't.'

'It's war, Mr Courtney.'

'I can see that. But where? Against whom?'

'On all the borders – Natal, the Cape.'

'Against?'

'The British Empire.' Goldberg shook his head as though he did not believe his own statement. 'We've taken on the whole British Empire.'

'We?' Sean asked sharply.

'The Transvaal Republic and the Orange Free State. Already we have won great victories – Ladysmith is besieged, Kimberley, Mafeking –'

'You, personally?'

'I was born here in Pretoria. I am a burgher.'

'Are you going to turn me in?'

'No, of course not. You've been a good customer of mine for years.'

'Thanks, Izzy. Look, I've got to get out of here as fast as I can.'

'It would be wise.'

'What about my money at the Volkskaas – can I get it out?'

Izzy shook his head sadly. 'They've frozen all enemy accounts.'

'Damn it, God damn it!' Sean swore bitterly, and then, 'Izzy, I've got twenty wagons and ten tons of ivory parked out there on the edge of town – are you interested?'

'How much?'

'Ten thousand for the lot; oxen, wagons, ivory – the lot.'

'It would not be patriotic, Mr Courtney,' Goldberg decided reluctantly. 'Trading with the enemy – besides I have only your word that it's ten tons.'

'Hell, Izzy, I'm not the British Army – that lot is worth twenty thousand quid.'

'You want me to buy sight unseen – no questions asked? All right. I'll give you four thousand – gold.'

'Seven.'

'Four and a half,' countered Izzy.

'You bastard.'

'Four and a half.'

'No, damn you. Five!' growled Sean.

'Five?'

'Five!'

'All right, five.'

'Thanks Izzy.'

'Pleasure, Mr Courtney.'

Sean described the location of his laager hurriedly.

'You can send someone out to pick it up. I am going to run for the Natal border as soon as it's dark.'

'Keep off the roads and well clear of the railway. Joubert has thirty thousand men in Northern Natal, massed around Ladysmith and along the Tugela heights.' Goldberg went to the safe and fetched five small canvas bags from it. 'Do you want to check?'

'I'll trust you as you trusted me. Good-bye, Izzy.' Sean dropped the heavy bags down the front of his shirt and settled them under his belt.

'Good luck, Mr Courtney.'

3

There were two hours of daylight left when Sean finished paying his servants. He pushed the tiny pile of sovereigns across the tailboard of the wagon towards the last man and went with him through the complicated ritual of farewell, the hand-clapping and clasping, the repetition of the formal phrases – then he stood up from his chair and looked around the circle. They squatted patiently, watching him with wooden black faces – but reflected back from them he could sense his own sorrow at this parting. Men with whom he had lived and worked and shared a hundred hardships. It was not easy to leave them now.

'It is finished,' he said.

'*Yebho*, it is finished.' They agreed in chorus and no one moved.

'Go, damn you.'

Slowly one of them stood and gathered the bundle of his possessions, a *kaross* (or skin blanket), two spears, a cast-off shirt that Sean had given him. He balanced the bundle on his head and looked at Sean.

'Nkosi!' he said and lifted a clenched fist in salute.

'Nonga,' Sean replied. The man turned away and trudged out of the laager.

'Nkosi!'

'Hlubi.'

'Nkosi!'

'Zama.'

A roll call of loyalty – Sean spoke their names for the

last time, and singly they left the laager. Sean stood and watched them walk away in the dusk. Not one of them looked back and no two men walked together. It was finished.

Wearily Sean turned back to the laager. The horses were ready. Three with saddles, two carrying packs.

'We will eat first, Mbejane.'

'It is ready, Nkosi. Hlubi cooked before he went.'

'Come on, Dirk. Dinner.'

Dirk was the only one who spoke during the meal. He chattered gaily, wrought up with excitement by this new adventure, while Sean and Mbejane shovelled fat Hlubi's stew and hardly tasted it.

Out in the gathering darkness a jackal yelped, a lonely sound on the evening wind, fitting the mood of a man who had lost friends and fortune.

'It is time.' Sean shrugged into his sheepskin jacket and buttoned it as he stood to kick out the fire, but suddenly he froze and stood with his head cocked as he listened. There was a new sound on the wind.

'Horses!' Mbejane confirmed it.

'Quickly, Mbejane, my rifle.' The Zulu leapt up, ran to the horses and slipped Sean's rifle from its scabbard.

'Get out of the light and keep your mouth shut,' Sean ordered as he hustled Dirk into the shadows between the wagons. He grabbed the rifle from Mbejane and levered a cartridge into the breech and the three of them crouched and waited.

The click and roll of pebbles under hooves, the soft sound of a branch brushed aside.

'One only,' whispered Mbejane. A pack-horse whickered softly and was answered immediately from the darkness. Then silence, a long silence broken at last by the jingle of a bridle as the rider dismounted.

Sean saw him then, a slim figure emerging slowly out

15

of the night and he swung the rifle to cover his approach. There was something unusual in the way the stranger moved, gracefully but with a sway from the hips, long-legged like a colt and Sean knew that he was young, very young to judge by his height.

With relief Sean straightened up from his crouch and examined him as he stopped uncertainly beside the fire and peered into the shadows. The lad wore a peaked cloth cap pulled down over his ears and his jacket was an expensive, honey-coloured chamois. His riding breeches were beautifully tailored and hugged his buttocks snugly. Sean decided that his backside was too big and out of proportion to the small feet clad in polished English hunting boots. A regular dandy, and the scorn was in Sean's tone as he called out.

'Stay where you are, friend, and state your business!'

The effect of Sean's challenge was unexpected. The lad jumped, the soles of his glossy boots cleared the ground by at least six inches, and when he landed again he was facing Sean.

'Talk up. I haven't got all night.'

The lad opened his mouth, closed it again, licked his lips and spoke.

'I was told you were going to Natal.' The voice was low and husky.

'Who told you that?' demanded Sean.

'My uncle.'

'Who is your uncle?'

'Isaac Goldberg.'

Sean digested this intelligence and while he did so he examined the face before him. Cleanshaven, pale, big dark eyes and a laughing kind of mouth that was now pursed with fright.

'And if I am?' Sean demanded.

'I want to go with you.'

'Forget it. Get back on your horse and go home.'

'I'll pay you – I'll pay you well.'

Was it the voice or the posture of the lad, Sean pondered, there was something very odd about him. He stood with a flat leather pouch held in both hands across the front of his hips – in an attitude of defence, as though he were protecting – protecting what? And suddenly Sean knew what it was.

'Take off your cap,' he ordered.

'No.'

'Take it off.'

A second longer the lad hesitated, then in a gesture that was almost defiance he jerked off the cap and two thick black braids of hair, shiny in the firelight, dropped and hung down almost to his waist and transformed him instantly from gawky masculinity into stunning womanhood.

Although he had guessed it, Sean was unprepared for the shock of this revelation. It was not so much her beauty, but her attire that caused the shock. Never in his life had Sean seen a woman in breeches, and now he gasped. Breeches, by God, she might as well be naked from the waist down – even that would be less indecent.

'Two hundred pounds –' She was coming towards him now, offering the pouch. At each step the cloth of the breeches tightened across her thighs and Sean dragged his eyes guiltily back to her face.

'Keep your money, lady.' Her eyes were grey, smoky grey.

'Two hundred on account, and as much again when we reach Natal.'

'I'm not interested.' But he was, those soft lips starting to quiver.

'How much then? Name your price.'

'Look, lady. I'm not heading a procession. There are

three of us already – one a child. There is hard riding ahead, plenty of it, and an army of Boers in between. Our chances are slim enough as it is. Another member to the party, and a woman at that, will make them prohibitive. I don't want your money, all I want is to get my son to safety. Go home and sit this war out – it won't last long.'

'I'm going to Natal.'

'Good. You go then – but not with us.' Sean could not trust himself longer to resist the appeal of those grey eyes and he turned to Mbejane. 'Horses,' he snapped and walked away from her. She stood watching him quietly as they mounted up, making no protest. She seemed very small and alone as Sean looked down at her from the saddle.

'I'm sorry,' he growled. 'Go home now like a good girl,' and quickly he wheeled away and trotted out into the night.

All night they rode, east through the open moonlit land. Once they passed a darkened homestead and a dog barked, but they sheered away and then turned east again and held the great crucifix of the Southern Cross at their right-hand. When Dirk fell asleep in the saddle and slipped sideways, Sean caught him before he hit the ground, pulled him across into his lap and held him there for the rest of the night.

Before dawn they found a clump of bush on the bank of a stream, hobbled the horses and made camp. Mbejane had the billycan boiling over a small well-screened fire and Sean had rolled Dirk unconscious into his blankets when the girl rode into camp and jumped down from her horse.

'I nearly lost you twice.' She laughed and pulled off the cap. 'Gave me a horrible fright.' She shook down the shiny braids. 'Coffee! Oh good, I'm famished.'

Menacingly Sean climbed to his feet and with clenched fists he glared at her, but undismayed she hobbled her horse and turned it loose before acknowledging him again.

'Don't stand on ceremony, please be seated.' And she grinned at him with such devilment in her grey eyes, aping so faithfully his stance with hands on those indecent hips, that Sean suddenly found himself smiling. He tried to stop it for he knew it was an admission of surrender, but his effort was so unsuccessful that she burst into delighted laughter.

'How's your cooking?' he demanded.

'So, so.'

'You'd better brush up on it because from now on you're working your passage.'

Later, when he had sampled it for the first time, he admitted grudgingly:

'Not bad – in the circumstances,' and wiped the plate with a crust of bread.

'You are too kind, sir.' She thanked him and lugged her blanketroll into the shade, spread it, pulled off her boots, wriggled her toes and lay back with a sigh.

Sean positioned his own bedroll with care so that, when he opened his eyes, without turning his head he could watch her from under the brim of the hat that covered his face.

He woke at midday and saw that she slept with one cheek in her open hand, the lashes of her eyes meshed together and a few loose strands of dark hair across a face that was damp and flushed in the drowsy heat. He watched her for a long time before silently rising and crossing to his saddle-bags. When he went down to the stream he took with him his flat canvas toilet-bag, the remaining pair of breeches that were neither patched nor too badly stained and a clean silk shirt.

Sitting on a rock beside the water, naked and freshly scrubbed, he regarded his face in the polished steel mirror.

'A big job.' He sighed and started snipping at the great bush of beard which had not felt the scissors in three years.

At dusk, self-conscious as a girl in her first party dress, Sean walked back into the camp. They were all awake. Dirk and the girl sat together on her blanket in such earnest conversation that neither of them noticed his arrival. Mbejane was busy at the fire; he rocked back on his heels and examined Sean without change of expression.

'We'd better eat and get going.'

Dirk and the girl looked up. Her eyes narrowed and then widened thoughtfully.

Dirk gaped at him, and then, 'Your beard's all funny –' he announced, and the girl tried desperately to quell her laughter.

'Get your blankets rolled up, boy.'

Sean tried to break Dirk's grip on the subject, but like a bulldog Dirk held on relentlessly.

'– and why are you wearing your best clothes, Dad?'

4

They rode three abreast in the darkness, Dirk between them and Mbejane trailing behind with the pack-horses. The land rose and fell beneath them like the swells of an endless sea and the way in which the grass moved with the night wind heightened the illusion of waves. Islands in the sea were the dark bulks of the kopjes they passed, and the yelp of a jackal was the voice of a seabird.

'Aren't we holding too far east?' The girl broke the silence and her voice blended with the soft sound of the wind.

'Intentionally,' Sean answered. 'I want to cross the tail of the Drakensberg well clear of the Boer concentrations around Ladysmith and the line of rail,' and he looked over Dirk's head at her. She rode with her face lifted to the sky.

'You know the stars?' he asked.

'A little.'

'So do I. I know them all.' Dirk accepted the challenge and swivelled towards the south. 'That's the Cross with the pointers, and that's Orion with his sword on his belt, and that's the Milky Way.'

'Tell me some others,' the girl invited.

'The others are just ordinary ones – they don't count. They haven't even got names.'

'Oh, but they have and most of them have got a story.'

There was a pause. Dirk was now in an invidious position; either he had to admit ignorance, and Dirk's pride was too large to swallow with ease, or else he would forgo what promised to be a choice series of stories. Large as was his pride, his appetite for stories was even larger.

'Tell me some,' he conceded.

'You see that little clump there underneath the big bright one? They are called the Seven Sisters. Well, once upon a time –'

Within minutes Dirk was completely absorbed. These were even better than Mbejane's stories – probably because they were new, while Dirk could recite from memory Mbejane's entire repertoire. He fell upon any weakness in the plot like a prosecuting attorney.

'But why didn't they just shoot the old witch?'

'They didn't have guns in those days.'

'They coulda used a bow and arrow.'

'You can't kill a witch with a bow and arrow. The arrow just goes – psst – straight through her without hurting her.'

'Hangs teeth!' That was really impressive, but before accepting it Dirk found it necessary to corroborate with expert opinion. He checked with Mbejane, translating the problem to the Zulu. When Mbejane supported the girl Dirk was convinced, for Mbejane was a celebrated authority on the supernatural.

That night Dirk did not fall asleep in the saddle and when they camped before dawn the girl's voice was hoarse with overwork, but her conquest of Dirk was complete and that of Sean was well advanced.

All night while he listened to her voice and the husky bursts of laughter that punctuated it Sean had felt the seed that was planted at their first meeting sinking its roots down into his lower belly and loins, spreading its tendrils up through his chest. He wanted this woman so violently that in her presence his wits failed him. Many times during the night he had attempted to join

22

the discussions, but each time Dirk had brushed his efforts aside with contempt and turned avidly back to the girl. By morning he had made the disturbing discovery that he was jealous of his own son – jealous of the attention Dirk was getting, and for which he hungered so strongly.

While they drank coffee after the morning meal lying on their blankets beneath a grove of syringa trees, Sean remarked:

'You haven't told us your name yet.' And of course it was Dirk that answered.

'She told me. Your name's Ruth – isn't it?'

'That's right, Dirk.'

With an effort Sean clamped down on the senseless anger that boiled up through him, but when he spoke his voice carried traces of it.

'We've heard enough from you for one night, my boy. Now get your head down, close your eyes and your mouth and keep them that way.'

'I'm not sleepy, Dad.'

'Do what I tell you.' Sean jumped up and strode out of the camp. He climbed the small kopje above them. By now it was full daylight and he searched the veld to the horizon on all sides. There was no trace of habitation or human. He climbed down again and fussed with the hobbles of the horses before returning to the grove of syringas.

Despite his protestations Dirk was curled like a sleeping puppy and, near the fire from a large bundle of blankets issued the unmistakable snoring of Mbejane. Ruth lay a little apart from them, a blanket thrown over her legs, her eyes closed and the front of her shirt rising and falling in a manner that gave Sean two good reasons for not sleeping. He lay propped on one elbow and fed his eyes and his imagination on her.

These four years past he had not seen a white woman, four years without the sound of a woman's voice or the comfort of her body. In the beginning it had worried him – the restlessness, the undirected fits of depression, and sudden bursts of temper. But gradually in the long days of hunting and riding, in the endless struggle with drought and storm, with beasts and the elements, he had brought his body under control. Women had faded into unreality, vague phantoms that plagued him only in the night so he twisted and sweated and cried out in his sleep until nature gave him release and the phantoms dispersed for a while to gather strength for their next visitation.

But this was no phantom that lay beside him now. By stretching out a hand he could stroke the faint down on her cheek and feel the blood-warm silk of her skin.

She opened her eyes, they were milky grey with sleep, slowly focusing until they levelled with his and returned his scrutiny.

Because of what she read there, she lifted her left hand from the blanket and held it out towards him. Her riding gloves were off. For the first time he noticed the slender gold ring that encircled her third finger.

'I see,' he muttered dully, and then in protest: 'But you are too young – you're too young to be married.'

'I'm twenty-two years old,' she told him softly.

'Your husband – where is he?' Perhaps the bastard was dead, his one last hope.

'I am going to him now. When war seemed inevitable he went to Natal, to Durban, to find a job and a home for us there. I was to follow him – but the war came earlier than we expected. I was stranded.'

'I see.' I am taking you to another man, he thought with bitterness, and put it in different words. 'So he is sitting in Durban waiting for you to make your own way through the lines.'

'He is with the army of Natal. A week ago he got a message through to me. He wanted me to stay on in Johannesburg and wait until the British capture the city. He says that with so great a force they will be in Johannesburg within three months.'

'Why didn't you wait, then?'

She shrugged. 'Patience is not one of my virtues,' and then the devilment was in her eyes again. 'Besides, I thought it would be fun to run away – it was so terribly dull in Johannesburg.'

'Do you love him?' he demanded suddenly. The question startled her and the smile died on her lips.

'He's my husband.'

'That doesn't answer my question.'

'It was a question you had no right to ask.' She was angry now.

'You have to tell me.'

'Do you love your wife?' she snapped at him.

'I did. She's been dead five years.' And her anger flickered out as swiftly as it had blazed.

'Oh, I'm sorry. I didn't know.'

'Forget it. Forget I ever asked.'

'Yes, that's best. We are getting into an awful tangle.' Her hand with the ring upon it was still held out towards him, lying between them on the soft carpet of fallen leaves. He reached out and lifted it. It was a small hand.

'Mr Courtney – Sean, it's best if – we mustn't – I think we'd better sleep now.' And she withdrew the hand and rolled away from him.

The wind woke them in the middle of the afternoon,

it roared in from the east, flattening the grass on the hills and thrashing the branches above their heads.

Sean looked up at the sky with the wind fluttering his shirt and ruffling his beard. He leaned forward against it, towering over Ruth so that suddenly she realized how big he was. He looked like a god of the storm, with long powerful legs braced apart and the muscles of his chest and arms standing out proudly beneath the white silk of his shirt.

'Clouds building up,' Sean shouted above the rush of the wind. 'No moon tonight.'

She stood up quickly and a sudden violent gust threw her off balance. She staggered against him and his arms closed about her. For a moment she was pressed to his chest, could feel the lean, rubbery resilience of his body and smell the man smell of it. It was a shock for both of them, this unexpectedly intimate contact and when she broke away her eyes were wide and grey with fear of the thing she had felt stir within her.

'I'm sorry,' she whispered. 'That was an accident.' And the wind caught her hair and streamed it across her face in a dancing, snapping black tangle.

'We'll upsaddle and ride with the daylight that is left,' Sean decided. 'We won't be able to move tonight.'

The clouds rolled in on the wind, spreading upon themselves, changing shape and dropping closer to the earth. Clouds the colour of smoke and bruises, heavy with the rain they carried.

The night came early, but still the wind roared and buffeted them in the gloom.

'It will drop in an hour or so, then we'll get the rain. We'll try and find shelter while there's still light enough to see.'

On the reverse slope of a kopje they found an overhang of rock and offloaded the packs beneath it. While Sean pegged the horses out on their head ropes to prevent them walking away before the storm, Mbejane cut grass and piled it into a mattress on the rock floor beneath the overhang. Huddled in their oilskins they ate biltong and cold mealie bread and afterwards Mbejane withdrew discreetly to the far end of the shelter and disappeared under his blankets. He had that animal knack of being able to sleep instantly and completely even under the most adverse conditions.

'All right, boy. Get into your blankets.'

'Can't I just . . . ' Dirk began his nightly protest.

'No, you can't.'

'I'll sing for you,' Ruth offered.

'What for?' Dirk was puzzled.

'A sleepy-time song – haven't you ever had a lullaby?'

'No.' But Dirk was intrigued. 'What you going to sing?'

'Into your blankets first.'

Sitting beside Sean in the darkness, very conscious of his bulk and the touch of his shoulder against hers, the muted roar of the wind as her accompaniment – Ruth sang.

First the old Dutch folksongs, 'Nooi, Nooi' and 'Jannie met die Hoepel been', then other old favourites like 'Frère Jacques'. Her voice meant something to each of them.

Mbejane woke to the sound of it and it made him remember the wind on the hills of Zululand and the singing of the young girls in the fields at harvest-time. It made him glad he was going home.

To Dirk it was the voice of the mother he had hardly known. A safe sound – and soon he slept.

'Don't stop,' whispered Sean.

So she sang for him alone. A love-song from two thousand years ago, filled with all the suffering of her people, but with joy in it also. The wind died away while she sang and her voice died away with it into the vast silence of the night.

The storm broke. The first thunder crashed and the lightning forked jagged-blue through the clouds. Dirk whimpered a little but slept on.

In the stark, blue light Sean saw that Ruth's cheeks were wet with tears and when the darkness closed around them again she started to tremble against him. He reached out for her and she clung to him, small and warm against his chest, and he could taste the salt of her tears on his lips.

'Sean, we mustn't.'

But he lifted her and held her across his chest as he walked out into the night. The lightning blazed again and lit the land with startling brilliance so he could see the horses huddling heads down, and the crisp outline of the kopje above them.

The first raindrops splashed against his shoulders and into his face. The rain was warm and he walked on carrying Ruth. Then the air was filled with rain, an encompassing pearly mist of it in the next flash of lightning, and the night was filled with the odour of rain on dry earth – a clean warm smell.

5

In a still morning, washed so clean by the rain that they could see the mountains, blue and sharp on the southern horizon, they stood together on the crest of the kopje.

'That's the tail of the Drakensberg, we've cleared it by twenty miles. There's very little chance of a Boer patrol this far out. We can ride by day now. Soon we'll be able to work in again and meet the railway beyond the battle lines.'

Because of the beauty of the morning, of the land that dripped away into the great, grassy bowl that was Natal, and of the woman that stood beside him, Sean was gay.

Because of the promise of an end to the journey and the promise of a new one with this woman as his companion, he was content.

When he spoke she turned slowly to look up at him, her chin lifting in acknowledgement of his superior height. For the first time Sean realized that his own mood was not reflected in her eyes.

'You are very lovely,' he said, and still she remained silent, but now he could recognize the shadows in her eyes as sorrow or something even stronger.

'Ruth, you'll come with me?'

'No.' She shook her head slowly, regretfully. The fat black python of hair rolled across her shoulder and hung down against the honey chamois leather of her jacket.

'You must.'

'I cannot.'

'But, last night.'

'Last night was madness . . . the storm.'

'It was right. You know that.'

'No. It was the storm.' She looked away from him towards the sky. 'And now the storm is ended.'

'It was more than that. You know it. It was from the first moment of our meeting.'

'It was a madness based upon deceit. Something that I will have to cover with lies – the way we had to cover it with darkness at the time.'

'Ruth. My God, don't talk about it like that.'

'Very well, I won't. I won't talk about it again, ever.'

'We can't leave it now. You know we can't.'

And in answer she held up her left hand so that the gold upon it caught the sun.

'We'll say good-bye here on a mountain in the sunlight. Though we'll ride together a little farther – it's here we'll say good-bye.'

'Ruth . . . ' he started, but she placed the hand across his mouth and he felt the metal of the ring on his lips and it seemed to him that the ring was as cold as his dread of the loss she was about to inflict upon him.

'No,' she whispered. 'Kiss me once more and then let me go.'

6

Mbejane saw it first and spoke quietly to Sean, perhaps two miles out on their flank, like a smudge of brown smoke rising beyond the fold of the nearest ridge, so faint that Sean had to search a moment before he found it. Then he swivelled away from it and hunted frantically for cover. The nearest was an outcrop of red stone half a mile away, much too far.

'What is it, Sean?' Ruth noticed his agitation.

'Dust,' he told her. 'Horsemen. Coming this way.'

'Boers?'

'Probably.'

'What are we to do?'

'Nothing.'

'Nothing?'

'When they show on the ridge I'll ride to meet them. Try to bluff our way through.' He turned to Mbejane and spoke in Zulu. 'I will go to them. Watch me carefully, but keep moving away. If I lift my arm let the pack-horses go and ride. I will hold them as long as I can, but when I lift my arm then it is finished.' Quickly he unbuckled the saddle-bag which held the gold and handed it to the Zulu. 'With a good start you should be able to hold them off until nightfall. Take the Nkosikazi where she wishes to go and then with Dirk return to my mother at Ladyburg.'

He looked again at the ridge just in time to see two horsemen appear upon it. Sean lifted the binoculars from his chest; in the round field of the glasses the two riders stood broadside, their faces turned towards him so he could make out the shape of their helmets. He saw the burnished sparkle of their accoutrements, the size of their mounts and their distinctive saddlery and he yelled with relief.

'Soldiers!'

As if in confirmation a squadron of cavalry in two neat ranks broke over the skyline with the pennants fluttering gaily on the forest of their lances.

Dirk hooting with excitement, Ruth laughing beside him and Mbejane dragging the pack-horses after them, Sean galloped standing in the stirrups and waving his hat above his head to meet them.

Unaffected by the enthusiasm of the welcome the lancers sat stolidly and watched them come and the subaltern at their head greeted Sean suspiciously as he arrived.

'Who are you, sir?' But he seemed less interested in Sean's reply than in Ruth's breeches and what they contained. During the explanations that followed Sean conceived for the man a growing dislike. Although the smooth, sun-reddened skin and the fluffy, yellow moustache aggravated this feeling, the central cause was the pair of pale blue eyes. Perhaps they always popped out that way, but Sean doubted it. They focused steadily on Sean only during the short period when Sean reported that he had made no contact with the Boer, then they swivelled back to Ruth.

'We'll not detain you longer, Lieutenant,' Sean grunted and gathered his reins to turn away.

'You are still ten miles from the Tugela River, Mr Courtney. Theoretically this area is held by the Boers and although we are well out on the flank of their main army it would be much safer if you entered the British lines under our protection.'

'Thank you, no. I want to avoid both armies and reach Pietermaritzburg as soon as possible.' The subaltern shrugged. 'The choice is yours. But if it were my wife and child . . . ' He did not finish, but turned in the saddle to signal the column forward.

'Come on, Ruth.' Sean caught her eye, but she did not move.

'I'm not going with you.' There was a flat quality in her voice and she looked away from him.

'Don't be silly.' It shocked him and gave his reply a harshness that lit sparks of anger in her eyes.

'May I travel with you?' she demanded of the subaltern.

'Well, ma'am.' He hesitated, glancing quickly at Sean before he went on. 'If your husband . . . '

'He's not my husband. I hardly know him.' She cut in and ignored the exclamation of protest from Sean. 'My husband is with your army. I want you to take me with you, please.'

'Well, now . . . ! That's a horse of another colour,' the officer drawled, but the lazy arrogance of his tone barely concealed his pleasure at the prospect of Ruth's company. 'I'd be delighted to escort you, ma'am.'

With her knees Ruth backed her mount and fell in beside the subaltern. This small manoeuvre placed her directly facing Sean – as though she were on the far side of a barrier.

'Ruth, please. Let me talk to you about this. Just a few minutes.'

'No.' There was no expression in her voice, nor in her face.

'Just to say good-bye,' he pleaded.

'We've said good-bye.' She glanced from Sean to Dirk and then away.

The subaltern raised his clenched first high and lifted

his voice. 'Column! Column, Forward!' and as his big, glossy hunter started he grinned maliciously at Sean and touched the brim of his helmet in ironical salute.

'Ruth!'

But she was no longer looking at Sean. Her eyes were fixed ahead and as she swept away at the head of the column her chin was up, that smiling type of mouth was drawn into two straight lips and the thick braid of hair thumped against her back with each thrust of the horse beneath her.

'Rough luck, matey!' called a trooper from the rear rank and then they were past.

Hunched in the saddle Sean stared after them.

'Is she coming back, Pa?' Dirk inquired.

'No, she's not coming back.'

'Why not?'

Sean did not hear the question. He was watching, waiting for Ruth to look back at him. But he waited in vain, for suddenly she was gone over and beyond the next fold in the land and a few seconds later the column had followed her. Afterwards there was only the vast emptiness of the land and the sky above – as vast as the emptiness within him.

7

Sean rode ahead. Ten yards behind they followed, Mbejane restraining Dirk from a closer approach for he understood that Sean must now be left alone. Many times in the years they had been together Mbejane and Sean had travelled in this formation – Sean riding ahead with his sorrow or his shame and Mbejane trailing him patiently, waiting for Sean's shoulders to straighten and his chin to lift from where it drooped forward on his chest.

There was no coherence in Sean's thoughts, the only pattern was the rise and swoop of alternate anger and despair.

Anger at the woman, anger almost becoming hatred before the plunge of despair as he remembered she was gone. Then anger building up towards madness, this time directed at himself for letting her go. Again the sickening drop as he realized that there was no means by which he could have held her. What could he have offered her? Himself? Two hundred pounds of muscle and bones and scars supporting a face like a granite cliff? Poor value! His worldly goods? A small sack of sovereigns and another woman's child – By God, that was all he had. After thirty-seven years that was all he had to show! Once more his anger flared. A week ago he had been rich – and his anger found a new target. There was at least somewhere he could seek vengeance, there was a tangible enemy to strike, to kill. The Boer. The Boer had robbed him of his wagons and his gold, had sent him scurrying for safety; because of them the woman had come into his life and because of them she had been snatched away from him.

So be it, he thought angrily, this then is the promise of the future. War!

He straightened in the saddle, his shoulders seemed to fill out wide and square. He lifted his head and saw the shiny snake of a river in the valley below. They had reached the Tugela. Without pause Sean pushed his horse over the lip of the escarpment. On its haunches, loose rock rolling and slithering beneath its hooves, they began the descent.

Impatiently Sean followed the river downstream, searching for a drift. But between the sheer banks it ran smooth and swift and deep, twenty yards wide and still discoloured with mud from the storm.

At the first place where the far bank flattened sufficiently to promise an easy exit from the water, Sean checked his horse and spoke brusquely.

'We'll swim.'

In reply Mbejane glanced significantly at Dirk.

'He's done this before,' Sean answered him as he dismounted and began to shed his clothing, then to the boy, 'Come on, Dirk. Get undressed.'

They drove the pack-horses in first, forcing them to jump from the steep bank and watched anxiously until their heads reappeared above the surface and they struck out for the far bank. Then all three of them naked, their clothing wrapped in oilskins and lashed to the saddles, they remounted.

'You first, Mbejane.'

A splash that rose above the bank.

'Off you go, Dirk. Remember to hang on to the saddle.'

Another high splash, and Sean flogged his mount as it baulked and danced sideways along the bank. A sudden lunge outwards and the long drop before the water closed over them.

Snorting water, they surfaced and with relief Sean saw Dirk's head bobbing beside that of his horse and heard his shouted excitement. Moments later they stood on the far bank, water streaming from their naked bodies, and laughed together at the fun of it.

Abruptly the laughter was strangled to death in Sean's throat. Lining the bank above them, grinning with the infection of merriment but with Mauser rifles held ready, stood a dozen men. Big men, bearded, festooned with bandoliers of ammunition, dressed in rough clothing and a selection of hats that included a brown derby and a tall beaver.

In imitation of Sean, both Mbejane and Dirk stopped laughing and stared up at the frieze of armed men along the bank. A complete silence fell on the gathering.

It was broken at last by the man in the brown derby as he pointed at Sean with the barrel of his Mauser.

'*Magtig*! But you'd need a sharp axe to cut through that branch.'

'Don't anger him,' warned the gentleman in the beaver. 'If he hits you over the head with it, it will crack your skull!' and they all laughed.

It was hard for Sean to decide which was the more discomforting; the intimate discussion of his nudity, or the fact that the discussion was conducted in the Taal (or Cape Dutch). In his impatience he had walked, or rather swum, into the arms of a Boer patrol. There was just a forlorn hope that he might be able to bluff his way through, and he opened his mouth to make the attempt. But Dirk forestalled him.

'Who are they, Pa, and why are they laughing?' he asked in clear piping English, and Sean's hope died as abruptly as did the Boer laughter when they heard that hated language.

'Oh, So!' growled the man in the beaver, and gestured eloquently with his Mauser. 'Hands up please, my friend.'

'Will you allow me to put my trousers on first?' Sean asked politely.

'Where are they taking us?' For once Dirk was subdued and there was a quiver in his voice that touched Beaver, who rode beside him. He answered for Sean.

'Now don't you worry, you're going to see a general. A real live general.' Beaver's English was intelligible and Dirk studied him with interest.

'Will he have medals and things?'

'*Nee*, man. We don't use such rubbish.' And Dirk lost interest. He turned back to Sean.

'Pa, I'm hungry.'

Again Beaver intervened. He pulled a long black stick of biltong, dried meat, from his pocket and offered it to Dirk.

'Sharpen your teeth on that, *Kerel*.'

With his mouth full Dirk was taken care of and Sean could concentrate on the other Boers. They were convinced they had caught a spy, and were discussing the impending execution. In a friendly manner Sean was admitted to the argument, and they listened with respectful attention to his defence. This was interrupted while they forded the Tugela and climbed the escarpment once more, but Sean continued it while they rode in a bunch along the crest. Finally, he convinced them of his innocence – which they accepted with relief, as none of them were really looking forward to shooting him.

Thereafter the talk turned to more pleasant topics. It was a glorious day, sunshine lit the valley in gold and green. Below them the river twisted and sparkled, working its devious way down from the smoky blue wall of the Drakensberg that stood along the far horizon. A few fat clouds dawdled across the sky, and a light breeze took the edge off the heat.

The youngsters in the party listened avidly as Sean spoke of elephant beyond the Limpopo, and of the wide land that waited for men to claim it.

'After the war . . . ' they said, and laughed in the sun. Then a change in the wind and a freak lie of the hills brought a faint but ugly sound down to them and the laughter died.

'The guns,' said one of them.

'Ladysmith.'

Now it was Sean's turn to ask the questions. They told him how the commandos had raced down on the town of Ladysmith and rolled up the force that stood to oppose them. Bitterly they remembered how old Joubert had held his horsemen and watched while the broken English army streamed back into the town.

'Almighty! Had he loosed us on them then! We would sweep them into the sea.'

'If Oom Paul had commanded instead of old Joubert, the war would be finished already – but instead we sit and wait.'

Gradually Sean filled in the picture of the war in Natal. Ladysmith was invested. General George White's army was bottled and corked within the town. Half the Boer army had moved forward along the railway and taken up a defensive line straddling the Escarpment, overlooking the river and the tiny village of Colenso.

Below them on the great plain of the Tugela, General Buller was massing his army for the breakthrough to relieve Ladysmith.

'But let him try – Oom Paul is waiting for him.'

'Who is Oom Paul – Surely not Kruger?' Sean was puzzled. Oom Paul was the affectionate nickname of the President of the South African Republic.

'*Nee*, man! This is another Oom Paul. This one is Vecht-General Jan Paulus Leroux of the Wynberg commando.' And Sean caught his breath.

'Is he a big man with red hair and a temper to go with it?'

Laughter, and then. '*Ja*! that's the one. Do you know him?'

'Yes. I know him.'

So my brother-in-law is now a general, Sean grinned to himself, and then asked:

'Is this the general we are going to visit?'

'If we can find him.'

Young Dirk will meet his uncle at last – and Sean found himself anticipating the reunion with a tingle of pleasure.

8

The canvas of the tent did little to moderate the volume of the voice within. It carried clearly to where Sean waited with his escort.

'Must I drink coffee and shake hands with every *rooinek* we catch? Have I not already enough work for ten men, but you must bring me more? Send him to one of the Field-Cornets! Send him to Pretoria and let them lock him up! Do whatever you like with him if he is a spy – but, in the name of a merciful providence, don't bring him to me.'

Sean smiled happily. Jan Paulus certainly hadn't lost his voice. There was an interval of comparative quiet while Beaver's voice mumbled within the tent. Then again the muted bellow.

'No! I will not! Take him away.'

Sean filled his lungs, cupped his hands about his mouth and shouted at the tent.

'Hey, you bloody Dutchman! Are you afraid to meet me again? You think I'll knock your teeth out like I did last time.'

A few moments of appalling stillness, then the clattering of an overturned stool and the flap of the tent was thrown open. Into the sunlight, blinking in the glare, but scowling, the red hair that fringed his bald pate burning like a bush-fire, and his shoulders hunched aggressively, came Jan Paulus. His face turned from side to side as he searched for the source of the insult.

'Here,' called Sean, and Jan Paulus stopped dead. Uncertainly he peered at Sean.

'You!' He took a pace forward and then, 'It is you, isn't it. Sean!' And he began to laugh. His right hand that had been clenched into a huge fist unfolded and was thrust forward.

'Sean! Hell, man! Sean!'

They gripped hands and grinned at each other.

'Come into the tent. Come on in, man.'

Once they were inside, Jan Paulus's first question was:

'Where's Katrina? Where is my little sister?' and immediately the smile was gone from Sean's face. He sat down heavily on the *reimpje* stool and took off his hat before he answered.

'She's dead, Paulus. She's been dead these last four years.'

Slowly the expression on Jan Paulus's face changed until it was bleak and hard.

'How?' he asked.

And what can I answer him, thought Sean. Can I tell him she killed herself for some reason that no one will ever know.

'Fever,' he said. 'Blackwater fever.'

'You did not send word to us.'

'I did not know where to find you. Your parents –'

'They too are dead,' Jan Paulus interrupted brusquely and turned away from Sean to stare at the white canvas wall of the tent. There was silence between them then as they remembered the dead in sorrow, made more poignant by its utter helplessness. At last Sean stood up and went to the entrance of the tent.

'Dirk. Come here.'

Mbejane pushed him forward and he crossed to Sean and took his hand. Sean led him into the tent.

'Katrina's son,' he said and Jan Paulus looked down at him.

'Come here, boy.' Hesitantly Dirk went to him. Suddenly Jan Paulus dropped into a squat so that his eyes were on a level with those of the child. He took Dirk's face between the palms of his hands and studied it carefully.

'Yes,' he said. 'This is the type of son she would breed. The eyes –' His voice stumbled and stopped. A second longer he looked into Dirk's eyes. Then he spoke again.

'Be proud,' he said and stood up. Sean motioned at the flap of the tent, and thankfully Dirk scampered out to where Mbejane waited.

'And now?' Jan Paulus asked.

'I want passage through the lines.'

'You are going over to the English?'

'I am English,' said Sean. Frowning a little, Jan Paulus considered this before he asked:

'You will give me your word not to take up arms with them?'

'No,' answered Sean and Jan Paulus nodded, it as the answer he had expected.

'There is a debt between us,' he decided. 'I have not forgotten the time of the elephant. This is full payment of that debt.' He crossed to the portable desk and dipped a pen. Still standing he wrote rapidly, fanned the paper dry and proffered it to Sean.

'Go,' he said. 'And I hope we do not meet again, for next time I will kill you.'

'Or I you,' Sean answered him.

9

That afternoon Sean led his party across the steel railway bridge over the Tugela, on through the deserted village of Colenso and out again across the plain. Far ahead, sown on the grass plain like a field of white daisies, were the tents of the great British encampment at Chievely Siding. But long before he reached it Sean came to a guard post manned by a sergeant and four men of an illustrious Yorkshire regiment.

"Ullo, Piet. And where the hell do you think you're off to?'

'I am a British subject,' Sean informed them. The sergeant ran an eye over Sean's beard and patched coat. He glanced at the shaggy pony he rode, and then considered the direction from which Sean had approached.

'Say that again,' he invited.

'I am a British subject,' Sean repeated obligingly in an accent that fell heavily on the Yorkshireman's ear.

'And I'm a ruddy Japanee,' agreed the sergeant cheerfully. 'Let's have your rifle, mate.'

Two days Sean languished in the barbed-wire prison compound while the Intelligence Department cabled the Registrar of Births at Ladyburg and waited for his reply. Two long days during which Sean brooded incessantly, not on the indignities which had been inflicted on him, but on the woman he had found and loved and lost again so quickly. These two days of enforced inactivity came at precisely the worst moment. By repeating over and over in his imagination each word that had passed between them, by feeling again each contact of their hands and bodies, by forming her face in his mind's eye and gloating over every detail of it – Sean burned her memory so deeply into himself that it was there for all time. Although he did not even know her surname, he would never forget her.

By the time he was released with apologies and given back his horses, rifle, moneybag and packs – Sean had driven himself into a mood of such overpowering depression that it could only be alleviated by liquor or physical violence.

The village of Frere, which was the first station south on the line to the coast, promised both of these.

'Take Dirk with you,' instructed Sean, 'beyond the town find a camp beside the road and make a big fire, so I can find you in the dark.'

'What will you do, Nkosi?'

Sean started towards the dingy little canteen that catered for the thirsty of Frere.

'I'm going there,' he answered.

'Come, Nkosizana.' As he and Dirk continued on down the street Mbejane was deciding how long he should give Sean before coming to fetch him. It was many years since the Nkosi had headed for a bar in such a determined fashion, but then there had been much to distress him these last few days. He will need until midnight, Mbejane decided, then he will be in a condition conducive to sleep.

From the door Sean surveyed the interior of the canteen. A single large room with a trestle bar counter along the back wall, and the room was comfortably full of warmth and men and the smell of liquor and cigars. Still standing in the entrance, Sean slipped his hand into the pocket of his trousers and surreptitiously counted his money– ten sovereigns he had allowed himself, more than sufficient for the purchase of the liquor he intended to consume.

As he worked his way through the crowd towards the bar, he looked at the men about him. Soldiers mostly, from a dozen different regiments. Colonials and Imperial troops, other ranks predominating, although a party of junior officers sat at a table against the far wall. Then there were a few civilians whom he judged to be transport drivers, contractors and business men, two women with the officers whose profession was never in doubt, and a dozen black waiters.

'What will it be, ducks?' the large woman behind the counter asked as he reached it and Sean regarded her moustache and her term of address with disfavour.

'Brandy.' He was in no mood for the niceties.

'You want the bottle, ducks?' She had recognized his need.

'That will do for a start,' he agreed.

He drank three large brandies, and with a faint dismay knew that they were having no effect – apart from sharpening his imagination to the point where he could clearly see Ruth's face before his eyes, complete in every detail down to the little black beauty spot high on her cheek and the way the corners of her eyes slanted upwards as she smiled. He would have to make a more active approach to forgetfulness.

Leaning back with both elbows on the counter and the glass clutched in his right hand, he studied the men about him once more. Evaluating each of them as a source of distraction and then discarding and moving his attention on, he was finally left with the small group around the gaming-table.

Seven players, the game draw poker, and from what he could see the stakes were modest. He picked up his bottle, crossed the room to join the circle of spectators and took up his position behind a sergeant of yeomanry who was receiving a battering from the cards. A few hands later the sergeant drew one to fill his flush, missed and pushed the bluff – raising twice until he was called by two pairs across the table. He threw his hand in and blew through his lips in disgust.

'That cleans me out.' He gathered the few coins left on the table in front of him and stood up.

'Rough luck, Jack. Anyone care to take his place?' The winner looked around the circle of spectators. 'Nice friendly little game, table stakes.'

'Deal me in.' Sean sat down, placed his glass and bottle strategically at his right hand and stacked five gold sovereigns in front of him.

'The man's got gold! Welcome.'

Sean ducked the first hand, lost two pounds to three queens on the next, and won five pounds on the third. The pattern of his luck was set, he played with cold single-mindedness – and when he wanted cards it seemed he had only to wish for them.

What was the old adage? – 'Unlucky in love, and the cards turn hot.' Sean grinned without amusement and filled a small straight with the five of hearts, beat down the three sevens that came against him and drew the pot towards him to swell the pile of his winnings. Up about thirty or forty pounds. He was enjoying himself now.

'A small school, gentlemen.' Three players had dropped out in the last hour leaving four of them at the table. 'How about giving the losers a chance to recoup?'

'You want to raise the stakes?' Sean asked the speaker. He was the only other winner, a big man with a red face and the smell of horses about him. Transport rider, probably.

'Yes, if everyone agrees. Make the minimum bet five pounds.'

'Suits me,' grunted Sean, and there was a murmur of agreement round the table. With heavy money out an air of caution prevailed at first, but slowly the game opened up. Sean's luck cooled a little, but an hour later he had built up his kitty on a series of small wins to a total of seventy-five pounds. Then Sean dealt a strange hand.

The first caller on Sean's left raised before the draw, and was raised in turn by the gentleman with the horsy smell, number three called and Sean fanned his cards open.

With a gentle elation he found the seven, eight, nine and ten of Clubs – with a Diamond six. A pretty little straight dealt pat.

'Call your twenty, and raise it twenty,' he offered, and there was a small stir of excitement among the onlookers.

'Call.' Number one was short of cash.

'Call,' echoed Horse Odour and his gold clinked into the pot.

'I'm dropping.' Number three closed his cards and pushed them away. Sean turned back to number one.

'How many cards?'

'I'll play with these.' Sean felt the first premonition of disaster.

'And you?' he asked Horse Odour.

'I'm also happy with what I have.'

Two pat hands against his small straight; and from the suit distribution, Sean's four Clubs, one of them would certainly be a flush. With a queasy feeling in his stomach Sean knew he was in trouble, knew his hand to be a loser.

Break the straight and go for the other Club, still not a certain winner, but the only thing worth trying.

'I'll draw one.' He tossed the six of Diamonds into the welter of discards, and dealt to himself from the top of the pack.

'My bet.' Number one's face was glowing with confidence. 'I'll raise the maximum – another forty. Cost you eighty pounds to look at me, boys. Let's see the colour of your money.'

'I'd like to push you – but that's the limit. I'll call.' Horse Odour's expression was completely neutral but he was sweating in a light sheen across his forehead.

'Let me go to the books.' Sean picked up his cards and, from behind the other four, pressed out the corner of the card he had drawn. It was black, he opened it a little more – a black six. Slowly he felt the pressure build up within him like a freshly fired boiler. He drew a long breath and opened the card fully.

'I'll call also.' He spoke on a gusty outgoing breath.

'Full house,' shouted number one. 'Queen's full – beat that, you bastards!'

Horse Odour slapped his cards down viciously, his red face crumbling in disappointment. 'Goddam it – of all the filthy luck. I had an ace-high flush.' Number one giggled with excitement and reached for the money.

'Wait for it, friend,' Sean advised him, and spread his cards face up upon the table.

'It's a flush. My full house beats you,' protested number one.

'Count the pips –' Sean touched each card as he named them, 'six, seven, eight, nine and the ten – all Clubs. Straight flush! You come second by a day's march.' He lifted number one's hands off the money, pulled it towards him and began stacking it in columns of twenty.

'Pretty hot run of luck you're having,' Horse Odour gave his opinion, his face still twisted with disappointment.

'Yes,' agreed Sean. Two hundred and sixty-eight pounds. Very pretty.

'Funny how it comes to you on the big hands,' Horse Odour went on. 'And especially when you're dealing. What did you say your profession was?'

Without looking up Sean began transferring the stacks of sovereigns to his pockets. He was smiling a little. The end to a perfect evening, he decided.

Satisfied that the money was secure Sean looked up at Horse Odour and turned that smile full upon him.

'Come along then, laddie,' he said.

'It will be a pleasure.' Horse Odour shoved his chair back and stood up.

'It will indeed,' agreed Sean.

Horse Odour led down the back-stairs into the yard, followed by Sean and the entire clientele of the canteen. At the bottom he paused, judging Sean's footstep on the wooden stairs behind him – then he spun and hit, swinging his body into the punch.

Sean rolled his head, but it caught him on the temple and he went over backwards into the crowd behind him. As he fell he saw Horse Odour jerk back the tail of his jacket and bring out the knife. It shone dull silver in the light from the canteen windows – skinning knife, curved, eight inches of blade.

The crowd scattered leaving Sean lying on the stairs, and Horse Odour came in to kill him, making an ugly sound, bringing the knife arching down from overhead, a clumsy, unprofessional blow.

Only slightly stunned, Sean followed the silver sweep of the knife with ease and the man's wrist slapped loudly into Sean's open left hand.

50

For a long moment the man lay on top of Sean, his knife-arm helpless in Sean's grip, while Sean assessed his strength – and with regret realized it was no match. Horse Odour was big enough, but the belly pressed against Sean's was flabby and large, and the wrist in Sean's hands was bony without the hard rubbery give of sinew and muscle.

Horse Odour started to struggle, trying to wrestle his knife-arm free, the sweat dewed on his face and then began to drip – it had an oily, unpleasant smell like rancid butter that blended poorly with the odour of horses.

Sean tightened his grip on the man's wrist, at first using only the strength of his forearm.

'Aah!' Horse Odour stopped struggling. Sean brought in the power of his whole arm, so he could feel his shoulder muscles bunching and writhing.

'Jesus Christ!' Shrieking, as bone cracked in his wrist, Horse Odour's fingers sprang open and the knife thumped on to the wooden stairs.

Still holding him, Sean sat up, then came slowly to his feet.

'Leave us, friend.' Sean flung him backwards into the dust of the yard. He was breathing easily, still feeling cold and detached as he looked down and watched Horse Odour scrabbling to his knees, nursing his broken wrist.

Perhaps it was the man's first movement towards flight that triggered Sean – or perhaps it was the liquor he had drunk that twisted his emotions, aggravated his sense of loss and frustration and channelled it into this insane outburst of hatred.

Suddenly it seemed to Sean that here before him on the ground was the source of all his ills – this was the man who had taken Ruth from him.

'You bastard!' he growled. The man sensed the change

in Sean and scrambled to his feet, his face turning desperately from side to side as he sought an avenue of escape.

'You filthy bastard!' Sean's voice rose, shrill with the strength of this new emotion. For the first time in his life Sean craved to kill. He advanced upon the man slowly, his fists opening and closing, his face contorted and the words that spilled from his mouth no longer making sense.

A great stillness had fallen upon the yard. In the shadows the watchers stood, chilled with the dreadful fascination of it. The man was frozen also, only his head moved and no sound came from his open lips – and Sean closed in with the weaving motion of a cobra in erection.

At the last moment the man tried to run, but his legs were slack and heavy with fear – and Sean hit him in the chest with a sound like an axe swung against a tree-trunk.

As he fell Sean went in after him, straddling his chest, roaring incoherently with only a single word recognizable – the name of the woman he loved. In his madness he felt the man's face breaking up under his fists, felt the warm splatter of blood thrown into his own face and on to his arms, and heard the shouts of the crowd.

'He'll kill him!'

'Get him off!'

'For Chrissake give me a hand – he's as strong as a bloody ox.'

Their hands upon him, an arm locked around his throat from behind, the shock as someone hit him with a bottle, the press of their bodies as they swarmed over him.

With men clinging to him, two of them riding his back and a dozen others on his arms and legs, Sean came to his feet.

'Pull his legs out from under him.'

'Get him down, man. Get him down.'

With a convulsive heave Sean swung the men on his arms into violent collision with each other. They released him.

He kicked his right leg free, and those on his other leg let go and scattered. Reaching over his shoulders he plucked the men off his back and stood alone, his chest swelling and subsiding as he breathed, the blood from the bottle gash in his scalp trickling down his face and soaking into his beard.

'Get a gun!' someone shouted.

'There's a shotgun under the bar.' But no one left the circle that ringed him in, and Sean glared around at them his eyes staring wildly from the plain of glistening blood that was his face.

'You've killed him!' a voice accused him. And the words reached Sean through the madness, his body relaxed slightly and he tried to wipe away the blood with the open palm of his hand. They saw the change in him.

'Cool down, mate. Fun's fun but the hell with murder.'

'Easy, now. Let's have a look what you've done to him.'

Sean looked down on the body, and he was confused and then suddenly afraid. The man was dead – he was certain of it.

'Oh, my God!' he whispered, backing away, wiping at his eyes ineffectually and smearing blood.

'He pulled a knife. Don't worry, mate, you've got witnesses.' The temper of the crowd had changed.

'No,' Sean mumbled; they didn't understand. For the first time in his life he had abused his strength, had used it to kill without purpose. To kill for the pleasure of it, to kill in the manner in which a leopard kills.

53

Then the man moved slightly, he rolled his head and one of his legs flexed and straightened. Sean felt hope leap within him.

'He's alive!'

'Get a doctor.'

Fearfully Sean approached and knelt beside the man, he unknotted the scarf from around his own throat and cleaned the bloody mouth and nostrils.

'He'll be all right – leave him to the Doc.'

The doctor came, a lean and laconic man chewing tobacco. In the yellow light of a hurricane lamp he examined and prodded while they crowded close about him craning to see over his shoulders. At last the doctor stood up.

'All right. He can be moved. Carry him up to my surgery.' Then he looked at Sean. 'Did you do it?'

Sean nodded.

'Remind me not to annoy you.'

'I didn't mean to – it just sort of happened.'

'Is that so?' The doctor shot a stream of yellow tobacco juice into the dust of the yard. 'Let's have a look at your head.' He pulled Sean's head down to his own level and parted the sodden black hair.

'Nicked a vein. Doesn't need a stitch. Wash it and a little iodine.'

'How much, Doc, for the other fellow?' Sean asked.

'You paying?' The doctor looked at him quizzically.

'Yes.'

'Broken jaw, broken collar-bone, about two dozen stitches and a few days in bed for concussion,' he mused, adding it up. 'Say two guineas.'

Sean gave him five. 'Look after him, Doc.'

'That's my job.' And he followed the men who were carrying Horse Odour out of the yard.

'Guess you need a drink, mister. I'll buy you one,' someone offered. The whole world loves a winner.

'Yes,' agreed Sean. 'I need a drink.'

Sean had more than one drink. When Mbejane came to fetch him at midnight he had a deal of difficulty getting Sean up on to the back of the horse. Half-way to the camp Sean slid off and subsided into the road, so Mbejane loaded him sideways – head and arms hanging over to port and legs dangling starboard.

'It is possible that tomorrow you will regret this,' Mbejane told him primly as he unloaded him beside the fire and rolled him still booted and bloody into his blanket.

He was correct.

10

In the dawn as Sean cleaned his face with a cloth dipped in a mug of hot water, regarding its reflection in the small metal mirror, the only fact that gave him the faintest satisfaction was the two hundred-odd sovereigns he had salvaged from the night's debauch.

'Are you sick, Pa?' Dirk's ghoulish interest in Sean's condition added substantially to his evil temper.

'Eat your breakfast.' Sean's tone was calculated by its sheer malevolence to dry up further questioning.

'There is no food.' Mbejane fell into the familiar role of protector.

'Why not?' Sean focused his bloodshot eyes upon him.

'There is one among us who considers the purchase of strong drink, and other things, more important than food for his son.'

From the pocket of his jacket Sean drew a handful of sovereigns. 'Go!' he ordered. 'Buy food and fresh horses. Go quickly so that in my grave illness I may not be afflicted with the wisdom of your counsel. Take Dirk with you.'

Mbejane examined the money, and grinned.

'The night was not wasted.'

When they had gone back to Frere, Dirk trotting beside the huge half-naked Zulu and his voice only fading at a distance of a hundred yards, Sean poured himself another mug of coffee and cupping it in his hands he sat staring into the ash and pink coals of the fire. He could trust Mbejane to use the money with care,

56

he had the bargaining patience peculiar to his race that could if necessary devote two days to the purchase of a single ox. These things did not concern Sean now. Instead he went over the events of the previous night. Still sickened by his display of murderous rage, he tried to justify it. Taking into account the loss of nearly all he owned, the accumulation of years of hard work that had been stripped from him in a single day; the hardship and uncertainty that had followed. And finally he had reached the flash point when liquor and poker-tensed nerves had snapped the last reserve in him and translated it all into that violent outburst.

But that was not all, he knew he had avoided the main issue. *Ruth*. As he came back to her a wave of hopeless longing overwhelmed him, a tender despair such as he had never experienced before. He groaned aloud, and lifted his eyes to the morning star which was fading on the pink horizon as the sun came up behind.

For a while longer he wallowed in the softness of his love, remembering the way she walked, the dark serenity of her eyes and her mouth when she smiled and her voice when she sang – until it threatened to smother him in its softness.

Then he sprang to his feet and paced restlessly in the grass beside the fire. We must leave this place, ride away from it – go quickly. I must find something to do, some way to keep from thinking of it, something to fill my hands which ache now from the need to hold her.

Along the road, going north to Colenso, a long column of infantry filed past him in the dawn. He stopped his pacing and watched them. Each man leaned forward against his pack and the rifles stood up behind their shoulders.

Yes, he thought, I will go with them. Perhaps at the place to which they march I can find what I could not

57

find last night. We will go home to Ladyburg, riding hard on fresh horses. I will leave Dirk with my mother, then come back to this war.

He began to pace again impatiently. Where the hell was Mbejane?

From the heights above, Sean looked down on Ladyburg. The village spread in a neat circle around the spire of the church. He remembered the spire as beacon-bright in its cladding of new copper, but nineteen years of weather had dulled it to a mellow brown.

Nineteen years. It did not seem that long. There were goods yards around the station now, a new concrete bridge over the Baboon Stroom, the blue gums in the plantation beyond the school were taller, and the flamboyants that had lined the main street were gone.

With a strange reluctance Sean turned his head and looked out to the right, across the Baboon Stroom, close in against the escarpment, to where he had left the sprawling Dutch gabled homestead of Theuniskraal with its roof of combed yellow thatch and the shutters of yellow-wood across the windows.

It was there, but not as he remembered it. Even at this distance he could see the walls were flaking and mottled with patches of dampness; the thatch was shaggy as the coat of an airedale; one of the shutters tilted slightly from a broken hinge; the lawns were brown and ragged where the bare earth showed through. The dairy behind the house had crumbled, its roof gone and the remains of its walls jutted forlornly upwards to the height of a man's shoulder.

'Damn the little bastard!' Sean's anger flared abruptly as he saw the neglect with which his twin brother had treated the lovely old house. 'He's so lazy he wouldn't get out of a bed he'd peed in.'

To Sean it was not just a house. It was the place his father had built, which had sheltered Sean on the day of his birth and through the years of his childhood. When his father died under the Zulu spears at Isandlawana, half the farm and the house had belonged to Sean; he had sat in the study at nights with the logs burning in the stone fireplace and the mounted buffalo head above it throwing distorted, moving shadows up on to the plaster ceiling. Although he had given his share away – yet it was still his home. Garry, his brother, had no right to let it decay and fall apart this way.

'Damn him!' Sean voiced his thoughts out loud – then almost immediately his conscience rebuked him. Garry was a cripple, his lower leg shot away by the blast of a careless shotgun. And Sean had fired that shotgun. Will I never be free of that guilt, how long must my penance continue? He protested at the goad of his conscience.

That is not your only trespass against your brother, his conscience reminded him. Who sired the child he calls his son? Whose loins sowed the seed that became man-child in the belly of Anna, your brother's wife?

'It has been a long time, Nkosi.' Mbejane had seen the expression on his face as Sean looked towards Theuniskraal and remembered those things from the past that were better forgotten.

'Yes.' Sean roused himself, and straightened in the saddle. 'A long road and many years. But now we are home again.'

He looked back towards the village, searching the quarter beyond the main street and the hotel for the roof of that little cottage on Protea Street. As he found it, showing through the tall, fluffy blue gum trees, there was a lift in his mood, a new excitement. Did she live there

59

still? How would she look – a little grey surely; had her fifty years marked her deeply, or had they treated her with the same consideration which she showed all those with whom *she* came in contact? Had she forgiven him for leaving without a farewell? Had she forgiven his long years of silence since then? Did she understand the reasons why he had never written – no word or message, except that anonymous gift of ten thousand pounds he had transferred to her bank account. Ten thousand miserable little pounds, which he had hardly noticed among all the millions he had won and lost in those days long ago when he was one of the lords of the Witwatersrand goldfields.

Again the sense of guilt closed in upon him. As he knew with utter certainty that she *had* understood, that she *had* forgiven. For that was Ada, the woman who was his stepmother – and whom he loved beyond the natural love one owes their own full-blooded mother.

'Let's go down,' he said and kicked his horse to a canter.

'Is this home, Pa?' Dirk shouted as he rode beside him.

'Yes, my boy. This is home.'

'Will Gran'ma be here?'

'I hope so,' Sean answered, and then softly, 'Beyond all other things, I hope that she will.'

Over the bridge above the Baboon Stroom, past the cattle-pens alongside the line of rail, past the old wood and iron station buildings with the sign, white and black faded to grey, 'Ladyburg. Altitude 2,256 ft. above sea level', swinging left into the dusty main street which was wide enough to turn a full span of oxen, and down to Protea Street rode Sean and Dirk, with Mbejane and the pack-mule trailing far behind.

At the corner Sean checked his mount to a walk,

drawing out the last few minutes of anticipation until they stopped outside the wicket fence of white that encompassed the cottage. The garden was neat and green, gay with beds of Barberton daisies and blue rhododendrons. The cottage had been enlarged, a new room built on the far side, and it was crisp-looking in a coat of new whitewash. A sign at the gate said in gold letters on a green ground.

'Maison Ada.
High-class Costumier'

Sean grinned. 'The old girl's gone all French, by God.' Then to Dirk, 'Stay here!'

He swung down from his horse, handed the reins to Dirk and went through the gate. At the door he paused self-consciously and adjusted his cravat. He glanced down at the severe dark broadcloth suit and new boots which he had purchased in Pietermaritzburg, slapped the dust from his breeches, stroked his newly trimmed beard into place, gave his moustache a twirl and knocked on the door.

It was opened at last by a young lady. Sean did not recognize her. But the girl reacted immediately, flushing slightly, attempting to pat her hair into place without drawing attention to its disarray, trying to dispose of the sewing in her hands, and exhibiting all the signs of confusion peculiar to the unmarried female who finds herself suddenly and unexpectedly in the presence of a large, well-dressed and attractive male. But Sean felt a twinge of pity as he looked at her scarred face, ugly with the purple cicatrice of acne.

Sean lifted his hat. 'Is Mrs Courtney here?'

'She's in the workroom, sir. Who shall I tell her is calling?'

'Don't tell her anything – it's a surprise,' Sean smiled at her, and she lifted her hands self-consciously in an attempt to mask the ruin of her face.

'Won't you come in, sir?' She turned her head aside, shyly – as though to hide it.

'Who is it, Mary?' Sean started at the voice from the depths of the cottage, it hadn't changed at all – and the years dropped away.

'It's a gentleman, Aunt Ada. He wants to see you.'

'I'm coming. Ask him to sit down, and please bring us coffee, Mary.'

Mary escaped thankfully and left Sean standing alone in the small sitting-room, twisting his hat in big brown hands, staring up at the daguerreotype print of Waite Courtney above the mantel. Although he did not recognize the fact, the face of his father in the picture was almost his own – the same eyes under heavy black brows, the same arrogance about the mouth, even the identical thrust of stubbornness in the jaw beneath the thick spade-shaped beard – and the big, hooked Courtney nose.

The door from the work-room opened and Sean swung quickly to face it. Ada Courtney came through it smiling, until she saw him, then she stopped and the smile died on her lips and she paled. Uncertainly her hand lifted to her throat and she made a small choking sound.

'Dear God,' she whispered.

'Ma.' Sean fidgeted his feet awkwardly. 'Hello, Ma. It's good to see you.'

'Sean.' The colour flooded back into her cheeks. 'For a moment I thought – you're grown so much like your father. Oh, Sean!' And she ran to him. He tossed his hat on to the sofa and caught her around the waist as she came.

'I've waited for you. I knew you'd come.'

62

Sean scooped her up and kissed her into a confusion of joy and laughter, swinging her while he did it, laughing himself.

'Put me down,' Ada gasped at last, and when he did she clung to him.

'I knew you'd come back. At first there were bits in the newspaper about you, and people told me things – but these last years there has been nothing, nothing at all.'

'I'm sorry.' Sean sobered.

'You're a bad boy.' She was sparkling with excitement, her hair had escaped from its bun and a wisp of it hung down her cheek. 'But it's so good to have you back –' and suddenly she was crying.

'Don't, Ma. Please don't.' He had never seen her cry before.

'It's just that . . . It's the surprise.' She brushed impatiently at her tears. 'It's nothing.'

Desperately Sean sought something to distract her. 'Hey!' he exclaimed with relief, 'I've another surprise for you.'

'Later,' she protested, 'One at a time.'

'This won't wait.' He led her to the door and out on to the front stoep with his arm around her shoulders.

'Dirk,' he shouted. 'Come here.'

He felt her standing very still as they watched Dirk coming up the garden walk.

'This is your Gran'ma.' He introduced them.

'Why is she crying?' Dirk eyed her with frank curiosity.

Later they sat at the table in the kitchen while Ada and Mary plied them with food. Ada Courtney believed that the first thing to do with a man was feed him.

Mary was almost as excited as Ada, she had taken full advantage of the few minutes she had been alone, and now her hair was freshly brushed and she wore a gay new apron, but the powder with which she had tried to cover the terrible disfiguration of the skin served only to call attention to it. In sympathy Sean refrained from looking at her, and Mary noticed. Shyly she devoted herself to winning Dirk's attention. She fussed over him quietly – and Dirk accepted this as the natural order of things.

While they ate Sean filled in the missing years for Ada with a brief outline of his activities, glossing over the death of Dirk's mother, and other things of which he had no reason to be proud. He came to the end of it.

'And so here we are.

"Home is the sailor, home from the sea,
And the hunter home from the hill."

Dirk, don't put so much in your mouth and keep it closed when you chew.'

'How long will you stay? Mary, see if there are any cream-puffs in the jar – Dirk is still hungry,' said Ada.

'You'll make him sick. I don't know; not long though – there's a war on.'

'You're going to join?'

'Yes.'

'Oh, Sean. Must you?' Knowing that he must. While he selected a cheroot from his case Sean studied her closely for the first time. There was grey now as he had known there would be, almost as much grey as black; long streaks of it across her temples and the texture of her skin had altered, losing the moisture of youth, drying out so that it creased around the eyes and stretched tight across her hands to show the knuckles more prominently and the blueness of veins beneath it. She was plumper also, her bosom was full and round,

64

each breast having lost its separate identity in the whole.

Yet the other qualities whose memories he had treasured so long ago still persisted, seemed indeed to have grown stronger; the composure which showed in the stillness of her hands and body, yet was given the lie by the humour that hovered around her lips; the eyes whose depths held compassion and a sure understanding of those things they looked upon. But mostly it was the indefinable aura of goodness about her – looking at her, he sensed again that behind those eyes no destructive thought could live for long.

Sean lit the cheroot and spoke while the smoke masked his face.

'Yes, Ma. I must go.'

And Ada, whose husband had ridden to war also, and not ridden home, could not prevent the sadness showing for an instant in her eyes.

'Yes. I suppose you must. Garry has gone already – and Michael has been agitating to follow him.'

'Michael?' Sean fired the question.

'Garry's son – he was born a short while after – after you left Ladyburg. He will be eighteen this winter.'

'What's he like?' Sean's voice was too eager. Michael – so that is what my son is named. My first-born. By God, my first-born, and I didn't even know his name until he was almost fully grown. Ada was looking at him with her own question unasked in her eyes.

'Mary, take Dirk through to the bathroom please. Try and get a little of that food from around his mouth.' When they had gone she answered Sean's question.

'He's a tall boy, tall and lean. Dark like his mother, but a serious lad. He doesn't laugh much. Always top of his class. I like him very much. He comes here often.' She was silent for a moment, then, 'Sean . . . '

Quickly Sean cut in. 'And how is Garry?' He sensed what she was going to ask.

'Garry has not changed very much. He has had a run of bad luck . . . Poor Garry, things have been bad on the farm. The rinder-pest ravaged his herds, he had to borrow money from the bank.' She hesitated an instant. 'And he is drinking a lot these days. I can't be sure of it – he never visits the hotel and I have never seen him take a drink. But it must be that.'

'I'll find out where he is when I go up to Colenso.'

'You'll have no difficulty finding him. Garry is a lieutenant-colonel on the General's staff. He was given promotion from major last week, and he has been awarded the Distinguished Service Order to go with his Victoria Cross. He is in charge of liaison between the Imperial and the Colonial troops.'

'Good God!' Sean was stunned. 'Garry a colonel!'

'General Buller thinks very highly of him. The General is also a holder of the Victoria Cross.'

'But,' Sean protested. 'You know how Garry got that decoration. It was a mistake. If Garry is on the General's staff – then Lord have mercy on the British Army!'

'Sean, you mustn't talk about your brother that way.'

'Colonel Garrick Courtney.' Sean laughed out loud.

'I don't know what there is between you and Garry. But it's something very nasty – and I don't want any of it in this house.' Ada's tone was fierce and Sean stopped laughing.

'I'm sorry.'

'Before we close the subject, I want to warn you. Please be very careful how you handle Garry. Whatever happened between you two – and I don't want to know what it is – Garry still hates you. Once or twice he started talking about you but I stopped him. Yet I know it from Michael – the boy has picked it up from his father. It's almost an obsession with him. Be careful of Garry.'

Ada stood up. 'And now about Dirk. What a lovely child he is, Sean. But I'm afraid you've spoiled him a little.'

'He's a tiger,' Sean admitted.

'What schooling has he been given?'

'Well, he can read a little –'

'You'll leave him here with me. I'll enrol him when the school term begins.'

'I was going to ask. I'll leave money with you.'

'Ten years ago there was a very large and mysterious deposit to my bank account. It wasn't mine – so I placed it out at interest.' She smiled at him and Sean looked guilty. 'We can use that.'

'No,' he said.

'Yes,' she contradicted. 'And now tell me when you are leaving.'

'Soon.'

'How soon?'

'Tomorrow.'

11

Since climbing the World's View road out of Pietermaritzburg, Sean and Mbejane had travelled in sunshine and in companionship. The feelings between them were solid, compacted by time and the pressure of trouble and shared laughter into a shield of affection – so that now they were happy as only men can be together. The jokes were old jokes, and the responses almost automatic – but the excitement between them was new, in the same way that each day's sun is new. For they were riding to war, to another meeting with death, so that everything else lost significance. Sean felt free, the thoughts and relationships with other people which had weighed him down over the past months slipped away. Like a ship clear for action he hurried with a new lightness to meet his chance.

At the same time he could stand aside from himself and grin tolerantly at his own immaturity. By God, we're like a couple of kids sneaking out of school. Then, following the thought further – he was suddenly thankful. Thankful that this was so; thankful that there was still this capacity to forget everything else and approach the moment in childlike anticipation. For a while this new habit of self-appraisal asserted itself; I am no longer young and I have learned much, gathered it brick by brick along the way and trimmed each brick and cemented it into the wall. The fortress of my manhood is not yet completed, but what I have built so far is strong. Yet the purpose of a fortress is to protect and hold safely those things that are precious; if, during the building, a man loses and expends those things which he wishes to protect, then the finished fortress is a mockery. I have not lost it all, a little I have used in barter. I have traded a little faith for the knowledge of evil; exchanged a little laughter for the understanding of death; a measure of freedom for two sons (and this was a good trade) – but I know there is still something left.

At his side Mbejane noticed the change of Sean's mood, and he moved in front of it to turn it once more into the sunshine.

'Nkosi, we must hurry if you wish to reach your drinking-place at Frere.'

With an effort Sean thrust his thoughts aside, and laughed. They rode on into the north, and on the third day they reached Chievely.

Sean remembered his innocent amazement when, as a youth, he had joined Lord Chelmsford's column at Rorke's Drift at the beginning of the Zulu War. He had believed then no greater accumulation of men was possible. Now he looked out across the encampment of the British Army before Colenso and smiled; Chelmsford's little force would have been lost in the artillery and ordnance park, yet beyond that the tents stretched away for two miles. Row upon row of white canvas cones with the horse lines in between – and to the rear the orderly acres of transport vehicles, thousands of them, with the draught animals scattered grazing across the veld almost to the range of the eye.

It was an impressive sight not only in its immensity but also in its neat and businesslike layout; so was the military precision of the blocks of men at drill, the massed glitter of their bayonets as they turned and marched and countermarched.

When Sean wandered into the camp and read the

names of the regiments at the head of each row of tents he recognized them as the sound of glory. But the new khaki uniforms and pith helmets had reduced them all to a homogeneous mass. Only the cavalry retained a little of the magic in the pennants that fluttered gaily at their lance-tips. A squadron trotted past him and Sean eyed their mounts with envy. Great shiny beasts, as arrogant as the men upon their backs. Horse and rider given an air of inhuman cruelty by the slender bright-tipped lance they carried.

A dozen times Sean asked his question, 'Where can I find the Guides,' and though the answer was given in the dialects of Manchester and Lancashire, in the barely intelligible accents of Scotland and Ireland, each had a common factor – they were all singularly unhelpful.

Once he stopped to watch a group training with one of the new Maxim machine-guns. Clumsy, he decided, no match against a rifle. Later he would remember this judgement and feel a little foolish.

All morning he trudged through the camp, with Mbejane trailing him, and at noon he was tired and dusty and bad-tempered. The Natal Corps of Guides appeared to be a mythical unit. He stood on the edge of the camp and looked out across the open veld, pondering his next move in the search.

Half a mile out on the grassy plain a thin drift of blue smoke caught his eye. It issued from a line of bush that obviously marked the course of a stream. Whoever had picked that spot to camp certainly knew how to make himself comfortable in the veld. Compared to the bleak surroundings of the main encampment it would be para-dise; protected from the wind, close to firewood and water, well away from the attention of senior officers. That was his answer, Sean grinned and set out across the plain.

His guess was proved correct by the swarm of black servants among the trees. These could only be Colonial troops, each with a personal retainer. Also, the wagons were drawn up in the circular formation of the laager. With a feeling of homecoming Sean approached the first white man he saw.

In an enamel hipbath beneath the shade of a mimosa tree this gentleman sat, waist deep, while a servant added hot water from a large black kettle.

'Hello,' Sean greeted him. The man looked up from his book, removed the cheroot from his mouth and returned Sean's greeting.

'I'm looking for the Guides.'

'Your search is ended, my friend. Sit down.' Then to the servant, 'Bring the Nkosi a cup of coffee.'

Thankful, Sean sank into the *reimpje* chair near the bath and stretched his legs out before him. His host laid aside the book and began to lather his hairy chest and armpits while he studied Sean with frank appraisal.

'Who's in charge here?' Sean asked.

'You want to see him?'

'Yes.'

The bather opened his mouth and yelled.

'Hey! Tim!'

'What you want?' The reply came from the nearest wagon.

'Fellow here to see you.'

'What's *he* want?'

'Says he wants to talk to you about his daughter.'

There was a long silence while the man in the wagon digested this, then:

'What's he look like?'

'Big bloke, with a shotgun.'

'You're joking!'

'The hell I am! Says if you don't come out he's coming in to get you.'

The canvas of the wagon canopy was lifted cautiously and an eye showed behind the slit. The ferocious bellow that followed startled Sean to his feet. The canvas was thrown aside and out of the wagon vaulted the Commanding Officer of the Guides. He moved in on Sean with his arms held like a wrestler. For a moment Sean stared at him, then he answered the bellow and dropped into a defensive crouch.

'Yaah!' The man charged and Sean met him chest to chest, locking his arms around him as they closed.

'Tim Curtis, you miserable bastard,' he roared in laughter and in pain as Tim tried to pull his beard out by the roots.

'Sean Courtney, you evil son of a bitch,' breathless as the air was forced from his lungs by Sean's hug.

'Let's have a drink.' Sean punched him.

'Let's have a bottle.' Tim caught his ears and twisted.

At last they broke apart and stood laughing incoherently in the pleasure of meeting again.

The servant returned with Sean's coffee and Tim waved him away disgustedly. 'None of that slop! Get a bottle of brandy out of my chest.'

'You two know each other, I presume.' The man in the bath interrupted them.

'Know each other! Jesus, I worked five years for him!' snorted Tim. 'Digging his dirty gold out of the ground. Worst boss I ever had.'

'Well, now's your chance,' Sean grinned, 'because I've come to work for you.'

'You hear that, Saul? The idiot wants to join.'

'*Mazeltov.*' The bather dunked the tip of his cheroot in his bath water, flicked it away and stood up. He offered Sean a soapy hand.

72

'Welcome to the legion of the lost. My name's Saul Friedman. I gather yours is Sean Courtney. Now where's that bottle and we'll celebrate your arrival.'

The commotion had summoned the others from their wagons and Sean was introduced to each of them. It seemed the uniform of the Guides was a khaki tunic without insignia or badges of rank, slouch hats and riding breeches. There were ten of them. A tough-looking bunch and Sean found their company to his liking.

Naked except for a towel draped round his waist, Saul did duty as barman, then they all settled down in the shade to a bout of drinking. Tim Curtis entertained them for the first twenty minutes with a biographical and biological account of Sean's career, to which Saul contributed comments that were met with roars of laughter. It was obvious that Saul was the Company wit, a function which he performed with distinction. He was the youngest of them all, perhaps twenty-five years old, and physically the smallest. His body was thin and hairy, and in a pleasant sort of way he was extremely ugly. Sean liked him.

An hour later when the brandy had taken them to the stage of seriousness which precedes wild and undirected hilarity, Sean asked,

'Captain Curtis . . . '

'Lieutenant, and don't forget it,' Tim corrected him.

'Lieutenant, then. What is our job, and when do we do it?'

Tim scowled at his empty glass, then looked across at Saul. 'Tell him,' he instructed.

'As mentioned earlier, we are the legion of the lost. People look on us with pity and a mild embarrassment. They pass us by on the far side of the street, making the sign of the Cross and murmuring a spell to avert the evil eye. We live here in our own little leper colony.'

'Why?'

'Well, first of all, we belong to the most miserable little runt in the entire army of Natal. An officer, who, despite a formidable array of medals, would not inspire confidence in a young ladies' choir. He is chief liaison officer for the Colonial troops on the general staff. Lieutenant-Colonel Garrick Courtney, V.C., D.S.O.' Saul paused and his expression changed. 'No relation of yours, I trust?'

'No,' lied Sean without hesitation.

'Thank God,' Saul continued. 'Anyway, this is why people pity us. The embarrassment arises from the fact that nobody recognizes our official existence. Even the drawing of rations must be preceded by a comic opera dialogue between Tim and the Quartermaster. But because we are called "Guides" everybody expects us to get out there and start doing a bit of guiding. So in some weird fashion the failure of General Buller to advance even one hundred yards in three months is laid at our door.' Saul filled his glass. 'Anyway, we haven't run out of brandy yet.'

'You mean we don't do anything?' Sean asked incredulously.

'We eat, we sleep and we drink.'

'Occasionally we go visiting,' Tim added. 'Now is as good a time as any.'

'Who do we visit?'

'There is a most enterprising woman in the area, not five miles distant. She owns a travelling circus — forty wagons and forty girls. They follow along behind the main army to comfort and encourage it. Let's go and get some comfort and encouragement. If we start now we'll get to the head of the line — first come, first served.'

'I'll leave you to it,' Saul stood up and drifted away.

'He's a good kid,' Tim observed as he watched him leave.

'Is it against his religion?'

'No. But he's married and takes it seriously. How about you?'

'I'm not married.'

'Let's go them.'

Much later they rode home together in the moonlight, both pleasantly melancholy with love and liquor. The girl who had taken Sean to her wagon was a friendly lass with a pair of fat maternal bosoms.

'I like you, mister,' she had told him afterwards.

'I like you also,' he replied truthfully.

Although Sean experienced no more shame or guilt than after satisfying any of his other bodily needs, yet he knew that half an hour with a stranger in a wagon bed was a very poor substitute.

He began to hum the tune that Ruth had sung on the night of the storm.

12

Lieutenant-Colonel Garrick Courtney removed his uniform jacket and hung it carefully on the dumb-valet beside his desk. The way a houseproud wife straightens a picture on her wall, he touched the purple watered silk on which was suspended the heavy, bronze cross, until it hung to his satisfaction. His lips moving, he read the inscription again. 'For Valour', and smiled.

The champagne he had drunk during lunch made his brain feel like a great brilliant diamond set in his skull, sharp and hard and clear.

He sat down, swivelled the chair sideways to the desk and stretched his legs out in front of him.

'Send him in, Orderly!' he shouted, and dropped his eyes to his boots. You couldn't tell the difference, he decided. No one could tell by looking at them which one was flesh and bone beneath the polished leather – or which leg was carved wood with a cunningly articulated ankle.

'Sir.' The voice startled him and he pulled his legs in guiltily, hiding them beneath his chair.

'Curtis!' He looked up at the man who stood before his desk. Tim stood rigidly to attention, staring stolidly over Garry's head, and Garry let him stand. He felt satisfaction that this hulking bastard must use those two powerful legs to pay respect to Garrick Courtney. Let him stand. He waited, watching him, and at last Tim fidgeted slightly and cleared his throat.

'At ease!' There was no doubt now as to who held the

power. Garry picked up the paper-knife from his desk and turned it in his hands as he spoke.

'You're wondering why I sent for you.' He smiled expansively. 'Well, the reason is that I have a job for you at last. I lunched with General Buller today.' He paused to let that absorb. 'We discussed the Offensive. He wanted my views on certain plans he has in mind.' Garry caught himself. 'Anyway, that is beside the point. I want you and your men to reconnoitre the river on both sides of Colenso. See here.' Garry spread a map on the desk in front of him. 'There are fords marked here and here.' He jabbed at the map with the paper-knife. 'Find them and mark them well. Check the bridges – both the railway and the road bridge, make certain they are intact. Do it tonight. I want your full report in the morning. You can go.'

'Yes, sir.'

'Oh, Curtis –' Garry stopped him as he stooped in the entrance of the tent. 'Don't fail. Find those fords.' The canvas flap dropped closed behind the American, and Garry opened the drawer of his desk and took out a silver flask set with carnelians. He unscrewed it and sniffed the contents before he drank.

With the dawn, in bedraggled pairs the Guides dribbled into camp. Sean and Saul were the last to return. They dismounted, turned their horses over to the servants and joined the group around the fire.

'Yes?' Tim looked up from where he squatted with a mug of coffee cupped in his hands. His clothing was soaked and steam lifted off it as it dried in the heat from the flames. 'They've blown the rail bridge – but the road bridge is still intact.'

'You're sure?'

'We walked across.'

'That's something anyway,' grunted Tim, and Sean raised a sceptical eyebrow.

'You think so. Hasn't it occurred to you that they've left the bridge because that is where they *want* us to cross?'

No one replied and Sean went on wearily:

'When we checked the bridges, Saul and I did a bit of exploring on the far side. Just beyond the railway bridge there is a series of little kopjes. We crawled around the bottom of them.'

'And?'

'There are more Boers sitting on those kopjes than there are quills on a porcupine's back. Whoever tries to cross those bridges in daylight is going to get the Bejesus shot out of him.'

'Lovely thought!' growled Tim.

'Charming, isn't it? Further contemplation of it will make me puke. What did you find?'

'We found plenty of water.' Tim glanced down at his sodden clothing. 'Deep water.'

'No ford,' Sean anticipated gloomily.

'None. But we found a ferryboat on the bank with the bottom knocked out of it. That could be the excuse for marking a ford on the map.'

'So now you can go and tell our beloved Colonel the glad tidings.' Saul grinned. 'But one gets you five that it has no effect. My guess is that Buller will attack Colenso within the next two days. He might just be able to get a couple of thousand men across that bridge, then we'd have a chance.'

Tim regarded him balefully. 'And the Guides will be the first across. All very well for you. The Rabbi has reduced your target area considerably – but what about us?'

'But it's marked on the map,' protested Lieutenant-Colonel Garrick Courtney. His head was bowed so that Tim could see the pink scalp through the furrows the comb had left in his sandy-brown hair.

'I've seen dragons and sea monsters marked on maps, sir,' Tim answered, and Garry looked up at him coldly with pale blue eyes.

'You're not paid to be a comedian, Curtis.'

'I beg your pardon, sir,' and Garry frowned. Curtis could make the 'sir' sound like an insult.

'Who did you send?' he demanded.

'I went myself, sir.'

'You could have missed it in the dark.'

'If there is a ford there, it would have a road or at least a path leading down to it. I wouldn't have missed that, sir.'

'But in the darkness you could have been mistaken,' insisted Garry. 'You might have missed something that would be obvious in daylight.'

'Well, sir . . . '

'Good.' Briskly Garry went on. 'Now, the bridges. You say these are still intact.'

'Only the road bridge, but . . . '

'But what?'

'The men I sent report that the hills beyond the river are heavily defended. Almost as though the bridge has been preserved to bait a trap.'

'Curtis.' Deliberately Garry laid his paper-knife upon the map before him. His nose was too large for the space between his eyes and when he pursed his lips this way

79

he looked, Tim thought, like a bird – a sparrow, a little brown sparrow.

'Curtis,' Garry repeated softly. 'It seems to me you have very little enthusiasm for this business. I send you out to do a job and you come back with a long list of excuses. I don't think you realize how important this is.'

Chirp, chirp – little sparrow. Tim smiled secretly and Garry flushed.

'For instance. Who did you send to reconnoitre these bridges – reliable men, I hope?'

'They are, sir.'

'Who?'

'Friedman.'

'Oh! The little Jewish lawyer. A wise choice, Curtis, a commendably wise choice.' Garry sniffed and picked up the paper-knife.

My God! Curtis marvelled. *He's a Jew-baiter as well, this little sparrow has all the virtues.*

'Who else did you send?'

'A new recruit.'

'A new recruit? A new recruit!' Garry dropped the knife and lifted his hands in appeal.

'I happen to have worked for him before the war. I know him well, sir. He's a first-class man. I'd trust him before anyone else you could name. In fact, I was going to ask you to approve his promotion to sergeant.'

'And what is the name of this paragon?'

'Funnily enough it's the same as yours, sir. Although he tells me you're not related. His name is Courtney. Sean Courtney.'

Slowly, very slowly, the expression of Garry's face altered. It became smooth, neutral. Pale also, the lifeless, translucent paleness of a corpse's face. All life died in his eyes as well – they were looking inwards, back into the secret places of long ago. The dark places. They saw a small boy climbing a hill.

He was climbing up through thick bush, young legs strong beneath him. Climbing in deep shade, with the smell of leaf-mould and the soft murmur of insects, sweating in the heat of a Natal summer's morning, eyes straining ahead through the dense green foliage for a glimpse of the bush buck they were hunting, the dog leaning eagerly against the leash and the same eagerness pumping in his own chest.

The dog barked once, and immediately the brush and stir of a big body moving ahead of them, the click of a hoof against rock, then the rush of its run.

The shot, a blunt burst of sound, and the buck bleating wounded as it thrashed through the grass, and Sean's voice high and unbroken: 'I got him. I got him first shot! Garry. Garry! I got him, I got him!'

Into the sunlight, the dog dragging him. Sean wild with excitement, running down the slope towards him with the shotgun. Sean falling, the gun flung from his hands, the roar of the second shot and the blow that knocked Garry's leg out from under him.

Sitting now in the grass and staring at the leg. The little white splinters of bone in the pulped flesh and the blood pumping dark and strong and thick as custard.

'I didn't mean it . . . Oh God, Garry, I didn't mean it. I slipped. Honest, I slipped.'

Garry shuddered, a violent almost sensual spasm of his whole body, and the leg beneath the desk twitched in sympathy.

'Are you all right, sir?' There was an edge of concern on Tim's voice.

'I am perfectly well, thank you, Curtis.' Garry smoothed back the hair from his temples. There were

81

deep bays of baldness there and his hairline was frayed and irregular. 'Please continue.'

'Well, I was saying – it looks like a trap. They've left those bridges because . . . '

'It is your duty to collect information, Curtis. It is the duty of the general staff to evaluate it. I think that completes your report? Good, then you may leave.'

He must have a drink now, already his hand was on the handle of the drawer.

'Oh, Curtis.' His voice croaked with the terrible dryness in his throat, but he spoke on through it. 'That promotion you spoke of is approved. Make the man a sergeant.'

'Very well, sir.'

'Of course, in the event of a frontal assault on the bridges he will act as guide for the first attack.'

'Sir?'

'You see the need for it, don't you?' Tim had never heard this wheedling tone from him before. It was almost as though he wanted Tim's approval. As though he were trying to justify his decision. 'I mean, he knows the bridges. He's been over them. He's the one who knows them, isn't he?'

'Yes, sir.'

'And after all, he's a sergeant. I mean, we should send someone with rank – we can't just send anybody.'

'I could go, sir.'

'No. No. We'll need you at the ford.'

'As you wish.'

'You won't forget, will you? You *will* send him, won't you?' Almost pleading now.

'I'll send him,' agreed Tim and stooped out of the tent. Garry jerked open the drawer and his fingernails scrabbled on the rough wood in their haste to find the flask.

13

To General Sir Redvers Buller, V.C.,
Officer Commanding,
British Expeditionary Army of Natal

At Chievely

December 19th 1899

Sir,

I have the honour to report that in accordance with orders received a reconnaissance was carried out by officers and men of the Natal Corps of Guides on the night of December 18th. The results of which are set out below:

Ford marked 'A' on attached Map: Although the ford promises passage for a large body of men, it is difficult to locate in darkness and a night crossing is not recommended.

Bridge marked 'B' on attached Map: This is a road bridge of metal construction. At present it is undamaged, probably due to its sturdy construction resisting demolition by the enemy.

Bridge marked 'C' on attached Map: This is a railway bridge also constructed of metal, but has been demolished by the enemy.

General: Limited penetration of the area beyond the Tugela River by elements of the N.C.G. revealed the presence of the enemy on the hills marked 'D' and 'E'. However, no evidence of artillery or excessive force was noted.

Courtney G., Lieutenant-Colonel
Officer Commanding N.C.G.,
In the Field.

EXTRACTS FROM THE BATTLE ORDERS OF GENERAL SIR REDVERS BULLER V.C. MADE AND SIGNED ON THE NIGHT OF DECEMBER 19TH 1899.

'. . . The force commanded by Brigadier Lyttelton will advance on and capture the village of Colenso. Thereafter it will seize and cross the metal bridge, and drive the enemy from the kopjes on the far bank. (See attached Map.)'

14

They lay in the grass, side by side, and the dew had soaked through the backs of their tunics. The night was still and silent. No clouds above and the fat stars were very bright. Ahead of them the silver smear of the Milky Way threw the silhouette of the Tugela heights into bold relief, gave it an aspect of brooding menace.

Saul yawned loudly, and immediately Sean was forced to do the same. Though they had not slept that night, it was not the weariness – but the symptom of nerves wound tight at the prospect of going in against the Boer guns . . .

'Another hour and a half until dawn,' Saul whispered, and Sean grunted. There was no profit in counting the hours. At forty-seven minutes past six the sun would rise, and from behind them the British Army would move forward across the brown grass plain.

Once more Sean rose to his knees and swept the ground before them with his eyes, letting them move slowly along the bank of the Tugela, picking up the loom of the steel road bridge a hundred paces ahead of them, accounting for each bush on this bank, that they had not multiplied or moved. Then satisfied, he sank down again.

'My God, it's cold!' He could feel Saul shivering beside him.

'It will warm up quite soon.' Sean grinned in the darkness as he answered. The clear night sky had allowed yesterday's warmth to escape, the grass and their clothing were wet, even the steel of the rifles was painfully cold to touch – but Sean had long ago learned to ignore physical discomfort. He could, when necessary, lie completely motionless while tsetse flies settled on his neck and sank their red-hot needles into the soft skin behind his ears. Nevertheless, it was a relief when the false dawn showed and it was time to move.

'I'll go in now,' he whispered.

'Good luck – I'll have breakfast ready when you come back.'

This was a job for one man. A job that Sean did not relish. They had made certain that there were no enemy on this side of the river, now at the last minute when it was too late for the Boers to alter their dispositions – someone had to cross and find out in what strength they were holding the bridge. A couple of Boer Maxims sited to command the bridge at short range, or even demolition charges set ready to blow, would mean that the chances of success instead of being slim would be nonexistent.

Sean slung his rifle across his back and began crawling forward through the grass. Twice he stopped to listen briefly, but there was little time – true dawn in an hour. He reached the bridge and lay in its heavy shadow, staring across at the far bank. Nothing moved. In the starlight the kopjes loomed like the backs of dark whales in the grassy sea. He waited five minutes – long enough for a restless sentry to fidget – still nothing.

'Here we go,' he whispered aloud, and suddenly he was afraid. For an instant he did not recognize the sensation, for he had experienced it only three or four times in his life, but never with so little cause. He crouched beside the steel girders of the bridge, with the weakness in his legs and his belly full of the oiliness. It was only when he caught the taste of it at the back of his throat, a taste a little like that of fish oil mixed with the efflu-ence of something long dead, that he knew what it was.

I'm afraid. His first reaction was of surprise, which changed quickly to alarm.

This was how it happened. He knew it happened to other men. He had heard them talk of it around the camp fires, remembered the words and the pity under-lying them.

'Ja, his gunboy led him back to camp. He was shaking like a man with fever, and he was crying. I thought he was hurt. "Daniel," I said, "Daniel, what is wrong?"

"'It broke," he said with the tears running into his beard. "It broke there in my head, I heard it break. I threw the gun away and I ran."

"'Did he charge, Daniel?" I asked.

"'No, man. I didn't even see him, just heard him feeding close by in the catbush. Then it broke in my head and I was running."

'He was no coward. I had hunted with him many times, seen him kill an elephant from a charge so that it fell close enough to touch with the gun-barrel. He was good, but he had lived too close to it. Then suddenly it broke in his head. He hasn't hunted again.'

I have accumulated fear the way an old ship collects barnacles and weed below the water-line, now it is ready to break in me also – Sean knew. Knew also that if he ran now, as the old hunter had run, he would never hunt again.

Crouching in the darkness, sweating in the cold of dawn with the iciness of his fear, Sean wanted to vomit. He was physically sick, breathing heavily through his open mouth, the warm oiliness in his belly coming close to venting itself, so weak with it that his legs began to tremble and he caught at one of the iron girders of the bridge for support.

A minute that seemed like all eternity, he stood like that. Then he began to fight it, bearing down on it, stiffening his legs and forcing them to move forward. Consciously he checked the relaxation of his sphincter muscle – that close he had come to the ultimate degradation.

He knew then that the old joke about cowards was true. And that it applied to him also.

He went up on to the bridge, picking up each foot deliberately, swinging it forward, laying it down and moving the weight of his body over it. His breathing was deliberate, each breath taken and expelled at the command of his brain. He couldn't trust his body now to perform even the simplest task – not after it had betrayed him so monstrously.

Had they been waiting at the bridge, the Boers would have killed him that morning. Without caution he paced slowly down the centre of it, big and heavily moving in the starlight and his footsteps rang on the metal.

Under his feet the metal gave way to gravel. He was across. He kept walking, down the middle of the road, following the gentle curve towards the dark hills.

He walked on with his terror and the sound of it roared in his head like the sound of the sea. The sling of his rifle slipped from his shoulder and the weapon clattered into the road. He stood for a full minute before he could gather himself to stoop and pick it up. Then he turned and went back. Pacing slowly, counting his footsteps, measuring them out – one each second – timing them carefully to prevent himself from running. Because if he ran he knew it was finished. He too would never hunt again.

'You all right?' Saul was waiting.

'Yes.' Sean sank down beside him.

'See anything?'

88

'No.'

Saul was staring at him. 'Are you sure you're all right?'

Sean sighed. Once before he had been afraid. Fear had come to him in a caved-in mineshaft, later he had gone back and left his fear in the same mineshaft, and had walked away from it alone. In the same way he had hoped to leave it now beyond the river, but this time it had followed him back. With a certainty he knew that it would never leave him from now onwards. It would always be near.

I will have to tame it, he thought. I will have to break it to the halter and the curb.

'Yes, I'm all right,' he answered Saul. 'What's the time?'

'Half-past five.'

'I'll send Mbejane back now.'

Sean stood up and went to where Mbejane waited with their horses. He handed Mbejane the small square of green cloth which was the prearranged signal that neither the bridge nor the town was defended in force. The red square he replaced in his breastpocket.

'I will come back,' Mbejane told him.

'No.' Sean shook his head. 'There is nothing for you here.'

Mbejane untied the horses. 'Stay in peace.'

'Go in peace.' Sean was thankful that Mbejane would not be there as witness, should he break under his new-found fear.

But I must not break, he decided grimly. Today will be the test. If I can last out this day, then perhaps I will have tamed it.

He went back to where Saul waited in the darkness, and together they lay and watched the dawn come on.

15

The darkness drew back, each minute enlarging the circle of their vision. Now the upper works of the bridge stood out, a neat geometrical pattern against the dark bulk of the heights. Then he could see the patterns of dark bush against pale grass and rock.

The new light distorted distance, made the high ground seem remote and no longer hostile. A flight of egrets flew in long formation above the course of the river, high enough to catch the sun so that they were birds of bright, glowing gold in a world of shadow. And the dawn brought with it a small cold wind whose voice in the grass blended with the murmur of the river.

Then the sun hit the heights as though to bless the army of the Republic. The mist in the gullies writhed in agony at its warmth, lifted into the wind and smeared away.

The rim of the sun pushed up over the edge of the land, and the day came bright and clean with dew.

Through his glasses Sean studied the crest of the high ground. At a hundred paces there were traces of smoke as the Boer Army brewed coffee.

'You think they'll spot us?' asked Saul.

Sean shook his head without lowering his glasses. Two small bushes and the thin screen of grass they had constructed during the night hid them effectively.

'Are you sure you are all right?' Saul asked once more. From the set of his face Sean seemed to be in pain.

'Stomach gripes,' Sean grunted. Let it start soon, please let it start. The waiting is the worst.

Then the ground trembled under his chest, the faintest vibration, and Sean felt relief flood through him. 'Here come the guns,' he said, and using the cover of one of the bushes, he stood up and looked behind him.

In a single column, following each other at strictly spaced intervals, the guns were moving into action. They were coming in fast, still tiny with distance but growing as the gunners astride the lead horses of each team urged them on. Closer now so that Sean could see the whip arms rising and falling, he heard the rumble and rattle of the carriages and faintly the shouts of the outriders.

Sixteen guns, one hundred and fifty horses to drag them, and a hundred men to serve them. But in the vastness of the great plain before Colenso the column seemed small and insignificant. Sean looked beyond them and saw the foot soldiers following them, line upon line, like the poles of a fence, thousands of them creeping forward across the plain. Sean felt the old wild elation begin. He knew the army was centred upon the line of markers which he and Saul had laid early the previous night, and that the two of them would be the first across the bridge – the first of all those thousands.

But it was elation of a different quality to anything he had experienced before. It was sharper and more poignant, seasoned by the red pepper of his fear. So that for the first time in his life Sean learned that fear can be a pleasurable sensation.

He watched the patterns of men and guns evolve upon the brown gaming-table – counters thrown down at chance, to be won or irretrievably lost at the fall of the dice of war. Knowing also that he was one of the counters, afraid and strangely jubilant in this knowledge.

The guns were close now. He could make sense of the shouting, see the features of the men and even recognize his own feelings in their faces.

Close, perhaps too close. Uneasily Sean glanced back at the forbidding heights beyond the river and gauged the range. Two thousand yards perhaps, long rifle shot. And still the guns came on.

'Jesus Christ! Are they mad?' Sean asked aloud.

'They must engage now.' Saul also saw the danger. 'They can't come closer.'

And still the guns came on. The sound of their charge was low thunder; dust from the dew-damp earth rose reluctantly behind them; horses with wide mouths throwing froth as they drove against the traces.

'They're in range now. They must stop, they must!' groaned Sean.

Then at last the column splayed open, alternate guns wheeling left and right still at full gallop. Swinging broadside to the waiting Boer rifles.

'My God! My God!' Sean mouthed the blasphemy in agony as he watched. 'They'll be massacred.'

Gunners rising in the stirrups, leaning back to check the carriages. The Gun-Captains jumping from their mounts, letting them gallop free as they ran to begin the unhitching and the pointing.

In this helpless moment while men swarmed over the guns, manhandling them to train upon the heights; while the horses still reared and whinnied in hysterical excitement; before the shells could be unloaded and stacked beside their pieces – in that moment the Boer rifles opened together. It was a sound that lacked violence, strangely unwarlike, muted by distance to the popping of a hundred strings of fireworks, and at first there was no effect. The grass was thick enough to hide the strike of the bullets, the dust too lazy with dew to jump and mark their fall.

Then a horse was hit and fell kicking, dragging its mate on to its knees also. Two men ran to cut it loose, but one of them never reached it. He sat down suddenly in the grass with his head bowed. Two more horses dropped, another reared and pawed wildly at the air with one front leg flapping loosely where a bullet had broken the bone above the knee.

'Get out!' roared Sean. 'Pull back while there's still time,' but his voice did not carry to the gun crews, could not carry above the shouting and the screaming of wounded horses.

There was a new sound now which Sean could not identify, a sound like hail on a tin roof, isolated at first then more frequent until it was a hundred hammers clanging together in broken rhythm – and he knew it was the sound of bullets striking the metal of the guns.

He saw:

A gunner fall forward and jam the breech of the piece until he was dragged clear;

A loader drop the shell he was carrying and stumble on with his legs folding until he subsided and lay still;

One of the horses break loose and gallop away across the plain dragging a tangle of torn traces behind it;

A covey of wild pheasant rise together out of the grass near the batteries and curve away along the river before dropping on stiff wings back into cover;

And behind the guns the infantry in neat lines advancing placidly towards the huddle of deserted cottages that was Colenso.

Then, with a crash that made the earth jump, and with sixteen long spurts of blue smoke, the guns came into action.

Sean focused his glasses on the ridge in time to see

the first shells burst along the crest. The evil blossoms of greenish-yellow lyddite fumes bloomed quickly in the sunlight, then drifted oily-thick on the wind.

Again the guns crashed, and again – each salvo more ragged than the last until it became a continuous stuttering, hammering roar. Until the stark outline of the ridge was blurred and indefinite in the dust and lyddite fumes. There was smoke also, a fine greyish mist of it banked along the heights – the smoke of thousands of rifles.

Quickly Sean set the rear sight of his Lee-Metford at a thousand yards, wriggled forward on his elbows, hunched down over his rifle and began shooting blindly into the smoke on the heights. Beside him Saul was firing also.

Twice Sean emptied his magazine before looking back at the guns. The tempo of their fire had slackened. Most of the horses were down in the grass. Dead men were draped across the gun carriages, others badly wounded crouched for cover behind the mountings, and where six men had served each piece before, now four or only three carried shell and loaded and fired.

'The fools, the bloody fools,' Sean whispered, and began to shoot again, concentrating his whole attention on the routine of jerking the bolt back, sliding it forward in the same motion, sighting up into the mist of gun smoke, and firing. He did not count the shots and each time the weapon clicked empty he groped for another clip from his bandolier and re-loaded. He was starting to sweat now, could feel it trickling down his armpits, his ears buzzed from the concussion of the rifle and his shoulder was beginning to throb.

Gradually a sense of unreality induced by the clamour of the guns and the smell of burnt powder came over him. It seemed that all he would ever do was lie and shoot at nothing, shoot at smoke. Then reality faded further so that all of existence was the vee and dot of a rifle sight, standing solid in mist. And the mist had no shape. In his ears was the vast buzzing silence that drowned all the other sounds of battle. He was alone and tranquil, heavy and dulled by the hypnotic drift of smoke and the repetitive act of loading and firing.

Abruptly the mood was broken. Over them passed a rustle like giant wings, then a crack as though Satan had slammed the door of hell. Startled he looked up and saw a ball of shimmering white smoke standing in the air above the guns, spinning and spreading, growing in the sky like a flower.

'What the . . .'

'Shrapnel,' grunted Saul. 'Now they're finished.'

Then crack and crack again as the Boer Nordenfeldts planted their cotton flowers of smoke above the plain, flailing the guns and the men who still worked them with a buzzing hissing storm of steel.

Then there were voices. Confused and dazed by the gunfire, it took Sean a minute to place them. He had forgotten the infantry.

'Close up there.'

'Close up on the right. Keep the line!'

'Don't run. Steady, men. Don't run.'

Long lines of men, lines that bulged and lagged and straightened again at the urging of their officers. Evenly spaced, plodding quietly with their rifles held across their chests, they passed the guns. Behind them they left khaki bundles lying on the plain, some of the bundles lay still but others writhed and screamed. As the gaps appeared in the lines they were quickly filled at the chant of 'Close up. Close up there on the flank.'

'They are heading for the railway bridge.' Sean felt the first premonition of disaster. 'Don't they know that it's been destroyed?'

'We'll have to stop them.' Saul scrambled to his feet beside Sean.

'Why didn't the fools follow our markers?' Angrily Sean shouted the question that had no answer. He did it to gain time, to postpone the moment when he must leave the flimsy cover of the grass shelter and go out into the open where the shrapnel and the Mausers swept the ground. Sean's fear came back on him strongly. He didn't want to go out there.

'Come on, Sean. We must stop them.' And Saul started to run. He looked like a skinny little monkey, capering out towards the advancing waves of foot soldiers. Sean sucked in his breath and held it a moment before he followed.

Twenty yards ahead of the leading rank of infantry, carrying a naked sword in one hand and stepping out briskly on long legs, came an officer.

'Hey, you!' Sean shouted at him, waving his hat to catch his attention. He succeeded. The officer fixed him with bright blue eyes like a pair of bayonets and the waxed points of his grey moustache twitched. He strode on towards Sean and Paul.

'You're heading for the wrong bridge,' Sean yelled at him, his voice high-pitched with agitation. 'They've blown the rail bridge, you'll never get across there.'

The officer reached them and checked his stride.

'And who the hell are you, if it's not a rude question?'

'We're the ground scouts . . . ' Sean started, then leapt in the air as a Mauser bullet flicked into the ground between his legs. 'And put that bloody sword away – you'll have every Boer on the Tugela competing for you.'

The officer, a colonel by the crowns on his shoulders, frowned at Sean.

'The correct form of address, Sergeant . . . '

'The hell with that!' Sean roared at him. 'Swing your

advance on to the road bridge.' He pointed with agitation at the metal superstructure of the bridge that showed on the left through the thorn trees. 'If you continue as you're going they'll cut you to pieces.'

A moment longer the Colonel fixed Sean with his bayonet eyes, then he lifted a silver whistle to his lips and blew a piercing blast.

'Take cover,' he shouted. 'Take cover!'

And immediately the first rank dropped into the grass. Behind them the other ranks lost their rigidity, as men hesitated.

'Get into the town,' a voice shouted. 'Take cover in the buildings.' And they broke and ran, a thousand men, jostling each other, racing for the security of the cottages of Colenso. Pouring into the single street, diving into doorways and windows. Within thirty seconds they had all gone to ground.

'Now, what's this all about?' demanded the Colonel, turning back to Sean. Impatiently Sean repeated himself, standing out in the open and uncomfortably aware that for absence of other targets the Boers were beginning to take a very active interest in them.

'Are you sure?'

'Dammit! Of course, I'm sure. The bridge is destroyed and they have torn up all the barbed wire fences and thrown them into the river. You'll never get across there.'

'Come along.' The Colonel set off towards the nearest cottage and Sean walked beside him. Afterwards he was never certain how he had managed to cover that hundred yards without running.

'For God's sake, put that sword away,' he growled at the Colonel as they walked with the flit, spang, flit, spang of bullets around them.

'Nervous, Sergeant?' And for the first time the Colonel grinned.

'You're damn right, I am.'

'So am I. But it would never do to let the men see that, would it?' He steadied the scabbard on his hips and ran the sword back into it. 'What's your name, Sergeant?'

'Sean Courtney, Natal Corps of Guides. What's yours?' Sean ducked instinctively as a bullet cracked past his head, and the Colonel smiled again at the familiarity.

'Acheson. John Acheson. 2nd Battalion, Scots Fusiliers.'

And they reached the cottage. No longer able to restrain himself, Sean dived thankfully through the kitchen door and found Saul already there. He handed Sean a cheroot and held a match for him.

'These crazy Souties!' he observed. 'And you're as bad as he is – strolling around in the middle of a battle.'

'Right, Courtney.' Acheson followed him into the kitchen. 'Let's go over the situation.'

He listened quietly while Sean explained in detail. He had to shout to lift his voice above the whistle and crack of the Boer artillery and the roar of a thousand Lee-Metford rifles as they replied from the windows and doorways of the village. Around them the kitchen was being used as a dressing-station and the moan and whimper of wounded men added to the hubbub of battle.

When Sean had finished Acheson turned away and strode to the window. He looked out across the railway tracks, to where the guns stood. They were drawn up in precise parade-ground formation. But now they were silent. Dribbling back towards the shelter of a deep donga – or gully – in the rear, the surviving gunners dragged their wounded with them.

'The poor bastards,' Sean whispered, as he saw one of the retreating gunners killed, shot in the head so that his helmet was thrown spinning upwards in a brief pink cloud of blood.

The sight seemed to rouse Acheson also.

'All right,' he said. 'We'll advance on the road bridge. Come on, Courtney.'

Behind him someone cried out, and Sean heard him fall. But he did not look round. He watched the bridge ahead of him. Although his legs moved mechanically under him it seemed to come no nearer. The thorn trees were thicker here beside the river and they gave a little cover from the merciless marksmen on the far bank. Yet men were falling steadily, and the shrapnel raged and cracked above them.

'Let's get across. Get the best seats on the other side,' Saul shouted beside him.

'Come on, then,' agreed Sean and they ran together. They were first on to the bridge, with Acheson just behind them. Bullets left bright scars on the grey painted metal, and then suddenly, miraculously, they were across. They had crossed the Tugela.

A drainage ditch beside the road and they dived into it, both of them panting. Sean looked back. Over the bridge poured a mass of khaki, all semblance of order gone as they crowded into the bottleneck and the fire from the Boers churned into them.

Once across, the leaders fanned out along the river, crouching below the dip in the bank, while behind them the slaughter on the bridge continued. A struggling mass of cursing, running, angry, frightened and dying men.

'It's a bloody abattoir.' Sean was appalled as he watched it. Dead and wounded men were falling over the low guard rail, splashing into the brown waters of the Tugela to sink or strike out clumsily for the banks.

But a steady stream of men was coming across and going to ground in the two-deep drainage ditches, and beneath the angle of the river bank.

It was clear to Sean that the attack was losing its impetus. As the men jumped down into the ditches he saw in their faces and in the way they flattened themselves into shelter that they had lost all stomach for the attack. The ordeal of the bridge had destroyed the discipline that had held their steady advance into those neatly controlled ranks. Officers and men were inextricably mixed into a tired and badly frightened rabble. There was no contact between the different groups in the drainage trenches and those lying in the lee of the river banks – and already there was little cover for the men who were still coming across. The fire from the Boer positions never faltered, and now the bridge was blocked with the bodies of the fallen, so that each new wave had to climb over them, stepping on dead and wounded alike, while the storm of Boer rifle-fire lashed them like wind-driven rain.

Rivulets of fresh bright blood dribbled down the supports of the bridge in ghastly contrast to the grey paint, and the surface of the river was stained by a chocolate-brown cloud of it spreading slowly downstream. Here and there a desperate rallying voice was lifted in the hubbub of incoherent shouts and groans.

'Here the 21st. Form on me the 21st.'

'Independent fire. On the heights. Ten rounds rapid.'

'Stretcher-bearer!'

'Bill. Where are you, Bill?'

'Jesus Christ! Jesus sobbing Christ!'

'Up, you men! Get up!'

'Come on the 21st. Fix bayonets.'

Some of them were head and shoulders out of the ditch returning the Boer fire, a few were drinking from their water-bottles already. A sergeant struggled with a jammed rifle and swore softly without looking up, while beside him a man sat with his back against the wall of the ditch, his legs sprawled open, and watched while the blood pumped from the wound in his belly.

Sean stood and felt the wind of a bullet slap against his cheek, while low in his stomach the slimy reptile of fear coiled itself tighter. Then he scrambled up the side of the ditch.

'Come on!' he roared and started running towards the hills. It was open here, like a meadow, and ahead of him an old barbed-wire fence sagged on rotten poles. He reached it, lifted his foot and kicked with his heel. The fence pole snapped level with the ground, the wire collapsed. He jumped over it.

'They're not coming,' Saul shouted beside him, and Sean stopped. The two of them were alone in the middle of the field – and the Boer rifles were seeking them eagerly.

'Run, Saul!' Sean shouted and snatched off his hat. 'Come on, you bastards.' He waved at the men behind him.

A bullet missed him so narrowly that he staggered in the wind of its passage.

'This way! Follow us! Come on!' Saul had not left him. He was dancing with excitement, and flapping his arms.

'Come back.' Acheson's voice floated across to them. He stood in the drainage ditch, showing clear from the waist up. 'Come back, Courtney!'

The attack was finished. Sean knew it in that instant, and saw the wisdom of Acheson's decision. Further advance over the open meadowland below the heights was suicide. The resolve that had carried him this far collapsed, and his terror snapped the leash he had held upon it. He ran back blindly, sobbing, leaning forward, his elbows pumping in time to his fear-driven feet.

Then suddenly Saul was hit beside him. It took him in the head, threw him forward, his rifle spinning from his hands, squawking hoarsely with pain and surprise as he went down skidding on his belly. And Sean ran on.

'Sean!' Saul's voice left behind him.

'Sean!' A cry of dreadful need, and Sean closed his mind against it and ran on towards the safety of the ditch.

'Sean. Please!' and he checked and stood uncertain with the Mausers barking above and the bullets clipping the grass around him.

Leave him, shrieked Sean's terror. *Leave him. Run! Run!*

Saul crawled towards him, blood on his face and his eyes fastened on Sean's face.

'Sean!'

Leave him. Leave him.

But there was hope in that pitiful blood-smeared face, and the fingers of Saul's hands clawed among the coarse grass roots as he dragged himself forward.

It was beyond all reason. But Sean went back to him.

Beneath the spurs of his terror Sean found the strength to lift him and run with him.

Hating him as he had never hated before, Sean blundered towards the drainage ditch carrying Saul. The acceleration of his brain slowed down the passage of time so that he seemed to run for ever.

'Damn you!' he mouthed at Saul, hating him.

'Damn you to hell!' The words came easily from his mouth, an inarticulate expression of his terror.

Then the ground gave way beneath his feet and he fell. Together they dropped into the drainage ditch and

Sean rolled away from him. He lay on his stomach and pressed his face into the earth and shook as a man shakes in high fever.

Slowly he came back from that far place where fear had driven him, and he lifted his head.

Saul sat against the bank of the ditch. His face was streaked with a mixture of blood and dirt.

'How are we doing?' Sean croaked and Saul looked at him dully. It was bright and very hot here in the sun. Sean unscrewed the stopper of his water-bottle and held it to Saul's lips. Saul swallowed painfully and water spilled from the corner of his mouth down his chin and on to his tunic.

Then Sean drank and finished panting with pleasure.

'Let's have a look at your head.'

He lifted Saul's hat from his head, and the blood that had accumulated around the sweat band poured in a fresh flood down Saul's neck. Parting the sodden black hair Sean found the groove in the flesh of his scalp.

'Grazed you,' he grunted and groped for the field dressing in the pocket of Saul's tunic. While he bound an untidy turban round Saul's head he noticed that a strange stillness had fallen on the field, a stillness accentuated rather than broken by the murmur of voices from the men around him and the occasional report of a rifle from the heights above.

The battle was over. At least we got across the river, he thought bitterly. The only problem that now remains is getting back again.

'How's that feel?' He had wet his handkerchief and wiped some of the blood and dust from Saul's face.

'Thank you, Sean.' Suddenly Sean realized that Saul's eyes were full of tears and it embarrassed him. He looked away from them.

'Thank you for . . . for coming back to get me.'

'Forget it.'

'I'll never forget it. Never as long as I live.'

'You'd have done the same.'

'No, I don't think so. I wouldn't have been able to. I was so scared, so afraid, Sean. You'd never know. You'll never know what it's like to be that afraid.'

'Forget it, Saul. Leave it alone.'

'I've got to tell you. I owe it to you – from now on I owe you . . . If you hadn't come back I'd be . . . I'd still be out there. I owe you.'

'Shut up, damn you!' He saw that Saul's eyes were different, the pupils had shrunk to tiny black specks and he was shaking his head in a meaningless idiotic fashion. The bullet had concussed him. But this could not prevent Sean's anger. 'Shut up,' he snarled. 'You think I don't know about fear. I was so scared out there – I hated you. Do you hear that? I hated you!'

And then Sean's voice softened. He had to explain to Saul and himself. He had to tell him about it, to justify it and place it securely in the scheme of things.

Suddenly he felt very old and wise. In his hands he held the key to the whole mystery of life. It was all so clear, for the first time he understood and he could explain it.

They sat close together in the sun, isolated from the men around them, and Sean's voice sank to an urgent whisper as he tried to make Saul understand, tried to pass on to him this knowledge that embraced all truth.

Beside them lay a corporal of the Fusiliers. He lay on his back, dead, and the flies swarmed over his eyes and laid their eggs. They looked like tiny grains of rice clustered in the lashes around his dead open eyes.

Saul leaned heavily against Sean's shoulder, now and then he shook his head in confusion as he listened to Sean. Listened to Sean's voice tripping and stumbling then starting to hurry as his ideas broke up and crumpled, heard the desperation in it as Sean strove to retain just a few grains of all that knowledge which had been his a few moment before. Heard it peter out into silence and sorrow as he found that it was gone.

'I don't know,' Sean admitted at last.

Then Saul spoke, his voice was dull and his eyes would not focus properly as he peered at Sean from beneath the blood-soiled turban of bandages.

'Ruth,' he said. 'You speak like Ruth does. Sometimes in the night when she cannot sleep she tries to tell me. Almost I understand, almost she finds it and then she stops. "I don't know," she says at last. "I just don't know."'

Sean jerked away from him, and stared into his face. 'Ruth?' he asked quietly.

'Ruth – my wife. You'd like her, Sean – she'd like you. So brave – she came to me through the Boer lines. All the way from Pretoria – riding alone. She came to me. I couldn't believe it. All that way. She just walked into camp one day and said, "Hello, Saul. I'm here!" just like that! You'll like her when you meet her, Sean. She's so beautiful, so serene ... '

In October when the big winds blow they come for the first time on a still day. It has been hot and dry for perhaps a month, then you hear them from far away, roaring softly. The roar mounts quickly, the dust races brown on the wind and the trees lean away from it, threshing and churning their branches. You see it coming but all your preparations are nothing when it hits. The vast roaring and the dust envelope you and you are numbed and blinded by the violence of it.

In the same way Sean saw it coming, he recognized it as the murderous rage which before had nearly killed a man, but still he could not prepare himself. And then it was upon him and the roaring filled his head and narrowed his vision so that all he could see was the face of Saul Friedman. The face was in profile for Saul was staring back across the plain of Colenso towards the English lines.

Sean lifted the dead corporal's rifle and laid it across his lap. With his thumb he slipped off the safety-catch, but Saul did not notice the movement.

'She's in Pietermaritzburg, I had a letter from her last week,' he murmured, and Sean shifted the rifle in his lap so that the muzzle aimed into the side of Saul's chest below the armpit.

'I sent her down to Pietermaritzburg. She's staying with her uncle there.' Saul lifted his hand and touched his head. Sean curled his finger on the trigger. 'I wish you could meet her, Sean. She'd like you.' Now he looked into Sean's face, and there was such pathetic trust in his eyes. 'When I write I am going to tell her about today – about what you did.'

Sean took up the slack in the trigger until he could feel the final resistance.

'We both owe you –' Saul stopped and smiled shyly. 'I just want you to know that I'll never forget it.'

Kill him, roared Sean's head. Kill him now – kill him quickly. Don't let him talk.

It was the first conscious command his instinct had issued.

Now! Do it now! But his trigger-finger relaxed.

This is all that stands between you and Ruth. Do it, do it now. The roaring in his head abated. The big wind had passed by and he could hear it receding. He lifted the rifle and slowly pushed the safety-catch across.

In the stillness after the wind he knew suddenly that from now on Saul Friedman was his special charge. Because he had come so close to taking it from him, Saul's life had become a debt of honour.

He laid the rifle aside and closed his eyes wearily.

'We'd better think about getting out of here,' he said quietly. 'Otherwise I might never get around to meeting this beauty of yours.'

16

'Hart has got himself into a mess out there!' General Sir Redvers Buller's voice matched the pompous jut of his belly and he leaned back against the weight of the telescope he held to his eye. 'What do you think, Courtney?'

'Well, he certainly hasn't reached the drift, sir. It looks to me as though he's been pinned down in the loop of the river,' Garry agreed.

'Damn the man! My orders were clear,' growled Buller. 'What can you make of the guns – can you see anything there?'

Every telescope in the party of officers swivelled back to the centre, to where the corrugated iron roofs of Colenso showed above the thorn trees, dimly through the dust and the smoke.

'I can't . . .' Garry started, then jumped uncontrollably as the naval 4·7 bellowed from its emplacement beside them. Every time that morning it had fired, Garry had jumped. *If only I knew when it was going to*, he thought and jumped again as it bellowed.

'They are not being served,' one of the other staff officers interposed and Garry envied him his composure and his calmness of voice. His own hands were trembling so that he must grip hard with both hands to keep his binoculars focused on the town. Each time the naval gun fired the dust of its recoil drifted over them, also the sun was fierce and he was thirsty. He thought of the flask in his saddle-bags and the next bellow of the gun caught him completely off guard. This time both his feet left the ground.

'. . . Do you agree, Courtney?' Buller's voice, he had not heard the beginning of the question.

'I do indeed, sir.'

'Good.' The General turned to his A.D.C. 'Send a rider to Hart. Tell him to pull out of there before he gets badly mauled. Quick as you can, Clery.'

At that moment Garry made a remarkable discovery. Behind the inscrutable mask of his face with its magnificent silver moustache, behind the bulging expressionless eyes – General Sir Redvers Buller was every bit as agitated and uncertain as was Garry Courtney. His continual appeals to Garry for support confirmed this. Of course, Garry did not consider that another reason why Buller addressed his appeals to him, rather than the regular officers of his staff, was because this was the one quarter from which Buller could rely on unquestioning support.

'That takes care of the left flank.' Buller was clearly relieved at his decision as he searched out towards the right, fixing the low round bulk of Hlangwane Kopje in the field of his telescope. 'Dundonald seems to be keeping his end up.' Earlier, there had been desultory rifle and pompom fire from the right flank. Now it was silent.

'But the centre . . . ' As though he had been delaying the moment, Buller at last turned his attention on the holocaust of dust and flame and shrapnel that enveloped Colenso.

'Come along.' He snapped his telescope closed. 'We'd better have a closer look at what they've accomplished there.' And he led his staff back to the horses. Careful that no one should usurp his place at the General's right hand, Garry limped along beside him.

At the headquarters of Lyttelton's Brigade, established

in a deep donga half a mile before the first scattered buildings of the town, it took Buller half a minute to find out what had been accomplished. It appalled him.

'We hold the town, sir. And three companies have advanced to the road bridge and seized it. But we cannot hope to hold it. I have sent a runner ordering them to withdraw on the town.'

'But why aren't the guns firing? What's happened to Colonel Long?'

'The guns have been silenced. Long is badly wounded.'

While Buller sat his horse, slowly absorbing this, a sergeant of the Transvaal Staats Artillerie jerked the lanyard of his quick-firing Nordenfeldt and fired the shell which changed a British reverse into a resounding defeat that would echo around the world.

From out of the broken and rocky complex of hills on the north bank the shell arched upwards; over the river with its surface churned to brown by shrapnel and short shell and blood; high over the deserted guns manned only by corpses; shrieking over the heads of the surviving gunners as they crouched in the rear with their wounded, forcing them to duck as they had ducked a thousand times before; plunging in its descent over the town of Colenso where weary men waited; down across thorn tree and mimosa and brown grass veld littered with dead men; falling at last in a tall jump of dust and smoke in the midst of General Buller's staff.

Beneath him Garry's horse dropped, killed instantly, pinning his leg so that had it been flesh and bone, not carved oak, it would have been crushed. He felt the blood soaking through his tunic and splattered in his face and mouth.

'I've been hit. Help me, God help me, I'm wounded.' And he writhed and struggled in the grass, wiping the blood on his face.

Rough hands freed his leg and dragged him clear of his horse.

'Not your blood. You're all right. Not your blood, it's his.'

On his hands and knees Garry stared in horror at the Surgeon-Major who had stood beside him and who had shielded him from the blast. Shrapnel had cut his head away, and the blood still spouted from his neck as though it were a severed hose.

Around him men fought their panic-stricken horses as they reared and whinnied. Buller was doubled up in the saddle, clutching the side of his chest.

'Sir, sir. Are you all right?' An A.D.C. had the reins and was bringing Buller's horse under control. Two officers ran to Buller and helped him down. He stood between them, his face contorted with pain, and his voice when he spoke was shaky, but hoarse.

'Disengage, Lyttelton! Disengage on your whole front!'

'Sir,' protested the Brigadier. 'We hold the town. Let me cover the guns until nightfall when we can retrieve them at our . . . '

'Damn you, Lyttelton. You heard me. Pull your brigade back immediately. The attack has failed.' Buller's breathing wheezed in his throat and he still clutched the side of his chest with both hands.

'To withdraw now will mean accepting heavier losses than we have suffered already. The enemy artillery is accurately ranged . . . '

'Pull them out, do you hear me!' Buller's voice rose to a shout.

'The guns . . . ' Lyttelton tried again, but Buller had already turned to his A.D.C.

'Send riders to Lord Dundonald's Brigade. He must retire immediately. I give him no latitude of discretion, he is to disengage his force at once and withdraw. Tell him . . . tell him the attack has failed on left and centre, tell him the guns are lost and he is in danger of being surrounded. Go. Ride fast.'

There was a murmur among them, horrified as they listened to these orders. Miserably every eye turned to Lyttelton, silently they pleaded with him, for he was the senior officer present.

'General Buller.' He spoke softly, but with an urgency that caught even Buller's shell-shocked attention. 'At least, let me try to recover the guns. We cannot abandon them. Let me call for volunteers. . . .'

'I'll go, sir. Please let me try.' A young subaltern elbowed Garry aside in his eagerness. Garry knew who he was, all of them did, for apart from being one of the most promising and popular youngsters in Buller's command – he was also the only son of the legendary Lord Roberts.

Assisted by his A.D.C., Buller moved to the shade of a mimosa tree and sank down heavily with his back against the rough bark of the trunk. He looked up at young Roberts, dully, without apparent interest.

'All right, Bobbie, Lyttelton will give you men. Off you go then.' He pronounced the sentence of death upon him, and Roberts laughed excitedly, gaily, and ran to his horse.

'I think we are all in need of refreshment. Will you join me in a sandwich and a glass of champagne, gentlemen?' Buller nodded to his A.D.C., who hurried to bring food and drink from his saddle-bags. A stray shell burst twenty yards away, scattering clods of earth over them. Stolidly Buller brushed a piece of dry grass from his whiskers and selected a smoked salmon sandwich.

17

Sean crawled down the drainage ditch towards the bank of the river. A shell burst on the edge of the ditch and scattered clods of earth over his back. He paused to brush a tangle of grass roots out of his whiskers and then crawled on to where Colonel Acheson squatted on his haunches in earnest conversation with a captain of the Fusiliers.

'Hey, Colonel Acheson. I doubt you'll need me again, will you?' The Captain looked shocked at Sean's term of address, but Acheson grinned briefly.

'A runner just got through. We have been ordered to withdraw.'

'What a pity!' Sean grunted sarcastically. 'Just when we were knocking the daylights out of old brother Boer,' and all three of them ducked as a machine-gun hammered lumps of dirt out of the bank above their heads. Then Sean took up from where he had been interrupted. 'Well, in that case – I'll be leaving you.'

'Where are you going?' the Captain demanded suspiciously.

'Not across that bridge.' Sean removed the stub of his cheroot from his mouth and pointed with it at the grey structure with its gruesome streaks of new paint. 'I've got a wounded man with me. He'll never make it. Have you got a match?'

Automatically the Captain produced a box of wax matches from his breast-pocket. 'Thanks. I'm going to swim him downstream and find a better place to cross.'

Sean re-lit his cheroot, blew a cloud of smoke and returned the Captain's matches.

'A pleasure meeting you, Colonel Acheson.'

'You have permission to fall out, Courtney.' A second longer they looked into each other's eyes, and Sean experienced a powerful desire to shake this man's hand but instead he started crawling back along the ditch.

'Courtney!' Sean paused and glanced over his shoulder. 'What's the name of the other Guide?'

'Friedman. Saul Friedman.'

Acheson scribbled briefly in his notebook, then returned it to his pocket.

'You'll hear more about today – good luck.'

'And to you, sir.'

From a tree that hung out over the brown water of the Tugela, Sean hacked a bushy green branch with his bayonet.

'Come on,' and Saul slid down the greasy clay of the bank, waist-deep into the river beside Sean.

'Leave your rifle.' Obediently Saul dropped it into the river.

'What's the bush for?'

'To cover our heads.'

'Why are we waiting?'

'For Acheson to create a diversion when he tries to get back across the bridge.'

At that moment a whistle shrilled on the bank above them. Immediately a fierce covering fire blared out and a party of khaki-clad figures stampeded out on to the bridge.

'Now,' grunted Sean. They sank together into the blood-warm water with only their heads, wreathed in leaves, above the surface. Sean pushed out gently and the current caught them. Neither of them looked back at the shrieking carnage on the bridge as they drifted away.

Twenty minutes later and a half-mile downstream, Sean edged across the current towards the remains of the railway bridge that hung like a broken drawbridge into the river. It offered a perfect access to the south and the embankment of the railway would cover them in their retreat across the plain.

Sean's feet touched mud bottom, then they were under the sagging bridge like chickens under the wing of a hen. He let the branch float away and dragged Saul to the bank between the metal girders.

'Five minutes' rest,' he told him and squatted beside him to rewind the bandage that had come down over Saul's ears. Muddy water streamed from sodden uniforms, and Sean mourned the cheroots in his tunic pocket.

There was another drainage ditch running beside the high gravel embankment of the railway. Along it, walking in a crouch, Sean prodded Saul ahead of him, yelling at him every time he attempted to straighten up and relieve his aching back. Once a sniper on the kopjes behind them thumped a bullet into the gravel near Sean's head, and Sean swore wearily and almost touched his knees with his nose. But Saul did not notice it. With his legs sloppy under him he staggered along in front of Sean, until finally he fell and lay in a sprawling, untidy heap in the bottom of the ditch.

Sean kicked him.

'Get up, damn you!'

'No, Ruth. Don't wake me up yet. It's Sunday. I don't have to work today.' Speaking quite clearly in a reasonable persuasive tone Saul looked up at Sean, but his eyes were matt and the pupils shrunken to black points.

'Get up. Get up!' The use of Ruth's name inflamed

Sean. He caught Saul's shoulder and shook him. Saul's head jerked crazily and fresh blood seeped through his bandage. Instantly contrite, Sean laid him back gently.

'Saul, please. You must try. Just a little farther.'

'Glossless,' whispered Saul. 'There is no gloss on it. I don't want it.' And he closed his eyes, his lips bulged open and his breath snored through them in tiny bubbles of spittle.

A suffocating despair drooped down over Sean as he studied Saul's face. The eyes had receded into dark plum-coloured cavities, leaving the skin stretched tight across his cheeks and across the gaunt bony nose.

Not because I nearly killed him, not because I owe it to him. But because – but because? How can you define your feelings for another man. All you can say is – because he is my friend. Then, because he is my friend I cannot leave him here.

Sinking down beside him, Sean lifted his slack body into a sitting position, draped one of Saul's arms around his shoulder and stood up. Saul hung beside him, his head lolled forward on his chest, and Sean looked ahead. He could see the survivors from the bridge struggling back through the village, dragging their wounded with them.

Across the whole breadth of the plain, singly and in twos and threes, harried by shrapnel, beaten, broken, Buller's mighty army was in retreat. And there, not a hundred yards from where Sean crouched in the railway ditch, drawn up neatly in the grass, deserted, forlorn, stood the field guns.

Quickly Sean averted his eyes from them and began plodding away from the river. Over his shoulder he held Saul's wrist, his free arm was wrapped around Saul's waist.

Then slowly he was aware that the Boer fire was

crescendoing once more. Shell that had fallen haphazard among the retreating men began to concentrate on an area directly ahead of Sean. Behind him the rifle-fire that had popped spasmodically on the heights now swelled into a fierce, sustained crackle like a bushfire in green forest.

Leaning against the side of the ditch Sean peered ahead through the mimosa trees and the storm of dust and bursting shell. He saw horses, two teams in harness, men with them racing in through the thorn trees, lifting pale dust in a cloud to mingle with the dust of the shells. Far ahead of them, brandishing his cane, leading them in towards the abandoned guns, galloped a figure on a big shiny bay.

'He's laughing.' In wonder, Sean watched the leading rider disappear behind a column of dust and high explosive, only to emerge again as he swerved his mount like a polo player. His mouth was open and Sean saw the glint of white teeth. 'The fool is laughing his head off!'

And suddenly Sean was cheering wildly.

'*Ride, man, Ride!*' he shouted and his voice was lost in the shriek and crash of the bombardment.

'They've come to fetch the guns,' howled Sean. 'Saul, they've come for the guns.' Without knowing how he had done it, mad with the excitement of it, Sean found himself out of the ditch, running with new strength, running with Saul's unconscious weight slung over his shoulder, running through the grass towards the guns.

By the time he reached the battery the first team was already there. The men were down struggling to back the horses up to the trail of the Number One gun. Sean slid the inert body from his shoulder and dropped it in the grass. Two of them were trying to lift the trail of the field gun, but this task required four men.

'Get out of the way!' Sean shouted at them and straddled the long wedge-shaped trail of steel. He locked his hands into the grips and heaved upwards, lifting it clear and high.

'Get the carriage.' Quickly they rolled the detachable axle and wheels in under the trail and locked them into position. Sean stepped back panting.

'Well done!' The young officer leaned forward in his saddle as he shouted at Sean. 'Get up on the carriage.'

But Sean turned and ran to Saul, he picked him up and stumbled with him to the carriage.

'Grab him!' he grunted at the two soldiers who were already aboard. Between them they dragged Saul up on to the carriage seat.

'No room for you, cock. Why don't you take Taffy's place on the right-hand wheeler?' one of them shouted down, and Sean saw he was correct. The drivers were mounting up, but one saddle was empty.

'Look after him,' he told the man who held Saul.

'Don't worry, I've got him,' the gunner assured him, and then urgently, 'You'd best grab a seat – we're pulling out.'

'Look after him,' Sean repeated and started forward.

In that moment the luck which had protected him all morning ran out. A shell burst beside him. He felt no pain but his right leg gave under him and he went down on his knees.

He tried to stand but his body would not obey.

'Forward!' shouted the subaltern, and the gun carriage trundled away, gathering speed, beginning to jolt and bounce as the drivers lashed the horses. Sean saw the gunner who held Saul staring back at him from the carriage, his face was contorted with helplessness.

'Look after him!' Sean shouted. 'Promise me you'll look after him.'

The gunner opened his mouth to reply, but another

shell burst between them, throwing up a curtain of dust that hid the carriage. This time Sean felt the shrapnel tear into his flesh. It stung like the cut of a razor and he sagged sideways. As he went down he saw that the Subaltern had been hit as well. Saw him throw up his arms and fall backwards over the rump of his horse, rolling from the saddle, hitting the ground with his shoulder, one foot caught in the stirrup so that he dragged over the rough ground until the stirrup leather snapped and left him lying. His horse galloped away in pursuit of the careering gun carriage.

Sean dragged himself after it. 'Look after him,' he shouted. 'For God's sake, look after Saul.' But nobody heard that shout for they were gone away amongst the trees, gone away in the dust with the shellfire escorting them like a troop of brown demons.

Still Sean crawled after them, using one hand to reach ahead and claw into the earth and inch his whole body belly down through the grass. His other arm dragged at his side, and he could feel his right leg slithering after him, until it caught and tethered him. He struggled against it, but his toe had hooked in a tuft of coarse grass and he could not free it. He wriggled on to his side and doubled up with his broken arm beneath him to look back at his leg.

There was much blood, a wet, slippery drag-mark of it across the flattened grass, and still it welled up out of his body. But there was no pain, only a dizziness and a weariness in his head.

His leg twisted at a ridiculous angle from his trunk, and the spur on his boot stood up jauntily. He wanted to laugh at the leg, but somehow the effort was too great and he closed his eyes against the glare of the sun.

Near him he heard somebody groaning and for a while he thought it must be Saul. Then he remembered that

Saul was safe, and it was the young subaltern. With his eyes closed Sean lay and listened to him die. It was an ugly sound.

18

Battle-General Jan Paulus Leroux stood upon the heights above the Tugela and removed his Terai hat. His head was bald with a fringe of ginger hair above the ears and thick around the back. The skin of his pate was smooth and creamy white where the hat had protected it from the sun, but his face had been weathered and sculptured by the elements until it looked like a cliff of red-stone.

'Bring my pony, Hennie.' He spoke to the lad who stood beside him.

'*Ja*, Oom Paul.' And he hurried away down the reverse slope to the pony laager.

From the firing trench at Jan Paulus's feet one of his burghers looked up at him.

'God has heard our prayers, Oom Paul. He has given us a great victory.'

Jan Paulus nodded heavily, and his voice as he replied was low and humble, without any trace of jubilation.

'*Ja*, Fredevik. In God's name, a great victory.'

But not as great as I had planned it, he thought.

Out of cannon shot, almost out of range of the naked eye, the last tattered remnants of the British were dwindling into the brown distance.

If only they could have waited, he thought with bitterness. So clearly I explained it to them, and they did not heed me.

His whole strategy had revolved upon the bridge. If only his burghers on the kopje below the heights had held their fire and let them cross. Then God would have delivered the enemy to them in thousands instead of hundreds. Caught in the amphitheatre of the heights with the river at their backs none of them would have escaped when his artillery destroyed the bridge behind them. Sadly he looked down upon the trap he had laid with such infinite care. From above he could see the trenches, each of them, masked and cunningly overlapped so that an unbearable fire could sweep the grassy bowl into which he had hoped to lure the British centre. The trap that would never be sprung, for he knew they would not come again.

Hennie climbed back to him, leading his pony, and Jan Paulus mounted quickly.

'Come, let us go down.'

At forty-two years of age, Jan Paulus Leroux was very young for the command he held. There had been opposition in Pretoria to his appointment when old Joubert retired, but President Kruger had ridden rough-shod over it and forced the Volkraad to accept. Ten minutes before, Jan Paulus had sent him a telegraphed message which had justified this confidence.

With long stirrup leathers, his massive body loose and relaxed in the saddle, his *sjambok* trailing from his wrist and the wide-brimmed hat shading his face, Jan Paulus went down to gather the harvest of war.

As he reached the kopjes and rode in among them, his burghers rose from their trenches on the slopes and cheered him. Their voices blended in a savage roar that echoed from the heights like the jubilation of lions on a new kill. Impassively Jan Paulus examined their faces as he passed. They were coated with red dust and burned powder, and sweat had run in dark lines through the grime. One man used his rifle as a crutch to balance himself against his wound, and there were harsh lines of pain around his mouth as he cheered. Jan Paulus checked his pony. 'Lie down, don't be a fool, man!' The man grinned painfully and shook his head.

'*Nee*, Oom Paul. I'm going with you to fetch the guns.'

Brusquely Jan Paulus motioned to the men who stood beside the wounded burgher. 'Take him away. Take him to the doctors.' And he trotted on to where Commandant Van Wyk waited for him.

'I told you to hold your men until they crossed,' he greeted him, and Van Wyk's grin faded.

'*Ja*, Oom Paul. I know. But I could not hold them. The young ones started it. When they saw the guns right there under their noses – I could not hold them.' Van Wyk turned and pointed across the river. 'Look how near they were.'

Jan Paulus looked across the river. The guns were standing in the open, so close and so lightly screened by the intervening thorn scrub that he could count the spokes of the wheels and see the sparkle of the brass breech fittings.

'It was too much temptation,' Van Wyk ended lamely.

'So! It is done, and we cannot undo it with words.' Grimly Jan Paulus determined that this man would never command again. 'Come, we will fetch them.'

At the road bridge Jan Paulus halted the long column of horsemen behind him. Although none of it showed on his face, yet his stomach heaved with horror at what he saw.

'Move them,' he ordered, and as the thirty burghers dismounted and went forward to clear the bridge he called out after them. 'Handle them gently, lift them – do not drag them away like mealie sacks. These were men. Brave men.' Beside him the boy, Hennie, was crying openly. The tears falling on to his patched tweed jacket.

'Be still, Jong,' Jan Paulus murmured gently. 'Tears

are for women.' And he urged his pony into the narrow passage between the dead. It was the dust and the sun and the lyddite fumes which had irritated his own eyes, he told himself angrily.

Quietly, lacking the triumphant bearing of victors, they came to the guns and spread out among them. Then a single rifle-shot cracked out and a burgher staggered and clutched the wheel of a gun carriage for support.

Whirling his pony, and flattening himself along its neck, Jan Paulus charged the donga beyond the guns from which the shot had come. Another shot hissed past his head, but by then Jan Paulus had reached the donga. Pulling his mount down from full gallop on to its haunches, he jumped from the saddle and kicked the rifle out of the British private's hands before dragging him to his feet.

'We have killed too much already, you fool.' Stumbling over the English words, his tongue clumsy with rage, he roared into the soldier's face. 'It is finished. Give up.' And then turning on the surviving gunners who huddled along the donga. 'Give up, give up, all of you!' None of them moved for a long minute, then slowly one at a time they stood up and shuffled out of the donga.

While a party of Boers led the prisoners away, and the others went about the business of hitching up the guns and the ammunition wagon, the British stretcher-bearers began filtering forward through the mimosa trees. Soon khaki figures were mingled everywhere with the burghers as they searched like bird-dogs for the wounded.

Two of them, dark-skinned Indians of the Medical Corps, had found a man lying out on the left flank. They were having difficulty with him, and Jan Paulus handed the reins of his pony to Hennie and walked across to them.

In semi-delirium the wounded man was cursing horribly and resisting all attempts by the two Indians to fix splints on his leg.

'Leave me alone, you bastards,' and a flying fist knocked one of them sprawling. Jan Paulus, recognizing the voice and the punch, started to run.

'You behave yourself, or I'll klop you one,' he growled as he reached them. Groggily Sean rolled his head and tried to focus on him.

'Who's that? Who are you? Get the hell away from me.'

Jan Paulus did not answer. He was looking at the wounds and they made him want to vomit.

'Give to me.' He took the splints from the shaken bearers and squatted down beside Sean.

'Get away!' Sean screamed at him. 'I know what you're going to do. You're going to cut it off!'

'Sean!' Jan Paulus caught his wrist and held it while Sean writhed and swore.

'I'll kill you, you filthy bastard. I'll kill you if you touch it.'

'Sean! It's me. Look at me!'

And slowly Sean relaxed, his eyes steadied.

'It's you? It's really you?' he whispered. 'Don't let them . . . don't let them take my leg. Not like they did to Garry.'

'Be still, or I'll break your stupid head,' growled Jan Paulus. Like his face, his hands were beefy and red, big hands with fingers like calloused sausages, but now they worked as gently as those of a mother on her child. At last, holding the ankle, he looked at Sean.

'Hold fast, now. I must straighten it.'

Sean tried to grin, but his face was grey beneath the

coating of battle filth, and sweat squeezed from his skin like a rash of tiny blisters.

'Don't talk so much, you bloody Dutchman. Do it!'

Bone grated on broken bone deep in the torn flesh and Sean gasped. Every muscle in his body convulsed and then relaxed again as he fainted.

'Ja,' grunted Jan Paulus. 'That's better,' and for the first time the set of his features betrayed his compassion. He finished with the bandages, and for a few seconds continued to squat beside Sean's unconscious body. Then he whispered so low that the two bearers could not catch the words.

'Sleep well, my brother. May God spare you your leg.'

And he stood, all trace of pity and sorrow locked away behind the red-stone of his face.

'Take him away,' he ordered, and waited while they lifted the stretcher and staggered away with it.

He went to his pony, and his feet dragged a little through the grass. From the saddle he looked once more towards the south but the two bearers had disappeared wth their burden among the mimosa trees. He touched spurs to his pony's flanks and followed the long procession of wagons, prisoners and guns back towards the Tugela. The only sound was the jingle of harness and the melancholy rumble of wheels.

19

Garrick Courtney watched the champagne spilling into the crystal bowl of his glass. The bubbles swirled in golden patterns, catching the lantern light. The mess corporal lifted the bottle, dexterously caught a drop of wine on his napkin and moved behind Garry to fill the glass of Brigadier Lyttelton, who sat beside him.

'No.' Lyttelton placed a hand over his empty glass to prevent him doing so.

'Come, come, Lyttelton.' Sir Redvers Buller leaned forward and looked down the table. 'That's an excellent wine.'

'Thank you, sir, but champagne is for victory – perhaps we should have a case sent across the river.'

Buller flushed slowly and looked down at his own glass. Once more an ugly silence descended on the mess. In an effort to break it Garry spoke up.

'I do think the withdrawal today was made in extremely good order.'

'Oh. I agree most heartily.' From across the table Lord Dundonald's icy sarcasm added to the gaiety. 'But in all fairness, Colonel, we were travelling very light on our return.'

This oblique reference to the guns sent every eye to Buller's face – Dundonald was showing a reckless disregard of that notorious temper. But as a peer of the realm he could take the chance. With a courteous insolence he met Buller's glare, and held it until the pale bulging eyes faded and dropped.

'Gentlemen.' Buller spoke heavily. 'We have had a most trying day, and for all of us there is still work to do.' He glanced at his A.D.C. 'Clery, will you be kind enough to propose the Queen?'

Alone, Garry limped from the huge marquee mess tent. The smaller tents, lit internally, were a vast field of luminous cones, and above them the night was black satin sown with silver stars. The wine that Garry had drunk during dinner hummed in his head so that he did not notice the dejected silence that smothered the encampment as he picked his way through it.

As Garry entered his headquarters a man stood up from the camp chair beside his desk. In the light of the lantern his features were gaunt, and weariness showed in every line of his body.

'Ah! Curtis.'

'Good evening, sir.'

'You've come to make your report?'

'I have, sir. For what it's worth.'

'Tell me, Curtis – how many casualties?' There was an eagerness behind the question which Tim found ghoulish. Speculatively he examined Garry's face before replying.

'We suffered heavily, out of a strength of twenty we had four killed, two missing and five wounded – three of them seriously.'

'Have you made out a list?'

'Not yet.'

'Well, tell me. Who were they?'

'Killed were Booth, Amery . . . '

No longer could Garry hold his impatience, he blurted out suddenly:

'What about that sergeant?'

'You mean Courtney?'

'Yes. *Yes.*' And now with his impatience was mingled a dread that made his stomach feel hollow.

'Wounded, sir.'

And Garry felt a lift of relief so intense that he must close his eyes and suck in his breath to ride it up.

Sean was still alive! Thank God. Thank God for that.

'Where is he now?'

'They've got him down at the railhead hospital. He's being sent out with the first batch of badly wounded.'

'Badly?' Garry's relief changed quickly to concern, and he demanded harshly, 'How badly? *How badly?*'

'That's all they told me. I went down to the hospital but they wouldn't allow me to see him.'

Garry sank into his chair and instinctively reached for the drawer before he checked himself.

'Very well, Curtis. You may go.'

'The rest of my report, sir?'

'Tomorrow. Leave it till tomorrow.'

With the liquor glowing hotly in his belly, Garry set off through the night towards the hospital. It did not matter now that he had planned and hoped that Sean would die. He no longer reasoned, but hurried through the sprawling camp, driven by his desperate need. Unrecognized but strong within him was the hope that he might again draw comfort and strength from that fountain as he had done so long ago. He started to run, stiffly, so the toe of his boot scuffed in the dust with each pace.

Desperately he searched through the hospital. He hurried along the rows of stretchers examining the faces of the wounded; he saw pain and mutilation and slow creeping death soaking like spilt red ink through the white bandages. He heard the moan and murmur and delirious laughter, he smelt the taint of agony-induced sweat blended with the heavy sweetness of corruption and disinfectant – and he hardly noticed them. One face, one face only, he wanted. And he did not find it.

'Courtney.' The medical orderly examined his list, tilting it to catch the lamplight. 'Ah! Yes. Here it is – let's see. Yes! He's gone already – left on the first train an hour ago . . . I can't say, sir, probably to Pietermaritzburg. They've established a big new hospital there. I can't tell you that either, I'm afraid, but they've got him listed here as *dangerous* . . . that's better than *critical* anyway.'

Wearing his loneliness like a cloak, Garry stumbled back to his quarters.

'Good evening, sir.' His servant was waiting for him. Garry always made them wait up. A new man this, they changed so fast. Never could keep a batman more than a month.

Garrick pushed past him, and half fell against the camp bed.

'Steady on, sir. Let's get you on to the bed, sir.' The man's voice was insidiously servile, the voice men used towards drunks. The touch of his hands infuriated Garry.

'Leave me.' He lashed out with a clenched fist across the man's face, throwing him back. 'Leave me. Get out and leave me!'

The servant rubbed his bruised cheek uncertainly, backing away.

'Get out!' Garry hissed at him.

'But, sir –'

'Get out, damn you. Get out!'

The man went out and closed the tent flap softly behind him. Garry stumbled across to it and laced it closed. Then he stood back. Alone. They can't see me now. They can't laugh now. They can't. Oh God, Sean!

He turned from the flap. The dummy leg caught on

130

the rough floor and he fell. One of the straps parted and the leg twisted under him. On his hands and knees he crawled towards the commode across the tent, and the leg jerked and twisted grotesquely behind him.

Kneeling beside the commode he lifted the china basin from its recess and reached into the space below it and he found the bottle. His fingers were too clumsy for the cork, he pulled it with his teeth and spat it on to the floor. Then he held the bottle to his lips and his throat jerked rhythmically as he swallowed. A little of the brandy spilled on to his tunic and stained the ribbon of the Victoria Cross.

He lowered the bottle and rested, panting from the sting of the liquor. Then he drank again more slowly. The trembling of his hands stilled. His breathing smoothed out. He reached up and took the tumbler from the top of the commode, filled it, then placed the bottle beside him on the floor and wriggled into a more comfortable position against the commode.

In front of him his artificial leg twisted on its broken straps at an unnatural angle below the knee. He contemplated it, sipping the brandy slowly and feeling it numb the taste-buds of his tongue.

The leg was the centre of his existence. Insensate, unmoving, still as the eye of a great storm upon which the whole turmoil of his life revolved. The leg – always the leg. Always and only the leg.

Now under the lulling spell of the liquor he had drunk, from the stillness at the centre where the leg lay, he looked outward at the gigantic shadows of the past, and found them preserved and perfect, not distorted or blurred by time, whole and complete in each detail.

While they paraded through his mind, the night telescoped in upon itself so that time had no significance. The hours endured for a few minutes and were gone while the level in the bottle fell and he sat against the commode sipping at the tumbler and watching while the night wasted away. In the dawn the final act was played out before him.

Himself on a horse in the darkness riding in cold soft rain towards Theuniskraal. One window showing a yellow oblong of lantern light, the rest dark in the greater dark mass of the homestead.

The unaccountable premonition of coming horror closing cold and soft as the rain around him, the silence spoiled only by the crunch of his horse's hooves in the gravel of the drive. The thump of his pegleg as he climbed the front steps and the chill of the brass doorknob in his hand as he turned it and pushed it in upon the silence.

His own voice slurred with drink and dread. 'Hello. Where's everybody? Anna! Anna! I'm back!'

The blue flare of his match and the smell of burnt sulphur and paraffin as he lit the lamp, then the urgent echoing thump of his pegleg along the passage.

'Anna, Anna, where are you?'

Anna, his bride, lay upon the bed in the darkened room, half-naked, turning quickly away from the light, but he had seen the dead-white face with swollen and bruised lips.

The lamp from the table threw bloated shadows on the wall as he stooped over and gently drew down the petticoats to cover the whiteness of her lower body, then turned her to face him. 'My darling, oh Anna, my darling. What's happened?' Through the torn blouse her breasts were engorged and darkly nippled with pregnancy. 'Are you hurt? Who? Tell me who did it?' But she covered her face and broken lips with her hands.

'My darling, my poor darling. Who was it – one of the servants?'

'No.'

'Please tell me, Anna. What happened?'

Suddenly her arms were about his neck and her lips close against his ear. 'You know, Garry! You know who did it.'

'No, I swear I don't. Please tell me.'

Her voice tight and hoarse with hatred, uttering that word, that one unbelievable horrible word. 'Sean!'

'Sean!' he said aloud in his desolation. 'Sean. Oh God!' and then savagely. 'I hate him. I hate him! Let him die – please God, let him die.'

He closed his eyes, losing his grip upon reality, and felt the first dizzy swing of vertigo as the liquor took firm hold upon him.

Too late now to open his eyes and focus them upon the bed across the tent, the giddiness had begun – now he would not be able to hold it down. The warm, acid-sweet taste of brandy welled up into his throat and mouth and nose.

20

When his servant found him it was the middle of the morning. Garry lay fully dressed but asleep upon the bed with his sparse hair ruffled, his uniform stained and grubby, and the leg lying derelict in the centre of the floor.

The servant closed the door softly and studied his master, his nostrils flaring at the sour smell of stale brandy and vomit.

'Had yourself one hell of a bust-out. Hey – Hop, Skip and Jump?' he murmured without sympathy. Then he picked up the bottle and examined the inch of liquor remaining in it. 'Your bloody good health, cock,' he saluted Garry and drained the bottle, patted his lips delicately and spoke again. 'Right! Let's get your sty clean up.'

'Leave me alone,' Garry groaned.

'It's eleven o'clock, sir.'

'Leave me. Get out and leave me.'

'Drink this coffee, sir.'

'I don't want it. Leave me.'

'I've got your bath filled, sir, and a clean uniform laid out for you.'

'What time is it?' Garry sat up unsteadily.

'Eleven o'clock,' the man repeated patiently.

'My leg?' Garry felt naked without it.

'One of the harness makers is stitching the straps, sir. It'll be ready by the time you've bathed.'

Even in a position of rest Garry's hands, laid upon the

desk in front of him trembled slightly, and the rims of his eyelids prickled. The skin of his face was stretched like that of a drum over the slow pain that throbbed within his skull.

At last he sighed and picked Lieutenant Curtis's report from the top of the slim sheaf of papers that waited for his attention. Garry skimmed through it dully, few of the names upon it meant anything to him. He saw Sean's name headed the list of wounded, and below him was the little Jewish lawyer. At last satisfied that the report contained nothing to the discredit of Colonel Garrick Courtney, he initialled it and laid it aside.

He picked up the next document. A letter addressed to him as Officer Commanding the Natal Corps of Guides, from a Colonel John Acheson of the Scots Fusiliers. Two pages of neat, pointed handwriting. He was about to discard it and leave it to his Orderly's attention when the name in the body of the text caught his eye. He leaned forward attentively and read quickly from the beginning.

'... pleasure in bringing to your attention ... conduct beyond the call of ... under intense enemy fire ... once more, initiated an advance ... although wounded ... disregard of personal danger ... two members of your Guides.

Sergeant Sean Courtney.

Pte. Saul Friedman.

... earnestly recommend ... Distinguished Conduct Medal ... great gallantry and powers of leadership.'

Garry dropped the letter and leaned back in his chair, staring at it as though it were his own death warrant. For a long while he did not move, while the pain kept beating in his head. Then he picked it up once more.

Now his hands trembled so violently that the paper fluttered like the wing of a wounded bird.

'Everything of mine, everything I've ever owned – he's taken it from me,' and he looked down at the ribbons on his breast. 'I've never had . . . Now this, the one thing.'

A drop of moisture fell on to the letter, blurring the ink.

'I hate him,' he whispered and tore the letter across. 'I hope he dies,' and he tore again and again, ripping it to shreds and at last screwing them into a ball in his clenched fist.

'No. You'll not get that from me. It's mine – it's the one thing you'll never have!' He hurled the crumpled ball against the canvas of the tent, and lowered his head on to his arms upon the desk. His shoulders shook as he sobbed:

'Don't die. Please, Sean, don't die.'

21

Simply by putting his shoulder against her and shoving her aside, Dirk Courtney cleared a small girl from the doorway and was first down the steps and out into the sun. Without looking back at the schoolhouse he headed for the hole in the back hedge, the others would be following.

They caught up with him while he was selecting a *klei-lat* from the hedge.

'Hurry up,' Dirk ordered. 'We got to get to the river first else they'll get the best place.'

They spread out along the hedge, small boys chattering like a troop of excited monkeys.

'Lend me your knife, Dirkie.'

'Hey, look at my lat.' Nick Peterson brandished the short rod of Port Jackson Willow he had cut and peeled. It whipped with a satisfying swish.

'It's not a lat,' Dirk informed him. 'It's a Lee-Metford.' He looked round at the rest of his team. 'You remember now – I'm Lord Kitchener, and you got to call me "My Lord".'

'And I'm General French,' announced Nick. This was fair enough, after all, he was Dirk's chief lieutenant. It had taken Dirk a mere two weeks and five bloody fist-fights to reach his position as unchallenged leader.

'And I'm General Methuen!' one of the lesser members yelped.

'And I'm General Buller!'

'And I'm General Gatacre!'

'You can't all be generals.' Dirk glared around. 'Only Nick and I are generals. You are all just privates and things.'

'Gee, man, Dirkie! Why you always got to spoil things?'

'You shut your mouth, Brian.' Dirk sensed mutiny, and quickly he diverted their attention. 'Come on, let's go and get ammo.'

Dirk took the long route down the sanitary lane. This way he was unlikely to meet adults and have any of his force seconded to serve elsewhere at wood chopping or gardening under parental control.

'Peaches are nearly ripe,' Nick commented as they passed the Pye orchard.

'Another week,' Dirk agreed, and crawled through the hedge into the Van Essen plantation that spread down to the Baboon Stroom.

'There they are!' someone shouted as they emerged from the trees.

'Boers, General!'

Out on the right, busy along the bank of the river was another bunch of small figures – sons of the Dutch families in the district.

'I'll go and talk to them,' Dirk said. 'You go for ammo.' They trotted off towards the river and Dirk called after them: 'Hey, Nick, get me a good dollop of clay.'

'All right, My Lord.'

With all the dignity of a general, officer and a peer of the realm, Dirk approached the enemy and stopped a short distance from them.

'Hey, Piet, are you ready yet?' he asked haughtily. Piet Van Essen was his second cousin twice removed. A chunky lad but not as tall as Dirk.

'Ja.'

'The same rules?' Dirk asked.

'*Ja*, the same rules.'

'No clothes,' Dirk warned him.

'And no throwing with stones,' Piet shot back.

'How many you got?' Dirk began counting the enemy suspiciously.

'Fifteen – same as you.'

'All right then,' Dirk nodded.

'All right then!'

Nick was waiting for him below the bank. Dirk jumped down beside him and accepted the large ball of blue clay that Nick handed him.

'It's just right, Dirkie, not too wet.'

'Good – let's get ready.'

Quickly Dirk stripped off his clothing, pulled the belt from the loops of his pants and buckled it around his waist to hold his spare lats.

'Hide the clothes, Brian,' Dirk ordered and surveyed his naked warriors. Nearly all of them still retained the almost womanly shape of youth; undeveloped chests, protruding stomachs and fat white buttocks.

'They'll come down the river like they do every time,' Dirk said. 'This time we're going to ambush them.' As he spoke he kneaded a handful of clay into a ball and spiked it on to the end of the lat. 'Me and Nick'll wait here – the rest of you on top of the bank in those bushes back there.'

He was looking for a target to practise on, and found it in a water tortoise which was laboriously climbing the far bank.

'Watch that old skilpad.' He interrupted himself; stepped forward with his right hand holding the lat thrown back, then whipped it through in an overhead swing.

The ball of clay flew from the end of the rod with a vicious hum and smacked onto the shiny black carapace with a force that left a white starshaped crack upon the shell. The tortoise jerked in its head and limbs and toppled backwards into the stream.

'Good shot!'

'There he is, let me have a shot.'

'That's enough! You'll get plenty shots just now.' Dirk stopped them. 'Now listen to me! When they come me and Nick will hold them here for a bit, then we'll run back along the river and they'll chase us. Wait until they are right underneath you – then give it to them.'

Dirk and Nick crouched side by side, close in against the bank with the water up to their noses. A tuft of reeds hid those parts of their heads still above the surface and within easy reach their loaded clay-lats lay on dry land.

Below water Dirk felt Nick's elbow nudge his ribs, and he nodded carefully. He also had heard the whisper of voices around the bend of the river, and the roll and plop of loose earth dislodged by a careless foot. He turned his head and answered Nick's grin with one just as bloodthirsty, then he peered around the reeds.

Twenty paces in front of him a head appeared cautiously around the angle of the bank and the expression on its face was set and nervous – and Dirk moved his own head back behind the bunch of reeds.

A long silence broken suddenly. 'They're not here.' The voice was squeaky with adolescence and tension. Boetie was a delicate child, small for his age, who insisted on joining the rest of them in games beyond his strength.

Another long silence and then the sound of a wholesale but stealthy approach. Dirk reached out and gripped Nick's arm – the enemy were committed, out in the open – he lifted his mouth above the surface.

'Now!' he whispered and they reached for their lats. The surprise was complete and devastating. As Dirk and Nick rose dripping, with throwing arms cocked, the attackers were bunched in such a way that they could neither run nor return the fire unhampered.

The clay pellets flew into them, slapping loudly on bare flesh, producing howls of anguish and milling, colliding confusion.

'Give it to them,' shouted Dirk, and threw again without picking his man, blindly into the mass of legs and arms and pink backsides. Beside him Nick worked in a silent frenzy of load and throw.

The confusion lasted perhaps fifteen seconds, before the howls of pain became shouts of anger.

'It's only Dirk and Nick.'

'Get them – it's only two of them.'

The first pellet flipped Dirk's ear, the second hit him full in the chest.

'Run!' he gasped through the pain, and floundered to the bank. Bent forward to climb from the stream he was frighteningly vulnerable, and a pellet thrown at point-blank range took him in that portion of his anatomy which he was offering to the enemy. The sting of it propelled him from the water and clouded his vision with tears.

'Chase them!'

'Hit them!'

The pack bayed after them, pellets hissed about them and slapped at them as they pelted back along the stream. Before they reached the next bend their backs and bottoms were dappled with the angry red spots which tomorrow would be bruises.

Without discretion, hot with the chase, shouting and laughing, the attackers poured into the trap and as they rounded the bend it closed upon them.

Dirk and Nick stood poised to meet them, and suddenly the bank above their heads was lined with squealing, dancing, naked savages, who hurled a steady stream of missiles into them.

For a minute they stood it, then completely broken they scrambled out of the river-bed with pellets flailing them and raced panic-stricken for the shelter of the plantation.

One of them remained below the bank, kneeling in the mud, sobbing softly. But according to the unspoken laws that goverened them this one was exempt from further punishment.

'It's only Boetie,' Nickie shouted. 'Leave him. Come on! Chase the others!' And he scrambled up the bank and led them after the flight. Yelling and shrilling with excitement they streamed away through the brown grass to where Piet Van Essen was desperately trying to stay the rout on the edge of the plantation, and gather his men to meet the charge.

But another of them remained below the bank – Dirk Courtney.

There were just two of them now. Screened by the bank, completely alone. Boetie looked up and through his tears saw Dirk coming slowly towards him. He saw the lat in Dirk's hand and the expression on his face. He knew he was alone with Dirk.

'Please, Dirk,' he whispered. 'I give up. Please. I give up.'

Dirk grinned. Deliberately he moulded the clay pellet onto his lat.

'I'll give you all my lunch tomorrow,' pleaded Boetie. 'Not just the sweets, I'll give you all of it.'

Dirk hurled the clay. Boetie's shriek thrilled his whole body. He began to tremble with the pleasure of it.

'I'll give you my new pocket-knife.' Boetie's voice was

muffled by sobs and his arms which he had crossed over his face.

Dirk loaded the lat, slowly so he could savour this feeling of power.

'Please, Dirkie. Please, man, I'll give you anything you –' and Boetie shrieked again.

'Take your hands off your face, Boetie.' Dirk's voice was strangled, thick with pleasure.

'No, Dirkie. Please no!'

'Take your hands away, and I'll stop.'

'You promise, Dirkie. You promise you'll stop.'

'I promise,' whispered Dirk.

Slowly Boetie lowered his arms, they were thin and very white, for he always wore long sleeves against the sun.

'You promised, didn't you. I did what you –' and the clay hit him across the bridge of his nose, spreading as it struck, jerking his head back. Immediately there was blood from both nostrils.

Boetie clawed at his face, smearing blood on to his cheeks.

'You promised,' he whimpered. 'You *promised*!' But Dirk was already moulding the next pellet.

Dirkie walked home alone. He walked slowly, smiling a little, with soft hair falling forward on to his forehead and a smear of blue clay on one cheek.

Mary was waiting for him in the kitchen of the cottage on Protea Street. She watched from the window while he slipped through the hedge and crossed the yard. As he came towards the door she noticed the smile on his face. There was hardly sufficient room in her chest for what she felt as she looked at the innocent beauty of his face. She opened the door for him.

'Hello, darling.'

'Hello, Mary,' Dirk greeted her, and his little smile became a thing of such radiance that Mary had to reach for him.

'My goodness, you're covered in mud. Let's get you bathed before your gran'ma gets home.'

Dirk extricated himself from her embrace and moved in on the biscuit-tin.

'I'm hungry.'

'Just one,' Mary agreed, and Dirk took a handful. 'Then I've got a surprise for you.'

'What is it?' Dirk was more interested in the biscuits. Mary had a surprise for him every evening and usually it was something silly like a new pair of socks she had knitted.

'I'll tell you when you're in the bath.'

'Oh, all right.' Still munching Dirk set off for the bathroom. He began to disrobe along the passage dropping first his shirt and then his pants for Mary to retrieve as she followed.

'What is the surprise?'

'Oh Dirk, you've been playing that horrible game again.' Mary knelt beside the tub and gently passed the soapy flannel down his bruised back and buttocks. 'Please promise me you'll never play it again.'

'All right.' It was a very simple matter to extract a promise from Dirk, he had made this particular one before. 'Now, what's your surprise?'

'Guess.' Mary was smiling now, a secret knowing smile which immediately caught Dirk's attention. He studied her scarred face, her ugly loving face.

'Sweets?' he hazarded, and she shook her head and caressed his naked body with the flannel.

'Not socks!'

'No.' She dropped the flannel into the soap-scummed water and clasped him to her chest. 'No, not socks,' she whispered.

He knew then.

'Is it . . . ? Is it . . .'

'Yes, Dirkie, it's about your father.'

Instantly he began to struggle.

'Where is he, Mary? Where is he?'

'Into your nightshirt first.'

'Is he here? Has he come home?'

'No, Dirk. He isn't here yet. He's in Pietermaritzburg. But you're going to see him soon. Very soon. Gran'ma has gone now to make reservations on the train. You're going to see him tomorrow.'

His hot, wet body began to tremble in her arms, quivering with excitement.

22

'In some respects, Mrs Courtney, it was possibly all to the good that we were unable to contact you before.' The Surgeon-Major tamped tobacco into his pipe, and began methodically searching all his pockets.

'Your matches are on the desk.' Ada came to his assistance.

'Oh! Thank you.' He got the pipe drawing, and continued, 'You see, your son was attached to an irregular unit – there was no record of next-of-kin, and when he came to us from Colenso six weeks ago he was, shall we say, in no condition to inform us of your address.'

'Can we see Pa now?' Dirk could no longer contain himself, for the past five minutes he had wriggled and fidgeted on the couch beside Ada.

'You'll see your father in a few minutes, young man.' And the surgeon turned back to Ada. 'As it so happens, Mrs Courtney, you have been spared a great deal of anxiety. At first there were grave doubts that we would be able to save your son's life, let alone his right leg. Four weeks it hung in the balance, so to speak. But now' – and he beamed at Ada with justifiable pride – 'well, you'll see for yourself.'

'He's well?' Quickly, anxiously she asked.

'What a formidable constitution your son has, all muscle and determination.' He nodded, still smiling. 'Yes, he's well on the road to recovery. There may be a slight limp in the right leg – but when you weigh that against what might have been . . . ' He spread his hands eloquently. 'Now the sister will take you through to him.'

'When can he come home?' Ada asked from the doorway.

'Soon – another month, perhaps.'

A deep veranda, cool with shade and the breeze that came in across the hospital lawns. A hundred high metal beds along the wall, a hundred men in grey flannel nightshirts propped against white pillows. Some of them slept, a few were reading, others talked quietly or played chess and cards on boards set between the beds. But one lay withdrawn, staring at, but not seeing, the pair of fiscal shrikes which squabbled raucously over a frog on the lawn.

The beard was gone, removed while he was too weak to protest on the orders of the ward sister who considered it unhygienic, and the result was a definite improvement that even Sean secretly admitted. Shielded for so long, the skin on the lower half of his face was smooth and white like that of a boy; fifteen years had been shaved away with that coarse black matt. Now emphasis was placed on the heavy brows which, in turn, directed attention to his eyes, dark blue, like cloud shadow on mountain lakes. Darker blue at this moment as he considered the contents of the letter he held in his right hand.

The letter was three weeks old, and already the cheap paper was splitting along the creases from constant refolding. It was a long letter, much of it devoted to detailed description of the clumsy sparring along the Tugela River in which Buller's army was now engaged. There was one reference to the headaches from which the writer periodically suffered as a result of his wound which was now externally healed, and many more to the deep gratitude that Saul felt for him. These embarrassed Sean to such an extent that when re-reading the letter he scowled and skipped each one as he came to it.

But there was one paragraph to which Sean returned each time, and read slowly, whispering it to himself so that he could savour each word:

I remember telling you about Ruth, my wife. As you know, she escaped from Pretoria and is in Pieter-maritzburg staying with relatives of hers. Yesterday I had a letter from her that contained the most wonderful tidings. We have been married four years this coming June, and now at last as a result of our brief meeting when she arrived in Natal – I am to become a father! Ruth tells me she has determined on a daughter (though I am certain it will be a son!) and she has selected a name. It is a most unusual name, to be charitable – I can see that it will require a great deal of diplomacy on my part to make her change her mind. (Among her many virtues is an obstinacy reminiscent of the rock of ages.) She wants to name the poor waif *'Storm'* – Storm Friedman – and the prospect appals me!

Although our faiths differ, I have written to Ruth asking her to agree to your election as 'Sandek' – which is the equivalent of godfather. I can foresee no objection from Ruth (especially in view of the debt which we both owe you) and it needs now only your consent. Will you give it?

At the same time I have explained to Ruth your present situation and address (c/o Greys Hospital!) and asked her to visit you there so that she can thank you personally. I warn you in advance that she knows as much about you as I do – I am not one to hide my enthusiasms!

Lying with the letter clutched in his hand, Sean stared out across the lawns into the sunlight. Beneath the bed-clothes, swelling up like a pregnant belly, was the wicker basket that cradled his leg. 'Storm!' he whispered, remembering the lightning playing blue and blinding white upon her body.

'Why doesn't she come?' Three weeks he had waited for her. 'She knows that I am here, why doesn't she come to me?'

'Visitors for you.' The sister paused beside him and straightened the bedclothes.

'Who?' He struggled up on to his good elbow, with the other arm still in its sling across his chest.

'A lady.' And he felt it surge through him. 'And a small boy.' The cold backwash of disappointment, as he realized it was not her. Then immediately guilt – Ada and Dirk, how could he hope it was someone else?

Without the beard Dirk did not recognize him until he was ten paces away. Then he charged, his cap flew from his head and his dark hair, despite the bonds of brilliantine, sprang up into curls as he ran. He was squeaking incoherently as he reached the bed, clambered up on to Sean's chest to lock both arms around his neck.

It was some time before Sean could prise him loose and look at him.

'Well, boy,' he said, and then again, 'well, my boy.' Unable to trust himself not to lay his love for the child

149

bare for all to see – there were a hundred men watching and grinning – Sean sought diversion by turning to Ada.

She waited quietly, as she had spent half her life waiting, but when he looked at her the tenderness showed in her smile.

'Sean.' She stooped to kiss him. 'What happened to your beard? You look so young.'

They stayed for an hour, most of which was taken up by a monologue from Dirk. In the intervals while he regained his breath Ada and Sean were able to exchange all their accumulated news. Finally, Ada stood up from the chair beside Sean's bed.

'The train leaves in half an hour, and Dirk has school tomorrow. We'll come up from Ladyburg each week-end until you are ready to return home.'

Getting Dirk out of the hospital was like evicting an unruly drunk from a bar. Alone Ada could not manage it and she enlisted a male hospital orderly to the cause. Kicking and struggling in tantrum, Dirk was carried down the veranda with his screams ringing back to Sean long after he had disappeared from view.

'I want my Dad. I want to stay with my Dad.'

23

Benjamin Goldberg was the executor of his brother's estate. This estate consisted of a forty-per-cent shareholding in Goldberg Bros. Ltd., a company which listed among its assets a brewery, four small hotels and a very large one situated on the Marine Parade at Durban, sixteen butcher shops, and a factory devoted to the manufacture of polony, pork sausages, bacon and smoked ham. The last products caused Benjamin some embarrassment, but their manufacture was too profitable to be discontinued. Benjamin was also the Chairman of the Board of Goldberg Bros., and a sixty-per-cent shareholder. The presence of an army of twenty-five thousand hungry and thirsty men in Natal had increased the consumption of beer and bacon in a manner that caused Benjamin further embarrassment, for he was a peaceable man. The huge profits forced upon him by the hostilities both troubled and delighted him.

These same two emotions were evoked by the presence in his household of his neice. Benjamin had four sons and not a single daughter, his brother Aaron had left one daughter for whom Benjamin would gladly have traded all four of his own sons. Not that the boys weren't doing very well, all of them settled into the business very nicely. One of them running the Port Natal Hotel, the eldest managing the brewery and the two others in the meat section. But – and here Benjamin sighed – but Ruth! There was a girl for a man's old age. He looked at her across the polished stinkwood breakfast table with its encrustation of silver and exquisite bone china, and he sighed again.

'Now, Uncle Ben, don't start again. Please.' Ruth buttered her toast firmly.

'So all I'm saying is that we need him here. Is that so bad?'

'Saul is a lawyer.'

'*Nu!* Is that so bad. He's a lawyer, but we need a lawyer with us. The fees I pay out to those other *schmoks!*'

'He doesn't want to come into the Company.'

'All right. We know he doesn't want charity. We know he doesn't want your money working for him. We know all about his pride – but now he's got responsibilities. Already he should be thinking about you – and the baby – not so much about what he wants.'

At the mention of the baby, Ruth frowned slightly. Benjamin noticed it, there were few things he did not notice. Young people! If only you could tell them. He sighed again.

'All right. We'll leave it until Saul comes back on leave,' he agreed heavily.

Ruth, who had never mentioned her uncle's offers of employment to Saul, had a momentary vision of living in Pietermaritzburg – close enough to be drowned in the tidal waves of affection that emanated from her Uncle Benjamin, caught like a tiny insect in the suffocating web of family ties and duties. She flashed at him in horror.

'You even mention it to Saul and I'll never speak to you again.'

Her cheeks flushed wondrously and fire burned in her eyes. Even the heavy braid of dark hair seemed to come alive like the tail of an angry lioness, flicking as she moved her head.

Oi Yoi Yoi! Benjamin hid his delight behind hooded lids. *What a temper! What a woman! She could keep a man young for ever.*

Ruth jumped up from the table. For the first time he noticed that she wore riding habit.

'Where are you going? Ruth, you're not riding again today.'

'Yes I am.'

'The baby!'

'Uncle Ben, why did you never learn to mind your own business?' And she marched out of the room. Her waist was not yet thickened with pregnancy and she moved with a grace that played a wild discord on the old man's heart strings.

'You should not let her treat you that way, Benjamin.' Mildly, the way she did everything, his wife spoke from across the table.

'There's something troubling that girl.' Carefully Benjamin wiped egg from his moustache, laid the napkin on the table, consulted the gold fob watch he drew from his waistcoat, and stood up. 'Something big. You mark my words.'

It was Friday, strange how Friday had become the pivot on which the whole week turned. Ruth urged the chestnut stallion, and he lengthened his stride under her, surging forward with such power that she had to check him a little and bring him down into an easy canter.

She was early and waited ten impatient minutes in the oak-lined lane behind Greys Hospital before, like a conspirator, the little nurse slipped out through the hedge.

'Have you got it?' Ruth demanded. The girl nodded, glanced around quickly and took an envelope out of her grey nursing cloak. Ruth exchanged it for a gold sovereign. Clutching the coin the nurse started back for the hedge.

'Wait.' Ruth stopped her. This was her only physical contact and she was reluctant to break it so soon. 'How is he?'

'It's all there, m'am.'

'I know – but tell me how he looks. What he does and says,' Ruth insisted.

'Oh, he's looking fine now. He's been up and about on his sticks all week, with that big black savage helping him. The first day he fell and you should have heard him swear. Lordy!' They both laughed together.

'He's a real card, that one. He and sister had another tiff yesterday when she wanted to wash him. He called her a shameless strumpet. She gave him what for all right. But you could see she was ever so pleased and she went around telling everybody about it.'

She burbled on and Ruth listened enchanted, until:

'Then yesterday, you know what he did when I was changing his dressing?' She blushed coyly. 'He gave me a pinch behind!'

Ruth felt a hot flood of anger wash over her. Suddenly she realized that the girl was pretty in an insipid fashion.

'And he said . . .'

'Thank you!' Ruth had to restrain the hand that held her riding-crop. 'I have to go now.' Usually the long skirts of her habit hampered her in mounting, but this time she found herself in the saddle without effort.

'Next week, m'am?'

'Yes,' and she hit the stallion across his shoulder. He lunged forward so violently that she had to clutch at the pommel of the saddle. She rode him as she had never ridden a horse before, driving him with whip and spur until dark patches of sweat showed on his flanks and froth spattered back along his shoulders, so that by the time she reached a secluded spot on the bank of the Umgeni River far out of town her jealousy had abated and she felt ashamed of herself. She loosened the stallion's girth and petted him a little before leaving him tethered to one of the weeping willows, and picking her way down the bank to her favourite log on the water's edge.

There she settled herself and opened the envelope. If only Sean could have known that his temperature chart, progress report, house-doctor's recommendations, and the sucrose content of his urine were being so avidly studied, he would probably have added a ruptured spleen to his other ills.

At last Ruth folded the pages into their envelope and tucked it away in the jacket of her habit. He must look so different without his beard. She stared into the pool below her and it seemed as though his face formed in the green water and looked back at her. She touched the surface with the toe of her riding-boot so that the ripples spread and shattered the image.

She was left with only the feeling of loneliness.

'I must not go to him,' she whispered, steeling the resolve which had kept her from him these past weeks since she had known he was there. So close – so terribly near.

Determinedly she looked down again into the pool and tried to conjure up the face of her husband. All she saw was a yellowfish, gliding quietly across the sandy bottom with the pattern of its scales showing like the teeth of a file along its sides. She dropped a pebble into the water and the fish darted away.

Saul. Merry little Saul with his monkey face, who

made her laugh the way a mother laughs at her child. *I love him*, she thought. And it was true, she loved him. But love has many shapes, and some are the shapes of mountains – tall and jagged and big. While others are the shape of clouds – which have no shape, no sharp outline, soft they blow against the mountain and change and stream away but the mountain stands untouched by them. The mountain stands for ever.

'My mountain,' she murmured, and she saw him again so vividly, standing tall above her in the storm.

'Storm,' she whispered and clasped her open hands across her belly that was still flat and hard.

'Storm,' she whispered and felt the warmth within her. It spread outwards from her womb, the heat rising with it until it was a burning madness she could no longer control. With her skirts flying about her legs she ran to the stallion, her hands trembled on the straps of the girth.

'Just once,' she promised herself. 'Just this once more.' Desperately she clawed up into the saddle.

'Just this once, I swear it!' and then brokenly, 'I can't help myself. I've tried – oh God, how I've tried!'

An appreciative stirring and hum of comment from the beds along the wall followed her as she swept down the hospital veranda. There was urgent grace in the way she held her skirts gathered in one hand, in the crisp staccato tap of her pointed boots along the cement floor and the veiled swing of her hips above. There was unrestrained eagerness in the sparkle in her eyes and the forward thrust of her breasts beneath the wine-coloured jacket. The wild ride which brought her here had flushed her cheeks and tumbled her hair glossy black down her temple and on to her forehead.

Those sick and lonely men reacted as though a goddess had passed them by, thrilled by her beauty, yet saddened because she was unattainable. She did not notice them, she did not feel their hungry eyes upon her nor hear the aching whisper of their voices – for she had seen Sean.

He came slowly across the lawns towards the veranda, using the stick awkwardly to balance the drag of his leg. His eyes were downcast and he frowned in thought. Her breath caught in her throat as she saw how wasted was his body. She had not remembered him so tall with shoulders gaunt and wide like the cross-tree of a gallows. Never before had she seen the bony thrust of his jawline, nor the pale smoothness of his skin faintly blue with new-shaved beard. But she remembered the eyes heavily overscored with black brows, and his great beaky nose above the wide sensuality of his mouth.

On the edge of the lawn he stopped with feet apart, set the point of the cane between them with both hands clasped over the head of it, and he lifted his eyes and looked at her.

For many seconds neither of them moved. He stood balancing on the cane with his shoulders hunched and his chin raised as he stared at her. She in the shadow of the veranda, her skirts still held in one hand – but the other at her throat, fingers trying to still the emotions that fluttered there.

Gradually his shoulders straightened until he stood tall. He hurled the cane aside and reached both hands open towards her.

Suddenly she was running over the smooth, green lawn. Into his arms, trembling in silent intensity, while he held her.

157

With both arms around his waist and her face pressed against his chest she could smell the man smell of him and feel the hard muscle of his arms as he enfolded her – and she knew she was safe. As long as she stayed like this – nothing, nobody could touch her.

24

On the slope of the table-topped mountain that crouches over the town of Pietermaritzburg there is a glade among the wattle trees. It is a secret place where even the timid little blue buck come out to graze in daylight. On a still day you can hear very faintly the pop of the wagon whips on the road below, or farther off the steam whistle of a train. But that is all that intrudes in this wild place.

A butterfly crossed the glade in uncertain wobbling flight, it came out of the sunlight into the dappled, moving shade along the edge, and settled.

'That's good luck,' Sean murmured lazily and Ruth lifted her head from the plaid rug on which they lay. As the butterfly moved its wings, fanning them gently, the iridescent green and yellow markings sparkled in the speck of sunlight that pierced the roof of leaves above them and fell upon it like a spotlight.

'It tickles,' she said, and the insect moved like a living jewel across the smooth white field of her belly. It reached her navel and paused. Then the tiny tendril of its tongue uncurled and dabbed at the fine sheen of moisture that their loving had left upon her skin.

'He's come to bless the baby.'

The butterfly skirted the deep, delicately chiselled pit and moved on downwards.

'Don't you think he's being just a little forward – he doesn't have to bless that as well?' Ruth asked.

'He certainly seems to know his way around,' Sean admitted dubiously.

The butterfly found its road southwards blocked by a forest of dark curls, so laboriously it turned and retraced its steps towards the north. Once more it detoured round her navel and then headed unerringly for the pass between her breasts.

'Keep right on, friend,' Sean cautioned, but it turned suddenly and climbed the steep slope until at last it sat triumphant on the peak.

Sean watched it throbbing its wings, blazing in oriental splendour upon her nipple, and he felt himself stirred once more.

'Ruth.' His voice was husky again. She rolled her head to look into his eyes.

'Go away, little butterfly,' and she brushed it from her breast.

Later, after they had slept a little, Ruth woke him and they sat facing each other on the rug with the open hamper between them.

While Sean uncorked the wine she worked over the hamper with the dedication of a priestess preparing a sacrifice. He watched her split the bread rolls and fill them with salty, yellow butter, then open the screw-topped jars of soused beans and pickled onions and beetroot. A heart of young lettuce rustled crisply as she plucked its leaves into a wooden bowl, and poured dressing over them.

Her hair, released from its braid, broke like a black wave over the marble of her shoulders, then rippled and swung with the small movements of her body. With the back of her hand she brushed it from her forehead, then looked up at him and smiled.

'Don't stare. It's bad manners.' She took the glass he

offered her and sipped the cool yellow wine, set it aside and went on to dismember the fat-breasted chicken. Pretending to ignore his eyes upon her body, she began to sing, softly, the love-song she had sung on the night of the storm and shyly her breasts peeped at him through the black curtain of her hair.

She wiped her fingers carefully on a linen napkin, took up the wineglass again and with elbows on her knees leaned forward slightly and returned his scrutiny with equal frankness.

'Eat,' she said.

'And you?'

'In a little while. I want to watch you.'

Then he was hungry.

'You eat the way you make love – as though tomorrow you die.'

'I'm taking no chances.'

'You're covered with scars, like an old tom-cat who fights too much,' and she leaned forward and touched his chest with one finger. 'What happened there?'

'Leopard.'

'And there?' She touched his arm.

'Knife.'

'And there?' his wrist.

'Burst shotgun.'

She dropped her hand and caressed the fresh purple cicatrice that twined around his leg like some grotesque parasitic vine.

'This one I know,' she whispered and her eyes were sad as she touched it.

Quickly, to change her mood, he spoke.

'Now it's my turn to ask the questions.' He reached across and laid his open hand upon her stomach where the first faint bulge pressed warmly into his palm.

'What happened there?' he demanded, and she giggled before she replied. 'Burst shotgun – or was it a cannon?'

When she had repacked the hamper she knelt beside him. He lay flat on his back with a long black cheroot between his teeth.

'Have you had sufficient?' she asked.

'My God, yes,' and he sighed happily.

'Well, I haven't.' She leaned over him, took the cheroot from his mouth and flicked it into the brambles.

With the first faint flush of evening in the sky a small breeze came down from the mountain and rustled the leaves above them. The fine hairs upon her forearms came erect, each on its tiny pimple of gooseflesh, and her nipples stood out dark and hard.

'You must not be late back to the hospital on the very first day they've let you out.' She rolled away from him and reached for her clothing. 'Matron will have me hung, drawn and quartered.' Sean agreed. They dressed quickly, and she was remote from him. All the laughter gone from her voice and her face cold and expressionless.

He stood behind her to lace the whalebone corset. He hated to cage that lovely body and was about to say so.

'Saul is coming tomorrow. A month's leave.' Her voice was harsh. His hands stilled and they stood without moving. It was the first time either of them had referred to Saul since that morning a month ago when she had come to him at the hospital.

'Why didn't you tell me sooner?' His voice also was harsh.

'I didn't want to spoil today.' She had not turned towards him, but stood staring out across the glade to the far hills beyond the town.

'We must decide what we are going to tell him.'

'There is nothing to tell him,' she answered flatly.

'But what are we going to do?' Now his voice was ugly with mingled dread and guilt.

'Do, Sean?' She turned slowly and her face was still cold and expressionless. 'We are going to do nothing – nothing at all.'

'But you belong to me!' he cried in protest.

'No,' she answered.

'The child – it's mine!'

At his words her eyes narrowed and the sweet line of her lips hardened in anger.

'No, damn you, it isn't! Not yours – although you sired it.' She flamed at him. It was the first time she had unleashed her temper at him. It startled Sean. 'The child belongs to Saul – and I belong to Saul. We owe you nothing.'

He stared at her. 'You don't mean that,' and the flames of her anger faded. Quickly he tried to press his advantage.

'We'll go away together.'

'*Run away* – you mean. *Sneak away* like a pair of thieves. What would we take with us, Sean? The happiness of a man who loves and trusts us both – that, and our own guilt. You'd never forgive me, nor I you. Even now when we talk of it you cannot meet my eyes. Already you are beginning to hate me a little'

'No! No!'

'And I would hate you,' she whispered. 'Call for my horse, please.'

'You don't love him.' The agonized accusal was wrung from him, but it was as though he had not spoken. She went on dressing.

'He'll want to see you. Half of every letter he writes is about you. I've told him that I've visited you at the hospital.'

'I'm going to tell him,' Sean shouted. 'I'll tell him everything.'

'No, you won't.' She answered him calmly. 'You did not save him at Colenso to destroy him now. You would destroy him – and us. Please call for my horse.'

Sean whistled and they stood together, not touching, not talking, not even looking at each other. Until Mbejane emerged from the bush below the glade leading the horses.

Sean lifted her into the saddle.

'When?' he asked quietly.

'Perhaps never,' she answered and swung the horse away. She did not look back so Sean never saw the tears that streamed down her face. The muffled drum of hooves drowned her sobs and she held her back and her shoulders stiff so that he would not know.

25

The War Council ended long after dark and when his commandants had unsaddled and ridden away to their laagers among the hills, Jan Paulus sat alone beside the fire.

He was tired, as though his brain was the cold, flabby body of an octopus and its tentacles spread out to every extremity of his body. He was lonely. Now at the head of five thousand men he was alone as he had never been in the vast solitude of the open veld.

Because of the loneliness and because of the companionship she had given him these past twenty years his thoughts turned to Henrietta, and he smiled in the darkness and felt the longing blunt the edge of his determination.

I would like to go back to the farm, for a week only. Just to see that they are all well. I would like to read to them from the Book and watch the faces of the children in the lamplight. I would like to sit with my sons on the stoep and hear the voices of Henrietta and the girls as they work in the kitchen. I would like . . .

Abruptly he stood up from beside the fire. *Ja*, you would like this and you would like that! Go, then! Give yourself leave of absence as you have refused it to so many others. He clenched his jaw, biting into the stem of his pipe. Or else, sit here and dream like an old woman while twenty-five thousand Englishmen pour across the river.

He strode out of the laager, and the earth tilted

upwards beneath his feet as he headed for the ridge. Tomorrow, he thought. Tomorrow.

God has been merciful that they did not rush the ridge two days ago when I had three hundred men to hold it. But now I have five thousand to their twenty-five – so let them come!

Suddenly, as he reached the crest, the valley of the Tugela lay below him. Soft with moonlight so that the river was a black gash in the land. He scowled as he saw the field of bivouac fires that straddled the drift at Trichardts farm.

They have crossed. May God forgive me that I had to let them cross, but I could not meet and hold them with three hundred. Two days I have waited in agony for my columns to cover the twenty miles from Colenso. Two days while the cannon bogged down in the mud. Two days while I watched their cavalry and their foot soldiers and their wagons crossing the drift and I could not stop them.

Now they are ready. Tomorrow they will come up to us. This is where they will come, to try at any other place is madness, a stupidity far beyond any they have shown before.

They cannot try the right, for to reach it they must march across our front. With little cover and the river fencing them in they would expose their flank to us at two thousand yards. No, they cannot try the right – not even Buller will try the right.

Slowly he turned his head and looked out to the left where the tall peaks rose sheer out of the heights. The formation of the ground resembled the back of a gigantic fish. Jan Paulus stood upon its head, on the relatively smooth slope of Tabanyama – but on his left rose the dorsal fin of the fish. This was a series of peaks – Vaalkrans, Brakfontein, Twin Peaks, Conical Hill and, the highest and the most imposing of all, Spion Kop.

Once again, he experienced the nagging prickle of doubt. Surely no man, not even Buller, would throw any army against that line of natural fortresses. It would be senseless as the sea hurling its surf at a line of granite cliffs. Yet the doubt remained.

Perhaps Buller, that pedestrian and completely predictable man; Buller who seemed eternally committed to the theory of frontal assault, perhaps this time he would know that the slopes of Tabanyama were *too* logically the only point at which he could break through. Perhaps he would know that the whole of the Boer Army waited for him there with all their guns. Perhaps he would guess that only twenty burghers guarded each of the peaks on the left flank – that Jan Paulus had not dared to spread his line so thin, and had risked everything on Tabanyama.

Jan Paulus sighed. Now it was past the time for doubt. He had made the choice and tomorrow they would know. Tomorrow, *van more*.

Heavily he turned away and started down towards the laager. The moon was setting behind the black massif of Spion Kop, and its shadow hid the path. Loose rock rolled under his feet. Jan Paulus stumbled and almost fell.

'*Wies Daar?*' The challenge from an outcrop of granite beside the path.

'A friend.' Jan Paulus saw the man now, he leaned against the rock with a Mauser held low across his hips.

'Tell me – what commando are you with?'

'The Wynbergers under Leroux.'

'So! Do you know Leroux?' the sentry asked.

'Yes.'

'What colour is his beard?'

'Red – red as the flames of hell.'

The sentry laughed.

'Tell Oom Paul from me I'll tie a knot in it next time I see him.'

'Best you shave before you try – he might do the same for you,' Jan Paulus warned him.

'Are you his friend?'

'And his kinsman too.'

'The hell with you then also.' The sentry laughed again. 'Will you drink coffee with us?'

It was an ideal opportunity for Jan Paulus to mingle with his men and gauge their temper for tomorrow. '*Dankie.*' He accepted the invitation.

'Good.' The sentry straightened up and Jan Paulus saw he was a big man, made taller by the homburg hat he wore. 'Karl, is there any coffee left in the pot?' He yelled into the darkness beyond the rocks and was answered immediately.

'In the name of God, must you bellow? This is a battlefield, not a political meeting.'

'The English are as loud. I've heard them all night.'

'The English are fools. Must you be the same?'

'For you, only for you.' The sentry dropped his voice to a sepulchral whisper, and then roared again suddenly: 'But what about that damned coffee?'

This one is not short of stomach, Jan Paulus grinned to himself, as the man, still chuckling happily, placed an arm about his shoulder and led him to the screened fire among the rocks. Three burghers squatted about it with blankets draped over their shoulders. They were talking among themselves as the sentry and Jan Paulus approached.

'The moon will be down in half an hour,' one of them said. '*Ja.* I will not be happy to see it gone. If the English plan a night attack, then they will come in the dark of the moon.'

'Who is with you?' Karl asked as they came towards the fire.

'A friend,' the sentry replied.

'From what commando?'

'The Wynbergers,' Jan Paulus answered for himself, and Karl nodded and lifted the battered enamel coffee-pot from the fire.

'So, you are with Oom Paul. And what does he think of our chances for tomorrow?'

'That of a man with one bullet left in thick catbush with a lungshot buffalo coming down in full charge.'

'And does it worry him?'

'Only a madman knows no fear. Oom Paul is afraid. But he tries not to show it, for fear spreads among men like the white sore throat diphtheria,' Jan Paulus replied as he accepted the mug of coffee and settled down against a rock out of the firelight so they would not recognize his face nor the colour of his beard.

'Show it or not,' grunted the sentry as he filled his mug. 'But I reckon he'd give one of his eyeballs to be back on his farm at Wynberg with his wife beside him in the double bed.'

Jan Paulus felt the glow of anger in his belly and his voice as he replied was harsh.

'You think him a coward?'

'I think I would rather stand on a hill a mile behind the fighting and send other men in to die,' the sentry chuckled again, but there was a sardonic note in it.

'I've heard him swear that tomorrow he will be in front wherever the fight is fiercest,' growled Jan Paulus.

'Oh, he said so? So that we fight more cheerfully? But when the Lee-Metfords rip your belly open – how will you know where Oom Paul is?'

'I have told you he is my kin. When you insult him you insult me.' Anger had closed Jan Paulus's throat so that his voice was hoarse.

'Good!' The sentry stood up quickly. 'Let us settle it now.'

'Be still, you fools.' Karl spoke irritably. 'Save your anger for the English,' and then more softly, 'all of us are restless, knowing what tomorrow will bring. Let your quarrel stand.'

'He is right,' Jan Paulus agreed, still choked with anger. 'But when I meet you again . . . !'

'How will you know me?' the sentry demanded.

'Here!' Jan Paulus jerked the wide-brimmed Terai hat from his head and flung it at the man's feet. 'Wear that and give me yours in exchange.'

'Why?' The sentry stood puzzled.

'Then if ever a man comes up to me and says, "You're wearing my hat", he will be saying, "Jan Paulus Leroux is a coward!"'

The man grinned so that his teeth glittered in the firelight, then he dropped his own black homburg into Jan Paulus's lap and stooped to pick up the Terai. In that instant, faintly on the wind, soft as the crackle of dried twigs, they heard the rifle-fire.

'Mausers!' shouted Karl and he leapt to his feet sending the coffee-pot flying.

'On the left,' moaned Jan Paulus in anguish. 'Oh, God help us! They've tried the left.'

The chorus of rifle-fire rose, swelling urgently; and now blending with the crisp crackle of the Mausers was the deep belling of the Lee-Metfords.

'Spion Kop! They're on Spion Kop,' and Jan Paulus ran, hurling himself down the path towards the laager with the black homburg jammed down over his ears.

26

The mist lay heavily on the peak of Spion Kop that morning, so that the dawn was a thing of liquid, pearly light. A soft uncertain thing that swirled about them and condensed in tiny drops upon the metal of their rifles.

Colonel John Acheson was breakfasting on ham sandwiches spread thickly with Gentleman's Relish. He sat on a boulder with his uniform cloak draped over his shoulders and chewed morosely.

'No sign of the jolly old Boer yet,' the captain beside him announced cheerfully.

'That trench is not deep enough.' Acheson glowered at the shallow ditch which had been scraped in the stony soil and which was now filled to capacity with men in all the various attitudes of relaxation.

'I know, sir. But there's not much we can do about it. We're down to bedrock and it would need a wagon-load of dynamite to sink another foot.' The captain selected a sandwich and upended the Relish bottle over it. 'Anyway, all the enemy fire will be from below and the parapets will cover that.' Along the front edge of the trench clods of earth and loose rock had been piled to a height of two feet. Pathetic cover for two thousand men.

'Have you ever been on this mountain before?' Acheson asked politely.

'No, sir. Of course not.'

'Well, what makes you so bloody certain how the land lies. You can't see a thing in this mist.'

'Well, sir, we *are* on the crest, and it *is* the highest . . . '
But Acheson interrupted him irritably. 'Where are those
damned scouts? Haven't they come in yet?' He jumped
up and with his cloak swirling about him strode along
the trench. 'You men. Can't you get that parapet higher
there!'

At his feet a few of them stirred and began half-heart-
edly piling stone. They were exhausted by the long night
climb and the skirmish which had driven the Boer garrison from the mountain, and Acheson heard them muttering sullenly behind him as he walked on.

'Acheson!' Out of the mist ahead of him loomed the
figure of General Woodgate followed closely by his staff.

'Sir!' Acheson hurried to meet him.

'Are your men entrenched?'

'As best they can.'

'Good. What of the enemy? Have your scouts reported
back yet?'

'No. They're still out there in the mist.' And Acheson
pointed into the smoky billows that limited the range
of their vision to fifty feet.

'Well, we should be able to hold until we are
reinforced. Let me know the moment . . . ' A small commotion in the mist behind them, and Woodgate paused.
'What is it?'

'My scouts, sir.'

Saul Friedman began delivering his report from a range
of twenty feet. His face was working with excitement
as he scurried out of the mist.

'False crest! We're on the false crest. The true summit
is two hundred yards ahead and there's a rise of ground
out on our right flank, like a little knoll all covered with
aloes, that enfilades our whole position. There are Boers
everywhere. The whole bloody mountain is crawling
with them.'

'Good God, man! Are you certain?'

'Colonel Acheson,' snapped Woodgate, 'turn your right flank to face the knoll,' and as Acheson strode away he added under his breath, 'if you have time!' and he felt the agitated swirl of the mist as it was swept away before the wind.

27

Jan Paulus stood beside his pony. The mist had dewed in his beard and set it a-sparkle in red-gold. Across both shoulders heavy bandoliers of ammunition drooped, and the Mauser rifle seemed like a child's toy in his huge hairy hands. His jaw was thrust forward in thought as he reviewed his dispositions. All night he had flogged his pony from laager to laager, all night he had roared and bullied and driven men up the slopes of Spion Kop. And now around him the mountain rustled and murmured with five thousand waiting burghers, and in an arc of 120 degrees behind it stood his guns. From Green Hill in the north-west to the reverse slopes of the Twin Peaks in the east, his gunners crouched beside their creusots and their Nordenfeldts, ready to range in upon the crest of Spion Kop.

All things are ready and now I must earn the right to wear this hat. He grinned and settled the homburg more firmly over his ears.

'Hennie, take my horse back to the laager.'

The boy led it away and he started up the last slope towards the summit. The light strengthened as he climbed and the burghers among the rocks recognized the flaming beacon of his beard.

'*Goeie Jag*, Oom Paul,' and, '*Kom saam om die Rooi Nekke te skiet*,' they called. Then two burghers ran down to meet him.

'Oom Paul. We've just been forward to Aloe Knoll. There are no English on it!'

'Are you sure?' It seemed too generous a gift of fortune.

'Ja, man. They are all on the back of the mountain. We heard them digging and talking there.'

'What commando are you?' Jan Paulus demanded of the men massed around him in the mist.

'The Carolina commando,' voices answered.

'Come,' ordered Jan Paulus. 'Come, all of you. We are going to Aloe Knoll.'

They followed. Skirting the summit, with the brush, brush, brush of hundreds of feet through the grass, hurrying so that their breathing steamed in the moist air. Until abruptly ahead of them humped the dark mound of Aloe Knoll and they swarmed over it and disappeared among the rocks and crevices like a column of ants returning to their nest.

Lying on his belly Jan Paulus lit his pipe and tamped down on the glowing tobacco with a fire-calloused thumb, sucked the smoke into his mouth and peered into the solid white curtain of mist. In the eerie silence that had fallen upon the mountain his stomach rumbled loudly and he remembered that he had not eaten since the previous noon. There was a stick of biltong in his coat pocket.

A lion hunts best on an empty stomach, he thought and drew again on his pipe.

'Here comes the wind,' a voice whispered near him, and he heard the rising sibilance of it through the aloes above his head. The aloes stood tall as a man, multi-headed, green candelabra tipped in crimson and gold, nodding slightly in the morning wind.

'Ja.' Jan Paulus felt it stirring deep in his chest, that blend of fear and exhilaration that drowned his fatigue. 'Here it comes.' He knocked out his pipe, stuffed it still

175

hot into his pocket and lifted his rifle from the rock in front of him.

Dramatically, as though unveiling a monument, the wind stripped the mists away. Beneath a sky of cobalt blue, soft golden brown in the early sunshine, lay the rounded peak of Spion Kop. A long uneven scar of red earth five hundred yards long was slashed across it.

'*Almagtig!*' Jan Paulus gasped. 'Now we have them.'

Above the crude parapet of the trench, like birds on a fence rail, so close that he could see the chinstraps and the button on each crown, the light khaki helmets contrasted clearly with the darker earth and grass. While beyond the trench, completely exposed from boots to helmets, standing in the open or moving leisurely forward with ammunition and water canteens, were hundreds of English soldiers.

For long seconds the silence persisted, as though the burghers who stared over their rifles at this unbelievable target could not bring themselves to press the triggers on which their fingers rested. The English were too close, too vulnerable. A universal reluctance held the Mausers silent.

'Shoot!' roared Jan Paulus. '*Skiet, Kerels, Skiet,*' and his voice carried to the English behind the trenches. He saw all movement among them suddenly paralysed, white faces turn to stare in his direction – and he sighted carefully into the chest of one of them. The rifle jumped against his shoulder, and the man went down into the grass.

That single shot broke the spell. Gunfire crackled in hysterical unison and the frieze of khaki figures along the trench exploded into violent movement as the bullets thudded amongst them. At that range most of Jan Paulus's burghers could be trusted to knock down four running springbok with five shots. In the few seconds that it took the English to dive into the trench, at least fifty of them went down, dead or wounded, and lay sprawled against the red earth.

Now there were only the helmets and heads above the parapet to shoot at and these were never still. They ducked and weaved and bobbed as Woodgate's men fired and reloaded, and seventeen hundred Lee-Metford rifles added their voices to the pandemonium.

Then the first shell, lobbed from a field gun on the reverse slope of Conical Hill, shrieked over the heads of the burghers and burst in a leap of smoke and red dust fifty feet in front of the English trench. A lull while Jan Paulus's heliograph team below the crest signalled the range correction to the battery, then the next shell burst beyond the trench; another lull and the third fell full upon the trench. A human body was thrown high, legs and arms spinning like the spokes of a wagon wheel. When the dust cleared there was a gap in the parapet and half a dozen men frantically trying to plug it with loose rock.

Together all the Boer guns opened. The constant shriek of big shells was punctuated by the vicious whine of the quick-firing pompoms. And once again a mist covered the peak, this time a thin sluggish mist of dust and lyddite fume which diluted the sunlight and clogged the nostrils and eyes and mouths of men for whom a long, long day had begun.

28

Lieutenant-Colonel Garrick Courtney was damnably uncomfortable. It was hot in the sun. Sweat trickled down under his tunic and moistened his stump so that already it was chafed. His field-glasses magnified the glare as he looked out across the Tugela River to the great hump of the mountain four miles away. The glare aggravated the ache behind his eyes, which was a memorial to last night's drinking.

'Woodgate seems to be holding very well. His reinforcements should be up to him soon enough.'

Sir Redvers Buller appeared to be satisfied, and none of his staff had any comment to add. Stolidly they stood and stared through their glasses at the peak which was now faintly blurred with the dust and smoke of battle.

Garrick was puzzling once more the devious lines of authority which Buller had established for the attack on Spion Kop. Commanding the actual assault was General Woodgate, who was now 'holding very well' on the peak, yet Woodgate was responsible not to Buller but to General Charles Warren, who had his headquarters beyond Trichardts Drift where the column had crossed. Warren was in turn responsible to Buller, who was well back behind the river, standing on a pleasant little hill called Mount Alice.

Everyone on the staff was aware that Buller hated Warren. Garrick was certain that Warren had been given command of an operation which Buller considered very risky, so that in the event it failed Warren would be discredited and goaded into resigning. Of course, if he succeeded, Sir Redvers Buller was still supreme Commander and the credit would therefore accrue to him.

It was a line of reasoning Garrick found easy to follow, in fact, had he been in Buller's position he would have done exactly the same thing. This secret knowledge gave Garry a deal of satisfaction, and standing beside Buller on the slope of Mount Alice he felt very much in tune with him. He found himself hoping that Spion Kop would soon be a bloody slaughter-house, and that Warren would retreat across the river in disgrace. He remembered the occasion in the mess when Sir Charles had referred to him as an 'irregular, and a damned *colonial* irregular – at that!' Garry's fingers tightened on his field-glasses and he glared out at the mountain. He was so deep in his resentment that he hardly noticed the signaller who came running from the mule wagon that housed the field telegraph which connected Buller's headquarters with those of Warren beyond the river.

'Sir! Sir! A message from General Warren.' The urgency of the man's tone caught all their attentions. As one man the entire general staff lowered their glasses and turned to him.

'Let's have it then, my man!' Buller snatched the sheet of notepaper and read it slowly. Then he looked up at Garry and there was something in those pale, bulging eyes, a pleasure, a conspiratory gleam that made Garry almost grin.

'What do you make of that, Courtney?' He handed the sheet across and waited while Garry read it.

'Message from Colonel Crofton on the Spion Kop. *Reinforce at once or all is lost. General Woodgate dead. What do you suggest. Warren.*'

'It seems to me, sir,' Garry spoke slowly, trying to

179

mask the fierce jubilation he felt, 'that Sir Charles Warren is on the verge of panic.'

'Yes, that's the way it looks.' Buller was openly gloating now.

'I would suggest sending him a message that will stiffen him, sir.'

'Yes, I agree.' Buller turned to the signaller and began to dictate. 'The mountain must be held at all costs. No withdrawal. I repeat no withdrawal. Reinforce with Middlesex and Dorset regiments.' Then he hesitated and looked around his staff. 'What do you know of this fellow Crofton. Is he the right man to command on the peak?'

There were non-committal sounds of negation from them until A'Court, Buller's A.D.C., spoke up.

'Sir. There is one excellent man up there – Acheson – Colonel John Acheson. You remember his showing at Colenso?'

Buller nodded thoughtfully and turning back to the signaller he went on with his dictation. 'You must put some really good hard fighting man in command on the peak. Suggest you promote Acheson to Major-General.'

29

In front of the trench the grass was flattened by the repeated counter-attacks that had swept across it, stained by the blood of those who had dragged themselves back from the Boer positions along the crest, and littered with the twisted corpses of those who had not. Every few seconds a shell exploded along the British line, so there was a continual moving forest of bursts, and the shrapnel hissed like the flails of threshing giants.

John Acheson forced himself to his feet and climbed on to the parapet and shouted, 'Come on, lads. This time they'll not stop us!' In the trench below him the dead and the wounded lay upon each other two and three deep, all of them coated with a layer of red dust. The same red dust coated the faces that looked up at him as he shouted again.

'Bugler, sound the charge. Come, lads, forward. Take the bayonet to them.'

The bugle started to sing, brassy and urgent. Acheson hopped like a gaunt, old stork from the parapet and flapped his sword. Behind him he heard laughter from a dozen throats, not the laughter of ordinary men, but the chilling discord of insanity.

'Follow me, the Lancs! Follow me!' His voice rose to a shriek and they scrambled from the trench behind him. Dusty spectres with bloodshot eyes, smeared with dust and their own sweat. Their laughter and their curses blended with the babbling of the wounded, outstripped it and climbed into a chorus of wild cheers. Without form, spreading like spilled oil, the charge flowed out towards the crest. Four hundred men staggering through the dust-storm of shell-fire and the tempest of the Mausers.

Acheson stumbled over a corpse and fell. His ankle twisted with a shock of pain that jolted his dulled senses. He recovered his sword, dragged himself up and limped grimly on towards the rampart of boulders that marked the crest. But this time they did not reach it to be thrown back as they had before. This time the charge withered before it had covered half the distance. In vain Acheson waved them forward, yelling until his voice was a hoarse croak. They slowed and wavered, then at last they broke and streamed back down the open bullet-swept slope to the trench. Tears of frustrated anger streaking his dusty cheeks, Acheson hobbled after them. He fell over the parapet and lay face down on the corpses that lined the trench.

A hand shaking his shoulder roused him and he sat up quickly and tried to control the breathing that shuddered up his throat. Dimly he recognized the man who crouched beside him.

'What is it, Friedman?' he gasped. But the reply was drowned in the arrival of another shell, and the delirious shrieks of a man wounded in the belly in the trench beside them.

'Speak up, man!'

'Heliograph message from Sir Charles Warren,' shouted Saul. 'You have been promoted General. You are in command of the peak.' And then with a dusty sweat-streaked grin he added: 'Well done, sir.'

Acheson stared at him aghast. 'What about General Woodgate?'

'He was shot through the head two hours ago.'

'I didn't know.' Since morning Acheson had known nothing that was happening outside his own small section of the line. His whole existence had closed down to a hundred yards of shrapnel-and-bullet-swept earth. Now he peered out at the holocaust around him and whispered, 'In command! No man commands here! The devil is directing this battle.'

'Sir Charles is sending up three more battalions to reinforce us,' Saul shouted into his ear.

'We can well use them,' Acheson grunted, and then, 'Friedman, I've sprained my ankle. I want you to lace up my boot as tight as you can – I'm going to need this foot again before the day is done.'

Saul knelt without argument and began working over his foot. One of the riflemen at the parapet beside him was thrown sideways. He fell across Acheson's lap, and from the wound in his temple the contents of his skull splattered them both. With an exclamation of surprise and disgust Saul pulled back and wiped his face, then he reached forward to drag the body from Acheson's legs.

'Leave him.' Acheson prevented him sharply. 'See to that boot.' While Saul obeyed, Acheson unwound the silk scarf from around his own neck and covered the mutilated head. It was a wound he had seen repeated a hundred times that day, all of them shot through the right side of the head.

'Aloe Knoll,' he whispered fiercely. 'If only we'd taken Aloe Knoll.' Then his tone dulled. 'My poor lads.' And gently he eased the shattered head from his lap.

30

'They are ripe now, let us pluck them!' With five hundred of his burghers Jan Paulus had left the shelter of Aloe Knoll and worked his way forward, crawling belly down through the jumble of rocks, until now they were crouched in a line along a fold of dead ground below the false crest. Twenty yards ahead of them was the right-hand extremity of the English trench. They could not see it, but clearly they heard the incoherent cries of the wounded; the shouts of 'Stretcher-bearer! Stretcher-bearer!' and 'Ammunition boys, here!' and above the splutter of musketry, the continuous metallic rattle of breech bolts reloading.

'You must signal to the guns, Oom Paul.' The burgher next to him reminded him.

'*Ja*,' Jan Paulus removed the homburg from his head and waved with it at the fat mound at Aloe Knoll behind them. He saw his signal briefly acknowledged and knew that the order to cease fire was being flashed by heliograph to the batteries.

They waited, tense to charge, a long line of men. Jan Paulus glanced along them and saw that each man stared ahead fixedly. Most of their faces masked by beards of fifty different hues, but here and there a lad too young for this work, too young to hide his fear. Thank God my eldest is not yet twelve, or he would be here. He stopped that train of thought guiltily, and concentrated his whole attention on the volume of shell-fire that raged just ahead of them. Abruptly it ceased, and in the comparative silence the rifle-fire sounded strangely subdued. Jan Paulus let the slow seconds pass, counting silently to ten, before he filled his lungs and roared:

'*Vrystaat!* Come on the Free Staters!'

Echoing his cry, yelling wildly, his burghers surged forward over the crest on to the English flank. They came from so close in, seeming to appear as a solid wall from under the English parapet, that the momentum of their charge carried them instantly into the depleted line of shell-shocked, thirst-tormented and dazed Lancashires. Hardly a shot was fired, and though a few individual scuffles rippled the smooth onward flow of the charge – most of the English responded immediately to the shouts of 'Hands Op! Hands Op!' by throwing down their rifles and climbing wearily to their feet with hands held high. They were surrounded by jubilant burghers and hustled over the parapet and down the slope towards Aloe Knoll. A great milling throng of burghers and soldiers spread over fifty yards of the trench.

'Quickly!' Jan Paulus shouted above the hubbub. 'Catch them and take them away.' He was well aware that this was only a very localized victory, involving perhaps a tenth of the enemy. Already cries of 'The Lancs are giving in!', 'Where are the officers?', 'Back, you men', were spreading along the English line. He had planted the germ of defeat among them, now he must spread it through them before he could carry the entire position. Frantically he signalled for reinforcements from the Boer positions along the crest, hundreds of his burghers were already running forward from Aloe Knoll. Another five minutes and complete victory would emerge from the confusion.

'Damn you, sir! What do you think you're doing!' The voice behind him was impregnated with authority, unmistakably that of a high-ranking officer. Jan Paulus wheeled to face a tall and enraged old gentleman, whose pointed grey whiskers quivered with fury. The apoplectic crimson of his countenance clashed horribly with its coating of red dust.

'I am taking your men hands-up away.' Jan Paulus struggled gutturally with the foreign words.

'I'll be damned if you are, sir.' Leaning heavily on the shoulder of a skinny little dark-haired man who supported him, the officer reached forward and shook a finger in Jan Paulus's face. 'There will be no surrender on this hill. Kindly remove your rabble from my trench!'

'Rabble, is it!' roared Jan Paulus. Around them the Boers and the British had ceased all activity and were watching with interest. Jan Paulus turned to the nearest burghers: '*Vat hulle weg!* Take them away!' His gesture that accompanied the order was unmistakable.

'We'll have none of that, sir!' Acheson glared at him before issuing his own order. 'You men, fall back and re-form on the Devonshires. Hurry it up, now. Come along. Come along.'

'Hey!' Jan Paulus held up his hand. 'These are my . . . ' He groped for the word. 'My captures.'

'Sir.' Acheson released his grip on Saul's shoulder, drew himself up to his full height and glared up into Jan Paulus's face. 'I will give you five minutes to vacate this trench – otherwise you will become my prisoner. Good day to you.' And he hobbled away through the grass. Jan Paulus stared in disbelief when fifty paces away Acheson turned, folded his arms across his chest, and waited grimly for the expiry of the five minutes. About him he had gathered a handful of battle-stained soldiers and it was clearly his intention to implement his threat with this pitiful little band. Jan Paulus wanted to laugh with frustration – the skinny old goat. But he realized with dismay that most of his prisoners were filtering away and hurrying to join Acheson. He must do something, but what? The whole position was deteriorating into a farce.

'Stop them!' he shouted at his burghers. 'Hold those men – they went hands-up. They cannot change their minds now.'

Then abruptly the whole position altered. Over the skyline behind Acheson and his tiny party poured a solid phalanx of fresh khaki-clad figures. The three battalions of reinforcements sent up from the foot of the mountain by Sir Charles Warren had at last arrived. Acheson glanced over his shoulder and saw them swarming forward. The brown parchment of his face tore laterally in a wide and wicked grin.

'Fix bayonets!' he shrieked, and drew his sword. 'Buglers sound the charge. Charge, men! Charge!'

Hopping and stumbling like a stork with a broken leg, he led them. Behind him, the glittering crest of a wave, a line of bayonets raced down on the trench. Jan Paulus's burghers hated naked steel. There were five hundred of them against two thousand. They broke and blew away like smoke on a high wind. Their prisoners ran with them.

Jan Paulus reached the crest and dropped behind a boulder that already sheltered three men.

'Stop them! Here they come!' he panted.

While the British wave slowed and expended itself against the reef of hidden Mausers, while they fell back with the shrapnel scourging them once more – Jan Paulus knew that he would not stand in the British trench again that day.

He could sense the despondency among his burghers. He knew that already the faint-hearted were slipping away to where their ponies waited at the foot of the mountain. He knew with sickened acceptance that he had lost Spion Kop. Oh! The English had paid a heavy price all right, there must be fifteen hundred of their dead and wounded strewn upon the peak, but they had torn a gap in his line. He had lost Spion Kop and through this breach would pour twenty-five thousand men to relieve Ladysmith, and to drive his burghers out of Natal and into the Transvaal. They had lost. It was finished.

John Acheson tried desperately to ignore the agony of his bloated foot, he tried to shut out the shrill chorus of the wounded pleading for water. There was no water on the peak. He turned his gaze away from the trench where men, drugged with exhaustion, oblivious to the thunder of the bombardment that still raged about them, lay in sleep upon the bodies of their dead and dying comrades.

He looked instead at the sun, that great, bloody orb lightly screened with long streamers of cloud. In an hour it would be dark – and he knew he had lost. The message he held in his hands admitted it, the grotesque piles of dead men that clogged the trench proved it. He re-read the message with difficulty for his vision jerked and swam giddily.

'If you cannot hold until tomorrow, retire at your discretion. Buller.'

Tomorrow. What would tomorrow bring, if not a repetition of today's horror? They had lost. They were going down from this mountain. They had lost.

He closed his eyes and leaned back against the rough stone of the parapet. A nerve in his eyelid began to twitch insistently, he could not stop it.

31

How many are there left? Half, perhaps. I do not know. Half my men gone, all night I heard their ponies galloping away, and the crack and rumble of their wagons, and I could not hold them.

Jan Paulus stared up at the mountain in the dawn.

'Spion Kop.' He mouthed the name with loathing, but its outline was blurred for his eyes could not focus. They were rimmed with angry red and in each corner was a lump of yellow mucus. His body seemed to have shrunk, dried out like that of an ancient mummy. He slumped wearily in the saddle, every muscle and nerve in his body screamed for rest. To sleep a while. Oh God, to sleep.

With a dozen of his loyal commandants he had tried all night to staunch the dribble of deserters that was bleeding his army to death. He had ridden from laager to laager, blustering, pleading, trying to shame them. With many he had succeeded, but with many he had not – and once he had himself been shamed. He remembered the old man with the long white beard straggling from his yellow, wizened face, his eyes glistening with tears in the firelight.

'Three sons I have given you today, Jan Paulus Leroux. My brothers have gone up your accursed mountain to beg for their bodies from the English. Three sons! Three fine sons! What more do you want from me?' From where he sat against the wheel of his wagon the old man struggled to his feet hugging the blanket around his shoulders, 'You call me coward, Leroux. You say I am afraid.' He stopped and struggled with his breathing, and when he went on his voice was a croak. 'I am seventy-eight years old and you are the first man to ever call me that – if God is merciful you'll be the last.' He stopped again. 'Seventy-eight years. Seventy-eight! and you call me that! Look, Leroux. Look well!' He let the blanket fall away and Jan Paulus stiffened in the saddle as he saw the bloody mess of bandages that swathed the old man's chest. 'Tomorrow morning I will be with my sons. I wait for them now. Write on our grave, Leroux! Write "Cowards" on our grave!' And through the old lips burst a froth of pink bubbles.

Now with red eyes Jan Paulus stared up at the mountain. The lines of fatigue and shame and defeat were etched deep beside his nostrils and around his mouth. When the mists cleared they would see the English on the crest and with half his men he would go back. He touched the pony with his spurs and started him up the slope.

The sun gilded the mountain mist, it swirled golden and began to dissipate.

Faintly on the morning wind he heard the cheering and he frowned. *The English cheer too soon*, he thought. *Do they think we will not come again?* He urged his pony upward, but as it scrambled over loose rock and scree he reeled drunkenly in the saddle and was forced to cling to the pommel.

The volume of cheering mounted, and he peered uncomprehendingly at the crest above him. The skyline was dotted with figures who danced and waved their hats, and suddenly there were voices all around him.

'They've gone.'

'The mountain is ours.'

190

'We've won! Praise God, we've won. The English have gone.'

Men crowded about his pony, and dragged him from the saddle. He felt his legs buckle under him, but rough hands were there to support him, and half dragging, half carrying him, they bore him up towards the peak.

Jan Paulus sat upon a boulder and watched them harvest the rich crop of battle. He could not sleep yet, not until this was done. He had allowed the English stretcher-bearers to come up his mountain and they were at work along the trench while his own burghers gleaned their dead from along the crest.

Four of them approached Jan Paulus, each holding the corner of a grey woollen blanket as though it were a hammock. They staggered under the load, until they reached the neat line of corpses already laid out on the grass.

'Who knows this man?' one of them called, but there was no reply from the group of silent men who waited with Jan Paulus.

They lifted the body out of the blanket and laid it with the others. One of the burghers who had carried him removed from his clutching, dead fingers a wide Terai hat and placed it over his face. Then he straightened and asked:

'Who claims him?' Unless a friend or a kinsman claimed the corpse it would be buried in a communal grave.

Jan Paulus stood up and walked across to stand over the body. He lifted the hat and replaced it with the homburg from his own head.

'Ja. I claim him,' he said heavily.

'Is he kin or friend, Oom Paul?'

'He is a friend.'
'What is his name?'
'I do not know his name. He is just a friend.'

32

Saul Friedman fidgeted impatiently. In his eagerness he had arrived half an hour before visiting-time began and for this he was doing penance in the bleak little waiting-room of Greys Hospital. He sat forward on the straight-backed chair, twisted his helmet between his fingers and stared at the large sign on the opposite wall.

'Gentlemen are requested *Not* to smoke'.

He had asked Ruth to come with him, but she had pleaded a headache. In a sneaking fashion Saul was glad. He knew that her presence would inhibit his reunion with Sean Courtney. He didn't want polite conversation about the weather and how was he feeling now, and he must come round to dinner some evening. It would have been difficult not to be able to swear if they wanted – it would have been even more difficult in view of Ruth's attitude.

Yesterday, the first day of his leave, he had spoken of Sean with enthusiasm. How many times had she visited him? How was he? Did he limp badly? Didn't Ruth think he was a wonderful person? Twice she replied and, well, no not badly, yes he was very nice. Just about then Saul perceived the truth. Ruth did not like Sean. At first he could hardly believe it. He tried to continue the conversation. But each of her monosyllabic replies confirmed his first suspicion. Of course, she had not said so, but it was so obvious. For some reason she had taken a dislike to Sean which was close to loathing.

Now Saul sat and pondered the reason. He discounted

the possibility that Sean had offended her. If that were the case Sean would have received as good as he gave and afterwards Ruth would have related the whole tale with glee and relish.

No, Saul decided, it was something else. Like a swimmer about to dive into icy water, Saul drew a metaphorical deep breath and plunged into the uncharted sea of feminine thought processes. Was Sean's masculinity so overpowering as to be offensive? Had his attention to her been below average (Ruth was accustomed to extravagant reactions to her beauty)? Could it be that . . . ? Or, on the other hand, did Sean . . . ? Saul was floundering heavily when suddenly, as a shipwrecked victim surfacing for the last time finds a tall ship close alongside with lifeboats being lowered from every derrick, the solution came to him.

Ruth was jealous!

Saul leaned back in the chair, astounded at the depth of his own perception.

His lovely, hot-tempered wife was jealous of the friendship between Sean and himself!

Chuckling tenderly, Saul laid plans to appease Ruth. He'd have to be less fulsome in his praises of Sean. He must get them together and in Sean's presence pay special attention to Ruth. He must . . .

Then his thoughts ricocheted off in another direction and he began to think about Ruth. As always when he thought too intensely about her, he experienced a feeling of bemusement similar to what a poor man feels on winning a large lottery.

He had met her at the Johannesburg Turf Club during the big Summer Meeting, and he had fallen in love at a range of fifty paces, so that when he was presented to her, his usually nimble tongue lay like a lump of heavy metal in his mouth and he squirmed and was silent.

The friendly smile she bestowed upon him licked across his face like a blow torch, heating it until he felt the skin would blister.

That night, alone in his lodging, he planned his campaign. To its conduct he allocated the sum of five hundred guineas, which was exactly half his savings. The following morning he began his intelligence work, and a week later he had collected a massive volume of information.

She was eighteen years old and was on a visit to relations in Johannesburg, a visit scheduled to last a further six weeks. She came from a rich Natal family of brewers and hotel-keepers, but she was an orphan and a ward of her uncle. While in Johannesburg she rode every day, visited the theatre or danced every night with an assortment of escorts, except Fridays when she attended the Old Synagogue in Jeppe Street.

His opening manoeuvre was the hire of a horse and he waylaid her as she rode out with her cousin. She did not remember him and would have ridden on, but at last his tongue, which was sharpened by three years of practice at the Johannesburg Bar, came to life. Within two minutes she was laughing and an hour later she invited him back to tea with her relatives.

The following evening he called for her in a splendid carriage and they dined at Candy's Hotel and went on to the Ballet in company with a party of Saul's friends.

Two nights later she went with him to the Bar Association Ball and found that he was a superb dancer. Resplendent in brand-new evening dress, with an ugly yet mobile and expressive face, an inch taller than her five feet six, with wit and intelligence that had earned him a wide circle of friends – he was the perfect foil for her own beauty. When he returned her home Ruth had a thoughtful but dreamy look in her eye.

The following day she attended Court and listened to him successfully defend a gentleman accused of assault with intent to do grievous bodily harm. She was impressed by his display and decided that in time he would reach the heights of his profession.

A week later Saul again proved his command of the spoken word in an impassioned declaration of love. His suit was judged and found worthy, and after that it was merely a case of informing the families and sending out the invitations.

Now, at last, four years later they were to have their first child. Saul grinned happily as he thought about it. Tomorrow he would begin his attempt to discourage the adoption of the name 'Storm'. It would be a difficult case to win, one worthy of his talents. In the preceding four years Saul had learned that once Ruth set her small white teeth into something she had a bulldog grip. A great deal of finesse was needed to loosen that grip without invoking her wrath. Saul had an awesome respect for his wife's wrath.

'It's four o'clock.' The little blonde nurse poked her head around the waiting-room door and smiled at him. 'You may go in now. You'll find him out on the veranda.'

Saul's eagerness returned in full flood and he had to restrain himself from bouncing too boisterously down the veranda.

He recognized Sean's bulk, clad in uniform khaki, reclining elegantly in a cane-backed chair and chatting to the men in the row of beds in front of him. He came up behind the chair.

'Don't stand up, Sergeant. Just toss me a salute from where you are.'

'Saul!' Lugging himself out of the chair and pivoting easily on his game leg, Sean gripped both Saul's shoulders in the old show of affection. The pleasure that fired Sean's expression was genuine and that was enough for Saul.

'Good to see you, you old bastard.' He returned Sean's grip, grinning happily. He did not notice how swiftly Sean's pleasure faded, and was replaced by a shifty, nervous smile.

'Have a drink.' They were the first words that came into Sean's mind. He must have time to feel his way. Had Ruth said anything to Saul, had he guessed?

'Water?' Saul grimaced.

'Gin,' whispered Sean, guilt making him garrulous and he went on in a clumsy attempt at humour. 'Water carafe is full of gin. For God's sake don't tell Matron. I smuggle it in. Argue with the nurse whenever she tries to change it – she says "Water stale, must change!" I say, "Like stale water, raised on stale water, stale water strongly indicated in all cases of leg injury!"'

'Give me stale water too,' laughed Saul.

While he poured Sean introduced Saul to the gentleman in the next bed, a Scotsman who agreed with them that stale water was a sovereign therapeutic for shrapnel wound in the chest – a complaint from which he was currently suffering. The three of them settled down to a course of intensive treatment.

At Sean's prodding Saul embarked on a long account of the battle of Spion Kop. He made it seem very funny. Then he went on to describe the final break through at Hlangwane, Buller's eventual relief of Ladysmith, and his cautious pursuit of Leroux's army which was now in full retreat into the Transvaal.

They discussed Lord Roberts's offensive that had driven up from the Cape, relieved Kimberley, swept on to take Bloemfontein and was now poised for the final thrust up through the belly of the Transvaal to Pretoria which was the heart.

'It will all be over in three months.' The Scotsman gave his opinion.

'You think so?' Sean sneered at him a little, and succeeded in provoking an argument whose flames were fed with gin.

As the level in the carafe fell the time for sober and serious discussion passed and they became sentimental. Tenderly Saul inquired after their injuries.

The Scotsman was being shipped home across the sea, and at the thought of parting they became sad.

Sean was returning the following day to Ladyburg for convalescent leave. At the end of which, if the doctors were satisfied that the pieces of shrapnel in his leg were satisfactorily encysted (two words which Sean had difficulty enunciating) he would be returned to duty.

The word '*duty*' aroused their patriotism and Sean and Saul with arms around each other's shoulders swore a mighty oath that together, comrades in arms, brothers in blood, they would see this war out. Never counting the cost in hardship and danger, together they would ride against the foe.

Suitable music was needed for their mood, and the Scotsman gave them 'The Wild Colonial Boy'. His eyes were moist and his voice quavered with emotion.

Deeply touching, but not entirely appropriate to the occasion, Sean and Saul did 'Hearts of Oak' as a duet, then all three launched into a lively rendition of 'Are you awake, Johnny Cope?'

The Matron arrived in the middle of the third chorus, by which time Johnny Cope and anybody else within a hundred yards could not possibly have been sleeping.

'Gentlemen, visiting hour ended at five o'clock.' She was a fearsome woman with a voice like a cavalry charge, but Saul who had pleaded before hanging judges rose undaunted to the defence.

'Madam.' He opened his address with a bow. 'These men – nay, let me speak with truth – these heroes have made great sacrifice in the name of freedom. Their blood has flowed like gin in defence of that glorious ideal – Freedom! All I ask is that a little of that precious stuff be granted unto them. Madam. In the name of honour, of fairness, and of gratitude I appeal to you.' He ended with one fist clenched above his heart and his head tragically bowed.

'Hoots, mon!'

'Oh good! Very good!'

The two heroes burst into spontaneous and heart-warming applause, but over the Matron's features descended a frosty veil of suspicion. She elevated her nose a little and sniffed.

'You're drunk!' she accused grimly.

'Oh, foul libel! Oh, monstrous untruth.' Saul backed hurriedly out of range.

'All right, Sergeant.' She turned grimly on Sean. 'Where is it?'

'What?' Sean was all helpless innocence.

'The bottle!' She lifted the bedclothes and began her search. Saul picked up his helmet, saluted them behind her back and tiptoed down the veranda.

33

Sean's leave in Ladyburg passed quickly, much too quickly. Mbejane had disappeared on a mysterious errand into Zululand. Sean guessed that it related to the two wives and their offspring that Mbejane had cheerfully sent to the kraals of their parents when he and Sean had left Ladyburg so many years before.

Dirk was incarcerated each morning in the schoolhouse, and so Sean was free to roam alone upon the hills and over the veld that surrounded the town. Most of his time he spent covering the huge derelict ranch called Lion Kop which spread above the escarpment. After a month he knew the course of every stream and each fold and slope of the land. His leg strengthened with the exercise. It no longer pained him and the scar lost its purple shine and dulled down to a closer match with his skin colour.

But as his strength returned and flesh filled out his shoulders and padded the gaunt bones of his face, so restlessness came back to him. His daily pilgrimage to Lion Kop Ranch became an obsession. He wandered through the bare rooms of the old homestead and saw them as they could be with the thatched roof replaced to keep out the rain and the flaking plaster renewed and freshly painted. He stood before the empty, smoke-blackened fireplace and imagined the glow and the warmth it could give. Stamping across the dusty floors he judged the yellow-wood planking as sound as the massive beams that supported the roof. Then he wandered out across the land, stooping now and then to take up a handful of earth and feel its rich loamy texture.

In the May of 1900 he went to the Deeds Registry at the Magistrate's office and surreptitiously inspected the title. He found that the fifteen thousand acres of Lion Kop Ranch had been purchased from the estate of the late Stephanus Johannes Erasmus by the Ladyburg Banking & Trust Co. Ltd. Transfer had been signed by Ronald Pye, Esq., in his capacity as Chairman of the Bank. Sean grinned. Ronny Pye was his most cherished childhood enemy. This could be very amusing.

Sean settled himself in the deep, soft nest of polished leather formed by the arm-chair and glanced curiously around the panelled office.

'A few changes since you were last here. Hey, Sean?' Ronny Pye interpreted his thoughts accurately.

'A few.' The Ladyburg Banking & Trust Co. was doing very prettily, judging by the furnishings. Some of its prosperity showed on the figure of its Chairman. Plenty of flesh under the solid gold watch-chain, dark but expensive jacket to offset the extravagant waistcoat, fifteen-guinea hand-made boots. Very nice until you looked at the face; pale so that the freckles showed like irregular gold coins, greedy eyes, ears like the handles of a shaving-mug – that much hadn't changed. But although Ronny was just two years Sean's senior, there was plenty of grey in his ginger sideburns and little wrinkles of worry around his eyes.

'Been out to Theuniskraal to visit your sister-in-law yet?' There was a sly expression in Ronny's face as he asked.

'No.'

'No, of course you wouldn't,' Ronny nodded under-standingly and managed to convey that the scandal, though old, was by no means dead. Sean felt a repug-nance that made him shift in his chair. The little ginger moustache heightened Ronny's resemblance to a bush rat. Now Sean wanted to end the business and get out into the fresh air again.

'Listen, Ronny. I've searched title on Lion Kop. You own it,' he began abruptly.

'Lion Kop?' The previous morning the clerk from the Registry had hurried down to Mr Pye with news that earned him a sovereign. There had been many others calling with the news that Sean had visited the ranch every day for a month. But now Ronny had to search his memory to place the name. 'Lion Kop? Ah, yes! The old Erasmus place. Yes, I do believe we picked it up from the estate. Paid too much for it, I'm afraid.' Here he sighed with resignation. 'But we can hold on to it for another ten years or so and get our money back. No hurry to sell.'

'I want it.' Sean cut short the preliminaries and Ronny laughed easily.

'You're in good company. Half the farmers in Natal want it – but not enough to meet our price.'

'How much?'

The established price of grazing land in the Ladyburg area was one shilling and sixpence an acre. Ten minutes before Ronny had set himself to ask two shillings. But now he was looking into Sean's eyes and remembering a fist crushing his nose and the taste of his own blood. He heard again Sean's arrogant laughter rejecting his overtures of friendship. No, he thought with hatred. No, you big cocky bastard, now you pay for those.

'Three shillings,' he said.

Sean nodded thoughtfully. He understood. Then sud-

202

denly he grinned. 'My God, Ronny, I heard you were a pretty sharp business man. But I must have heard wrong. If you paid three shillings for Lion Kop they really caught you with your skirts up.' And Ronny flushed. Sean had probed deep into his pride.

'I paid ninepence,' he snapped. 'I'm selling for three shillings.'

'Make out the deed of sale for £2,250. I'll take it.'

Damn it! Damn it to hell! Ronny swore silently. *He would have paid five.*

'That's for the land only. An extra £1,000 for the improvements.'

'Anything else?' Sean inquired.

'No.'

Sean calculated quickly, with transfer tax he could meet the price with a few hundred spare.

'I'll still take it.'

Ronny stared at him while his brain wriggled like a snake. *I didn't realize he wanted it that badly – I could have had his soul!*

'Of course, my Board will have to approve the sale. It depends on them really.' Ronny's Board of Directors consisted of himself, his little sister Audrey, and her husband Dennis Petersen. Ronny held eighty per cent of the shares, and Sean knew this. He had examined the Company's Articles that were lodged with the Registrar.

'Listen to me, dear friend of my youth.' Sean leaned forward across the stinkwood desk and picked up a heavy silver cigar-box. 'You made an offer. I accepted it. I'll be here at four o'clock this afternoon with the money. Please have the documents ready.' Sean lifted the cigar-box in one fist and started to squeeze. The muscles in his forearm writhed like mating pythons and the box crumpled and burst open at the seams. Sean placed the distorted lump of metal on the blotter in front of Ronny.

'Don't misunderstand me, Sean.' Ronny grinned nervously and dragged his eyes away from the box. 'I'm certain I'll be able to convince my Board.'

34

The following day was a Saturday. No school for Dirk and Sean took him along on the daily ride out to the ranch. Almost beside himself with joy at being alone with his god, Dirkie raced his pony ahead and then circled at full gallop to fall in beside Sean once more. Laughing with excitement, chattering ecstatically for a while, then he could no longer contain his high spirits and he galloped ahead. Before Sean reached the cross-roads below the escarpment he met a small caravan of travellers coming in the opposite direction.

Sean greeted the leader solemnly. 'I see you, Mbejane.' Mbejane had the jaded and slightly sheepish look of a tom-cat returning from a busy night out. 'I see you also, Nkosi.'

There was a long, embarrassed silence while Mbejane took a pinch of snuff and stared fixedly at the sky above Sean's head. Sean was studying Mbejane's travelling companions. There were two in their middle age, which is about thirty-five years old for a Zulu woman. Both of them wore the tall head-dress of clay which denotes matronhood. Though they retained the proud, erect carriage, their breasts were pendulous and empty and the skin of their bellies above the brief aprons was wrinkled with the marks of child-bearing. There were also two girls just beyond puberty, moon-faced, skins glowing with youth, straight and well-muscled, buttocks like ripe melons and firm, round breasts. They hung their heads and giggled shyly.

'Perhaps it will rain tonight,' Mbejane remarked.

'Perhaps.'

'It will be good for the grazing.' Mbejane ploughed on doggedly.

'Who the hell are these women?' Sean could contain his curiosity no longer and Mbejane frowned at this breach of etiquette. Observations on the weather and the grazing should have continued another five minutes.

'Nkosi, these two are my wives.' He gestured at the matrons.

'The other two your daughters?'

'No.' Mbejane paused, then went on gravely: 'It is not fitting that a man of my years should have but two women who are old for work and the bearing of children. I have purchased two younger wives.'

'I see,' said Sean, and kept the grin off his face. Mbejane had invested a large percentage of his capital. 'And what do you propose doing with all your wives, you know we must soon return again to fight?'

'When the time comes they will go to the kraals of their fathers and wait for me there.' Mbejane hesitated delicately. 'I bring them with me until I am certain that I have trodden on the moon of each of them.'

Treading on a woman's moon was the Zulu expression for interrupting her menstrual cycle. Mbejane was making sure his investment bore interest.

'There is a farm upon the hills up there.' Sean seemed to be changing the subject.

'Many time, Nkosi, you and I have spoken of it.' But Mbejane understood and there was an anticipatory gleam in his eyes.

'It is a good farm?' Sean held him a little longer in suspense.

'It is truly an excellent and beautiful farm. The water is sweeter than the juice of the sugar-cane, the earth is richer than the flesh of a young ox, the grass upon it as thick and as full of promise as the hair on a woman's pudendum.' Now Mbejane's eyes were shining with happiness. In his book a farm was a place where a man sat in the sun with a pot of millet beer beside him and listened to his wives singing in the fields. It meant cattle, the only true wealth, and many small sons to herd them. It meant the end of a long weary road.

'Take your wives with you and select the place where you wish to build your kraal.'

'Nkosi.' There is no Zulu equivalent of *thank you*. He could say *I praise you*, but that was not what Mbejane felt. At last he found the word. '*Bayete! Nkosi, Bayete!*' The salute to a King.

Dirk's pony was tethered to the hitching-post in front of the homestead. Using a charred stick Dirk was writing his name in big crude capitals on the wall of the front veranda.

Although the entire house would be replastered and painted Sean found himself quivering with anger. He jumped from his horse roaring and brandishing his *sjambok* and Dirk disappeared round the corner of the house. By the time Sean had regained self-control and was sitting on the veranda wall revelling in the pride of ownership, Mbejane arrived. They chatted a while and then Mbejane led his women away. Sean could trust him to build the beehive huts of his kraal on the richest earth of Lion Kop.

The last girl in the line was Mbejane's youngest and prettiest wife. Balancing the large bundle on her head, her back straight, her buttocks bare except for the strip of cloth that covered the cleft, she walked away with such unconsciously regal grace that Sean was instantly and forcibly reminded of Ruth.

His elation subsided. He stood up and walked away

from the old building. Without Ruth in it, this house would not be a home.

He sat alone on the slope of the hills. Again he was reminded of Ruth. This place was so much like their secret glade. Except, of course, there were no wattle trees here.

35

'Wattle!' exclaimed Ronny Pye and glared at his sister and his brother-in-law. 'He's planting wattle.'

'What for?' Dennis Petersen asked.

'For the bark, man. The bark! There's a fortune in it. Twenty pounds a ton!'

'What do they use it for?'

'The extract is used in tanning leather.'

'If it's so good why haven't other people –' Dennis began, but Ronny brushed him aside impatiently.

'I've gone into it thoroughly. Lion Kop is ideal wattle ground, high and misty. The only other really good ground in the district is Mahobo's Kloof Ranch and Theuniskraal. Thank God you own Mahobo's Kloof! Because that's where we're going to plant our own wattle.' He looked at Dennis but without seeing him as he went on. 'I've spoken to Jackson at Natal Wattle Company. He'll sell us the saplings on the same terms as he's supplying that bastard Courtney, and he'll buy our bark – every scrap of it at a guaranteed twenty pounds a ton. I've hired two men to supervise the planting. Labour will be our big problem, Sean has grabbed every native within twenty miles. He's got an army of them up there.' Suddenly Ronny stopped. He had seen the expression on Dennis's face. 'What's wrong with you?'

'Mahobo's Kloof!' Dennis moaned. 'Oh God! Oh my God!'

'What do you mean?'

'He came to see me last week. Sean . . . He wanted an option to purchase. A five years' option.'

'You didn't give it to him!' Ronny screamed.

'He offered three shillings an acre – that's six times as much as I paid for it. How could I refuse.'

'You fool! You blithering bloody idiot! In five years that land will be worth . . . ' Ronny gulped, 'It will be worth at least ten pounds!'

'But nobody told me!' Dennis wailed the age-old cry of the might-have-been, the lament of those that never quite succeed.

'Nobody told Sean either.' Audrey spoke softly for the first time and there was that in her voice that made Ronny turn savagely on his handsome sister.

'All right – we all know about you and Sean. But he didn't stay around long enough for you to get your hooks into him, did he?' Ronny stopped himself and glanced guiltily at Dennis. It was years before Audrey had abandoned all hope of Sean's return to Ladyburg and succumbed to Dennis's gentle but persistent courtship. Now Dennis coughed awkwardly and looked at his hands on the desk in front of him.

'Well, anyway,' he murmured, 'Sean's got it and there's nothing we can do about it.'

'Isn't there – hell!' Ronny pulled a notebook towards him and opened it. 'This is how I see it. He's borrowed that ten thousand from his mother – you know the money we tried to get her to invest in the Burley deal.' They all remembered the Burley deal and looked a little ashamed. Ronny hurried on. 'And he's borrowed another five thousand from Natal Wattle – Jackson let it slip out.' Ronny went on with his calculations. When he finished he was smiling again. 'Mr Sean Courtney is stretched about as thin as he can get without breaking.

Just one slip, one little slip and – Pow!' He made a chopping motion with his open hand. 'We can wait!'

He selected a cigar from the leather box which had replaced the silver one and lit it before he spoke again. 'By the way – did you know he hasn't been discharged from the army yet? The way the war is going they certainly need good fighting men. That leg of his looks all right to me. Perhaps a word in the right ear – a little pressure somewhere.' Ronny was positively grinning now. His cigar tasted delicious.

36

The doctors at Greys Hospital had given Sean his final examination a week before Christmas. They had judged his disability as roughly one per cent, a slight limp when he was physically tired. This disqualified him from a war wound pension and had made him available for immediate return to duty.

A week after New Year's Day of 1901 the first letter from the army arrived. He was to report immediately to the Officer Commanding the Natal Mounted Rifles – the regiment which had now swallowed up the old Natal Corps of Guides.

The war in South Africa had entered a new phase. Throughout the Transvaal and Orange Free State the Boers had begun a campaign of guerilla warfare alarming in its magnitude. The war was far from over and Sean's presence was urgently required to swell the army of a quarter of a million British troops already in the field.

He had written begging for an extension of his leave, and had received in reply a threat to treat him as a deserter if he wasn't in Johannesburg by February 1st.

The last two weeks had been filled with frantic activity. He had managed to finish the planting of ten thousand acres of wattle begun the previous May. He had arranged a further large loan from Natal Wattle to pay for the tending of his trees. The repairs and renovation of the Homestead on Lion Kop were completed and Ada had moved from the cottage in Protea Street to act as caretaker and manager of the estate during his absence.

Now, as he rode alone over his land in a gesture of farewell, he had an opportunity to think of other things. The main one of these was his daughter. His first and only daughter. She was two months old now. Her name was Storm and he had never seen her. Saul Friedman had written a long, joyous letter from the front where Sean was soon to join him. Sean had sent hearty congratulations and then tried once again to contact Ruth. He had written her without result and, finally, had abandoned his work on Lion Kop and gone up to Pietermaritzburg. Four days he waited, calling morning and afternoon at the Goldberg mansion – and each time Ruth was either out or indisposed. He had left a bitter little note for her and gone home.

Deep in gloom he rode through his plantations. Great blocks of young trees, row upon endless row, covered the hills of Lion Kop. The older wattle planted ten months before had started to come away. Already it was waist high with fluffy green tops. It was an achievement of almost superhuman proportion, ten months of ceaseless gruelling labour by two thousand native labourers. Now it was done. He had retained a gang of fifty Zulus, who would work under Ada's supervision, clearing the undergrowth between the rows and guarding against fire. That was all there was to it; four years of waiting until the trees reached maturity and were ready for stripping.

But now he was so completely absorbed in thought that he passed over the boundary of Lion Kop without noticing, and rode on along the foot of the escarpment. He crossed the road and the railway line. From ahead the murmur of the White Falls blended with the wind whisper in the grass, and he glimpsed the flash of water cascading down from the high rock in the sunshine. The acacia trees were in bloom, covered with the golden mist of their flowers above, gloomy with shadows beneath.

He crossed the river below the pool of the falls. The escarpment rose steeply above him, striped with dark dense bush in the gulleys, a thousand feet high so it blocked out the sunlight. The pool was a place of fern and green moss, and the rocks were black and slippery with the spray. A cold place, out of the sun – and the water roared as it fell in a white, moving veil like smoke.

Sean shivered and rode on, ambling up the slope of the escarpment. Then he knew that instinct had directed him. In his distress he had come back to the first home he had ever known. This was Courtney land beneath his feet, and spreading down and out towards the Tugela. The nostalgia came upon him more strongly as he climbed, until at last he reached the rim and stood looking down upon the whole of Theuniskraal.

He picked out the landmarks below him; the homestead with the stables and the servants' quarters behind it; the paddocks with the horses grazing heads down and tails swinging; the dip-tanks among the trees – and each of them had some special memory attached to it.

Sean dismounted and sat down in the grass. He lit a cheroot, while his mind went back and picked over the scrap-heap of the past. An hour, and then another, passed before he came back to the present, pulled his watch from the front pocket of his waistcoat and checked the time.

'After one!' he exclaimed, and stood to dust the seat of his pants and settle his hat on to his head before beginning the descent of the escarpment. Instead of crossing the river at the pool, he stayed on Theuniskraal and keeping to higher ground aimed to intersect the road on this side of the bridge. Occasionally he found cattle feeding together in herds of less than a dozen; they were all in condition, fat on the new grass, for the land was not carrying nearly its fully capacity. As he passed they lifted their heads and watched him with vacant, bovine expressions of unsurprise.

The forest thickened, then abruptly ended and before him lay one of the small swampy depressions that bellied out from the river. From his look-out on the escarpment this area had been screened by trees, so now for the first time Sean noticed the saddled horse tethered on the far edge of the swamp. Quickly Sean searched for its rider, and found him in the swamp – only his head visible above the bright poisonous green field of papyrus grass. The man's head disappeared again and there was a commotion in the grass; a wild thrashing and the sudden panic-ridden bellow of a beast.

Sean worked his way quickly round the edge of the swamp until he reached the horse. The head and shoulders of the man in the swamp reappeared and Sean could see that he was splattered with mud.

'What's the trouble?' Sean shouted, and the head turned towards him.

'There's a beast bogged down here.'

'Hold on, I'll give you a hand.' Sean stripped his jacket, waistcoat and shirt and hung them with his hat on a branch before going in. Ploughing knee-deep through ooze that bubbled and belched gas as he disturbed it, using both arms to part the coarse tangle of reeds and march grass, Sean finally reached them.

The beast was an old black cow; her hindquarters completely submerged in a mudhole and her front legs twisted helplessly under her chest.

'She's just about finished,' said the man. Sean looked at him and saw he was not a man but a youth. Tall for his age, but lightly built. Dark hair, cropped short and the big nose to show he was a Courtney.

With an unnatural tightness in his gut and a shortening of his breath, Sean knew that he was looking at his son.

'Don't just stand there,' snapped the boy. He was covered from the chest down in a glistening evil-smelling coat of mud, sweat pouring down his face and dissolving the spots of mud on his forehead and cheeks, breathing heavily through open mouth, crouching over the animal to hold its head above the surface.

'Have to roll her,' said Sean. 'Keep her head up.' He waded to the hindquarters and the mud bubbled greasily up around his waist. He thrust his arms down through it – groping for the trapped legs.

Sean's hands could only just encompass the thick bone and sinew of the hock. He settled his grip and leaned back against it, straining upwards, gradually bringing the full strength of his body into the pull until he knew that something in his belly was on the point of tearing. He held like that, his whole face contorted, mouth wide open so that his breathing rattled hoarsely up his throat, the great muscles of his chest and arms locked in an iron convulsion.

A minute, two minutes, he held the stance while the boy watched him with a mingled expression of alarm and wonder. Then suddenly there was a squelching popping escape of swamp gas around Sean's chest, and the beast began to move. Slowly at first, reluctantly up through the ooze showed the swell of its rump – then faster, as the mud lost its hold, until, with a final belch and sigh, it yielded and Sean came to his feet holding the legs above the surface – the cow lying exhausted on her side.

'Hell's teeth!' breathed the boy in open admiration.

For a moment the beast lay quiescent, then realizing that its legs were free, it began to struggle, thrashing wildly to regain them.

'Hold the head,' shouted Sean, and blundered sideways until he could grab its tail and prevent it from attempting to stand. When the animal was quiet again he began to drag it, moving backwards, towards the firm ground. Like a bobsleigh the carcass slid easily over the carpet of mud and flattened reeds until it grounded. Then Sean jumped clear while she struggled up, stood a moment and then lumbered unsteadily away into the trees.

Sean and his son stood together, gasping, covered with filth, still ankle-deep in mud, watching the cow disappear.

'Thanks. I'd never have done it on my own, sir.' The form of address and the boy's tone touched something deep in Sean.

'It needed two of us,' he agreed. 'What's your name?'

'Courtney, sir. Michael Courtney.' He held out his hand towards Sean.

'Nice to meet you, Mike.' Sean took the hand.

'I know you, don't I, sir? I'm sure I've seen you before – it's been worrying me.'

'I don't think so.' With an effort Sean kept his feelings from showing in his voice and face.

'I'd . . . I'd count it an honour to know *your* name.' As Michael spoke a shyness came upon them both.

What can I tell him? thought Sean. For I must not lie – and yet I cannot tell him the truth.

'My God, what a bloody mess,' he laughed instead. 'We stink like we've been dead ten days.'

Michael seemed to notice their condition for the first time. 'Ma will have a hernia when she sees me,' he laughed also, then, 'Come up to the house. It's not far from here. Have lunch with us and you can clean up – the servants will wash your clothes for you.'

'No.' Sean shook his head. 'I must get back to Lady-burg.'

'Please. I'd like you to meet my mother. My father's not here – he's at the war. But, please come home with me.'

He really wants me to. As Sean looked into his son's eyes the warm feeling that he had been struggling to suppress flooded up from his chest and he felt his face flush with the pleasure of it.

'Mike,' he spoke slowly, groping for the right words. 'Things are a bit difficult right now. I can't take you up on the invitation. But I'd like to see you again and I'll be through this way one day. Shall we leave it until then?'

'Oh!' Michael made no attempt to hide his disappoint-ment. 'Anyway, I'll ride with you as far as the bridge.'

'Good.' Sean picked up his shirt and wiped off the surplus mud, while Michael unhitched their horses.

They rode slowly, in silence at first with the shyness still on them. Then they started to talk, and quickly the barriers between them crumbled. With a feeling of pride that was ridiculous in the circumstances, Sean became aware of the quickness of Michael's brain, the ease of expression unusual in one so young, and the maturity of his views.

They spoke of Theuniskraal.

'It's a good farm.' There was pride in Michael's voice. 'My family has owned it since 1867.'

'You're not running much stock,' Sean grunted.

'Pa has had a run of bad luck. The rinderpest hit us but we'll build it up again – you wait and see.' He was silent a moment, then, 'Pa's not really a cattleman, instead of putting money into stocks he spends it on horses – like Beauty here.'He patted the neck of his magnificent golden mare. 'I've tried to argue with him, but –' Then he realized that he was steering close to the leeshore of disloyalty, and he checked himself then went on hurriedly: 'Don't misunderstand me, my father is an unusual man. Right now he's on the army staff – a colonel, and one of General Buller's right-hand men. He is a holder of the Victoria Cross for bravery, and he has been awarded the D.S.O. for the job he is doing now.'

Yes, thought Sean, I have defended Garry also, many times, as often as you will by the time you reach my age. In understanding he changed the direction of the conversation.

They spoke of the future:

'So you want to be a farmer, then?'

'I love this place. I was born here. To me it is not just a piece of land and a house. It is part of a tradition to which I belong – built by men of whom I am proud. After Pa, I will be the only one left to continue it. I won't fail that trust. But . . . '

They had reached the rise above the road, and Michael stopped and looked at Sean as though trying to make up his mind how much he should tell this stranger.

'But?' Sean prompted him gently. For a moment longer Michael stared at him, trying to account for his certainty in this man – for the conviction he had that he could trust him beyond all other men on earth. He felt that he had known him all his life, and between them was something so strong – so good and strong as to be almost tangible.

'But,' he jerked himself back to their conversation, 'that is not all. I want something beyond just land and cattle. It's so difficult to explain. My grandfather was a big man; he worked with people as well as animals. He had . . . you do understand me, don't you?'

219

'I think so,' Sean nodded 'You feel you'd like to make a place for yourself in the scheme of things.'

'Yes, that's it. I'd like to make decisions other than when to cull and when to brand, or where to build a new dip-tank.'

'What are you going to do about it then?'

'Well, I'm at Cape Town University. This is my third year – I'll have my degree by Christmas.'

'Then what?'

'I don't know, but I'll find something.' Then Michael smiled. 'There's a lot to learn first. Sometimes when I realize how much it frightens me a little.'

They walked their horses down towards the road, so completely absorbed in each other that neither of them noticed the buggy coming towards them from the direction of Ladyburg until it was almost on them.

Then Michael glanced up. 'Hey! Here comes my mother. Now you can meet her.'

With a sense of dread numbing him, Sean realized he was trapped. There was no escape – the buggy was less than fifty yards away, and he could see Anna sitting up behind the coloured driver staring at them.

Michael shouted, 'Hello, Ma!'

'Michael! Whatever have you been doing? Look at you!' There was a shrewishness in her voice now. The years had treated Anna in the manner she deserved, had sharpened her features and exaggerated the catlike set of her eyes. She turned those eyes on Sean and she frowned. The frown cut deep grooves in her forehead and showed the heavy lines of flesh beneath her chin.

'Who's that with you?' she asked Michael.

'A friend. He helped me free a bogged animal. You should have seen him, Ma. He lifted it clean out of the mud.'

Sean saw that she was expensively dressed, ostentatiously so for a farmer's wife on a working day. Velvet and ostrich feathers – those pearls must have cost Garry a small fortune. The rig was new, polished black lacquer picked out with scarlet, and brass fittings – another few hundred pounds' worth. Sean ran his eyes over the horses, matched bays, blood stock – Jesus! he thought.

Anna was still frowning at him, recognition and doubt mixed in her expression. She was starting to flush, her lips trembling.

'Hello, Anna.'

'Sean!' She spat the word.

'It's been a long time. How are you?'

Her eyes slanted venomously. She hardly moved her lips as she snapped at Michael, 'Get away from that man!'

'But . . . ' The bewildered look on Michael's face hurt Sean like a spear thrust.

'Do as your mother says, Michael,' Sean told him.

'Are you . . . are *you* my Uncle Sean?'

'Yes.'

'Get away from him,' shrilled Anna. 'Don't you ever speak to him again. Do you hear me, Michael? He's evil – evil! Don't ever let him near you. He'll destroy you.' Anna was panting, shaking with rage and hatred, babbling like a madwoman. 'Get off our land, Sean Courtney. Get off Theuniskraal and don't come on again.'

'Very well, Anna. I'm going.'

'Michael. Get on your horse!' she screamed at him. 'Hurry. Come away from him.'

Michael swung up into the saddle.

'Drive on. Drive quickly,' she ordered the coloured coachman. At the touch of the whip the big bays jumped forward and Anna was thrown back against the padded seat. 'Come on, Michael. Come home immediately.'

Michael looked across at Sean. He was bewildered, uncertain. 'I don't . . . I don't believe that you . . . '

'We'll talk again some other time, Mike.'

And suddenly Michael's expression changed, the corners of his mouth drooped and his eyes were dark with regret at having found, and lost, so soon.

'No,' he said, lifted his hand in a gesture of farewell, and wheeled his horse. Crouched forward on its neck he drove in savage pursuit of the buggy.

'Michael,' Sean called after him, but he did not seem to hear.

37

And so Sean went back to war. The farewell was an ordeal. Ada was so brave about it that Sean wanted to shake her and shoud, 'Cry, damn you! Get it over with!' Dirk threw one of his more spectacular fits. He clung to Sean and yelled until he almost suffocated himself. By the time the train pulled out Sean was in a towering rage that lasted until they reached Pietermaritzburg four hours later.

He took his anger into the saloon on the station and sedated it with half a dozen brandies. Then, with Mbejane carrying his luggage, he worked his way through the crowd on the platform, searching for an empty compartment on the northbound express. As all traffic was on military permit only, his fellow-travellers were exclusively clad in khaki. A vast, drab throng speckled with gay spots of colour, women who were sending men to war and not very happy about it. The sound of weeping blended with the roar of loud voices, men's laughter and the occasional squeal of a child. Suddenly, above it all Sean heard his name called. He peered about and saw an arm waving frantically above the heads of the crowd.

'Sean! Hey, Sean!' Saul's head bobbed into view and then disappeared as he hopped up and down. Sean fought his way through to him and they shook hands delightedly.

'What the hell are you doing here?' Saul demanded.

'Heading back to duty – and you?'

'A week's leave just ended. Came down to see the baby. My God, what luck I spotted you!'

'Is Ruth here?' Sean could not contain the question.

'She's waiting in the carriage outside.'

'I'd like to have a look at this infant.'

'Of course. Let's find a couple of seats first and dump our luggage, then we've got twenty minutes before the train leaves.'

Sean saw her as they came out on to the front steps of the station building. She sat in an open carriage while a coloured coachboy held a parasol over her. She was dressed in dove-grey with big leg-o'-mutton sleeves slashed with pink and a huge hat piled with pink roses. Her face was in profile as she leaned forward over the bundle of white lace on her lap. Sean felt the leap in his chest as he looked at the calm lines of her face. He stopped and whispered,

'My God, she's lovely,' and beside him Saul laughed with pleasure.

'Wait until you meet my daughter!'

She did not see them approach the carriage, she was too intent on her child.

'Ruth, I've a surprise for you,' bubbled Saul. She looked up and Sean was watching her. She went rigid with shock, staring at him while all colour drained away from her face.

'Hello, Ruth.'

She did not reply immediately. Sean saw her mask her face with a pale impassivity.

'Hello, Sean. You startled me.'

Saul had missed the interplay of their emotions. He was climbing up into the carriage beside her.

'Come, have a look.' Now he was opening the lace shawl, leaning over the infant, his face alight with pride.

Silently Sean climbed up into the carriage and sat opposite them.

'Let Sean hold her, Ruth.' Saul laughed. 'Let him get a good look at the loveliest girl in the world.' And he did not notice the way in which Ruth froze again and hugged the child to her protectively.

'Take her, Sean. I promise she'll not wet you too badly, though she might sick up a little,' Saul went on happily.

Sean held out his hands for the infant, watching Ruth's face. It was defiant, but afraid.

'Please,' he said. The colour of her eyes seemed to change a darker bluer grey. The hard lines around her mouth dissolved and her lips quivered pink and moist. She leaned forward and placed her daughter in his arms.

38

It was a long, slow journey up to Johannesburg – a journey broken by interminable halts. At every siding there was a delay, sometimes of half an hour but usually of three times that length. Occasionally, without apparent reason, they groaned to a stop in the middle of the veld.

'What the hell is the trouble now?'

'Somebody shoot the driver.'

'Not again!'

Protest and comment were shouted by the angry heads that protruded from the windows of every coach. And when the guard trotted up along the gravelled embankment towards the front of the train, he was followed by a chorus of catcalls and hooting.

'Please be patient, gentlemen. We have to check the culverts and bridges.'

'The war's over.'

'What are you worried about?'

'The jolly old Boer is running so hard he hasn't got time to worry about bridges.'

Men climbed down beside the tracks, and stood in small impatient groups until the whistle blew and they scrambled aboard as the train jolted and began crawling forward again.

Sean and Saul sat together in a corner of a crowded compartment and played Klabrias. Because the majority regarded the cold clean highveld air with the same horror as if it had been a deadly cyanide gas, the windows were tightly closed. The compartment was blue with pipe-smoke and fetid with the smell of a dozen unwashed bodies. The conversation was inevitable. Confine a number of men in a small space and they'll get round to it in under ten minutes.

This company had a vast experience in matters pornographic.

A sergeant had served three years in Bangkok, but it took him two hours to convince his companions that what rumour placed horizontally, nature, in fact, had maintained at the vertical. He carried his point only after an expedition down the corridor from which he returned with another old China hand. This expert produced photographic evidence which was studied minutely and deemed conclusive.

It served also to remind a corporal who had done a tour of duty in India of his visit to the Temple of Konarak. A subject which was good for another hour and paved the way for a smooth entry into a discussion of the famous Elephant House in Shanghai.

They kept it up from noon until nightfall.

In the meantime, Saul had lost interest in the cards and taken a book from his bag and started reading. Sean was bored. He cleaned his rifle. Then he picked his teeth with a match and stared out of the window at the small herds of springbok that grazed along the line of rail. He listened to a detailed account of the pleasures provided by the proprietress of the Elephant House, and decided to give it a wide berth if he ever visited Shanghai.

'What are you reading?' he demanded of Saul at last.

'Huh?' Saul looked up vaguely and Sean repeated the question. '*The Westminster System of Government*'. Saul held the book so that Sean could see the title.

'Jesus!' grunted Sean. 'What do you read that stuff for?'

227

'I am interested in politics,' Saul explained defensively and returned to reading.

Sean watched him for a while then, 'Have you got any other books with you?'

Saul opened his bag again. 'Try this.'

'*The Wealth of Nations*'. Sean handled the book dubiously. 'What's it about?' But Saul was reading again.

Sean opened the heavy volume and glanced idly at the first page. He sighed with resignation for it was a long time since he had read anything but a letter or a bank statement – then his eyes started moving back and forth across the page like the shuttle of a loom. Without knowing it, they were weaving the first threads into a fabric that would cover a part of his soul which until now had been naked.

After an hour Saul looked across. 'What do you make of it?' he asked.

Sean grunted without looking up. He was completely absorbed. This was important. The language of Adam Smith had a certain majestic clarity. With some of his conclusions Sean did not agree but the reasoning evoked a train of thought in Sean's own brain, stimulating it to race ahead and anticipate – sometimes correctly, but often reaching a point wide of where the author was aimed.

He read quickly, knowing that he would go back and read it all again for this was only a scouting party into the unknown territory of economics. With his eyes still fixed on the pages, he groped in the pockets of his tunic, found a stub of pencil and underlined a passage to which he wanted to return. Then he left it and went on. Now he used the pencil frequently.

'No!' he wrote in the margin at one place.

'Good,' at another.

Saul looked up again and frowned as he realized Sean

was defacing the book. Then he noticed Sean's expression, saw its scowling concentration and his own face relaxed. He watched Sean from under lowered eyelashes. His feeling for this man of muscle and moods and unexpectedly soft places had passed affection and now reached the borders of adulation. He did not know why Sean had placed protecting wings above him, nor did he care. But it was good to sit quietly, no longer reading, and watch the face of this big man who was more than just a friend.

Alone in the midst of a multitude they sat together. The train snaked northwards across the grassland, spreading a long trail of silver-grey smoke behind it and the sun sank exhausted to the earth and bled on to the clouds. After it was gone the darkness came quickly.

They ate canned meat spread on coarse bread with the blade of a bayonet. There was no lighting in the compartment, so after they had eaten they sat together wrapped in their blankets and talked in darkness. Around them all other conversation died and was replaced by the sounds of sleep. Sean opened one of the windows and the cold sweet air cleaned their minds and sharpened them so that they talked in quietly suppressed excitement.

They talked of men and land and the welding of the two into a nation; and how that nation should be governed. They spoke a little of war and much of the peace that would follow it; of the rebuilding of that which had been destroyed into something stronger.

They saw the bitterness ahead that would flourish like an evil weed nourished on blood and the corpses of the dead, and they discussed the means by which it should be rooted out before it strangled the tender growth of a land that could be great.

They had never spoken like this before. Saul hugged

his blankets about his shoulders and listened to Sean's voice in the darkness. Like most of his race his perception had been sensitized and sharpened so that he could pick up a new quality, a new sense of direction in this man.

I have had a hand in this, he thought, with a stirring of pride. He is a bull, a wild bull, charging anything that moves; charging without purpose, then breaking his run and swinging on to something new; using his strength to destroy because he had never learned to use it in any other way; confused and angry, roaring at the barbs in his shoulders; chasing everything and as a consequence catching nothing. Perhaps I can help him, show him a purpose and a way out of the arena.

And so they talked on into the night. The darkness added another dimension to their existence. Unseen, their physical forms no longer limited them and it seemed that their minds were freed to move out and meet in the darkness, to combine into a cushion of words that carried each idea forward. Until abruptly, the whole delicate pattern was shattered and lost in the concussion of dynamite and the shriek of escaping steam, the roar of breaking timber and glass, and the confusion of equipment and sleeping bodies thrown violently together as the train reared and twisted and plunged from the tracks. Almost immediately a further sound blended into it all – the crackling of musketry at close range and the steady hammering beat of a Maxim machine-gun.

Sean was pinned helplessly in the complete darkness, unable to breathe under an immense weight. He struggled wildly, tearing at the men and baggage above him, his legs bound by loose blankets. The weight eased enough for him to drag air into his lungs, but a knee was driven into his face with such force that his lip burst open and the blood oozed saltily into his mouth. He lashed out and felt the stinging rake of broken glass along his arm.

In the darkness men screamed in terror and in pain, leading the hideous chorus of groans and oaths and gunfire.

Sean dragged his body free of the press, felt men thrashing under him as he stood.

Now he could hear the repeated splintering thud of bullets into woodwork much louder than the guns that fired them.

Someone reeled against him and Sean caught him.

'Saul?'

'Leave me, let me go.' A stranger, Sean released him.

'Saul. Saul. Where are you?'

'Sean.'

'Are you hurt?'

'No.'

'Let's get out of here.'

'My rifle.'

'Bugger your rifle.'

'Where's the window?'

'Blocked.'

At last Sean was able to get some idea of their situation. The coach was on its side with the windows against the earth and the whole welter of dead and broken men piled upon them. The door was high above them, probably jammed.

'We'll have to break out through the roof.' He groped blindly, then swore and jerked his hand back as a splinter of wood knifed up under a fingernail, but he felt a draught of cold air on his face.

'There's a hole.' He reached out again eagerly and felt the torn timber. 'One of the planks is sprung.'

Immediately there was a rush of bodies in the darkness, hands clawed at him as half a dozen men fought to find the opening.

'Get back, you bastards.' Sean struck out with both fists and felt them connect. He was panting and he could feel the sweat sliding down his back. The air was heavy with the body warmth and breath of terrified men.

'Get back. I'll work on it.' He forced his hands into the crack and tore the loose plank out. For an instant he struggled with the temptation to press his face to the narrow opening and suck in the clean air. Then he locked his hands on to the next plank, braced his legs against the roof and heaved back with all his strength. It wouldn't budge. He felt the panic mounting in him once more.

'Find me a rifle, somebody,' he shouted above the uproar.

'Here.' Saul's voice, and the rifle was thrust into his hands. He ran the barrel into the opening and using it as a lever flung his weight on to it. He felt wood tearing, moved the barrel and pulled again. It gave and he cleared the plank and started on the next.

'All right. One at a time. Saul, you first.' With his panic just below the surface, Sean shoved each man unceremoniously through the jagged opening. A fat one stuck and Sean put a boot behind him and pushed. The man squeaked and went out like a champagne cork.

'Is there anyone else?' he shouted in the darkness.

'Sean,' Saul's voice from outside. 'Get out of there.'

'You get under cover,' Sean roared back at him.

The Boer fire still flailed the wrecked train. Then he asked again, 'Is there anyone else?' and a man groaned at Sean's feet.

Quickly Sean found him. Hurt badly, his head twisted. Sean cleared the tangle of baggage from above his body and straightened him out. Can't move him, he decided, safer here until the medicos come. He left him and stumbled over another.

'Damn them,' he sobbed in his dreadful anxiety to get out. This one was dead. He could feel the reptilian clamminess of death on his skin, and he left him and scrabbled his way out into the open night.

After the utter blackness of the compartment, the stars lit the land with a pearly light and he saw the fog of steam hanging above the locomotive in a high, hissing bank, and the leading coaches telescoped into each other, and the others jack-knifed and twisted into a weird sculpture of destruction. At intervals along the chain a few rifles winked a feeble reply to the Boer fire that poured down upon them.

'Sean,' Saul called from where he was crouched beside the overturned coach. Sean ran to him and lifted his voice above the clamour.

'Stay here. I'm going back to look for Mbejane.'

'You'll never find him in this lot. He was with the horses – listen to them.'

From the horse-boxes at the rear of the train came such a sound that Sean hoped never to hear again. Two hundred trapped and frenzied animals – it was far worse than the sound of those men still in the wreckage.

'My God!' whispered Sean. Then his anger rose higher than his fear. 'The bastards,' he grated and looked up at the high ground above them.

The Boers had chosen a place where the line curved along the bank of a river. The watercourse cut off escape on that side, and on the other the ground rose steeply in a double fold that commanded the full length of the railway line.

Along the first fold lay their riflemen, two hundred of them at least, judging by the intensity of their fire, while from above them on the summit ridge the muzzle

233

flashes of the Maxim gun faded and flared as it traversed relentlessly back and forth along the train. Sean watched it hungrily for a moment, then he lifted the rifle that he still carried and emptied the magazine, firing at the Maxim. Immediately the flashes grew brighter as it came questing back to find him, and around Sean's head the air was filled with the swishing crack of a hundred whips.

Sean ducked down while he reloaded, then stood up again to shoot.

'You bastards,' he shouted at them, and his voice must have carried for now the riflemen up there were helping the Maxim to search him out. They were getting very close.

Sean crouched down once more, and beside him Saul was firing also.

'Where did you get the rifle?'

'I went back for it.' Saul punctuated his reply with gunfire and Sean grinned as his fingers fumbled with the reload. 'You're going to get hurt one day,' he said.

'You taught me how to go about it,' Saul retorted.

Once more Sean emptied his magazine to no effect, except that the recoil of the rifle invoked the old high madness in him. It needed only Mbejane's voice beside him to trigger it completely.

'Nkosi.'

'Where the hell have you been?' Sean demanded.

'My spears were lost. I spent much time finding them in the darkness.'

Sean was silent for a moment while he peered up at the ridge. Out on the left there was a gap in the line of riflemen where a narrow donga ran through them and down towards the railway. A small party might be able to go up that gully and pass through the rear of the Boer firing-line. From there the solitary Maxim on the ridge would be very vulnerable.

'Bring your spears, Mbejane.'

'Where are you going?' Saul asked.

'I'm going to try for that machine-gun. Stay here and keep these gentlemen's minds on other things.'

Sean started off along the train towards the outlet of the donga. He covered fifty yards before he realized that not only Mbejane but Saul was with him.

'Where do you think you're going?'

'With you.'

'The hell you are!'

'Watch me.' There was that peculiar note of obstinacy in Saul's voice that Sean had come to recognize, and there was no time to argue. He ran on until he was opposite the donga where again he sought shelter in the lee of an overturned coach while he made his final assessment of the position.

The donga looked narrow but deep, and the scrub-bush that filled it would give them cover to the top where there was a definite gap in the Boer line.

'It'll do,' he decided aloud, and then to the other two, 'I'll go first, then you follow me, Saul, and watch those big feet of yours.'

He was vaguely aware that some show of resistance was being organized among the survivors of the wreck. He could hear the officers rallying them and now a hundred rifles were returning the Boer fire.

'All right. I'm off.' Sean stood up. 'Follow me as soon as I get across.'

At that moment a new voice hailed them. 'What are you men up to?'

'What's it to you?' Sean flashed impatiently.

'I'm an officer,' and then Sean recognized the voice

and the lanky figure with a bared sabre in one hand. 'Acheson!'

A second's hesitation before Acheson recognized him. 'Courtney. What are you doing?'

'I'm going up that donga to attack the Maxim.'

'Think you can reach it?'

'I can try.'

'Good fellow – off you go then. We'll be ready to support you if you make it.'

'See you at the top,' said Sean and ran out towards the mouth of the donga.

They moved quietly in single file upwards and the guns and the shouting cloaked the soft sounds of their advance. Sean could hear the voices of the burghers above them growing closer and louder as they approached – very close now – on the side of the donga just above their heads – then behind them, and they were through.

The donga was shallower here, starting to flatten out as it neared the crest. Sean lifted his head above the side and looked out. Below him he could just make out the lumpy shapes of the Boers in the grass but their rifles threw long orange spouts of flames when seen from above – while the British replies were mere pinpricks of light from around the dark tangle of coaches.

Then Sean's attention focused on the Maxim and he could see why the rifle-fire from below had made no effect on it. Sited just below the crest of the ridge on a forward bulge of the slope, it was protected by a scharnz of rock and earth that had been thrown up in front of it. The thick water-jacketed barrel protruded through a narrow opening and the three men that served it crouched low behind the wall.

'Come on,' whispered Sean, and wriggled up out of the donga on to his belly to begin the stalk.

One of the gunners saw him when he was a few yards from the gun. '*Magtig! Pasop, daars 'n –*' and Sean went in with the rifle clubbed in both hands and the man never finished his warning. Mbejane and Saul followed him in, and for a few seconds the emplacement was filled with a struggling mass of bodies. Then it was over and the three of them panted heavily in the stillness.

'Do you know how to work this thing, Saul?'

'No.'

'Nor do I.' Sean squatted behind the gun and settled his hands on to the twin grips, his thumbs automatically resting on the firing-button.

'*Wat makeer julle daar bo? Skiet, man, skiet!*' a Boer shouted from below, and Sean shouted back, '*Wag maar 'n oomblik – dan skiet ek bedonderd.*'

'*Wie's dar? Who's that?*' the Boer demanded and Sean depressed the gun.

It was too dark to use the sights, so he took a vague aim over the barrel and thrust his thumbs down on the button. Immediately his shoulders shook like those of a man using a jack hammer and he was deafened by the harsh beat of the gun, but he swung the barrel in a low, sweeping arc across the ridge below him.

A storm of shouts and cries of protest broke out along the Boer line, and Sean laughed with savage delight. The Boer fire upon the train withered miraculously as men jumped up and scattered beneath the spray of bullets. Most of them streamed back to where their horses waited behind the crest, keeping well out on the flanks of the Maxim, while a line of cheering British infantry followed them up from the train – giving the support that Acheson had promised.

Only a tiny but determined group of Boers came up the slope towards Sean, yelling angrily and shooting as they came. There was dead ground directly below the

237

emplacement where Sean could not reach them with the Maxim.

'Get out of here. Run out to the sides,' Sean shouted back at Saul and Mbejane as he hoisted the heavy gun on to the rock wall in front of him to improve its field of fire. But the movement twisted the belt of ammunition and after the first burst the gun jammed hopelessly. Sean lifted it above his head, stood like that for an instant and then hurled it among the men below him. It knocked two of them down into the grass. Sean snatched up a pumpkin-sized rock from the top of the wall and sent it after the gun – and another, and another. Howling with the laughter of fear and excitement, he rained rocks upon them. And they broke. Most of them veered out to the sides and joined the general rush for the horses.

Only one man kept coming, a big man who climbed quickly and silently. Sean missed him with three rocks, and suddenly he was too close – not ten feet away. There he paused and lifted his rifle. Even in the dark, at that range, the Boer could hardly miss and Sean sprang from the top of the wall. For an instant he dropped free, and then with a shock that knocked the wind from both of them, he drove into the burgher's chest. They rolled down the slope, kicking and grappling, bouncing over the rocky ground, until a small thorn bush held them.

'Now, you bloody Dutchman!' rasped Sean. He knew there was only one possible outcome to this encounter. With supreme confidence in his own strength Sean reached for the man's throat, and with a sense of disbelief felt his wrist held in a grip that made the bone creak.

'*Kom, ons slaat aan*,' the burgher's mouth was an inch from Sean's ear, and the voice was unmistakable.

'Jan Paulus!'

'Sean!' The shock of recognition eased his grip for an instant, and Sean broke his hand loose.

Only once in his life had Sean met a man whose strength matched his own – and now again they were pitted against each other. He drove the heel of his right hand up under Jan Paulus's chin, forcing his head back against the encircling left arm. It should have broken Jan Paulus's neck. Instead he locked his arms around Sean's chest below the level of his armpits – and squeezed. Within seconds Sean felt his face swelling and congesting with blood, his mouth opened and his tongue came out between his teeth.

Without breath, yet he maintained the pressure on Jan Paulus's neck, felt it give fractionally – and knew that another inch of movement would snap the vertebrae.

The earth seemed to tilt and turn beneath him, he knew he was going for his vision was blotched with moving patches of deeper darkness – the knowledge gave him a little more strength. He flung it all on to Jan Paulus's neck. It moved. Jan Paulus gave a wild muffled cry and his grip on Sean's chest eased a fraction.

Again, Sean told himself, again. And he gathered all of what was left for the final effort.

Before he could make it, Jan Paulus moved quickly under him, changing his grip, lifting Sean clear of his chest. Then his knees came up under Sean's pelvis and with a convulsive heave drove Sean's lower body forward and over – cartwheeling him so that he was forced to release Jan Paulus's neck and use his hands to break his own fall.

A rock caught him in the small of the back and agony flared in him like sheet lightning in a summer sky. Dimly through it he heard the shouts of the British infantry very near, saw Jan Paulus scramble up and glance down the slope at the starlight on the bayonets, and saw him take off up the slope.

Sean dragged himself to his feet and tried to follow him but the pain in his back was an effective hobble and Jan Paulus reached the crest ten paces ahead of him. But as he ran, another dark shape closed on his flank the way a good dog will quarter on a running rybuck. It was Mbejane and Sean could see the long steel in his hand as he lifted it above Jan Paulus's back.

'No!' shouted Sean. 'No, Mbejane! Leave him! Leave him!'

Mbejane hesitated, slowed his run, stopped and looked back at Sean.

Sean stood beside him, his hands clasped to his back and his breathing hissing in his throat. Below them from the dark rear slope of the ridge came the hoof-beats of a single running pony.

The sounds of Jan Paulus's flight dwindled, and they were engulfed in the advance of the lines of the bayonet men from the train. Sean turned and limped back through them.

39

Two days later, on the relief train, they reached Johannesburg.

'I suppose we should report to somebody,' Saul suggested as the three of them stood together on the station platform beside the small pile of luggage they had been able to salvage from the train wreck.

'You go and report, if that's what you want,' Sean answered him. 'Me, I'm going to look around.'

'We've got no billets,' Saul protested.

'Follow your Uncle Sean.'

Johannesburg is an evil city, sired by Greed out of a dam named Gold. But it has about it an air of gaiety, of brittle excitement and bustle. When you are away from it you can hate it – but when you return you are immediately re-infected. As Sean was now.

He led them through the portals of the railway building into Eloff Street and grinned as he looked up that well-remembered thoroughfare. It was crowded. The carriages jostled for position with the horse-drawn trams. On the sidewalks beneath the tall three- and four-storeyed buildings the uniforms of a dozen different regiments set off the butterfly colours of the women's dresses.

Sean paused on the station steps and lit a cigar. At that moment the sounds of carriage wheels and human voices were drowned by the plaintive wail of a mine hooter and immediately others joined in signalling the noon. Automatically Sean reached for his pocket-watch to check the time, and noticed the same general movement in the crowded street. He grinned again.

Jo'burg hasn't changed much – still the old habits, the same feeling about it. The mine dumps higher than he remembered them, a few new buildings, a little older and a little smarter – but still the same heartless bitch beneath it all.

And there on the corner of Commissioner Street, ornate as a wedding-cake with its fancy ironwork and corniced roof, stood Candy's Hotel.

With rifle and pack slung over each shoulder, Sean pushed his way through the press on the sidewalk with Saul and Mbejane in his wake. He reached the hotel and went in through the revolving glass doors.

'Very grand.' He looked about the lobby as he dumped his pack on the thick pile of the carpet. Crystal chandeliers, velvet curtains roped with silver, palms and bronze urns, marble tables, fat plush chairs.

'What do you think, Saul. Shall we give this flophouse a try?' His voice carried across the lobby and stilled the murmuring of polite conversation.

'Don't talk so loudly,' Saul cautioned.

A general officer in one of the plush chairs hoisted himself and slowly turned his head to train a monocled stare upon them, while his aide-de-camp leaned across and whispered, '*Colonials*'.

Sean winked at him and moved across to the reception desk.

'Good afternoon, sir.' The clerk regarded them frostily.

'You have reservations for my chief of staff and myself.'

'What name, sir?'

'I'm sorry, I can't answer that question. We are travelling incognito,' Sean told him seriously, and a helpless expression appeared on the man's face. Sean dropped his voice to conspiratory level. 'Have you seen a man come in here carrying a bomb?'

'No.' The man's eyes glazed a little. 'No, sir. No, I haven't.'

'Good.' Sean appeared relieved. 'In that case we'll take the Victoria Suite. Have our luggage sent up.'

'General Caithness has the Victoria Suite, sir.' The clerk was becoming desperate.

'What?' Sean roared. 'How dare you!'

'I didn't . . . We had no . . .' Stuttering, the clerk backed away from him.

'Call the owner,' ordered Sean.

'Yes, sir.' And the clerk disappeared through a door marked 'Private'.

'Have you gone mad?' Saul was fidgeting with embarrassment. 'We can't afford to stay at this place. Let's get out of here.' Under the concentrated scrutiny of every guest in the lobby he was very conscious of their grubby travel-stained uniforms.

Before Sean could answer a woman came through the 'Private' doorway, a very lovely but very angry woman with eyes that blazed like the blue sapphires at her throat.

'I am Mrs Rautenbach – the owner. You asked to see me.'

Sean just smiled at her, and her anger withered slowly as she began to recognize him beneath the creased ill-fitting tunic and without the beard.

'Do you still love me, Candy?'

'Sean?' She was still uncertain.

'Who else?'

'Sean!' And she came to him on the run. Half an hour later General Caithness had been evicted and Sean and Saul were settling comfortably into the Victoria Suite.

Freshly bathed, with only a towel round his waist, Sean lay back in his chair while the barber scraped away his three-day growth of beard.

'Some more champagne?' Candy had not taken her eyes off him for the last ten minutes.

'Thanks.'

She filled his glass, replaced it at his right hand and then touched the thick muscles of his upper arm. 'Still hard,' she murmured. 'You've kept ahead of the years.' Her fingers moved on to his chest. 'Just a little grey here and there – but it suits you,' and then to the barber, 'Haven't you finished yet?'

'One moment more, madam.' He again scissored along the line of Sean's temple, stood back and studied his masterpiece – then, with modest pride, held the mirror for Sean's approval.

'Excellent. Thank you.'

'You may go now. See to the gentleman next door.' Candy had waited long enough. As the door closed behind the barber she turned the key. Sean stood up from the chair and they faced each other across the room.

'My God, but you're big.' Her voice was husky, unashamedly hungry.

'My God, but you're beautiful,' Sean answered her, and they moved slowly to meet in the centre of the floor.

Later, they lay quietly while the darkness gathered in the room as evening fell. Then Candy moved her mouth across his shoulder and, the way a cat cleans its kittens, she began gently to lick the long red scratches upon his neck.

When the room was truly dark Candy lit one of the shaded gas-lights and sent down for biscuits and a bottle of champagne. They sat together upon the rumpled bed and talked.

At first there was a shyness between them because of what they had done together – but soon it passed – and they sat up far into the night.

Rare it is for a man to have a friend as well as a lover in one woman – but with Candy this was possible. And to her he released all those things that had been bottled and fomenting within him.

He told her of Michael, and the strange bond between them.

He told her of Dirk, and hinted at his misgivings for the boy.

He spoke of the war and of what he would do when it finished.

He told her of Lion Kop and his wattle.

But one thing he could not tell her. He could not speak of Ruth or the man who was her husband.

40

During the next few days Sean and Saul reported to the headquarters of the Regional Commander and were assigned neither billets nor duties. Now that they had arrived no one seemed very interested in them. They were told to report daily, and turned loose again. They returned to Candy's Hotel and spent most of the days playing billiards or cards and most of the evenings eating and drinking and talking.

A week of this and Sean was getting bored. He began to feel like a stud stallion. Even a solid diet of heavenly manna begins to pall after a while – so when Candy asked him to escort her to a reception and dinner with which Lord Kitchener was celebrating his promotion to Supreme Command of the Army in South Africa, Sean accepted with relief.

'You look like some sort of god,' Candy told him as he entered her suite through the concealed doorway which connected it with his own bedroom in the Victoria rooms. When she had shown him this discreet little panel and demonstrated how at a touch it slid silently aside, Sean had thrust down the temptation of asking how many others had used it. It was senseless to resent the nameless host who had passed through the panel to tteach Candy all those little tricks with which she now delighted him.

'You don't look too bad yourself.' She was dressed in blue silk, the colour of her eyes, and she wore diamonds at her throat.

'How gallant you are!' She came to him and stroked the silk lapels of his newly tailored evening jacket. 'I wish you'd wear your medals.'

'I haven't any medals.'

'Oh Sean! You must have! With all those bullet holes in you, you must have medals.'

'I'm sorry, Candy.' Sean grinned. At times she was so far from being the glittering sophisticated woman of the world. Although she was a year older than he was, time had not destroyed that fragile quality of skin and hair that most women lose so quickly. There was no thickening of her body, no coarsening of her features.

'Never mind – even without medals, you'll be the handsomest man there tonight.'

'And you the loveliest girl.'

As the carriage rolled down Commissioner Street towards the Grand National Hotel, Sean lay back against the yielding support of soft polished leather. His cigar was drawing evenly with an inch of firm grey ash, the single brandy he had drunk before leaving glowed beneath the starched front of his dress-shirt, a faint aura of bay rum clung and hovered around him – and Candy's hand lay lightly upon his leg.

All these things induced in him a mood of deep contentment. He laughed easily at Candy's chatter and let the smoke of his cigar trickle through his lips – tasting it with an almost childlike pleasure. When the carriage stopped before the entrance to the hotel and rocked gently on its superb springing, he climbed down and stood by the big rear-wheel to guard Candy's skirt as she descended.

Then, with her fingers on his forearm, he guided her up the front steps and through the glass doors into the lobby of the hotel. The splendour of the place did not equal Candy's own establishment. But it was impressive

247

enough – and so was the reception line that awaited them. While they took their places among those waiting to meet the Commander-in-Chief, Sean spoke quietly to an aide-de-camp.

'My Lord, may I present Mr Courtney and Mrs Rautenbach.'

Lord Kitchener had a formidable presence. His hand was cold and hard and he stood as tall as Sean. The eyes that stared for an instant into Sean's held a disquieting ridigity of purpose. Then he turned to Candy and his expression softened momentarily as he bowed over her hand.

'Very kind of you to come, madam.'

Then they were past and into the gaudy of uniforms and velvet and silk. The whole was dominated by dress scarlet of the Guards and Fusiliers, but there was also the gold-frogged blue of the Hussars, the green of the Foresters, kilts of half a dozen Highland regiments, so that Sean's black dress suit was conspicuously conservative. Among the glitter of orders and decorations shone the jewellery and white skins of the women.

Here assembled were the prize blooms of the huge tree that was the British Empire. A tree grown strong above the rest of the forest. Two centuries of victory in war had nurtured it, two hundred million persons were its roots that sucked in the treasures of half the world and sent them up along the shipping lanes to that grey city astride the Thames that was its heart. And there this rich sap was digested and transmuted into men. These were the men whose lazy speech and careful nonchalance reflected the smugness and arrogance which made them hated and feared by even the trunk of the great tree that gave them flower. While the lesser trees crowded closer and sent their own roots out to divert a little of its sustenance to themselves, the first disease had already eaten into the wood beneath the bark of the giant. America, India, Afghanistan, and South Africa, had started the dry rot that one day would bring it crashing down with a force that would shatter its bulk into so many pieces as to prove it not teak but soft pine.

Watching them now, Sean felt himself apart from them, closer in spirit and purpose to those shaggy men whose Mausers still shouted desperate defiance at them from the vast brown veld.

These thoughts threatened to spoil his mood and he thrust them down, exchanged his empty glass for another filled with bubbling yellow wine and attempted to join the banter of the young officers who surrounded Candy. He succeeded only in conceiving a burning desire to punch one of them between his downy moustaches. He was savouring the idea with increasing relish when a touch on his arm turned him.

'Hello, Courtney. Seem to find you everywhere there is either a fight or a free drink.' Startled, Sean turned to look into the austere face and incongruously twinkling eyes of Major-General John Acheson.

'Hello, General. I notice you frequent the same areas.' Sean grinned at him.

'Bloody awful champagne. Old K. must be economizing.' Then he ran his eyes over Sean's immaculate evening dress. 'A bit difficult to tell whether you have received the awards for which I recommended you.'

Sean shook his head. 'Still a sergeant. I didn't want to embarrass the General Staff by appearing in my chevrons.'

'Ah!' Acheson's eyes narrowed slightly. 'Must be some hold up. I'll look into it.'

'I assure you I'm quite happy this way.'

Acheson nodded and changed the subject. 'You haven't met my wife?' This was patronage on the grand scale. Sean was not to know that Acheson considered him his personal good luck charm. His own rapid promotion dated from their first meeting. Sean blinked in surprise before answering,

'I haven't yet had the honour.'

'Come along them.'

Sean excused himself from Candy, who dismissed him with a tap of her fan and Acheson steered him through the press towards a group at the end of the room. A dozen paces from it Sean stopped abruptly.

'Something wrong?' Acheson asked.

'No. Nothing.' Sean started forward again, but now his eyes were fastened with fascination on one of the men who was a part of the group towards which they were headed.

A slim figure in the dark blue dress uniform of the Natal Mounted Rifles. Sandy brown hair brushed straight back from his high forehead, nose too big for the mouth and the chin beneath it, slightly round-shouldered but with the highest reward for bravery showing purple and bronze beside the striped ribbon of the Distinguished Service Order on his chest, while on his shoulders the silver crowns and lace proclaimed him a colonel.

Slowly, with a new awakening of his guilt, Sean let his eyes move down to this man's legs. With incomprehension he saw them perfectly matched, booted in polished black leather. Only when the man moved slightly, shifting his weight, Sean saw the leadenness in one of them and understood.

'My dear – I would like to present Mr Courtney. I think you have heard me speak of him. He was with me at Colenso, and on the train a few weeks ago.'

'Indeed. Mr Courtney, this is a great pleasure.' She was plump and friendly but Sean was hardly able to murmur the correct response so conscious was he of the other eyes upon his face.

'And this is Major Peterson of my staff.'

Sean nodded.

'Colonel Courtney you will probably know – seeing that you bear the same name, and not to mention the fact that he is your Commanding Officer.'

For the first time in nineteen years Sean looked into the face of the man he had crippled.

'Hello, Garry,' he said and held out his hand. He stood with it out and waited.

Garry Courtney's lips moved. He hunched his shoulders and his head swung slightly from side to side.

Take it, Garry. Please take my hand. Sean tried silently to urge him. Realizing the forbidding setf of his own countenance, Sean forced his lips into a smile. It was an uncertain thing that smile, it trembled a little at the corners of his mouth.

In response Garry's own lips relaxed and for a moment Sean saw the terrible longing in his brother's eyes.

'It's been a long time, Garry. Much too long.' Sean prodded forward with his open right hand. *Take it. Oh God, please make him take it.*

Then Garry straightened. As he did so the toe of his right book scraped softly, awkwardly on the marble floor. The naked longing in his eyes was glazed over, the corners of his mouth lifted upwards in something close to a sneer.

'Sergeant,' his voice was too loud, too high. 'Sergeant, you are incorrectly dressed!' Then he turned, pivoting on the dead leg, and limped slowly away through the throng.

Sean stood with his hand still out and the smile frozen on his mouth.

*You shouldn't have done that to us. We both wanted
— I know you wanted it as much as I.*

Sean let his hand fall empty to his side and balled it
into a fist.

'You know him?' Acheson asked softly.

'My brother.'

'I see,' Acheson murmured. He saw many things —
and one of them was the reason why Sean Courtney was
still a sergeant.

Major Peterson coughed and lit a cigar. Mrs Acheson
touched the General's arm. 'My dear, Daphne Langford
arrived yesterday. There she is with John — we must
have them to dinner.'

'Of course, my dear. I will ask them this evening.'

They turned their attention on each other, giving Sean
the respite he needed to recover from his snubbing.

'Your glass is empty and so is mine, Courtney. I
suggest we go on to something more substantial than
K's cooking champagne.'

Brandy, fiery Cape brandy, very different from that
soapy liquor they make in France. A dangerous spirit to
take in his present mood. And only one mood was possible for Sean after what Garry had done to him — cold,
murderous rage.

His face was impassive, politely he responded to Mrs
Acheson's charm, once he smiled at Candy across the
room, but always he sent brandy after brandy down to
feed the rage that seethed in his belly; his eyes followed
the figure in dark blue as it limped from group to group.

The aide-de-camp who arranged the dinner seating
could never have known that Sean was a mere sergeant.
As Mrs Rautenbach's guest he believed him to be an
influential civilian and placed him high at the long
table, between Candy and Mrs Acheson, with Major

Peterson below him and a brigadier and two colonels opposite. One of the colonels was Garrick Courtney.

Beneath the almost uninterrupted stare which Sean fastened on him, Garry became nervously garrulous. Never once meeting Sean's eyes, he aimed his remarks higher up the table, and that bronze cross suspended on he ribbon of shot purple silk that bumped against his chest each time he leaned forward gave a weight to his opinions that was evident in the attention they received from the officers of general rank.

The food was excellent. Rock lobster that had run the gauntlet of Boer blockade from the Cape, plump young pheasant, venison, four assorted sauces – even the quality of the champagne had improved. But Sean ate little, instead he gave permanent employment to the wine steward who hovered behind his chair.

'And so,' said Garrick as he selected a cigar from the cedarwood box that was offered him, 'I cannot see hostilities continuing another three months at the outside.'

'I agree with you, sir,' Major Peterson nodded. 'We'll be back in London for the season.'

'Poppycock!' Sean made his first contribution to the discussion. It was a word he had learned only recently – but he liked it. Besides, there were ladies present.

Peterson's face chameleoned to a creditable match with the scarlet of his dress coat, Acheson started to smile then changed his mind, Candy wriggled in anticipation for she had reached the edge of boredom, and a chilly stillness fell over that area of the table.

'I beg your pardon?' Garry looked at him for the first time.

'Poppycock,' Sean repeated, and the wine steward stepped forward to cascade champagne into the crystal bowl of his glass, an operation which he had repeated at least a dozen times during the course of the evening – but this time it commanded the attention of the entire company.

'You don't agree with me?' Garry challenged.

'No.'

'Why not?'

'Because there are still eighteen thousand Boers in the field, because they are still an organized army, because not once have they had a decisive defeat inflicted on them – but mainly because of the character of these eighteen thousand that are left.'

'You don't –' Garry's voice was petulant, but Acheson interrupted smoothly. 'Excuse me, Colonel Courtney.' Then he turned to Sean. 'I believe you know these people –' he hesitated and then went on, 'you are even related through marriage.'

'My brother-in-law leads the Wynberg commando,' Sean affirmed. The old boy knew more of his past than he suspected – must have made a few inquiries. Sean was flattered and the harshness gone from his voice.

'What, in your opinion, will be their course of action from now on?' Acheson pursued the subject and Sean tasted his champagne while he considered his reply.

'They will scatter – break up into their traditional fighting units, the commando.' Acheson nodded, from his position on the General Staff he knew this had already happened.

'In so doing they will avoid the necessity of dragging a supply column with them. Once the rainy season begins these small units will find grazing less of a problem for their horses.'

'Yes.' Sean saw they were all listening now. He thought quickly, cursing the wine that had dulled his brain. 'They will avoid battle, run from it and swing round to jab at the flanks, then run again.'

'Supplies?' asked the Brigadier.

254

'The veld is their storeroom, each farm upon it a haven.'

'Ammunition, weapons, clothing?' persisted the Brigadier.

'Every British soldier they capture or kill will provide a brand-new Lee-Metford rifle and a hundred rounds of ammunition.'

'But how long can they live like that?' Garry spoke indulgently, as though to a child. 'How far can they run?' He glanced around at the others seeking their support, but everyone was watching Sean.

'How wide is the veld – that is how far they can run.' Sean turned on him, stung by the tone of his voice. 'My God, you know them. Hardship is a way of life with them. Pride, the watchword that will carry them on.' ·

'You paint a pretty picture.' Garry smiled easily. 'It is unusual to find such appreciation of grand strategy among the rank and file.' Then he looked higher up the table once more with an emphasis that excluded Sean from the conversation. 'As I was saying, General Acheson, I believe –'

'One moment please, Colonel.' Acheson in turn excluded him and put his question to Sean. 'If you had the running of it, what plan of action would you adopt?'

Across the table Garrick Courtney coughed in a manner intended to inform the company that his brother was about to make a fool of himself.

It was not lost on Sean. 'The problem revolves around one single fact. The mobility of the enemy,' he stated grimly.

'Your perception does you great credit,' murmured Garry.

'Our first problem is to contain him and then to wear him down,' Sean went on, trying to ignore the taunts of his brother.

'Contain him?' The Brigadier fired the question.

'Hold him into a limited area,' Sean explained.

'How?'

'Say, by a series of set fortifications,' Sean suggested.

'Correct me if I'm wrong – but you propose to divide the whole of the highveld into paddocks and farm the enemy as one would dairy cattle?' Garry was still smiling.

'The new blockhouse lines along the line of rail are proving effective. It should be possible to extend them across the open veld – every time the enemy had to pass through them he would be subjected to a mauling by the garrisons and his position would immediately be pin-pointed.'

'The cost would be enormous,' Acheson pointed out.

'Not as great as supporting an army of a quarter of a million men in the field for another five years,' Sean brushed his objection aside, he was well set on his run of ideas. 'Then, within the defined areas small well-mounted bodies of men, unimpeded by supply wagons and artillery, could be used to raid the commandos – hitting them in an unrelenting series of raids and ambushes. Driving them on to the blockhouse lines, wearing down their horses, giving them no chance to rest, employing exactly their tactics of skirmishing. Against the commandos use counter-commandos.'

Acheson nodded thoughtfully. 'Go on,' he said.

'Then, clear out the farms,' Sean went on recklessly. 'Bring in the women and old men whose crops keep the commandos fed. Force them to operate in a vacuum.'

In the years ahead Sean was to regret the impulse that made him say it. Perhaps Kitchener would have scorched the land without Sean's suggestion, perhaps he had no hand in the formation of the concentration camps that bred bitterness Sean would spend the rest of his life trying to sweeten. But he could never be certain. He was drunk and angry – but later this knowledge would not comfort him.

Now suddenly he felt empty as though in a premonition of the monstrous seed he had sown and he sank into brooding silence while the others passed his ideas back and forth, building on them, already beginning to plan.

When the dinner party broke up and they drifted through to drink coffee, Sean made one more attempt to tear down the barrier between his brother and himself. He went to him with his pride in his hands and offered it. 'I was in Ladyburg last month. All's well there. Ada writes to say –'

'I receive a weekly letter not only from my wife but from my stepmother and my son. I am fully aware of the latest news from home. Thank you.' Garry stared over Sean's shoulder as he replied.

'Garry . . .'

'Excuse me.' Garry nodded briefly and limped away to speak to a brother officer. He kept his back towards Sean.

'Let's go home, Candy.'

'But, Sean . . .'

'Come on.'

Sean slept very little that night.

41

The Headquarters of the General Officer Commanding the eastern sector were tastefully situated in the offices of a brewery company in Plein Street. Major Peterson was waiting for Garry when he arrived.

'I sent for you two hours ago, sir.'

'I was indisposed,' Garry told him.

'Old Ach is not in a very good mood today – we'd better not keep him waiting any longer. Come along.'

Down the passage, where orderlies bustled, Peterson led him, and to a door at the far end. He knocked once and then opened it. Acheson looked up from his paperwork.

'Colonel Courtney is here, sir.'

'Thank you, Peterson. Come in, Courtney.'

Peterson closed the door and left Garry standing alone on the thick Persian rug in front of Acheson's desk.

'I sent for you two hours ago, Courtney.' Acheson used the same reprimand, and Garry shifted his leg uncomfortably.

'I wasn't too well this morning, sir. Had to get the doctor in.'

Acheson fingered his white moustache as he examined the dark circles beneath Garry's eyes, and the chalky colour of his face. 'Sit down,' he ordered.

Acheson was silent, watching him. Bur Garry avoided his eyes. He felt brittle from the previous night's drinking, his skin dry and sensitive, and he fidgeted in the chair, clasping and unclasping the hand that lay in his lap.

'I want one of your men,' Acheson spoke at last.

'Of course, sir,' Garry nodded.

'That sergeant – Courtney. I want to give him an independent command.'

Garry sat very still.

'You know who I mean?' Acheson persisted.

'Yes, sir.'

'You should,' Acheson murmured dryly. 'I have personally recommended him to you on two occasions for recognition.' He flicked through the sheaf of papers in front of him.

'Yes, sir.' Garry's right hand was opening and closing again.

'I notice you took no action on either of my recommendations.'

'No, sir.'

'May I ask why?'

'I didn't have . . . I didn't think the occasions merited further action.'

'You thought that my judgement was in error?' Acheson asked politely.

'No, sir. Of course not, sir.' Garry answered quickly.

'Well, then?' Acheson's eyes were pale blue, but cold.

'I spoke to the man. Congratulated him. After Colenso I gave him leave.'

'Very decent of you – in view of the wounds he received there.'

'I didn't want to . . . You see – he's my brother. It was difficult – favouritism. I couldn't really do much.' Garry wriggled sideways in his chair, his hands came up pawing the air as though to pluck words from it.

'Your brother?' Acheson demanded.

'Yes. My brother. I know him, I know him – you

don't. You can't have any idea.' Garry could feel the pattern of his thoughts disintegrating, his voice sounded shrill in his own ear. He had to explain, he had to tell Acheson. 'My leg,' he shrilled, 'my leg. You see it. look at it! He did that. he took my leg. You don't know him. He's evil. He's evil, evil. I tell you he's evil.'

Acheson's expression had not changed, but his eyes were colder, more watchful. Garry had to reach him and make him understand.

'Anna.' Garry's lips were wet and blubbery. 'My wife, Anna. He did that to her. Everything he touches – you can't know how he is. I know. He's evil. I tried, I hoped at Colenso – but you can't destroy him. He is the destroyer.'

'Colonel Courtney!' Acheson's voice cut into his tirade, and Garry jerked at the crack of it. He covered his lips with his fingers and slowly he subsided into the chair.

'I just want to explain. You don't understand.'

'I think I do,' Acheson clipped the words short and harsh. 'I am granting you indefinite leave on grounds of ill-health.'

'You can't do that – I won't resign my commission.'

'I have not asked you to,' Acheson snapped. 'I will send the papers to your hotel this afternoon. You can take tomorrow's train south.'

'But – but, sir –'

'That will be all, Courtney. Thank you.'

Acheson turned his attention once more to his papers.

42

That afternoon Sean spent two hours with Acheson, then he returned to Candy's Hotel and found Saul in the billiard room. Sean selected a cue. Saul laid both balls against the far cushion and straightened.

'Well?' he asked, as Sean chalked his stick.

'You'll never believe it.'

'Tell me, and let me be the judge.'

Grinning secretly Sean cannoned twice and then sank the red.

'From sergeant without portfolio, to a full-blown major and an independent command,' he announced.

'*You?*'

'Me.' Sean chuckled and missed a cannon.

'They must be crazy.'

'Crazy or not. From now on you will stand in my presence, adopt a respectful tone of speech – and miss that shot.'

Saul missed.

'If you're an officer and a gentleman why don't you behave like one and keep your mouth shut when I'm making a play.'

'You also have changed your status.'

'How?'

'You're now a lieutenant,' Sean informed him.

'No!'

'With a gong.'

'A gong?'

'A medal, you fool.'

'I'm overcome. I am speechless.' At last Saul broke down and began to laugh. It was a sound which Sean enjoyed. 'What kind of a gong – and what for?'

'Distinguished Conduct Medal – for the night of the train.'

'But, Sean, you . . . '

Sean interrupted. 'Yes, they gave me one also. Old Acheson got quite carried away. He started hanging medals and promotions on everything that moved, with the same dedicated fervour as a bill-poster putting up advertisements for Bovril. He damned nearly pinned a medal on the orderly who brought in the coffee.'

'He gave you coffee?'

'And a cigar,' Sean answered. 'He counted not the cost. It was like two lovers on an assignation. Repeatedly he addressed me as *My dear fellow*.'

'And what is this command he gave you?'

Sean racked his cue and stopped laughing.

'You and I are to head one of the first counter-commandos. Small, lightly equipped units to ride in and ginger up the Boer. Harass him, wear him down, chase the guts out of his horses and keep him moving until he runs on to one of the big columns.'

The following morning they rode out with Major Peterson to inspect the band of volunteers he had assembled for them.

'A mixed bag I'm afraid, Courtney. We've scratched together three hundred and fifteen.' Peterson was gloating a little behind the apology. He had not forgotten that *poppycock*.

'It must have been difficult,' Sean agreed. 'You only

had a quarter of a million to choose from. What about officers?'

'Sorry. Only Friedman here. But I have got you an absolute gem. Sergeant-major. Snaffled him from the Dorsets. Fellow by the name of Eccles. First-class, absolutely first-class.'

'And Tim Curtis – the one I asked for?'

'Sorry again. They've reopened the gold mines. All engineers are being pulled out and sent back to work.'

'Damn it, I wanted him. What about machine-guns?'

'Four Maxims. Bloody lucky to get them.'

'Horses?'

'A bit of a struggle – but you can go down to remount and take your pick.'

Sean went on relentlessly with his demands and questions during the ride out towards Randfontein. His excitement for the challenge of this venture rose steadily as they argued and talked. At last he was taking it seriously. He asked the final and crucial question as they trotted past the sentries into the great army camp on the outskirts of Johannesburg.

'Has Acheson decided in which area I will be operating?'

'Yes.' Peterson dropped his voice. 'South-east Transvaal.'

'That's where Leroux is!'

'That's right. The gentleman who met your train the other day.'

Jan Paulus again!

'Here you are, Courtney.'

A little apart from the main camp stood three lines of white canvas tents. A field kitchen smoked at the far end and around it were clustered Sean's warriors.

'My God, Peterson. You said a mixed bag! You've

263

robbed the army of cooks and batmen. And what are those – *sailors*, Bejesus!'

Peterson smiled thinly and shifted in the saddle.

'Press-ganged them,' he admitted. 'Gunnery detail from *Repulse*. Ah, here comes your sergeant-major.'

Eccles approached in column of fours; bull-built, black moustache, a few inches over six feet and all of it held stiffly erect. Peterson introduced them and they appraised each other.

'A right scruffy lot we got here, sir.'

'We've got a bit of work to do, Eccles.'

'That we 'ave, sir.'

'Let's get started than.' And they glowered at each other in mutual respect and liking.

A week later they were ready to go. Saul had named them 'Courtney's Fighting Scouts'. They were all well mounted, although there were some interesting styles of horsemanship evident – especially among the delegates from the Royal Navy. By bullying the quartermaster Sean had arrived at a standard uniform similar to that of the Imperial Light Horse; slouch hats, khaki tunics and riding breeches, bandoliers, puttees and issue boots. They had forty fat and healthy pack-mules, four Maxim machine-guns and Eccles had trained teams to serve them.

Acheson had approved Sean's request to use Charlestown as a base. He had arranged rail transport south to this tiny village near the Natal border, promised support from the big flying columns in the area, and informed Sean that he was expecting *big things* from him. He made it sound like a threat.

43

'But, darling, you haven't even been given a real uniform. You look so drab.' Candy, who was watching him dress from the double bed, held very definite views on what constituted a real uniform. It had gold lace and frogging with, say a Star of the Garter on a rich scarlet ground. 'Look at those buttons – they're not even shiny.'

'Boers like shiny things – makes for good shooting in the sun.' Sean glanced over his shoulder at her. Her hair was fluffed into golden disorder and the blue gown was arranged to provoke rather than conceal. Hastily Sean returned his eyes to his own reflection in the full-length mirror and brushed the hair back along his temples. A touch of grey in it now. Quite dignified, he decided. Pity about the nose. He took it between his fingers and straightened it, a hell of a nose, but when he released his grip it returned immediately to a half-cock position.

'Well, I'll be leaving you now,' he said, and she stood up quickly and the laughter was gone from her lips, they trembled a little.

'I'll come down with you.' She rearranged the gown quickly.

'No.'

'Yes, I have a farewell present for you.'

In the hotel yard, hitched behind four fat mules, was a scotch cart. She led him to it and lifted the tarpaulin cover.

'A few things I thought you might need.'

Against the cold she had provided a sheepskin coat,

six fine woollen blankets and a silk eiderdown, two feather pillows and a mattress; a case of Courvoisier brandy and a case of Veuve Clicquot champagne. Against starvation there was potted salmon, strawberry jam, caviar in little glass jars, tinned delicacies all carefully packed in wooden boxes. For his health a medicine chest complete with a set of surgical instruments. Against the Boer there was a Toledo steel sabre in a leather scabbard worked with silver and a matched pair of Colt revolvers in a mahogany presentation case.

'Candy . . . ' Sean stumbled. 'I don't know what to say.'

She smiled a little and took his arm, hugging it. 'There's something else also.' She nodded to one of the grooms, who disappeared into the stables and led out a full-blooded Arab stallion with an English hunting saddle on its back.

'My God!' exclaimed Sean, and the stallion danced sideways so that the early sun glowed on the sheen of its coat. It flared the great pink pits of its nostrils and rolled its eyes before rearing high and dragging the groom off his feet.

'Candy, my dear,' Sean repeated.

'Good-bye, Sean.' She lifted her lips for his kiss and then broke away and almost ran back to the hotel.

While Saul shouted ribald encouragement, Mbejane and the groom held its head. Sean mounted the stallion, then they turned it loose and Sean fought to quieten it. At last he brought it under a semblance of control and, crabbing and prancing with arched neck and dainty high-stepping gait, persuaded it to head off in the general direction of Johannesburg railway station.

Eccles watched his approach impassively.

'What the hell are you laughing at, Sergeant-Major?'

'I wasn't laughing, sir.'

Sean dismounted and, with relief, gave the stallion into the care of two of his troopers.

'Nice bit of horseflesh, sir."

'What do you think he'll fetch?'

'You're going to sell him, sir?' Eccles could not hide his relief.

'You're damn right, I am. But it's a gift, so no sale here in Johannesburg.'

'Well, Colonel Jordan at Charlestown is usually in the market for a good nag. I should be able to get you a price, sir. We'll see what we can do.'

Colonel Jordan purchased not only the stallion but the pistols and the sabre as well. The secretary of the Charlestown garrison officers' mess frothed at the mouth with excitement when Eccles drew back the tarpaulin cover from the scotchcart.

When Sean's column rode out into the brown open winter grassland towards the jagged line of the Drakensberg, the little scotchcart trotted behind with the Maxims and a dozen ammunition cases making a full load.

44

There was cold that first night, and the stars were brilliant, clear and very far away. In the morning the land lay white and brittle in the grip of frost; each blade of grass, each twig and fallen leaf transformed into a white-jewelled wonder. A thin scum of ice covered the pool beside which the column had camped.

Mbejane and Sean squatted together. Mbejane with his monkey-skin kaross draped over his shoulders and Sean with the sheepskin coat buttoned to the throat.

'Tonight we will camp below that mountain.' Sean pointed away towards the west at the blue cone that stood out against the lighter blue of the dawn sky. 'You will find us there.'

'Nkosi,' Mbejane nodded over his snuffbox.

'These others.' Sean pointed with his chin at the group of four natives who waited quietly with the spears beside the pool. 'Are they men?'

Mbejane shrugged. 'I know little of them. The best of those I spoke with, perhaps. But they work for gold – and of their hearts I do not know.' Before going on, he regarded their clothing; tattered European cast-offs which were everywhere replacing the traditional tribal costume. 'They dress without dignity. But beneath the rags it is possible that they are men.'

'They are all we have so we must use them. Yet I wish we had those others who now grow fat in the company of their women.'

Mbejane smiled. A week before he had put the message into the grapevine and he knew that both Hlubi and Nonga were at that moment dissipating their accumulations of fat as they trotted north from their kraals along the Umfolozi River. They would be here soon.

'This is the way we will hunt,' Sean told him. 'Your men will spread out ahead of us and search for sign. The horses of those we seek will carry no steel on their hooves. If you find it fresh, then follow it until the run and direction of it is clear. Then return to me in haste.'

Mbejane nodded and sniffed a pinch from his snuffbox.

'While you search, stop at the kraals you find along the way. Speak with the people there, clearly, if the Mabune are here these people will know of it.'

'It will be as you say, Nkosi.'

'The sun comes.' Sean looked up at the glow of it upon the high places while the valleys were blue with shadow. 'Go in peace, Mbejane.'

Mbejane folded his kaross and tied it with a strip of leather. He picked up his stabbing spear and slung the great oval war shield on his shoulder. 'Go in peace, Nkosi.'

Sean watched while he talked with the other trackers, listening to the sonorous rise and fall of his voice. Then they scattered, trotting away into the veld, dwindled and were gone.

'Eccles.'

'Sir.'

'Finished breakfast?'

'Yes, sir.'

The men stood to their horses, blanket-rolls and carbines on the saddles, slouch hats pulled well down and the collars of their greatcoats turned up against the cold. Some were still eating with their bayonets from the cans of shredded beef.

'Let's go, then.'

The column clos'd up, riding four abreast, the pack-mules and the scotchcart in the centre, the outriders fanning out ahead to screen the advance. It was a tiny command, not a hundred and fifty paces long even with the pack animals, and Saul smiled as he remembered the massive fifteen-mile column that had marched from Colenso to Spion Kop.

Yet it was enough to tickle his pride. Courtney's Fighting Scouts. The task now was to justify the second word of their title.

Saul hooked one leg over the saddle, balanced his notebook upon it – and while they rode he and Sean planned a thorough reorganization of the column.

When they halted at midday the planning was put into effect. A patrol of ten men in charge of the mules, for this duty Sean picked those who were fat, old or ungainly in the saddle. These men would also act as horseholders when the unit went into fight on foot.

From among his sailors, Sean selected the gunners to captain the four Maxim teams. The riflemen were divided into patrols of ten with the most likely men promoted Sergeant Patrol Leaders, and their warrants noted in Saul's little book.

It was well after nightfall when they offsaddled that night below the dark massif of the mountain. Mbejane was waiting with his men beside a small, well-screened fire.

'I see you, Mbejane.'

'I see you, Nkosi.'

In the firelight Mbejane's legs were coated with dust to the knees and his face was grey with fatigue.

'What news?'

'Old sign. Perhaps a week ago, many men camped over there below the river. Twenty fires not in lines as the soldiers make them. They left no little tin pots as the soldiers do when they have emptied them of meat. No tents, but beds of cut grass – many beds.'

'How many?' It was an idle question for Mbejane could not count as a white man counts. He shrugged.

'As many beds as there are men with us?' Sean sought a comparison.

'More.' Mbejane thought carefully before answering.

'As many again?' Sean persisted.

'Perhaps as many again – but no more than that.'

Probably five hundred men, Sean guessed. 'Which way were they moving?'

Mbejane pointed south-west.

Back towards Vryheid and the protection of the Drakensberg mountain. Yes, it was part of the Wynberg commando without doubt.

'What news from the kraals?'

'There is fear among them. They tell little, and that of no importance.' Mbejane made no attempt to hide his disgust, the contempt that the Zulu feels for every other tribe in Africa.

'You have done well, Mbejane. Rest now for we ride before the dawn.'

Four more days they moved south-west, Sean's trackers sweeping the ground ten miles on each side of their path and finding it empty.

The Drakensberg reared up like a serrated back of a prehistoric monster along the south horizon. There was snow on the peaks.

Sean exercised his men in the counters to a surprise attack. Riflemen wheeling out and dismounting in line to cover the Maxims as they galloped wildly for the nearest high ground. Holders gathering the loose horses and pelting away to the cover of the nearest donga or kopje. Again and again they repeated this manoeuvre.

Sean worked them until they leaned forward in their

saddles to nurse aching backsides and cursed him as they rode. He worked them to the edge of exhaustion and then on to a new physical fitness. They sprouted beards, their faces reddened and peeled, then darkened with the sun, their uniforms darkened also, but with dirt. Now they no longer cursed him. There was a new feeling among them, they laughed more and sat solid in the saddle, slept soundly at night despite the cold and woke with eagerness.

Sean was moderately satisfied.

On the morning of the tenth day Sean was scouting ahead of the column with two of his troopers. They had just dismounted to rest among an outcrop of boulders when Sean picked up movement out on the plain ahead. With a savage lift of anticipation he scrambled down from the boulder on which he was sitting and ran to his horse for his binoculars.

'Damn it!' he mouthed his disappointment as he saw the lance blades glitter in the round strangely fore-shortened field of the glasses. 'Cavalry.'

Half an hour later they met the small patrol of lancers from one of the big columns that were driving south from the line of blockhouses. The young subaltern in command gave Sean a cigar, and the latest news of the war.

De la Rey and Smuts were rampaging north of Johannesburg in the Magaliesberg with forty thousand men chasing their three thousand. South in the Free State another of the great De Wet hunts was in full swing. But this time they would catch him, the subaltern assured Sean. Fifty thousand foot and horse had driven his commando into the angle between the blockhouse line and the flooded Riet River. In the east it was quieter.

The commandos there lacked leadership and were lying up in the mountains around Komatipoort.

'So far it's quiet here also, sir. But I don't like the looks of it. This man Leroux is a nasty piece of work, clever man too. So far he's limited his activities to a few raids. Ten days ago about five hundred of his men hit one of our supply columns near Charlestown. Wiped out the guard and collected enough ammunition to fight a full-scale battle, then made off towards the mountains.'

'Yes,' Sean nodded grimly. 'We found one of his camps.'

'No sign of him since then, sir. We've been scouring the ground for him, but so far without luck.'

'What's his force?' Sean asked.

'He can muster three thousand, so they say. My guess is that he's getting himself poised for something really big.'

That night Mbejane came into camp well after midnight. He came to where Sean slept under the scotchcart and with him were two other men.

'Nkosi.'

Sean rolled on his side, instantly awake at the touch. 'Mbejane?' He crawled out from under the cart and stood up.

The moon was up, silver and round and bright. By its light he recognized the men with Mbejane and exclaimed with pleasure:

'By God! Hlubi! Nonga!' Then remembering his manners, 'I see you.'

He stepped forward grinning broadly to clasp their shoulders in turn. And each replied gravely as they returned his embrace. 'I see you, Nkosi.'

'Are you well?'

273

'I am well. Are you well?'

The catechism of Zulu greeting can be carried on for as long as there is time available. More than a year had passed since Sean had discharged them from his service outside Pretoria, and so Sean must ask each of them for news of his father, his brothers, his herds, and the journey they had made, before he could put his own question.

'You came through Ladyburg?'

'We came that way,' agreed Hlubi.

'You saw the Nkosana Dirk?'

Now for the first time they both smiled, white teeth in the moonlight.

'We sat in council with the Nkosizana,' Hlubi chuckled. 'He grows like a bull calf. Already he wears scars of battle, honourable blackening of one of his eyes.'

'He grows in wisdom also,' Nonga boasted. 'Saying aloud to us those things which are written in the book.'

Hlubi went on: 'He sends greetings to the Nkosi, his father, and asks that he be allowed now to leave his school and join with him once more. For now he is skilled in the matter of books and numbers.'

Sean laughed. 'And what of the Nkosikazi, my mother?' he asked.

'She is well. She sends you this book.' Hlubi produced a travel-stained envelope from his loin-cloth. Sean tucked it away inside his coat to be read at leisure.

'Now.' The formula of greeting completed, Sean could come to the present. 'What news of Mabunu? Have you found sign?'

Mbejane squatted on his haunches and laid his spear and shield beside him. The other followed his example. The meeting came to order.

'Speak,' Mbejane ordered Hlubi.

'We came through the mountains, this being the shorter way,' Hlubi explained. 'In the hills below the mountains we found the road made by many horses, and following it we came upon a level place surrounded by rock. The Mabunu are there with cattle and wagons.'

'How far is this place?' Sean asked eagerly.

'A day's long journey.' Thirty miles.

'How many Mabunu?' Sean asked and Mbejane explained, 'As many as camped at the place I told you of.'

It made sense, Sean decided. Jan Paulus would have split his force into smaller units, for reasons of supply and concealment, until such time as he needed them.

'We will go then,' he said and stood up.

Eccles woke quickly.

'Sergeant-Major. The guides have found a small Boer commando in laager below the mountains. Get the men mounted up.'

'Sir!' Eccles's moustache, rumpled with sleep, quivered like the whiskers of a hunting dog.

While around him the commotion of upsaddling began, Sean kicked life into the fire and in its yellow flickering light he tore a page from his notebook and licked the point of a pencil.

To all British troops in the field:

I am in contact with a Boer commando of 500. Will attempt to contain them pending your arrival. The bearer will act as a guide.

S. Courtney (Major).

5th August, 1900. Time 00.46 hours.

275

'Hlubi,' he called.

'Nkosi!'

'Take this book,' he handed him the note. 'There are soldiers out there.' He swept his arm towards the north. 'Give it to them.'

45

Bunched into a compact column with the gallant little scotchcart bouncing and jolting in the rear, Courtney's Fighting Scouts cantered southwards with the brown winter grass brushing their stirrups.

With Saul beside him and the two Zulus ranging ahead like hunting dogs, Sean rode in the van. He slouched easily in the saddle and tried with both hands to steady Ada's letter as it fluttered in the wind of his passage. It was strange to read the gentle reassuring words as he hurried into battle.

All was well at Lion Kop. The wattle grew apace — free from fire, drought or pestilence. She had hired an assistant manager who worked afternoons only; his mornings required attendance at Ladybury School. Dirk was earning his princely salary of two shillings and sixpence a week and seemed to be enjoying the work. The arrival of his school report for the period ended at Easter was the occasion for some concern. His average high marks for each subject were followed by the notation, 'Could do much better' or 'Lacks concentration'. The whole was summarized by the Headmaster, 'Dirk is a high-spirited and popular boy. But he must learn to control his temper and to apply himself with more diligence to those subjects he finds distasteful.'

Dirk had recently fought an epic bout of fisticuffs with the Petersen boy, who was two years his senior, and had emerged blooded and bruised, but victorious. Here Sean detected a note of pride in Ada's prim censure.

There followed half a page of messages dictated by Dirk in which protestations of filial love and duty were liberally punctuated with requests for a pony, a rifle, and permission to terminate his scholastic career.

Ada went on tersely to say that Garry had recently returned to Ladyburg, but had not yet called upon her.

Finally, she instructed him to take pains with his health, invoked the Almighty to his protection, anticipated his swift return to Lion Kop – and ended with love.

Sean folded the letter carefully and tucked it away. Then he let his mind drift, lolling in the saddle while the brown miles dropped steadily behind his horse. There were so many loose or ravel threads to follow – Dirk and Ada, Ruth and Saul, Garrick and Michael – and all of them made him sad.

Then suddenly he glanced sideways at Saul and straightened in the saddle. This was not the time to brood. They had entered the mouth of one of the valleys that sloped upwards towards the massive snow-plastered ramparts of the Drakensberg, and were following a stream whose banks dropped ten feet to the water that gurgled and tinkled over the polished round boulders in its bed.

'How much farther, Nonga?' he called.

'Close now, Nkosi.'

In another valley that ran parallel to the one Sean was following, separated from it by two ridges of broken rock, a young Boer asked the same question.

'How much farther, Oom Paul?'

But before answering, Vecht-Generaal Jan Paulus Leroux eased himself around in the saddle and looked back along the commando of one thousand burghers he was leading to a rendezvous at his laager in the mountains. They rode in a solid mass that clogged the floor of the valley, bearded men in a motley of dark homespun clothing, on ponies shaggy in their winter coats – yet Jan Paulus felt pride swell in his chest as he looked at them. These were the bitter-enders, veterans of half a hundred fights, men forged and tempered in the furnace of battle, razor-sharp and resilient as the finest steel. Then he looked at the boy beside him – a boy in years only for his eyes were old and wise.

'Close now, Hennie.'

'Eccles, we'll halt here. Water the horses. Loosen the girths but don't offsaddle. No fires but the men can rest and eat.'

'Very well, sir.'

'I am going forward to have a look at the laager. While I am away I want you to issue an extra hundred rounds of ammunition to each man. Check the Maxims. I should be back in two hours.'

'When will it be, sir?'

'We'll move forward at dusk, I want to be in position to attack as soon as the moon rises. You can tell the men now.'

As Sean and Nonga left the column and moved on foot up the valley, two men watched them from the ridge. They lay on their bellies among the rocks. Both of them were bearded. One of them wore a British officer's Sam Browne belt over his patched leather jacket, but the rifle that rested on the rock in front of him was a Mauser.

'They send spies to the laager,' he whispered, and his companion answered in the Taal.

'*Ja*, they have found it.'

'Go! Ride quickly to Oom Paul and say for him that we have three hundred khaki ripe and ready for the plucking.'

The other Boer grinned and wriggled backwards, working his way off the skyline. Once below it he ran to his pony and led it down into the grass which would muffle its hoof-beats, before he mounted.

An hour later Sean returned from his reconnaissance.

'We've got them, Eccles,' he grinned savagely at Saul and Eccles.

'They're about two miles ahead in a hidden basin of hills.' He squatted down and smoothed a patch of earth with the palm of his hand. 'Now here is the way we'll do it.' With a twig he drew quickly in the dirt. 'This is our valley. Here we are. This is the laager, hills here and here and here. This is the entrance to the basin. Now, we'll place two Maxims here, with a hundred men below and in front of them like this. I want you –'

Abruptly his earthen map exploded, throwing dirt into his eyes and open mouth. 'What the bloody –' he mouthed as he clawed at his face but the rest of it was lost in the blast of the Mausers.

Through streaming eyes Sean looked up at the ridge. 'Oh my God!' A fire haze of gunsmoke drifted across it like sea spray on a windy day, and he sprang to his feet.

'Into the river. Get the horses into the river,' he roared above the murderous crackle, the shrill fluting whine of ricochets and the continuous slapping of bullets into earth and flesh.

'Into the river. Get into the river!' He ran down the

column shouting at the men who were struggling to clear their rifles from the scabbards of plunging, rearing horses. The Boer fire flogged into them, dropping men and horses screaming in the grass. Loose horses scattered along the valley, reins trailing and empty stirrups bouncing against their flanks.

'Leave them! Let them go! Get into the river!' Two of the mules were down, kicking, wounded in the traces of the scotchcart. Sean tore the tarpaulin loose and lifted out one of the Maxims. A bullet splintered the woodwork under his hands.

'You!' he shouted at one of his sailors. 'Grab this!' He passed the gun to him and the man ran with it cradled in his arms and jumped over the river bank. With a case of ammunition under each arm Sean followed him. It seemed as though he ran waist-deep in water, each pace dragging with painful deliberation and his fear came strongly upon him. A bullet flipped his hat forward over his eyes, the ammunition cases weighted him down, and he blundered panic-stricken towards the river. The earth was gone abruptly from under his feet and he fell, dropping free until, with a shock that jarred his spine, he struck and toppled forward face-down into the icy water.

Immediately he scrambled up and, still clutching the Maxim ammunition, floundered to the steep bank. Above him the Boer fire whipped and sang, but the bed of the river was crowded with his men, and others still fell and jumped from the bank to add to the congestion.

Panting and streaming water from his clothing Sean leaned against the bank while he gathered himself. The stream of survivors into the river-bed dwindled and stopped. The Boer fire also stuttered out and a comparative quiet fell over the field, spoiled only by the groaning and cursing of the wounded.

Sean's first coherent thought was for Saul. He found him holding two pack-mules under the bank with Nonga and Mbejane beside him holding another pair. He sent Saul to take command at the far end of the line.

'Sergeant-Major!' Sean shouted, and with relief heard Eccles's reply from close at hand.

'Here, sir.'

'Spread them out along the bank. Get them to cut firing platforms.'

'Very good, sir,' and immediately he began. 'Here you lot, you heard the Major! Up off your backsides!'

Within ten minutes there were two hundred rifles lining the bank and the Maxim was sited and manned behind a scharnz of stone and earth. Those men who had lost their weapons were tending the wounded. This pitiful little group were gathered in the middle of the line, they were propped against the bank, sitting waist-deep in slush and their blood stained the water pinky-brown.

Sean climbed up on to one of the firing platforms beside Eccles and lifted his head to peer cautiously over the bank. The area in front of him was a sickening sight. Dead mules and horses with their packs burst open littering the grass with blankets and provisions. Wounded animals flopping helpless or standing quietly with their heads hanging.

'Is there anyone out there still alive?' Sean called, but the dead men gave him no answer. A sniper on the ridge ploughed a bullet into the ground in front of Sean's face and he ducked down quickly.

'Most of them managed to crawl in, sir. Those that didn't are better out there than in the mud here.'

'How many did we lose, Eccles?'

'About a dozen dead, sir, and twice as many wounded. We got off very lightly.'

'Yes,' Sean nodded. 'Most of their initial fire went high. It's a mistake even the best shots make when shooting downhill.'

'They fair caught us with our pants down,' mused Eccles and Sean did not miss the censure in his tone.

'I know. I should have placed look-outs on the ridge,' he agreed. You're no Napoleon, he told himself, and you've got casualties to prove it.

'How many of them lost their weapons?' he asked.

'We've got two hundred and ten rifles and one Maxim, sir, and I issued an extra hundred rounds to each man just before the attack.'

'Should be enough,' Sean decided. 'Now all that remains is to sweat it out until my native guide brings up reinforcements.'

For half an hour nothing happened beyond a little desultory sniping from the ridge. Sean moved along the line talking to the men.

'How's it going, sailor?'

'Me old ma would have a fit, sir. "George," she'd say, "sitting in the mud is not going to do your piles no good," she'd say, sir.' The man was shot through the stomach and Sean had to force his chuckle through his throat.

'I could use a smoke, though. That I could.'

Sean found a damp cigar in his pocket for him and moved on. A youngster, one of the Colonials, was crying silently as he held against his chest the blood-soaked bundle of bandages that was his hand.

'Giving you pain?' Sean asked gently. The boy looked up at him, the tears smearing his cheeks. 'Go away,' he whispered. 'Please go away.'

Sean walked on. I should have put look-outs on the ridge, he thought again. I should have –

'Flag of truce on the ridge, sir,' a man shouted excitedly and Sean clambered up beside him.

Immediately a hum of comment ran along the line.

'They're hanging out their washing.'

'The bastards want to surrender. They know we've got them licked.'

Sean climbed out of the river-bed and waved his hat at the speck of white that fluttered on the ridge, and a horseman trotted down towards him.

'*Middag, Menheer*,' Sean greeted him. He received only a nod in reply and took the note the man proffered:

Menheer,

I expect the arrival of my Hotchkiss gun at any moment. Your position is not safe. I suggest you lay down your guns to prevent further killing.

J.P. Leroux, Vecht-Generaal,
Wynberg commando.

It was written on an irregular scrap of brown wrapping paper in High Dutch.

'My greetings to the General, *Menheer*, but we will hold out here a little longer.'

'As you wish,' the Boer acquiesced, 'but first you must see if any of these' – he pointed at the khaki figures that were scattered among the dead mules and horses – 'you must see if any of them are still alive. And you must destroy the wounded animals.'

'It is kind of you, *Menheer*.'

'You will, of course, make no attempt to pick up weapons or ammunition.'

'Of course.'

The Boer stayed with them while Eccles and half a dozen men searched the field, destroying the maimed animals and examining the fallen troopers. They found one man still alive. The air hissed softly from his sev-

284

ered windpipe and a froth of blood bubbles writhed about the hole. On a blanket they carried him down to the river-bed.

'Eleven dead, sir,' Eccles reported to Sean.

'Eccles, as soon as the truce ends we are going to recover another Maxim and the two cases of ammunition.'

They stood beside the scotchcart and Sean inclined his head to indicate the bulky, blue-metalled weapon that showed from beneath the tarpaulin.

'Very good, sir.'

'I want four men ready below the lip of the bank. Make sure each man has a knife to cut the pack ropes.'

'Yes, sir.' Eccles grinned like a playful walrus and drifted back towards the river, and Sean strolled across to the mounted Boer.

'We have finished, Menheer.'

'Good. As soon as I cross the skyline up there – then we'll start again.'

'I agree.' Sean walked back to the river, picking his way through the dead. Already the flies were there, swarming green and metallic, rising like a migrating hive of bees as he passed, then settling again.

Sean reached the bank and below him Saul crouched at the head of a bunch of unarmed men. Behind them stood a very disgruntled Eccles, his moustache drooping in disappointment. Instantly Sean saw what had happened – Saul had used his superior rank to take over command of the volunteers. 'What the hell do you think you're doing?' Sean demanded, and Saul answered him with an obstinate stare.

'You'll stay where you are. That's an order!' He turned to Eccles. 'Take over, Sergeant-Major,' and Eccles grinned.

This was no time to argue. Already the Boer horseman

285

was half way up the ridge. Sean raised his voice and shouted at the long line of men below the bank.

'Listen, all of you. No one is to fire until the enemy do. That way we may be able to spin it out a little longer.' Then less loudly as he spoke to Eccles. 'Don't run, just walk out casually.' Sean jumped down the bank and stood between Eccles and Saul. All three of them peered up at the ridge and saw the Boer reach the crest, wave his hat and disappear.

'Go!' Sean said, and all of them went. Eccles, the four volunteers – and Saul. Flabbergasted, Sean stared at the six of them as they strolled out towards the scotchcart. Then his anger flared. *The stupid little bastard*, and he went also.

He caught up with them as they reached the scotch-cart, and in the strained silence of the suspended storm he growled at Saul:

'I'll fix you for this!' and Saul grinned triumphantly.

Still there was a puzzled silence from the ridge – but it could not last much longer.

Together Saul and Eccles slashed at the ropes that held the tarpaulin, and Sean pulled it back and reached for the gun.

'Take it.' He passed it to the man behind him. At that moment a warning shot cracked over their heads.

'Grab one each and run!'

From the ridge and the river came gunfire like a long roll of drums, and they ran doubled beneath their loads and dodging, back towards the river.

The man carrying the Maxim fell headlong. Sean threw the ammunition case he carried, it dropped short of the bank, but skidded forward and toppled over the edge. Hardly pausing in his run, he stopped and gathered the fallen Maxim and went on. Ahead of him first

Eccles, then Saul jumped into safety and Sean followed them with the three surviving troopers.

It was over, Sean sat waist-deep in the icy water with the machine-gun clutched to his chest, and all he could think of was his anger at Saul. He glared at him, but Saul and Eccles knelt facing each other grinning and laughing.

Sean handed the gun to the nearest trooper and crossed to Saul. His hand fell heavily on his shoulder and he pulled him to his feet.

'You –' He could not find words cutting enough. If Saul had been killed out there, Ruth would never have believed Sean had not ordered it so. 'You fool,' he said and might have hit him, but he was distracted by the cries from the firing platform beside him.

'The poor bastard!'

'He's up.'

'Lie down, for God's sake, lie down.'

Sean released Saul, jumped up on to the platform and stared through the loophole in the scharnz.

Out in the open the trooper who had carried the Maxim was on his feet. He was moving parallel to the ban, shambling with a curious idiot gait, his hands hanging loosely by his sides. They were shooting at him from the ridge.

Held in the paralysis of horror, none of them went to him. He was hit and he lurched but tottered on with the Boer rifles hunting him, staggering in a circle away from the river. Then, suddenly they killed him and he dropped on to his face.

The gunfire stopped and in the silence the men in the river-bed began to move around, and talk of trivial things, avoiding each other's eyes, ashamed to have watched such a naked intimate thing as that man's dying.

Sean's anger was gone, replaced by guilty thankfulness that it had not been Saul out there in the open.

46

In the long period of stagnation that followed, Sean and Saul sat together against the bank. Though they talked little, the old sense of companionship was restored.

With a rush and rattle the first shell ripped the air above their heads, and with everyone else Sean ducked instinctively. The shell burst in a tall brownish-yellow spurt on the far slope. Consternation bushfired along the river.

'Lummy, they've got a gun!'

'Book me on the next train, mate!'

'Nothing to worry about, boys,' Sean shouted reassuringly. 'They can't reach us with that piece.'

And the next shell burst on the lip of the bank, showering them with earth and pebbles. One startled second they stood dazed and coughing in the fumes, and the next they fell on the bank like a band of competitive grave-diggers. Dust from their exertions rose in a pale brown mist over the river to puzzle the Boers on the ridge. Almost before the arrival of the next shell, each man had hacked out a small earthen cupboard into which he could squeeze himself.

The Boer gunners were alarmingly inconsistent. Two or three rounds would fly wildly overhead and burst in the open veld. The next would land squarely in the river spraying mud and water high in the air. When this happened the sound of sustained cheering drifted faintly down from the ridge, followed by a long pause – presumably while the gunners received the congratulations of their fellows. Then the bombardment would recommence with enthusiastic rapidity, which slowly wound down into another long pause while everybody rested.

During one of these intervals Sean peered through his loophole. From a dozen points along the ridge rose pale columns of smoke.

'Coffee break up there, Eccles.'

'The way they do things we can expect another white flag and a couple of their lads coming down with coffee for us as well.'

'I doubt it,' Sean grinned. 'But I think we can expect them to come down though.' Sean pulled out his watch. 'Half-past four now. Two hours to sundown. Leroux must try for a decision before dark.'

'If they come, they'll come from behind,' Saul announced cheerfully and pointed to the slope of ground that menaced their rear. 'To meet a charge from there, we would have to line the far bank and expose our backs to sniping from the ridge.'

Sean considered the problem for a minute. 'Smoke! That's it!'

'I beg yours, sir?'

'Eccles, get the men to build fireplaces of stone along the bed and set grass and branches ready to light,' Sean ordered. 'If they do come from behind we'll screen ourselves with smoke.'

Fifteen minutes of furious activity completed the work. At intervals of ten paces along the river-bed they built flat-topped cairns of stone that rose above the level of the water. On each was piled a large heap of grass and wild hemlock branches gathered from where they overhung the bank of the river.

*

A little before sunset, in that time of shadows and deceptive light, with a haze rising in the still, cold air to mask them, Leroux charged his horsemen at the river.

Sean heard a low drumming of hooves as though a train passed in the distance and started to his feet.

'Here they come!' somebody shouted. 'The bastards are coming from behind.'

With the low sun at their backs throwing big, distorted shadows ahead of them, they swept down in a long line from the west.

'Light the fires!' bellowed Sean. They were lying flat on their horses, five hundred of them coming in at full gallop and shooting as they came.

'Maxims!' Sean shouted. 'Get the Maxims across!' The teams dragged the heavy unwieldy weapons from their emplacements and floundered with them across the stream. From each of the fires blue smoke spread and lifted. Men coughed and swore and splashed to their new positions. From the ridge a furious covering fire raked the river and then the field-piece crashed shell after shell amongst them.

'Fire at will!' Sean shouted. 'Hit the bastards. Hit them. Hit them hard.'

The din was appalling – gunfire and bursting shells, the hammering beat of the Maxims, shouts of defiance and pain, the thunder of charging hooves, crackling of the flames. Over it all a dense fog of smoke and dust.

With elbows on the rough shale of the bank, Sean aimed and fired and a horse went down, throwing rider and rifle high and clear. Without taking the butt from his shoulder he worked the bolt and fired again. Got him! swaying and twisting in the saddle. Drop, you bastard! That's it – slide forward and fall. Shoot again, and again. Empty the magazine. Hitting with every shot.

Beside him the matelot traversed the Maxim in a deliberate hammering arc. Fumbling, as he reloaded, Sean watched the Maxim scythe its slow circle of destruction, leaving a shambles of downed horses and struggling men, before its beat stopped abruptly and the matelot crouched over it to fit a fresh belt from the wooden case. A bullet from the ridge, fired blindly into the smoke, hit him in the back of the neck and he fell forward, jamming the gun, blood gushing from his open mouth over the jacketed barrel. His limbs twitched and jerked in the epilepsy of death.

Sean dropped his rifle and dragged the matelot off the gun, levered the first round of the belt into the breech and thrust his thumbs down on the buttons.

They were close now. Sean bore down on the firing handles to raise his fire, aiming at the chests of the horses. The sailor's blood fried and sizzled on the hot barrel, and the grass in front of the muzzle flattened and quivered in the continuous blast.

Above him a solid frieze of milling horses was outlined against the darkening sky, the men upon them pouring their bullets into the crowded river-bed. Wounded horses plunged down the bank, rolling and kicking into the mud.

'Dismount! Dismount! Go in after them!' an old burgher with a neat blond beard yelled.

Sean dragged the gun around to get him. The man saw him in the smoke but his right leg was out of the stirrup, his rifle held in the left hand, helpless in the act of dismounting. Sean saw his eyes were grey and without fear as he looked down into the muzzle of the Maxim. The burst hit him across the chest, his arm windmilled, his left foot caught in the stirrup as he went backwards and his pony dragged him away.

The attack broke. The Boer fire slackened, ponies wheeled away, and raced back for the shelter of the hills. The old burgher Sean had killed went with them, dragged upon his back with his head bouncing loosely over the broken ground, leaving a long slide mark of flattened grass.

Around him Sean's men cheered and laughed and chattered with jubilation. But in the mud there were many who did not cheer and with a guilty shock Sean realized he had been standing on the corpse of the sailor who had died over the gun.

'Our round, that one!' Eccles beamed. Callous among the dead as only an old soldier can be.

'Yes,' Sean agreed.

Out in the open a horse heaved itself up and stood shivering, one leg hanging broken under it. A wounded burgher started to cough in the grass, choking and gasping as he drowned in his own blood.

'Yes, our round, Eccles. Put up the flag. They must come down and collect the wounded.'

They used lanterns in the darkness to find the wounded and kill the horses.

'Nkosi, at a place where the river turns and the banks are low, they have placed men,' Mbejane reported, back from the reconnaissance on which Sean had sent him. 'We cannot escape that way.'

'I thought as much,' Sean nodded, and held out the open can of bully beef to Mbejane. 'Eat,' he said.

'What's he say, sir?' Eccles asked.

'The river is held in force downstream.' Sean lit one of the cheroots that he had recovered in the darkness from the saddle-bag of his dead horse.

'Ruddy cold sitting here in the mud,' Eccles hinted.

'Patience, Sergeant-Major,' Sean smiled. 'We'll give

them until midnight. By them most of them will be down the other side of the ridge drinking coffee around the fires.'

'You are going to rush the ridge, sir?' Eccles obviously approved.

'Yes. Tell the men. Three hours' rest and then we'll take the ridge.'

'Very good, sir.'

Sean lay back and closed his eyes. He was very weary, his eyes felt gritty from the dust and smoke, his lower body was wet and cold, his boots heavy with mud. Lyddite fumes had given him a blinding headache.

I should have put a look-out on the ridge, he thought again. My God! What a mess I've made of this. My first command and already I've lost all the horses and damnnigh half of my men. I should have put a look-out on the ridge.

47

They took the ridge a few minutes after midnight with hardly any opposition. The few Boer sentries made good time down the far slope and Sean looked down upon the Boer laagers. The camp fires glimmered in an irregular line along the valley. Men stood around them staring up at the ridge. Sean scattered them with a dozen lusty volleys, and then yelled, 'Cease firing. Eccles, get the men settled in. We are going to have visitors fairly soon.'

The Boers had built scharnzes along the crest which saved Sean's men much inconvenience and within ten minutes the Maxims were emplaced and Sean's two hundred unwounded men waited behind walls of rough rock for the situation necessitated a hurried War Council in the valley below. But at last they heard the first stealthy approach of the attackers.

'Here they come, Sergeant-Major. Hold your fire, please.'

The burghers worked their way up cautiously and when Sean could hear their voices whispering among the rocks he decided they were close enough and discouraged further intimacy with volleyed rifle-fire and the use of all his Maxims. The Boers replied with heat and at the height of the exchange the Hotchkiss gun joined in from the valley. Its first shell passed but a few feet over Sean's head, then burst in the valley behind him. The second and third shots dropped neatly among the attacking Boer riflemen and raised such a howl of protest that the gunners, their efforts not appreciated, maintained an aloof and offended silence for the rest of the night.

Sean had expected a determined night attack but it soon became clear that Leroux was fully aware of the danger of closely engaging an inferior force in the dark. He contented himself with keeping Sean awake all night, his burghers taking it in turn to come up and keep the short-range rifle duel going – and Sean began to have qualms about the wisdom of his offensive. Dawn would find him on a rocky ridge, facing a numerically superior force, with his line anchored at neither end, and short enough to be easily flanked and enfiladed. He remembered Spion Kop – and there was little comfort in the memory. But the alternative was to fall back on the river, and his hackles rose at the thought. Unless relief came soon, defeat was certain – better here on the high ground than in the mud. We'll stay, he decided.

In the dawn there was a lull but although the gunfire dwindled to an occasional crack and flash on the lower slope yet Sean could sense an increase of activity among the Boers. Ominous rustlings and the muted sounds of movement on his flanks confirmed his misgivings. But now it was too late to retreat on the river, for already the mountains were showing stark silhouettes against the dawn sky. They seemed very close, as close and unfriendly as the unseen multitude of the enemy waiting out there for the light to come.

Sean stood up. 'Take the gun,' he whispered to the man beside him as he relinquished the Maxim.

All night he had fought with that wicked clumsy weapon and now his hands were claws shaped to the firing grips, and his shoulders ached intolerably. He flexed them as he moved down the line, stopping to chat with the men who lay belly-down behind the scharnz,

296

trying to make his words of encouragement sound convincing.

In their replies he sensed the respect they were forming for him as a fighting man. It was more than respect – closer to a tolerant affection. The same feeling old General Buller had evoked amongst his men. He made mistakes, a lot of men died when he led, but they liked him and followed cheerfully. Sean reached the end of the line.

'How's it going?' he asked Saul softly.

'Fair enough.'

'Any sign of the old Boer?'

'They're pretty close – we heard them talking a few minutes ago. My guess is they're as ready as we are.'

'We've got enough to finish this business.'

To finish the business! That would be his decision. When the massacre began, how much must he make then endure before he called for quarter, and they stood up with arms raised in the most shameful of all attitudes?

'You'd better get under cover, Sean. Light's coming fast.'

'Who the hell is looking after whom,' Sean grinned at him. 'I want no more heroics from you,' he said, and walked quickly to his station on the other flank.

The night lifted quickly from the land, and morning came as abruptly as it does only in Africa. The Boer laagers were gone. The Hotchkiss gun was gone. Sean knew that the gun and the Boer horses had been moved back behind the new ridge which now faced their position. He knew also that the rocky ground below him was crawling with the enemy, that they were on his flanks and probably in his rear as well.

Slowly, the way a man looks at a place before he begins a long journey, Sean looked around him at the mountains and the sky and the valley. In the soft light is was very beautiful.

He looked down the gut of the valley towards the grass plains of the highveld. His head jerked with surprise. He felt excitement lift the hair on his forearms. The mouth of the valley was blocked by a dark mass. In the uncertain light it could have been a plantation of wattle trees – oblong and regular and black against the pale grass. But this plantation was moving, changing shape, elongating. Birnam Wood to Dunsinane.

The first rays of the sun slanted in across the crest of the ridge and lit the lance-heads into a thousand minute dazzles.

'Cavalry!' roared Sean. 'By Jesus, look at them.'

The cry was taken up and thrown along the line, yelling, cheering wildly they fired down upon the tiny brown figures that were scurrying away to meet the Boer pickets who galloped in across the floor of the valley, each of them dragging a bunch of a dozen horses after him.

Then above the cheering and the gunfire, high above the sounds of hooves and the cries of panic, a bugle began to sing: 'Bonnie Dundee' – sharp and clear and urgently it commanded the charge.

Sean's rifles fell silent. The cheering faltered and stopped. One by one his men stood up to watch as the lines of lancers moved forward. Walk. Trot. Canter. Gallop. The lance heads dropped. Belly-high they flitted like fireflies in front of the solid dark ranks, and that terrible thing swept down upon the tangle of men and frenzied, struggling horses.

Some of the Boers were up now, wheeling away, breaking like game before the beaters.

'My God!' breathed Sean, tensing himself for the burst of sound as the charge struck home. But there was only the drum of hooves – no check, no distortion as the dark squadrons drove through the Boers. Precisely they wheeled, and came back. Broken lances thrown aside, sabres unsheathed, bright and long.

Sean watched a burgher dodging desperately as a lancer followed him. Saw him turning at the last moment and crouching with his arms covering his head. The lancer stood in his stirrups and swung his sabre backhanded. The burgher dropped. Like a polo player the trooper pivoted his horse and rode back of the Boer, leaning low out of the saddle to sabre him again as he knelt in the grass.

'Quarter!' growled Sean, the his voice rising shrilly in horror and disgust, 'Give them quarter. For the love of God, give them quarter!'

But cavalry gives no quarter. They butchered with dispassionate parade-ground precision. Hack and cut, turn and trample until the blades blurred redly – until the valley was strewn with the bodies of men wounded a dozen times.

Sean tore his eyes away and saw the remains of Leroux's commando scattered into the broken ground where the big cavalry mounts could not follow.

Sean sat down on a rock and bit the end off a cheroot. The rank smoke helped cleanse his mouth of the taste of victory.

Two days later Sean led his column into Charlestown. The garrison cheered them and Sean grinned as he watched his men react. Half an hour before they had bumped along, hunched unhappily on their borrowed mounts. Now they sat erect and jaunty, eating the applause and liking the taste.

Then the grin faded from Sean's face as he saw how his band was depleted, and he looked back and the fifteen crowded wagons that carried the wounded.

If only I'd put look-outs on the ridge.

48

There was an urgent summons from Acheson waiting for Sean. He caught the northbound express twenty minutes after arriving in Charlestown, hating Saul for the hot bath in which he left him, and for the uniform which Mbejane had persuaded a plump Zulu maid to wash and iron, hating him still more venomously for the invitation to be guest of honour at the officers' mess that night – and knowing that Saul would drink deep on Veuve Clicquot and Courvoisier which had once belonged to Sean.

When Sean arrived in Johannesburg the following morning, with soot from the locomotive adding a subtle touch to the fragrance he had gathered from two unwashed weeks in the veld, there was an orderly to meet him and conduct him to Acheson's suite in the Grand National Hotel.

Major Peterson was patently taken aback by Sean's turn-out, he eyed the stains and tears and dried mud with genteel horror at the contrast they afforded to the breakfast table's crisp white linen and splendid silver. The ripeness of Sean's odour impaired Peterson's appetite and he dabbed at his nose with a silk handkerchief. But Acheson seemed not to notice, he was in festive mood.

'Damned fine show, Courtney. Oh, damned fine. Proved your point entirely. We'll not have much trouble from Leroux for some time, I warrant you. Have another egg? Peterson, pass him the bacon.'

Sean finished eating and filled his coffee cup before he made his request. 'I want to be relieved of this command, I made a bloody mess of it.'

Both Acheson and Peterson stared in horror. 'Good God, Courtney. You've achieved a notable success – the most spectacular in months.'

'Luck,' brusquely Sean interrupted. 'Another two hours and we would have been wiped out.'

'Lucky officers are more valuable to me than clever ones. Your request is refused, Colonel Courtney.' So it's Colonel now, a bribe to get me into the dentist's chair. Sean was mildly amused.

A knock at the door prevented Sean continuing his protestation, and an orderly came into the room and handed Acheson a message.

'Urgent dispatch from Charlestown,' he whispered. Acheson took the paper from him and used it like a conductor's baton as he went on talking.

'I have got three junior officers for you, men to replace your losses. You catch them for us and hold them for my cavalry. That's all I want from you. While you're doing your bit the columns are going to start a series of new drives. This time we are going to sweep every inch of the ground between the blockhouse lines. We are going to destroy the crops and the livestock; burn the farms; take every woman, man and child off the land and put them in detainment camps. By the time we're finished there will be nothing but bare veld out there. We will force them to operate in a vacuum, while we wear them down with a relentless series of drives and raids.' Acheson slapped the table so that the crockery jingled. 'Attrition, Courtney. From now on it's a war of attrition!'

Those words had an uncomfortable familiarity for Sean. And suddenly a picture of desolation formed in his mind. He saw the land – his land – blackened with fire, and the roofless homesteads standing in the wastes. The sound of the empty winds across the land was the wailing of orphans, and the protest of a lost people.

'General Acheson –' he began, but Acheson was reading the dispatch.

'Damn!' he snapped. 'Damn and blast! Leroux again. He doubled back and caught the transport column of those same lancers who cut him up. Wiped it out and disappeared into the mountains.' Acheson laid the message on the table in front of him and stared at it. 'Courtney,' he said, 'go back and, this time, catch him!'

49

'Breakfast is ready, Nkosi.' Michael Courtney looked up from his book at the servant. 'Thank you, Joseph, I'm coming now.'

These two hours of study each morning passed so quickly. He checked the clock on the shelf above his bed – half-past six already – closed the book and stood up.

While he brushed his hair he watched his reflection in the mirror without attention. His mind was fully occupied with events that would fill this new day. There was work to do.

His reflection looked back at him with serious grey eyes from a face whose lean contours were marred by the big Courtney nose. His hair was black and springy beneath the brush.

He dropped the brush and while he shrugged into his leather jacket he flipped open the book to check a passage. He read it through carefully, then turned and went out into the corridor.

Anna and Garrick Courtney were seated at opposite ends of the long dining-table of Theuniskraal and they both looked up expectantly as he entered.

'Good morning, Mother.' She held up her face for his kiss.

'Good morning, Pa.'

'Hello, my boy.' Garry was wearing full dress, complete with crowns and decorations, and Michael felt a flare of irritation. It was so damned ostentatious. Also it reminded him that he was nineteen years old and there was a war going on while he sat at home on the farm.

'Are you going into town today, Pa?'

'No, I'm going to do some work on my memoirs.'

'Oh,' Michael glanced pointedly at the uniform and his father flushed slightly and applied himself to his meal.

'How are your studies, darling?' Anna broke the silence.

'Well enough, thank you, Mother.'

'I'm certain you'll have as little trouble with the final examinations as you had with the others.' Anna smiled at him possessively and stretched out to touch his hand. Michael withdrew it quickly and laid down his fork.

'Mother, I want to talk to you about enlisting.' Anna's smile froze. At the end of the table Garry straightened in his chair.

'No,' he snapped with unusual violence. 'We've been over this before. You're still a minor and you do as you're told.'

'The war is almost over, darling. Please think of your father and me.'

It began then. Another of those long wheedling, pleading arguments that sickened and frustrated Michael until he stood up abruptly and left the room. His horse was waiting saddled for him in the yard. He threw himself on to its back and swung its head at the gate, lifting it over, and scattering chickens as he landed. He galloped furiously away towards the main dip-tank.

From the dining-room they heard the hooves beat away until they had dwindled into silence. Garry stood up.

'Where are you going?' snapped Anna.

'To my study.'

'To the brandy bottle in your study,' she corrected him contemptuously.

'Don't, Anna.'

'Don't, Anna,' she mimicked him. 'Please don't, Anna. Is that all you can say?' Her voice had lost the genteel inflexion she had cultivated so carefully. Now it contained all the accumulated bitterness of twenty years.

'Please, Anna. I'll stop him going. I promise you.'

'You'll stop him!' She laughed. 'How will you stop him? Will you rattle your medals at him? How will you stop him – you, who have never done one useful thing in all your life?' She laughed again, shrilly. 'Why don't you show him your leg and say, "Please don't leave your poor crippled Daddy".'

Garry drew himself up. His face had gone very pale. 'He'll listen to me. He's my son.'

'Your son!'

'Anna, please –'

'Your son! Oh, that's choice! He's not your son. He's Sean's son.'

'Anna.' He tried to stop her.

'How could you have a son?' She was laughing again, and he could not stand it. He started for the door but her voice followed him, cutting into the two most sensitive places in his soul; his deformity and his impotence.

He stumbled into his study, slammed the door and locked it. Then he crossed quickly to the solid cabinet that stood beside his desk.

He poured the tumbler half-full and drank it. Then he sank into his chair and closed his eyes and reached for the bottle behind him. He poured again carefully and screwed the cap back on to the bottle. This one he would sip slowly, making it last perhaps an hour. He had learned how to keep the glow.

He unbuttoned and removed his tunic, stood up and hung it over the back of the chair, seated himself once more, sipped at the tumbler, then drew towards him the pile of handwritten sheets, and read the one on top.

'Colenso: An account of the campaign in Natal under General Buller.' By Colonel Garrick Courtney, V.C., D.S.O.

He lifted it, laid it aside, and began to read what followed. Having read it so many times before, he had come to believe in it. It was good. He knew it was good. So too did Messrs William Heinemann in London, to whom he had sent a draft of the first two chapters. They were anxious to publish as soon as possible.

He worked on quietly and happily all morning. At midday old Joseph brought a meal to the study. Cold chicken and salads on Delft-ware china, with a bottle of white Cape wine wrapped in a snowy napkin. He worked as he ate.

That evening when he had altered the last paragraph on the final page and laid his pen on the inkstand, he was smiling.

'Now, I will go and see my darling.' He spoke aloud and put on his tunic.

The homestead of Theuniskraal sat on the crest of a rise below the escarpment. A big building of white-washed walls, thatch and Dutch gables. In front of it the terraced lawns sprawled away, contoured by beds of azaleas and blue rhododendrons and bounded on the one side by the horse paddocks: two large paddocks for the brood mares and the yearlings, where Garry paused beside the low fence and watched the foals nuzzling upwards at the udders.

Then he limped on along the fence towards the smaller enclosure with its nine-foot fence of thick, canvas-padded gumpoles that contained his stud stallion.

307

Gypsy was waiting for him, nodding his almost snake-like head so that his mane flared golden in the late sunlight, flattening his ears, then pricking them forward, dancing a little with impatience.

'Hey, Boy. Hey there, Gypsy,' Garry called and the stallion thrust his head between the poles to nibble with soft lips at Garry's sleeve.

'Sugar, is that what you're after.' Garry chuckled and cupped his hands while the stallion fed delicately from them.

'Sugar, my darling,' Garry whispered in sensual delight at the touch of the soft muzzle on his skin and Gypsy cocked his ears to listen to his voice.

'That's all. All finished.' The stallion nuzzled his chest and Garry wiped his hands on its neck, caressing the warm and silky coat.

'That's all, my darling. Now run for me. Let me watch you run.' He stepped back and clapped his hands loudly. 'Run, my darling, run.'

The stallion pulled his head back between the poles and went up on his hind legs, whinnying as he reared, cutting at the air with his fore-hooves. The veins stood out along the belly and upon the tight double-swollen bag of its scrotum.

Swift and virile and powerful, it pivoted upon its quarters.

'Run for me!' shouted Garrick. The stallion came down into full gallop along the track worn by its hooves, sweeping around the paddock with loose dirt flying and the light dancing on his coat as the great muscles bulged beneath.

'Run.' Leaning against the poles of the fence, Garrick watched him with an expression of terrible yearning.

When he stopped again with the first dark patches of

sweat dulling his shoulders, Garrick straightened up and shouted across the stable yard.

'Zama, bring her now!'

On a long rein two grooms led the brood mare down towards the paddock. Gypsy's nostrils flared into dark pink caverns and he rolled his eyes until the whites showed.

'Wait, my darling,' whispered Garrick in a voice tight with his own excitement.

50

Michael Courtney dismounted among the rocks on the highest point of the escarpment. For a week he had denied the impulse to return to this place. Somehow it seemed a treachery – a disloyalty to both his parents.

Far below and behind him in the forest was the tiny speck of Theuniskraal. Between them the railway angled down towards the sprawled irregular pattern of rooftops that was Ladyburg.

But Michael did not look that way. He stood behind his mare and gazed along the line of bare hills to the gigantic quilt of trees that covered them in the north.

The wattle was tall now, so that the roads between the blocks no longer showed. It was a dark smoky green that undulated like the swells of a frozen sea.

This was as close as he had ever been to Lion Kop. It was a forbidden land, like the enchanted forest of the fairy-tale. He took the binoculars from his saddle-bag and scanned it carefully, until he came to the roof of the homestead. The new thatch, golden and unweathered, stood out above the wattle.

Grandma is there. I could ride across to visit, there would be no harm in that. *He* is not there. *He* is away at the war.

Slowly he replaced the binoculars in the saddle-bag, and he knew he would not go to Lion Kop. He was shackled by the promise he had made to his mother. Like so many other promises he had made.

With dull resignation he remembered the argument

at breakfast that morning, and knew that they had won again. He could not leave them, knowing that without him they would wither. He could not follow *him* to war.

He smiled ironically as he remembered the fantasies he had imagined. Charging into battle with *him*, talking with *him* beside the camp fire in the evenings, throwing himself in front of a bayonet meant for *him*.

From the look-out on the escarpment Michael had spent hours each day of the last Christmas holidays waiting for a glimpse of Sean Courtney. Now with guilt he remembered the pleasure he had experienced whenever he picked up that tall figure in the field of his binoculars and followed it as it moved between the newly planted rows of wattle.

But he's gone now. There would be no disloyalty if I rode across to see Grandma. He mounted the superb golden mare and sat deep in thought. At last he sighed, swung her head back towards Theuniskraal – and rode away from Lion Kop.

I must never come up here again, he thought determinedly, especially after *he* comes home.

51

They are tired, tired to the marrow of their bones. Jan Paulus Leroux watched the lethargy of his burghers as they off-saddled and hobbled their horses. They are tired with three years of running and fighting, sick-tired in the certain knowledge of defeat, exhausted with grief for the men they have buried, with grief also for the children and the women with them in the camps. They are wearied by the sight of burned homes scattered about with the bones of their flocks.

Perhaps it is finished, he thought and lifted the battered old Terai from his head. Perhaps we should admit that it is finished, and go in to them. He wiped his face with his scarf and the cloth came away discoloured with the grease of his sweat and the dust of the dry land. He folded the scarf into the pocket of his coat and looked at the fire-blackened ruins of the homestead on the bluff above the river. The fire had spread into the gum trees and the leaves were sere and yellow and dead.

'No,' he said aloud. 'It is not finished – not until we try for this last time,' and he moved towards the nearest group of his men.

'Ja, Hennie. How goes it?' he asked.

'Not too bad, Oom Paul.' The boy was very thin, but then all of them were thin. He had spread his saddle-blanket in the grass and lay upon it.

'Good.' Jan Paulus nodded and squatted beside him. He took out his pipe and sucked on it. There was still the taste of tobacco from the empty bowl.

'Will you take a fill, Oom Paul?' One of the others sat up and proffered a pouch of springbok skin.

'*Nee, dankie.*' He looked away from the pouch, shutting out the temptation. 'Keep it for a smoke when we cross the Vaal.'

'Or when we ride into Cape Town,' joked Hennie, and Jan Paulus smiled at him. Cape Town was a thousand miles south of them, but that was where they were going.

'*Ja*, keep it for Cape Town,' he agreed and the smile on his face turned bitter. Bullets and disease had left him with six hundred ragged men on horses half-dead with exhaustion to conquer a province the size of France. But it was the last try. He started to speak then.

'Already Jannie Smuts is into the Cape with a big commando. Pretorius also has crossed the Orange, De la Rey and De Wet will follow – and Zietsmann is waiting for us to join him on the Vaal River. This time the Cape burghers must rise with us. This time . . . '

He spoke slowly, leaning forward with his elbows on his knees, a gaunt giant of a man with his unkempt, ginger beard wiry with dust and streaked about the mouth with yellowish grey. The cuffs of his sleeves were stained with the discharge from the veld sores on his wrists. Men came across from the other groups and squatted in a circle about him to listen and take comfort.

'Hennie, bring my Bible from the saddle-bag. We will read a little from the Book.'

The sun was setting when he closed the Book and looked around at them. An hour had gone in prayer that might more profitably have been spent in rest, but when he looked at their faces he knew the time had not been wasted.

'Sleep now, *Kerels*. We will upsaddle early tomorrow.' If they do not come in the night, he qualified himself silently.

But he could not sleep. He sat propped against his saddle and for the hundredth time re-read the letter from Henrietta. It was dated four months earlier, had taken six weeks to reach him along the chain of spies and commandos which carried their mail. Henrietta was sick with dysentery and both the younger children, Stephanus and baby Paulus, were dead from the *witseerkeel*. The concentration camp was ravaged by this disease and she feared for the safety of the older children.

The light had failed so he could not read further. He sat with the letter in his hands. With such a price as we have paid, surely we could have won something.

Perhaps there is still a chance. Perhaps.

'Upsaddle! Upsaddle! Khaki is coming.' The warning was shouted from the ridge across the river where he had placed his pickets. It carried clearly in the still of the evening.

'Upsaddle! Khaki is coming.' The cry was taken up around the camp. Jan Paulus leaned over and shook the boy beside him, who was too deep in exhaustion to have heard.

'Wake up, Hennie. We must run again.'

Five minutes later he led his commando over the ridge and southward into the night.

52

'Still holding southwards,' Sean observed. 'Three days' riding and they haven't altered course.'

'Looks like Leroux has got his teeth into something,' agreed Saul.

'We'll halt for half an hour to blow the horses.' Sean lifted his hand and behind him the column lost its shape as the men dismounted and led their horses aside. Although the entire unit had been remounted a week before, the horses were already losing condition from the long hours of riding to which they had been subjected. However, the men were in good shape, lean and hard-looking. Sean listened to their banter and watched the way they moved and laughed. He had built them into a tough fighting force that had proved itself a dozen times since that fiasco a year ago when Leroux had caught them in the mountains. Sean grinned. They had earned the name under which they rode. He handed his horse to Mbejane and moved stiffly towards the shade of a small mimosa tree.

'Have you got any ideas about what Leroux is up to?' he asked Saul as he offered him a cheroot.

'He could be making a try at the Cape railway.'

'He could be,' Sean agreed as he lowered himself gratefully on to a flat stone and stretched his legs out in front of him. 'My God, I'm sick of this business. Why the hell can't they admit it's finished – why must they go on and on?'

'Granite cannot bend.' Saul smiled dryly. 'But I think that now it is very near the point where it must break.'

'We thought that six months ago,' Sean answered him, then looked beyond him. 'Yes, Mbejane, what is it?'

Mbejane was going through the ritual which preceded serious speech. He had come and squatted half a dozen paces from where Sean sat, had laid his spears carefully beside him in the grass, and now he was taking snuff.

'Nkosi.'

'Yes?' Sean encouraged him and waited while Mbejane tapped a little of the dark powder on to his fingernail.

'Nkosi, this porridge has an unusual taste.' He sniffed and sneezed.

'Yes?'

'It seems to me that the spoor has changed.' Mbejane wiped the residual snuff from his nostrils with the pink palm of his hand.

'You speak in riddles.'

'These men we follow ride in a different manner from the way they did before.'

Sean thought about that for a few seconds before he saw it. Yes! He was right. Where previously Leroux's commando had spread and trampled the grass in a road fifty feet wide, since this morning they had ridden in two files as though they were regular cavalry.

'They ride as we do, Nkosi, so the hooves of the horses fall in the tracks of those that lead. In this way it is difficult to tell how many men we follow.'

'We know there are about six hundred. . . . Hold on! I think I see what you . . . '

'Nkosi, it comes to me that there are no longer six hundred men ahead of us.'

'My God! You could be right.' Sean jumped up and began to pace restlessly. 'He is splitting his commando again. We've crossed a dozen rocky places where he could have detached small groups of his men. By evening we'll be following less than fifty men – when that happens they'll break up into individuals, lose us in the dark and head separately for a pre-arranged rendezvous.' He punched his fist into the palm of his hand. 'That's it, by God!' He swung round to face Saul.

'You remember that stream we crossed a mile back – that would have been an ideal place.'

'You're taking a big risk,' Saul cautioned him. 'If we go back now and it turns out you're wrong – then you've lost him for good.'

'I'm right,' Sean snapped. 'I know I am. Get them mounted up – we're going back.'

Sean sat his horse on the bank of the stream and looked down into the clear water that sparkled over gravel and small round boulders.

'They will have gone downstream, otherwise the mud they stirred up would have washed down across the ford.' He turned to Saul. 'I'm going to take fifty men with me so as not to raise too much dust. Give me an hour's start and then follow with the rest of the column.'

'*Mazeltov.*' Saul grinned at him.

With a Zulu tracker on each bank Sean and Eccles and fifty men followed the stream towards the northwest. Behind them the mountains of the Drakensberg were an irregular pale blue suggestion against the sky and around them the brown winter-sere veld spread away in the folded complexity of ridges and the shallow valleys. In the rocky ground along the ridges grew the squat little aloe plants, holding up their multiple flowers like crimson candelabra while in the valleys the stunted thorn bushes huddled along the course of the stream.

High, cold cloud obscured the sky. There was no warmth in the pale sunlight, and the wind had a knife-edge to it.

Two miles below the ford Sean was showing his anxiety by leaning forward in the saddle and checking the ground that Mbejane had already covered. Once he called, 'Mbejane, are you sure you haven't missed them?'

Mbejane straightened from his crouch and turned slowly to regard Sean with a look of frigid dignity. Then he shifted his war shield to the other shoulder and, not deigning to answer, he returned to his search.

Fifty yards farther on he straightened again and informed Sean.

'No, Nkosi. I have not missed them.' He pointed with his assegai at the deeply scarred bank up which horses had climbed, and the flattened grass which had wiped the mud from their legs.

'Got them!' Sean exulted in his relief; behind him he heard the stir of excitement run through his men.

'Well done, sir.' Eccles's moustache twitched ferociously as he grinned.

'How many, Mbejane?'

'Twenty, not more.'

'When?'

'The mud has dried.' Mbejane considered the question, stooping to touch the earth and determine its texture. 'They were here at half sun this morning.'

The middle of the morning; they had a lead of five hours.

'Is the spoor fat enough to run upon?'

'It is, Nkosi.'

'Then run, Mbejane.'

The spoor bellied towards the west then swung and steadied in the same persistently southward direction,

318

and Sean's column closed up and cantered after Mbejane.

Southward, always southward. Sean pondered the problem – what could he hope to accomplish with a mere six hundred?

Unless! Sean's brain started to harry a vague idea. Unless he intended slipping through the columns of infantry and cavalry that lay before him and trying for a richer prize.

The railway, as Saul had suggested? No, he discounted that quickly. Jan Paulus would not risk his whole command for such low stakes.

What then? The Cape? By God, that was it – the Cape! That rich and lovely country of wheatlands and vineyards. That serene and secure land, lazing in the security of a hundred years of British rule – and yet peopled by men of the same blood as Leroux and De Wet and Jan Smuts.

Smuts had already taken his commando across the Orange River. If Leroux followed him, if De Wet followed him, if the Cape burghers broke their uneasy neutrality and flocked to join the commandos – Sean's mind baulked at the thought. He left the wider aspect of it and came back to the moment.

All right then, Jan Paulus was riding to the Cape with only six hundred men? No, he must have more. He must be riding to a rendezvous with one of the other commandos. Who? De la Rey? No, De la Rey was in the Magaliesberg. De Wet? No, De Wet was far south – twisting and turning away from the columns that harried him. Zietsmann? Ah, Zietsmann! Zietsmann with fifteen hundred men. That was it.

Where would they meet? On a river obviously, for they must have water for two thousand horses. The Orange was too dangerous – so it must be the Vaal, but whereabouts on the Vaal? It must be a place easily recognizable. One of the fords? No, cavalry used the fords. A confluence of one of the tributaries? Yes, that was it.

Eagerly Sean unbuckled his saddle-bag and pulled from it his map-case. Holding the heavy cloth map folded against his thigh he twisted sideways in the saddle to study it.

'Here we are now,' he muttered and ran his finger south. 'The Padda River!'

'I beg your pardon, sir.'

'The Padda, Eccles, the Padda!'

'Very well, sir,' agreed Eccles with stolid features covering his bewilderment.

In the dark valley below them the single fire flared briefly, then died to a tiny glow.

'All ready, Eccles,' Sean whispered.

'Sir!' Without raising his voice Eccles placed affirmative emphasis on the monosyllable.

'I'll go down now.' Sean resisted the impulse to repeat his previous orders. He wanted to say again how important it was that no one escaped, but he had learned that once was enough with Eccles. Instead he whispered, 'Listen for my signal.'

The Boers had only one sentry. Secure in the knowledge that their stratagem had thrown off all pursuit, they slept around the poorly screened fire. Sean and Mbejane moved down quietly and squatted in the grass twenty paces from the high rock on which the sentry sat. The man was outlined darkly against the stars and Sean watched him intently for a full minute before he decided.

'He sleeps also.'

Mbejane grunted.

'Take him quietly,' Sean whispered. 'Make sure his rifle does not fall.' Mbejane moved and Sean laid a hand on his shoulder to restrain him. 'Do not kill – it is not necessary.' And Mbejane moved silently as a leopard towards the rock.

Sean waited straining his eyes into the darkness. The seconds dragged by – and suddenly the Boer was gone from the rock. A gasp, a soft sliding sound and stillness.

Sean waited, and then Mbejane was back as silently as he had left.

'It is done, Nkosi.'

Sean laid his rifle aside and cupped his hands over his lips, filled his cheeks and blew the long warbling whistle of a nightbird. At the fire one of the sleepers stirred and muttered. Farther off a horse stamped and blew softly through its nostrils. Then Sean heard a pebble click and the cautious swish of feet through grass, small sounds lost in the wind.

'Eccles?' Sean murmured.

'Sir.'

Sean stood up and they closed in on the camp.

'Wake up, gentlemen. Breakfast is ready.' Sean shouted in the Taal, and each burgher woke to find a man standing over him and the muzzle of a Lee-Metford pressing into his chest.

'Build up that fire,' Sean ordered. 'Take their rifles.' It had been too easy, he spoke roughly in the irritation of anti-climax.

'Mbejane, bring the one from the rock – I want to see how gently you dealt with him.'

'Mbejane dragged him into the firelight and Sean's lips tightened as he saw the way the man's head lolled and his legs hung.

'He's dead,' Sean accused.

'He sleeps, Nkosi,' Mbejane denied.

Sean knelt, beside him and twisted his face to catch the light. Not a man, a lad with a thin bitter face and the fluff of pale, immature beard on his cheeks. In the corner of his eye a stye had burst to matt the closed lashes with yellow pus. He was breathing.

Sean glanced up at the other prisoners. They were being herded away out of earshot.

'Water, Mbejane.' And the Zulu brought a canteen from the fire while Sean explored the hard swelling above the boy's temple.

'He'll do,' Sean grunted, and curled his lips in distaste at what he must do as soon as the lad recovered. He must do it while he was still groggy and bemused by the blow. From his cupped hand he splashed cold water into his face and the boy gasped and rolled his head.

'Wake up,' Sean urged quietly in the Taal. 'Wake up.'

'Oom Paul?' The Boer mumbled.

'Wake up.' The lad struggled to sit.

'Where . . . You're English!' As he saw the uniform.

'Yes,' Sean snapped. 'We're English. You've been caught.'

'Oom Paul?' The boy looked round wildly.

'Don't worry about him. He'll be with you on the boat to St Helena. Leroux and Zietsmann were both caught on the Vaal yesterday. We were waiting for them at the Padda and they walked right into the trap.'

'Oom Paul caught!' The boy's eyes were wide with shock, still dazed and out of focus. 'But how did you know? There must have been a traitor – someone must have told. How did you know about the meeting-place?' He stopped abruptly as his brain caught up with his tongue. 'But how . . . Oom Paul couldn't be on the Vaal yet, we left him only yesterday.' Then sickeningly he

322

realized what he had done 'You tricked me,' he whispered. 'You tricked me.'

'I'm sorry,' Sean said simply. He stood up and walked across to where Eccles was securing his prisoners.

'When Captain Friedman arrives tell him to bring the column in to the garrison at Vereeniging and wait for me there. I am going ahead with my servant,' he said abruptly, then called across to Mbejane.

'Mbejane, bring my horse.' He would trust no one else to carry the news to Acheson.

The following afternoon Sean reached the railway line guarded by its blockhouses and flagged a northbound train. The next morning he de-trained with soot-inflamed eyes, tired and filthy, at Johannesburg station.

53

Jan Paulus Leroux checked his horse and behind him the tiny fragment of his commando bunched up and all of them peered eagerly ahead.

The Vaal is a wide, brown river, with sandbanks through which it cuts its own channel. The banks are steep and along them are scattered a few of the ugly, indigenous thorn trees which provide no cover for an army of three thousand men and horses. But Leroux had chosen the rendezvous with care. Here the tiny Padda River looped down through a complex of small kopjes to join the Vaal and among these kopjes an army might escape detection – but only if it exercised care. Which Zietsmann was not doing.

The smoke from a dozen fires hazed out in a long pale smear across the veld, horses were being watered on one of the sandbanks in the middle of the river, and a hundred men were bathing noisily from the bank, while laundry decked the thorn trees.

'The fool,' snarled Leroux and kicked his pony into a run. He stormed into the laager, flung himself off his horse and roared at Zietsmann.

'*Menheer*, I must protest.'

Zietsmann was nearly seventy years old. His beard was pure white and hung to the fifth button of his waistcoat. He was a clergyman, not a general, and his commando had survived this long because it was so ineffectual as to cause the British no serious inconvenience. Only great pressure from Delarey and Leroux had forced him to take part in this wild plan. For the last three days, as he waited for Leroux to join him, he had been harassed by doubts and misgivings. These doubts were shared by his wife – for he was the only Boer general who still had his woman with him in the field.

Now he stood up from his seat by the fire and glared at this red-bearded giant Leroux, whose face was mottled with fury.

'*Menheer*,' he growled. 'Please remember you are speaking not only to your Elder, but also to a Dominie of the Church.'

In this way was set the tone for the long discussions which were to fill the next four days. During this time Leroux saw his bold design bog down in a welter of trivialities. He did not resent the loss of the first day which was spent in prayer, indeed he realized that this was essential. Without God's blessing and active intervention the enterprise must fail, so the sermon he delivered that afternoon lasted a little over two hours and the text he selected was from Judges – 'Shall I yet again go out to battle against the children of Benjamin, my brother, or shall I cease?' and the Lord said, 'Go up; for tomorrow I will deliver them into thine hand.'

Zietsmann bettered his time by forty minutes. But then, as Leroux's men pointed out, Zietsmann was a professional while Oom Paul was only a lay-preacher.

The next and most critical question was the election of the Supreme Commander for the combined enterprise. Zietsmann was the older by thirty years, a factor heavily in his favour. Also, he had brought sixteen hundred men to the Vaal against Leroux's six hundred. Yet Leroux was the victor of Colenso and Spion Kop, and since then he had fought consistently and with not a little success, including the wrecking of eight trains and the annihilation of four British supply columns.

Zietsmann had been second in command at Modder River, but since then he had done nothing but keep his commando intact.

For three days the debate continued with Zietsmann dourly refusing to bring the matter to the vote until he sensed that opinion had swung to his side. Leroux wanted command; not only for personal satisfaction, but also because he knew that under this cautious and stubborn old man they would be lucky to reach the Orange River, let alone force an effective entry into the Cape.

The card that won the hand belonged to Zietsmann, and it was ironic that he had it simply because of his inactivity over the last eighteen months.

When Lord Roberts had marched into Pretoria two years before, his entry had been offered only token resistance, for the Government of the South African Republic had withdrawn along the eastern railway line to Komatipoort. With them went the entire contents of the Pretoria Treasury, which totalled two million pounds in gold Kruger sovereigns. Later, when old President Kruger left for Europe, a part of this treasure went with him, but the balance had been shared out among the remainder of the commando leaders as their war chests to continue the fight.

Months before most of Leroux's share had been expended on the purchase of supplies from the native tribes, on ammunition from the Portuguese gun runners and on payment to his men. During a desperate night action with one of the raiding British columns he had lost the balance along with his Hotchkiss gun, twenty of his best men and a hundred irreplaceably precious horses.

Zietsmann, however, had come to the meeting with a pack-mule carrying thirty thousand sovereigns. The successful invasion of the Cape would depend largely upon this gold. On the evening of the fourth day he was duly elected Commander by a majority of two hundred, and within twelve hours he had demonstrated how well-equipped he was for the task.

'So we start in the morning, then,' one of the burghers beside Leroux grunted.

'About time,' another commented. They were break-fasting on biltong – sticks of hard dried meat – for Leroux had succeeded in convincing Zietsmann that cooking-fires were dangerous.

'No sign of Van der Bergh's men?' asked Leroux.

'Not yet, Oom Paul.'

'They are finished, or else they would have been here days ago.'

'Yes, they are finished,' agreed Leroux. 'They must have run into one of the columns.' Twenty good men, he sighed softly, and Hennie was with them. He was very fond of the boy, all of them were. He had become the mascot of the commando.

'At least they are out of it now – the lucky thunders.' The man had spoken without thinking, and Leroux turned on him.

'You can go too hands-up for the British, there is no one to stop you.' The softness of his voice did not cover the ferocity in his eyes.

'I didn't mean it that way, Oom Paul.'

'Well, don't say it then,' he growled, and would have continued, but a shout from the sentry on the kopje above them brought them all to their feet.

'One of the scouts coming!'

'Which way?' Leroux bellowed upwards.

'Along the river. He's riding to burst!'

And the sudden stilling of voices and movement was the only outward sign of the dread that settled upon all of them. In these days a galloping rider carried only evil tidings.

They watched him splash through the shallows and slide from the saddle to swim beside his horse across the deep channel. Then pony and rider, both streaming water, came lunging up the near bank and into the camp.

'Khaki,' shouted the man. 'Khaki coming!'

Leroux ran to catch the pony's head and demanded, 'How many?'

'A big column.'

'A thousand?'

'More than that. Many more – six, seven thousand.'

'Magtig!' swore Leroux. 'Cavalry?'

'Infantry and guns.'

'How close?'

'They will be here before midday.'

Leroux left him and ran down the slope to Zietsmann's wagon.

'You heard, *Menheer*?'

'*Ja*, I heard.' Zietsmann nodded slowly.

'We must mount up,' Leroux urged.

'Perhaps they will not find us. Perhaps they will pass us by.' Zietsmann spoke hesitantly, and Leroux stared at him.

'Are you mad?' he whispered, and Zietsmann shook his head – a confused old man.

'We must mount up and break away towards the south.' Leroux grabbed the lapels of Zietsmann's frock coat and shook them in his agitation.

'No, not the south – it is finished. We must go back,' the old man muttered, then suddenly his confusion cleared. 'We must pray. The Lord will deliver us from the Philistine.'

'*Menheer*, I demand . . . ' Leroux started, but another urgent warning shouted fromt he kopje interrupted him.

'Riders! To the south! Cavalry!'

Running to one of the horses Leroux vaulted on to its bare back, with a handful of its mane he turned it towards the kopje and flogged it with his heels, driving it up the steep rocky side, scrambling and sliding in the loose rock until he reached the top and jumped down beside the sentry.

'There!' The burgher pointed.

Like a column of safari ants, tiny and insignificant in the immensity of brown grass and open sky, still four or five miles distant, the squadrons were strung out in extended order across the southern hills.

'Not that way. We cannot go that way. We must go back.' He swung round to the north. 'We must go that way.'

Then he saw the dust in the north also and he felt his stomach slide sickly downwards. The dust drifted low, so thin it might have been only heat haze or the passing of a dust devil – but he knew it was not.

'They are there also,' he whispered. Acheson had thrown his column in from four directions. There was no escape.

'Van der Bergh!' whispered Leroux bitterly. 'He has gone hands-up to the English and betrayed us.' A moment longer he stared at the dust, then quickly he adjusted to the problem of defence.

'The river is our one line,' he muttered. 'With the flanks anchored on this kopje and that one there.' He let his eyes run back up the little valley of the Padda River, carefully memorizing the slope and lay of the land, storing in his mind each of its salient features, already siting the captured Maxims, picking the shelter of the hills and river bank for the horses, deciding where the reserves should be held.

'Five hundred men can hold the north kopje, but we will need a thousand on the river.' He vaulted up on to the pony and called down to the sentry, 'Stay here. I will send men up to you. They must build scharnzes along the ridge – there, and there.'

Then he drove the pony down the slope, sliding on its haunches until it reached the level ground.

'Where is Zietsmann?' he demanded.

'In his wagon.'

He galloped across to it and jerked open the canvas at the entrance.

'*Menheer*,' he began and then stopped. Zietsmann sat on the wagon bed with his wife beside him. A Bible was open on his lap.

'*Menheer*, there is little time. The enemy closes from all sides. They will be upon us in two hours.'

Zietsmann looked up at him, and from the soapy glaze of his eyes Leroux knew he had not heard.

'Thou shalt not fear the arrow that flieth by day, nor the terror that walketh by night,' he murmured.

'I am taking command, *Menheer*,' Leroux grunted. Zietsmann turned back to the book and his wife placed an arm round his shoulders.

We can hold them for this day, and perhaps tomorrow, Leroux decided from where he lay on the highest kopje. They cannot charge their cavalry against these hills, so they must come for us with the bayonet.

It is the guns first that we must fear, and then the bayonet.

'Martinus Van der Bergh,' he said aloud. 'When next we meet I will kill you for this.' And he watched the batteries unlimbering out of rifle-shot across the river, forming their precise geometrical patterns on the brown grass plain.

'*Nou skiet hulle,*' muttered a burgher beside him.

'*Ja,*' agreed Leroux. 'Now they will shoot,' and the smoke gushed from the muzzle of one of the guns out on the plain. The shell burst thunderously on the lower slopes and for an instant the lyddite smoke danced like a yellow ghost, swirling and turning upon itself, before the wind drifted it up to them. They coughed in the bitter-tasting fumes.

The next shell burst on the crest, throwing smoke and earth and rock high into the air, and immediately the rest of the batteries opened together.

They lay behind their hastily constructed earthworks while the shellfire battered the ridge. The shrapnel buzzed and hummed and struck sparks from the rocks, the solid jarring concussions made the earth jump beneath their bellies and dulled their ears so they could hardly hear the screaming of the wounded, and slowly a great cloud of dust and fumes climbed into the sky above them. A cloud so tall that Sean Courtney could see it from where he waited fifteen miles north of the Vaal.

'It looks as though Acheson has caught them,' murmured Saul.

'Yes, he's caught them,' Sean agreed, and then softly, 'The poor bastards.'

'The least they could have done was to let us be in at the kill,' growled Sergeant-Major Eccles. The distant rumble of the guns had awakened his blood lust and his great moustache wriggled with frustration. 'Don't seem right to me, seeing as how we been following the old

Boer for going on a year and a half – the least they could have done was to let us be there at the end.'

'We are the cover guns, Eccles. General Acheson is trying to drive them south on to his cavalry, but if any of the birds break back through his line of beaters then they're ours,' Sean explained.

'Well, it just don't seem right to me,' Eccles repeated, then suddenly remembering his manners, he added, 'Begging your pardon, sir.'

54

Exultantly General Acheson traversed his binoculars across the group of hills. Vaguely through the dust and smoke he could pick out their crests.

'A fair cop, sir!' Peterson grinned.

'A fair cop indeed,' Acheson agreed. They had to shout above the thunder of the guns and beneath them their horses fidgeted and trembled. A dispatch-rider galloped up, saluted and handed Peterson a message.

'What is it?' Acheson asked without lowering his glasses.

'Both Nichols and Simpson are in position for the assault. They seem anxious to engage, sir.' Then Peterson looked up at the holocaust of dust and flame upon the hills. 'They'll be lucky if they find anyone left to fight up there.'

'They will,' Acheson assured him. He was not misled by the deceptive fury of the barrage. They had survived worse at Spion Kop.

'Are you going to let them go, sir?' Peterson insisted gently. For another minute Acheson watched the hills, then he lowered his glasses and pulled his watch from his breast pocket. Four o'clock – three hours more of daylight.

'Yes!' he said. 'Send them in.'

And Peterson scribbled the order and handed it to Acheson for his signature.

*

'*Hier Kom Hulle.*' Leroux heard the shout in the ceaseless roar of the shells, heard it take up and passed along the line.

'Here they come.'

'*Pasop!* They are coming.'

He stood up and his stomach heaved at the movement. Poisoned by the lyddite fumes, he fought his nausea and when he had controlled it he looked out along the river. For a second the veil of dust opened so he could see the tiny lines of khaki moving in towards the hills. Yes, they were coming.

He ran down his own line towards the river, shouting as he went.

'Wait until they are certain! Don't shoot until they reach the markers!'

From this corner of the kopje he could look out over every quarter of the field.

'*Ja*, I thought so!' he muttered. 'They come from two sides to split us.' Advancing on the frontage of the river were those same lines of tiny figures. The lines bulged and straightened and bulged again, but always they crept slowly nearer. Already the leading rank was moving up on his thousand-yard markers, in another five minutes they would be in range.

'They stand out well,' Leroux muttered as he ran his eyes along the rows of markers. While most of his men were building the earthworks along the kopjes and the river, others had paced out the ranges in front of these defences. Every two hundred and fifty yards they had erected those small cairns of stones, and over each they had smeared whitish grey mud from the river. It was a trick the British never seemed to understand, and as they advanced the Boer rifles had their range almost to the yard.

'The river is safe,' he decided. 'They cannot break

through there,' and he allowed himself time to grin. 'They never learn. Every time they come against the worst side.' Then he switched his attention to the assault on his left flank. This one was dangerous, this was where he must command in person, and he ran back to his original position while around him and overhead the storm of shrapnel and lyddite roared on unabated.

He dropped on his belly between two of his burghers, wriggled forward unbuckling the bandolier from around his chest and draped it over the boulder beside him.

'Good luck, Oom Paul,' a burgher called.

'And to you, Hendrik,' he answered as he set the rear sight of his Mauser at a thousand yards, then laid the rifle on the rock in front of him.

'Close now,' the burgher beside him muttered.

'Very close. Good luck and shoot straight!'

Suddenly the storm lifted and there was silence. A vast aching silence, more shocking than the buzzing, howling roar of the guns. The dust and the smoke drifted away from the crests and after its gloom the sunshine burned down brightly on the hills and the golden brown plain, it sparkled with dazzling brilliance on the sweeping waters of the Vaal, and it lit each tiny khaki figure with stark intensity, so their shadows lay dark on the earth beneath them. They reached the line of markers.

Leroux picked up his rifle. There was one man he had been watching, a man who walked a little ahead of his line. Twice Leroux had seen him pause as if to shout an order to those who followed him.

'You first, my friend,' and he took the officer in his sights, holding him carefully in the notch with the bead obscuring his trunk. Gently he took up the slack in the trigger and the recoil slammed back into his shoulder. With the vicious and characteristic crack of the Mauser stinging his eardrums, Leroux watched the man go down into the grass.

'*Ja!*' he said and reloaded.

Not in simultaneous volley, not with the continuous wild crackle which they had used at Colenso – but in a careful, steady stutter which showed that each shot was aimed – the Boer rifles started the hunt.

'They have learned,' Leroux muttered as he worked the bolt of his rifle, and the empty case pinged away among the rocks. 'They have learned well,' and he killed another man. At two places on the ridge the Maxim guns began their frenzied hammering bursts.

Before it reached the second row of markers, the first line of infantry no longer existed, it was scattered back in the grass, completely annihilated by the terrible accuracy of the Boer fire. The second line walked over them and came on steadily.

'Look at them come,' shouted a burgher farther down the line. Though they had seen it a dozen times before, all of these ragged farmers were awed by the passive, impersonal advance of British infantry.

'These men fight not to live but to die!' muttered the man who lay beside Leroux.

'Then let us help them to die,' Leroux shouted. And below him on the plain the slow inexorable ranks moved forward towards the third row of markers.

'Shoot, *Kerels*. Shoot straight,' Leroux roared, for now he could see the bayonets. He pressed a clip full of ammunition down into the magazine, and with the back of his hand brushed the clinging drops of sweat from his eyebrows, pushed the rifle forward and knocked down four men with his next six shots. Then he saw the change. At one place the line bulged as men began to hurry forward, while on the flanks it wavered and disintegrated as others hung back or crouched down behind pitifully inadequate cover.

'They are breaking!' Leroux howled excitedly. 'They won't reach the slopes.'

The forward movement faltered, no longer able to stand the mauling they were receiving, men turned back or went to ground while their officers hurried along the ranks goading them on. In so doing they proclaimed to the Boer riflemen that they were officers and at that range they did not survive long.

'They're finished!' shouted Leroux, and a thin burst of cheering ran along the ridge while the Boer fire increased in volume, flailing into the milling confusion of a broken infantry assault.

'Hit them, *Kerels*. Keep hitting them!' The following ranks overran the leaders, then in turn faltered and failed as the Maxim and Mauser fire churned into them.

Out on the plain a bugle began to lament, and as it mourned, the last spasmodic forward movement of the assault ceased, and back past the dead and the wounded streamed the retreat.

A single shell rushed overhead to burst in the valley beyond and immediately, as if in frustrated fury, the guns lashed the kopje once more. But in the jump and flash of the shells five hundred Boers cheered and laughed and waved their rifles at the retreating infantry.

'What happened on the river?' Leroux called in the tumult, and after a while the answer came back.

'They did not reach the river. They are broken there also.'

Leroux lifted his hat from his head and wiped the sweat and the dust from his face. Then he looked at the sunset.

'Almighty God, we give you thanks for this day. We

337

ask your mercy and guidance in the days that are to come.'

The shellfire lashed the hills like the surf of a storm-driven sea until the night came. Then in the darkness they saw the fires of the British bivouacs spread like a garden of yellow flowers on the plains around them.

55

'We must break out tonight.' Leroux looked across the fire at Zietsmann.

'No.' The old man spoke softly, not looking at him.

'Why?' demanded Leroux.

'We can hold these hills. They cannot drive us from them.'

'*Ja!* We can hold them tomorrow – two days, a week – but then it is finished. We lost fifty men today from the guns.'

'They lost many hundreds. The Lord smote them and they perished.' Zietsmann looked up at him now and his voice gathered strength. 'We will stay here and place our trust in the Lord.' There was a murmur of agreement from those who listened.

'*Menheer.*' Leroux covered his eyes for a moment, pressing fingers into them to still the terrible aching. He was sick from the lyddite, and tired – tired to the depths of his soul. It would be easier to stay. There would be no dishonour in it for they had fought like no men before them. Two more days and then it would be over without dishonour. He removed his hands from his face. '*Menheer*, if we do not break out tonight we never will. By tomorrow we will not have the strength.' He stopped for the words came slowly, slurred a little from a brain dulled by the lyddite and the hammering of big guns. He looked at his hands and saw the suppurating sores on his wrists. There would be no dishonour. They would fight this last time and then it would be finished.

'But it is not a matter of honour,' he mumbled. Then he stood up and they watched him in silence for he was going to speak. He spread his hands out in appeal, and the firelight lit his face from below leaving his eyes in shadow, dark holes like the sockets of a skull. He stood like that for a while and his rags hung loosely on the gaunt wasted body.

'Burghers . . . ' he started. But the words were not there. There was nothing except the need to fight on. He dropped his hands to his sides.

'I am going,' he said with simplicity. 'When the moon goes down I ride,' and he walked away from the fire. One by one other men rose and followed him, and all of them were men of his own commando.

Six men squatted in a circle and watched the moon as it touched the hills. Behind them the horses were saddled and the rifles stuck up from their scabbards. By each of the six hundred horses a burgher lay fully clothed, wrapped in his blanket and trying to sleep. Though the horses stamped and moved restlessly there was no jingling of bits for all of them were carefully muffled.

'We will say it again, so that each of us knows his part.' Leroux looked around the circle. 'I will go first with a hundred men and follow the river towards the east. What is your route, Hendrik?'

'South, through the cavalry until the dawn, then round towards the mountains.'

Leroux nodded and asked the next man:

'And yours?'

'West along the river.'

'Ja, and yours?'

He asked each in turn and when all had answered – 'The place of meeting is the old laager by the Hill of Inhlozana. Is this agreed?'

And they waited, watching the moon and listening to

the jackals squabbling over the British corpses on the plain. Then the moon went down below the hills and Leroux stood up stiffly.

'*Totsiens, Kerels*. Good luck to all of us.' He took the reins of his pony and led it down towards the Vaal, while in silence a hundred men led their horses after him. As they passed the single wagon beside the Padda, old Zietsmann was waiting and he came forward leading a pack-mule.

'You are going?' he asked.

'*Ja, Menheer*. We must.'

'God go with you.' Zietsmann thrust out his hand and they gripped briefly.

'The mule is loaded. Take the money with you. We will not need it here.'

'Thank you, *Menheer*.' Leroux motioned to one of his men to take the mule. 'Good luck.'

'Good luck, General.' For the first time Zietsmann used his title, and Leroux went down to the perimeter of their defences and out into the veld where the British waited.

With the first pale promise of dawn in the sky, they were through and clear. Though twice during the night heavy outbursts of firing in the darkness far behind them showed that not all of the escaping bands had been so fortunate.

56

Sean and Saul stood beside the little scotchcart and Mbejane brought them coffee.

'My God, it's cold enough to freeze the hanger off a brass monkey.' Sean cupped his hands around the mug and sipped noisily.

'At least you've got a hood to keep your tip warm,' Saul retorted. 'We'd better get moving before we all freeze to the ground.'

'Dawn in an hour,' Sean agreed. 'Time to start walking our beat,' and he called across to Mbejane, 'Kill the fire and bring my horse.'

In double file with the scotchcart bumping along in the rear they started on the outward leg of their patrol. In the last four days they had covered the same ground as many times, tacking backwards and forwards across the beat that Acheson had assigned them. The grass was brittle with frost and crunched under the horses' hooves.

While ahead of them the Zulu trackers ranged like gundogs, and behind the troopers huddled miserably in their greatcoats, Sean and Saul picked up their endless discussion from the point at which they had left it the previous evening. Already they had reached so far into the future that they were talking of a federation under responsible government that would encompass all the territories south of the Zambesi.

'That's what Rhodes has proposed for the last ten years,' Saul pointed out.

'I don't want any part of that wily bastard.' Sean spoke

emphatically. 'He'll keep us tied for ever to the apron strings of Whitehall – the sooner we get rid of him and Milner the better, say I.'

'You want to get rid of Imperial rule?' Saul asked.

'Of course, let's end this war and send all of them back across the sea. We can run our own affairs.'

'Colonel, it seems to me you are fighting on the wrong side,' Saul remarked, and Sean chuckled.

'But seriously, Saul . . . ' He never finished. Mbejane came out of the darkness, running with silent purpose so that Sean checked his horse and felt the skin along his arms prickle with nervous excitement.

'Mbejane?'

'Mabuna!'

'Where? How many?'

He listened to Mbejane's hurried explanation, then swung round to face Sergeant-Major Eccles, who was breathing heavily down his neck.

'Your birds, Eccles. A hundred or so of them, only a mile ahead and coming straight towards us.' Sean's voice was tight with the same excitement that made Eccles's moustache wriggle like an agitated caterpillar on the impassive oval of his face. 'Deploy in single line. They'll walk right on top of us in the dark.'

'Dismounted, sir?'

'No,' Sean answered. 'We'll gun charge them as soon as they show. But for God's sake keep it quiet.'

As Sean sat his horse with Saul beside him, the two files of troopers opened on each side of them. There was no talking; only the clicking of iron-shod hooves on rock, the rustling of men struggling out of their heavy greatcoats, and the soft rattle and snick of breech-bolts opening and closing.

'Once more into the breach, dear friends,' whispered Saul, but Sean did not answer because he was wrestling

343

with his fear. Even in the cold of dawn his hands were damp. He wiped them on the thighs of his breeches and slid his rifle from the scabbard.

'What about the Maxims?' Saul asked.

'No time to set them up.' Sean knew his voice was hoarse and he cleared his throat before he went on. 'We won't need them – it's six to one.'

He looked along the silent line of his men. A dark line against the grass that was paling in the dawn. He could see that each of his troopers leaned forward in the saddle with his rifle held across his lap. The tension was a tangible thing in the half-darkness; even the horses were infected, they moved beneath their riders, shifting their bodies, nodding with impatience. Please God, let none of them whicker now.

And he peered ahead into the darkness. Waiting with his own fear and the fear of his men so strong that the Boers must surely smell it.

A patch of greater darkness in the dawn, ahead and slightly to the left of centre. Sean watched it for a few seconds and saw it move, slowly, like the moonlit shadow of a tree on the open veld.

'Are you sure they're Boers?' Saul whispered, and the doubt startled Sean. While he hesitated the shadow spread towards them and now he could hear the hooves.

Are they Boers? Desperately he searched for some sign that would allow him to loose his charge. Are they Boers? But there was no sign – only the dark advance and the small sounds of it, the click and creak in the dawn.

They were close now, less than a hundred yards, although it was impossible to tell with certainty for the dark, moving mass seemed to float towards them.

'Sean . . . ' Saul's whisper was cut off by the shrill nervous whinny of his horse. The sound was so unexpected that Sean heard the man beside him gasp. Almost immediately came the sign for which Sean waited.

'*Wie's daar!*' The challenge from ahead was in the guttural of the Taal.

'Charge!' yelled Sean and hit his horse with his heels. Instantly the whole of his line jumped forward to hurl itself upon the Boers.

Forward in the pounding hooves, forward in the shouting, in the continuous crackle of rifle-fire that sparkled along the line – with his fear left behind him, Sean spurred at them. Steadying the butt of his rifle under his right armpit, firing blind, blending his voice with the yelling of six hundred others, leading slightly in the centre of the line; he took his commando down upon the Boers.

They broke before the charge. They had to break for they could not hope to stand against it. They swung and drove their exhausted horses back towards the south.

'Bunch up!' roared Sean. 'Bunch on me!' And his line shortened so they charged knee to knee in a solid wall of men and horses and gunfire before which the Boers fled in wild despair.

Directly in Sean's path lay a stuggling, badly wounded horse with its rider pinned underneath it. Jammed into the charge he could not swerve.

'Up, Boy!' he shouted and lifted his horse with his knees and his hands, clearing the tangle and stumbling as they landed. Then forward again in the urgent, jostling clamour of the charge.

'We're gaining!' yelled Saul. 'This time we've got them.'

The horse beside him hit a hole and went down with its leg breaking like a pistol-shot. The trooper was thrown from it high and clear, turning in the air as he fell. The line closed to fill the gap, and pounded on over the grassland.

'There's a kopje ahead,' Sean shouted as he saw the ragged loom of it against the dawn sky. 'Don't let them reach it!' And he raked his spurs along his horse's ribs.

'We won't catch them,' warned Saul. 'They'll get into the rocks.'

'Damn it! God damn it!' groaned Sean. In the past few minutes the light had strengthened. Dawn in Africa comes quickly once it starts. Clearly he could see the leading Boers ride into the rocks, throw themselves from their ponies and duck into cover.

'Faster!' shouted Sean in agony. 'Faster!' as he saw the chance of quick success slip from his grasp. Already Mausers were talking back from the lower slopes of the kopje, and the last burghers were down and scurrying into the rocks. Loose ponies turned wildly into his line, empty stirrups flapping, eyes wide with terror – forcing his men to swerve into each other, dissipating the force of the charge. A loose pack-mule with a small leather pack upon its back climbed up through the rocks until a stray bullet killed it and it rolled into a deep crevice. But nobody saw it fall.

Sean felt the horse between his legs jerk and he was thrown with such violence that the stirrup leathers snapped like cotton and he went up and out, hung for a sickening moment and then swooped down to hit the ground with his chest and shoulder and the side of his face.

While he lay in the grass the charge spent itself like a wave on the kopje, then eddied and swirled into confusion. Dimly Sean was aware of the hooves that trampled about his head, of the sound of the Mausers and the shouts of the men who were swept by them.

'Dismount! Get down and follow them.' Saul's voice

and the tone of it roused Sean. With his hands under his chest he pushed himself into a sitting position. The side of his face burned where the skin had been smeared away, his nose was bleeding and the blood turned the earth in his mouth to a gritty paste. His left arm was numb to the shoulder and he had lost his rifle.

Dully he tried to spit the filth from his mouth while he peered at the chaos about him, trying to make sense of it. He shook his head, to joggle the apathy from his brain, while all around him men were being cut down at point-blank range by the Mausers.

'Dismount! Dismount!' The urgency of Saul's voice brought Sean unsteadily to his feet.

'Get down, you bastards!' He took up the cry. 'Get down and chase them.' A horse brushed against him and he staggered but kept his balance. The trooper slid down from its back beside Sean.

'Are you all right, Colonel?' He reached out to steady Sean, but a bullet took him in the chest below his raised arm and killed him instantly. Sean stared down at the body and felt his brain click back into focus.

'The bastards,' he snarled and snatched up the man's rifle, then, 'Come on!' he roared. 'Follow me!' and he led them out of the shambles of struggling horses into the rocks.

In the next half-hour, grimly and irresistibly, they used their superior numbers to drive the Boers back up the kopje. Each outcrop of rocks was a strongpoint that had to be assaulted and carried, and paid for in blood. On a front of perhaps two hundred yards, the attack became a series of isolate skirmishes over which Sean could not maintain command. He gathered those men who were near him and boulder by boulder they fought their way towards the top, while the burghers in front of him held each position until the last moment and then fell back on the next.

The top of the kopje was flattened into a saucer with fifty feet of steep open ground falling away on all sides, and finally sixty burghers reached this natural fortress and held it with the determination of men who knew that they fought for the last time. Twice they threw the British from the lip of the saucer and sent them scrambling and sliding back into the shelter of the broken rock below. After the second repulse a heavy unnatural silence settled on the kopje.

Sean sat with his back to a rock and took the water-bottle that a corporal offered him. He rinsed the slime of blood and congealing saliva from his mouth and spat it pink on to the ground beside him. Then he tilted the bottle and swallowed twice with his eyes tightly closed in the intense pleasure of drinking.

'Thanks.' He passed the bottle back.

'More?' the corporal asked.

'No.' Sean shook his head and looked back down the slope. The sun was well up now, throwing long shadows behind the horses that were grazing far out across the veld below. But at the foot of the slope lay the dead animals, most of them on their sides with legs thrust stiffly out. Blanket-rolls had burst open to litter the grass with the pathetic possessions of the dead men around them.

The men in their khaki and brown were as inconspicuous as piles of dead leaves in the grass, mostly British but with here and there a burgher lying amongst them in the fellowship of death.

'Mbejane.' Sean spoke softly to the big Zulu who squatted beside him. 'Find Nkosi Saul and bring him to see me here.'

He watched the Zulu crawl away. Mbejane had been

left behind at the start of that wild gallop, but before Sean was half-way up the kopje he had glanced back to find him kneeling two paces behind, ready with a bandolier of ammunition for the moment when Sean needed it. Neither of them had spoken until this moment. Between them words were seldom necessary.

Sean fingered the raw graze on his face and listened to the murmured conversation of the men around him. Twice he heard clearly the voices of Boers from the saucer above them and once he heard a burgher laugh. They were very close, and Sean moved uneasily against the rock.

Within minutes Mbejane was back with Saul crawling behind him. When he saw Sean, Saul's expression changed quickly.

'Your face! Are you all right?'

'Cut myself shaving.' Sean grinned at him. 'Have a seat. Make yourself comfortable.'

Saul crawled the last few yards and settled himself against Sean's rock. 'Now what?' he asked.

'Ten minutes' rest, then we're going up again,' Sean told him. 'But this time with a little more purpose. I want you to work around the back of the kopje with half the men. Take Eccles with you. We'll rush their whole perimeter at the same moment. When you're in position fire three shots in quick succession then count slowly to twenty. I'll back you from this side.'

'Good.' Saul nodded. 'It'll take me a little while to get round – don't be impatient.' And he was smiling as he rose to his knees and leaned forward to touch Sean's shoulder.

Sean would always remember him like that: big mouth creased at the corners, smiling with white teeth through three days' growth of beard, slouch hat pushed to the back of his head, so his hair fell forward on to his forehead, and sunburned skin flaking from the tip of his nose.

The rock behind them was cracked through. If Saul had not leaned forward to make that gesture of affection he would not have exposed himself.

The sniper on the ridge had seen the brim of his hat above the rock and he held his aim into the crack. At the moment that Saul's fingers touched Sean's shoulder his head moved across the gap and the Boer fired.

The bullet hit Saul in the right temple, slanted diagonally back through his head and came out behind his left ear.

Their faces were but eighteen inches apart and Sean was smiling into Saul's eyes as the bullet hit. Saul's whole head was distorted by the impact, swelling and bursting like a balloon. His lips stretched so that for an instant his smile was a hideous rubbery thing and then he was snatched away and thrown sideways down the slope. He slid to a stop with his head and shoulders mercifully covered by a tuft of the coarse grey grass that grew among the rocks, but his trunk shivered and his legs danced and kicked convulsively.

For a slow count of ten Sean did not move nor did his expression alter. It took him that long to believe what he had seen. Then his face seemed to crumple.

'Saul!' His voice was a croak.

'Saul!' It rose higher, sharp with the realization of his loss.

He came slowly to his knees. Now Saul's body was still, very still and relaxed.

Again Sean opened his mouth but this time the sound he uttered was without form. The way an old bull buffalo bellows at the heart shot, that way Sean gave expression to his grief. A low shuddering cry that carried to the men in the rocks around him and to the Boers in the saucer above.

He made no attempt to touch Saul. He stared at him. 'Nkosi.' Mbejane was appalled at what he saw on Sean's face. His tunic was stiff with his own dried blood. The graze across his cheek was swollen and inflamed and it wept pale lymph. But it was the eyes that alarmed Mbejane.

'Nkosi.' Mbejane tried to restrain him, but Sean did not hear. His eyes were glazing over with the madness that had taken the place of his grief. His head hunched down on his shoulders and he growled like an animal.

'Take them! Take the bastards!' And he went up and over the rock in a twisting leap with the bayoneted rifle held against his chest.

'Come on!' he roared and went up the slope so fast that only one bullet hit him. But it did not stop him and he was over the lip, roaring and clubbing and hacking with the bayonet.

From the rocks four hundred of his men swarmed up after him and boiled over the lip of the saucer. But before they reached Sean he was face to face with Jan Paulus Leroux.

This time it was no match. Jan Paulus was wasted and sick. A gaunt skeleton of the man he had been. His rifle was empty and he fumbled with the reload. He looked up and recognized Sean. Saw him tall and splattered with blood. Saw the bayonet in his hands and the madness in his eyes.

'Sean!' he said and lifted the empty rifle to meet the bayonet. But he could not hold it. With Sean's weight behind it the bayonet glanced off the stock and went on. Jan Paulus felt the tingling slide of the steel through his reluctant flesh and he went over backwards with the bayonet in him.

'Sean,' he cried from his back. Sean stood over him and plucked the bayonet out. He lifted it high with both hands, his whole body poised to drive it down again.

They stared at each other. The British charge swept past them and they were alone. One man wounded in the grass and the other wounded above him with the bayoneted rifle and the madness still on him.

The vanquished in the grass, who had fought and suffered and sacrificed the lives of those he loved.

The victor above him, who had fought and suffered and sacrificed the lives of those he loved.

The game was war. The prize was a land. The penalty for defeat was death.

'Maak dit klaar! Make it finished!' Leroux told him quietly. The madness went out in Sean like the flame of a candle. He lowered the bayoneted rifle and let it drop. The weakness of his wound caught up with him and he staggered. With surprise he looked down at his belly and clasped his hands over the wound, and then he sank down to sit beside Jan Paulus.

In the saucer the fight was over.

57

'We're ready to move, sir.' Eccles stood beside the scotch-cart and looked down at Sean. A massive scowl concealed his concern. 'Are you comfortable?'

Sean ignored the question. 'Who is in charge of the burial details, Eccles?'

'Smith, sir.'

'You have told him about Saul – about Captain Friedman?'

'Yes, sir. They will bury him separately.'

Sean lifted himself painfully on to an elbow and for a minute stared at the two gangs working bare to the waist on the communal graves. Beyond them lay the rows of blanket-wrapped bundles. A fine day's work, he thought bitterly.

'Shall we start, sir?' Eccles asked.

'You've given Smith my orders? Burghers to be buried with their comrades – our men with theirs?'

'It's all taken care of, sir.'

Sean lay back on the bedding that covered the floor of the scotchcart.

'Please send my servant to me, Eccles.'

While he waited for Mbejane, Sean tried to avoid contact with the man who lay beside him in the scotchcart. He knew Jan Paulus was watching him.

'Sean – *Menheer*, who will say the words for my men?'

'We have no Chaplain.' Sean did not look at him.

'I could say them.'

'General Leroux, it will be another two hours before

the work is completed. You are wounded, and it is my duty to get this column with the other wounded back to Vereeniging as soon as I can. We are leaving the burial detail and when they're finished they'll catch us up.' Sean spoke lying on his back staring up at the sky.

'*Menheer*, I demand —' Jan Paulus began, but Sean turned angrily towards him.

'Listen, Leroux. I've told you what I'm going to do. The graves will be carefully marked, and later the War Graves Commission will send a Chaplain.'

There was very little room in the scotchcart and they were both big men. Now, as they glared at each other their faces were a foot apart. Sean would have said more, but as he opened his mouth the wound in his guts caught him and he gasped. The sweat broke out heavily across his forehead.

'Are you all right?' Jan Paulus's expression altered.

'I'll feel better once we get to Vereeniging.'

'*Ja*, you're right. We must go,' agreed Leroux.

Eccles came back with Mbejane.

'Nkosi, you sent for me?'

Mbejane, I want you to stay here and mark the place where they bury Nkosi Saul. Remember it well, for later you must be able to bring me back to it,' Sean mumbled.

'Nkosi.' Mbejane went away.

'Very well, Eccles. You can start.'

It was a long column. Behind the van rode the prisoners, many of them mounted two up. Then followed the wounded, each in a horse litter of poles and blankets, behind them the scotchcart, and finally Eccles and two hundred troopers of the rearguard. Their progress was slow and dismal.

In the scotchcart neither of them spoke again. They lay in pain, bracing themselves against the jolt and lurch, with the sun beating down mercilessly upon them.

In that dreamlike state induced by pain and loss of blood, Sean was thinking of Saul. At times he would convince himself that it had not happened and he would experience a rush of relief as though he had woken from a nightmare to find it was not reality. Saul was alive after all. Then his mind would focus with clarity and Saul was dead again. Saul was wrapped in a blanket with the earth above him, and they all had planned was down there with him. Then Sean would grapple once more with the unanswerable.

'Ruth!' he cried aloud, so that Jan Paulus beside him stirred uneasily.

'Are you all right, Sean?'

But Sean did not hear him. Now there was Ruth. Now there was Ruth alone. He felt joy then in his loss, joy quickly swamped with guilt. For an instant he had been glad that Saul was dead, and his treachery sickened him and ached like the bullet in his guts. But still there was Ruth, and Saul was dead. I must not think of it like that. I must not think! and he struggled up into a sitting position and clung to the side of the scotchcart.

'Lie down, Sean,' Jan Paulus told him gently. 'You'll bleed again.'

'You!' Sean shouted at him. 'You killed him.'

'Ja.' Leroux nodded his red beard into his chest. 'I killed them, but you also – all of us. Ja, we killed them.' And he reached up and took Sean's arm and drew him down into the blankets. 'Now lie still or we'll bury you also.'

'But why, Paul. Why?' Sean asked softly.

'Does it matter why? They are dead.'

'And now what happens?' Sean covered his eyes from the sun.

'We go on living. That is all, we just go on.'

'But what was it about. Why did we fight?'

'I don't know. Once I knew clearly, but now I have lost the reason,' Leroux answered.

They were silent for a long time and then they began to talk again. Groping together for the things that must take the place of that which had filled these last three years.

Twice that afternoon the column halted briefly while they buried men who had died of their wounds. And each of these deaths – one a burgher and the other a trooper – gave poignancy and direction to the talk in the scotchcart.

In the evening they met a patrol that was scouting ahead of the big columns returning from the Padda River. A young lieutenant came to the scotchcart and saluted Sean.

'I have a message for you from General Acheson, sir.'

'Yes?'

'This fellow Leroux got away from us at the Padda. Zietsmann, the other Boer leader, was killed, but Leroux got away.'

'This is General Leroux,' Sean told him.

'Good God!' He stared at Leroux. 'You caught him. I say – well done, sir. Jolly well done.' In the past two years Jan Paulus had become a legend to the British, so that the lieutenant examined him now with frank curiosity.

'What is your message?' Sean snapped.

'Sorry, sir.' The youngster dragged his eyes away from Jan Paulus. 'All the Boer leaders are meeting at Vereeniging. We are to give them safe conduct into the garrison. General Acheson wanted you to try to contact Leroux with the offer – but, that won't be difficult now. Jolly good show, sir.'

356

'Thank you, Lieutenant. Please tell General Acheson that we'll be in Vereeniging tomorrow.'

They watched the patrol ride away and disappear over a fold in the land.

'So!' growled Leroux. 'It's surrender then.'

'No,' Sean contradicted him. 'It's peace!'

58

The primary school at Vereeniging had been converted into an officer's hospital. Sean lay on his field cot and regarded the picture of President Kruger on the wall opposite him. In this way he was putting off the moment when he must continue with the letter he was writing. So far he had written the address, the date and the salutation: 'My dear Ruth'.

It was ten days since the column had returned from the veld. It was also ten days since the surgeons had cut him open and tied together those parts of his alimentary canal that the bullet had disrupted. He wrote:

I am at this moment well on the way to recovering from a small wound received two weeks ago near the Vaal River – so please take no notice of my current address. [He started a new paragraph.]

God knows I wish the circumstances in which I write were less painful to both of us. You will by now have received an official notification of Saul's death, so there is nothing I can add but to say that he died in circumstances of great personal gallantry. While about to lead a bayonet charge he was shot and killed *instantly*.

I know you will want to be alone in your grief. It will be some weeks before the doctors allow me to travel. By the time I reach Pietermaritzburg I hope you will be sufficiently recovered to allow me to call on you in the hope that I may be able to give you some comfort.

I trust that small Storm continues to increase in weight and beauty. I look forward to seeing her again.

A long while he pondered the ending, and finally decided on 'Your true friend'. He signed it, folded it into its envelope and laid it on the locker beside his bed for posting.

Then he lay back on his pillows and surrendered himself to the ache of loss and the dull pain in his belly.

After a while his physical pain dominated, and he glanced surreptitiously around the ward to ensure there were no nurses about.

Then he lifted the sheet, pulled up his nightshirt and began picking at the bandage until he had exposed the edge of the wound with the black horsehair stitches standing stiffly out of it like the knots in a strand of barbed wire. An expression of comical disgust curled his lips. Sean hated sickness – but especially he hated it in his own flesh. The disgust gave way slowly to a helpless anger and he glared at the wound.

'Leave it stand, old Sean. Looking won't make it better.' Sean had been so intent on the evil gash in his stomach that he had not heard the speaker approach. Despite the cane and the limp that dragged his right leg, Leroux moved silently for a big man. He stood now beside the bed and smiled shyly down at Sean.

'Paul!' Guiltily Sean covered himself.

'*Ja*, Sean. How goes it?'

'Not too bad. And you?'

Leroux shrugged. 'They tell me I will need this for a long time to come.' He tapped the ferrule of the cane on the floor. 'May I sit down?'

'Of course.' Sean moved to give him the edge of the

bed and Leroux lowered himself with his bad leg stretched stiffly in front of him. His clothing was newly washed and the cuffs of his jacket darned; patches on the elbows, and a long tear in the knee of his breeches had been cobbled together with crude, masculine stitches.

His beard had been trimmed and squared. There were iodine-stained bandages covering the open sores on his wrists, but a red mane of hair hung to the collar of his jacket and the bones of his forehead and cheeks made harsh angles beneath the skin that was desiccated and browned by the sun.

'So!' said Sean.

'So!' Leroux answered him and looked down at his hands. Both he and Sean were silent then, awkward and inarticulate, for neither of them dealt easily in words.

'Will you smoke, Paul?' Sean reached for the cheroots on his locker.

'Thank you.' They made a show of selecting and lighting, then silence overwhelmed them again and Leroux scowled at the tip of his cheroot.

'This is good tobacco,' he growled.

'Yes,' agreed Sean and regarded his own cheroot with equal ferocity. Leroux coughed and rolled his cane between the fingers of his other hand.

'*Toe maar*, I just thought I'd come and see you,' he said.

'I'm glad of it.'

'So, you're all right then, hey?'

'Yes. I'm all right,' Sean agreed.

'Good.' Leroux nodded sagely. 'Well, then!' He stood up slowly. 'I had better be going. We are meeting again in an hour. Jannie Smuts has come up from the Cape.'

'I heard so.' Even the hospital was penetrated by rumours of what was happening in the big marquee tent pitched on the parade-ground near the station. Under the chairmanship of old President Steyn the Boer leaders were talking out their future. De Wet was there, and Niemand and Leroux. Botha was there and Hertzog and Strauss and others whose names had echoed across the world these last two years. And now the last of them, Jannie Smuts, had arrived. He had left his commando besieging the little town of O'Kiep in the Northern Cape and travelled up the British-held railway. Now they were all assembled. If they had gained nothing else in these last desperate years, they had at least won recognition as the leaders of the Boer people. This tiny band of tired and war-sick men was treating with the representatives of the greatest military power on earth.

'*Ja*, I have heard so,' Sean repeated, and impulsively he thrust out his hand. 'Good luck, Paul.'

Leroux seized his hand and held it hard, his mouth moved with the pressure of his emotion.

'Sean, we must talk. We have to talk!' he blurted.

'Sit down,' Sean told him and Leroux freed his hand and sank on to the bed once again.

'What must I do, Sean?' he asked. 'It's you who must advise me. Not these . . . not these others from over the sea.'

'You have seen Kitchener and Milner.' It was not a question, for Sean knew of the meeting. 'What do they ask of you?'

'They ask everything.' Leroux spoke bitterly. 'They ask for surrender without terms.'

'Will you agree to that?'

For a minute Leroux was silent, and then he lifted his head and looked full into Sean's face.

'So far we have fought to live,' he said and what Sean saw in those eyes he would never forget. 'But now we will fight to die.'

'And by this, what will you achieve?' Sean asked softly.

'Death is the lesser evil. We cannot live as slaves.' Leroux's voice rose sharply. 'This is my land,' he cried.

'No,' Sean told him harshly. 'It is also my land, and the land of my son,' and then his voice softened. 'And the blood of my son is your blood.'

'But these others – this Kitchener, this devil Milner.'

'They are a people apart,' Sean said.

'But you fought with them!' Leroux accused.

'I have done many foolish things,' agreed Sean. 'But, from them I have learned.'

'What are you saying?' demanded Leroux, and Sean could see the sparkle of hope in his eyes. I must say this carefully, thought Sean, I must be very careful. He drew a long breath before he spoke.

'As it stands this moment your people are scattered but alive. If you fight on, the British will stay until you have found the annihilation you seek. If you stop now, then soon they will leave.'

'Will you leave?' demanded Leroux savagely.

'No.'

'And you are British! The British will stay – you and those like you.'

Then Sean grinned at him. It was so sudden, so irresistible that grin, that it threw Leroux off balance.

'Do I look and talk like a *rooinek*, Paul?' he asked in the Taal. 'Which half of my son is burgher and which half British?'

Confused by this sneak attack Leroux stared at him for a long time before he dropped his eyes and fiddled with his cane.

'Come on, man,' Sean told him. 'Make an end to this foolishness. You and I have a lot of work to do.'

'You and I?' Leroux asked suspiciously.

'Yes.'

Leroux laughed, a sudden harsh bellow of laughter.

'You are a *slim Kerel*,' he roared.

'I'll have to think about what you have said.' He rose from the bed and seemed to stand taller now. The laughter filled out his gaunt features and wrinkled his nose.

'I'll have to think very carefully about it.' He reached out his hand again and Sean took it. 'I will come and talk with you again.' He turned away abruptly and limped down the ward with his cane tapping loudly.

Jan Paulus kept his word. He visited Sean daily, an hour or so at a time, and they talked. Two days after the Boer surrender he brought another man with him.

Jan Paulus stood a good four inches over him, but though he was slimly built the visitor gave the impression of size.

'Sean, this is Jan Christian Niemand.'

'Perhaps I am lucky we did not meet before, Colonel Courtney.' Niemand's voice, high in timbre, was crisp and authoritative. He spoke the perfect English he had learned at Oxford University. 'What do you think, *Oubas*?' He addressed Jan Paulus by the title which was obviously a private joke between them, and Jan Paulus chuckled.

'Very lucky. Otherwise you also might be using a stick.'

Sean examined Niemand with interest. Hard years of war had muscled his shoulders and he walked like a soldier, yet above the pointed blond beard was the face of a scholar. The skin had a youthful clarity which was almost maidenly, but the eyes were a penetrating blue, the merciless blue of a Toledo steel blade.

His mind had the same resilience, and before many minutes Sean was using all his wits to meet and answer questions that Niemand asked him. It was clear that he

363

was being subjected to some sort of test. At the end of an hour he decided he had passed.

'And now, what are your plans?'

'I must go home,' Sean answered, 'I have a farm and a son – soon, perhaps, a wife.'

'I wish you happiness.'

'It is not yet settled,' Sean admitted. 'I still have to ask her.'

Jannie Niemand smiled. 'Well, then, I wish you luck with your suit. And strength to build a new life.' Suddenly he was serious. 'We also must rebuild what has been destroyed.' He stood up from the bed and Jan Paulus stood with him.

'There will be need of good men in the years ahead.' Niemand held out his hand and Sean took it. 'We will meet again. Count on that.'

59

As the train ran in past the great white mine dumps and Sean leaned from the window of the coach to look ahead at the familiar skyline of Johannesburg, he wondered how such an unlovely city still had the power to draw him back each time. It was as though he was connected to it by an elastic umbilical cord which allowed him a wide range. But when he reached its limit it pulled him back.

'Two days,' he promised himself. 'Two days I'll stay here. Just long enough to hand old Acheson my formal resignation and tell Candy Good-bye. Then I'll head south to Ladyburg – and leave this town to stew in its own evil juices.'

Near at hand a midday hooter howled from one of the mines, and immediately its cry was taken up and answered by the other mines. It sounded as though a pack of hungry wolves were hunting across the valley, the wolves of greed and gold. Those mines that had been forced to close during the hostilities were now back in production, and the black smoke from their stacks sullied the sky and drifted in a dirty mist across the crest of the ridge.

The train slowed, and the unexpected clatter and lurch of the points broke the rhythm of its run. Then it was sliding in along the concrete platform of Johannesburg Station. Sean lifted his luggage down from the rack above his head and passed it out of the open window to Mbejane. The exertion of lifting and carrying no longer caught in his guts; except for the irregular scar near his navel he was completely healed. When he strode down the platform towards the exit he held himself erect, no longer stooping to favour his stomach.

A horsedrawn cab deposited them on the pavement outside Acheson's headquarters, and Sean left Mbejane guarding the luggage while he pushed his way across the crowded lobby and climbed the staircase to the first floor.

'Good afternoon, Colonel.' The orderly sergeant recognized him immediately and jumped to attention with such alacrity that he overturned his stool.

'Afternoon, Thompson,' Sean told him. The honours of his rank still embarrassed him. Thompson relaxed and inquired with more than just the formal concern:

'How are you, sir? Sorry to 'ear about your belly, sir.'

'Thank you, Thompson, I am fine now. Is Major Peterson in?'

Peterson was delighted to see him. He made tender inquiries after the movement of Sean's bowels, for irregularity was often one of the unpleasant aftermaths of a stomach wound. Sean reassured him and Peterson went on:

'Have some tea. The old man is busy right now but he'll see you in ten minutes,' and he shouted for Thompson to bring tea before he returned to the subject of Sean's wound. 'Much of a scar, old chap?' he asked.

Sean loosened his Sam Browne belt, unbuttoned his tunic and pulled his shirt out from his trousers. Peterson came round the desk and inspected Sean's hairy stomach at close range.

'Very neat. Damn good job they did on you.' Peterson gave his expert opinion. 'I got one at Omdurman – one of those fuzzy wuzzies pegged me with his dirty great spear.' And he in turn partially disrobed and displayed his pale hairless chest. From common courtesy Sean was forced to cluck and shake his head at the small triangular cicatrice on Peterson's bosom, although secretly he was not impressed. The attention went to Peterson's head.

'Got another one – damn painful it was too!' and he unbuckled his belt and had his trousers half down when the interleading door opened.

'Hope I'm not interrupting anything, gentlemen?' General Acheson inquired politely. There were a few moments of confusion while they both attempted to dress and make the correct military salutations. Peterson had the nicest decision to make, one not covered by the Articles of War. It was one of the few occasions in history where a divisional commander was received by a senior field officer standing at rigid attention with his trousers round his ankles. Major Peterson affected a rather startling line in scarlet flannel underwear. Once Acheson had understood the reason for this irregularity of dress among his officers, he was strongly tempted to join in the exhibition, for he also had some fine scars, but he restrained himself admirably. He led Sean through to the inner office and gave him a cigar.

'Well, Courtney. I hope you haven't come looking for a job.'

'On the contrary – I want to get the hell out of this business, sir.'

'I think we can arrange that. The Paymaster will be relieved.' Acheson nodded. 'I'll get Peterson to draw up your papers.'

'I want to leave tomorrow,' Sean insisted, and Acheson smiled.

'You're in a big hurry. All right. Peterson can post them to you for your signature – your unit has already been disbanded so there is no point in kicking your heels around here.'

'Good!' Sean had anticipated resistance, and he laughed with relief.

'There are just three other items,' Acheson went on, and Sean frowned with quick suspicion.

'Oh?'

'Firstly, a parting gift from His Majesty. A Distinguished Service Order for catching Leroux – there will be an investiture next week. Lord K. would like you to attend personally.'

'Hell, no! If I've got to stay in Johannesburg – I don't want it.'

And Acheson chuckled. 'A surprising lack of gratitude! Peterson can post it to you also. Secondly, I've been able to bring a little influence to bear on the War Claims Adjustment Board. Although Parliament hasn't passed the Bill, they've gone ahead and sanctioned your claim.'

'Good God!' Sean was stunned. At Acheson's suggestion he had registered a claim for ten thousand pounds, his deposit in the Volkskaas Bank, which had been seized by the Boers at the outbreak of war. He had expected nothing from it, and had promptly forgotten about it. 'They haven't made a full award, have they?'

'Don't be naïve, Courtney.' Acheson chuckled. 'Only twenty per cent against a possible further adjustment once the Bill is through the House. Still, two thousand is better than a poke in the eye with a blunt stick. Here's their cheque. You'll have to sign for it.'

Sean examined the slip of paper with rising delight. It would go a little way towards paying off his loan from Natal Wattle. He looked up quickly.

'And the third item?' he asked.

Acheson slipped a small square of cardboard across

368

the desk. 'My card – and a standing invitation to visit and stay as long as you like whenever you are in London.' He stood up and extended his hand. 'Good luck, Sean. And I'd like to think it isn't good-bye.'

In a rosy state of elation induced by freedom and the prospect of a loving farewell with Candy Rautenbach, Sean stopped the cab first at the railway station to reserve a seat on the following morning's southbound train, and to cable Ada of his homecoming. Then, on to Commissioner Street and the lobby of Candy's Hotel to ask for the proprietress.

'Mrs Rautenbach is resting, sir, and cannot be disturbed,' the clerk informed him.

'Good man!' Sean passed him half a guinea and ignored his squawks of protest as he climbed the marble staircase.

He let himself silently into Candy's suite and crossed to her bedroom. He wanted to surprise her; and there could be no doubt that he succeeded beyond his wildest expectations. Candy Rautenbach was not resting. In fact she was most strenuously employed in the entertainment of a gentleman whose tunic, hanging over the back of one of the gilt and red velvet chairs, showed him to be a subaltern in one of His Majesty's regiments.

Sean supported his subsequent actions on the hypothesis that Candy was his exclusive property. In the flood of righteous indignation that overwhelmed him, he took no account of the fact that his visit was a farewell gesture, that his relationship with Candy had been at best vague and intermittent, and that he was the following morning leaving to propose matrimony to someone else. All he saw was the cuckoo in the nest.

369

So that no discredit may reflect on the courage of the subaltern of the honour of his regiment, we must remember that his knowledge of Candy's domestic arrangements, if not those of her anatomy, was incomplete. She had been introduced to him as *Mrs Rautenbach* and now in this terrible moment as he returned to reality he assumed that the large and angry man who bore down on the bed, roaring like a wounded bull, was the one and only Mr Rautenbach come home from the wars. He made preparation for departure, which began with a rapid descent from the high four-poster bed on the opposite side to that of Sean's approach. In a condition of stark mental clarity induced by a super-abundance of adrenalin in the blood stream, the subaltern became aware of his own nudity which prevented flight into the public gaze, of the fact that Mr Rautenbach's threatening advance made such flight imperative, and finally that Mr Rautenbach wore the uniform and insignia of a full colonel. This last consideration weighed most heavily with him, for despite his age he came from an old and respected family with an impressive record of military service and he understood the decencies and orders of society of which one of the strictest was that you did not unite with the wife of an officer who outranked you.

'Sir,' he said, and drew himself up with dignity. 'I think I can explain.'

'You little bugger!' Sean answered him in a tone that suggested his explanation would have little consequence. Taking the shortest route, which was over the bed, Sean went for him. Candy, who had in these first few seconds been too preoccupied with pulling the coverlets over herself to take any active part in the proceedings, now shrieked and lifted the silk eiderdown in such a way that it wrapped around Sean's boots as he leaped over her, and became tangled in his spurs. Sean fell with a crash that reverberated through the whole building and startled the guests in the lobby below, and he lay for the moment stunned with his feet on the bed and his head and shoulders on the floor.

'Get out!' Candy shouted at the subaltern, as Sean began to stir ominously. Then she gathered up an armful of bedclothes and spread them over Sean, winding him and smothering him.

'Hurry up. For God's sake, hurry!' she entreated as her friend hopped with one leg in his breeches. 'He'll tear you to pieces.' And she pounced on top of the struggling, cursing mound of sheets and blankets.

'Don't worry about the boots,' and the subaltern tucked them under one arm, slung his tunic over his shoulders and placed his helmet on the back of his head.

'Thank you, ma'am,' he said, and then with gallantry, 'I sincerely regret any inconvenience I have caused you. Please give my apologies to your husband.'

'Get out, you fool,' she pleaded, clinging desperately to Sean as he heaved and swore. After he had left she stood up and waited for Sean to emerge.

'Where is he? I'll kill him. I'll murder the little bastard!' Sean threw off the bedclothes, scrambled to his feet and glared wildly around him. But the first thing he saw was Candy, and Candy was shaking with laughter. There was a lot of Candy to shake and most of it was white and round and smooth, and even if the laughter was a little hysterical it was still a very pleasing spectacle.

'Why did you stop me?' Sean demanded, but he was fast transferring his interest from the subaltern to Candy's bosom.

'He thought you were my husband,' she gasped.

'The little bastard,' growled Sean.

'He was sweet.' And abruptly she stopped laughing.

'And who the hell are you to come barging in here, anyway? Do you think you own the world and everything in it?'

'You belong to me.'

'Like hell, I do!' Candy exploded. 'Now get out of here, you big lumbering ox.'

'Put some clothes on.' Things were taking an unforeseen turn. Sean had expected her to be guilty and contrite.

'Get out of here,' she yelled, as her temper started to run. Sean had never seen her like this and he only just managed to field the large vase she hurled at his head. Frustrated in her desire to hear breaking china, Candy grabbed another missile, an ornamental mirror, which crashed with satisfying violence against the wall behind him. Her boudoir was furnished in splendid Victorian taste and provided an almost unlimited supply of ammunition. Despite Sean's nimble footwork, he could not remain unscathed for ever and finally he was hit by a gilt-framed picture of some nameless officer. Candy's taste leaned rather heavily towards martial men.

'You little bitch!' roared Sean in pain, and he launched a counter-attack. Candy fled, naked and squealing, but he caught her at the door, lifted her on to his shoulder and carried her kicking to the bed.

'Now, my girl,' he grunted as he arranged her, pink bottom up, across his lap. 'I'm going to teach you some manners.'

The first slap left a perfect red print of his hand upon her chubby cheeks, and stilled her struggles. The second slap had considerably less force behind it, and the third was an affectionate pat. But Candy was sobbing pitifully.

With his right hand raised, Sean realized with dismay that for the first time in his life *he was striking a woman!* 'Candy!' He spoke uncertainly, and was amazed that she twisted and sat up in his lap, clasped him about the neck and pressed a damp cheek against him.

Words welled up in his throat, words of apology, a plea for forgiveness – but his good sense prevented them from emerging and instead he demanded huskily, 'Are you sorry for your behaviour?'

Candy gulped and nodded shakily. 'Please forgive me, darling. I deserved that.' And her fingers fluttered at his throat and across his lips. 'Please forgive me, Sean. I'm so terribly sorry.'

They ate dinner in bed that evening. In the early morning, while Sean soaked lazily in the sunken bath and the hot water stung the scratches on his back, they talked.

'I'm catching the morning train home, Candy. I want to be home for Christmas.'

'Oh, Sean! Can't you stay – just a few days?'

'No.'

'When will you come back?'

'I don't know.'

There was a long silence before she spoke again.

'I take it then that I am not included in your plans for the future?'

'You are my friend, Candy,' he protested.

'Now, isn't that nice.' And she stood up. 'I'll order your breakfast.'

In the bedroom she paused and regarded herself slowly in the full-length mirror. The blue silk of her gown matched the blue of her eyes, but at this time of the day there were tiny creases in the skin of her throat.

I am rich, she thought, *I don't have to be lonely.* She walked on past the mirror.

60

Sean walked slowly up the gravel drive towards the Goldberg mansion. He walked between an avenue of 'Pride of India' trees and around him the green lawns climbed in a series of terraces towards the rococo façade of the house. It was a morning of drowsy warmth and the doves in the Pride of Indias cooed sleepily.

Faintly from among the ornamental shrubbery he heard the tinkle of laughter. He stopped and listened to the sound of it. Suddenly he was shy, loth to meet her again – unable to know how she would receive him for she had not replied to his letter.

At last he left the drive and crossed the carpet of lawn until he reached the lip of an amphitheatre. In the bowl below him stood a miniature replica of the Parthenon temple. Clean, white, marble columns in the sunshine, with a circular fish-pond like a moat around it. He could see the shapes of carp gliding slowly through the green water below the lily pads. The lily blossoms were white and gold and purple.

Ruth sat upon the raised marble edge of the pond. She was dressed all in black from her throat to her toes, but her arms were bared and she held them out and cried:

'Walk, Storm. Walk here to me.'

Ten paces away, her solid bottom solidly planted on the lawn, Storm Friedman regarded her mother seriously from under a bang of dark hair.

'Come on, baby,' Ruth urged her, and very deliberately the child leaned forward. Slowly she elevated her plump

374

posterior until it was pointed towards the sky, displaying a laced and be-ribboned pair of pantaloons beneath the short skirt. She remained like that for a few seconds and then, with an effort, came up on to her feet and stood balanced precariously on her fat, pink legs. Ruth clapped her hands in spontaneous delight, and Storm smiled in triumph, displaying four large white teeth.

'Come here to Mummy,' laughed Ruth and Storm completed a dozen unsteady paces before abandoning this form of locomotion as impractical. Dropping to her hands and knees she finished the course at a canter.

'You cheated!' Ruth accused, and jumped up to catch her under the arms and swing her high. Storm squealed ecstatically. 'More!' she commanded. 'More!'

Sean wanted to laugh with them. He wanted to run down to them and gather them both in his arms. For suddenly he knew that here was the whole meaning of life, his excuse for existing. A woman and a child. *His* woman, and *his* child.

Ruth looked up and saw him. She froze with the child held to her chest. Her face was without expression as she watched him come down the steps into the amphitheatre.

'Hello.' He stopped in front of her, twisting his hat awkwardly between his hands.

'Hello, Sean,' she whispered, then the corners of her mouth lifted in a shy, uncertain smile and she flushed. 'You took so long. I thought you weren't coming.'

A great grin split Sean's face and he stepped forward, but at that moment Storm, who had been staring at him with solemn curiosity, began a series of convulsive leaps accompanied by yells of:

'Man! Man!' Her feet were anchored against Ruth's stomach, which gave power to her thrusts. She leaned out towards Sean determined to reach him, and Ruth

375

was taken by surprise. Sean had to drop his hat and catch Storm before she fell.

'More! More!' yelled Storm, continuing to bounce in Sean's arms. One of the few things Sean knew about babies was that they have a soft pulsing spot on the top of their heads which is very vulnerable, so he clung to his daughter in terror that he drop her and in equal terror that he crush her. Until Ruth stopped laughing, relieved him of his burden and said,

'Come up to the house. You're just in time for tea.'

They crossed the lawn slowly, each of them holding one of Storm's hands, so that the child need no longer concentrate on balancing and could devote her whole attention to the fascinating manner in which her feet kept alternately appearing and disappearing under her.

'Sean. There is one thing I have to know before anything else.' Ruth was looking down at her child, not at him. 'Did you . . . ' She paused. 'Saul – Could you have prevented what happened to him. I mean, you didn't . . . ' Her voice trailed off.

'No, I didn't,' he said harshly.

'Swear it to me, Sean. As you hope for salvation, swear it to me,' she pleaded.

'I swear it to you. I swear on . . . ' He sought for an oath, not on his own life, for that was not strong enough. 'I swear on the life of our daughter.'

And she sighed with relief. 'That was why I did not write to you. I had to know first.'

He wanted to tell her then that he was taking her away with him, he wanted to tell her about Lion Kop and the huge empty house that waited for her to make it into a home. But he knew it was not the moment –

not immediately after they had spoken of Saul. He would wait.

He waited while he was introduced to the Goldbergs and was left with them when Ruth took the child into the house to deliver her into the care of the nurse. She returned and he made small conversation during tea and tried not to let them see it in his eyes when he looked at Ruth.

He waited until they were alone together on the lawn and then he blurted it out:

'Ruth, you and Storm are coming home with me.'

She stopped over a rosebush and picked a butter-yellow blossom, then with a slight frown on her face she broke each of the tiny red thorns off the stem before she looked at him.

'Am I, Sean?' she asked innocently, but he should have been warned by the chips of diamond brightness in her eyes.

'Yes,' he said. 'We can be married within the next few days. It will take that long to arrange a special licence and for you to pack. Then I'll take you to Lion Kop – I haven't told you about . . . '

'Damn you,' she said softly. 'Damn your conceit. Damn your arrogance.' And he gawked at her.

'You stroll in with your whip in your hand, crack it once and expect me to bark and jump through the hoop.' She was working herself into a fury now. 'I don't know what dealings you've had with women before – but I for one am not a camp-follower, nor do I intend being treated like one. Did it ever occur to you for one single second that I might not be prepared to accept this favour you intend bestowing on me? How long did it take you

377

to forget that I have been a widow for three short months? What supreme lack of perception made you believe I would run from one man's grave and throw myself into your condescending arms?'

'Buth, Ruth, I love you.' He tried to stop her outburst, but she shouted at him.

'Then prove it, damn you. Prove it by being gentle. Prove it by treating me like a woman and not a chattel – by *understanding*.'

Now his surprise gave way to an anger every bit as intense as hers, and in his turn he shouted at her.

'You weren't so bloody fussy on the night of the storm – or afterwards!'

As though he had struck her, she stepped back a pace and the mutilated rosebud dropped from her hand.

'You swine,' she whispered. 'Get out, and don't come back.'

'Your servant, ma'am.' He clapped his hat on to his head, swung round and strode away across the lawn. When he reached the gravel drive his steps slowed and he stopped and wrestled with his anger and his pride.

Then slowly he turned. The lawn was an empty sweep of smooth green. She was gone.

Ruth ran up the wide marble staircase, but by the time she reached her bedroom window he was half-way down the drive. From the height of the second floor his figure was foreshortened so he appeared massive, and his dark suit stood out clearly against the pale gravel of the drive. He reached the gates and stopped, she leaned forward eagerly across the sill of the window so he could see her more easily when he turned to look back. She saw him deliberately light a long black cheroot, flick away the match, adjust the hat on his head, square his shoulders – and walk away.

In disbelief she stared at the twin columns of the gate, and the dark green hawthorn hedge behind which he had disappeared. Then slowly she left the window and crossed to the bed and sat down.

'Why didn't he understand?' she asked softly.

She knew she would cry later, in the night when the real loneliness began.

61

Sean returned to Ladyburg in the middle of a misty Natal winter's day. As the train huffed over the rim of the escarpment, he stood on the balcony of his coach and looked out at the vast green stain upon the hills of Lion Kop. The sight of it moved him, but his elation was toned with dark colours.

This is the middle of the way. This year I will be forty-one years old. Out of all that striving and folly something must have emerged. Let me total my assets.

In cash I have a little over two thousand pounds (compliments of the War Claims Adjustment Board). In land I have fifteen thousand acres, with an option to purchase as many more. I have ten thousand acres of standing wattle which, in another year, will be ready for cutting. My loans against this are heavy but not oppressive, so I am a wealthy man.

In things of the flesh I have a number of grey hairs, a fine collection of scars and a broken nose. But I can still lift and carry a two-hundred-pound sack of mealies under each arm, I can eat half a young sheep at a sitting; without field-glasses I can count the number of head in a herd of springbok at a distance of two miles, and Candy who knows about these things made no complaint about my stamina. I am not yet old.

Apart from these things I have a son who belongs to me (and a son and a daughter who do not). Although I have lost the best of them, I have friends – perhaps more friends than enemies.

But as important as any of these is the purpose and direction I have at last achieved. I know what I want. My course is plotted and the wind stands fair.

These are my assets. These are mine to use and enjoy.

What are my liabilities? Borrowed money, the hatred of a brother and a son, and Ruth.

Ruth is gone! Ruth is gone! Clattered the crossties under the coach. Ruth is gone! Ruth is gone! They mocked him.

Sean scowled and forcibly changed the words in his mind.

'The wind is fair! The wind is fair!'

Over the months that followed Sean used his whole energy in the development of Lion Kop. He planned the cutting of his standing bark and decided to reap one-third of it a year before maturity, and another third in each of the subsequent two years. To replace it he used his two thousand pounds not to pay off his loans, but to plant the rest of his land to wattle. When this was done he had to keep busy. He bought himself a theodolite and a book of instruction in elementary survey, and mapped his lands, laid out his block of trees, pegged new roads for access to his plantations when the cutting began.

Once again he had nothing to do, so he went to see Dennis Petersen and spent a long day arguing the purchase of Mahobo's Kloof Ranch on which he had bought an option. He had no cash, and Jackson at Natal Wattle baulked at the suggestion of further loans. When Dennis refused to consider extended terms of payment, Sean called on Ronny Pye at the Ladyburg Banking & Trust. It was a forlorn chance and Sean was genuinely surprised when Ronny gave him a cup of coffee and a cigar, then listened politely to his proposition.

'You're putting it all on one horse, Sean,' Ronny warned him.

'There's only one horse in this race. It can't lose.'

'Very well.' Ronny nodded. 'Here's what I will do with you. I will advance you the full purchase price of Mahobo's Kloof, plus a further ten thousand pounds to develop it. In return you will give me a first bond on Mahobo's Kloof, and a second bond on Lion Kop after Natal Wattle Company's loan.'

Sean took it. A week later Ronny Pye called on Jackson in Pietermaritzburg. After the preliminary sparring Ronny asked him:

'Are you quite happy about those Notes you have out to Courtney?'

'The security is good.' Jackson hesitated. 'But he seems to be going a little wild.'

'I might be willing to take them over from you,' Ronny hinted delicately, and Jackson rubbed his nose thoughtfully to mask his relief.

Happily Sean flung his army of Zulus at the virgin grasslands of Mahobo's Kloof. He delighted in the long ranks of sweating, singing blackmen as they opened the rich, red earth and placed the fragile little saplings.

Dirk was Sean's constant companion in these days. His attendance in the schoolhouse became more sporadic. Convinced that Dirk would never become a scholar, Sean tacitly condoned the gastric disturbances that prevented Dirk leaving for school in the mornings, but cleared miraculously a few minutes later and allowed him to follow Sean out into the plantations. Dirk aped

Sean's stance, his seat in the saddle, and his long reaching walk. He listened carefully to Sean's words and repeated them later without omitting the oaths. In the late afternoons they hunted quail and pheasant and guinea-fowl along the slopes of the escarpment. On Sunday when Sean rode across to his neighbours for a bush buck shoot, or a poker session, or merely to drink brandy and talk, then Dirk went with him.

Despite Sean's protest, Ada returned with her girls to the cottage on Protea Street. So the homestead of Lion Kop was a vast empty shell. Sean and Dirk used only three of the fifteen rooms, and even these were sparsely furnished. No carpets on the floor, nor pictures on the walls. A few leather-thonged chairs, iron bedstead, plain deal tables, and a cupboard or two. Piled in odd corners were the books and fishing-rods; a pair of shotguns and a rifle on the rack beside the fireplace. The yellow-wood floor was unpolished with dust and bits of fluff beneath the chairs and beds, dark stains left by the litter of pointer puppies; and in Dirk's bedroom, which Sean never visited, there was a welter of old socks and soiled shirts, school exercise books and trophies of the hunt.

Sean had no interest in the house. It was a place to eat and sleep, it had a roof to keep the rain out, a fireplace for warmth, and lamp-light so that he could indulge his new appetite for reading. With reading glasses purchased from a travelling salesman on his nose, Sean spent his evenings wading through books on politics and travel, economics and surveying, mathematics and medicine, while Dirk, ostensibly preparing his schoolwork, sat across the fireplace from him and watched him avidly. Some nights when Sean was engaged in correspondence, he would forget that Dirk was there and the boy would sit up until after midnight.

Sean was now corresponding with both Jannie

Niemand and Jan Paulus Leroux. These two had become a political team in the Transvaal, and were already bringing gentle pressure to bear on Sean. They wanted him to organize the equivalent of their South Africa Party, and to lead it in Natal. Sean hedged. Not yet, perhaps later he told them.

Once a month he received and answered a long letter from John Acheson. Acheson had returned to England and the gratitude of the nation. He was now Lord Caisterbrook and from his seat in the House of Lords he kept Sean informed of the temper and mood of the English people and the affairs of State.

Sometimes, more often than was healthy, Sean thought about Ruth. Then he became angry and sad and desperately lonely. Slowly it would build up within him until he could not sleep, then he would go down at night to a friendly widow who lived alone in one of the gangers' cottages beside the new railways yards.

Yet he counted himself happy, until that day at the beginning of September 1903, when he received an embossed card. It said simply:

> Miss Storm Friedman requests the pleasure of the company of Colonel Sean Courtney, D.S.O., D.C.M., at a party to celebrate her third birthday.
> 4 p.m., September 26th.
> *R.S.V.P.*
> The Golds, Chase Valley,
> Pietermaritzburg.

In the bottom right-hand corner was an inky fingerprint about the size of a threepenny-piece.

62

On the 24th, Sean left by train for Pietermaritzburg. Dirk came back from the station with Ada to his old room in the cottage on Protea Street.

That night Mary lay awake and listened to him cry for his father. Only a thin wooden partition spearated them. Ada's cottage had not been designed as a workshop and hostel for her girls. She had solved the problem by enclosing the wide, back veranda and dividing it into cubicles each large enough to hold a bed, a cupboard and a washstand. One of these was Mary's and tonight Dirk was in the cubicle next to hers.

For an hour she lay and listened to him weep, praying quietly that he would exhaust himself and fall asleep. Twice she thought he had done so, but each time after a silence of only a few minutes the tear-muffled sobs started again. Each of them drove needles of physical pain deep into her chest, so that she lay rigid in her bed with her fists clenched until they ached.

Dirk had become the central theme of her existence. He was the one bright tower in the desolation. She loved him with obsessive devotion, for he was so beautiful, so young and clean and straight. She loved the feel of his skin and the springy silk of his hair. When she looked at Dirk her own face did not matter. Her own scarred ruin of a face did not matter.

The months she had been separated from him had been an agony and a dark lonely time. But now he was back and once again he needed her comfort. She slipped from her bed and stood taut with her love, her whole attitude portraying her compassion. The moonlight that filtered in through the mosquito-screened window treated her with the same compassion. It toned down the mottled cicatrice that coarsened the planes of her face and it showed them as they might have been. Her twenty-year-old body beneath the thin nightgown was slender but full-breasted, innocent of the marks that marred her face. A young body, a soft body clad in moon-luminous white like that of an angel.

Dirk sobbed again and she went to him.

'Dirk,' she whispered as she knelt beside his bed. 'Dirk, please don't cry, please, my darling.'

Dirk gulped explosively and rolled away from her, folding his arms across his face.

'Shh! my darling. It's all right now.' She began to stroke his hair. Her touch evoked a fresh outburst of grief from him, liquid choking grief that spluttered and throbbed in the darkness.

'Oh Dirk, please . . . ' And she went into his bed. The sheets were warm and moist where he had lain. She gathered him, held his hot body to her bosom and began to rock him in her arms.

Her own loneliness at last overwhelmed her. Her voice took on a husky quality as she whispered to him. She strained to him – her need growing much greater than his.

One last covulsive sob and Dirk was silent. She felt the tension go out of his back and out of his hard round buttocks that were pressed into her stomach. Straining him even closer, her fingers moved down across his cheek to caress his throat.

Dirk turned towards her, turning within the circle of her arms. She felt his chest heave and subside as he sighed, and his voice stifled with misery.

'He doesn't love me. He went away and left me.'

'I love you, Dirk,' she whispered. 'I love you – we all love you, darling.' And she kissed his eyes and his cheeks and his mouth. The taste of his tears was hot salt.

Dirk sighed again and bowed his head until it was on her bosom. She felt his face nuzzling into the softness and her hands went to the back of his head and drew it closer.

'Dirkie . . .' Her voice dried up in the strange new heat within her.

In the morning Dirk woke slowly, but with a feeling of wonder. He lay a while and thought about it, unable at first to place the formless shimmering sense of well-being that possessed him.

Then he heard Mary moving about behind the partition of her cubicle. The gurgle and splash of water poured from jug to basin, the rustle of cloth. finally, the sound of her door softly opened and closed, and her steps moving away towards the kitchen.

The events of the previous evening came back to him, crisp and stark in every detail. Not fully understood, but looming large to overshadow all else in his mind.

He threw the sheets aside and lifted himself on both elbows, drew up his nightshirt and contemplated his body as though he had never seen it before.

He heard footsteps approaching. Quickly he covered himself, pulled the bedclothes over and feigned sleep.

Mary came in quietly and placed a cup of coffee, with a rusk in the saucer, on the bedside table.

Dirk opened his eyes and looked at her.

'You're awake,' she said.

'Yes.'

'Dirk . . . ' she started, and then she blushed. It mottled the puckered skin of her cheeks. Her voice fell to a whisper, scratchy with her shame. 'You mustn't ever tell anybody. You must forget about . . . what happened.'

Dirk did not reply.

'Promise me, Dirkie. Please promise me.'

He nodded slowly. Not trusting himself to speak, his throat filled with a knowledge of domination over her.

'It was wrong, Dirkie. It was a terrible thing. We mustn't even think about it again.'

She walked to the door.

'Mary.'

'Yes.' She stopped without turning, her whole body poised like a bird on the point of flight.

'I won't tell anyone – if you come again tonight.'

'No,' she hissed violently.

'Then, I'll tell Granny.'

'No. Oh, Dirkie. You wouldn't.' She was beside the bed now, kneeling, reaching for his hand. 'You mustn't – you mustn't. You promised me.'

'Will you come?' he asked softly. She peered into his face, into the serene perfection of warm brown skin and green eyes with the black silk of his hair curling on to the forehead.

'I can't – it's a terrible, terrible thing that we did.'

'Then I'll tell,' he said.

She stood up and walked slowly out of the cubicle, her shoulders slumped forward in the attitude of surrender. He knew she would come.

63

In a hired carriage Sean arrived punctually at the Goldberg residence. He arrived like a column of wise men
from the east. The seats of the carriage were piled with
fancy-wrapped packages. However, Sean's limited
knowledge of a three-year-old female's tastes were
reflected in his choice of gifts. Every single package
contained a doll. There were large china dolls that closed
their eyes when reclining, small rag dolls with blonde
plaits, a doll that passed water, a doll that squawked
when its stomach was squeezed, dolls in a dozen
national costumes and dolls in swaddling clothes.

Mbejane followed the carriage leading the gift which
Sean considered a master stroke of originality. It was a
piebald Shetland pony, complete with a hand-fashioned
English saddle and a tiny martingale and reins.

The gravel drive was crowded with carriages. Sean
was forced to walk the last hundred yards, his arms
filled with presents. Under these circumstances navi-
gation was a little difficult. He took a fix on the hid-
eously ornamented roof of the mansion, which he could
just see over the top of his load, and set off blind across
the lawns. He was aware of the continuous and piercing
shrieking which grew louder as he proceeded, and finally
of an insistent tugging on his right trouser leg. He
stopped.

'Are those *my* presents?' a voice from somewhere
above the level of his knee asked. He craned his head
out to one side and looked down into the upturned face

of a miniature Madonna. Large shining eyes in an oval of innocent purity framed with shiny dark curls. Sean's heart flipped over.

'That depends what your name is,' he hedged.

'My name is *Miss* Storm Friedman of The Golds, Chase Valley, Pietermaritzburg. *Now* are they my presents?'

Sean bent his knees until he squatted with his face almost on a level with that of the Madonna.

'Many happy returns of the day, Miss Friedman,' he said.

'Oh, goody!' She fell on the packages, trembling with excitement while from the mass of fifty children who ringed them in the shrieking continued unabated.

Storm demolished the wrappings in very short order, using her teeth when her fingers were inadequate for the task. One of her small guests attempted to assist her, but she flew at him like a panther kitten with a cry of 'They're *my* presents!' He retired hastily.

At last she sat in a litter of wrappings and dolls and pointed at the single remaining package in Sean's hands.

'That one?' she asked.

Sean shook his head. 'No, that one is for your Mummy. But if you look behind you, you might find something else.'

Mbejane, grinning widely, was holding the Shetland. For seconds Storm was too overcome to speak and then with a sound like a steam-whistle she flew to her feet. Deserting her newly adopted children, she ran to the pony. Behind her a flock of small girls descended on the dolls, vultures when a lion leaves the kill.

'Lift me! Lift me!' Storm was hopping with delirious impatience. Sean took her up and the warm, wriggling little body in his hands made his heart flip again. Gently he set her on the saddle, handed her the reins and led the pony towards the house.

A queen riding in state, followed by an army of her attendants, Storm reach the upper terrace.

Ruth was standing beside the delicacy-laden trestle table with the parents of Storm's guests. Sean handed the lead rein to Mbejane. 'Look after her well,' and he crossed the terrace, very conscious of the many adult eyes upon him, thankful for the hour he had spent that morning at the barber's shop, and for the care he had taken with his attire – a brand-new suit of expensive English broadcloth, boots burnished to a gloss, solid gold watch chain across his belly and a white carnation in his buttonhole.

He stopped in front of Ruth and removed his hat. She held out her hand, palm downwards. Sean knew that he was *not* expected to shake that hand.

'Sean, how good of you to come.'

Sean took her hand. It was a measure of his feelings that he bowed to touch it with his lips – a gesture which he considered French, foppish and undignified.

'It was good of you to ask me, Ruth.'

He produced the box from under his arm and held it out to her. She opened it without a word and her cheeks flushed with pleasure when she saw the long-stemmed roses it contained.

'Oh, how sweet of you!' And Sean's heart did its trick again as she smiled full into his eyes, then slipped her hand into the crook of his arm.

'I'd like you to meet some friends of mine.'

That evening when the other guests had left and Storm, prostrated with nervous and physical exhaustion, had been put to bed, Sean stayed on to dinner with the Goldbergs. By now both Ma and Pa Goldberg were fully aware that Sean's interest in Ruth was not on account of his previous friendship with Saul. All afternoon Sean had followed Ruth around the lawns like a huge St Bernard behind a dainty poodle.

During dinner Sean, who was extremely pleased with himself, Ruth, the Goldbergs and life in general, was able to endear himself to Ma Goldberg and also dull Ben Goldberg's suspicions that he was a penniless adventurer. Over brandy and cigars Sean and Ben discussed the ventures on Lion Kop and Mahobo's Kloof. Sean was completely frank about the financial tightrope which he was walking, and Ben was impressed with the magnitude of the gamble and Sean's cold appraisal of the odds. It was just such a *coup* as this that had put Ben Goldberg where he was today. It made him feel nostalgic and vaguely sentimental of *the old days*, so that when they went through to join the ladies he patted Sean's arm and called him 'My boy'.

On the front steps, while he was preparing to leave, Sean asked, 'May I call on you again, Ruth?' and she answered,

'I'd like that very much.'

Now began what was for Sean a novel form of courtship. To his surprise he found he rather enjoyed it. Every Friday night he would entrain for Pietermaritzburg and install himself in the White Horse Hotel. From this base he conducted his campaign. There were dinner parties, either at The Golds or with Ruth's friends or at one of the local hostelries where Sean played host. There were balls and dances, days at the races, picnics and rides over the surrounding hills with Storm on her Shetland bouncing along between them. During Sean's absences from Ladyburg, Dirk moved into the cottage on Protea

Street and Sean was relieved that he seemed to accept it with better grace.

The time arrived when at last the first blocks of wattle were ready for the axe. Sean determined to use this as an excuse to inveigle Ruth away to Ladyburg. The Goldbergs froze up solid at the suggestion and only thawed when Sean produced a written invitation from Ada for Ruth to be her guest for the week. Sean went on to explain that it was to be a celebration of his first cutting of bark, which would begin at the end of the week, and that thereafter he could not leave Ladyburg for months.

Ma Goldberg, who was secretly delighted at having Storm all to herself for a whole week, exerted a subtle influence on Ben, and very grudgingly he gave his approval.

Sean decided that Ruth would be treated like visiting Royalty – the grand climax to his suit.

64

As one of the biggest landowners in the district and because of his war honours, Sean ranked high in the complicated social structure of Ladyburg. Therefore, preparations for Ruth's visit produced an epidemic of excitement and curiosity that affected the entire Lady-burg district. The flood of invitations he released sent women to their wardrobes and sewing-baskets, while the outlying farmers begged accommodation from rela-tives and friends nearer town. Other leading members of the community, jealous of their social status, rode out to Lion Kop with offers to provide entertainment on those three days of the week which Sean had left empty. Reluctantly Sean agreed – he had private plans for those three days.

Ada and her girls were inundated with orders for new clothing, but they still made one afternoon free and came up to the Lion Kop homestead armed with brooms and dusters and tins of polish. Sean and Dirk were driven from the house. They spent that afternoon riding over Sean's estate, looking for the best place to hold the big bush-buck shoot which would be the climax of the week.

With a gang of his Zulus, Mbejane hacked down the jungle of undergrowth around the homestead and dug the barbecue pits.

The Village Management Board met in secret con-clave, infected by the general excitement and armed with strict instructions from their wives, they voted unanimously for a civic reception of Ruth Friedman at the station and a formal Ball that night. Dennis Petersen, who had Sean's consent to a barbecue on the night of Ruth's arrival, was placated with the promise that he would be allowed to make a short speech of welcome at the station.

Sean called upon Ronny Pye and was again surprised when Ronny agreed cheerfully to a further loan of one thousand pounds. Ronny signed the cheque with the satisfied air of a spider putting the final thread into his web, and Sean left immediately for Pietermaritzburg to visit a jeweller. He returned home five hundred pounds poorer, with a packet in his breast-pocket that contained a huge square-cut diamond set in a band of platinum. Dirk was at the station to meet him. Sean took one look at him and ordered him to the village barber.

The night before Ruth's arrival Sean and Mbejane fell upon Dirk in a surprise attack and dragged him protesting to the bathroom. Sean was astounded by the large quantities of foreign matter that he removed from Dirk's ears, and by the way in which Dirk's suntan dissolved so readily under an application of soap.

The following morning as her railway coach ground to a jerky halt in front of the station building, Ruth looked down on a mass of strangers surrounding the roped-off area in front of her. Only one family was not represented in the crowd, which included the young ladies and gentlemen of Ladyburg High School in their church clothes.

She stood uncertainly on the balcony of the coach and heard the hum of appreciative 'comment and speculation. Ruth had relieved the plain black mourning with a wide ribbon of pink around the crown of her hat, pink gloves and gauzy pink veil, which shrouded her face in a misty and mysterious fashion. It was very effective.

Convinced that there was some misunderstanding, Ruth was about to withdraw into the coach, when she noticed a deputation approaching along the roped-off passageway. It was headed by Sean and she recognized the thunderous scowl he wore as his expression of acute embarrassment. She felt an inexplicable urge to burst out laughing, but managed to keep it to a smile as Sean climbed up on to the balcony and took her hand.

'Ruth, I'm terribly sorry. I didn't plan all this – things got a little out of control,' he whispered hurriedly, then he muttered an introduction to Dennis Petersen, who had ponderously mounted the steps behind him. Now Dennis turned to face the crowd and spread his arms in the gesture that Moses might have employed on his return from the mountain.

'Ladies and gentlemen, citizens of Ladyburg, friends –' he began, and from the way he said it Sean knew he was good for another half-hour. He glanced sideways at Ruth and saw that she was smiling. It came as a surprise to him when he realized she was enjoying herself. Sean relaxed a little.

'It gives me great pleasure to welcome to our fair town this lovely lady, friend of one of our foremost . . . ' Ruth's fingers found their way surreptitiously into Sean's hand, and Sean relaxed a little more. He saw the wide brim of Ada's hat standing out in the crowd and he smiled at her. She replied with a nod of approval towards Ruth.

By some curious twist of oratory, Dennis was now talking about the new water filtration plant and its benefit to the community.

'— But, my friends, this is only the first of a series of projects planned by your Board.' He paused significantly.

'Hear, hear,' Sean interjected loudly and clapped his hands. The applause was taken up by the crowd, and Sean stepped past Dennis to the rail of the balcony.

'On behalf of Mrs Friedman and myself, I thank you for your friendship and your hospitality.' Then, leaving Dennis on the balcony making helpless little movements with his hands and silently opening and closing his mouth, Sean spirited Ruth away, ran her through a rapid fire series of introductions and handshakes, gathered Ada and Dirk and got them all into the carriage.

While Sean and Mbejane fussed with the luggage, Ruth and Ada settled their skirts and adjusted their hats before meeting each other's eyes again.

'Although Sean warned me, I didn't expect you to be quite so lovely,' Ada said. Flushing with pleasure and relief, Ruth leaned impulsively across to touch her arm.

'I've been longing to meet you, Mrs Courtney.'

'If you promise to call me Ada, then I'll call you Ruth.'

Sean scrambled into the carriage, flustered and perspiring. 'Let's get the hell out of here.'

That week was to be remembered for many years. The usual Christmas festivities paled into insignificance beside it.

Matrons competed fiercely to provide food, mountains of it, prepared from their closely guarded recipe books. In between cooking they conducted old feuds, began new ones and worried about their daughters.

The young bucks competed on the gymkhana and polo field, then again on the dance floor. Dirk Courtney won the junior tent-pegging event. Then against a visiting team from Pietermaritzburg College he captained the school rugby team to an inglorious 30–0 defeat.

The young ladies competed with equal ferocity, covering it with giggles and blushes. The success of their efforts was measured in the outbreak of betrothals and scandals during the week.

The older men smiled indulgently, until, fortified with bottled spirit, they discarded their dignity and capered and panted around the dance floor. There were three bouts of fisticuffs – but these were between old enemies and none of them were really worth watching.

Only one family held aloof from the festivities. There were many of the young ladies who missed Michael Courtney.

During one of the infrequent lulls of the week, Sean managed to separate Ruth from Ada, and take her out to the homestead at Lion Kop. She moved silently through the empty rooms, appraising each with narrowed thoughtful eyes while Sean hovered anxiously behind her, certain that her silence was disapproval. In fact, Ruth was in ecstasy; a shell, a magnificent shell of a house, with no trace of another woman in it, waiting for her to bring it to life. She could imagine exactly the curtains she wanted, her Persian carpets sent down by Uncle Isaac from Pretoria and now in storage, would look just right once she had the yellow-wood floors polished to a gloss. The kitchen, of course, would have to be completely rebuilt – with a new double Agar stove. The bedroom . . .

Unable to contain himself, Sean blurted out:

'Well, do you like it?'

She turned slowly to him, the mists of thought clearing from her eyes.

'Oh, Sean! It's the most beautiful house in all the world.'

In this emotional moment, Sean put forward the proposition he had planned for that evening.

'Ruth, will you marry me?'

And Ruth, who had planned to hesitate and ask for a little time to consider, replied instantly:

'Oh, yes please!'

She was truly impressed with the ring.

65

The finale to the week was Sean Courtney's bush-buck shoot.

Sean and Dirk arrived at Protea Cottage with the dawn. They were dressed in rough hunting clothes and the leather gun-cases lay on the floor of the mule-wagon under Sean's feet. It took nearly fifteen minutes for Sean to transfer Ruth, Ada and her girls from the cottage to the carriage. In the same way a man might drive a flock of chickens towards the door of a henhouse. He would get them all moving slowly in front of him, down the path towards the carriage, clucking and fussing. Almost there when suddenly one of them would shriek softly and double back towards the cottage for a forgotten parasol or work-basket and the general movement would break down again.

The third time this happened Sean felt something snap inside his head. He bellowed. A vast hush fell over the ladies and two of them looked as though they might cry.

'Now don't get worked up, dear.' Ada tried to soothe him.

'I am not getting worked up.' Sean's voice quivered with the effort of restraint. 'But if everybody is not in the carriage by the count of ten – then I might easily get that way.'

They were all seated by the count of five and he drove out to the stockpens – a very ruffled rooster.

Carriages and mule-wagons carrying the entire population of the Ladyburg district were waiting in a disorderly tangle in the field beside the stockpen. Sean trotted past in a babble of greeting and comment. One at a time the waiting carriages wheeled into line behind him and the long convoy wound out towards Mahobo's Kloof Farm. The big shoot had begun.

In the middle of the line someone was playing a concertina and the singing started. It spread to each carriage in turn and blended with the sound of wheels and hooves and laughter.

Gradually Sean's irritation smoothed out. Ada's girls were singing *Boland Se Nooinentje* in the back seat. Dirk had jumped down from the carriage and with half a dozen of the youngsters from the village ran ahead of the horses. Ruth's hand touched Sean's leg uncertainly and as he turned and grinned at her he saw the relief in her answering smile.

'What a beautiful day, Sean.'

'Sorry I nearly spoiled it –' he answered.

'Oh, nonsense!' She moved closer to him and suddenly he was happy. All the preparation was worth it. Beside him Ruth laughed softly.

'What's the joke?' Sean reached out and took her hand.

'No joke. I just felt like laughing,' she answered. 'Look how green everything is.' She said it to distract him, to make him look away so that she could study his face. The subterfuge worked.

'The land seems so young now.' His eyes, as he looked at it, took on that gentleness she knew so well. By now she knew many of his moods and she was learning how to induce or redirect each of them. He was such a simple man, yet in that simplicity lay his strength. He is like a mountain, she thought. You know how it will be with the sun on it in the early morning. You know that when the wind is in the south there will be mist covering the crest, and in the evening the shadows will fall in certain patterns across the slopes and the gorges will look dark and blue. Yet also you know the shape of the mountain is unchanged, that it will never change.

'I love you, my mountain,' she whispered, and anticipated the startled expression before it flashed across his face.

'Hey?'

'I love you, my man,' she amended.

'Oh! I love you too.'

And now he is vaguely embarrassed. Oh, God, I could eat him! If I were to reach over and kiss him now in front of everybody . . . ! Secretly she savoured the idea.

'What devilment are you planning?' he demanded gruffly. He wasn't supposed to read her so accurately. Taken off balance she stared at him. Suddenly the mountain had shown that it understood exactly the way she felt when she looked at it.

'Nothing,' she denied in confusion. 'I wasn't . . . ' Before she realized fully what he was about, he had turned half-way in his seat towards her and lifted her bodily into his lap.

'Sean, no!' she gasped and then her protests were muffled. She heard the laughter of Ada's girls, the hoots of encouragement and applause from the other carriages, and she kicked and struggled, pushing with one hand against his chest and trying to keep her hat on with the other.

By the time he replaced her on the seat beside him, her hair had come down behind, her hat was off and her cheeks and ears were flaming red. She had been very thoroughly kissed.

'Nice shot, Sean!'

'Author! Author!'

'Arrest that man!' The cries and the laughter added to her confusion.

'You're terrible!' Ruth used her hat as a screen behind which she tried to control her blushes. 'In front of all those people, too!'

'That should keep you out of mischief for a while, me lass!'

And suddenly she wasn't so sure of the shape of her mountain.

The cavalcade turned off along the rough track from the main road, splashed through the drift, climbed the far bank and spread out among the trees. Servants, who had been waiting since the previous evening, ran to their masters' horses as they halted. Each vehicle disgorged a noisy blast of children and dogs, and then a more dignified trickle of adults. The women moved without hesitation towards the two huge marquees that had been erected among the trees, while the men unloaded the gun-cases and began assembling their weapons.

Still sitting on the front seat of the wagon, Sean opened the leather case at his feet and while his hands automatically fitted the barrels into the breech piece of his shotgun he allowed himself to review his preparations with a certain amount of satisfaction.

He had selected this site not only for the cool grove of syringa trees which provided shade above and a soft carpet of fallen leaves below, nor for the proximity of the tinkling stream where all the animals could be watered, but also because it was situated within fifteen minutes' walk of the first beat.

Days before a gang of Zulus working under Mbejane had cleared out all the undergrowth beneath the trees, had erected the marquee tents and the trestle tables, dug the cooking pits and even built two grass-walled pit latrines discreetly out of view of the main camp.

Huge log fires were burning in the cooking pits now, but by noon they would have burned down to glowing coal beds. The trestle tables about which the women had already begun working were laden with food. There was a great deal of activity going on in that direction at the moment – most of it talking.

From the other wagons men were starting to drift towards him, buckling on their cartridge belts, hefting shotguns, chatting together nonchalantly in an attempt to disguise their excitement. Under instruction from Sean, Dirk had assembled a rabble of those males who were too young to handle shotguns but too old to stay with the women. These were making no effort to hide *their* excitement. Armed with *sikelas* (the Zulu fighting sticks) they were showing every indication of getting out of hand. Already one small boy was weeping loudly and massaging the welt he had received from a playful *sikela*.

'All right – shut up, all of you,' Sean shouted. 'Dirk will take you up to the beaters. But remember! Once the hunt starts, keep in the line and listen to what you're told. If I catch anybody running about or getting ahead of the line – I'll personally wallop the tar out of him. Do you understand?' It was a long speech to shout and Sean ended with his face flushed ferociously. This gave weight to his words and resulted in a respectful chorus of:

'Yes, Mr Courtney.'

'Off you go, then.'

Whooping, racing each other they poured away through the trees and a comparative peace descended on the camp.

'My God, let alone bush buck, that lot would drive elephant, buffalo and lion panic-stricken ahead of them,'

404

observed Dennis Petersen dryly. 'How about our positions, Sean?'

Aware that he had their complete attention, Sean drew the moment out a little.

'We are going to drive the Elands' Kloof first,' he announced. 'Mbejane and two hundred Zulus are waiting at the head of the Kloof for the signal. The guns will take station at the tail of the Kloof.' Sean paused.

'How about our positions?'

'Patience. Patience.' Sean chided them. 'I know I shouldn't have to repeat the safety rules, but . . . ' and he immediately went on to do so. 'No rifles – shotguns only. You'll shoot only in an arc of 45 degrees directly ahead of you – no passing shots to either side. Especially you, Reverend!' That gentleman, who was notoriously trigger-happy, looked suitably abashed. 'My whistle will mean the beaters are too close – all guns up and unloaded immediately.'

'It's getting late, Sean.'

'Let's get on with it.'

'Right,' Sean agreed. 'I'll take centre gun.' There was a murmur of agreement. That was fair enough, the plum to the man who provided the hunt, no one could grudge that. 'On my left flank in this order, Reverend Smiley – since the Almighty will obviously send most of the game his way, I might as well profit by it.' A burst of laughter as Smiley wavered between horror at the blasphemy and delight at his own good fortune. 'Then Ronny Pye, Dennis Petersen, Ian Vermaak, Gerald and Tony Erasmus (you two fight it out in a brotherly fashion), Nick . . . ' Sean read from the list in his hand. This in strict order of seniority was the social register of Ladyburg, a proper and exact balancing of wealth and influence, of popularity and age. Apart from placing himself in the centre of the line, Sean had not taken much part in the preparation of the list – quite correctly Ada had not trusted his sense of social perception.

'That takes care of the left flank.' Sean looked up from the list. He had been so engrossed in reaching that he had not sensed the air of tension and expectancy which had fallen over his audience. A single horseman had crossed the drift and walked his magnificent thoroughbred into the camp. He had dismounted quietly and servants had led his horse away. Now, carrying a shotgun, he was walking towards Sean's wagon.

Sean looked up and saw him. He stared in surprise, while slowly elation mounted within him until it reached his face in a wide grin.

'Garry, glad you could make it!' he called out spontaneously, but Garry's face remained without expression. He nodded a curt greeting. At least he's come, exulted Sean. This is the first overture. Now it's up to me.

'You can take the first position on my right, Garry.'

'Thank you.' Now Garry smiled, but it was a curiously cold grimace and he turned away to talk with the nearest man. A small shiver of disappointment moved the crowd. They had expected something spectacular to happen. All of them knew of the feud between the Courtney brothers and the mystery that surrounded it. But now, with a feeling of anti-climax they turned their attention back to Sean's reading. Sean finished and jumped down from the wagon, and immediately the crowd moved away. Sean sought Garrick and saw him far ahead near the head of the long file of men that was strung out along the footpath that led to Elands' Kloof.

The file moved fast as the hunters stepped out eagerly. Unless he ran, Sean knew he would not be able to pass the men ahead of him and catch up with Garry. I'll wait until we reach the beat, he decided. My God, what a wonderful ending to this week. I have Ruth, now if only I can get back my brother and with him Michael!

From the shoulder of the gorge Sean looked down across Elands' Kloof. A deep slot of a valley, two miles long and five hundred yards wide at this end, but it tapered slowly upwards until it lost its identity in the high ground. The full length of it was clogged solid with dark green bush, a seemingly impenetrable mass above which a few tall trees reared up in a desperate attempt to reach the sunlight. Like the tentacles of a giant squid, creepers and vines lifted from the dark bush to over-power them and drag them down. Here on the shoulder the air was dry and wholesome – down there it would stink of damp earth and rotting vegetable matter.

Lingering as though suddenly reluctant to go down into the humid discomfort of the Kloof, the hunters gathered on the shoulder. Shading eyes against the glare, they peered up towards the head of the gorge where the beaters were a line of dark specks against the green spring grass.

'There go the kids,' someone pointed. Dirk was lead-ing his band along the high ground above the Kloof.

Sean moved across to his twin brother.

'Well, Garry, how are things out at Theuniskraal?'

'Not bad.'

'I read your book – I think it's excellent. It certainly deserved the reception it got in London. Lord Caister-brook wrote to me to say that your concluding chapter is giving the War Office much food for thought. Well done, Garry.'

'Thank you.' But there was an evasive lack of warmth in Garry's reply. He made no attempt to continue the conversation.

'Michael didn't come out with you today?'

'No.'

'Why not, Garry?' And Garry smiled for the first time, a cool, spiteful smile.

'He didn't want to.'

'Oh!' The hurt showed in Sean's face for an instant, then he turned to the men around him. 'Right, gentlemen, let's get down there.'

In position now, a line of men standing quietly in the gloom and stagnant heat. Each man's neighbour visible only as an indefinite shape among the leaves and vines and fallen trees. Few things sharp – the outline of a hatbrim, the glint of a random beam of sun on gun-metal, a human hand framed in a hole of dark green leaves. The silence heavy as the heat – spoiled by the nervous rustle of a branch, a hastily smothered cough, the click of a shotgun breech.

Sean hooked his thumb across both hammers of his gun and pulled them back to full cock, lifted the twin muzzles to the roof of leaves above his head and fired in rapid succession. He heard the deep booming note of the gun bouncing against the sides of the valley, echoing and fragmenting as it was thrown back upon itself. Then swiftly the silence closed in again.

He stood motionless, tuning his hearing as finely as was possible, but his reward was the thin drone of an insect and the harsh startled cry of a bush lourie. He shrugged, two miles of distance and the mass of vegetation would blanket completely the cries of the beaters and the clatter of their sticks as they thrashed the bush. But they were coming now, of this he was certain, they would have heard his signal shots. He could imagine them moving down the line, two hundred black men interspersed with the small white boys, chanting the rhetorical question which was as old as the drive hunt itself.

'*E'yapi!* Repeated over and over again, the accent on the first half of the word, shrilling it.

'*E'yapi!* Where are you going?'

And between him and the beaters, in that wedge of tangled bush, there would be the first uneasy stirring. Dainty bodies, dappled with grey, rising from the secret beds of fallen leaves. Hooves, pointed and sharp, splayed and driven deep into soft leaf-mould by the weight of tensed muscle. Ears pricked forward, eyes like wet black satin, shiny moist muzzles quivering and snuffling, corkscrew horns laid back. The whole poised on the edge of flight.

With the taint of gunsmoke in his nostrils, Sean opened the action of his shotgun and the empty shells ejected crisply, pinging out to leave the eyes of the breech empty. He selected two fresh cartridges from his belt and slid them home, snapped the gun closed and thumbed the hammers on to half-cock.

Now they would be moving. The does first, gingerbrown and dappled like roe-deer, slipping away down the valley with their fawns long-legged beside them. Then the bucks, the Inkonka, black and big and silent as shadows; crouching as they moved, horns flat against their shoulders. Moving away from the faint cries and the commotion, moving their mates and their young away from danger – down towards the waiting guns.

'I heard something then!' The Reverend Smiley's voice sounded as though he were being strangled, probably by the dog collar which showed as a pale spot in the gloom.

'Shut up, you fool!' Sean gambled his chance of salvation on the rebuke, but he need not have worried for the endearment was drowned by the double blast of Smiley's shotgun – so indecently loud and totally unexpected that Sean's feet left the ground.

'Did you get him?' Sean asked, his voice a little shaky from the fright. No reply.

'Reverend, did you get one?' Sean demanded. He had seen nothing, and heard nothing that might by the most generous stretch of imagination lead anyone to suspect the presence of a bush buck.

'My goodness, I could have sworn . . . ' Smiley's reply was in the kind of voice you would expect from beyond the grave. 'Oh dear, I think I must have been mistaken.'

Here we go again, thought Sean with resignation.

'If you run out of cartridges let me know,' he called softly and grinned at Smiley's injured silence. The shots would have turned the game back towards the beaters, they would be starting to mill now as they sought an avenue of escape. Perhaps moving out on the flanks. As if in confirmation of Sean's thoughts, a shotgun thudded out on the left, then another, then two more on the right.

The fun had started in earnest.

In the brief silence he heard the beaters now, their excited cries muffled but urgent.

A blur of movement ahead of him through the screen of branches, just a flick of dark grey and he swung the gun and fired, wallop of the butt on to his shoulder, and thud and scuffle and roll and kick in the undergrowth.

'Got him!' exulted Sean. Still kicking, the head and shoulders of a half-grown ram emerged from under a bramble bush. It was down, mouth open, bleeding, crabbing against the earth, leaving a drag mark through the dead leaves. Boom again, the mercy stroke, and it lay still. Head speckled with tiny buckshot wounds, eyelids quivering into death and the swift rush of blood from the nostrils.

The din of gunfire all about, cries of the beaters and

the answering shouts of the gunners, the panic-stricken run and crackle in the bush ahead.

Inkonka, big one, black as a hellhound, three twists in the horn, eyes staring, lunging into the clearing to halt with head up and front legs braced wide, hunted, panting, wild with terror.

Lean forward against the gun, hold the pip on his heaving chest and fire. The bounce of the gun and the long blue gush of smoke. Knock him down with the solid charge of short range buckshot. Cleanly, quickly, without kicking.

'Got him!'

Another one, blundering straight into the gun line, blind with panic, bursting out of the undergrowth almost on top of Sean. Doe with fawn at her heels – let her go.

The doe saw him and wheeled left to take the gap between Sean and Garrick. As it dashed through, Sean looked beyond and saw his brother. Garrick had left his position and closed in on Sean. He was crouched slightly, the shotgun held in both hands, hammers fully cocked – and his eyes were fastened on Sean.

Garrick waited quietly during the initial stages of the beat. The tree-trunk on which he sat was soft and rotten, covered with moss and the orange and white tongues of fungus. From the inside pocket of his jacket he took the silver flask inlaid with carnelians. The first mouthful started his tears and numbed his tongue, but he swallowed it painfully and lowered the flask.

He has taken from me everything I ever had of value:

My leg: Garry looked down at the way it stuck out stiffly ahead of him with the heel buried in the damp

411

leaf-mould. He drank again quickly, closing his eyes against the sting of brandy.

My wife: In the dark redness behind his eyelids he saw her again, as Sean had left her, lying in torn clothing with bruised and swollen lips.

My manhood: Because of what he did to her that night, Anna has never let me touch her body. Until then there was hope. But now I am forty-two years old and I am virgin. It is too late.

My position: That swine Acheson would never have thrown me out – but for Sean.

And now he will take Michael from me.

He remembered again the premonition of disaster that he had experienced when Anna reported to him how she had found Michael and Sean together on Theuniskraal. It had started then, each little incident building up. The day Michael had stared at the faded but bold entries in the leather-bound stock register. 'Is that Uncle Sean's handwriting?'

That battered saddle Michael had found in the loft above the stables; he had polished it lovingly and restitched the seams, fitted new stirrup leathers, and used it for a year. Until Garry had noticed the crude initials cut into the leather of the flap. 'S.C.' That night Garry had taken the saddle and thrown it into the furnace of the hot-water boiler.

Eight months ago, on Michael's twenty-first birthday, Garry had called him into the panelled study of Theuniskraal, and reluctantly told him of Sean's legacy to him. Michael had held the dog-eared sheet and read it through with his lips moving silently. Then at last he looked up and his voice was shaky. 'Uncle Sean gave me a half-share in Theuniskraal even before I was born. Why, Dad? Why did he do that?' And Garry had no answer for him.

This last week had been the climax. It had taken all

Anna's and Garrick's combined influence and entreaties to prevent Michael responding to the invitations Sean had sent. Then the Zulu herdboy, whose duty was to follow Michael and come to Garrick immediately Michael crossed the boundary of Theuniskraal, reported that each evening Michael rode up to the high ground on the escarpment and sat there until after dark staring in the direction of Lion Kop ranch.

I am going to lose him. He is my son, even if Sean sired him. But he is my son, and unless I prevent it Sean is going to take that away from me also.

Unless I prevent it. He lifted the flask to his lips once more and found with surprise that it was empty. He screwed the stopper down and returned the flask to his pocket.

Around him the gunfire and the shouting began. From the log beside him he picked up the shotgun and loaded it. He stood up and cocked the hammers.

Sean saw him, coming slowly, limping a little, crouching, making no attempt to fend off the branches that dragged across his face.

'Don't bunch up, Garry. Stay in your position, you're leaving a gap in the line.'

Then he noticed Garry's expression. It seemed that the skin had been stretched tight across the cheek-bones and the nose, so the rims of his nostrils were white. His jaws were chewing nervously and there was a fine sheen of sweat across his forehead. He looked sick or deadly afraid.

'Garry, are you all right?' Alarmed, Sean started towards him – then stopped suddenly. Garry had lifted the shotgun.

413

'I'm sorry, Sean. But I can't let you have him,' he said. The blank double eyes of the muzzles were all Sean saw of the gun, and below them, Garry's knuckles white with pressure, as he gripped the stock. One finger was hooked forward around the triggers.

Sean was afraid then. He stood without moving for his legs were heavy and numb under him.

'I've got to.' Garry's voice was a croak. 'I have to do it – otherwise you'll take him. You'll destroy him also.'

With fear making his legs clumsy and slow, Sean turned deliberately away from him and walked back to his station. The muscles of his back were stiff with anticipation, knotted so tightly that they ached.

The beaters were close now, he could hear them shouting and thrashing the bush just ahead. He lifted the whistle to his lips and blew three shrill blasts. The shouting died away, and in the comparative silence Sean heard a sound behind him, a sound half-way between a sob and a cry of pain.

Slowly, inchingly, Sean turned his head to look back. Garry was gone.

Beneath him Sean's legs began to tremble, and a muscle in his thigh twitched spasmodically. He sank down and sat on the carpet of soft damp leaves. When he lit a cheroot he used both hands to steady the fluttering flame of the match.

'Dad! Dad!' Dirk came pelting out into the tiny clearing. 'Dad, how many did you get?'

'Two,' said Sean.

'Only two?' And Dirk's voice went flat with disappointment and shame. 'Even Reverend Smiley beat you hollow. He got four!'

66

Ruth returned to Pietermaritzburg the afternoon following the hunt, Sean insisted on accompanying her home. Ada, Dirk and a dozen of the friends Ruth had made during the week were at the station to see them leave. Sean was trying to detach Ruth from the earnest discussion into which all women seem to fall on the eve of a major parting. His repeated, 'You'd better get aboard, my dear,' and 'The flag's up, Ruth', were studiously ignored by all of them until he found it necessary to take Ruth's arm and bundle her up into the coach. Her head reappeared instantly at the window to take up the discussion at the exact point where Sean had interrupted it. Sean was about to follow her when he saw Dirk. With a stab of guilt Sean realized how blatantly he had neglected Dirk during the week.

'Cheerio, Dirkie,' Sean called gruffly and the boy flew to him and wound his arms tightly around Sean's neck.

'Come on, Dirk. I'll be back tomorrow morning.'

'I want to go with you.'

'You have school tomorrow.' Sean tried to loosen Dirk's hold. The women were watching in silence now, and Sean felt himself flushing with embarrassment. *My God, he's not a baby any more – he's nearly fifteen.* He tried to keep his irritation from showing in his voice as he whispered:

'Stop that now. What will people think of you?'

'Take me with you, Dad. Please take me,' and Dirk quivered against him. The whistle blew and with voluble relief the women turned away and began talking at once.

'Do you think I'm proud of you when you act like this?' Sean hissed at him. 'Now, behave yourself and shake hands properly.'

Dirk clutched his hand, with the tears filling his eyes.

'Stop it this instant!' Sean turned abruptly and swung himself up into the coach as the train jerked forward and started sliding out of the platform.

Dirk took a few indeterminate paces after it and then stopped with his shoulders shaking uncontrollably, his eyes still fastened on Sean's face as it protruded from the window.

'Your father will be back tomorrow, Dirkie.' Ada laid her hand consolingly on Dirk's shoulder.

'He doesn't love me,' whispered Dirk. 'He never even . . .'

'Of course he does,' Ada interrupted quickly. 'It was just that he was so . . .' But Dirk did not wait her to finish. He shrugged her hand away, spun round and jumped blindly from the platform on to the tracks, ducked through the barbed-wire fence beyond and ran out across the fields to intercept the train as it made its first long turn on to the slope of the escarpment.

He ran with his face contorted, and the harsh grass brushing his legs, he ran with his arms pumping the rhythm of his racing feet – and ahead of him the train whistled mournfully and crawled out from behind the Van Essen plantation.

It was crossing his front, still fifty yards away, slowly gathering speed for its assault on the escarpment. He would not reach it – even though Sean's coach was the last before the guard's van – he would not reach it.

He stopped, panting, searching wildly for a glimpse of

his father – but the window of Sean's compartment was blank.

'Pa!' He waved both arms wildly above his head. 'Pa! It's me. Me – Dirk.'

Sean's compartment moved slowly across his line of vision. For a few brief seconds he looked into the interior.

Sean stood sideways to the window, he was leaning forward with his shoulders hunched and Ruth was in his arms. Her head thrown back, the hat gone from her head and her dark hair in abundant disarray. She was laughing, white teeth and eyes asparkle. Sean leaned forward and covered her open mouth with his own. And then they were past.

Dirk stood like that with his arms raised. Then slowly they sank to his sides. The tension in his lips and around his eyes smoothed away. All expression faded from his eyes and he stood and watched the train puff and twist up the slope until with a last triumphant spurt of steam it disappeared over the skyline.

Dirk crossed the railway line and found the footpath that climbed the hills. Once he lifted his hands and with his thumbs wiped the tears from his cheeks. Then he stopped listlessly to watch a scarab beetle at his feet. The size of a man's thumb, glossy black and horned like a demon, it struggled with a ball of cow-dung three times its own size. Standing on its back legs, thrusting with its front, it rolled the perfect sphere of dung before it. Oblivious of everything but the need to spawn, to bury the ball in a secret place and deposit its eggs upon it, it laboured in silent dedication.

With the toe of his boot Dirk flicked the ball away into the grass. The beetle stood motionless, deprived of the whole purpose of its existence. Then it began to search. Back and forth, clicking and scraping its shiny body armour across the hard, bare earth of the path.

Watching its frenzied search dispassionately, Dirk's face was calm and lovely. He lifted his foot and brought his heel down gently on the beetle.

He could feel it wriggling under his boot until with a crunch its carapace collapsed and it spurted brown as tobacco juice. Dirk stepped over it and walked on up the hill.

In the night Dirk sat alone. His arms were clasped around his legs and his forehead rested on his knees. The shafts of moonlight through the canopy of wattle branches had a cold white quality, similar to the emotion that held Dirk's body rigid. He lifted his head. Moonlight lit his face from above, accentuating the perfection of his features. The smooth, broad depth of his forehead, the flaring dark lines of his brows set off the large but delicately formed plane of his nose. But now his mouth was a line of pain, of cold white pain.

'I hate him.' His mouth did not lose the shape of pain as he whispered the words, 'and I hate her. He doesn't care about me any more – all he cares about is that woman.'

'The vicious hiss of breath through his lips was the sound of despair.

'I always try to show him . . . No one else but him, but he doesn't care. Why doesn't he understand – Why? Why? Why?'

And he shivered feverishly.

'He doesn't want me. He doesn't care.'

The shivering ceased, and the shape of his mouth changed from pain to hatred.

'I'll show him. If he doesn't want me – then I'll show him.' And the next words he spat as though they were filth from his mouth, 'I hate him.' Around him the wattle branches rustled in the wind. He jumped to his feet and ran, following the moonlit road deeper into the plantations of Lion Kop.

A *meerkat* hunting alone along the road saw him and scampered into the trees like a small grey ferret. But Dirk ran on, faster now as his hatred drove him and his breathing sobbed in rhythm with his feet. He ran with the dry west wind into his face – he needed the wind. His revenge would ride on the wind.

'Now, we'll see,' he shouted suddenly as he ran. 'You don't want me – then have this instead!' And the wattle and wind answered him with a sound like many voices far away.

At the second access road he turned right and ran on into the heart of the plantations. He ran for twenty minutes and when he stopped he was panting wildly.

'Damn you – God damn you all.' His voice came catchy from his dried-out mouth.

'Damn you, then.' And he walked off the road and fought his way into the trees. They were two-year growth not yet thinned, and the branches interlaced to dispute his passage – hands trying to hold him, small desperate hands clutching at him, tugging at his clothing like the supplicating hands of a beggar. But he shrugged them away and beat them off until he was deep in amongst them.

'Here!' he said harshly and dropped to his knees in the soft crackling trash of small twigs and dry leaves that carpeted the earth. Hooking his fingers he raked a pyramid of the stuff, and he sobbed as he worked so that his muttering was broken and without coherence.

'Dry, it's dry. I'll show you then – you don't want –

419

Everything I've done you've . . . I hate you . . . Oh, Pa! Why? Why don't you – what have I done?'

And the matchbox rattled. Twice he struck and twice the match broke in his fingers. The third flared blue, spitting tiny sparks of sulphur, burning acrid, settling down to a small yellow flame that danced in the cup of his hands.

'Have this instead!' And he thrust the flame into the pile of kindling. It fluttered, almost died and then grew again as a wisp of grass caught it.

Consumed instantly, the grass was gone and the flame died, gone – almost, but then a leaf and it jumped brightly, orange points of flame in the twigs. The first tiny popping and it spread sideways, a burning leaf swirled upwards.

Dirk backed away as the flame leapt jubilantly into his face. He was no longer sobbing.

'Pa,' he whispered and the flame fastened on to the living leaves of a branch that hung above it. A gust of wind hit it and sprayed sparks and golden orange flame against its neighbour.

'Pa.' Dirk's voice was uncertain, he stood up and wiped his hands nervously against his shirt.

'No.' He shook his head in bewilderment, and the sapling bloomed with fire and the fire whispered softly.

'No.' Dirk's voice rose. 'I didn't really mean . . . ' but it was lost in the pistol-shots of flame and the whisper that was now a drumming roar.

'Stop it,' he shouted. 'Oh God, I didn't mean it. No! No!' And he jumped forward into the heat of it, into the bright orange glare, kicking wildly at the flaming kindling, scattering it so that it fell and caught again in fifty new points of fire.

'No, stop it. Please stop it!' And he clawed at the burning tree until the heat drove him back. He ran to another sapling and tore a leafy branch from it. He rushed at the fire, beating at it, sobbing again in the smoke and the flame.

Riding joyously on the west wind, roaring red and orange and black, the flames spread out among the trees and left him standing along in the smoke and the swirling ash.

'Oh Pa! I'm sorry, I'm sorry – I didn't mean it.'

67

A shutter kept slamming softly in the wind, but this was not the only reason Michael Courtney could not sleep. He felt trapped, chained by loyalties he could not break; he was aware of the dark oppressive bulk of the Theuniskraal homestead around him. A prison, a place of bitterness and hatred.

He moved restlessly on his bed and the shutter banged and banged. He threw back the single sheet and the floorboards creaked as he stood up from the bed.

'Michael!' The voice from the next room was sharp, suspicious.

'Yes, Mother.'

'Where are you going, darling?'

'There's a loose shutter. I'm going to close it.'

'Put something on, darling. Don't catch cold.'

Stifling, beginning to sweat now in physical discomfort, Michael knew he must get out of this house into the cool freedom of the wind and the night. He dressed quickly but silently, then carrying his boots he crept down the long passage and out on to the wide front stoep.

He found the shutter and secured it, then he sat upon the front steps and pulled on his boots before standing again and moving out across the lawns. He stood on the bottom terrace of Theuniskraal's gardens and around him the west wind soughed and shook the trees.

The restlessness of the wind increased his own, so he must get out of the valley – get up on to the high ground of the escarpment. He started to walk, hurrying past the paddocks towards the stables. In the stable yard he stopped abruptly, his tall lean body caught in mid-stride. There was a glow, a soft orange glow on the far hills of Lion Kop.

Then Michael ran, shouting as he passed the grooms' quarters. He threw open the half-door of one of the stalls and snatched the bridle from its peg as he ran to his horse. Hands clumsy with haste, he forced the bit between the animal's teeth and buckled the cheek strap. When he led it out into the yard two of the grooms were standing there, bewildered with sleep.

'Fire!' Michael pointed along the hills. 'Call everybody and bring them to help.' He went up on to the bare back of his horse and looked down at them. 'Bring every man from the location, come in the mule-wagon. Come as fast as you can.' Then he hit his heels into the mare's flanks and drove her out of the yard, laying forward across her back.

Twenty minutes later Michael checked her on the crest of the escarpment. She was blowing heavily between his knees. Still five miles ahead, bright even in the bright moonlight, a circle of fire lay on the dark plantations of Lion Kop. Above it a black cloud, a cloud that climbed and spread on the wind to hide the stars.

'Oh God – Uncle Sean!' The exclamation wrung from Michael was a cry of physical pain, and he urged the mare forward again. Charging her recklessly through the ford of the Baboon Stroom so that the water flew like exploding glass, then lunging up the far bank and on along the hills.

The mare was staggering in her gallop as Michael kneed her through the gates into the yard of the Lion Kop homestead. There were wagons and many blackmen carrying axes. Michael hauled the mare back so violently that she nearly fell.

'Where is the Nkosi?' he shouted at a big Zulu he recognized as Sean's personal servant.

'He has gone to Pietermaritzburg.'

Michael slid down from his horse and turned her loose.

'Send a man to the village to ask for help.'

'It is done,' the Zulu replied.

'We must move all the livestock from the top paddocks, get the horses out of the stables – it may come this way,' Michael went on.

'I have sent all the wives to do these things.'

'You have done well, then. Now let us go.'

The Zulus were swarming up on to the wagons, clutching the long-handled axes. Michael and Mbejane ran to the lead wagon. Michael took the reins. At that moment two horsemen galloped into the yard. He could not see their faces in the night.

'Who's that?' Michael shouted.

'Broster and Van Wyk!' The nearest neighbours.

'Thank God! Will you take the other wagons?'

They dismounted and ran past Michael.

Michael stood with his legs braced apart, he threw his shoulders open as he wielded the whip and then sent it snaking forward to crack an inch above the ears of the lead mules. They lunged forward into the traces and the wagon bounced and clattered out of the yard.

As they galloped in frantic convoy along the main access road towards the plantations they met the Zulu women with their children from the location streaming down towards the homestead, their soft voices calling greeting and speed to their men as they passed.

But Michael hardly heard them, he stood with his

eyes fastened on the pillar of red flame and smoke that rose from the heart of Sean's trees.

'It is in the trees we planted two years ago.' Mbejane spoke beside him. 'But already it will be close upon the next block of older trees. We cannot hope to stop it there.'

'Where then?'

'This side there are more young trees and a wide road. We can try there.'

'What is your name?' Michael asked.

'Mbejane.'

'I am Michael. The Nkosi's nephew.'

'I know.' Mbejane nodded, then went on, 'Turn off where next the roads meet.'

They came to the cross-roads. In the sector ahead were the young trees – ten feet high, thick as a man's arm, massed dark leaves and interlacing branches. Far out beyond them in the tall mature wattle was the line of flame. Above it a towering wall of sparks and dark smoke, coming down swiftly on the wind. It would be upon them in less than an hour at its present rate of advance.

A fire like this would jump a thirty-foot road without checking – they must cut back into the young wattle and increase the gap to sixty feet at the least.

Michael swung the wagon off the road and hauled the mules to a halt. He jumped down to meet the other wagons as they came up.

'Go on for two hundred yards – then start your boys in chopping out the wattle towards the fire – we've got to widen the road. I'll start my gang here,' he shouted at Van Wyk.

'Right.'

'Mr Broster – go on to the end of the block and start

425

working back this way – cut the timber out another thirty feet.'

Without waiting to hear more, Broster drove on. These two men, twice Michael's age, conceded him the right of command without argument.

Snatching an axe from the nearest Zulu, Michael issued his orders as he ran to the young wattle. The men crowded after him and Michael selected a tree, took his stance and swung the axe in a low arc from the side. The tree quivered and rained loose leaves upon him at the blow. Smoothly he reversed his grip on the shaft of the axe and swung again from the opposite side. The blade sliced through the soft wood, the tree sagged wearily away from him and groaned as it subsided. He stepped past it to the next. Around him the Zulus spread out along the road and the night rang with the beat of their axes.

Four times during the next half-hour fresh wagons galloped in, wagons loaded with men and driven by Sean's neighbours, until almost three hundred men were using the axe on Sean's lovingly planted and tenderly nursed wattle.

Shoulder to shoulder, chopping in wordless frenzy, trampling the fallen saplings as they moved forward.

Once a man yelled in pain and Michael looked up to see two Zulus dragging another back to the road with his leg half severed by the slip of a careless axe. Dark blood in the moonlight.

One of the neighbours hurried to tend the injured man and Michael turned back to the destruction of the wattle.

Swing, change hands and swing again, the solid *thunk!* and the tree swaying. Shove it over and struggle through the fallen tangle of branches to the next. Swing again, and smell the sweet bleeding sap – feel the ache in the shoulders and the sting of sweat in the burst blishers of the palms.

Then suddenly the other smell, acrid on the wind. Smoke. Michael paused and looked up. The men on each side of him stopped work also and the firelight danced on their naked, sweat-greased bodies as they leaned on their axes and watched it come.

On a front four hundred yards wide, ponderously it rolled down towards them. Not with the explosive white heat of a burning pine forest, but in the awful grandeur of orange and dark red, billowing smoke and torrential sparks.

Gradually the sound of axes died along the line as men stopped and watched this appalling thing come down towards them. It lit their faces clearly, revealing the awe that was on all of them. They could feel the heat now, great gusts of it that shrivelled the tender growth ahead of the flames – and suddenly a freak of the wind sent a bank of black smoke billowing down over the motionless line of men and blotted them out from each other. It cleared as swiftly as it came, and left them coughing and gasping.

'Back! Get back to the road!' yelled Michael and the cry was taken up and thrown along the line. They waded back through the morass of waist-high vegetation and assembled in small subdued groups along the road, standing together helplessly with the axes idle in their hands, fearful in the face of that line of flame and smoke.

'Cut branches to beat with!' Michael whipped their apathy. 'String out along the edge.' He hurried along the road, pushing them back into line, bullying them, cursing in his own fear. 'Come on, the flames will drop when they reach the fallen trees. Cover your faces – use your shirts. Hey, you – don't just stand there.'

With renewed determination each man armed himself with a green branch, and they re-formed along the road.

Quietly they stood in the daylight glare of the flames – black faces impassive, white ones flushed with heat and working anxiously.

'Do you think we'll be able to . . .' Michael started as he reached Ken Broster, and then he stopped. The question he had been about to ask had no answer. Instead he said, 'We've lost three thousand acres already – but if it gets away from us here!'

Involuntarily both of them glanced back at the tall mature wattle behind them.

'We'll hold it here,' Broster stated with a certainty he did not feel.

'I hope you're right,' whispered Michael, then suddenly Broster shouted:

'Oh Christ – look!'

For a moment Michael was blinded by the red glare and unsighted by the smoke. The fire burned unevenly. In places it had driven forward in great wedge-shaped salients of flame and left behind bays of standing wattle that were withering and browning in the heat.

From out of one of these bays, into the springy matt of fallen and trampled branches staggered a man.

'Who the hell . . .' started Michael. The man was unrecognizable. His shirt ripped to shreds by branches that had also scourged his face into a bloody mask. He floundered forward towards the road, two slack exhausted paces before he fell and disappeared under the leaves.

'The Nkosana.' Mbejane's voice boomed above the thunder of the flames.

'Dirk! It's Dirk Courtney!' Michael started forward.

The heat was painful in Michael's face. How much more intense must it be out there where Dirk was lying. As if they knew their prey was helpless the flames raced

428

forward eagerly, triumphantly to consume him. Whoever went in to rob them would meet the full fury of their advance.

Michael plunged into the brush and ploughed his way towards where Dirk thrashed feebly, almost encircled by the deadly embrace of the flames – and the heat reached out ahead of the flames to welcome him. Mbejane ran beside him.

'Go back,' shouted Mbejane. 'It needs only one of us.' But Michael did not answer him and they crashed side by side through the brush, racing the fire with Dirk as the prize.

Mbejane reached him first and lifting him, turned back for the road. He took one step before he fell and rose again unsteadily from the mass of branches. Even his vast strength was insufficient in this vacuum of heat. His mouth was open, a pink cave in the glistening black oval of his face, wide open and his chest heaved strenuously as he hunted air, but instead sucked the scalding heat into his throat.

Michael threw himself forward against the heat to reach him. It was almost a solid thing, a barrier of red shimmering glare. Michael could feel it swelling and tightening the skin of his face and drying the moisture from his eyeballs.

'I'll take his legs,' he grunted and reached for Dirk. A patch of brown appeared miraculously on the sleeve of his shirt – singed by the flames as though it had been carelessly ironed. Beneath it the heat sunk a barb of agony into his flesh.

Half a dozen paces together with Dirk between them before Michael tripped and fell, dragging Mbejane down with him. They were a long time rising, all movement slowing down – but when they did they were surrounded.

Two prongs of flame had reached the area of fallen saplings on either side of them. This had slowed them and diminished their fury. But a chance gust of the wind and fuel had forced them to curl inwards on each other, spreading horns of fire ahead of Michael and Mbejane and leaving them enclosed by a dancing, leaping palisade of flame.

'Go through!' croaked Michael, his throat scalded and swollen. 'We must break through.'

And they churned their way towards the encircling wall. Through it, vague and unreal, he could see men beating at the flames – distorted phantoms trying desperately to open a path for them. Mbejane wore only a loin cloth, no breeches, coat nor boots to protect him, as Michael had. He was very near the limit of his strength.

Now looking at Michael across the body of the boy they carried, Mbejane saw a curious thing. Michael's hair crinkled slowly and then began to smoke – smouldering like an old sack.

Michael screamed at the agony of it, a hideous sound that shrilled above the roar and crackle of the flames. But agony was the key that unlocked the last storehouse of his strength. As though it were a rag doll he snatched Dirk's body from Mbejane's grasp and lifting it with both hands on to his shoulders he charged into the fire.

The flames reached to his waist, clawing greedily at him as he ran and the smoke eddied and swirled about him – but he was through.

'Help Mbejane!' he shouted at the Zulu beaters and then he was out on to the road. He dropped Dirk and beat at his clothing with his bare hands. His boots were charred and his clothing was alight in a dozen places. He fell and rolled wildly in the dusty road to smother it.

Two Zulus went in to help Mbejane. Two nameless

blackmen, two labourers – men of no distinction. Neither of them wore boots. Both of them reached Mbejane as he tottered weakly towards them. One on each side they urged him back towards the road.

At this moment Michael rolled to his knees in the road and despite his own agony watched them with a sickened fascination.

Leading Mbejane between them as though he were a blind man, they stumbled barefooted into the flames and stirred up a great cloud of sparks around them. Then the smoke rolled down over them and they were gone.

'Mbejane!' croaked Michael, and pushed himself to his feet to go to him – then:

'Oh God – Oh, thank God.' Mbejane and one of the Zulus stumbled out of the smoke into the arms of the men who waited for them.

No one went back for the other Zulu. No one went back for him until two hours later when the dawn had broken and the fire had been stopped at the road and the mature wattle had been saved. Then Ken Broster led a small party gingerly into the wilderness of still smouldering ash, into the black desert. They found him on his face. Those parts of him that had lain against the earth were still recognizable as belonging to a human being.

68

'Ladyburg in twenty minutes, Mr Courtney.' The conductor put his head round the door of the compartment.

'Thanks, Jack.' Sean looked up from his book.

'I see from this morning's paper that you're engaged to be married?'

'That's right.'

'Well, then, break clean, no hitting low – let's have a good clean fight and good luck to both of you.' Sean grinned and the man went down the passage. Sean packed his book into the briefcase, stood up and followed him.

On the balcony of the coach he stopped and lit a cheroot, then he leaned on the railings and looked out across the veld for his first glimpse of Lion Kop. This had become a ritual whenever he returned to Ladyburg.

This morning he was as happily content as he had ever been in his life. Last night, after conferring with Ma and Pa Goldberg, Ruth had set the wedding date for March next year. By then Sean would have completed his first cutting of bark, and they would take a month to honeymoon in the Cape.

Now, at last, I have everything a man could reasonably ask for, he thought, and smiled and in that moment he saw the smoke. He straightened up and flicked the cheroot away.

The train snaked up towards the rim of the escarpment, slowing as the gradient changed beneath it. It reached the crest and the whole vista of the Ladyburg valley opened below it. Sean saw the great irregular blot upon his trees, with the thin grey streams of smoke drifting wearily away across the hills.

He opened the balcony gate and jumped down from the train. He hit and slid and rolled down the gravel embankment. The skin was scraped from his knees and the palms of his hands. Then he was on his feet, running.

Along the road where the fire had been stopped men waited. Sitting quietly or sprawled in exhausted sleep, all of them were coated with ash and soot. Their eyes were smoke-inflamed and their bodies ached with fatigue. But they waited while the black acres smouldered and smoked sullenly – for if the wind came up again it would fan the ashes to life.

Ken Broster lifted his head from his arm, then sat up quickly.

'Sean's here!' he said. The men around him stirred and then stood up slowly. They watched Sean approaching, he came with the sloppy, blundering legs of a man who has run five miles.

Sean stopped a little way off and his breathing wheezed and heaved in his throat.

'How? How did it happen?'

'We don't know, Sean.' In sympathy Ken Broster dropped his eyes from Sean's face. You do not stare at a man in anguish. Sean leaned against one of the wagons. He could not bring himself to look again at the vast expanse of smouldering desert with the skeletons of the treetrunks standing out of it like the twisted and blackened fingers of an arthritic hand.

'One of your men was killed,' Ken told him softly. 'One of your Zulus.' He hesitated – then went on firmly. 'Others were hurt, badly burned.'

Sean made no reply, he did not seem to understand the words.

'Your nephew and your boy – Dirkie.' Still Sean stared at him dully.

'Mbejane also.' This time Sean seemed to cringe away from him.

'I sent them down to the homestead – the doctor's there.'

Still no reply from Sean, but now he wiped the palm of his hand across his mouth and eyes.

'Mike and Dirk aren't too bad, skin burns – but Mbejane's feet are in a hell of a mess.' Ken Broster spoke quickly now. 'Young Dirk got trapped in front of the flames. Mike and Mbejane went to get him ... surrounded ... down ... picked him up ... tried to help ... useless ... badly burned ... meat off his feet ...

To Sean the words were disjointed, meaningless. He leaned against the wagon. There was looseness in him, a lack of will. *It was too much. Let it go. Let it all go.*

'Sean, are you all right?' Broster's hands on his shoulders. He straightened up and looked around him again.

'I must go to them. Lend me a horse.'

'You go ahead, Sean. We'll stay on here and watch it for you. Don't worry about it, we'll make bloody sure she doesn't start again.'

'Thank you, Ken.' Then he looked around the circle of anxious compassionate faces. 'Thank you,' he said again.

Sean rode slowly into the stable yard on Lion Kop. There were many carriages and servants, black women and children, but a hush came upon them when they recognized him. Surrounded by women, a crude litter lay near the far wall of the yard and Sean walked across to it.

'I see you, Mbejane.'

434

'Nkosi.' Mbejane's eyelashes were burned away giving his face a bland and slightly puzzled expression. His hands and his feet were bound loosely in bundles of crisp white bandages through which ointment had soaked in yellow patches. Sean squatted behind him. He could not speak. He reached out almost hesitantly and touched Mbejane's shoulder.

'Is it bad?' he asked then.

'No, Nkosi. It is not too bad. My wives have come for me. I will return when I am ready.'

They spoke together a little while, and Mbejane told him of Dirk and how Michael had come. Then he murmured, 'This woman is the wife of the one who died.'

Sean noticed her for the first time. She sat alone in the crowded yard, on a blanket against the wall. A child stood beside her, leaning forward, naked, holding one of her fat, black breasts with both hands as he fed from it. She sat impassively with her legs folded under her, a cloak of ochre-dyed leather draped loosely over her shoulders, but open at the front for the child. Sean moved across to her. The child watched him with large dark eyes, but without removing the nipple from his mouth and the corners of his mouth were wet with spilled milk.

'He was a man,' Sean greeted the woman.

She inclined her head gravely. 'He was a man!' she agreed.

'Where will you go?' Sean asked.

'To my father's kraal.' The high headdress of red clay enhanced the quiet dignity of her reply.

'Select twenty head of cattle from my herds to take with you.'

'*Ngi Yabonga* – I praise you, Nkosi.'

'Go in peace.'

'Stay in peace.' She stood, lifted the child on to her

435

hip and walked slowly from the yard without looking back.

'I will go now, Nkosi.' Mbejane spoke from the litter. The colour of his skin was grey with pain. 'And when I return we will plant again. It was only a small fire.'

'It was only a small fire.' Sean nodded. 'Go in peace, my friend. Drink much beer and grow fat. I will visit you.'

Mbejane chuckled softly and signalled his wives to their places around the litter. They lifted him, young women strong from their work in the fields.

'Stay in peace, Nkosi.' Mbejane lay back painfully upon the soft mattress of fur, and they carried him out of the yard. They began to sing as they passed the gates, moving in double file on each side of the litter, stately and tall, their naked backs glistening with oil, rumps swaying together beneath the brief loin cloths, and their voices joined high and proud in the ancient song of welcome to the warrior returned from battle.

Gathered on the stoep of Lion Kop were many of his neighbours and their wives, come with sympathy and offers of assistance.

Ada was waiting for him as Sean climbed the steps.

'Dirk?' he asked.

'He is well, asleep now. Laudanum.'

'Michael?'

'He is waiting for you. He refused the drug. I've put him in your room.'

On his way down the passage Sean stopped at Dirk's room and looked in. Dirk lay on his back with bandaged hands folded across his chest. His face was swollen and laced with ugly red lines where the wattle branches had

436

clawed him. On the chair beside his bed Mary sat in patient vigil. She looked at Sean and made to rise. Sean shook his head.

'No. I will come back when he is awake.' He went on down the passage to his own room.

Three of Ada's girls hovered and chirruped about Michael's bed like birds whose nests are endangered. They saw him and stopped their chatter. All Ada's girls held Sean in unexplained awe.

'Oh, Mr Courtney. His poor hands . . . ' one little lass began, then blushed crimson, dropped a hurried curtsy and escaped from the room. The others followed quickly.

Sean moved across to the bed.

'Hello, Mike.' His voice was gruff, as he saw the blister that hung like a pale grape on Michael's cheek.

'Hello, Uncle Sean.' The raw places of his face and lips were smeared with yellow ointment. Sean sat down gingerly on the edge of the bed.

'Thank you, Michael,' he said.

69

Ronny Pye called early the following morning. With him came Dennis Petersen and both of them were wearing suits.

'Very fancy turn-out,' Sean greeted them. 'Business or social?'

'Well, you might say a little of each.' Ronny paused at the top of the veranda steps. 'May we come in?'

Sean led them to the end of the veranda, and they seated themselves before anyone spoke again.

'I heard about the fire, Sean. Terrible business. I heard there was a native killed and both Dirk and Michael were hurt. Terrible business.' Ronny shook his head in sympathy.

'Did you also hear that I lost four thousand acres of timber?'

Sean inquired politely.

'Heard that also.' Ronny nodded solemnly. 'Terrible business.'

Ronny and Dennis glanced at each other furtively, and then looked down at their hands.

'Very nasty,' Ronny repeated and a silence fell upon them.

'Anything else worrying you?' Sean inquired politely.

'Well, now that you've brought it up –' Ronny reached inside his jacket and withdrew a long folded document tied with a red ribbon. 'Mind you, we don't have to discuss it today. Leave it until you feel better?'

'Talk!' Sean grunted.

'Clause eight.' Ronny spread the document between the coffee-cups on the table. 'In the event of the said security, namely, a certain block of wattle known as No. 2 block of Lion Kop Estates in extent approximately . . . ' Ronny hesitated. 'Guess there's no sense in me reading it all. You know what it says. That wattle was part of the collateral for the loan.'

'How long will you give me to raise the money?' Sean asked.

'Well, Sean, you understand there is no period of grace allowed in the contract. Seems to me you'll have to put it up right away.'

'I want a month,' Sean told him.

'A month!' Ronny was shocked and hurt by the request. 'See here now, Sean. I don't honestly – I mean, surely you've got the money. I mean why do you need a month. Just let us have your cheque.'

'You know damned well I haven't got it.'

'Seems to me –' Ronny offered delicately. 'Seems to me if you haven't got it now, there's not much chance you'll have it in a month. No offence, Sean, but we have to look at this thing from a business angle. If you follow me.'

'I follow you.' Sean nodded. 'And I want a month.'

'Give it to him,' blurted Dennis Petersen, his first contribution, and Ronny turned on him instantly with his face twisting into a snarl. The struggle he had within himself to smooth out his features and to restore his voice to its level and reasonable tone lasted fully five seconds.

'Well now, Dennis,' he murmured. 'That's an unusual way to look at it. Seems to me –'

'I spoke to Audrey before we came up here. I promised her . . . Anyway, we both agreed.' Dennis was staring out across the valley, unable to meet his partner's eyes.

Suddenly Ronny Pye chuckled. Yes, by God! It would be even better that way – watching this big arrogant bastard crawling round begging, with his hat in his hands. Sean would go to Jackson first and Ronny had telegraphed Jackson the previous afternoon. He had also telegraphed Nichols at the Standard Bank. By now the message would be spreading swiftly along the network of South African banking channels. Sean Courtney would find it difficult to borrow the price of a meal.

'All right then, Sean. As a special concession you can have a month.' Then all the laughter was gone and he leaned forward in his chair. 'You've got exactly thirty days. Then, by Christ, I am going to sell out under you.'

After they were gone Sean sat alone on the wide veranda. The sunlight on the hills was bright and hot, but in the shade it was cool. He heard Ada's girls chattering somewhere in the house, then one of them giggled shrilly. The sound irritated Sean, his frown deepened and he drew a rumpled envelope from his jacket pocket and smoothed it out on the arm of his chair. Awhile he sat in thought nibbling the stub of a pencil.

Then he wrote: 'Jackson. Natal Wattle'. And again, 'Standard Bank'. Then 'Ben Goldberg'. He paused and considered this last name on his list. Then he grunted aloud and scratched it out with two hard strokes of the pencil. Not from the Goldbergs. Leave them out of this.

He wrote again quickly, scrawling a single word – 'Candy' and below it 'Tim Curtis'.

That was all. John Acheson was in England. It would take two months to receive a reply from him.

That was all. He sighed softly and folded the envelope into his pocket. Then he lit a cheroot, sank down in the chair and placed his feet on the low veranda wall in front of him. I'll leave on tomorrow morning's train, he thought.

The windows behind him were open. Lying beyond them in the bedroom Michael Courtney had heard every word of their conversation. Now he stood up painfully from the bed and began to dress. He went out the back way and nobody saw him leave. His mare was in the stables, and on a borrowed saddle he rode back to Theuniskraal.

Anna saw him coming and ran out into the yard to meet him. 'Michael! Oh, Michael. Thank God you are safe. We heard . . . ' Then she saw his face and the raw, swollen burns on it and she froze. Michael dismounted slowly and one of the grooms led his horse away.

'Michael, darling. Your poor face.' And she embraced him quickly.

'It's nothing, Mother.'

'Nothing!' She pulled away from him, lips drawn into a tight, hard line. 'You run away in the middle of the night to that . . . that . . . Then you come home days later with your face and your hands in a terrible mess – is that nothing!'

'I'm sorry, Mother. Gran'ma looked after me.'

'You knew I'd be half-dead with worry, sitting here imagining all sorts of things. You didn't send word to me, you just let me . . . '

'You could have come to Lion Kop,' he said softly.

'To the home of that monster? Never!' And Michael looked away from her.

'Where's Father?'

'In his study, as usual. Oh, darling, you don't know how I've missed you. Tell me you love me, Michael.'

'I love you,' he repeated automatically and the sensation of suffocating was on him again. 'I must see Dad. It's very urgent.'

'You've just arrived. Let me fix something to eat – let me see to your poor face.'

'I have to see Dad now. I'm sorry.' And he went past her towards the house.

Garry was sitting at his desk when Michael walked into the study. Michael hated this room. He hated the high smoke-stained ceiling, the oppressive darkness of the panelled walls, the massive hunting trophies, he hated even the carpets and the smell of old paper and dust. From this room had issued the decrees and the pronouncements which had restricted and predetermined his life. This room was the symbol of everything from which he wished to escape. Now he glared around it definatly, as though it were a living thing – I've come back to extract from you what you owe me, he thought, you've had value from me, now pay me back!

'Michael!' Garrick's boot scraped on the wooden floor as he stood to greet him, and Michael winced at the sound.

'Hello, Dad.'

'Your mother and I, we have been so worried. Why didn't you send word to us?' The hurt was there in Garrick's voice. Michael opened his mouth to apologize in automatic guilt, but the words came out differently from the way he had intended.

'I was busy. I didn't have a chance.'

'Sit down, my boy.' Garrick gestured to one of the polished leather arm-chairs. He removed the metal-framed spectacles from his nose, but he did not look at Michael's injured face again. He would not think about Sean and Michael together.

'I'm glad you've come back. I was just working on the opening chapters of my new book. It's a history of our

442

family from the time of your great-great-grandfather's arrival at the Cape. I'd very much like your opinion. I'd value it immensely. The considered opinion of a graduate from the South African College.'

The trap was closing. It was so obvious that Michael squirmed. He could almost feel the panelled walls moving in on him. He started to protest: 'Dad, I have to speak to you.' But already Garrick was adjusting his spectacles and shuffling through the papers on his desk, talking quickly.

'I think you'll like it. It should interest you.' Garrick glanced up and smiled at Michael with the eagerness of a child that brings a gift. 'Here we are. I'll start at the beginning. You must allow for it being the first rough draft. It's not polished yet.' And he began to read. At the end of each paragraph he searched for Michael's approval, smiling in anticipation of it. Until Michael could bear it no longer, until he shouted suddenly in the middle of a sentence.

'I want you to pay me out my share of Theuniskraal.'

There was a momentary break in Garrick's reading, just a flutter in his voice to acknowledge Michael's request and then he went on steadily, but his voice had lost its timbre and was now a lifeless monotone. He finished the paragraph, laid the sheet aside, removed his spectacles and placed them in their case. The lid of the case snapped shut against the tension of its spring and Garry lifted his head slowly.

'Why?'

'I need the money.'

'What for?'

'I need it.'

Garry stood up and moved across to the window. He stood before it with his hand clasped behind him. The green lawns flowed down to the fence that bounded the gardens, and upon them the poinsettia bushes were vivid patches of scarlet. Beyond, the land lifted into the first long roll, golden grass and scattered forest with the cattle feeding beneath and the massive silver and blue clouds piled above.

'It will rain tonight,' Garrick murmured, but Michael did not answer. 'We need it. Three weeks of dry, and the pasture is withering.' Still no reply and Garry returned to his desk.

'I hear there was a fire on Lion Kop last night.'

'There was.'

'They say that your uncle is finished. They say the fire finished him.'

'No!' Michael denied it quickly. 'That's not true.'

'Is that why you want the money, Michael?'

'Yes.'

'You want to give it to Sean?'

'I want to buy a share in Lion Kop Wattle. I don't want to give anything – it will be a business offer.'

'And what about Theuniskraal – it's your home. You were born here.'

'Please, Dad. I've made up my mind.'

'Did Sean suggest this?'

'He did not. He knows nothing about it.'

'It's your idea then. You thought it up all on your own. You're going to sell out your own parents for him. My God, what sort of hold has he over you that you would do that for him.'

Flushing a dusty brick colour, Michael kicked back his chair and jumped to his feet.

'You make it sound like treachery.'

'That's exactly what it is!' shouted Garrick. 'It's Judas's work. Your mother and I – we raised you with everything. We scraped to send you to University, we built our whole lives around you. We worked for the day you would return here to Theuniskraal and . . . ' He stopped, panting, and wiped from his chin the bubble of saliva that had burst through his lips. 'Instead you ran off to join that . . . that swine. How do you think we liked that? Don't you think it nearly broke our hearts? Of all people you had to go to him! And now, now you want half of Theuniskraal to take him as a gift – to buy his . . . '

'Stop that!' Michael warned him sharply. 'And before you go on remember where I got my half of Theuniskraal. Remember who made the original gift.' He picked up his hat and riding-crop and strode towards the door.

'Michael.' The terrible appeal in Garry's voice checked him.

'What is it?'

'Your share – it isn't very much. I hadn't told you before, but there was a time – when you were very young. The rinderpest. I had to –' He couldn't go on.

'What are you trying to tell me?'

'Sit down, Michael. Sit down and I'll show you.' Reluctantly, afraid of what he was about to hear, Michael returned and stood beside his chair.

Garry selected a key from the bunch on his watch-chain and opened the top drawer of his desk. He selected a rolled document, slipped it from its retaining ribbon and handed it without speaking to his son.

Michael spread it and read the words upon the cover. 'Deed of Mortgage'.

With a sliding sensation in his stomach, he turned the page. He did not read it all. Words and groups of words stood out in bolder print, and they were sufficient:

'The Ladyburg Trust & Banking Co.' . . . 'A certain piece of land in extent approx. 25,000 morgen situate in the district of Ladyburg, Magisterial Division of Pietermaritzburg, known as the farm Theuniskraal' . . . 'All constructions, erections and improvements thereon . . . Plus interest at eight and one half per cent.'

'I see.' Michael handed the document back to his father and stood up.

'Where are you going?'

'Back to Lion Kop.'

'No!' Garry whispered. 'No, Michael. Please, my son. No – O God – No!' Michael left the room and closed the door softly behind him.

When Anna came into the room Garry was sitting behind the desk, sitting quietly with his shoulders slumped forward.

'You let him go!' she hissed. Garry did not move, he did not seem to hear.

'He's gone. Gone to your brother – and you let him.' Her voice was very low, but now it rose harshly and she shrieked at him. 'You useless drunken animal. Sitting here playing with your little books. You were not man enough to breed him – your brother had to do that for you! And you are not man enough to keep him – again your brother! You let him go. You've taken my son from me.'

Garry sat unmoving. He saw nothing. He heard nothing. In his head was a soft, misty greyness, and the mist blotted out all sight and sound. It was warm in the mist – warm and safe. No one could reach him here for it wrapped and protected him. He was safe.

'This is all you are good for.' Anna snatched a handful of the manuscript sheets from the desk in front of him. 'Your little pieces of paper. Your dreams and stories of other men – real men.'

She ripped the pages through and through again, then flung them at him. The pieces fluttered and swirled, then settled like dead leaves on his shoulders and in his hair. He did not move. Panting in her grief and anger, she took up what remained of the manuscript and shredded that also, scattering the tiny white scraps about the room.

70

The two of them stood together on the station platform. They did not speak. Most of the previous day and night had been spent talking and now there was nothing more to say. They stood together in quiet companionship – and a stranger looking at them would have known immediately they were father and son. Though Michael was not as tall, and he was lean beside Sean's bulk – yet the tone of the skin and the colour of the hair were the same. Both had the big Courtney nose and their mouths were wide and full-lipped.

'I'll telegraph as soon as I hit gold.' Sean had explained to Michael in detail the financial structure of Lion Kop. He had told him how he intended to find the money which would keep it from collapsing.

'I'll hold this end up.' Michael was to begin cutting the wattle which had survived the fire. They had ridden the previous afternoon through the plantations and marked the blocks which were ripe for the axe. 'Good luck, Uncle Sean.'

'Since we are working together now, Mike, I suggest you drop the "Uncle". It's too clumsy for everyday use.'

Michael grinned. 'Good luck, Sean.'

'Thanks, Mike.' They clasped hands, gripping hard, then Sean climbed up into the coach.

Jackson was friendly but firm and Nichols at the Standard Bank was very polite and full of sympathy. Sean caught the northbound train for Johannesburg to fire his last two bullets.

'Colonel Courtney. How good to see you.' The reception clerk at Candy's Hotel came round from behind his desk to greet Sean. 'We were only talking about you last week. Welcome back to Johannesburg.'

'Hello, Frank. Putting on a little weight there, aren't you?' Sean prodded his waistcoat and the man chuckled. 'Tell me, Frank, is Candy . . . is Mrs Rautenbach in?'

'Ah! There've been some changes since you left, sir.' The clerk grinned with just a trace of malice. 'It's not Mrs Rautenbach any longer. No, sir. Mrs Heyns – Mrs Jock Heyns now!'

'Good God! She married Jock!'

'That she did. Two weeks ago – biggest wedding in Jo'burg since the war. Two thousand guests.'

'Where is she now?'

'On the water. Off to England and the Continent for six months' honeymoon.'

'I hope she'll be happy,' Sean murmured softly, remembering the loneliness he had seen in her eyes when he left.

'With all Mr Heyns's money? How can she be otherwise?' the clerk asked in genuine surprise.

'Will you be staying, Colonel?'

'If you have a room.'

'We always have a room for our friends. How long, sir?'

'Two days, Frank.'

Tim Curtis was Chief Engineer on the City Deep. When Sean spoke to him about a loan he laughed.

'Christ! Sean, I only work there – I don't own the bloody mine.'

Sean had dinner with him and his bride of two years' standing. At their urging Sean examined their newborn infant and secretly decided that it looked like an unweaned bulldog.

Extending his stay in Johannesburg, Sean visited the banks. He had dealt with most of them long ago, but the personnel had changed, so he was puzzled that the manager of each institution seemed to have heard of him.

'Colonel Courtney. Now would you be Colonel Sean Courtney of Lion Kop Wattle Estates down in Natal?' And when he nodded he saw the shutters come down in their eyes, like windows barred by a prudent householder against burglars.

On the eighth night he ordered liquor to be sent to his suite – two full bottles of brandy. He drank steadily and desperately. The brandy would not quieten the violent struggles of his brain, but seemed to goad it, distorting his problems and deepening his melancholia.

He lay alone until the dawn paled out the yellow gaslight of the lamps. The brandy hummed giddily in his head and he longed for peace – the peace he had found only in the immense silence and space of the veld. Suddenly a picture formed in his mind of a lonely grave below a little hill. He heard the wind moan over it and saw the brown grass sway. That was peace.

He sat up unsteadily.

'Saul,' he said, and the sadness was heavy on him for the pilgrimage he had promised himself and had not made.

'It is finished here. I'll go now,' and he stood up. The giddiness caught him and he clutched at the head-rail of the bed to steady himself.

71

He recognized the kopje from four miles off. Into his memory its shape was indelibly etched; the symmetrical slope of the sides cobbled with boulders that glinted dully in the sunshine like the scales of a reptile, the flattened summit ringed by a bolder stratum of rock, the high altar on which the sacrifice to greed and stupidity had been made.

Closer he could discern the aloe plants upon the slopes, fleshy leaves spiked like crowns and jewelled with scarlet blooms. On the plain below the kopje, in the short brown grass, stood a long line of white specks. Sean rode towards them and as he approached each speck evolved into a cairn of whitewashed stones and on each stood a metal cross.

Stiff from the long day in the saddle Sean dismounted slowly. He hobbled the horses, dropped saddle and pack from their backs and turned them loose to feed. He stood alone and lit a cheroot, suddenly reluctant to approach the line of graves.

The silence of the empty land settled gently upon him, a silence not broken but somehow heightened by the sound of the wind across the plain. The harsh tearing as his mount cropped at the dry brown grass seemed sacrilegious in this place, but it roused Sean from his thoughts. He walked towards the double line of graves and stood before one of them. Stamped crudely into the metal of the cross the words 'Here lies a brave burgher'.

He moved along the line of crosses and on each he

read those same words. On some of them the printing was irregular, on one the 'r' in burgher had been replaced by a 'g'. Sean stopped and glared at it, hating the man who in his haste and unconcern had made the epitaph an insult.

'I'm sorry.' He spoke aloud, apologizing to the man who lay beneath it. Then he was embarrassed, angry at himself for the weakness. Only a madman speaks aloud to the dead. He strode away towards the second row of crosses.

'Leading Seaman W. Carter, R.N.' The fat one.

'Corporal Henderson C.F.S.' Twice in his chest and another in the belly.

He walked along the line and read their names. Some were just names, others he saw instantly and vividly. He saw them laughing, or frightened, saw the way they rode, remembered the sound of their voices. This one still owed him a guinea, he remembered the bet.

'Keep it.' He spoke and immediately checked himself again.

Slowly he went on to the end of the line, his momentum running down as he approached the grave that stood separate from the others – the way he had ordered it.

He read the inscription. Then he squatted down comfortably on his haunches beside it and stayed there until the sun settled and the wind turned cold and plaintive. Only then he went to his saddle and loosened the blanket-roll. There was no firewood and he slept fitfully in the cold of the night and the icier cold of his thoughts.

In the morning he went back to Saul's grave. For the first time he noticed that grass was growing up between the stones of the cairn and that the cross sagged a little to one side. He shrugged off his coat and went down on his knees, working like a gardener over the grave, weeding out the grass with his hunting knife, making certain the roots were removed. Then he went to the head and lifted the rocks away from around the cross. He tore the cross from the ground and re-dug the hole for it, setting it up again carefully, plugging the base with pebbles and earth and at last packing the whitewashed rocks firmly around it once more.

He stood back, brushed earth and flakes of whitewash from his hands and surveyed his handiwork. It still was not right, there was something missing. He thought about it, frowning heavily until he found the answer.

'Flowers,' he grunted and lifted his head towards the aloes on the kopje above him. He set off up the slope, picking his way through the litter of boulders towards the summit. His knife slipped easily through the soft thick stems and the juice oozed heavily from the wounds. With an armful he started back down the slope. Out to one side a patch of colour caught his eye, a sprinkling of pink and white among the boulders. He detoured towards it. Hottentot Daisies, each one a perfect trumpet with a pink throat and a fragile yellow tongue. Delighted with his find, Sean laid aside his burden of aloe blooms and went in amongst them. Stooping like a reaper he worked through them towards the lip of a narrow ravine, gathering the flowers into posies and binding the stems together with grass. Finally, he reached the ravine and straightened up to rest his aching back.

The ravine was narrow, he could have jumped across it with little effort – but it was deep. He peered down into it without much interest. The cleft was floored with rainwashed sand, and his interest quickened as he made out the half-buried bones of a large animal. But what made him climb down into the ravine was not the bones, but the bulky leather object entangled with them.

Sliding on his backside the last few feet of the descent

he reached the bottom, and examined his find. A leather mule-pack, double pouches, and the buckles of the harness almost rusted away. He tugged the whole lot loose from the sand and was surprised at the weight of it.

The leather was dry and brittle, faded almost white with exposure and the locks of the pouches were rusted solid. With his knife he slit the flap of one pouch and out of it cascaded a stream of sovereigns. They fell into the sand, clinking upon each other in a heap that glittered with merry golden smiles.

Sean stared at them in disbelief. He dropped the pack and squatted on his haunches over the pile. Timidly he picked up one of the discs and examined the portrait of the old President, before lifting the coin to his mouth and biting down upon it. His teeth sank into the soft metal and he removed it from his mouth.

'Well, damn me sideways,' he invited, and he laughed out loud. Rocking back on his haunches and lifting his face to the sky he roared out his jubilation and his relief. It went on and on until his laughter dried suddenly, and he sobered.

Cupping a double handful of the gold he asked it:

'Now, where the hell did you come from?' And his answer was in the grim face embossed upon each coin. Boer Gold.

'And who do you belong to?'

The answer was the same, and he let the coins trickle through his fingers. Boer Gold.

'The hell it is!' he growled angrily. 'Starting this minute it's Courtney Gold.' And he began to count it.

As his fingers worked so did his brain. He prepared his case against his own conscience, they owed him the balance outstanding on a train of wagons filled with ivory, they owed him his deposits in the Volkskaas Bank. They owed him for a shrapnel wound in the leg

454

and a bullet in the belly, they owed him for three years of hardship and danger, and they owed him for a friend. As he stacked the sovereigns into piles of twenty he considered his case, found it good and proven, justified it and gave judgement in his own favour.

'I find for the appellant,' he announced, and concentrated his whole attention on the counting. An hour and a half later he reached the total.

There was a huge pile of coins upon the flat rock he had used as a desk. He lit a cheroot and the smoke he drew into his lungs made him lightheaded. His conscience had surrendered unconditionally and in its place was a sense of well-being. All the more intense for the period of depression through which he had come.

'Sean Courtney accepts from the Government of the one-time Republic of the Transvaal an amount of twenty-nine thousand, two hundred pounds, in full discharge of all debts and claims.' He chuckled again and began shovelling the gold back into the leather pouches.

With the heavy pack slung over his shoulders and with his arms full of wild flowers, Sean went down the kopje. He saddled his horse and loaded the pack on to his mule before he went to pile the flowers on Saul's grave. They made a brave show of colour against the brown grass.

He lingered another hour, fussing over his floral arrangements and resisting the temptation to thank Saul. For now he had decided the gold was not a gift from the Republican Government – but from Saul Friedman. This made it even easier to accept.

At last he mounted and rode away. As the man and his horses dwindled into insignificance on the great brown plain, a dust devil came dancing up from the south. A tall, spinning column of heated air and dust and fragments of dry grass, it weaved and swayed towards the graveyard below the kopje. For a time it seemed as though it would pass wide of it, but suddenly it changed direction and dashed down upon the double row of crosses. It snatched up the flowers on Saul's grave, lifted them, ripped their petals and scattered them widely across the plain.

72

With Michael beside him lugging the carpet-bag which was the heaviest item of luggage, Sean left the buggy and crossed the side-walk into the offices of the Ladyburg Banking & Trust Co.

'Oh! Colonel Courtney,' the young lady at the reception desk enthused. 'I'll tell Mr Pye you are here.'

'Please don't bother. I'll carry the glad news myself.'

Ronny Pye looked up in alarm as the door of his office flew open and the two of them walked in.

'Good morning, Ronny,' Sean greeted him cheerfully. 'Have you bled any good stones today, or is it still too early?'

Guardedly Ronny murmured a reply and stood up.

Sean selected a cigar from the leather box on the desk and sniffed it.

'Not a bad line in horse-dung you've got here,' he remarked and bit the end off. 'Match please, Ronny, I'm a customer, where are your manners?'

Reluctantly, suspiciously, Ronny lit the cigar for him. Sean sat down and placed his feet on the desk with ankles neatly crossed.

'How much do I owe you?' he asked. The question heightened Ronny's suspicion and his eyes settled on the carpet-bag in Michael's hands.

'You mean altogether? Capital *and* interest?'

'Capital *and* interest,' Sean affirmed.

'Well, I'd have to work that out.'

'Give it to me in round figures.'

'Well, very roughly, you understand, it would be around – oh, I don't know – say . . . ' He paused. That carpet-bag looked confoundedly heavy. Its sides bulged and he could see the tension in Michael's arm muscles as he held it. 'Say, twenty-two thousand, eight hundred and sixteen pounds, fifteen shillings.' As he named the exact figure Ronny dropped his voice in veneration the way a primitive tribesman might invoke the name of his god.

Sean lowered his feet. Then he leant forward and swept the papers that covered the desk to one side.

'Very well. Pay the man, Michael.'

Solemnly Michael placed the bag in the cleared space. But when Sean winked at him his solemnity cracked and he grinned.

Making no attempt to hide his agitation, Ronny plunged both hands into the mouth of the bag and withdrew two pouches of unbleached canvas. He loosened the draw string of one and spilled gold on to his desk.

'Where did you get this?' he demanded angrily.

'At the end of the rainbow.'

'There's a fortune here,' Ronny protested, as he dipped into the carpet-bag again.

'A goodly amount, I'll admit.'

'But, but . . . ' Ronny was scratching in the pile of coins, hunting for the secret of their origin like a hen for a worm. However, Sean had spent a week in Johannesburg and another two days in Pietermaritzburg visiting every bank and exchanging small parcels of Kruger coin for Victorian and Portuguese, and the coin of half a dozen other States. For a minute Sean watched his efforts with a smile of happy contempt. Then he excused himself.

'We'll be getting on home now.' Sean placed an arm around Michael's shoulder and led him to the door.

'Deposit the balance to my account, there's a good fellow.'

Further protest stillborn on his lips, and despair mingled with frustration, Ronny Pye watched through the window as Lion Kop Wattle Estates climbed up into the buggy, settled its hat firmly, waved a whip in a courteous farewell and trotted sedately out of his clutches.

All that summer the hills of Lion Kop echoed to the thud of axes and the singing of hundreds of Zulus. At each tree toppled and fell in a froth of heaving branches, men with cane-knives moved forward to strip the rich bark and tie it in bundles. Every train that left for Pietermaritzburg towed truckloads of it to the extract plant.

Each long day together strengthened the bonds between Sean and Michael. They evolved a language of their own, notable only for its economy of words. Without lengthy discussion each took charge of a separate sphere of Lion Kop activity. Michael made himself responsible for the maintenance of equipment, the loading and dispatch, all the paperwork and the ordering of material. At first Sean surreptitiously checked his work, but when he found no fault in it he no longer bothered. They parted only at the end of each week; Sean to Pietermaritzburg for obvious reasons, and Michael to Theuniskraal in duty. Michael hated those returns home, he hated Anna's endless accusations of disloyalty and her occasional fits of weeping. But even worse was the silent reproach in Garry's face. Early each Monday morning, with the joy of a released convict he set off for Lion Kop and Sean's welcome:

'What about those bloody axe handles, Mike?'

Only in the evenings they talked freely sitting

together on the stoep of the homestead. They spoke of money and war and politics and women and wattle – and they talked as equals, without reserve, as men who work together with a common purpose.

Dirk sat quietly in the shadows and listened to them. Fifteen years old, but Dirk had a capacity for hatred out of all proportion to his age, and he used it all on Michael. Sean's handling of Dirk was in no way different; his school attendance was still spasmodic, he trailed Sean about the plantations and received his full share of rough affection and even rougher discipline – yet he sensed in the relationship between Sean and Michael a terrible threat to his security. Merely by reason of age and experience he was excluded from the evening discussions on the stoep. His few contributions were received with indulgent attention, then the talk would be resumed as though he had not spoken. Dirk sat quietly planning in lurid detail his assassination of Michael. On Lion Kop that summer there were small thefts and unexplained acts of vandalism, all of which affected only Michael. His best riding-boots vanished, his single dress shirt was ripped down the back when he came to don it for the monthly dance at the schoolhouse, his pointer bitch whelped a litter of four puppies, which survived only a week before Michael found them dead in the straw of the barn.

Ada and her young ladies began preparing for the Christmas of 1904 in the middle of December. As their guests, Ruth and Storm came down from Pietermaritzburg on the twentieth and Sean's frequent absences from Lion Kop left a heavy burden of work on Michael. There was an air of mystery in the Protea Street cottage. Sean was strictly excluded from the long sessions in Ada's private rooms, where she and Ruth retired to plan the wedding dress, but this was not the only secret. There was something else, which was keeping all the young ladies in fits of suppressed giggles and excitement. With a little eavesdropping Sean gathered it was something to do with his Christmas present from Ruth. However, Sean had other worries, chief of which was maintaining his position in the fierce competition for Miss Storm Friedman's favours. This included a heavy expenditure on sweetmeats, which were delivered to Storm without Ruth's knowledge. The Shetland pony had been left in Pietermaritzburg and Sean was required to substitute at the cost of his dignity and grass stains on the knees of his breeches. As reward he was invited to take tea each afternoon with Storm and her dolls.

Favourite among all Storm's dolls was a female child with human hair and an insipid expression on its large china face. Storm wept with a broken heart when she found that china head shattered into many pieces. With Sean's help she buried it in the back yard and they stripped Ada's garden of flowers for the grave. Sullenly Dirk watched the funeral. Storm was now completely reconciled to her loss and so thoroughly enjoyed the ceremony that she insisted Sean exhume the body and start again. In all the doll was buried four times and Ada's garden looked as though a swarm of locusts had descended upon it.

73

Christmas Day started early for Sean. He and Michael
supervised the slaughter of ten large oxen for the Zulu
labour force, then distributed pay and gifts. To each man
a khaki shirt and short pants, and for each of their wives
a double handful of coloured beads. There was much
singing and laughter. Mbejane, risen from his sickbed for
the occasion, made a speech of high dramatic content.
Unable to prance on his freshly healed legs, yet he shook
his spears, postured and roared his questions at them.

'Has he beaten you?'

'*Ai-bho!*' They hurled the negative back at him.

'Has he fed you?'

'*Yhe-bho!*' explosive accent.

'Is there gold in your pockets?'

'*Yhe-bho!*'

'Is he our father?'

'He is our father!'

All to be construed not too literally, Sean grinned.
Then he stepped forward to accept the large earthenpot
of millet beer that Mbejane's senior wife presented to
him. It was a matter of honour that this be emptied
without removing it from the lips, a feat which Sean and
then Michael both accomplished. Then they climbed up
into the waiting buggy, Mbejane took the reins and with
Dirk on the seat beside him drove them down to Ladyburg.

After the first flurry of greeting and good wishes, Ruth
led Sean into the back yard followed by everyone else.

There stood a large object covered by a tarpaulin which was ceremoniously removed and Sean gaped at what Ruth had given him.

Its paintwork burnished to a high gloss, metal parts and polished leather upholstery sparkling in the sun – stood a motor vehicle.

Stamped in the huge metal wheel hubs, and below the mascot on the radiator were the words 'Rolls-Royce'.

Sean had seen these fiendishly beautiful machines in Johannesburg, and now he was overcome by the feeling of unease they had given him then.

'My dear Ruth, I haven't the words to thank you.' He kissed her heartily to delay the moment when he must approach the monster.

'Do you really like it?'

'Like it? It's the most magnificent thing I have ever seen.' Over her shoulder Sean noticed with relief that Michael had taken over. As the only engineer present, he was seated behind the wheel and speaking authoritatively to the crowd about him.

'Get in!' Ruth ordered.

'Let me look at it first.' With Ruth on his arm, Sean circled the Rolls, never approaching closer than half a dozen paces. The great headlights glared at him malevolently and Sean averted his eyes. His unease was slowly becoming genuine fear as he realized that he was expected not only to ride in the thing, but to direct its course and speed.

Unable to delay longer, he approached and patted the bonnet.

'Hey there!' he told it grimly. With an unbroken animal you must establish mastery from the first contact.

'Get in!' Michael was still in charge and Sean obeyed, placing Ruth in the middle of the front seat and himself

463

nearest the door. On Ruth's lap Storm bounded and squealed with excitement. The delay while Michael consulted the handbook at length did nothing for Sean's confidence.

'Ruth, don't you think it wise to leave Storm behind – just this first time?'

'Oh, she isn't any trouble.' Ruth regarded him quizzically, then smiled. 'It's really quite safe, darling.' Despite her assurance, Sean stiffened in terror when the motor finally roared into life; and he held that pose, staring fixedly ahead, during the whole of their triumphal progress through the streets of Ladyburg. Citizens and servants boiled from the houses along their route and lined the road to cheer in wonder and delight.

At last they were back in Protea Street and when Michael stopped outside the cottage Sean escaped from the vehicle like a man waking from a nightmare. He firmly vetoed the suggestion that the family motor to church, on the grounds that it was irreverent and in bad taste. The Reverend Smiley was flattered that Sean remained awake throughout his sermon, and judged by Sean's worried expression that at last he was in fear for his soul.

After church Michael went out to Theuniskraal to eat Christmas dinner with his parents, but returned early in the afternoon to begin Sean's instruction. The entire population of Ladyburg turned out to watch Sean and Michael circling the block at a walking pace. By early evening Michael decided that Sean was ready for a solo circuit and accordingly he disembarked.

Alone at the wheel, sweating nervously, Sean looked at the sea of expectant faces around him and saw Mbejane grinning hugely in the background.

'Mbejane!' he bellowed.

'Nkosi!'

'Come with me,' and Mbejane's grin dissolved. He backed away a little. It was unnatural that a vehicle should move of its own accord – and Mbejane wanted no part of it.

'Nkosi, there is much pain still in my legs.'

Among the crowd were many of the Zulu labourers from Lion Kop, who had come down from the hills when news of the miracle reached them. Now one of these laughed in such a manner as to cast doubt on Mbejane's courage. Mbejane drew himself to his full height and withered the man with his eyes, then he stalked proudly to the Rolls, sat on the seat beside Sean and folded his arms across his chest.

Sean drew a deep breath and gripped the steering-wheel with both hands, his eyes narrowed and he scowled ahead down the road.

'Clutch in!' he muttered to himself. 'In gear! Brake off! Throttle down! Clutch out!'

The Rolls leapt forward so violently that both he and Mbejane were nearly thrown over the back of the seat. Fifty yards farther on the machine expired from lack of fuel, a stroke of good fortune because it was unlikely that Sean would have been able to remember the procedure for stopping it.

Grey of face and unsteady of limb, Mbejane alighted from the Rolls for the last time. He never rode in it again – and secretly Sean envied him his freedom. He was greatly relieved to hear that it would be weeks before more fuel could be sent up from Cape Town.

74

Three weeks before Sean's wedding Ada Courtney went into her orchard one morning early to pick fruit for breakfast. She found Mary there, dressed in her white nightgown, and hanging by her neck from the big avocado tree. Ada cut her down and sent one of the servants to call Doctor Fraser.

Between them they carried the dead girl to her cubicle and laid her on her bed. While Doc Fraser made a hasty examination Ada stood staring down at the face that death had made more pitiful.

'What depths of loneliness drove her to this,' she whispered, and Doc Fraser pulled the sheet over the corpse and looked across at Ada.

'That wasn't the reason – in fact, it might have been better if she were a little more lonely.' He pulled out his tobacco pouch and began to load his pipe. 'Who was her boy friend, Aunt Ada?'

'She had none.'

'She must have.'

'Why do you say that?'

'Aunt Ada, this girl was four months pregnant.'

It was a small funeral, just the Courtney family and Ada's girls. Mary was an orphan and she had no other friends.

Two weeks before the wedding, Sean and Michael

finished the season's cut of bark and switched the Zulus to planting out the blocks destroyed by the fire. Together they drew up a draft Profit and Loss Account. Combining their rudimentary knowledge of accounting and arguing far into the night, they finally agreed that from fifteen hundred acres of wattle they had cut fourteen hundred and twenty tons of bark, to gross a little over twenty-eight thousand pounds sterling.

But here all agreement ended. Michael insisted that the stocks of material and expenditure on planting of new trees be carried forward, giving a net profit for the year of nine thousand pounds. Sean wanted to write all expenditure off against income and show a profit of one thousand, so they deadlocked and finally sent all the books to a qualified accountant in Pietermaritzburg. This gentleman sided with Michael.

They then considered the prospects for the coming season and were a little awed when they realized that there would be four thousand acres of wattle to reap and an expected gross of eighty thousand pounds sterling – always providing there were no more fires. That evening, without Sean's knowledge, Michael wrote two letters. One to a manufacturer of heavy machinery in Birmingham, whose name and address Michael had furtively copied from one of the huge boilers in the Natal Wattle Estate Company's plant. The other to the firm of Foyle's booksellers in Charing Cross Road, London, requesting the immediate dispatch of all and any literature on the processing of wattle bark. Michael Courtney had caught from Sean the habit of dreaming extravagantly. He had also acquired the trick of setting out to make those dreams become reality.

*

Three days before the wedding Ada and her young ladies set out for Pietermaritzburg by train and Sean, Michael and Dirk followed in the Rolls.

The three of them arrived dusty and bad-tempered outside the White Horse Hotel. It had been a nerve-racking journey. Sean had enlivened it by shouting incessant warnings, instruction and blasphemy at Michael, the driver.

'Slow down, for God's sake, slow down! Do you want to kill us all!'

'Look out! Watch that cow!'

'Don't drive so close to the verge!'

Dirk had done his share by demanding halts for urination, hanging over the sides, climbing tirelessly between the front and back seats and urging Michael to exceed the speed-limit set by Sean. Finally, in anger, Sean had Michael stop the car and administered corporal punishment with the birch of a melkbos tree cut from beside the road.

On arrival Dirk was met by Ada, and led away snivelling. Michael took the Rolls and disappeared in the direction of the Natal Wattle Company's plant, where he was to spend most of the following three days snooping and asking questions, and Sean went to find Jan Paulus Leroux, who had come down from Pretoria in response to Sean's wedding invitation. By the day of the wedding Michael Courtney had compiled a small volume of notes on wattle processing, and Jan Paulus had given Sean a minute account of the aims and objects of the South African Party. But in response to his urgings Sean had promised only to 'think about it'.

The wedding ceremony had given everybody much cause for thought. Although Sean had no qualms about marrying in a synagogue, yet he steadfastly refused to undergo the painful little operation which would enable him to do so. His half-hearted suggestion that Ruth should convert to Christianity was met with a curt rejection. Finally, a compromise was agreed, and Ben Goldberg persuaded the local Magistrate to perform a civil ceremony in the dining-room of The Golds.

Ben Goldberg gave the bride away and Ma Goldberg wept a little. Ruth was magnificent in Ada's creation of green satin and seed pearls. Storm wore an exact miniature of Ruth's dress and sparked off a minor brawl with the other flower girls during the ceremony. Michael as Best Man conducted himself with aplomb. He quelled the riot among the flower girls, produced the wedding ring on cue and prompted the groom when he muffed his lines.

The reception on the lawns was attended by a huge crowd of the Goldbergs' friends and business associates and by half the population of Ladyburg, including Ronny Pye, Dennis Petersen and their families. Garrick and Anna Courtney were not there, nor had they acknowledged the invitation.

Brilliant sunshine blessed the day and the lawns were smooth and green as expensive carpets. There were long trestle tables laden with the fruits of Ma Goldberg's kitchen and the products of Ben Goldberg's brewery.

Storm Friedman went from group to group of guests, boosting up her skirts to display the pink ribbons in her pantaloons, until Ruth caught her at it.

Having found his first taste of champagne very much to his liking, Dirk went on to drink six glasses of it behind the rose bushes. He was then copiously ill. Fortunately Michael found him before Sean did, and spirited him away to one of the guest bedrooms and left him there to languish.

With Ruth on his arm, Sean inspected the display of wedding gifts and was impressed. He then circulated among the crowds on the lawn until he reached Jan Paulus and fell into an earnest political discussion. Ruth left them to it and went to change into her going-away clothes.

The prettiest and most blonde of Ada's young ladies caught the bouquet. Immediately thereafter she caught Michael's eye and blushed to match the crimson carnations in her hand.

Amid a hum of appreciative comment and a snowstorm of confetti Ruth returned and, a queen ascending the throne, took her seat in the Rolls. Beside her Sean, in dustcoat and goggles, steeled himself, muttered his usual incantations and gave the Rolls its head. Like a wild horse the machine seemed to rear on its hind wheels and then tear down the driveway scattering gravel and guests. Ruth clutching desperately at a large hatful of ostrich feathers and Sean shouting at the Rolls to 'Whoa! There, girl,' – they headed out along the road that led through the Valley of a Thousand Hills to Durban and the sea, and disappeared in a tall column of dust.

75

Three months later, having picked up Storm from Ma Goldberg *en passant*, they reappeared at Lion Kop homestead. Sean had put on weight and both of them had that smugly complacent look found only in the faces of couples returning from a successful honeymoon.

On the front stoep and in the outbuildings of Lion Kop were the crates and packing-cases which contained wedding gifts, Ruth's furniture and carpets, and the additional furniture and curtains they had purchased in Durban. Ruth, ably assisted by Ada, threw herself joyously into the task of unpacking and moving in. Meanwhile Sean began a tour of inspection of the estate to determine how much of it had suffered in his absence, and he felt vaguely cheated when he found that Michael had managed very well without him. The plantations were trim and cleared of undergrowth, the vast black scar through their centre was nearly obliterated with freshly planted rows of saplings, the labour force was half as productive again under the new incentive payment scheme which Michael, in consultation with the Accountant, had introduced. Sean gave Michael a lecture on 'not getting too bloody clever' and 'learning to walk before you run' which he ended with a few words of praise.

Thus encouraged, Michael approached Sean one night when he was alone in his study. Sean was in a state of deep contentment induced by a meal from an enormous roast sirloin which he was digesting, by the fact that

Ruth had finally agreed to his adoption of Storm and the change of her name from Friedman to Courtney, and by the prospect of joining Ruth in their gargantuan double bed just as soon as he finished his brandy and his hand-rolled Havana cigar.

'Come in, Michael. Sit down. Have a brandy.' Sean greeted him genially, and almost defiantly Michael crossed the Persian carpet and laid a thick sheaf of papers on the desk in front of him.

'What's this all about?' Sean smiled at him.

'Read it and you'll see.' Michael retreated to a chair across the room. Still smiling Sean glanced at the heading on the top sheet.

'Preliminary estimates and ground plan for proposed Tannin Extraction Plant. Lion Kop Estates.'

The smile faded. Sean turned the page and as he read he began to frown and then to scowl. When at last he finished he relit his dead cigar and sat in silence for five minutes while he recovered from the shock.

'Who put you up to this?'

'Nobody.'

'Where would you sell your extract?'

'Page 5. The outlets are listed there – and the ruling prices over the last ten years.'

'This plants needs 20,000 tons of bark a year – if we planted every foot of Lion Kop and Mahobo's Kloof to wattle we could only supply half of that.'

'We'd buy the rest from the new estates along the valley – we could offer a better price than Jackson, because we'd save railage to Pietermaritzburg.'

'Who would run the plant?'

'I'm an engineer.'

'On paper you are,' Sean grunted. 'What about water?'

'We'd damn, the Baboon Stroom above the falls.'

For an hour Sean poked and prodded at the scheme,

472

seeking for a soft spot. His agitation mounted as Michael calmly met each of his queries.

'All right,' Sean growled. 'You've done your homework. Now answer me this one. How the hell do you propose finding seventy thousand pounds to finance this little lot?'

Michael closed his eyes as though he were praying, his jaw was a hard, thrusting line. And suddenly Sean wondered why he had never noticed the strength in that face, the stubborn almost fanatical determination. Michael opened his eyes again and spoke softly.

'A loan on Lion Kop and Mahobo's Kloof for twenty-five thousand, a notarial bond on the plant for as much again – and a public share issue on the balance.'

Sean jumped up from his desk and roared.

'No!'

'Why not?' still calmly and reasonably.

'Because I've spent half my life in debt up to here!' Sean grabbed his own throat. 'Because now at last I'm in the clear and I want to stay that way. Because I know what it feels like to have more money than I need, and I don't like the feeling. Because I'm happy just the way things are now – and I don't want to catch another lion by the tail and have him turn round and claw the hell out of me.' He stopped panting and then shouted: 'Because a certain amount of money belongs to you, but more than that you belong to it. Because I don't want to be that wealthy again!'

Lean and fast as an angry leopard, Michael came out of his chair and smashed a balled fist on to the top of the desk. He glared across at Sean, flushed angry red under his tan, quivering like an arrow.

'Well, I do! Your only objection to my plan is that it's sound,' he blazed. Sean blinked in surprise and then rallied.

473

'If you get it, you won't like it!' he bellowed, and Michael matched his volume.

'Let me be the judge of that!'

At that moment the door of the study opened and Ruth stood on the threshold and stared at them. They looked like a pair of game cocks with their hackles up.

'What on earth is going on?' she demanded. Both Michael and Sean looked up guiltily, then slowly they relaxed. Michael sat down and Sean coughed awkwardly.

'We are just having a discussion, my dear.'

'Well, you've woken Storm and just about torn the roof off.' Then she smiled and crossed to take Sean's arm. 'Why don't you leave it until tomorrow. Then you can continue your discussion at twenty paces with pistols.'

The pygmies of the Ituri Forests hunt elephant with tiny arrows. Once the barb is lodged they follow quietly and doggedly, camping night after night on the spoor until at last the poison works its way to the animal's heart and brings it down. Michael had placed his arrowhead deep in Sean's flesh.

76

At Lion Kop Ruth found a happiness she had never expected, had not believed existed.

Up to this time her existence had been ordered and determined by an adoring but strict father, and then in the same manner by Ben Goldberg. The few short years with Saul Friedman had been happy, but now they were as unreal as memories of childhood. Always she had been wrapped in a cocoon of wealth, hemmed in by social taboos and the dignity of the family. Even Saul had treated her as a delicate child for whom all decisions must be made. Life had been placid and orderly, but deadly dull. Only twice she had rebelled, once to run away from Pretoria and again when she had gone to Sean in the hospital. Boredom had been her constant companion.

But now suddenly she was mistress of a complex community. The sensation had been a little overpowering at first and from habit she had appealed to Sean for him to make the fifty decisions that each day brought forward.

'I'll make a bargain with you,' he answered. 'You don't tell me how to grow wattle and I'll not tell you how to run the house – put the damn sideboard where it looks best.'

Hesitantly at first, then with growing confidence and at last with sureness and pride she made Lion Kop into a home of beauty and comfort. The coarse grass and scrub around the homestead fell back to make room for lawns and flower-beds, the outer walls of Lion Kop gleamed in a crisp new coat of whitewash. Inside, the yellow-wood floors shone like polished amber setting off the vivid Bokhara carpets and draped velvet curtains.

After a few disastrous experiments the kitchens began to yield a succession of meals that moved Michael to raptures, and even Sean pronounced them edible.

Yet, with a dozen servants, she had time for other things. To read, to play with Storm and to ride. Sean's wedding gift to her was a string of four golden palaminos. There was time also for long visits from and with Ada Courtney. The two of them established an accord stronger than that of mother and daughter.

There was time for dancing and barbecues, there was time for laughter and for long quiet evenings when she and Sean sat alone on the wide front stoep or in his study and talked of many things.

There was time for love.

Her body, hard from riding and walking, was also healthy and hot. It was a sculpture sheathed in velvet and fashioned for love.

There was only one dark place in her happiness – Dirk Courtney.

When her overtures were met with sullenness and her small specially cooked gifts were rejected, she realized the cause of his antagonism. She sensed the bitter jealousy which was eating like a canker behind those lovely eyes and the passssionately beautiful face. For days she prepared what she would say to him. The she found the opportunity when he came into the kitchens while she was alone. He saw her and turned quickly to leave, but she stopped him.

'Oh, Dirk, please don't go. I want to discuss something with you.' He came back slowly and leaned against the table. She saw how tall he had grown in the last year, his shoulders were thickening into the shape of manhood and his legs were strong and tapered from the narrow hips that he thrust forward in a calculated insolence.

'Dirk ... ' she began and paused. Suddenly she was unsure of herself. This was not a child as she had imagined; there was a sensuality in that beautiful face she found disturbing – he carried his body with awareness, moving like a cat. Suddenly she was afraid, and she swallowed jerkily before she went on:

'I know how difficult it has been for you – since Storm and I came to live here. I know how much you love your father, how much he means to you. But ... ' She spoke slowly, her carefully prepared speech forgotten so that she had to grope for the words to explain. She tried to show him that they were not in competition for Sean's love; that all of them – Ruth, Michael, Storm and Dirk – formed a whole; that their interests did not overlap, but that each of them gave to Sean and received from him a different kind of love. When at last she faltered into silence she knew he had not listened nor tried to understand. 'Dirk, I like you and I want you to like me.'

With a thrust of his buttocks against the table, Dirk straightened up. He smiled then and let his eyes move down over her body, slowly.

'Can I go now?' he asked, and Ruth stiffened. Then she knew there was no compromise, that she would have to fight him.

'Yes, Dirk. You may go,' she answered. She knew with sudden clarity that he was evil, and if she lost this contest he would destroy her and her child. In that moment she was no longer afraid.

Catlike, Dirk seemed to sense the change in her. For a moment she thought she saw a flicker of doubt, of uncertainty in his eyes – then he turned away and sauntered out of the kitchen.

She guessed that it would come soon, but not as soon as it did.

Every afternoon Ruth would ride out into the plantations with Storm's pony on a lead rein beside her. They made a game of finding Sean and Michael, following the labyrinth of roads that criss-crossed through the blocks of trees, guided by the vague directions of the gangs of Zulus until finally they ran them down and delivered the canteens of coffee and the hamper of sandwiches. Then, all four of them would picnic on the soft carpet of dead leaves beneath the trees.

This afternoon, dressed in riding habit and carrying the hamper, Ruth came out into the kitchen yard. The young Zulu nursemaid was sitting in the shade of the kitchen wall flirting with one of the groms. Storm was nowhere in sight, and Ruth asked sharply:

'Where is Miss Storm?'

'She went with Nkosana Dirk.' And Ruth felt the tingling premonition of danger.

'Where are they?' and the nursemaid pointed vaguely in the direction of the stables and outbuildings that sprawled away down the back slope of the hill.

'Come with me.' Ruth dropped the hamper and ran with her skirts gathered in one hand. She reached the first row of stables and hurried down them, glancing into each stall as she passed. Then into the feed rooms with the big concrete bins and the smell of oats and molasses and chopped lucerne mixing with the sharp tang of dung and dubbined leather, out again into the sunlight, running for the barns.

Storm screamed in terror, just once, but high and achingly clear, so the silence afterwards quivered with the memory of it.

478

The harness room. Ruth swirled in her run. *God, please No! Don't let it happen. Please! Please!*

She reached the open door of the harness room. It was gloomy and cool within the thick stone walls, anf for a moment the scene made no sense to Ruth.

Her back wedged into the far corner, Storm stood with hands lifted to shield her face – small fingers rigid, splayed open, spread like the tip feathers of a bird's wing. Her body shook silently with her sobs.

In front of Storm, squatting on his heels, Dirk leaned forward with one hand outstretched as though he offered a gift. He was laughing.

Then Ruth saw the thing in Dirk's hand move and she froze with horror. It uncoiled from around his wrist, and slowly reached out towards Storm, its head cocked back in a half-loop of its body, tiny black tongue vibrating between the grinning pink lips.

Ruth screamed, and Dirk jumped to his feet and spun to face her with his right hand hidden behind his back.

From the corner Storm darted across the room and buried her face in Ruth's skirts, weeping piteously. Ruth picked her up and held her tight against her shoulder, but she never took her eyes off Dirk's face.

'It's only a *rooi-slang*.' Dirk laughed again, but nervously. 'They're harmless – I was only having a joke.' He brought the snake out from behind his back, dropped it on to the stone-flagged floor and crushed its head under the heel of his riding-boot. He kicked it away against the wall, then with an impatient gesture he brushed the black curls from his forehead and made to leave the room. Ruth stepped across to block his path.

'Nannie, take Miss Storm back to the house.' Gently Ruth handed the child to the Zulu nursemaid and closed the door after them and slid the bolt across.

Now it was darker in the room, two square shafts of

sunlight filled with moving dust motes fell from the high windows, and the quiet was spoiled only by the sound of Ruth's laboured breathing.

'I was only having a joke,' Dirk repeated, and grinned defiance at her. 'I suppose you'll run and tell my father?'

The walls of the room were studded with wooden pegs from which were suspended the harness and saddlery. Beside the door hung Sean's raw-hide stockwhips, eight foot of braided leather tapering from the butt handle into nothingness. Ruth lifted one down from the rack and flicked the lash out to lie upon the floor between them.

'No, Dirk, I'm not going to tell your father. This thing is between you and me alone.'

'What are you going to do?'

'I'm going to settle it.'

'How?' Still grinning, he placed his hands on his hips. Beneath rolled sleeves his upper arms bulged smooth and brown as though they had been freshly oiled.

'Like this.' Ruth flicked her skirt aside and stepped forward, using the whip underhand she sent the lash snaking out to coil around Dirk's ankle and immediately she jerked back on it. Taken completely off balance, Dirk went over backwards. His head hit the wall as he fell and he lay stunned.

To give herself space in which to wield the whip, Ruth moved into the centre of the room. Her anger was cold as dry ice, it gave strength to arms already finely muscled from riding, and it seared away all mercy. Now she was a female animal fighting for the survival of herself and her child.

She had learned to use a stockwhip in the process of becoming an expert horsewoman, and her first blow split Dirk's shirt from the shoulder to the waist. He shouted with anger and rolled on to his knees. The next blow cut down from the base of his neck along his spine, paralysing him in the act of rising. The next, across the back of both knees, knocked his legs out from under him.

On his belly Dirk reached for the pitchfork against the wall, but braided leather exploded around his wrist. He shouted again and rolled on his side to nurse the hand against his chest.

Ruth hit him and he writhed across the floor towards her like a wounded leopard with its hindquarters shattered by buckshot. Step by step Ruth retreated before him, and the long lash hissed and cracked.

Without mercy she beat him until his shirt hung in tatters from his waist and shoulders, exposing the smooth white skin with the fat crimson welts superimposed upon it.

She beat him until his shouts turned to shrieks and finally to sobbing.

She beat him until he lay shivering, moaning, moving feebly with his blood sprinkled in dark blobs on the stone paving around him.

Then she folded the whip and turned to open the door. In the stable yard, standing in silent curiosity, were gathered all the grooms and the household servants.

Ruth selected four of them.

'Take the Nkosana to his room.'

Then to one of the grooms,

'Ride to the Nkosi. Tell him to come quickly.'

Sean came quickly; he came wild with anxiety and nearly tore the door off Dirk's bedroom in his haste. He stopped dead on the threshold and stared aghast at Dirk's back.

Stripped to the waist, Dirk lay face downwards on his bed and Ruth worked over him with a sponge. On the table beside her stood a steaming basin and the pungent reek of antiseptic filled the room.

'Good God! What happened to him?'

'I beat him with a stockwhip.' Ruth answered him calmly and Sean gaped at her, then dropped his gaze to Dirk.

'You did that?'

'Yes.'

The anger tightened Sean's mouth.

'Jesus God! You've cut him to pieces. You've half killed him.' And he glanced at Ruth. 'Why?'

'It was necessary.' The absolute assurance and lack of remorse in her reply, confused Sean. He was suddenly uncertain in his anger.

'What did he do?'

'I can't tell you that. It is something private between us. You must ask Dirk.'

Sean crossed quickly to the bed and knelt beside it.

'Dirk. Dirkie, my boy, what happened. What did you do?' And Dirk lifted his face from the pillow and looked at his father.

'It was a mistake. It doesn't matter.' Then he buried his face in the pillow once more, and his voice was muffled, so Sean had excuse for not believing that he had heard correctly.

'What did you say?' he demanded, and there was a short delay before Dirk replied quite distinctly,

'I said – it was my fault.'

'That's what I thought you said.' Sean stood up with a puzzled expression on his face. 'Well, I don't know why you sent for me, Ruth. You seem to have the situation fairly well in hand.' He moved to the door, looked back as though he were going to speak, then, changing his mind, he shook his head and went out.

That night in the quiet, exhausted minutes before sleep, Sean murmured against her cheek, 'I think you did today what I should have done years ago.' and then, with a sleepy chuckle, 'At least there's no doubt in anyone's mind as to who is the mistress of Lion Kop.'

77

There was a guileless simplicity in Sean's approach to life – in his mind any problem when met with direct action disintegrated.

If you became obsessed with a woman, you tumbled her. If that didn't produce the desired effect, then you married her.

If you wanted a piece of land or a horse or a house or a gold mine, then you paid your money and took it. If you didn't have the money, you went out and found it.

If you liked a man you drank with him, hunted with him, laughed together. If you disliked him, you either punched him in the head or subjected him to a ponderous sarcasm and mockery. Either way you left him in no doubt of your feelings.

When a son got out of hand you whaled the tripe out of him, then gave him an expensive present to demonstrate your affection. Now he admitted he had been tardy in the matter of Dirk; but Ruth had done a most effective job. It only remained for him to call Dirk into the study and shout at him a little. A week later he returned from a trip to Pietermaritzburg and with an embarrassed scowl presented to Dirk his peace offerings. The first was a brass-bound leather case, which contained a handmade shotgun by Greener of London; tooled silver inlay, glossy walnut stock and butt, and interchangeable Damascus barrels. The other was a two-year-old filly from the Huguenot stud at Worcester in the Cape. By Sun Lord out of Harvest Dance, Sun Dancer was an animal of the most distinguished blood in Africa and of surpassing beauty and speed. Sean paid a thousand guineas for her and considered he had got the best of the bargain.

As far as he was concerned there was no longer any problem with Dirk, and Sean could devote all his energy to furthering the three major ventures in which he was engaged.

Firstly, there was the matter of putting Ruth with child. Here he had her wholehearted co-operation. But their efforts, apart from providing a deal of healthy exercise and pleasure, were singularly unproductive. Sean remembered the deadly skill he had shown in their first encounter and was puzzled. Ruth suggested they keep in training until the rainy season began; she had developed a superstitious belief in the power of thunder. On one of his trips to Pietermaritzburg Sean saw a carved wooden statue of Thor in a junk dealer's window. He bought it for her, and from then on the god stood on their bedside table clutching his hammer and overlooking their strivings with such a knowing expression that at last Ruth turned him face to the wall.

Then there was Michael's Tannin Extract Plant. He had resorted to a piece of underhand villainy that shocked Sean and, he professed, killed his belief in the essential decency of mankind. Michael had visited each of the new growers along the valley, men who had followed Sean's lead in the planting of wattle, and after swearing them to secrecy had offered them shares in the Company. They were enthusiastic and with Michael at the head they visited Lion Kop in formal deputation. The meeting was conducted with so much verbal thunder and lightning thrown about that the Great God Thor might have been in the Chair. At the end Sean, who had teased the idea all the months since Michael had approached him and who was now as enthusiastic as

485

any of them, allowed himself to be persuaded. He spoke for seventy per cent of the shares and the balance was allotted to the other growers. A Board of Directors, with Sean as Chairman, was elected and the Accountant was instructed to proceed with the registration of The Ladyburg Wattle Co-operative Ltd. For the first time Sean exercised his majority vote to crush the misgivings of the other shareholders and appoint Michael Courtney as Plant Engineer. Then, with an older director to act as a steadying influence, Michael was put aboard the next Union Castle mailship for England, a letter of authority in his pocket and Sean's warnings and words of wisdom in his head. Remembering himself at the age of twenty-three, Sean decided it necessary to point out to Michael that he was being sent to London to buy machinery and increase his knowledge of it, not to populate the British Isles nor to tour their hostelries and gaming establishments.

There was swift reaction from Jackson at Natal Wattle, who regretted that the contracts between the Tugela Valley growers and his company would not be renewed – and that owing to heavy demands from elsewhere he could no longer supply seed or saplings. But Sean's seedbeds were now well enough established to meet the needs of the whole valley – and, with luck, their plant would be in production by the beginning of the next cutting season.

Before Michael and his chaperon returned flushed with the success of their mission, Sean had another visitor. Jan Paulus Leroux, weary of the three-year argument he and Sean had conducted with the aid of the postal authority, arrived at Ladyburg and expressed his intention of staying until Sean agreed to head the Natal branch of the South African Party and to contest the Ladyburg seat at the next Legislative Assembly elections. Two weeks later, after he and Sean had hunted and killed a number of guinea-fowl, pheasant and bush buck; had consumed huge quantities of coffee and more moderate quantities of brandy; had talked each other hoarse and had closed the last gap between them, Jan Paulus left on the Johannesburg train with the parting words:

'*Toe Maar!* It is settled then.'

The South African Party's platform was a Federation of the Cape, the Transvaal, the Orange Free State and Natal, under government responsible to Whitehall. It was opposed by extreme English and Dutch opinion – the jingoes who shouted 'God Save the King', and the Republicans who wanted the Almighty to treat the King differently.

After meeting with the men on the list Jan Paulus had given him, Sean began the campaign. His first convert was Ruth Courtney, won over by the prospect of the excitement associated with an election battle rather than by Sean's oratory. Now a week or more of every month was spent in travelling about Natal to attend political gatherings. Ruth rehearsed Sean in his speech – he had only one – until he was word perfect. She kissed the babies and played hostess to the wives, tasks in which Sean showed no special aptitude. She sat beside him on the platform and restrained him from going down into the audience to engage in hand-to-hand combat with hecklers. The way she smiled and the way she walked certainly lost no votes for the South African Party. From London Lord Caisterbrook promised his support, and it looked as though Sean could count on twenty-two seats out of the Assembly's thirty.

*

On the level ground below the escarpment, hard by the Baboon Stroom, the plant of the Ladyburg Wattle Co-operative took shape. It covered ten acres of ground and beyond it the cottages of the employees were laid out in neat blocks.

Despite Michael's vehement protests, Sean bowed to the will of his fellow directors and a consulting engineer was employed until such time as the plant was in production. Without him they would have lost a year's harvest of bark, for although Michael was eager and tireless, yet he was a young man with no practical experience. Even with the older man to help him, the plant was still a long way from ready before the season's cutting began. When at last the tall silver smoke stack began spewing smoke and the furnaces lit the night with a satanic glow, there were thousands of tons of bark piled up in the open-sided warehouses around the factory.

It was a wonderful season. Good rains had filled the bark with rich sap and when the year ended the Co-operative had shown a profit of ten thousand pounds on its first year's operation – Lion Kop Estates a profit four times greater. Sean had been in and out of debt as swiftly as a small boy visits the bathroom when sent to wash his face.

Despite the good rains, there were only three spectacular storms that summer. On each occasion Sean was away from Lion Kop on business. While the lightning leapt across the hills and the hammer strokes of thunder broke over the valley, Ruth stood at the window of their bedroom and lamented another wasted opportunity. Mbejane did much better – all his seed brought forth fruit and he reaped four fat sons that season.

78

It was a busy year for Dirk Courtney also. After his resounding defeat at the thin end of the stockwhip, Dirk and Ruth fell into a state of wary neutrality – but he conceded control of Lion Kop to her.

Storm Courtney he ignored, unless she was in Sean's lap or riding on his shoulder. Then he watched them covertly until he could find an excuse to interrupt their play or to get away from Lion Kop. His absences became more frequent; there were trips to Pietermaritzburg and the surrounding districts to play rugby and polo; there were mysterious night excursions to Ladyburg, and in the day he rode away at dawn each morning – Sean believed he rode to school until he received a note from the headmaster asking him to call.

After showing him the attendance register and a copy of Dirk's academic record, the headmaster leaned back in his chair and waited for Sean's comments.

'Not so good, hey?'

'I agree, Mr Courtney. Not so good.'

'Couldn't we send him to a boarding establishment somewhere, Mr Besant?'

'Yes, you could do that,' Besant agreed dubiously, 'but would it serve any real purpose – apart from providing him with expert coaching in rugby football?'

'How else will he get his University entrance?' Sean was impressed with what higher education had done for Michael. He looked upon it as a sovereign alchemy for all the ills of youth.

'Mr Courtney . . . ' The headmaster hesitated delicately. He had heard of Sean's temper and did not want a personal demonstration of it. 'Some young men are not really suited for University training.'

'I Want Dirk to go,' Sean interjected.

'I doubt that either Stellenbosch or Cape Town Universities share your ambitions.' The schoolroom manner re-asserted itself for a moment, and Besant spoke with dry sarcasm.

'You mean he's stupid?' Sean demanded.

'No, no.' Hurriedly Besant soothed him. 'It's just that he's not, shall we say, academically inclined.'

Sean pondered on that awhile. It seemed a very nice distinction, but he let it go and asked:

'Well, what do you suggest?'

Besant's suggestion was that Dirk Courtney get the hell out of his school — but he phrased it gently.

'Although Dirk is only sixteen — he is very mature for his age. Say you were to start him at the Wattle Company . . . ?'

'You recommend I take him away from school, then?' Sean asked thoughtfully, and Besant suppressed a sigh of relief.

Dirk Courtney was apprenticed to the foreman boilermaker at the factory. His first action was to inform his journeyman that he'd be running this show one day and what was he going to do about it? That gentleman, forewarned by Dirk's reputation, regarded him dolefully, spat a long squirt of tobacco juice an inch from Dirk's gleaming toecap, and replied at some length. He then pointed to a kettle on the workshop forge and told Dirk to make him a cup of coffee, and while he was about it to remove his thumb from his posterior orifice. Within a week the two of them were cronies and the man, whose name was Archibald Frederick Longworthy, began to instruct Dirk in arts other than the fabrication of steelplate. Archy was thirty-six years old. He had come out to Africa after completing a five-year term in Leavenworth Prison for the intriguing offence of *Crimen Injuria* – and when he explained the meaning Dirk was delighted.

Archy introduced Dirk to one of his friends, Hazel, a plump and friendly girl who worked at the Ladyburg Hotel as a barmaid and dispensed her favours in the same cheerful manner that she did her liquor – but Dirk quickly became her favourite, and he learned some pretty little tricks from her.

Shrewdly, Archibald Longworthy examined the situation and decided that nothing but profit could come from friendship with Sean Courtney's heir. Besides which the boy was a lot of fun. He could tumble a tart and swig gin with the best of them – also he had a seemingly inexhaustible supply of sovereigns.

In exchange Dirk hero-worshipped Archy, diverting much of his feelings from his father to his first real friend. Ignoring the grey wrists and neck which bespoke Archy's disaffection for soap and water, the pale wispy hair through which pink scalp showed, ignoring also the black tooth in the front of his mouth – Dirk invested him with the glamour and excitement of an old-time pirate.

When Dirk found himself to be suffering from a painless but evil-smelling condition, it was Archy who assured him it was only 'whites' and went with him to a doctor in Pietermaritzburg. On the train coming home they planned their revenge with much laughter, comradely banter – and rising anticipation.

Hazel was surprised to see them in the middle of a Sunday afternoon, she sat up quickly as they came into her room overlooking the back yard of the hotel.

'Dirkie, you shouldn't come here in the daytime – your Pa will find out.' It was warm in the shabby little room, and the smell of cheap scent and a half-filled chamber-pot blended harshly with the odour of female perspiration. Hazel's thin chemise clung damply to her body and outlined the heavy hang of her breasts and the deep lateral fold around the level of her navel. There were dark smudges below her eyes and a curl was sweat-plastered down her cheek where the pillow had left little creases in the skin. The two of them stood in the door-way and grinned at her, from many experiences Hazel recognized the wolfish eagerness those grins masked.

'What do you want?' Suddenly she was afraid and instinctively she covered the deep cleft of her bosom with one hand.

'Dirkie here wants to have a little chat with you.' Carefully Archy closed the door and turned the key in the lock, then he ambled towards the bed. Manual labour had sheathed his arms in hard, knotty muscle and the hands that hung at his sides were disproportionately large and coated with coarse, blond hair.

'You keep away from me, Archy Longworthy.' Hazel swung her legs off the bed, the chemise pulled up to expose fat white thighs. 'I don't want no trouble, you just leave me alone.'

'You give Dirkie here a clap. Now Dirkie here is my friend and he don't like what you give him.'

'I didn't! It couldn't have been me. I'm clean – I tell you.' She stood up, still holding the front of her chemise closed and backed away before him. 'You keep away from me.' Then as Archy jumped forward, 'No – don't! I'll ...' And she opened her mouth to scream, but

Archy's hand closed over it like a great hairy spider. She struggled desperately, clawing at the hand over her face.

'Come on, Dirk.' Archy chuckled, as he held her easily with one arm around her waist. Uncertainly Dirk hesitated at the door, no longer grinning.

'Come on, man. I'll hold her.' With a sudden swing of his arm Archy hurled the girl face down on the bed, the jumped across to keep her mouth smothered in the pillow. 'Come on, Dirk, use this!' With his free hand Archy unbuckled the wide belt he wore. The leather was studded with blunt metal spikes. 'Double it over!'

'Hell's teeth, Arch – you reckon we should?' Dirk still hesitated, the belt hanging limply from his hands.

'You scared, or something?' And Dirk's mouth hardened at the gibe. He stepped forward and swung the belt in a full overarm stroke across the wriggling body. Hazel froze at the sting of it and she gasped explosively into the pillow.

'That's the stuff – hold on a second.' Archy hooked his thumb into the thin fabric of her chemise and ripped it down from the shoulder-blades to the hem. Her fat woman's buttocks bulged through, dimpled and white. 'Now, give it hell!'

Again Dirk lifted the heavy doubled leather, he stood poised like that while a sensation of giddy power buoyed him upwards to the level of the gods, then he swung his body down into the next stroke.

79

'He's unopposed,' Ronny Pye murmured, and beside him Garrick Courtney stirred uneasily.

'Have you heard him speak?' Ronny persisted.

'No.'

'He wants to throw in Natal with that bunch of Dutchmen up in the Free State and Transvaal.'

'Yes, I know.'

'Do you agree with him?'

Garry was silent, he seemed to be engrossed with the antics of the small herd of foals in the paddock in front of them as they chased each other on legs that seemed to have too many joints, clumsy in their fluffy baby coats.

'I'm sending twenty yearlings up to the show sales in Pietermaritzburg – should average about four, five hundred a head because they're all first-class animals. Be able to let you have a sizeable payment on the bond.'

'Don't worry about that now, Garry. I didn't come out here looking for money.' Ronny offered his cigar-case, and when Garry refused he selected one himself and began preparing it carefully. 'Do you agree with this idea of a Union?'

'No.'

'Why not?' Ronny did not look up from his cigar, he did not want to show his eagerness prematurely.

'I fought them – Leroux, Niemand, Botha, Smuts. I fought them – and we won. Now they're sitting up there in Pretoria calmly plotting to take over the whole

494

country – not just the Free State and Transvaal, but Natal and the Cape as well. Any Englishman who helps them is a traitor to his King and his country. He should be put against the wall and shot.'

'Quite a few people round here think that way – quite a few. And yet no one is opposing Sean Courtney – he's just going to walk into the Assembly.'

Garry turned and began limping slowly along the paddock fence towards the stables, and Ronny fell in beside him.

'Seems to me and the others we need a good man to put against him – someone with a lot of prestige. Good war record, man who has written a book and knows what's going on – knows how to use words. If we could find someone like that, then we'd be happy to put up the expense money.' He struck a match and waited for the sulphur to clear before he lit his cigar and spoke through the smoke. 'Only three months to election time – we got to get organized right away. He's holding a meeting at the schoolhouse next week.'

Sean's political campaign, which had been ambling along mildly without causing much interest, suddenly took on new dramatic quality.

His first meeting in Ladyburg was attended by most of the local population – all of them so starved for entertainment that they were prepared to listen to Sean reel off the little speech that they had already read reported verbatim in most of the Natal newspapers. With hardy optimism they hoped that question time might be more rewarding – and some of them had prepared queries on such momentous matters as the price of hunting licences, the public library system, and the control of foot and mouth disease. At the very least it was an opportunity to meet friends from the outlying areas.

But, apart from Sean's employees, friends and neighbours, others arrived at the schoolhouse and filled the first two rows of desks. All of them were young men Sean had never seen before, and he eyed them with heavy disapproval while they laughed and joked loudly during the preliminaries.

'Where did this bunch come from?' he demanded of the Chairman.

'They came in on the afternoon train – all in one party.'

'Seems as though they're looking for trouble.' Grimly Sean sensed in them the slightly feverish excitement of men steeling themselves to violence. 'Most of them have been on the bottle.'

'Now, Sean.' Ruth leaned across and laid her hand on his knee. 'You must promise not to get worked up. Don't antagonize them.' Sean opened his mouth to reply, then left it like that as Garry Courtney came in through the crowd around the doorway and moved across to sit with Ronny Pye in the back row.

'Close your mouth, darling,' Ruth murmured and Sean obeyed, then smiled and waved a greeting to his brother. Garry replied with a nod, and immediately fell into deep discussion with Ronny Pye.

Amid coughing and feet shuffling the Chairman rose to introduce Sean to men who had been his schoolmates, who had drunk his brandy and hunted with him. He went on to tell them how Sean had won the Anglo-Boer war virtually single-handed, how he had brought prosperity to the district with his factory and his wattle. Then he ended with a few remarks that had Sean squirming in his seat and trying to get two fingers into his collar.

496

'So, ladies and gentlemen of our fair district – I give you a man of vision and foresight, a man with a heart as big as his fists – your candidate and mine, Colonel Sean Courtney!'

Sean stood up smiling, to be rocked by a blast of jeers and catcalls from the front rows. The smile faded and his fists curled into great bony hammers on the table in front of him. He scowled down on them, beginning to sweat with anger. A light tug on the tail of his coat steadied him and his fists opened a little. He began to speak, bellowing above the shouts of 'Sit down!', 'Speak up!', 'Give him a chance!', 'Stand down!', and the thunder of booted feet stamping in unison on the wooden floor.

Three times in the uproar he lost the run of his speech and had to turn to Ruth for prompting, scarlet in the face with anger and mortification, while waves of derisive laughter broke over him. He ended up reading out the last half from his notebook – it made little difference that he stumbled and lost his place repeatedly for no one more than three feet away could hear a word. He sat down and a sudden silence descended on the hall, an air of expectancy that made Sean realize that this must have been carefully planned – and that the main entertainment was still to follow.

'*Mr* Courtney.' At the back of the hall Garry Courtney was on his feet, and every head was craned around towards him. 'May I ask you a few questions?'

Sean nodded slowly. So that is it! Garry planned this reception.

'My first question, then. Can you tell us what the name is for a man who sells his country to the enemies of his King?'

'Traitor!' howled the hecklers.

'Boer!' They stood up in a mass and roared at him. The pandemonium lasted perhaps five minutes.

'I'm taking you out of here,' Sean whispered to Ruth and reached for her arm, but she pulled away.

'No, I'm staying.'

'Come on, do as I tell you. This is going to get rough.'

'You'll have to carry me out first,' she flared at him, angry and beautiful.

Sean was about to accept the challenge, when suddenly the uproar ceased abruptly. Again, all heads turned towards Garrick Courtney, where he stood ready with his next question. In the silence he grinned maliciously.

'One other thing, do you mind telling us the nationality and faith of your wife?'

Sean's head jerked back. He felt the sickening physical jolt of it in his stomach, and he started to struggle to his feet. But Ruth was already standing, and she laid a hand on his shoulder to prevent him rising.

'I think I will answer that one, Garry.' She spoke clearly with just that trace of huskiness in her voice.

'I am a Jewess.'

The silence persisted. Still with her hand on Sean's shoulder, standing straight and proud beside him, she held Garry's stare across the room. Garry broke first. Flushing up along his neck, he dropped his eyes and shifted clumsily on his bad leg. Among the men in the front rows the same guilty reaction followed her words. They glanced at each other and then away, moving awkwardly in shame. A man stood up, and started down the aisle towards the door. Half-way there he stopped and turned.

'Sorry, Missus. I didn't know there'd be any of that,' and he went on towards the door. As he passed Ronny Pye he tossed a sovereign into his lap. Another man stood up, grinned uneasily at Ruth and hurried out.

498

Then in twos and threes the others followed him. The last of them trooped out in a bunch, and Sean noted with relish that not all of them returned Ronny's sovereigns.

At the end of the schoolroom Garry dithered, uncertain whether to leave or to stay and attempt to brazen his way out of a situation he had so seriously misjudged.

Sean stood up slowly and encircled Ruth's waist with one arm, he cleared his throat for it was choked with his pride of her.

'Not only that,' he called, 'but she's one of the best goddamned cooks in the district also.' In the laughter and cheers that followed Garry stumbled and pushed his way out of the room.

80

The following day Garrick Courtney announced his intention of contesting the Ladyburg seat as an Independent, but not even the Loyalist newspapers gave him an outside chance of winning – until six weeks before polling-day.

On that evening, long after dark, Dirk hitched Sun Dancer at the rail outside the hotel. After he had loosened the girth and slipped the bit from her mouth, he left her to drink at the trough and went up on to the sidewalk. As he sauntered past the bar he peered in through the large window with its gold-and-red-lettered slogan, 'Got a thirst, drink a Goldberg Beer!'

Quickly he checked the clientele at the bar for informers. There were none of his father's foremen – they were always dangerous, nor were Messrs Petersen or Pye or Erasmus present this evening. He recognized two of the factory mechanics, a couple of railway gangers, a bank clerk, a counter-hand from the Co-operative Society among the half-dozen strangers – and he decided that it was safe. None of these ranked high enough in Ladyburg society to carry news to Sean Courtney of his son's drinking habits.

Dirk walked to the end of the block, paused there for a few seconds, and then strolled casually back. But his eyes were restlessly checking the shadows for tale carriers. Tonight the main street was deserted, and as he came level with the swing doors of the bar he stepped sideways through them and into the warm yellow lamplight of the saloon. He loved this atmosphere – he loved the smell of sawdust, liquor, tobacco smoke and men. It was a place of men. A place of rough voices and laughter, of crude humour and companionship.

A few of the men along the bar glanced up as he entered.

'Hey, Dirk!'

'We've missed you – where have you been all week?'

Dirk returned Archy's greeting self-consciously and when he walked to take the stool beside him at the end of the bar counter he held himself erect and swaggered a little – for this was a place of men.

'Good evening, Dirk. What will it be?' The barman hurried across to him.

'Hello, Henry – is it all right tonight?' Dirk dropped his voice to a whisper.

'Should be – we aren't expecting any snoopers,' Henry reassured him. 'But the door behind you isn't locked.'

Dirk's seat in the corner had been selected with care. From it he could survey each newcomer to the room while being screened himself by the drinkers along the counter. Behind him a door led through the washup into the back yard – a necessary precaution when you're seventeen and both the law and your father forbid you liquor.

'Very well, then – give me the usual,' Dirk nodded.

'You're out late tonight,' Henry remarked as he poured gin into a tumbler and filled it with bottled gingerbeer. 'You been out hunting again?' Henry was a small man in his early fifties, with a pale unsunned face and little blue eyes, and now as he asked the question he winked one of them at Archy Longworthy.

'Did you get it tonight?' Archy took over the catechism.

Dirk laid a finger along the side of his nose. 'What do you think?' He grinned and they all laughed delightedly.

'Who was it? *Madame?*' Archy drew him out, playing for the other listeners, who were leaning forward still chuckling.

'Oh, her!' Dirk shrugged contemptuously. *Madame* was the code name of the wife of one of the railway drivers. Her husband ran the night train to Pietermaritzburg every alternate day. She was not considered much of a conquest.

'Who them?' Henry kidded softly.

'I'll let you know when I'm finished nesting there myself,' Dirk promised.

'A pretty one?' they insisted. 'Young, hey?'

'She's all right – not too bad.' Dirk tasted his gin.

'Man, you get so much you don't hardly 'preciate it any more,' Archy chided him, grinning at his audience, and Dirk bridled with pleasure. 'Come on, Dirk – tell us, man. Is she hot?'

For answer Dirk extended one finger cautiously and touched his glass, hissed sharply as though he had touched red hot steel and jerked his hand back with an exclamation of pain. They roared with appreciation and Dirk laughed with them, flushing, eager for their acceptance.

'Give us the story –' Henry insisted. 'You don't have to give us the name, just give us the details. Where did you take her?'

'Well –' Dirk hesitated.

'Come on, Dirk. Tell us about it.'

And of course he obliged. Telling it in detail so that the indulgent quality of their laughter changed and they leaned closer to him listening hungrily.

'Jesus! Did she say *that!*'

'Then what did you do?' they encouraged him.

And Dirk told them. He was a natural storyteller and he built up the suspense until there was a small island of attentive silence around him. But the rest of the bar-room was louder with laughter and voices than it had been when he entered. One group in particular were feeling their liquor.

'– So I took her hand,' Dirk went on, 'and I said, "Now I've got a little surprise for you." "What is it?" she asked, as though she didn't know. "Close your eyes and I'll show you." I told her ... ' And a voice rang loudly from across the room:

'– You take that big ugly bastard Courtney. What does he do except drive round in a big motor-car and make speeches.'

Dirk stopped in the middle of a sentence and looked up. Suddenly his face was pale. The man who had spoken was one of the group at the far end of the bar. He was dressed in a shabby overall of blue denim. A man no longer young, with the lines of hardship etched deep around his eyes and mouth.

'You know who gives him his money? I tell you – we give it to him. Without these he'd be finished – he wouldn't last a month.' The man held up his hands, they were calloused and the nails were split and ragged, encrusted with dark semi-circles of dirt. 'That's where he gets his money. Colonel Bloody Courtney.'

Dirk was staring across at the speaker; his hands lay clenched on the counter in front of him. Now suddenly the room was very quiet – so that the man's next words seemed even louder.

'You know what he pays – thirty-two pounds a month top journeyman's wages! Thirty-two pounds a month!'

'The minimum rate is twenty-five –' one of his companions observed dryly. 'I reckon you're free to move on to a better job – if you can find it. Me, I'll stay on here.'

'That's not the point. That big idle bastard's making a fortune out of us – I reckon he can afford to pay more. I reckon . . . '

'Do you reckon you're worth that much?' Dirk jumped up from his stool and shouted the question down the length of the counter. There was a stir of interest and every head turned towards him.

'Leave him, Dirk, he's drunk. Don't start anything,' Henry whispered in agitation, and then raising his voice and turning to the other, 'You've had enough, Norman. Time you were on your way. You old lady will be waiting dinner for you.'

'Good God!' Norman was peering in Dirk's direction, his eyes focusing blearily.

'Good God! It's Courtney's pup.'

And Dirk's face set into nervous rigidity. He began to walk slowly down the room towards the man.

'Leave him, Dirk.' To restrain him Archy caught his arm as he passed. But Dirk shrugged it off.

'You insulted my father. You called him a bastard!'

'That's right.' Norman nodded. 'Your daddy's a bastard all right. Your daddy's a big lucky bastard who's never done a full day's work in his life – a big, lucky, bloodsucking bastard. And he's whelped an equally useless pup, who spends his time . . . '

Dirk hit him in the mouth, and he went over backwards off the stool, flailing his arms as he fell. He hit the floor with his shoulders and rolled on to his knees spitting blood and a broken tooth from his mouth.

'You little bastard –' he mouthed through the blood. Dirk stepped forward with his left foot and swung his boot with the whole weight of his body behind it. The toe of his boot thudded into the man's chest and flung him on to his back.

'Christ, stop him,' shouted Henry from behind the bar. But they sat paralysed as Dirk stooped for the bar stool, lifted it above his head and then brought it down, swinging his body with it as though he were chopping a log. The heavy wooden seat hit the man in the centre of his forehead, it hit solidly for the back of his head was against the floor and could not give with the blow. It split his skull cleanly and twin spurts of blood shot from his nostrils into the sawdust on the floor.

'You've killed him.' A single voice broke the long silence that followed.

'Yes.' Dirk agreed. *I've killed him. I've killed a man.* It sang within him savagely. It came up and filled his chest so that he could hardly breathe. And he stood over the corpse not wanting to miss a moment of it. He felt his legs trembling under him, the muscles of his cheeks so tight with excitement they felt they must tear.

'Yes, I killed him.' His voice was choked with the violence of the pleasure that gripped him. His vision narrowed down so that the dead man's face filled the whole field of it. The forehead was deeply dented and the eyes bulged from their sockets.

Around him there was a sudden bustle of consternation.

'You'd better send for his father.'

'I'm getting out of here!'

'No, stay where you are. Nobody must leave.'

'My God, call Doc Fraser.'

'Doc's not wanted – get the police.'

'He was so quick – like a bloody leopard –'

'Christ, I'm getting out of here.'

Two of them stooped over the body.

'Leave him!' snapped Dirk. Don't touch him.' Jealous

505

as a young lion of its kill. And instinctively they obeyed. They stood up and moved away. With them everyone else drew back, leaving Dirk standing alone.

'Get his father,' repeated Henry. 'Someone ride out and call Sean Courtney.'

An hour later Sean strode into the room. He wore an overcoat over his nightshirt and his boots had been pulled hurriedly over his bare feet. He stopped on the threshold and glared around the room, his hair in wild disorder from sleep – but when he entered, the atmosphere in the room changed. The tense silence relaxed and every face turned eagerly towards him.

'Mr Courtney – thank God you've come,' blurted the young police constable who was standing beside Dr Fraser.

'How bad is it, Doc?' Sean asked.

'He's dead, Sean.'

'Pa, he insulted . . . ' Dirk started.

'Shut up!' Sean ordered him grimly. 'Who is he?' he fired at the constable.

'Norman Van Eek – one of your fitters from the mill.'

'How many witnesses?'

'Fourteen of them, sir. They all saw it.'

'Right,' Sean ordered, 'get the body down to the police station. You'll be able to take statements from them tomorrow morning.'

'What about the accused . . . I mean what about your son, sir?' The constable corrected himself.

'I'll be responsible for him.'

'I'm not sure that I shouldn't . . . ' He saw the expression on Sean's face. 'Well, that will be all right, I suppose,' he agreed reluctantly.

'Pa . . . ' Dirk started again.

'I told you to keep your mouth shut – you've done

enough damage for one night.' Sean spoke without looking at him, then to the barman,

'Fetch a blanket.' Then to the police constable, 'Get some of them to help you,' and he pointed towards the window which was lined four deep with curious faces.

'Very well, Mr Courtney.'

After they had shuffled out with the blanket-wrapped body, Sean glanced significantly at Dr Fraser.

'I'd better get down there – complete my examination.'

'You go ahead,' Sean agreed and the doctor packed his bag and went. Sean closed the door behind him and slammed the shutters across the window. Then he turned to the men who stood anxiously along the bar.

'What happened?' They stirred restlessly and looked everywhere but at him.

'You, George?' Sean selected one of his mechanics.

'Well, Mr Courtney, your Dirk went up to Norman and hit him off the stool. Then he kicked him as he was trying to get up, then he picked up the stool and hit him with it.' The mechanic stumbled hoarsely through his explanation.

'Did this man provoke him?' Sean demanded.

'Well, he called you a – begging your pardon, Mr Courtney – he called you a big, idle, bloodsucking bastard.'

Sean frowned quickly. 'Did he now! What else did he say?'

'He said you were a slave owner – that you starved your men. He said that he was going to get even with you sometime.' Archy Longworthy took over the telling of it with a note of interrogation in his voice as he glanced round at the others for support. After a few seconds there was a guilty nodding of heads and a few murmurs of agreement. Archy took courage from it. 'He

507

sort of hinted that he was going to wait for you one night and get even.'

'Did he say that in so many words?' Sean's presence dominated the room with such an obvious air of authority that when Archy looked again for support he found it in their faces.

'He said: "One night I'm going to wait for that big bastard – then I'll show him a few things."' Archy gave them the exact words. No one protested.

'Then what happened?'

'Well then he sort of picked on young Dirk. And "here's Courtney's brat," he said. "Yellow as his old man, I reckon!"'

'What did Dirk do?' Sean asked.

'Well, Mr Courtney, he just laughed – like a gentleman, sort of, nice and friendly. "Forget it," he said – "you've had too much to drink."'

A sudden thought occurred to Sean. 'What was Dirk doing in here, anyway?'

'Well, it's like this, Mr Courtney – a few weeks ago he lent me a couple of pounds. I asked him to call round here tonight so I could give it back to him – that's all it was.'

'He wasn't drinking then?' Sean asked suspiciously.

'Good Lord, no!' Archy was so obviously shocked at the suggestion that Sean nodded.

'All right, what happened then?' he pursued.

'Well, Norman went on ribbing him. Called him a coward and all that – I can't remember the exact words. But at last young Dirk lost his temper. He walked across and hit him off the stool. Well, I guess Norman deserved that – what do you think, boys?' Archy looked at them again.

'That's right – fair made my blood boil to hear him

508

picking on Dirk like that.' The mechanic backed him up and the others murmured agreement.

'Well, then,' Archy took up the tale again, 'Norman's lying on the floor and pulls out his knife.' There was a rustle of astonishment from along the bar. One man opened his mouth and lifted his hand in protest, but suddenly embarrassed, he carried the gesture through and massaged his neck.

'Knife. What knife – where's it now?' Sean leaned forward eagerly. Standing beside him Dirk began to smile softly. When he smiled his face was beautiful.

'Here's the knife.' Henry, the barman, reached under the counter and brought out a large bone-handled clasp knife. Everybody in the room stared at it blankly.

'How did it get there?' Sean asked, and now for the first time he was aware of the sickly guilt-ugly faces in front of him. He knew then for certain it was a lie.

'I took it off Norman afterwards. We thought it best you should be the first one to know the truth – you being his father, and all.' Archy wriggled his shoulders ingratiatingly and smiled around at his witnesses.

Slowly Sean turned to the man nearest to him, the bank clerk.

'Is this the knife with which Norman Van Eek threatened my son?'

'Yes, Mr Courtney.' The man's voice squeaked unnaturally.

Sean looked at the man beyond him and repeated the question exactly.

'Yes, that's the one, sir.'

'That's it.'

'Yes.'

'No doubt about it – that's it.'

He asked each man in turn and each answered the same.

'Dirk.' Sean came last to him. He asked it slowly and heavily. Looking into the clear innocent eyes of his son. 'As God is your witness – did Norman Van Eek draw this knife on you?'

Please, my son, deny it now. Say it so they all can hear you. If you value my love – tell me the truth now. Please, Dirk, please. All this he tried to say, tried to convey it with the sheer force of his gaze.

'As God is my witness, Pa,' Dirk answered him and was silent again.

'You have not answered,' Sean insisted. *Please, my son.*

'He drew that knife from the hip pocket of his overalls – the blade was closed. He opened it with the thumbnail of his left hand, Pa,' Dirk explained softly. 'I tried to kick it out of his hand, but hit his chest instead. He fell on to his back and I saw him raise the knife as though he were going to throw it. I hit him with the stool. It was the only way I could stop him.'

All the passion went out of Sean's face. It was stony and hard.

'Very well,' he said. 'We'd better get home now.' Then he addressed the rest of the bar-room. 'Thank you, gentlemen.' And he walked out through the door to the Rolls. Dirk followed him meekly.

The next afternoon Dirk Courtney was released by the local magistrate into his father's custody on bail of fifty pounds, pending the visit of the Circuit Court two weeks later, when he was to stand trial on a charge of manslaughter.

His case was set down at the head of the Court list. The whole district attended the trial, packing the tiny Courthouse and clustering at each of its windows.

After a retirement of seven minutes the jury brought back its verdict and Dirk, walking out of the dock, was surrounded by the laughing, congratulating crowd and borne out into the sunlight.

In the almost deserted Courtroom Sean did not rise from his seat in the front row of chairs. Peter Aaronson, the defence lawyer Sean had imported from Pietermaritzburg, shuffled his papers into his briefcase, made a joke with the Registrar, then walked across to Sean.

'In and out again in seven minutes already – that's one for the record book.' When he smiled he looked like a koala bear. 'Have a cigar, Mr Courtney.' Sean shook his head and Peter thrust a disproportionately large cigar into his own mouth and lit it. 'I tell you truly, though, I was worried by the knife business. I expected trouble there. I didn't like that knife.'

'No more did I,' Sean agreed softly, and Peter held his head on one side examining Sean's face with bright, birdlike eyes.

'But I liked those witnesses – a troupe of performing seals. "Bark," you say to them – Woof! Woof! Just like magic. Someone trained them pretty well.'

'I don't think I understand you,' Sean said to him grimly, and Peter shrugged.

'I'll post my account – but I warn you I'm going to hit you with a big one. Say, five hundred guineas?'

Sean lay back in his seat and looked up at the little lawyer.

'Say, five hundred,' he agreed.

'Next time you need representation – I recommend a bright youngster name of Rolfe. Humphrey Rolfe,' Peter went on.

'You think I'll need a lawyer again?'

'With your boy – you'll need a lawyer,' Peter told him with certainty.

'And you don't want the job?' Sean leaned forward with sudden interest. 'At five hundred guineas a throw?'

'Money I can get anywhere.' Peter took the cigar from his mouth and inspected the fluffy grey ash at its tip. 'Remember the name, Mr Courtney – Humphrey Rolfe. He's a bright boy – and not too fussy.'

He walked away down the aisle lugging his heavy briefcase, and Sean stood up and followed him slowly. Pausing on the steps of the Courthouse he looked across the square. The centre of a small knot of men, Dirk stood laughing, with Archy Longworthy's arm around his shoulder. Archy's voice carried to where Sean stood.

'Don't let any of you get the idea you can tangle with Dirkie here – you'll end up with your teeth busted clean out the back of your head.' Archy grinned so that the blackened tooth showed. 'I say it so you can all hear me. Dirkie here is my friend – and I'm proud of him.'

You alone, thought Sean. He looked at his son and saw how tall he stood. Shaped like a man – broad in the shoulders with muscle in his arms, no fat on the belly and long legs dropping away clean from hips.

But he is only sixteen. He's a child – perhaps there is still time to prevent him setting hard. Then with truth he knew he was deceiving himself, and he remembered what a friend had said to him long ago:

'Some grapes grew in the wrong soil, some were diseased before they went to the press, and others were spoiled by a careless vintner – not all grapes make good wine.'

And I am the careless vintner, he thought.

Sean walked across the square. 'You're coming home,' he told Dirk harshly, knowing as he looked at the lovely face that he no longer loved his son. The knowledge nauseated him.

'Congratulations, Colonel. I knew we'd win,' Archy Longworthy beamed, and Sean glanced at him.

512

'I'll be in my office ten o'clock tomorrow morning. I want to talk to you.'

'Yes, sir!' grinned Archy happily, but he was not grinning when he left Ladyburg on the following evening's train with a month's pay in lieu of notice to compensate him.

81

With the storm of adverse editorial comment raised by Dirk's trial, Garry Courtney's chances in the coming election increased significantly. The jingo press spoke darkly of a 'surprise outcome, which thinking men will welcome as a true assessment of the worth of the two candidates for the Ladyburg constituency'. Only the Liberal papers reported the generous pension which the Ladyburg Wattle Co-operative Co. voted to Norman Van Eek's widow and orphan.

But everyone knew that Sean Courtney was still a long way ahead. He could be certain of the vote of the two hundred men employed at the factory and on his estates, the other wattle producers of the valley and their employees, as well as a good half of the townsfolk and ranchers – that was until the *Pietermaritzburg Farmer & Trader* devoted a full front page to the exclusive story of one Archibald Frederick Longworthy.

Mr Longworthy related how, by the threat of physical violence and loss of employment, he had been forced to perjure himself in court. How, after the case, he had been summarily dismissed from his work. The exact nature of his perjury was not revealed.

Sean cabled his lawyers in Pietermaritzburg to begin immediate proceedings against the *Farmer & Trader* for defamation of character, libel, contempt, treason, and anything else they could think of. Then, reckless of his own safety, he climbed into the Rolls and raced at thirty miles an hour in pursuit of his cable. He arrived in

Pietermaritzburg to find that Mr Longworthy, after signing a sworn statement and graciously accepting a payment of fifty guineas, had departed without leaving a forwarding address. Legal advice was against Sean visiting the editor of the *Farmer & Trader* and laying himself open to a counter-suit of assault and battery. It would be two months before the defamation trial was heard in court, and the election was to be held in ten days' time.

All Sean could do was publish a full-page denial in each of the Liberal papers, then return to Ladyburg at a more sedate pace. There a telegram awaited him from Pretoria. Jan Paulus and Jan Niemand suggested that in the circumstances it might be better if Sean withdraw from nomination. Sean's reply went sizzling back over the wires.

Like a pair in harness, Garry and Sean Courtney swept up to the polling-day finishing line.

The actual voting took place in the Ladyburg Village Management offices under the beady eyes of two Government registration officers. Thereafter, the ballot boxes would be removed to Pietermaritzburg, where on the following day in the City Hall the votes would be counted and the official results announced.

On opposite sides of the square the opposing candidates set up the large marquee tents from which free refreshments would be served to the voters. Traditionally the candidate who fed the largest number would be the loser. Nobody wished to put *their* choice to additional expense, so they patronized the other man's stall. This day, however, both candidates served an almost equal amount of food.

It was a day that threatened the approach of the wet

season, humid heat lay trapped beneath grey overcast clouds and the occasional bursts of sunlight stung like the blast of an open furnace door. Sean, suited and waist-coated, sweated with anxiety as he greeted each visitor to his stall with a booming, false *camaraderie*. Beside him Ruth looked like a rose petal, and smelled as sweet. Storm, demure for once, stood between them. Dirk was not there – Sean had found work for him on the far side of Lion Kop. Many sly eyes and snide sallies remarked his absence.

Ronny Pye had persuaded Garry not to wear his uniform. Anna was with him, pretty in mauve and artificial flowers. It was only at closer range that the ugly little lines around her mouth and eyes, and the grey hairs that were woven into the shiny black mass of her hair showed up. Neither she nor Garry let their eyes wander across the square.

Michael arrived and spoke first with his father, kissed his mother dutifully, then crossed to resume the argument Sean had broken off the night before. Michael wanted Sean to buy ten thousand acres of the coastal lowlands around Tongaat and plant it to sugar-cane. Within a few minutes he realized that this was not the best time to push his idea; Sean greeted each of his points with hearty laughter and offered him a cigar. Discouraged but not resigned, Michael went into the ballot office and, settling his problem of divided loyalty, deliberately spoiled his paper. Then he returned to his office at the wattle factory to whip his sugar estimates into shape for the next attack on Sean.

Ada Courtney never left the Protea Street cottage all that day. She had steadfastly denied appeals to join either camp, and refused to allow any of her girls to help in the preparations. She had prohibited any political discussion in her house – and ordered Sean to leave when he had disregarded this rule. Only after Ruth had interceded and Sean had made an abject apology, was he allowed to return. She disapproved of the whole business and considered it undignified and common that members of her family should not only be standing for public office but actually competing for it. Her deep distrust of and contempt for officialdom stemmed from the time the Village Board had wanted to place street lamps along Protea Street. She had attended their next meeting armed with an umbrella, and in vain they had tried to convince her that street lights did not attract mosquitoes.

However, Ada was the only person in the district who did not attend. From mid-morning until polling closed at five o'clock the square was jammed solid with humanity, and when the sealed ballot boxes were borne in state to the railway station, many of them climbed on the same train and went up to Pietermaritzburg for the official counting.

It had been a day of unremitting nervous tension, so a very short time after entering their suite in the White Horse Hotel, Ruth and Sean fell into exhausted sleep in each other's arms. When, in the early morning a brilliant electrical storm raged down upon the town, Ruth moved restlessly in her sleep, coming slowly back to consciousness – and to the realization that she and Sean were already engaged in the business that had been delayed so long. Sean woke at the same time and, for the few seconds that it took him to understand what was happening, was as bewildered as she – then both of them went to it with a will. By dawn Ruth knew that she would bear a son, though Sean felt it was a little soon to tell for certain.

After bathing, they ate breakfast in bed together with a renewed sense of intimacy. Ruth in a white silk gown, with her hair loosed into a shiny mass on her shoulders and her skin glowing as though she had been freshly scrubbed, was extreme provocation to Sean. Consequently they arrived late at the City Hall, much to the agitation of Sean's supporters.

The counting was well advanced. In a roped-off section of the hall ballot officers sat in silent industry at the tables piled with the small pink slips of paper. On a placard above each table was printed the name of the district and the candidates, and between the tables scrutineers paced watchfully.

The body of the hall was filled with a milling, humming swarm of men and women. Before it engulfed them Sean caught a glimpse of Garry and Anna moving through the press, then for the next ten minutes he was subjected to an orgy of hand-shaking, back-slapping and well wishes – interrupted by a bell and a complete silence.

'The result for the legislative assembly seat of Newcastle . . . ' a high thin voice announced in the hush ' . . . Mr Robert Sampson 986 votes. Mr Edward Sutton 423 votes . . . ' And the rest was lost in a burst of cheers and groans. Sampson was the South African Party candidate, and Sean fought his way through the pack that surrounded him.

'Well done, you old son of a gun,' shouted Sean and beat him between the shoulder-blades.

'Thanks, Sean. It looks as though we are home and dry – I never expected a majority that size!' and they wrung each other's hands deliriously.

The morning went on with intervals of excited, buzzing tension exploding into applause as each result was announced. Sean's confidence rose as his party captured each seat they had expected, and one that they were resigned to lose – but then the bell rang again and in

the same impersonal tone the Chief Registration Officer
at last announced:

'The result for the legislative assembly seat of Ladyburg and the lower Tugela –' he felt the cold emptiness
of apprehension in his stomach, and his breath burning
up the back of his throat. Standing beside him he could
sense the rigidity of Ruth's body and he groped for her
hand.

'Colonel *Garrick* Courtney 638 votes. Colonel *Sean*
Courtney 631 votes.'

Ruth's hand squeezed hard, but Sean did not reply to
the pressure. The two of them stood very still, a tiny
island of quiet in the surge and roar – in the triumphant
cheers and despairing groans – until Sean said softly: 'I
think we'll go back to the hotel, my dear.'

'Yes,' she answered as softly, and the sound of her
voice was helpless pity. Together they started across the
floor and a way opened for them. A passage lined by
faces that bore expressions of regret, happiness, curiosity, indifference and triumphant malice.

Out into the sunlight and across the street to the rank
of hire-cabs they walked together, while behind them
the uproar was muted – sounding at this distance like
the voices of wild animals.

Sean handed Ruth up into the coach and was about
to join her before he remembered what there was still
to be done. He spoke to the driver and gave him money
before coming back to Ruth.

'Please wait for me at the hotel, my dear.'

'Where are you going?'

'I must offer Garry our congratulations.'

Through the screen of bodies that surrounded him

Garry saw Sean approaching, and he felt his body tensing involuntarily – racked by that conflict of hatred and love he bore for this man.

Sean stopped in front of him and smiled. 'Well done, Garry!' he said and offered his right hand. 'You beat me in a hard straight fight – and I'd like to shake your hand.'

Garry took the words up with temerity, examined them with growing realization of their meaning and found that they were true. He had fought Sean and beaten him. This was something that could not be destroyed – something that Sean could never take away from him. *I've beaten him.* For the first time – the very first time in all my life!

It was an emotional orgasm so intense that for a long moment Garry could not move or make any reply.

'Sean . . . ' His voice choked up. He caught Sean's out-stretched hand in both of his and held it with desperate strength.

'Sean, perhaps now . . . ' he whispered, 'I'd like to . . . I mean, when we get back to Ladyburg . . . ' Then he stopped and blushed scarlet with embarrassment. Quickly he released Sean's hand and stepped back. 'I thought you might like to come out to Theuniskraal,' he mumbled, 'some day when you're not busy. Look around the old place.' Then more eagerly, 'It's been a long time. I've still got Pa's old . . . '

'Never!' Anna Courtney hissed the word. Neither of them had noticed her cross the hall, but now she appeared suddenly at Garry's side. Her eyes were bright gems of hatred set in their patterns of wrinkles, and her face was white as she glared at Sean. 'Never.' She hissed again, and took Garry's arm. 'Come with me,' she commanded, and Garry followed her meekly. But he glanced back at where Sean still stood, and there was a desperate plea in his eyes. A plea for understanding, for forgiveness of this weakness.

82

Like one who lives in a hurricane belt, and recognizes the shape of clouds and the breathless hush that precedes high wind – Ruth knew she would have to deal with the brooding undirected rage which would be Sean's reaction to this failure of his plans. His moods came at widely spaced intervals and did not last long – but she feared those moods of his, and like the prudent householder forewarned of the hurricane's approach, she took precautions to minimize its wrath.

When she reached the hotel she sent an urgent summons to the Manager.

'In half an hour I want lunch served in the suite – not your ordinary bill of fare. Something really good.' The Manager thought a moment. 'Oyster! We have a barrel just arrived from Umhlanga Rocks.'

'Excellent.' Ruth liked the man's response to the emergency.

'Then I could do a smoked ham, cold venison, cold rock lobster, salads?'

'Excellent again. What about cheese?'

'Gruyère. Danish Blue. Camembert.'

'Wine?'

'Champagne?'

'Yes,' Ruth agreed instantly. She would shamelessly exploit Sean's weakness for it. 'A bottle of Veuve Clicquot – no, on second thoughts, three bottles.'

'I'll send the wine up first?'

'Immediately – with your best glass and a silver bucket,' Ruth told him.

Then she fled to her toilet. Thank the Lord for French perfume and this morning dress of grey silk she had been saving for just such an occasion. She worked quickly, but with skill, upon her face and hair, and when she was finished she sat quietly before the mirror and composed her features into an expression of peace. The effect was very satisfactory, she decided after critical contemplation. Since it was the way he had first seen it, Sean could never resist her hair in braids. It made her look like a little girl.

'Shall I open the wine, Madam?'

'Yes, please.' She called into the sitting-room, then went through to await the onslaught of the hurricane.

Ten minutes later it came wafting in like a gentle zephyr, with a cigar clamped between its teeth, its hands thrust deep into trousers pockets and a bemused expression on its face.

'Hey, now!' Sean stopped when he saw her, and removed the cigar. 'That's nice!'

The fact that he had noticed her appearance was proof that her weather forecast was hopelessly incorrect and she burst out laughing.

'What's so funny?' Sean asked mildly.

'Nothing and everything. You and me. Have a glass of champagne.'

'Mad woman,' Sean said and kissed her. 'I like your hair like this.'

'Aren't you disappointed?'

'About the result, you mean? Yes, I suppose I am.' He went to the central table and poured wine into the crystal glasses, handed one to her and took up the other.

'I give you a toast – the short, exciting political career of Sean Courtney.'

'You wanted to win so badly – but now . . . ?'

Sean nodded. 'Yes, I always want to win. But now that the game is lost . . . ' He shrugged. 'Shall I tell you something? I was getting a bit sick of all the speechifying and hand-shaking. I feel that even in my sleep I have a vacant grin on my face.' He crossed to one of the leather arm-chairs and sank down into it gratefully. 'There is something else also. Come here and let me tell you about it.'

She went to him, sat in his lap and slid her hand into the front of his shirt so that she could feel the soft springy hair of his chest, and the hard rubbery flesh beneath.

'Tell me,' she said, and he told her about Garry. He spoke slowly, telling her everything – about the leg, how it was when they were children, and finally, about Michael. She was quiet for a while, and he could see the hurt in her eyes that Sean had been another woman's lover. At last she asked:

'Does Garry know that Michael is your son?'

'Yes. Anna told him one night. She told him the night I left Ladyburg – he wanted to kill me.'

'Why did you leave?'

'I couldn't stay on. Garry hated me for siring his son – and Anna hated me because I would not go to her.'

'She still wanted you, then?'

'Yes. That night – the night I left, Anna came to me and asked me to . . . ' Sean paused. 'You know what I mean.'

'Yes.' Ruth nodded, hurt still and jealous, but making the effort to understand.

'I refused her – and she went to Garry and, in spite, she told him about the child. My God, what a poisonous bitch she is!'

'But if she wanted you, why did she marry Garry?'

'She was with child. She thought I had been killed in the Zulu war – she married him to provide a father for her child.'

'I see,' Ruth murmured. 'But why do you tell me this?'

'I wanted you to understand how I feel about Garry. After what he did to you at that meeting I can't expect you to have much sympathy for him – but he wasn't trying to hurt you, he was aiming at me. I owe him so much, I never seem able to pay him. That's why . . . '

'That's why you are glad he won today?' Ruth finished for him.

'Yes,' Sean answered eagerly. 'You see, don't you, how important this must have been to him. For the first time he was able to . . . able to . . . ' Sean fluttered his hands in frustration as he sought the words.

'He was able to compete with you on equal terms,' Ruth supplied them for him.

'Exactly!' Sean struck the arm of his chair with clenched fist. 'When I went to congratulate him, he was ready to meet me. He invited me out to Theuniskraal – just then that evil, bloody woman interfered and took him away. But somehow I know it's going to be all right now.'

A knock on the outer door interrupted him, and Ruth jumped up from his lap.

'That will be the waiter with the lunch,' but before she was half-way across the room, the knock was repeated with such insistence that it threatened to loosen the plaster.

'I'm coming.' Irritated, Ruth raised her voice and swung the door open.

Led by Bob Sampson a flood of men rushed into the room; jabbering and gesticulating they bore down on Sean.

'What the hell's going on?' he demanded.

'You've won!' shouted Bob. 'A recount, you won on a recount – by ten votes!'

'My God!' breathed Sean, and then so softly that only Ruth heard him, 'Garry. Poor Garry!'

'Open that champagne – send for another case. We're in solidly – all of us!' exulted Bob Sampson. 'So let's drink to the Union of South Africa!'

83

'Not even this once. Out of so many times, so many things – not even this once.' Already Garry Courtney was drunk. He lay deep in his chair with a tumbler held in both hands, stirring the brown liquid with a circular movement so a few drops slopped over the rims an stained the cloth of his trousers.

'No,' agreed Anna. 'Not even this once.' She stood with her back to him, staring out of the window of their suite into the gaslit street below, for she did not want him to see her face. But she could not control the harsh, gloating quality of her voice. 'Now you can go back to writing your little books. You've made your point – you've proved to yourself and the rest of the world how effective you are.'

Moving her hands slowly, she began to massage her own upper arms with sensual pleasure. A tiny shudder thrilled her so she moved restlessly and her skirts rustled like leaves in the wind. God, how close it had been – and she had been afraid.

'You're a loser, Garry Courtney. You *have* always been – and you *will* always be.'

Again she shuddered with the memory of her fear. He had so nearly escaped. She had seen it begin from the moment the first result was announced, every minute it had grown stronger. Even his voice had changed, deeper with the first hint of confidence in it. He had looked at her strangely, without submission, with the beginning of his contempt. Then the flare of rebellion when he had spoken to Sean Courtney. She had been truly afraid then.

'You are a loser,' she repeated, and heard the sound he made – half-gulp, half-sigh. She waited and when she heard the soft gurgle of brandy poured from bottle to glass she hugged herself tighter and now she smiled as she remembered the announcement of the recount. The way he had shrunk, the way he had crumpled and turned to he with all of it gone – the confidence and contempt wiped away. Gone! Gone for ever. Sean Courtney would never have him. She had made that oath – and now it would be kept.

As so many times before, she played over in her mind the details of that night. The night she had made the oath.

It was raining. She was standing on the wide stoep of Theuniskraal, and Sean was leading his horse up across the lawns of Theuniskraal. The damp linen of his shirt clung to his shoulders and chest, the rain had made his beard break out in tiny curls so he looked like a mischievous pirate.

'Where's Garry?' Her own voice, and his voice answering.

'Don't worry. He's gone into town to see Ada. He'll be back by supper-time.'

Then he was coming up the steps towards her, standing tall above her, and his hand on her arm was cold from the rain.

'You must take better care of yourself now. You can't stand in the cold any more.' And he led her through the french doors. The top of her head was on a level with his shoulders, and his eyes as he looked down at her were gentle with masculine awe of pregnancy.

'You're a damn fine woman, Anna. And I'm sure you're going to make a fine baby.'

528

'Sean!' She remembered how his name had come up her throat like an involuntary exclamation of pain. The fierce forward surge that had flattened her body against his, back arching to send her hips forward searching for his manhood. The coarse electric feeling of his hair in her hands as she pulled his face down and the taste of his mouth opened warm and moist.

'Are you mad!' As he tried to break away from her, her arms locked around his body and her face pressed to his chest.

'I love you. Please, Sean, please. Just let me hold you, that's all. I just want to hold you.'

'Get away from me!' And she felt herself thrown roughly on to the couch beside the fireplace.

'You're Garry's wife and you'll soon be the mother of his child. Keep your hot little body for him.' And his face thrust forward, close to hers. 'I don't want you. I could no more touch you than I could go with my own mother. You're Garry's wife. If ever again you look at another man I'll kill you. I'll kill you with my bare hands.'

Love congealing instantly, transformed to hatred by his words. Her fingernails raking across his cheek so the blood slid down into his beard, and he caught her wrists. Holding her while she struggled and screamed at him.

'You swine, you dirty, dirty swine. Garry's wife you say. Garry's baby you say! Now hear the truth. What I have within me you put there. It's yours – not Garry's!'

Then he was backing away from her. 'You're lying. It can't be.'

Following him now, speaking those cruel words softly. 'You remember how we said good-bye when you went to war? You remember that night in the wagon?'

'Leave me, leave me alone. I've got to think. I didn't

know.' And he was gone. She heard the door of his study slam, and she stood in the centre of the floor while the storm surf of her anger abated and exposed the black reefs of hatred beneath.

Then she was alone in her bedroom, standing before the mirror – making her oath.

'I hate him. There's one thing I can take from him. Garry belongs to me now. Mine, not his. I will take that away from him.'

The pins pulled from her hair, so it tumbled to her shoulders. Her fingers tangling it into confusion. Teeth closing on her own lips so she could taste the blood.

'Oh God, I hate him,' she whispered through the pain. Tearing open the blouse of her dress, watching in the mirror the great pink bosses of her nipples already darkening with the promise of fruition.

'I hate him.' Pantaloons torn and discarded, bowls of face powder and cosmetics swept from the dressing-table to burst and fill the room with the pungent reek of perfume.

Then lying alone in the darkening room. Waiting for Garry to come.

Now she turned away from the window and looked down at Garry, triumphantly, knowing he could never escape again.

I have kept my oath, she thought, and crossed to the chair.

'Poor Garry.' She forced her voice to croon gently, and she stroked the hair back from his forehead. He looked up at her, surprised, but eager for affection. 'Poor Garry. Tomorrow we'll go home to Theuniskraal.'

She moved the bottle on the side table closer to his hand. Then she kissed his cheek lightly, and went on into the bedroom of the suite – smiling again, secure and safe in his weakness.

84

Four months passed quickly. Sean, distracted by the responsibilities of his office, the mountains of correspondence, the meetings and sessions, the petitioners and the schemers – offered only a token resistance to Michael's sugar plans. Michael went off to the coast, purchased the land, and became deeply involved with the seller's eldest daughter. This young lady had the dubious distinction of being one of the few divorcees in Natal. When the scandal reached his ears, Sean, secretly pleased that Michael's chastity was at last shed, boarded the Rolls and went off on a flying mission of rescue. He returned to Ladyburg with a penitent Michael in tow. Two weeks later the young lady married a travelling salesman and moved from Tongaat to Durban, whereupon Michael was allowed to return to Tongaat and begin the development of the sugar estate.

Ruth no longer accompanied Sean on all of his absences from Ladyburg. Her swiftly increasing girth and a mild malady which assailed her in the mornings kept her at Lion Kop, where she and Ada spent much time in the design and fabrication of babywear. In this Storm rendered assistance. The matinée jacket, which took three months to knit, was certain to fit the infant perfectly – provided it was a hunchback with its one arm twice as long as the other.

Kept busy from early morning to nightfall in the capacity of overseer on Mahobo's Kloof, Dirk found little time for distraction. Ladyburg was now well covered by Sean's espionage system, and Dirk's few visits were reported in detail.

But on the far side of Ladyburg, derelict and shabby from want of love, brooded the great homestead of Theuniskraal. In the night a single window showed a pale yellow square of light as Garry Courtney sat alone at his desk. In front of him lay a pathetically thin sheaf of papers. Hour after hour he stared at it – but no longer seeing it. He was dry inside, deprived of the juice of life and seeking its substitute in the bottle, which was always near him.

The days drifted into weeks, and they in turn became months – and he drifted with them.

Each afternoon he would go down to the paddocks, then, leaning against the heavy wooden paling, he would watch his bloodstock. Hour after hour he stood unmoving and it seemed that, in time, he left his own body and lived within those richly gleaming skins, as though his own hooves drove deep into the turf as he ran, as though his own voice squealed and his muscles bunched and moved in the savage mating of heaving bodies.

Ronny Pye found him there one afternoon; without Garry being aware of his presence, he came up silently and stood beside him, studying the pale intense face with the chisel-marks of pain and doubt and terrible yearning sculptured deep around the mouth and below the pale blue eyes.

'Hello, Garry.' He spoke softly, but recognizing the pity in his own voice he thrust it aside. There was no room for softness now, and ruthlessly he hardened his resolve.

'Ronny.' Vaguely, Garry turned to him, and when he smiled it was shyly. 'Business or social?'

'Business, Garry.'

'The bond?'

'Yes.'

'What do you want me to do?'

'How about coming into town – we can go over things in my office.'

'Now?'

'Yes, please.'

'Very well.' Garry straightened up slowly. 'I'll come with you.'

They rode together over the crest of ground and down towards the concrete bridge over the Baboon Stroom. Both of them silent – Garry because there was nothing in him, nothing to give voice to; Ronny Pye because of his sense of shame for the thing he was about to do. He was going to take a man's home from him and turn him loose upon a world in which he would have no chance of survival.

At the bridge they stopped automatically to rest their horses, and they sat without speaking, an incongruous pair. One man sitting quietly, slim and wasted, his clothing slightly rumpled, his face austere with suffering; the other plump, red-faced below bright ginger hair, dressed in expensive cloth, fidgeting in the saddle.

There was little sign of life across the river. A long, tired smear of smoke from the wattle factory stack rising straight into the still hot air, a black boy moving cattle down to drink at the river, the huff and clatter and clang of a locomotive shunting in the goods-yards – but otherwise the town of Ladyburg lay slumbering in the heat of a summer afternoon.

Then on the open grassy plain below the escarpment, urgent movement caught Ronny's eye, and he focused his attention upon it with relief.

A horseman riding fast, and even at this distance Ronny recognized him.

'Young Dirk,' he grunted, and Garry roused himself

533

and peered out across the river. Horse and rider blended into one unit, seeming to touch the earth so lightly they were bound to it only by a pale feather of dust that drifted low behind them.

'My God, that little bastard can ride.' In reluctant admiration Ronny shook his head solemnly and a drop of perspiration broke from his hairline and slid down his cheek. The horse reached the road and pivoted neatly, flattening into the increased speed of its run. Movement of such rhythmic grace and power that the watchers were stirred.

'Look at him go!' whistled Ronny. 'Don't reckon there's anything to catch that horse in the whole of Natal.'

'You think so?' Garry's voice was suddenly alive, and his lips were pursed in anger.

'I'm damned certain of it.'

'Mine. My colt – Grey Weather. Over a point-to-point course, I'd match him against any of Sean Courtney's stud.'

And those words gave Ronny Pye the idea. He turned it over in his mind while with slightly narrowed eyes he watched Dirk Courtney race Sun Dancer down towards the wattle factory. When horse and rider had disappeared through the tall gates, Ronny spoke softly:

'Would you back your colt with money?'

'I'd back him with my life.' There was savagery in Garry's voice.

Yes, thought Ronny, this way at least I will give him a chance. This way the fates will make the decision – there will be no blame to my account.

'Would you back him with Theuniskraal?' he asked, and the silence drew out.

'How do you mean?' whispered Garry.

'If you win, the bond on Theuniskraal is set aside.'

'And if I lose?'

'You lose the farm.'

'No,' snapped Garry. 'Christ, no! That's too much.'

Ronny shrugged indifferently. 'It was just an idea – you're probably wise. You wouldn't have much of a chance against Sean.'

Garry gasped sharply, that challenge had wounded deep as a lance. Made it a direct competition between Sean and himself; to ignore it would be to admit he could never win.

'I'll take the bet.'

'The whole bet? You'll cover my money with what you have left of Theuniskraal?'

'Yes, damn you. Yes. I'll show you how much chance I have against him.'

'We'd better get it down in writing,' Ronny suggested gently. 'Then I'll see if I can arrange it with Sean.' He touched his mount with his spurs and they moved forward across the bridge. 'By the way, I think it best we tell nobody about our little bet. We'll pretend it's just an honour match.'

Garry nodded his agreement. But that night when he wrote to Michael he told him about it, then went on to plead with Michael to ride Grey Weather in the race.

Two days before the competition Michael confided in his grandmother. Ada went out to Theuniskraal to try and dissuade Garry from this reckless gamble, without success. Garry was almost fanatical in his determination. The stake meant nothing to him – it was the prospect of winning.

And now he had Grey Weather and Michael to run for him. This time he would win. This time!

85

In the dark Sean walked with Dirk down the lane to the stables. The clouds banked along the escarpment were fired red by the hidden sun and the wind fretted through the plantations, so that the wattle moaned and shook.

'North wind,' grunted Sean. 'It'll rain before nightfall.'

'Sun Dancer loves the rain,' Dirk answered him tensely, and Sean glanced at him.

'Dirk – if you lose today . . . ' he started, but Dirk cut him short.

'I won't lose,' and again as though it were a vow, 'I won't lose!'

'If you'd only show as much determination in other things – the more important . . . '

'Important! Pa, this is important. This is the most important thing I've ever done.' Dirk stopped and turned to his father. He caught Sean's sleeve, clinging to him. 'Pa, I'm doing this for you – for you, Pa!'

Sean looked down and what he saw in his son's face, in that beautiful face, silenced the retort that he was about to make. Where did I go wrong with you, he asked himself with love stained by loathing. Where did you get this blood, why are you this way, demanded his pride and his contempt.

'Thanks,' he said dryly, freed his arm and walked on towards the stables.

Sightless in his deep preoccupation with Dirk, Sean was into the stable yard before he noticed Mbejane.

'Nkosi. I see you.' Mbejane rose solemnly from the hand-carved stool on which he sat.

'I see you also,' Sean cried with pleasure, and then controlled himself. A display of emotion in front of lesser persons would embarrass Mbejane. 'You are well?' he asked gravely, and restrained the desire to prod the swelling dignity of Mbejane's stomach, reminding himself that Mbejane's abundant flesh and fat had been carefully cultivated as a sign to the rest of the world of his prosperity.

'I am well,' Mbejane assured him.

'That you have come gives me pleasure.'

'Nkosi, on a day of importance it is right that we should be together – as it was before.' And Mbejane allowed himself to smile for the first time, a smile that within seconds became a mischievous grin that Sean gave back to him. He should have guessed that Mbejane would never miss a fight, or a hunt, or a contest.

Then Mbejane turned to Dirk.

'Do us honour today,' he commanded, as though he spoke to one of his own sons. 'Your father and I will be watching you.' He placed a huge black hand upon Dirk's shoulder as though in benediction, then he turned to gesture with his fly-whisk at the stable-boys waiting behind him.

'Bring the horse!'

Two of them led her out, her hooves ringing on the paving of the yard as she danced a little. Head up, moving greyhound-bellied, pricking her ears forward and back, she saw Dirk and wrinkled the soft velvet of her nostrils as she whickered.

'Hey, girl!' Dirk walked towards her. At his approach she rolled her eyes until the whites showed and her small dainty ears flattened wickedly against her neck.

'Stop that nonsense,' Dirk admonished, and she bared

yellow teeth menacingly and reached with her slender snakelike neck. He put out his hand to her and she took his fingers between those terrible teeth and nibbled them tenderly. Then, finished with pretence, she snorted, pricked her ears and nuzzled his chest and neck.

'Where is her blanket? Has she eaten? Put the saddle and bridle in the car.' Dirk snapped a chain of questions and instructions at the stable-boys as he caressed Sun Dancer's face with the gentle hands of a lover.

So many contradictions in one person. Sean watched his son with sadness heavy upon him, oppressive as this red dawn. Where did I go wrong?

'Nkosi, I will walk down with the horse.' Mbejane sensed his mood and sought to end it.

'Better that a man of your station should ride with me in the motor-car,' Sean demurred, and took a fiendish pleasure in the shifty glance that Mbejane cast at the great gleaming Rolls parked at the far end of the yard. It has eyes like a monster, thought Mbejane and looked quickly away.

'I will walk with the horse and see that it comes to no harm,' he announced.

'As you wish,' Sean agreed. The small procession set off towards Ladyburg. The two grooms leading Sun Dancer in her red tartan blanket, and Mbejane following sedately with his small black sons carrying his carved stool and his spears behind him.

Two hours later Sean drove the Rolls into the field behind the stockyards. Staring straight ahead, both hands gripping the wheel so that the knuckles of his hands gleamed white – Sean did not hear the shouted greetings nor see the gala crowds and the bunting until

538

the Rolls bumped to a halt in the grass and his hands unfroze slowly from the wheel. Then he exhaled gently and the rigid muscles of his face softened into a grin of uncertain triumph.

'Well, we made it!' He spoke as if he were not quite certain.

'You did very well, my dear.' Ruth's voice was also a little scratchy and she relaxed her protective hold on Storm.

'You should let me drive, Pa.' Dirk was lounging against the saddlery on the back seat. Sean turned furiously upon him, but Dirk was too quick. He flung open the door and was absorbed into the crowd that had gathered around the Rolls before Sean could assemble his words. Sean glowered after him.

'Hello, Sean. Nice to see you.' Dennis Petersen had opened the door at his elbow and Sean hastily rearranged his features into a smile.

'Hello, Dennis. Nice turn-out.'

'Everybody in the district,' Dennis assured him, as they shook hands, and then looked with satisfaction around the field. There were at least fifty carriages parked haphazard along the stockyard fence, an open wagon had been arranged as a refreshment stall with silver urns of coffee and piles of cakes laid out upon it. A dog fight was in progress near the gate, while small boys in already wilted church clothes shrieked and whooped and chased each other through the crowd.

'Who's responsible for the decorations?' Sean asked, surveying the flags and bunting that fluttered from the poles that marked the finishing line and from the wide roped-off lane that led up to them.

'The Board — we voted it last week.'

'Very nice.' Sean was looking now at the stockpen where the horses were. A solid barricade of humanity lined the railings, but he saw Dirk climb over and jump down beside Sun Dancer amid a splatter of applause from the onlookers.

'Good-looking lad.' Dennis was watching Dirk also, but there was something in his tone that added, *but I'm glad he's not mine.*

'Thanks.' The defiance in Sean's voice was not lost on Dennis and he smiled ironically.

'We'd better go across and talk to the other judges, Garrick is waiting.' Dennis jerked his head towards the carriage at the end of the line, and although he had been painfully aware of it, Sean looked at it for the first time.

Together with Pye, Erasmus and his father, Michael was standing beside it watching them. Tall and lean in tight black riding-boots, and an open shirt of white silk accentuating the breadth of his shoulders, he leaned against the wheel. Above him Ada and Anna sat together on the rear seat and suddenly Sean felt a twist of anger in his stomach that Ada should be there with *them.*

'Mother.' He greeted her without smiling.

'Hello, Sean.' And he could not fathom the tone of her voice nor her expression. Was it regret, or perhaps a reluctant rejection? For a long minute they held each other's eyes – until at last Sean had to break, because now, instead of anger, he felt guilty. But he did not understand the source of his guilt – it was only the sorrowful accusation in Ada's eyes that had given it to him.

'Anna.' He greeted her and received in exchange a stiff nod.

'Garry.' Sean tried to smile. He made a movement to lift his right hand, but as he did so he knew it would be rejected, for the same accusation that he had seen in Ada's eyes was also in Garry's. He turned with relief to Michael.

540

'Hello, Mike. You know you're going to get the pants thrashed off you?'

'I'm going to make you eat those words without salt!' And they laughed together easily, laughed with such obvious joy in each other that Anna moved restlessly in her seat and spoke sharply.

'Can't we get this over with, Ronny?'

'Yes,' Ronny Pye agreed hastily. 'Well, then. Where is young Dirk? We'd better go and find him.'

In a group they left the women and moved through the crowd towards the stockpen where Dirk stood laughing with two girls that Sean recognized as daughters of one of the factory foremen. They were both looking up at Dirk and reacting with such unashamed adoration that Sean felt a lift of indulgent pride. Casually Dirk dismissed the girls and came across to meet them.

'All set, Pa.'

'So I see,' Sean gruffed, and waited for Dirk to show courtesy to the men with him, but Dirk ignored them and spoke only to Ronny Pye.

'Let's hear it.'

'Well, then. A contest between Garry Courtney's colt Grey Weather and Sean Courtney's filly Sun Dancer. An honour match with no stake put up by the owners. Agreed?'

'Right,' said Sean.

Garry opened his mouth and then closed it firmly and nodded. He was sweating a little. He unfolded the handkerchief in his hand and wiped his forehead.

'The distance approximately five miles around four points. The points being firstly the posts that have been erected on this field, secondly the north-eastern boundary marker of the farm Theuniskraal.' Ronny pointed at the crest of the escarpment that stood above them, its slope golden with grass in the morning sun and smeared with streaks of dark green bush. 'Thirdly, the No. 3 dip-tank of Mahobo's Kloof farm, which you can't see from here as it is behind those trees.' Ronny's arm described a long arc along the crest of the escarpment and stopped pointing at the spires of a clump of saligna gums. 'But both of you know it?' 'Sure,' agreed Dirk, and Michael nodded. 'The fourth and finishing-point is the same as the starting-point – here.' He jerked his thumb at the two posts that fluttered gay with flags.

'Stewards have been posted at the Theuniskraal boundary and the dip-tank – make sure you pass on the far side of them. The judges are Messrs Petersen, Erasmus and myself. All and any dispute regarding the running or interpretation of the rules will be decided by us. . . . ' Ronny went on talking and Sean felt his excitement mounting from his stomach and beginning to tingle along his forearms. It was taking a hold on all of them now, even Ronny's voice had an edge to it. Though Sean did not understand that the foxlike eagerness of his face came from the knowledge that this was a contest in which he stood to gain more than any of them. But Garrick understood fully, and his eyes watched Ronny's lips hypnotically.

'That's it, then,' Ronny finished and then to the riders, 'Get saddled up, and bring your horses to the start.'

The judges walked away and left the four Courtneys standing together.

'Sean . . . ' Garry spoke first, his eyes were stricken. 'I think you should know . . . ' but he did not finish.

'What?' Sean asked abruptly, and at the tone of his voice Garrick straightened up. The thing in his eyes changed shape, and became what Sean had never expected to see there – pride.

'It doesn't matter.' Garry turned away and walked

purposefully towards his horse, and there was a spring in his stride and a set to his shoulders.

'Good luck, Mike.' Sean punched his arm.

'And the same to you.' Michael started after Garrick, then stopped and turned back to Sean. 'Whatever anyone else says, Sean, I know you didn't plan this.' Then he was striding away.

'What the hell did he mean by that?' puzzled Sean, but Dirk cut into his thoughts.

'Why did you have to do that, Pa?' he demanded.

'What?' Sean looked at him uncomprehendingly.

'Give him luck. Why did you have to give him luck? I'm riding for you – not him. I'm your son – not him!'

The two riders moved together towards the start, and buzzing with excitement the crowd went with them.

Sean walked beside Sun Dancer, with Dirk leaning attentively from the saddle to listen to him.

'Take it gently to the swamp, don't push her for she'll need all her steam in the mud. Michael will gain there, that colt is strong in the leg, but heavy. Follow him and let him break a path for you. Out of the swamp you can catch up and pass him on the slope, push hard there. You must lead him to the top and hold your lead along the crest to the dip-tank.'

'All right, Pa.'

'Now, when you start down again keep well out beyond the Van Essen plantation on to hard ground – that way you can cut the edge of the swamp. My guess is that Mike will come straight down and plough through the middle – but you must take the longer route – and use Sun Dancer's speed against Grey Weather's strength.'

543

They had reached the starting-posts and the crowd scattered and spread away to line the ropes. An open funnel of humanity faced the two horsemen, then the swamp with its deceptively lush papyrus grass concealing the glutinous mudholes. Beyond it the great soar of the escarpment. A long course. A hard course.

'Are both of you ready?' called Ronny Pye from the sidelines. 'Clear the field, please, Sean.'

Sean put his hand on Dirk's knee.

'Let's see what you can do, boy.' Then he ducked under the ropes into the crowd.

Sun Dancer was skittering nervously, coming up on her back legs and throwing her head so that the mane flew red-gold in the sunlight. She was sweating in dark patches on her shoulders. Michael was circling Grey Weather, keeping him moving gently, leaning forward and patting his neck, talking to him so that he switched his ears, cocking them half back to listen.

'Quiet, please, everybody!' Dennis was using a megaphone, and the buzz of voices descended into an expectant rustling.

'You're under starter's orders now,' he shouted at the riders, 'Turn wide, and walk up together.'

They swung away from the posts, and came together. Dirk touched Sun Dancer with the spur and she jumped back thrusting her quarters into Michael's leg.

'Keep your bloody animal under control,' he snarled at Michael. 'Don't crowd me!'

'Are you nervous, Dirkie?' Obediently Michael wheeled his mount aside.

'Damn you! – I'll show you who's nervous,' and Sun Dancer threw her head in protest, as Dirk sawed her with the curb.

'Come round, swing them round.' Dennis's voice through the megaphone boomed distortedly.

They turned in line and started walking up, twenty yards from the start, two horses with the sunlight glowing on their polished skins. Pale gold and dark red. The crowd sighed softly like wind in the grass.

Ten paces and Sun Dancer was pushing forward, lengthening her stride, crabbing a little.

'Hold your line! Keep together,' Dennis cautioned them, and Dirk yanked her back roughly. The rims of his nostrils were flared and white with tension.

Michael moved up beside him, holding his hands low. The big red colt stepping high in the exaggerated action of an animal under restraint.

Quickening together over the last five paces, their riders hunching lower in the saddles, they came to the posts.

'Go!' bellowed Dennis, and 'Go!' roared a hundred voices. Still in line, matching each other's stride, they changed from a walk into an easy, free, swinging canter. Both Dirk and Michael rising slightly in their stirrups to hold them from headlong flight. Half a mile ahead lay the swamp and beyond it five miles of mountain and rough, rocky ground, of donga and thornbush. They cantered down between the yelling lines and out of the funnel into the open.

The crowd broke and scattered to various points of vantage and Sean ran with them, unslinging his binocular-case, chuckling with excitement in the general confusion of shouts and laughter.

Ruth was waiting for him beside the Rolls and he caught her around the waist and lifted her on to the bonnet.

'Sean, you'll scratch the paintwork,' she protested, as she clutched at her hat and teetered dangerously on the high, round bonnet.

'The hell with the paintwork,' he laughed as he

545

climbed up beside her and she clung to him for support. 'There they are!'

Far out across the field the two horses ran down towards the bright green of the swamp. Sean lifted and focused his binoculars, and suddenly they were so close he expected to hear the drumming of the hooves. Grey Weather was pulling ahead, forcing powerfully with his great shoulders lunging into each stride – and Sun Dancer trailed him with her neck arched against the pressure of the bit. On her back Dirk sat upright with his elbows pressed into his flanks as he held her.

'The little bugger is listening to advice,' Sean growled. 'I quite expected him to be using the whip already.'

Across the distance that separated them Sean could feel as a tangible thing Dirk's determination to win, he could see it in the way he held his shoulders, he could see it in the rigid lines of his arms. But what he did not see were the harsh lines of hatred in Dirk's face as he stared at Michael's back ahead of him.

The beat of hooves changed its tone, no longer ringing on hard ground, but dulling as they reached the swamp. Now lumps of damp clay flew from Grey Weather's hooves and a piece hit Dirk's chest and sprayed dirt on the white silk of his shirt. Sun Dancer's gait altered as she felt the soft ground.

'Easy, girl. Hey there, girl,' Dirk whispered and held her firmly with his knees to give her confidence. The grass brushed his stirrups and ahead of him Grey Weather splashed into the first mudhole, plunged through it and into the swamp proper. The tall papyrus engulfed him.

'The old man was right,' Dirk smiled for the first time. Michael was forcing a path through the reeds, flattening them for Dirk to follow with half the effort. Twice Grey Weather sunk to his belly in potholes of black glue, rearing and struggling to free himself while Dirk skirted them.

Both horses were shiny with mud, and their riders were soaked to the waist and splattered above. The swamp stank like an animal cage and marsh gas erupted sullenly as they disturbed it. Clouds of insects rose about them, a sakabula bird fled shrieking as they ploughed through the papyrus. One of the razor leaves lashed Michael's cheek and a thread of blood ran down his jaw washing the blobs of mud with it and dripped on to his shirt.

Then suddenly the ground firmed under them, the solid papyrus broke into clumps, thinned and was left behind and Grey Weather led them out on to the first slope of the escarpment. He was running heavily now, and grunting with each stride, while Sun Dancer moved up beside him.

'You're finished!' Dirk shouted at Michael as they drew level. 'I'll see you at the finish-line,' and he leaned forward in the saddle and gave Sun Dancer the spurs and the whip together.

Without pressing his horse Michael angled him off towards the right, letting him move under slack rein to pick his own way and he began the first leg of the series of zigzags that would take him to the top.

On the steep ground below the crest Dirk used the whip incessantly, and Sun Dancer went up in a series of scrambling leaps with the loose rock rolling under her hooves. The sweat had washed away the mud from her shoulders and she landed with less control at each jump. 'Pull, you bitch. Pull!' Dirk shouted at her, and looked back in agony at Michael's sedate ascent. He was two hundred yards below and coming steadily. Dirk's movement caught Sun Dancer off balance and she landed awkwardly at the next jump, her hooves scrab-

547

bled and she started to fall. Dirk kicked his feet from the stirrups and jumped with the reins still in his hands. The instant he landed he leaned back on the reins to hold her, but she was down on her knees now, sliding back and she pulled Dirk down with her on to the level place below.

They struggled together and when at last he got her on her feet she was trembling with terror, dust and pieces of dry grass coated her muddy legs.

'Damn you! Damn you, you clumsy bitch,' whispered Dirk as he ran his hands over her hocks to check for damage. He glanced back at Michael and found him much closer now.

'Oh, God!' he blurted, snatched up Sun Dancer's reins and ran at the slope dragging her after him. Dirk came out on the crest with sweat pouring down his face and soaking through his shirt. Saliva had dried to a thick gummy froth in his mouth and he was panting harshly – but he had held on to his lead and Sun Dancer was over her trembling fit. She had recovered sufficiently to cavort a little as he mounted.

'This way, Dirkie!' The two stewards standing on the pile of stones that marked the Theuniskraal boundary were waving and shouting wild encouragement. Dirk clouted the spurs into her and was off again, galloping along the ridge, sweeping past them and on towards the clump of gums three miles ahead.

'Catch him, Mike. Ride, man, ride!' Faint shouts behind him – and Dirk knew without looking back that Mike had reached the top and was chasing him. He rode on, grimly mourning the time lost on the ascent and hating both Sun Dancer and Michael for it. At this point he should have led by four hundred yards – not fifty.

Directly ahead now was the gorge through which the Baboon Stroom dropped down the escarpment, its side choked with dark green river bush. Dirk found the path and turned away from the skyline aiming upstream at the ford. Without grass to muffle them Sun Dancer's hooves hammered in staccato rhythm on the hard-packed earth of the path, but also he could hear behind him like an echo the beat of other hooves – Michael was on to the path behind him. Dirk looked back under his own arm. Michael was so close that he could see the laughter lines creasing the corners of his mouth, and the mockery inflamed him.

'I'll show him –!' And Dirk started with the whip again, cracking it across Sun Dancer's flanks and shoulders so that she jumped forward with a new urgency. Down the steep bank of the river and out on to the white sandbank, he plunged with Grey Weather's nose drawing level with his boot. Into the dark green water they rode abreast, throwing up a veil of spray that sparkled in the sunlight, slipping from their saddles to swim beside the horses through the deep, while the current moved them down towards the falls. Up into the saddles again the instant the horses found the bottom and splashed towards the far bank. Out on to the sand, with water streaming from sodden clothing, shouting with excitement as they raced for the narrow path that climbed the far bank. First man on to it would hold the advantage.

'Give way! I'm leading – give me way,' screamed Dirk furiously.

'Make your own way!' Michael laughed back at him.

'You bastard!' Dirk used his knees and reins to thrust Sun Dancer's shoulder into Michael, trying to force him clear.

'None of that!' Michael warned him.

'You bastard – I'll show you.'

They rode knee to knee now. Dirk sat up quickly and

twisted his foot, placing his booted toe under Michael's instep. With a sudden vicious lift of his leg he slipped Michael's foot from the stirrup and threw him sideways. As he felt himself going over Michael clutched desperately at the pommel, pulling the saddle with him so it slid on to Grey Weather's flank and the shift of weight forced the horse to disengage and slew away from the path. Michael went down on his shoulder into the sand and rolled with his knees drawn up against his stomach.

'That's for you!' Dirk yelled in defiance as he went up the bank and out into the open veld again. Behind him in the river-bed Michael staggered to his feet, his wet clothing coated white with sand, and ran after Grey Weather who was trotting back towards the water with the saddle hanging under his chest.

'The dirty little swine. My God, if only Sean knew!' Michael caught the horse before it started to drink, wrestled the saddle on to his back again and clinched the girth.

'Now, I can't let him win!' He jumped up on to Grey Weather and booted him towards the bank. 'I can't let him win.'

Two hundred yards ahead Dirk's shirt was a white blob against the brown grass. As he rounded the dip-tank and pointed Sun Dancer's head at the ridge for the last leg, one of the stewards shouted:

'What happened to Michael?'

'He fell in the river,' Dirk called back. 'He's finished!' And his voice rang with triumph.

'He's leading – Dirk's leading!' Sean stood on the Rolls with his glasses trained on the clump of gum-trees, and

550

now he was the first to spot the tiny figure of the horseman as it showed on the crest of the escarpment.

'Where's Michael?' Ruth asked.

'He can't be far behind,' Sean muttered and waited anxiously for him to appear. He had fretted while he watched Dirk's reckless ascent of the slope, and cursed him loudly for his brutal treatment of Sun Dancer. Then he had entreated him to *get a bloody move on* during the run along the ridge with Michael gaining steadily on him. When the two horsemen had veered away from the skyline to cross the Baboon Stroom they had disappeared from view and this was the first glimpse the spectators had received of either competitor since that moment.

'The little idiot's riding too wide. I told him to cut the edge of the swamp – not ride round it altogether.'

'Where's Michael?' Ruth repeated. Sean swung the glasses back and scanned the crest with the first twinges of concern.

'Not showing yet – he must have run into trouble.'

'Do you think he's all right? Has he been hurt?'

'How should I know?' Sean's anxiety made him irritable, but immediately he was penitent and encircled Ruth's waist with his arm. 'He can look after himself, that one. No sense fussing about him.'

Dirk was well down the slope now, leaving a thin trail of dust, for Sun Dancer skidded on her haunches most of the way.

'Still no sign of Michael?' Ruth moved restlessly against him.

'No. Not yet,' Sean grunted. 'Dirk can afford to miss the swamp – he's leading by a quarter of a mile.'

Suddenly a sigh of relief moved the crowd like a gust of wind through a field of wheat.

'There he is!'

'He's coming straight down the slope.'

'He can't make it unless he flies!'

Sean swung his glasses from Dirk to Michael and back, estimating their speeds and positions, allowing for Michael's delay in the swamp, but setting against that the additional distance that Dirk had to cover.

'It's going to be close –' he decided aloud. 'Dirk's got the edge, but it's going to be very close.'

Ada did not see it that way. Dirk was leaading and Dirk was going to win. She looked across at Garrick. He stood beside the finishing-post a hundred yards away, but even at that distance there was no mistaking the droop of his shoulders and the air of misery that surrounded him like an aura of defeat. Sun Dancer's hooves were slashing his life to threads.

Unable to bear it a moment longer, Ada jumped down from the carriage and ran through the crowd to where Sean stood like a triumphant colossus on the bonnet of the Rolls.

'Sean.' She reached up and touched his leg, but he was so engrossed he did not feel or hear her.

'Sean,' she shouted and tugged at his trouser-leg.

'Mother?' He turned vaguely to look down at her.

'I must talk to you,' Ada shouted above the sound of the crowd that was rising with excitement.

'Not now. They're coming in to the finish – climb up here where you can see it.'

'Now. I must speak to you now. Come down this instant!' Her tone shocked him, for a second he wavered and peered furtively back at the race. Then he shrugged with resignation and jumped down beside her.

'What is it? Please be quick – I don't want to miss –'

'I'll be quick.' Sean had never seen such a cold fury on her before. 'I wanted to say that I never thought I'd see that day when I had nothing left for you but contempt. Thoughtless you've been often – but never down-right merciless.'

'Mother, I . . .' He was bewildered.

'Listen to me. You set out to destroy your brother and you've done it. Well, I hope you have the pleasure of it. You've got Theuniskraal now. Enjoy it, Sean. Sleep well at night.'

'Theuniskraal! What do you mean?' He shouted at her now in his confusion. 'I didn't wager for the farm!'

'Ah, no,' Ada scoffed at him. 'Of course you didn't – you let Ronny Pye do that for you.'

'Pye? What's he got to do with it?'

'Everything! He helped you plan it. He helped you provoke Garry into this stupidity. He holds the mort-gage on Theuniskraal.'

'But . . .' Slowly the enormity of it all began to shape up in Sean's mind.

'You took his leg – now take Theuniskraal, but pay for it with my love.' She looked steadily into his eyes, but the pain was there clouding her own. 'Good-bye, Sean. We won't speak to each other again.' And she walked slowly away. She walked like an old woman at last, a tired and worn old woman.

Sean understood and began to run towards the finish-ing-line. He drove through the crowd like a shark through a shoal of sardines. Over their heads he saw the two horsemen galloping in across the field.

Dirk was leading, standing in the stirrups to thrash Sun Dancer with the whip. His black hair fluttered in the wind, and his shirt filthy with thrown mud. Under him the filly danced on flying hooves and the beat of them drummed above the rising roar of the crowd. Her body was black and shiny with sweat, and froth flew from her gaping pink mouth to form white lace on her chest and flanks.

553

Fifty hopeless yards behind her plunged the colt with Michael flogging his heels into him with despair. Michael's face was twisted in an agony of frustration. Grey Weather was finished, his legs loose with exhaustion and his breath sawing hoarsely with each stride.

Sean tore his way through the press of bodies that lined the guide ropes. He reached the front rank and shouldered two women from his path. Then he stooped and ducked under the rope into the open.

Sun Dancer was almost up to him, hammering down in a crescendo of hooves, her head nodding with each stride.

'Dirk! Stop her!' roared Sean.

'Pa! Pa! Get out of the way . . .' Dirk screamed back at him, but Sean sprang to intercept him.

'Pa!'

Sean was in front of him, crouching with arms extended. Too close to swing Sun Dancer's head away from him, too late to stop her charge.

'Jump, girl, jump,' shouted Dirk and gathered the horse with his knees, feeling her respond with a bunching of her quarters; feeling her lift her forelegs against her chest and drive upwards in a high parabola. But sensing also the sluggishness of her exhausted body and knowing she had not gone high enough to clear Sean's head.

An aching moment as Sun Dancer lifted clear of the ground, the horrified groan of the crowd as her forelegs smashed into Sean and she twisted in the air, falling. Dirk thrown, his stirrup leathers parting like whip cracks. Then all of them down together in the grass. Shrill screams of women in the crowd.

Sun Dancer struggling up again with a foreleg swinging loosely from the knee, whinnying in the pain of broken bone.

Sean on his back, his head twisted to the side and blood from his torn cheek dribbling into his nose and mouth so that his breathing snored hoarsely.

Dirk with the skin smeared from elbows and one cheek, crawling towards Sean, kneeling beside him, raising both hands clenched, hammering down with them so that his fists splattered the blood, beating them into the chest and slack, unconscious face of his father.

'Why did you? Oh, God, I hate you.' Shock and fury and despair. 'For you! You stopped me, you stopped me.'

Michael dragging Grey Weather down on his haunches, flinging from the saddle, running to them, holding Dirk's arms, dragging him off, fighting him.

'Leave him, you little bastard.'

'He didn't want me to. He stopped me, I hate him. I'll kill him.'

The crowd surging forward, flattening the guide ropes, two men helping Michael hold Dirk, the rest of them ringing Sean's body.

The cries and questions:

'Where's Doc Fraser?'

'Jesus, he's badly hurt!'

'Catch that horse. Get a gun.'

'What about the bets?'

'Don't touch him. Wait . . . .'

'Got to straighten his arm.'

'Get a gun. For Christ sake, get a gun.'

Then a new silence on them, their ranks opening quietly and Ruth coming through to him running – Mbejane behind her.

'Sean.' She knelt beside him, clumsy in her pregnancy. 'Sean,' she began again, and the men about her could not look at her face.

'Mbejane, bring him to the car,' she whispered.

He slipped the monkey-skin cloak from his shoulder

555

and let it drop, stooped over Sean and lifted him. The great black muscles of his chest and arms swelled, and he stood with his legs braced wide against the weight.

'His arm, Nkosikazi.'

She arranged the hanging arm comfortably across his chest.

'Bring him,' she repeated and together they walked through the crowd. Sean's head lolled against Mbejane's shoulder like that of a sleeping child. Mbejane laid Sean gently on the back seat with his head in Ruth's lap.

'My daddy,' she kept repeating, her face screwed up with horror at the blood and her tiny body trembling like that of a frightened rabbit.

'Will you drive us please, Michael?' Ruth looked up at him as he stood beside the Rolls. 'Take us to Protea Street.'

With Mbejane loping alongside, the big car bumped across the field through the throng of anxious watchers, then swung on to the main road and moved away towards Ladyburg.

86

While about him the crowds scattered slowly and drifted to their carriages, Dirk Courtney stood alone and watched the Rolls disappear in its own blown dust.

Waves of reaction shivered up his legs and turned to heavy nausea in his gut. The open gravel rash on his face burned like acid spilled upon the skin.

'You'd better go in and have Doc Fraser put something on your face.' Coming from his carriage with a heavy service revolver, Dennis Petersen paused beside him.

'Yes,' Dirk answered dully, and Dennis walked on to where two native grooms held Sun Dancer. Unsteadily on three legs, but quiet now, she stood between them with her head hanging dejectedly.

Dennis touched the muzzle of the revolver to her forehead, and at the shot she recoiled violently and dropped, shuddering. Her legs stiffened in one last convulsion, then she lay still.

Watching, Dirk shuddered in sympathy and then leaned forward to vent his nausea in the grass. It came up sour and scalding hot. He wiped it from his mouth with the palm of his hand, then he began to walk. Without direction, blindly, from the field towards the escarpment.

Over in his mind, keeping pace with his legs like the refrain of a marching song:

He doesn't want me. He doesn't want me.

And then savagely:

I hope he dies. Please let him die.

'Please let him die.' Anna Courtney said it softly, so that Garry standing below her seat in the buggy did not hear her. He stood with his shoulders hunched, and his head thrust forward in thought, hands hanging at his sides slowly folding and unfolding, then he raised one of them and squeezed the fingers into his closed eyelids.

'I'm going to him,' he said. 'God help me, but I'm going to him.'

'No! I forbid it. Leave him – let him suffer as I suffered.'

Slowly, bewildered, Garry shook his head.

'I must. It's too long, too much. I must. Pray God it's not too late.'

'Let him die.' Then suddenly it snapped in her head, broke under the weight of the hatred so long sustained.

She rose screaming in her seat. 'Die! Damn you. Die!' And Garry uncovered his eyes, and looked at her in alarm.

'Compose yourself, my dear.'

'Die! Die!' Her face was blotched with flaming spots of red, and her voice squawked as though she were being strangled. Garry scrambled up beside her and flung his arms around her protectively.

'Get away from me. Don't touch me.' She screamed at him; fighting from his embrace. 'Because of you I lost him. He was so big, so strong. He was mine – and because . . .'

'Anna, Anna. Please don't.' He tried to soothe her raving. 'Please stop it, my dear.'

'You, you crawling, crippled thing. Because of you.' And suddenly it had to come out, like pus from a canker. 'But I paid you back. I took him from you also – and now he's dead. You'll never have him.' She laughed, gloating, demented.

'Anna, Stop it.'

'That night – do you remember that night? Will you or he ever forget it? I wanted him, I wanted him big like a bull on top of me, I wanted him rutting deep like it was before – I begged him. I pleaded – but because of you. Because of his crippled little weakling brother. Christ, I hated him!' She laughed again, a shriek of pain and hatred. 'I tore my clothing and bit into my own lips, as I had wanted him to do. When you came – I wanted you to . . . but you, I had forgotten you were only half a man! I wanted you to kill him – *kill him!*'

Pale, so that the sweat on his face shone like water on white marble, Garry pulled away from her with loathing.

'All this time I thought he – I believed you.' And he half fell from the buggy, leaning against it for a moment to steady himself. '. . . All this time wasted.' Then he launched himself and began to run, his bad leg jerking and catching under him.

'You want a lift, Garry?' Dennis Petersen drew level with him and called down from the carriage.

'Yes. Oh, yes.' Garry caught the handrail and dragged himself up beside Dennis. 'Take me to him, please, as fast as you can.'

87

Silent, deserted, the great house crouched over her. Dark with the shutters closed against the sun, brooding and immense, smelling musty as though old passions had died within its walls.

Anna stood alone in the huge central room and screamed its name.

'Theuniskraal!'

And the thick stone walls smothered the sound of her madness.

'He is dead! Do you hear me? I took him away from all of you.' And she shrieked in triumphant laughter, with the tears greasing her cheeks. 'I won! Do you hear me? I won!' And her grief distorted the laughter.

She picked up the heavy glass lamp and hurled it across the room; it burst and the paraffin sprayed wide, glistening on the walls and soaking into the carpet.

'Theuniskraal! Hear me! I hate you also. I hate him. I hate you all – all of you.'

She raged through the room, tearing down the gilt-framed pictures and smashing them so that the glass sparkled like tiny jewels in the gloom; she used a chair to smash in the front of the display cabinet and wreck the old china and glassware in it; she swept the books from the shelves into fluttering heaps, and threw their torn pages in the air.

'I hate!' she screamed. 'I hate!' And the great house waited silent. Exhausted with worn-out emotions – old and sad and wise.

'I hate you – all of you.' And she ran out into the passage, through the kitchens to the pantries. On the lowest shelf stood a four-gallon drum of methylated spirit and she panted as she struggled with the stopper. The stopper came out, the clear liquid welled and ran down the metal sides, and she picked the drum up across her chest and stumbled back into the kitchen. It spilled down her skirts, soaking in, drenching the heavy cloth, forming a spreading pool on the stone flags.

'I hate!' She laughed and stumbled, staggering off balance, still clutching the drum she fell against the kitchen range. Hot metal scorched her clothing and burned through to the flesh of her hip, but she did not feel it. Her sodden skirts brushed over the fire-box, a tiny point of flame caught and grew. So when she ran on into the house a fiery train swept behind her.

Back in the central room, she poured from the drum over the books and the carpet, laughing as she splashed the long-draped velvet curtains.

Oblivious of the flames that followed, until her petticoats caught and burned against her legs. Then she screamed again at the agony of her tortured flesh and brain. She dropped the metal drum and it exploded, showering her with liquid blue flame, turning her hair and her face and her whole body into a living torch, a torch that fell and writhed and died before the flames reached the thatch of the roof of Theuniskraal.

88

They faced each other across the waist of the dhow, and the bright sunlight threw their shadows along the filthy planking of the deck. Two tall young men, both dark-haired and burned rich brown by the sun, both with the big Courtney nose – both angry. From the poop three of the Arab crew watched with mild curiosity.

'So, you won't come home, then?' Michael asked. 'You're going through with this childishness?'

'Why do you want me to?'

'Me? Good God, if I never see you again it would be too soon. Ladyburg will be a cleaner town without you.'

'Then why did you come?'

'Your father asked me.'

'Why didn't he come himself?' Dirk's bitterness echoed in his voice.

'He's still a sick man – his head. Hurt badly.'

'If he wanted me, he would have come.'

'He sent for you, didn't he?'

'But why did he want you to win – why did he stop me?'

'Listen to me, Dirk. You're young yet. There are many things you don't understand.'

'Don't I!' And Dirk threw back his head and laughed scornfully. 'Oh, I understand all right. You'd better get off this boat, we're just about to sail.'

'Listen, Dirk . . . '

'Get off. Run back to him – you can have my share.'

'Dirk, listen to me. He said if you refused to come –

562

then I was to give you this.' From inside his coat Michael drew an envelope and offered it.

'What is it?'

'I don't know – but I expect that it's money.'

Dirk came slowly across the deck and took the envelope from him.

'Have you a message for him?' Michael asked, and when Dirk shook his head he turned and jumped down on to the wooden jetty. Immediately a bustle began behind him as the Arab crew cast off the lines.

Standing on the edge of the jetty, Michael watched the stubby little craft drift out on the waters of Durban Bay. He could smell the stench of her bilges, her sides were streaked with human filth, and the single sail that rose slowly as the crew hoisted the long teak boom was stained and patched like a quilt.

The wind took her and the pregnant belly of the sail bulged out, she heeled and thrust forward through the chop of dirty green water – headed towards the bar, where a low surf broke in languid lines of white.

The two half-brothers stared at each other across the widening gap. Neither of them lifted an arm or smiled. The dhow bore away. Dirk's face was a tiny brown fleck above the white of his tropical suit, then suddenly his voice.

'Tell him . . .' Small in the distance. 'Tell him . . .' and the rest of it was lost on the wind, in the soft lap and sigh of the wavelets beneath the jetty.

89

Below where they sat on the lip of the escarpment, the walls of Theuniskraal stood up like smoke-browned tombstones marking the burial ground of hatred.

'About time you started rebuilding,' Sean grunted, 'you can't stay on at Protea Street for ever.'

'No.' Garry paused before going on: 'I've picked out the new site for the homestead – there, beyond the number two dip.'

Both of them looked away from the roofless ruins, and they were silent again until shyly Garry asked, 'I'd like you to have a look at the plans. It won't be as big as the old house now that there is just Michael and I. Could you . . . ?'

'Good,' Sean cut in quickly. 'Why don't you bring them across to Lion Kop tomorrow evening? Ruth will want you to stay for dinner.'

'I'd like that.'

'Come early,' said Sean, and started to stand up from the rock on which he sat. He moved heavily, awkwardly – and Garry jumped up to help him. Hating the weakness of his slowly mending body, Sean would have brushed Garry's eager hands away. But he saw the expression on his brother's face and instead he submitted meekly.

'Give me an arm over the rough ground, please.' He spoke gruffly.

Side by side, with Sean's arm across Garry's shoulder, they moved to where the buggy waited.

Further Wilbur Smith Titles Available from Mandarin

While every effort is made to keep prices low, it is sometimes necessary to increase prices at short notice. Mandarin Paperbacks reserves the right to show new retail prices on covers which may differ from those previously advertised in the text or elsewhere.

The prices shown below were correct at the time of going to press.

☐ 7493 0638 6	**When the Lion Feeds**	£4.99
☐ 7493 0639 4	**Cry Wolf**	£4.99
☐ 7493 0373 5	**Men of Men**	£5.99
☐ 7493 0635 1	**The Sound of Thunder**	£4.99
☐ 7493 0633 5	**The Diamond Hunters**	£4.99
☐ 7493 0551 7	**A Sparrow Falls**	£4.99
☐ 7493 0628 9	**Hungry as the Sea**	£4.99
☐ 7493 0552 5	**The Angels Weep**	£4.99
☐ 7493 0543 6	**Dark of the Sun**	£4.99
☐ 7493 0624 6	**The Leopard Hunts in Darkness**	£4.99
☐ 7493 0621 1	**Wild Justice**	£4.99
☐ 7493 0622 X	**Eagle in the Sky**	£4.99
☐ 7493 0615 7	**Gold Mine**	£4.99
☐ 7493 0616 5	**Shout at the Devil**	£4.99
☐ 7493 0613 0	**Sunbird**	£4.99
☐ 7493 0611 4	**The Burning Shore**	£4.99
☐ 7493 0608 4	**The Eye of the Tiger**	£4.99
☐ 7493 0609 2	**A Falcon Flies**	£4.99

All these books are available at your bookshop or newsagent, or can be ordered direct from the publisher. Just tick the titles you want and fill in the form below.

Mandarin Paperbacks, Cash Sales Department, PO Box 11, Falmouth, Cornwall TR10 9EN.

Please send cheque or postal order, no currency, for purchase price quoted and allow the following for postage and packing:

UK including BFPO	£1.00 for the first book, 50p for the second and 30p for each additional book ordered to a maximum charge of £3.00.
Overseas including Eire	£2 for the first book, £1.00 for the second and 50p for each additional book thereafter.

NAME (Block letters) ....

ADDRESS ....

....

☐ I enclose my remittance for ....

☐ I wish to pay by Access/Visa Card Number

Expiry Date

Ponderously Sean climbed up and settled himself into the padded leather seat.

'Thanks.' He gathered up the reins and smiled down at Garry, and Garry flushed with pleasure and looked away to the infinite lines of young wattle trees that covered the hills of Theuniskraal.

'Looks good, doesn't it?' he asked.

'You and Michael have done wonders up here,' Sean agreed, still smiling.

'Courtney Brothers and Son.' Softly Garry spoke the name of the new company which had merged the lands of Theuniskraal and Lion Kop into one vast estate. 'Now at last it is the way it should have been long ago.'

'Until tomorrow, Garry.' Sean flipped the reins and the buggy rolled forward, rocking gently over the uneven surface of the new road.

'Until tomorrow, Sean.' Garry called after him, and watched until the buggy was lost to sight among the blocks of dark mature wattle. Then he walked to his horse and mounted. He sat a while watching the distant ranks of Zulu labourers singing as they worked. He saw Michael moving on horseback amongst them, stopping occasionally to lean from the saddle and urge them on.

And Garry began to smile. The smile smoothed away the lines from around his eyes. He touched the horse with his spurs and cantered down to join Michael.